Corporate Investigations

Second Edition

Compiled By
Reginald J. Montgomery, CPP, PSP, CLI, CFE, CP, CST
William J. Majeski

Contributing Authors

John S. Belrose
Julius Bombet, CLI, CFE
Gerald R. (Gary) Brown
Matthew Buchert
James R. Buckley
James P. Carino, CPP, CFC, VSM
Grace Elting Castle, CLI
Paul J. Ciolino, CFE, BCFE, CII
Steven Cooper
Harold F. Coyne, Jr., PPS
Robert J. DiPasquale, CPA, CFE
Robert Dudash, CFE
Jay L. Groob
Kitty Hailey, CLI
Bruce Hulme, CFE
Don C. Johnson, CLI, CII
Robyn R. Mace, Ph.D.
Michael C. McDermott
Kevin D. Murray, CPP, CFE, BCFE
Tom Owen
John J. Palmatier, Ph.D.
Edwin H. Petersen
Raymond M. Pierce
Jeffery Richardson, Sr.
Al Ristuccia
David Roberts, FIPI
Ben Scaglione, CPP, CHSP
Todd Scheffer, CFE
Herbert Simon, CPP
Larry R. Troxel, CLI, REA
Jonathan Turner, CFE, CII
Peter F. Wade

Tucson, Arizona

This publication is designed to provide accurate and authoritative information in regard to the subject matter covered. It is sold with the understanding that the publisher is not engaged in rendering legal, accounting, or other professional service. If legal advice or other expert assistance is required, the services of a competent professional should be sought.

—From a *Declaration of Principles* jointly adopted by a committee of the American Bar Association and a committee of publishers and associations.

Lawyers & Judges Publishing Company, Inc.
P.O. Box 30040 • Tucson, AZ 85751-0040
(800) 209-7109 • FAX (800) 330-8795
e-mail: sales@lawyersandjudges.com

Library of Congress Cataloging-in-Publication Data

Corporate investigations / compiled by Reginald Montgomery, William Majeski.-- 2nd ed.
p. cm.
Includes bibliographical references and index.
ISBN-13: 978-1-933264-02-8 (hardcover)
ISBN-10: 1-933264-02-0 (hardcover)
1. White collar crime investigation. 2. Corporations--Corrupt practices.
I. Montgomery, Reginald J. II. Majeski, William J.
HV8079.W47C666 2005
658.3'8--dc22

2005010237

ISBN 1-933264-02-0
ISBN 978-1-933264-02-8
Printed in the United States of America
10 9 8 7 6 5 4 3 2 1

Contents

Part II
Due Diligence and Forensic Accounting

Part IV
Dealing with Threats and Violence

Part V
Geographics and Cultural Considerations

Acknowledgments

I would like to thank the original and new contributors to this second edition who have written their best. The experience and knowledge shared here makes all who read this book, better investigators.

We thank all our clients who finance our training by hiring us to guide them through the landmines of corporate investigation.

Finally, there are many corporate security professionals who have been constant mentors, teachers, and supporters of this art we call corporate investigations.

Reginald J. Montgomery

I would like to personally thank all of the contributing authors. They have graciously shared their knowledge and expertise. They unselfishly took time from their busy schedules to help prepare a text that will benefit all those involved in the corporate security arena. These ladies and gentlemen are among the most talented professional investigators in their respective fields.

I would like to add a very special note of thanks to my dear friend Reggie Montgomery. Without his insistence I would not have been a part of this project. He had the foresight to recognize the need for this book and the fortitude to relent.

William J. Majeski

Dedication

I want to dedicate the 2nd Edition of this book to my wife Antoinette! She shows me every day that things are much better the second time around.

Reginald J. Montgomery

As with any endeavor which takes a great deal of effort, time becomes a precious and limited commodity.

I would like to thank my wife Evelyn, and my daughter Nicole for so graciously sharing their time during this project. I would also like to acknowledge my departed parents Mary and Ziggy, for having given me a solid foundation from which to build my life.

I would like to add a special note of thanks to my daughter Julie Fritzsch, for her editorial skills and her insight. Her wisdom is always appreciated.

William J. Majeski

Preface

Some of the most complex and thorough investigations are conducted in the corporate arena by some of the world's finest investigators. Corporate investigators' mind-sets are much different than those of civil or legal defense investigators. In corporate investigations the rules and guidelines an investigator must follow also diverge from civil and legal. New and revised government regulations, case law, and legislative decrees have increased the corporate investigator's responsibilities.

Corporate clients demand and deserve the very best. Corporate investigators can deliver consummate results. *Corporate Investigations, 2nd Edition*, has been comprised by the nation's very finest corporate investigators. Almost a thousand years of collective knowledge and experience have been consolidated and are offered as text for clients as well as practitioners.

Presenting individual expertise, the authors illuminate an overview, followed by identifying the obstacles one will encounter and how to address them. In-depth explanations are afforded. Hints for successfully incorporating this newfound knowledge are demonstrated.

Law enforcement has an obligation to protect people and property. Conversely, corporate security has those responsibilities on a greater scale with added concerns regarding intellectual property, conception, research and development, production, shipping, receiving, asset protection, physical and financial security, and a myriad of related issues.

Asset protection encompasses:

1. Personnel—the most important
2. Product

3. Intellectual property
4. Physical facilities
5. Professional and business reputations

Every corporate investigative assignment involves one or more of these assets. The more intricate and heterogeneous the corporation, the greater the challenges. Imagination, creativity, and greed drive an ever-expanding corporate crime arena. Corporate investigative specialization is one of the finest weapons available to the corporate world.

Most often corporate entities are held to higher standards by the courts and society. Loss of public confidence and negative press are critical concerns which competent corporate investigators can prevent. Corporations have an obligation to protect their assets and maintain their ability to conduct business. Publicly owned companies are held to even more strict standards as they are responsible to their stockholders, employees and the public. Corporate entities have often found themselves being held responsible for activities that are currently unacceptable, yet were normal business practices when they were committed.

Corporate investigators are sometimes limited in expertise associated with specific disciplines. They are only as good as the knowledge of the collective network. To best serve the clients, investigators have to obtain knowledge from their expert colleagues.

Corporate Investigations, 2nd Edition, contains assets that we have gathered over the past thirty-five years. The chapters in this book will give the reader a view of our experience and knowledge. This is a solid representation of available corporate investigative talent. It is our hope that this revised edition will be an asset to all investigators and clients.

Reginald J. Montgomery
William J. Majeski

Part I

Investigative Tools, Techniques, and Working Relationships

Chapter 1

The FCRA and Corporate Investigations

Bruce H. Hulme, CFE

Synopsis

1.1 Introduction

In 1970, Congress enacted the Fair Credit Reporting Act, commonly referred to as the "FCRA" or the "Act," 15 U.S.C.§§1681 et seq. The present FCRA includes the amendments to the FCRA set forth in the Consumer Credit Reporting Reform Act of 1996 (Public Law 104-208, the Omnibus Consolidated Appropriations Act for Fiscal Year 1997, Title II, Subtitle D, Chapter 1), Section 311 of the Intelligence Authorization Act for Fiscal Year 1998 (Public Law 105-107), the Consumer Reporting Clarification Act of 1998 (Public Law 105-347), Section 506 of the Gramm-Leach-Bliley Act (Public Law 106-102), Sections 358(g) and 505 (c) of the Uniting and Strengthening America by Providing Appropriate Tools Required to Intercept and Obstruct Terrorism Act of 2001 (USA Patriot Act) (Public Law 107-56), and the Fair and Accurate Credit Transactions Act of 2003 (Fact Act) (Public Law 108-159). The FCRA may be subject to other legislation enacted after the printing of this text. Thus, readers should refer to the most recent statute when determining the legal implications of the FCRA relative to corporate investigations.

The FCRA primarily governs the accumulation and distribution of information that bears on an individual's creditworthiness by regulating consumer reporting agencies, such as credit bureaus, and establishing protections for consumers with regard to the privacy of their sensitive financial information. The FCRA was enacted, in part, to address privacy concerns associated with the sharing of consumers' financial and credit history contained in consumer credit reports. The Act limits the disclosure of consumer reports only to entities with specified "permissible purposes" (such as evaluating individuals for credit, insurance, employment, or similar purposes), and under specified conditions (including certification of the permissible purpose by the user of the report). It generally limits disclosure of consumer reports primarily to instances where a consumer initiates a transaction, such as an application for credit, employment, or insurance. The FCRA also provides consumers with certain rights in connection with the information maintained by consumer reporting agencies. The Federal Trade Commission (FTC) is the agency responsible for the enforcement of the federal FCRA.

In addition to regulating the manner in which the disclosure of personal information by consumer credit reporting agencies is regulated, the Act requires such services to adopt reasonable procedures to ensure the accuracy of the personal information contained in their credit reports. It also gives consumers a process for reviewing and correcting inaccurate information in a credit report.

This chapter will provide an overview of the FCRA in relation to third-party investigations occurring in the workplace, conflicts arising out of compliance with the FCRA and other statutes, investigations that affect an employee's work status, pre-employment background investigations, and due diligence investigations. Video surveillance and the "transactions or experiences" exception to the FCRA will be covered. In addition, there will be some comment on the significance of the FCRA and the increasing role of the Federal Trade Commission (FTC), the agency responsible for enforcement of the Fair Credit Reporting Act (FCRA), with respect to federal privacy legislation that affects investigators and security professionals. Enactment of important implications under the Fair and Accurate Credit Transactions Act of 2003 "FACT Act" will be covered as well.

1.2 Definitions

The implications of the FTC's expansion of their definition of what defines one as a *consumer reporting agency*, their interpretation of what constitutes an *investigative consumer report* and their analysis of the meaning *for employment purposes*, not only encompass the activities of private investigators, fraud examiners and security professionals, but may include outside counsel, attorneys, independent consultants, forensic specialists, auditors, and accountants. For the most part, they do not include in-house investigations, loss prevention or security investigations conducted by the employer's own personnel within the workplace.

A. Terminology

Investigators should not only have a general understanding of the FCRA, and its amendments, but should be familiar with the terms *disclosure, consent, certification, accuracy of information collected, adverse action, permissible purpose, obligations and liability*, and, to a limited extent, *immunity* from certain legal actions. Additional terms or phrases that will be covered are *regularly engaged* for *monetary fees* in the practice of *assembling or evaluating* consumer reports or *other information*" and *furnishing consumer reports to third parties.* These are all "terms of art" that are statutorily defined and subject to interpretation by the FTC and the courts.

B. Historical application

The U.S. Public Interest Research Group and the National Consumer Law Center present a slant on the historical application of the FCRA to investigative reports for employment purposes. They comment on the fact that its purpose was not to correct errors in standardized factual credit reports but to rein in the investigative reporting industry, pointing out what Senator William Proxmire, who had introduced the bill, had called devastating impacts on consumers in employment related investigations.

According to the 1969 *Congressional Record*, the senator commenting on malicious gossip and hearsay, stated:

> Perhaps the most serious misinformation in credit reporting files is malicious gossip and hearsay. This type of information is the most prevalent in the files of credit reporting agencies which specialize in investigating people who apply for insurance and employment. The information is often obtained from neighbors and coworkers where the opportunity is ripe for anonymous character assassination. These kinds of investigations usually include detailed information on highly personal items. . . . Considering the gossipy information included in . . . insurance investigations it is frightening to think such information could affect a consumer's entire career. It is bad enough to be turned down for insurance. It is much worse to lose a job on the basis of an erroneous piece of information in a credit file.[1]

Consumer advocates note that the 1996 amendments to the FCRA came about as a result of such abuses and claim that Congress clearly realized that consumer reports on current employees were being used in the context of workplace misconduct, such as *"where the employer believes that fraudulent or criminal activity [of an employee] is ongoing and directly related to the employment involved."*[2]

These advocates cite a 1991 *Newsday* article as being representative of horror stories that Congress sought to address in their amendment, but which caused unintended consequences:

> Consider what happened to James Russell Wiggens of Washington, D.C. He was fired after Equifax told his employer he had been convicted of possession of cocaine. Equifax's report was erroneous, but it took Wiggens two years to get his job back.

> When Pan Am flight attendants applied to work for Delta Airlines, Equifax was working for Delta. Flight attendants say Equifax quizzed acquaintances of applicants about their sexual preferences, use of alcohol and financial circumstances. Now New York City's Human Rights Commission is trying to determine whether Delta's job-interviewing practices violated city anti-discrimination laws. Fine, but Wiggens' experience, and the charges by former Pan Am flight attendants, ought to be enough to persuade Congress to define clearly the line between legitimate background checks and Big Brother tactics.[3]

The 1996 amendments to the FCRA expanded privacy safeguards, primarily for employees, and imposed new requirements on users of consumer reports for employment purposes. They became effective September 30, 1997, and created additional obligations for employers and prospective employers that obtain, and utilize, either consumer reports or investigative consumer reports for employment purposes.

Disclosure requirements created unintended consequences that affect the manner in which investigations may be conducted and thus undermine the ability of an employer that retains outside investigators to investigate allegations of criminal activity and other types of misconduct related to employment, such as sexual harassment, employment discrimination, violence, theft, embezzlement or allegations of drug use.

Additional obligations were placed on the provider of investigative services that hinder the manner in which an investigation may be conducted, such as alerting the target employee in advance of undertaking the investigation by requiring notification and possibly furnishing the subject with unredacted investigative reports.

Passage of the FACT Act in 2003 was to eliminate some of the more onerous provisions relative to workplace investigations.

1.3 Pre-employment and Workplace Investigations

Investigations that commonly fall under the purview of the FCRA are pre-employment and workplace investigations. The manner in which the investigation is conducted, the party to whom the results of the investigation are given, the status of the investigator in relation to the client and subject of the investigation, are all factors in determining whether or not the investigation falls under the provisions of the FCRA.

A. FCRA provisions

In conducting corporate investigations, there are a number of provisions in the FCRA of which an investigator should be aware:

1. The investigator should have knowledge of the definitions of terms referred to in the FCRA, such as consumer, consumer report, investigative consumer report, consumer reporting agency, and investigative consumer reporting agency. The investigator should not only read the FCRA in its entirety, but should also study relevant important portions of the Act itself. For example, there are seventeen sections applicable to investigations conducted in the workplace. It is important to note that all requirements applicable to consumer reports are also applicable to investigative consumer reports. The FCRA, as amended, may be viewed on-line in its entirety in PDF format at http://www.ftc.gov/os/statutes/fcrajump.htm.
2. The investigator should know the permissible purposes for which a consumer report may be accessed and, equally important, know if such information is actually a consumer report once it is obtained. In addition, he or she must possess knowledge of the authorizations that must be executed and the disclosure statements that must also be made.
3. The investigator must know the nuances of the use of the report that come into play when determining if the information obtained actually falls under the purview of the FCRA.
4. The investigator and client should be aware of the sanctions imposed in violation of the provisions of the FCRA that are a legal mine field.
5. The investigator should be familiar with the Federal Trade Commission's letter opinion rulings, issued periodically, that have significant impact on whether or not an investigation falls under the Act. Some key letter opinions are appended for review. A complete index of all FCRA staff opinion letters may be found at http://www.ftc.gov/os/statutes/fcra/index.htm.
6. Both the investigator and client should be familiar with the types of investigations that may conceivably fall under the FCRA, and which, after complying with the provisions of the

FCRA in the course of the investigation, may conflict with provisions of other federal or state statutes mandating the manner in which certain investigations need to be conducted.

7. The investigator should look at consumer reports and FCRA provisions in light of other public records that are routinely accessed or obtained.
8. The investigator should be aware of the functions of the Federal Trade Commission not only under the FCRA but also in light of regulations governing personally identifiable information, financial information, and acts that the FTC regards as deceptive practices—such as the use of pretexts—and the way in which the FCRA is being used to propose or enact privacy legislation, and the increased jurisdiction being given to the FTC that affects the manner in which corporate investigations are undertaken.
9. The investigator should have some familiarity with key court decisions affecting the FCRA.

B. FCRA terms

1. Consumer

The definition of a "consumer" according to the FCRA is an "individual." If the definition were to have been limited to just an individual who is the subject of a credit report, or to the person seeking credit, there would be little need in this chapter for commenting upon the extent that the FCRA provisions must be considered when undertaking investigations in the workplace or conducting an inquiry that affects a person's employment status. Unfortunately, the act does not limit its applicability to just a consumer's creditworthiness, credit standing, or credit capacity.

2. Consumer report

The term "consumer report" means any written, oral or, other communication of any information by a consumer reporting agency bearing on a consumer's credit worthiness, credit standing, credit capacity, character, general reputation, personal characteristics, or mode of living which is used, or expected to be used, or collected in whole or in part for the purpose of serving as a factor in establishing the consumer's eligibility for:

(a) credit or insurance purposes, (b) employment purposes, or (c) any other purpose authorized under Section 604. [15 U.S.C. §1681 a(d)(1)]

3. Employment purposes

The report must have been prepared for one of the foregoing listed purposes, which in this case would be for an "employment purpose." The term "employment purpose" means that the report is being "used for the purpose of evaluating an individual for employment, promotion, reassignment, or retention as an employee." [§1681a(h)] In contrast, a third party retained to defend a lawsuit who undertakes an investigation to prepare the client company's defense is generally not producing a "consumer report." Investigations for purposes of litigation, in most cases, according to verbal FTC staff attorney opinions, fall outside the purview of the FCRA.

Of importance to the investigator are letter rulings of the Federal Trade Commission related to conducting investigations by a third party in the workplace; the most notable being commonly referred to as the *Judith A. Vail staff opinion*. Although that opinion addressed the issue of sexual harassment, it actually applied to all employee misconduct investigations. It affected investigations of theft, embezzlement, fraud, workplace threats and violence, safety hazards, misuse of property, disclosure of trade secrets, and other types of employee misconduct such as drug or alcohol abuse.

1.4 The Opinion Letter

Until the passage of the Fair and Accurate Credit Transactions Act in 2003, the 1999 amendments to the FCRA presented an obstacle in properly conducting investigations that remotely affected a person's employment status. Strict compliance with the FCRA by the retained private investigator, fraud examiner, or security consultant and their clients, created a conflict of law with the manner in which one had to investigate allegations of sexual harassment. It failed to provide protection for an employee of the client with a legitimate case against his or her supervisor and posed greater threat of physical harm or retaliation by an employee suspected of engaging in violent or threatening behavior in the workplace.

The FTC, on April 5, 1999, issued the *Judith Vail* opinion letter. Its position was that when a third party (i.e., private investigator, fraud examiner, or security consultant) undertook a workplace investigation involving any type of employee misconduct, or an investigation of alleged wrongdoing by a current employee, the investigator (or third party) was a "consumer reporting agency" and as such was preparing an "investigative consumer report."

The FTC broadly interpreted the FCRA as applying to cases where an employer retains a third party to conduct an investigation in the workplace. According to the *Vail* letter, the investigation was regarded as an "adverse action" and the entity conducting the investigation was a "consumer reporting agency" that compiles an "investigative consumer report" for the client-employer's use.

Third-party investigators are generally hired to conduct a thorough investigation because of their special expertise, independence, and resources. In-house investigations do not fall under the onerous restrictions of the FCRA, but many employers lack the resources to conduct them. The FTC interpretations of the FCRA in relation to outside investigators discouraged an employer from conducting an investigation.

In a fraud or theft investigation, had a suspect employee failed to give consent after receiving the FTC-mandated notice from the employer, he or she could prevent the investigation (by an outside investigator) taking place. The suspect employee then also had the opportunity to destroy incriminating evidence and conspire with coworkers who might also be involved in the fraud or theft to collaborate on their cover stories. Thus, the element of surprise was completely eliminated from the arsenal of the investigator. Although the required advanced notice and disclosure aspects of the *Vail* letter were to be addressed by Congress with passage of the FACT Act in 2003 the reasoning of the *Vail* opinion letter reflects the position of the FTC with regard to interpreting the FCRA. For this reason the implications of *Vail* remain in this edition for future reference.

1.5 Best Evidence Requirement

A little-known aspect of the FCRA is what is referred to as the "best evidence" requirement. FCRA provisions require that information contained in an investigative consumer report adverse to the interest of the employee, that is based on personal interviews, must either be confirmed from sources with independent knowledge or the person interviewed must have been the best possible source. This impediment to a third-party investigation may hamper investigations that are based primarily on circumstantial evidence. An interview that yields adverse information may be supported by independent facts or evidence only and not corroborated by any other individual. Thus the best possible source of evidence may be unavailable to the investigator.

1.6 Mandated Disclosure

The provision of the FCRA that mandates disclosure of information to the employee creates a doubly chilling effect. First, a complainant or whistle-blower advising the employer of illegal activity on the part of a suspect employee consumer loses his or her anonymity. Second, the investigator cannot report with full candor in the written report knowing that the suspect employee may obtain access to it at a later date.

Finally, there is also the added burden of possibly having to resolve disputes with the suspect employee over the contents of the investigator's report should its completeness or accuracy be questioned. This provision of the FCRA may very well be warranted in the case of information that remains in someone's credit file. However, this is an overly burdensome requirement on outside investigations that produce a report that involved an analysis of voluminous records, dead-end leads, and numerous interviews.

Complex outside investigations concerning an employee for a single client employer should not be compared with credit-related investigations of credit reporting agencies that primarily collect information from publicly available documents and commercial databases and which, in turn, sell their report to multiple customers.

> On March 30, 2004, FACT Act, the Fair and Accurate Credit Transactions Act, became effective and amended Section 603 of the FCRA to provide that employers or their investigators need not provide notice or obtain employee permission to order the investigation of suspected employee misconduct, nor no longer need obtain the employer's certification that the requisite notices have been given to the suspect(s).
>
> The changes also provide that the employer need not provide the employee with a copy of the investigative report but rather, after taking adverse action, " . . . *the employer shall disclose to the consumer a summary containing the nature and substance of the communication upon which the adverse action is based, except that the sources of information*

acquired solely for use in preparing what would be but for subsection (d)(2)(D) an investigative consumer report need not be disclosed."[4]

It should be noted however that the above change to the FCRA in no way altered the requirements for employers ordering a Consumer Report on job applicants or on existing employees for promotional purposes.

Employers must still make the requisite disclosure to the applicant or employee of their intent to order a consumer report or investigative consumer report and obtain permission. Investigators acting as consumer reporting agencies must still obtain certification from the employer indicating the disclosures have been made and written permission obtained before commencing the investigation.

1.7 Civil Liability

The FCRA imposes civil liability for both willful and negligent noncompliance by consumer reporting agencies and parties who procure reports from (or furnish information to) such agencies. It grants civil enforcement authority to the Federal Trade Commission, other federal agencies, and the states to seek both monetary and injunctive relief for violations of the Act. The potential monetary penalties include, for those who knowingly violate the FCRA, up to $2,500 per violation in a civil action brought by the Commission in district court, or damages incurred by residents of a state in an action brought by the attorney general (or other official or agency designated by the state) on their behalf. The FCRA also provides for criminal sanctions against parties who infringe on consumer privacy by unlawfully obtaining consumer reports. Some of the sanctions can be Draconian. Sections 616 and 617 of the Act allow the aggrieved plaintiff in a civil cause of action no limit on actual and punitive damages.

For negligent noncompliance, the aggrieved party may recover attorney fees and costs, in addition to the actual damages. Civil damages for willful noncompliance may include the greater of $1,000 or the actual damages, punitive damages, attorney fees, and costs.

Prior to the 2003 passage of FACT Act it had been pointed out by attorneys specializing in employment law that the FTC's broad interpretation under the *Vail* opinion letter could increase the risk of further litigation in lawsuits that were brought against employers and in which investigators were also named as defendants. Plaintiffs' attorneys could just add an additional cause of action, in boilerplate fashion, alleging failure to comply with the FTC's notice and disclosure requirements in order to fall under the unlimited actual and punitive damages that may be recovered under the FCRA.

One such example was the 1999 case of *Shane Salazar v. Golden State Warriors*, United States District Court for the Northern District of California (C994825), wherein the plaintiff sued his former employer for over $1,000,000. The undercover operation of an investigative firm was a key factor in the litigation. The plaintiff was observed using cocaine by the third-party investigator, and was fired by the Golden State Warriors. Salazar's use of an illegal substance was not at issue. His complaint alleged that the surveillance should not have been performed without his consent under the FCRA. Fortunately for the investigator, the court ruled that the surveillance fell under the "transactions or experiences" exclusion of the FCRA. A third-party investigator's direct questioning of the employee would not have fallen under the FCRA either.

That decision also commented on the investigator's method of obtaining leads while conducting the investigation which could have caused the plaintiff to prevail. Apparently the investigator accessed a third-party database of information concerning the plaintiff but did not provide the information in the investigative report submitted to the employer. In addition, motor vehicle plate searches were also run on vehicles observed while holding the plaintiff under surveillance but did not include any motor vehicle bureau information concerning Salazar. Since the information pertained only to other persons, the court ruled that the information did not constitute the creation of a consumer report. Thus, the court ruled that the investigator's report was solely a report of transactions or experiences and not an investigative consumer report. The FCRA is silent about sharing "transactional, experiential information."

Although this decision favored the investigator one should keep in mind that *oral reports fall under the restrictions of the FCRA*. In many instances an investigator provides oral interim reports during the course of handling an investigation and such information might easily create the existence of a record by the person taking the verbal report on behalf of the client employer.

1.8 Enforcement Powers

It should also be noted that the FTC under the FCRA has procedural, investigative, and enforcement powers and may bring an action to enforce any violation as an "unfair or deceptive act or practice" in violation of the Federal Trade Commission Act.

1.9 Consumer Reporting Agencies

The FCRA directly affects a company's ability to obtain background information on applicants and current employees through consumer reporting agencies after being amended in 1997 and again in 1998.

The FTC *Vail* letter opinion, and others, have insisted that the definition of "employment purposes" is to be "interpreted liberally."

The FCRA regulates the circumstances under which employers can use reporting agencies to obtain background information and to rely on that information in making hiring, promotion, transfer, and other employment decisions.

A consumer reporting agency is defined as

> any person which for monetary fees, dues or on a cooperative nonprofit basis, regularly engages in whole or in part in the practice of assembling or evaluating consumer credit information or other information on consumers for the purpose of furnishing consumer reports to third parties, and which uses any means or facility of interstate commerce for the purpose or furnishing consumer reports. [See §1681a(f)]

The private investigator, fraud examiner or security consultant conducting his or her first workplace investigation by definition cannot be a consumer reporting agency. He or she must "regularly" engage in conducting workplace investigations. However, what this definitively means is uncertain. Definitions of this term were commented upon by the judge in the federal case of *Rebecca Johnson v. Federal Express Corp.*, as covered later in this chapter.

Investigators, fraud examiners, and security professionals should familiarize themselves with the FCRA requirements for a "consumer reporting agency." They should review and be certain that their clients are familiar with the applicable FCRA requirements, including consent and disclosure requirements, additional disclosures required for "investigative consumer reports," pre-adverse action requirements, and adverse action requirements. One must be aware of the practical impact of the client using a third party to conduct the sensitive, often confidential, workplace investigation.

For example, prior to the FACTA Act, in an objective investigation involving allegations of sexual harassment, the client employer must have at a minimum obtained the consent of the alleged harasser prior to the commencement of the investigation. [15 U.S.C. §1681b(b)(2)] For typical investigations unrelated to suspected employee misconduct, which include personal interviews, investigative consumer reports are thus created which result in additional disclosure requirements. [§1681d(a)(1)]

In a non-suspected workplace misconduct investigation, within three days of requesting the investigation the client must provide the appropriate disclosure to the employee about the use of a third party to conduct the investigation and provide the FTC's prepared Summary of Rights. [§1681d(a)(1)]

The employer client must also provide a complete and accurate disclosure of the nature and scope of any investigative consumer investigation if the employee requests such report.

The client is required to advise the alleged harasser, in writing, about the nature and the scope of the investigation, if it was requested, within five days of the request or within five days of requesting the investigation. [§1681d(b)]

Finally, should the employer decide to take adverse action against the employee based upon a consumer report, it must first provide the employee with a full, unredacted copy of the report. [§1681b(b)(3)]

1.10 Legislative Relief

The National Council of Investigation & Security Services (NCISS), together with the American Society for Industrial Security (ASIS) and the National Association of Legal Investigators, Inc. (NALI), worked diligently during three sessions of Congress to gain passage of legislation to rectify the unintended consequences of the 1996 amendments to the FCRA. In 1999, a proposal was introduced by Republican Congressman Pete Sessions of Texas, as the Fair Credit Reporting Act Amendments of 1999 to enact amendments to § 603(d)(2)(A) of the Fair Credit Reporting Act [15 U.S.C. § 1681a(d)(2)(A)]. Although it had bipartisan support, it was not passed in the 106th Congress. It was reintroduced in 2001 in the 107th Congress with the bipartisan co-sponsorship of Representative Sheila Jackson-Lee, Democrat of Texas, as H.R. 1543, the Civil Rights and Employee Investigation Clarification Act. It failed to pass in that session as well. In 2003 Congressman Sessions reintroduced an identical bill and its beneficial provisions eventually became a part of the FACT Act, which was signed into law by President George W. Bush in December 2004.

This bill corrects the blatant, although unintended, defect in the original Fair Credit Reporting Act by affording confidentiality to investigations into such matters as sexual harassment or potential violence in the workplace, employee fraud, embezzlement or dishonesty, and workplace safety. Congress finally recognized that these types of investigations, conducted by third parties, had been rendered largely useless because of the notification and consent requirements that were originally intended to apply to credit reports.

A third-party investigative report falling under the FCRA had to be furnished to the employee suspect in an unredacted form if it resulted in adverse actions relating to the affected employee. This effectively provided a target list to an employee about to go "postal."

In addition, the prior FCRA requirements had been in conflict with EEOC provisions relating to the release of information provided by complainants.

In essence the enactment of FACTA, strongly supported by our profession, has now excluded communications "made to an employer in connection with an investigation of suspected misconduct relating to employment, or compliance with federal, state, or local laws, the rules of a self-regulatory organization, or any preexisting written policies of the employer"

Presently, FACTA provides that after taking any adverse action based in whole or in part on such a communication the employer shall disclose to the consumer [i.e., employee] a summary containing the nature and substance of the communication upon which the adverse action is based.

1.11 Law Enforcement Issues

The U.S. Department of Justice had also expressed concern about the implications of applying the FCRA for law enforcement investigations and about corporate compliance and self-reporting programs that are encouraged by the government. Although recognizing the importance of the FCRA in protecting consumers' and employees' rights against the dissemination of inaccurate or misleading personal information, the Justice Department believes that applying the previous provisions of the FCRA to the use of outside entities by employers to conduct good faith investigations of allegations of civil or criminal wrongdoing posed serious negative consequences for law enforcement and corporate compliance programs.

Such provisions as interpreted by the *Vail* opinion letter could lead to the "premature disclosure of law enforcement investigations, inhibit the voluntary disclosure of criminal activities, create potential procedural rights for criminal defendants, and lead to needless litigation." If the FTC's interpretations had ever been accepted by the courts, "employers would be subject to the full panoply of disclosure obligations under the FCRA, including that the employer must provide a complete, unredacted copy of any report, including the names of witnesses and their statements, to the employee before taking any adverse employment action."[5]

Complainants and witnesses would hesitate to give complete statements or fail to come forward if they knew that their identities and the complete contents of their statements would be disclosed to the subject of the investigation, thus exposing them to intimidation or retaliation by the subject.

Companies might refrain from retaining an outside experienced professional investigator or decline to conduct an investigation out of fear that having to "disclose the results to any wrongdoing employee may cause them to place limits on the contents of the report, thus affecting their ability to properly evaluate the results of the investigation and limiting the content and completeness of any resulting disclosure to law enforcement."

Since the FCRA required the disclosure of the contents of an investigative report prior to taking an adverse employment action, another possible unintended consequence of the Act might be the question of whether or not a referral itself to a law enforcement agency constituted an adverse employment action.

From a law enforcement perspective, disclosures deprived their investigators of the opportunity to properly conduct surveillance or running an undercover operation hoping to obtain admissions from the employee subject and identifying others in criminal activity. Also of concern was the possibility that the subject, by the very fact of the disclosure, might be afforded the opportunity to destroy evidence or tamper with witnesses.

1.12 Attorney-Client Privilege

Some lawyers have argued that investigations performed under the "attorney work product" rule will not fall under the FCRA. Others argue that, under *Vail*, there is no such exemption. They hold that the FTC opinion compromises privileges recognized by the Federal Rules of Civil Procedure and most states' rules of civil procedure with regard to attorney-client privilege, work product, and third-party reports prepared by investigators in anticipation of litigation. Although, as indicated earlier, the FTC has informally stated that in most instances such would be exempt, a literal interpretation of *Vail* would seem to be otherwise.

A federal court decision in the 2001 case of *Hazel Hartman v. Lisle Park District* [United States District Court, Northern District of Illinois, (01 C 1904)] concerned a plaintiff who had reported alleged misconduct of a district park director. The case involved First Amendment protection issues as well as the Illinois Whistleblower Reward and Protection Act. Hartman claimed that during the course of an investigation conducted by the co-defendant law firm representing her employer (the park district) that their investigation of her resulted in their preparing a "consumer report" within the meaning of the FCRA. Furthermore it was claimed that they did not notify her that they were investigating her, nor did they obtain her consent or furnish her with a copy of their report. The above fact situation certainly would have been the scenario under *Vail*.

The court held that under

> [t]he prevailing principles of administrative law, Federal Trade Commission opinion letters (referring to *Vail*) interpreting the Fair Credit Reporting Act are entitled to respect by [the] district court to the extentthat FTC interpretations have the power to persuade on issue, but opinion letters are not entitled to deference.

If the decision had been limited to just this conclusion, third-party investigators might have felt some hope that their reports would escape the

FCRA restrictions. However, the court went further. Surprisingly the co-defendant law firm's report of that law firm's

> [i]nvestigation of dealings by the public employee [Hartman] of the park district with district did not allegedly concern employee's credit history, her character, her general reputation, or her personal characteristics or mode of living, and thus report was not within the scope of the Fair Credit Reporting Act.

Furthermore, the alleged report prepared by the law firm concerned the employee's transactions or experiences with the firm's client employer and was not a "consumer report" within the meaning of the FCRA and, although the report was prepared by the law firm and not the employer, the firm had an attorney-client relationship with the employer when the report was prepared and was not acting as a consumer reporting agency. The court also held that an attorney is an agent of his or her client and the client is bound by the attorney's acts and statements made within the scope of their relationship.

The court also went further, stating:

> Even if alleged report by [the] law firm, which investigated alleged workplace misconduct by [the] public employee, was within the scope of the FCRA, [the] firm was not [a] "consumer reporting agency" within [the] meaning of FCRA. [The] firm was not [a] "third party" in the same way that [a] credit bureau or detective agency was, in that [the] firm acted as fiduciary and agent for [the] employer, their client.

The court had also noted that the then FTC Chairman Robert Pitofsky, in a letter of March31, 2000, to Rep. Pete Sessions, concerning proposed amendments at that time to the FCRA, had stated that

> [i]n the employment context, an outside agency (such as a private investigator or law firm) that regularly conducts investigations of alleged workplace misconduct by employees is very likely a "consumer reporting agency" and the report it makes to an employer is likely to be a 'consumer report' within the meaning of the FCRA.

It would probably be a wise course of action for a third-party investigator first to attempt to be retained by the employer's outside counsel and submit all reports as attorney work product with the caveat that they are privileged and confidential. Some states also have provisions under their licensing statutes indicating that disseminating reports of private investigators to anyone other than the client, absent a court order or subpoena, or in some cases to regulatory bodies or law enforcement, as being unlawful.

In the *Hartman* decision the court, in referring both to the credit bureau or a detective agency, wrote:

> Unlike those types of contract workers, the attorney has a relationship, of trust, confidence, and confidentiality with his client and owes a duty of loyalty that among other things precludes the attorney from taking on engagements that would give rise to a conflict with the client's interest.

Although such relationships are nonexistent between a credit bureau and its clients that gain information that is sold for specific reasons to multiple customers, licensed private investigators certainly are held to a standard under various state laws that would invariably result in the loss of licensure if any of the above stated standards that the court ascribed to attorneys were violated by the licensed private investigator.

There was another 2001 significant court decision, *Rebecca Johnson v. Federal Express Corp.* [United States District Court, M.D. Alabama, Northern Division (CIV A. 00-D-354-N)] which, like *Salazar v. Golden State Warriors*, fell under the "transactions or experiences" provision. This decision also covered the definition of "regularly engaging in assembling or evaluating consumer information," which term is used to bring most third-party outside investigators under the restrictions of the FCRA when conducting workplace investigations.

FedEx had terminated their employee, the plaintiff, after a forensic document examiner had compared handwriting exemplars from her to an anonymous note that had been sent to management threatening to "come in here one day and shoot up this place" and found it very likely that she had written the note. She claimed discrimination, violation of the FCRA, and a number of state law torts. Her claims (including the FCRA claim) were dismissed, except for one involving false imprisonment (FedEx security had questioned her at their offices for over seven hours). Here we are only concerned with the FCRA implications.

The plaintiff in her claim that FCRA provisions had been violated, relied on the *Vail* opinion as well as the letter ruling *Susan R. Meisinger opinion of August 31, 1999*, which is included in the Appendix at the end of this chapter. The letter writers happened to be two employment law attorneys, the latter having been executive vice-president and chief operating officer of the Society of Human Resource Management and a former deputy undersecretary of labor. They had sought an opinion from the FTC and asked that agency to assume that an employer wished to investigate a charge of sexual harassment leveled against an employee. The issues presented in the letters were whether an investigative report, relying on company documents and conversations with employees compiled by an outside agency, constituted an "investigative consumer report" under the FCRA. Both of the FTC's *Vail* and *Meisinger* letters opined that they did and that the employer does indeed trigger the FCRA if it uses such information to take adverse employment action.

Johnson contended that the forensic document examiner was a "consumer reporting agency" and that his handwriting analysis was a "consumer report" or an "investigative report," and that FedEx violated the Act by procuring the report and relying on it for "employment purposes" without complying with the statute's numerous notice-and-delay requirements which the court described as "onerous." [15 U.S.C. §§ 1681a(d)-(f),(h), 1681b(b) 1681d.] Under the FCRA, FedEx would have been obligated to notify the plaintiff employee that a report was being obtained, provide her a copy of it before taking any adverse action, and afford her reasonable time to challenge the report's accuracy.

The report from the forensic document examiner who had tested the employees' writing samples firsthand "drew conclusions based on his personal knowledge therefrom [and] was based entirely on information supplied by employees, and, thus, not [a] 'consumer reporting agency' within the meaning of the FCRA." The provision thus exempts any report based on the reporter's firsthand experience with the subject (i.e., the handwriting).

The court also pointed out that neither the FCRA nor its legislative history define the term "regularly," necessitating the court to look for guidance in the Fair Debt Collection Practices Act (FDCPA) which has statutes similar to the FCRA and which also protects consumers. The FDCPA defines a debt collector "as any person . . . who regularly collects or attempts to collect debts owed to others." The court quoted a Sixth Circuit opinion on the definition of "regularly" by quoting *Black's Law Dictionary*, stating that "[t]he term 'regularly' means 'at fixed and certain intervals, regular in point of time. In accordance with some consistent or periodical rule of practice.' The term 'regular' means 'usual, customary, normal or general. . . . Antonym of 'casual' or 'occasional'." Thus, the court concluded that a debt collector "must have more than an 'occasional' involvement with debt collection activities to qualify as a 'debt collector' under the FDCPA."

The court in the Johnson case stated:

> That by regulating only those consumer reporting agencies that "regularly engage" in reporting, Congress opted for incomplete coverage of the industry. Therefore, the court holds that a consumer reporter must provide consumer reports as a part of his usual, customary, and general course of his business if he is to qualify as a "consumer reporting agency" under the FCRA.

The forensic document examiner had indicated that he rarely evaluated consumer information, that he performed document analysis on behalf of various types of clients that included criminal prosecutors, public defenders, police departments, plaintiff and defendant civil attorneys, and corporations, and that approximately 85 to 90 percent of his business involved criminal matters or consultation in ongoing litigation matters. In addition to stating that he did not regularly engage in assembling or evaluating consumer information, he indicated that less than 10 percent of his business related to employment matters. The court determined that it need not know precisely at what point an outside investigator becomes a reporting agency to find that this forensic examiner did not qualify as being one but did point out that reporting was not the examiner's usual and customary and general course of business and was less than 10 percent of his work.

The court had also found the opinion letters not binding and not persuasive and agreed with other commentators that "the application of the FCRA's notice-and-delay provisions would undermine the efficiency and efficacy of employers' legitimate workplace investigations." In addition, the court noted that the

> FTC appears to have drawn a false analogy between employment decisions, by a present or prospective employer, based on information about a consumer's general status (such as credit, criminal or family history and the like) and a decision by a present employer about consumer's particular workplace conduct (such as his threats of violence).

Unfortunately, the court stated that it "need not enter this thicket, however, to find that Johnson has offered no evidence that [forensic examiner] is a 'consumer reporting agency,' or that Johnson's handwriting sample does not fall within FCRA's exception to its otherwise capacious definition of 'consumer report.'" [15 U.S.C. § 1681a(d)(2).] It would have been enlightening to have the ruling address the issue of a third-party investigation entity, with a wide range of clients, experiences, and objectives other than establishing the employee's work status, as being a consumer reporting agency or an investigative consumer agency.

1.13 Protection

Even with the passage of FACT Act, which remedied most defects in the FCRA as regards to workplace misconduct, there are some steps that employers might still consider to protect themselves and the outside investigator. They are:

1. Provide those mandatory disclosures to all employees at the time of their hiring.
2. Instruct the outside investigator to omit from the report the identities of all witnesses and parties interviewed.

The foregoing suggestions were offered in the *Meisinger* opinion letter authored by the then associate director of the FTC's Division of Financial Practices. However, previously informal verbal FTC staff opinions had indicated that disclosure and consent forms signed by an applicant would be insufficient to cover subsequent investigations and that the new hires would have to sign another form at the time of the ensuing investigation.

Even though the courts were basically rejecting the *Vail* opinion, the issues regarding workplace employee misconduct investigations as regards to reporting and disclosure requirements were not resolved until the passage of FACT Act, effective March 31, 2004.

1.14 Outside Investigators

Third-party outside investigators are often called upon to determine whether or not a crime was committed, determine the responsible party, or recover the stolen goods. The purpose of the investigation is not for an "employment purpose in determining an employee's future retention or employment status," although the results of the investigation may eventually be a determining factor. There are many reasons that workplace investigations may be conducted and their initial purposes relate to federal statutes other than the FCRA.

Although the labor movement has gone on record as favoring workplace investigations by third-party investigators, they basically seek to limit such to Title VII-related investigations and still retain some of the FCRA restrictions. They are fearful of those employers that use surveillance as a tool to deter workers from exercising their rights under the Fair Labor Standards Act and the National Labor Relation Act to organize unions.

They acknowledge that in-house investigators often lack the skill that outside third-party investigators possess; viewing them as a far greater threat. In written testimony in 2000 by the AFL-CIO regarding amending the FCRA for workplace investigation they wrote:

> Under the pretext of investigating allegations of theft, product tampering, drug use, racial or sexual harassment, and other illegal misconduct, third party investigators gain access to a wide range of information about workers. Some investigations focus on particular individuals. Others cast a much broader net under the guise of enforcing anti-theft or anti-drug policies. Regardless of which type of investigation the employer conducts, much of the information remains unverified, and much of it is the product of coercive and deceptive techniques.
>
> Improper third party investigators present a particular threat to workers' rights that is significantly greater than that posed by employer investigations. Professional investigators are adept at mining the wealth of infor-

> mation available on the Internet that can be obtained on individuals. They have resources and expertise to conduct wide ranging interviews outside the workplace that lie beyond the capabilities of the typical employer. They often have operatives trained to pose as employees for the purpose of collecting information from other employees. They have access to surveillance technology that the typical employer does not have. It is entirely appropriate that the FCRA seeks to provide certain protection for consumers in as well out of the workplace against the abuse of these formidable tools.

As noted in the court decisions mentioned previously, those concerns described by the AFL-CIO, related to surveillance and the use of undercover operatives, would not fall under the FCRA in most cases. Although in certain types of workplace investigations they are willing to concede that advance notice to a target employee may be a problem, their greater concern is that at some point the employee be at least notified that an investigation has taken place, whether or not any adverse action has been taken. They do not want employers building dossiers on their employees under the ruse of conducting a workplace investigation for nebulous safety purposes when they are actually attempting to curtail union organizing or collective bargaining activities. Of course, the concerns of the unions can already be address by means other than the FCRA.

1.15 EEOC and Other Federal Laws

A. EEOC

The FCRA and the FTC's opinion letters directly conflict with other federal laws. The Equal Employment Opportunity Commission was troubled by the FTC's conclusion and concerned that the FCRA's specific requirements controlling third-party discrimination investigations would have unintended consequences for the enforcement of civil rights laws in the workplace. Employers are charged with the duty of maintaining a workplace free from discrimination and harassment. Having to provide the harasser or wrongdoer with the identity and complete unredacted complaint of the victim or complainant as indicated earlier would have a chilling effect and would deter witnesses from coming forward.

B. Drug-Free Workplace Act and Occupational Safety and Health Act

The Drug-Free Workplace Act imposes a duty on employers to investigate and eliminate drug use in the workplace. OSHA requires employers to provide a safe workplace, and there are regulations imposing a duty on the employer to investigate potential hazards including exposure to workplace violence.

C. Department of Health and Human Services Office

There are many statutes and regulations with respect to self-reporting programs that encourage corporations to hire outside investigators. For example, the Department of Health and Human Services Office of the Inspector General issued a compliance guidance program for managed care companies which "discovers from any source evidence of misconduct related to payment or delivery of health care items or services under the Medicare+Choice Contract should conduct a timely, reasonable inquiry into the misconduct . . ."

D. Foreign Corrupt Practices Act

Other professions may fall under the outside third-party investigator mandates. The U.S. Attorney General's Office noted in a consent agreement in a Foreign Corrupt Practices Act case that a company must designate officers with "the authority and responsibility to implement and utilize monitoring and auditing systems reasonably designed to detect criminal conduct by the company's employees and other agents, including where appropriate, the retention of outside counsel and independent auditors to conduct investigations and audits."

E. Food, Drug and Cosmetic Act

Under the Food, Drug and Cosmetic Act, drug and device manufacturers engage in extensive testing of products being brought to market. They are concerned with falsification of test data and product tampering by employees. The advance notice requirement about the scope of the investigation would make it unlikely to detect error during research and would allow the destruction of evidence. The government contends that any FCRA procedures that impede a thorough investigation into drug or device testing pose a threat to the public's health and safety.

F. Whistle Blower Act

There are also "whistle blower" statutes that encourage employees to come forward with information without fear of reprisal. The FCRA notice provisions deter informants from providing evidence due to the disclosure of their identities in the final report. Other programs that encourage self-reporting include the AntiKickback Act of 1986 and the False Claims Act.

G. Privacy issues

Issues involving credit header access, identity theft, pretexting of financial institutions and their customers, acquisition of personally identifiable information, and the use of social security numbers as a national identifier have contributed to the emergence of legislation restricting investigators use of heretofore recognized investigative techniques. Such legislation often either directly affects the implementation of the FCRA or at a minimum requests oversight in some manner from the FTC.

Unions, consumer groups, and privacy advocates are of the opinion that it was a mistake when the 1994 consent decree between the FTC and TRW (subsequently known as Experian) allowed for certain "sensitive personal information," commonly referred to "credit header" information contained in credit reports, to be exempt from the definition of a credit report. Such advocacy groups have sought to close what they term a loophole in the FCRA.

The credit header, a term that initially defined the top portion of a credit report, limits the information to name, addresses, date of birth, social security number, and telephone numbers. Places of employment were at one time often revealed as well; credit standing and such information was not. The "big three" have sold credit header information in bulk. In 1997 the FTC issued the *Individual Reference Services, A Report to Congress*. An extensive workshop was held, with all sides of the credit header issue heard, after which the FTC allowed computerized database services that sell personally identifiable information about consumers—referred to as the individual reference services group (IRSG)—to put forth proposals for self-regulation.

Principles were established regarding control, access, and dissemination of credit header information. A time period was set to monitor self-regulation of the information broker industry (at least, those who were members of the IRSG). Audit trails and a three-tiered customer category scheme were implemented. Law enforcement and private investigators were allowed the highest access of record procurement. For example, the individual's social security number was to be provided in full and not truncated.

The FTC acknowledged that there were permissible uses for such information by private investigators for many purposes, such as locating witnesses, identifying parties and witnesses with a financial stake in the outcome of cases, finding assets to satisfy judgments, conducting due diligence investigations of financial representations, and locating pension fund beneficiaries. Each of the forgoing purposes at some point might be a part of a corporate investigation.

Some of the factors that have contributed to the plethora of restrictive legislation include

- abuses by information brokers, primarily those with an Internet website presence, as well as by unscrupulous private investigators;
- notorious incidents involving stalkers causing death or injury to victims located using information purchased from either info-brokers or private investigators; and
- the increasing identity theft crime wave.

In the 108th Congress, H.R. 2971 and S. 2801, the Social Security Number Privacy and Identity Theft Prevention Act, sponsored by Republican Representative E. Clay Shaw of Florida and Democrat Senator Dianne Feinstein of California, would have outlawed the use of credit headers. It failed to pass due to strong opposition lobbying efforts by the National Council of Investigation and Security Services. The beneficial sections of the bill were added to H.R. 10, the 9/11 Recommendations Implementation Act. This factor, combined with other ID theft legislation previously passed in 2004, negated the importance of passage of H.R.2971/S. 2901. However, similar detrimental legislation is expected to be introduced during the 109th Congress in 2005 and 2006 at the request of privacy advocates. NCISS is presently working closely with Senator Feinstein's staff to put forth legislation that will protect consumers from having their personal information sold over the Internet to the general public while still allowing such information to be obtained for legitimate business purposes by investigators.

H. Gramm-Leach-Bliley Act

The Gramm-Leach-Bliley Act, commonly referred to as GLBA, not only imposed restrictions on pretexting financial institutions and their customers, but the FTC interpreted the act as eliminating unrestricted acquisition and dissemination of credit headers.

1.16 A Review of the FCRA—Consumer Reports and Investigative Consumer Reports

With respect to pre-employment investigations, the following is an overview of some applicable provisions of the FCRA regulating the use of both "consumer reports" and "investigative consumer reports."

The Act directly affects an employer's ability to obtain background information on job applicants and current employees using consumer reporting agencies and investigative consumer reporting agencies. It regulates the circumstances under which such agencies obtain information that is relied upon by the employer in making hiring, promotion, transfer, and other employment decisions.

Prior to an employer retaining an outside investigator to conduct a pre-employment or background investigation on a current employee, the employer must certify to the consumer reporting agency (or for practicable purposes in this illustration, the investigator) that it has provided the applicant or employee a "clear and conspicuous" written disclosure that a report may be obtained for employment purposes. There was a time that such disclosure could be incorporated into an application for employment form. However, now such must be a "stand alone" document. That person must also provide the employer written authorization to procure the report.

When it appears that a third-party investigator will be used, background investigation consent requirements will probably be best met if the job applicant or employee signs a combined disclosure and consent form incorporating the consumer report and investigative consumer report notice and disclosure requirements. This is because a request for a consumer report will become a request for an investigative consumer report if the credit reporting agency does more than just "verify the facts."

Investigative consumer reports are consumer reports that include information obtained from personal interviews. It is the FTC's contention that one is not an investigative consumer reporting agency if merely verifying the accuracy of the information contained in an applicant's employment form because they do not consider such to be a personal interview.

However, once a question is posed such as "what was the person's reason for termination?" it is the position of the FTC that the inquiry is a personal interview and any response to such question that was contained in a consumer reporting agency's report is an investigative consumer report.

The employer is also mandated to certify to the investigator that before it will take any adverse action based in whole or in part on the investigator's report, it will furnish the applicant or employee with a copy of the report and provide a description of his or her rights under the FCRA, a FTC document. Included in the certification must be a statement that the information obtained will not be used in violation of any federal or state equal opportunity law or regulation.

After receiving the investigator's report, but before any adverse action is taken, the employer must provide the applicant or employee with a copy of the report and a written description of that person's rights under the law.

There are special provisions relating to disclosure of investigative consumer reports. Such a report may not be procured or caused to be prepared on any consumer "unless it is clearly and accurately disclosed to the consumer that an investigative consumer report including information as to his character, general reputation, personal characteristics and mode of living, whichever are applicable, may be made." [15 U.S.C. § 1681d]

Such disclosure must be either mailed or delivered to the consumer, no later than three days after the report was first requested and must include a statement advising the recipient of the right to request additional disclosures and also provide a list of all federal agencies responsible for enforcing any provision of this title, along with their addresses and telephone numbers.

The FCRA says that a consumer report is

> [a]ny written, oral or other communication of any information by a consumer reporting agency bearing on a consumer's (person's) creditwor-

> thiness, credit standing, credit capacity, character, general reputation, personal characteristics, or mode of living which is used or expected to be used or collected in whole or in part for the purpose of serving as a factor in establishing the consumer's eligibility for employment purposes.

Criminal background checks, motor vehicle bureau reports, and credit checks are typical examples of consumer reports when a consumer reporting agency furnishes such information to an employer.[6]

An investigative consumer report is

> [a] consumer report in which information on a consumer's character, general reputation, personal characteristics, or mode of living is obtained through personal interviews with neighbors, friends, or associates of the consumer reported on, or with others with whom he is acquainted or who may have knowledge concerning any such items of information.

Thus, when an investigative consumer reporting agency (an investigator) interviews a job applicant's or employee's friends, neighbors, associates, acquaintances, or others with knowledge, and provides this information to an employer to use in making employment decisions, the information is likely an investigative consumer report. The common example of such a report is when the consumer reporting agency contacts an applicant's or an employee's former employers, and reports this information to a prospective or current employer.

One must be aware of the fact that the Act states that

> [a] consumer reporting agency shall not prepare or furnish an investigative consumer report on a consumer that contains information that is adverse to the interest of the consumer and that is obtained through a personal interview with a neighbor, friend, or associate of the consumer or with another person with whom the consumer is acquainted or who has knowledge of such items of information, unless that agency has followed reasonable procedures to obtain confirmation of the information, from an additional source that has independent and direct knowledge of the information. or the person interviewed is the best source of the information.

In addition to the FCRA, which is federal, many states have enacted their own fair credit reporting laws, some of which are different from and, in some instances, more restrictive than the FCRA. This chapter does not attempt to cover the various state laws applicable to pre-employment investigations.

The Consumer Reporting Clarification Act of 1998 further amended the FCRA and brought about a significant change in the manner in which records of criminal convictions are reported. Previously, consumer reporting agencies were precluded from providing employers with "records of arrest, indictment, or conviction of a crime, which date of disposition, release, or parole, [that] antedate the report by more than seven years." An employer may now obtain from the consumer reporting agency records of criminal conviction without any time limitations imposed. However, under the FCRA, criminal arrest information remains limited to the past seven years, unless the pre-employment investigation pertains to a position where the annual salary is, or is expected to equal, $75,000 or more. *Investigators should check their state laws prior to obtaining and disclosing arrest conviction information.*

Cases under Title 11 or under the Bankruptcy Act that, from the date of entry of the order of relief or the date of adjudication, as the case may be, antedate the report by more than ten years may not be reported and must be excluded from consumer reports. If the applicant or employee, prior to final judgment, withdrew the bankruptcy then the investigator's report must indicate "that such case or filing was withdrawn upon receipt of documentation certifying such withdrawal."

Suits and judgments from date of judgment, paid tax liens from date of payment, accounts placed for collection or charged to profit and loss, and any other adverse items of information which antedate the report by seven years may not be reported and is information that must be excluded from consumer reports. Investigators conducting employment background checks should also review their respective state laws regarding reporting prohibitions, restrictions, and additional time limitations.

In due diligence investigations the permissible use under the category of having a legitimate need for the information was at one time often used in accessing credit reports. However, that permissible purpose was amended to read that a consumer reporting agency might furnish a consumer report

> [t]o a person which it has reason to believe . . . intends to use the information, as a potential investor or servicer, or current insurer, in connection with a valuation of, or an assessment of the credit or prepayment risks associated with, an existing credit obligation. or otherwise has a legitimate business need for the information in connection with a business transaction that is initiated by the consumer. . . .

Thus, the individual subject of the due diligence investigation must have initiated the business transaction to allow the investigator access to a consumer report. However, no such requirement exists for obtaining reports about a business when conducting a due diligence investigation.

> There is a limitation of liability. Except as provided in 15 U.S.C. §§ 1681n and 1681o of the FCRA, no consumer (employee) "may bring any action or proceeding in the nature of defamation, invasion of privacy, or negligence with respect to the reporting of information against any consumer reporting agency, any user of information, or any person who furnishes information to a consumer reporting agency, based on information disclosed pursuant to Sections 1681g, 1681h, or 1681m of the Act or based on information disclosed by a user of a consumer report to or for a consumer against whom the user has taken adverse action, based whole or in part on the report, except as to false information furnished with malice or willful intent to injure such consumer."

Endnotes

1. 115 Cong.Rec.2411 (Jan 31, 1969).

2. Testimony of the National Consumer Law Center and the U.S. Public Interest Research Group (PIRG) before the U.S. House of Representatives Committee on Banking and Financial Services, Subcommittee on Financial Institutions and Consumer Credit regarding Employer Investigations of Employee Misconduct in Relation to the Fair Credit Reporting Act. May 4, 2000.

3. "Real Bad Vibes," Newsday, December 10, 1991, p. 50.

4. Statement of James K. Robinson, Assistant Attorney General, Commercial Division, before the U.S. House of Representatives Committee on Banking and Financial Services, Subcommittee on Financial Institutions and Consumer Credit concerning the Application of the Fair Credit Reporting Act to

Investigations of Workplace Misconduct. May 4, 2000.

5. 2001 U.S. Dist. Lexis 12414. Memorandum Opinion and Order. Matthew F. Kennedy, District Judge.

6. 2001 WL936165 (N.D.III).

Appendix

Appended is the FCRA required notice to inform users of consumer reports of their legal obligations and responsibilities. It outlines the permissible purposes, certifications, adverse action requirements, and obligations of users and resellers of consumer reports.

Also appended are FTC opinion letters relating to third-party workplace investigations, public record searchers, and the "legitimate business need for information in connection with a business transaction that is initiated by a consumer."

There is no single comprehensive law that addresses the use of personal consumer information. Appended is a list of federal privacy laws currently dealing with personal privacy in the commercial context that investigators should be aware of in addition to the FCRA.

Chapter 2

Assessing Credibility: ADVA Technology, Voice and Voice Stress Analysis

John J. Palmatier, Ph.D.

Synopsis

2.1 Introduction

In a recent investigation, in which I played a small role by testing the credibility of several suspect's stories, employees and a supervisor from one of the big three automakers stole automobile parts valued in excess of $1 million.

The investigation eventually focused in part on a refuse company that had been contracted to remove scrap from one of the automobile manufacturer's warehouses. An innovative employee working for the automobile manufacturer befriended one of the refuse drivers asking him how he would like to make some extra money. The automotive employee then, with a supervisor's knowledge, began tagging brand-new auto parts, such as entire engine assemblies, which were valued from $3,000 to $10,000 each, and other expensive parts, as scrap. Knowing the friendly refuse driver's schedule, the employee would move the parts to the refuse removal area where the refuse driver would load the parts onto his truck.

Later, the refuse driver would deliver the parts to a designated drop-off point where the parts were distributed by being sold or sent to other participants.

Although crimes of this magnitude are not perpetrated every day, the frequency with which they do occur is surprising. In the above case, certainly due in part to the dollar amount involved, and the stature of the automobile manufacturer, law enforcement agents quickly agreed to assist in conducting an investigation. Unfortunately, this is not always the case. Law enforcement resources are limited. In fact, many people are unaware that law enforcement agencies, and district attorney offices, routinely establish "law enforcement priorities," meaning they will not *investigate or prosecute crimes in which the amount lost, that is the dollar value of the crime, does not meet a specific threshold.*

An example of this practice is in part evidenced by looking at the number of grand jury proceedings and criminal cases filed and then terminated by U.S. attorneys. For instance, the most recent *Sourcebook of Criminal Justice Statistics* (Bureau of Justice Statistics, 2001), Table 5.5 shows that in the year 2000 there were 52,887 cases filed by U.S. Attorney offices with 46,308 terminated. Although cases may be terminated for any of several reasons, conversations with federal, state and local law enforcement officials, and personal experience over a twenty-six-year law enforcement career, repeatedly found that many cases are not prosecuted because they do not meet a required threshold generally defined by some monetary value, which often differs from one jurisdiction to another. Or as a note following Table 5.5 explains: "Each U.S. attorney, under the direction of the U.S. Attorney General, is responsible for establishing law enforcement priorities . . ."

Even though a police officer may go to the scene of a crime and take an initial report, the chance that a meaningful investigation or follow-up to the initial report will be conducted is relatively remote. Many businesses and corporations have learned this lesson and increasingly employ security professionals to establish crime prevention programs, monitor employee activity in the workplace, and to investigate internal crimes (Marx, 1987).

Like society, the corporate landscape continues to evolve. Today more than ever before, businesses merge to form larger corporations with whom medium-sized and smaller businesses must compete. Although it is stating the obvious, businesses must depend on people to represent them and to conduct their business; without individuals to perform necessary day-to-day tasks, business would cease to exist.

The last decade (1990–2000) witnessed unprecedented economic growth. This is evidenced by the U.S. Department of Labor's statistics, which show that throughout the five-year period, 1995 to 2000, unemployment remained at near record low levels. In this environment, many business managers experienced at least some difficulty employing sufficient numbers of qualified personnel. Consequently, employees were often asked to "fill in" and complete tasks that would normally be done by someone else. In these types of situations employees could often increase their salaries substantially by simply working additional hours. However, as FBI statistics show (Bureau of Justice Statistics, 2001) there is always a group of employees who feel that, for one reason or another, they are not fully or justly compensated and therefore entitled to more. These are the individuals found in almost every business or corporate setting who, when given an opportunity, will rationalize why it is appropriate for them to abscond with goods or funds from their employers.

Writing about corporate investigations, Bologna and Shaw (1997) note that fraud, embezzlement, and on the job theft are among the most common types of crimes employees committed. The investigation of these crimes often proves difficult because of the lack of physical evidence.

Investigation of this kind of crime often consists of collecting circumstantial evidence and then confronting a suspect with this in the hope that he will confess, provide a tacit admission, or possibly implicate others. One problem with circumstantial evidence is that it can often be denied, or explained away by a quick-thinking suspect. An investigator's success often depends on his or her ability to assess the credibility of witnesses and suspects. Unfortunately, research (Ekman, 1992; Vrij, 2000) shows that the ability to detect deception, even by trained investigators, varies greatly from individual to individual, and often the accuracy of those decisions are no better than chance.

2.2 Deception and the Voice

A. Overview

In business, profit margins are often quite small. Corporate leaders and business managers often go to extraordinary lengths in the hope of increasing profits by only a few percentage points. Given this fact, it is surprising that very experienced business leaders will frequently overlook what should be an obvious opportunity to increase revenue. More important, this potential increase in revenue does not require marketing, needs little advertising, and a minimal allocation of resources. Every business can expect to lose goods and revenue due to theft, fraud, embezzlement, and other crimes carried out by customers, potential clients, and their own employees. Consequently, it should take very little thought to see the potential increase in profits if an organization could effectively decrease such losses by 10 percent, 15 percent or maybe even 25 percent.

Savings like those just mentioned are within reason. To achieve these benefits however, requires a concerted effort by security specialists, investigators, and other responsible business leaders, to recognize, embrace, and then within the realm of their responsibility, to use technologies that permit them to assess individual credibility.

The potential uses for credibility assessment in the private sector are many. For example, investigators may use this technology to interview witnesses and potential suspects in internal and other types of investigations; human resource specialists could use this ability to interview potential employees, to verify education, past employment, and to ferret out information purposely withheld from an employment application; supervisors and managers could use this technology to assist them in assessing employee performance, or as a supplement to promotional interviews; sales or marketing personnel could use this technology to verify credit references and other information needed to close a deal. Whenever knowing the truth would be of importance, there would be one more possible use for this type of technology.

In the past, credibility assessment was synonymous with the polygraph. The polygraph process however, is complicated and requires a great deal of education, and experience in order for the person using this technology to achieve an acceptable level of proficiency and accuracy. Consequently, the training and maintenance of a competent polygraph examiner also requires a significant financial investment. These facts, coupled with an increasing necessity to accurately discriminate between those who are telling the truth, and those who do not tell the truth, has sparked a search for alternatives to the polygraph. Today, one possible technology focuses on the monitoring and measurement of changes in vocal communication.

A great deal of research has focused on the voice in attempting to find meaningful indicators of deception. For example, researchers have examined factors such as vocal pitch (Ekman, O'Sullivan, Friesen, Wallace and Scherer, 1991; Rockwell, Buller and Burgoon, 1997), response latencies, the time between the asking of a question and the giving of a response (Stiff, Corman, Krizek and Snider, 1994), and nervous vocalizations (Burgoon, Buller, Dillman and Walther, 1995), in an effort to more accurately label people as truthful or deceptive in many different settings.

To date, researchers have found that the voice is much more complicated than one would believe. For instance, in two different studies (O'Hair, Cody and Behnke, 1985; O'Hair, Cody, Wang and Chao, 1990) researchers found that a prepared lie, a false response to an anticipated question, elicited higher levels of vocal stress, defined as a change in the presence or absence of modulation of the fundamental frequency of a vocal signal (for a more detailed explanation see section B), compared to truthful answers given to other questions. O'Hair et al. (1985) also found that in telling a prepared lie there were other individual differences. When individuals with higher levels of communication apprehension told a prepared lie, they exhibited increased levels of vocal stress compared to the amount of vocal stress present when they were asked to tell another type of lie, such as a spontaneous lie. Concurrently, other subjects in that study, those exhibiting low communication apprehension, showed no significant differences in vocal stress levels when telling either a prepared or a spontaneous lie. These findings are of interest because in an investigative setting witnesses and suspects have generally thought about the questions an investigator may ask them, and likely already prepared or rehearsed some type of response. O'Hair et al.'s (1985) findings would suggest that if an investigator were able to monitor the level of vocal stress present in a person's voice as they were interviewed it could be used to aid in discriminating between people telling the truth and those who would lie.

B. The detection of deception by voice stress analysis: the literature

Voice stress analysis (VSA) traces its lineage back to the mid-1960s when the United States Army was looking for a less intrusive alternative to the polygraph process. Those advocating the development of an instrument for VSA noted that the primary purpose of the human voice is to communicate, and that "it is also probable that the voice is an indicator of the psychological and physiological state of the speaker" (Ruiz, Legros and Guell, 1990). Reviewing the relevant literature, Ruiz et al. (1990) noted that a vocal message carries much more information than just its semantic content; and that research suggests that physical fatigue and psychological stress may be detected as acoustic modifications in the fundamental frequency of a speaker's voice.

Ruiz et al. (1990) wrote that the fundamental frequency of the vocal signal is slowly modulated (8–14 Hz) during speech in an emotionally neutral setting. It was theorized that this modulation, if it exists, would be the product of the natural trembling of the muscles controlling the vocal cords (vocal folds); similar to the natural trembling in the striated muscles explored by Lippold (1970). It was believed that in situations demanding increased "mental or psychomotor" activity, the 8–14 Hz modulation would then decrease as the striated muscles surrounding the vocal cords contracted in response to the arousal, thus limiting the natural trembling (Ruiz et al., 1990).

After reviewing the literature, Ruiz et al. (1990) concluded that the research was incomplete as far as efforts to identify and measure the acoustic characteristics of the voice were concerned. He believed that the conditions used in many laboratory experiments, that is, the conditions chosen to heighten arousal and induce subject's stress, as measured by increased mental or psychomotor activity, were highly subjective. The findings of the studies reviewed suggested that the acoustic indicators used were closely related to the type of condition and arousal studied. Therefore, the study of artificial or simulated conditions and arousal (stress) in laboratory settings may have little value when used to study the presence or absence of stress in actual or field settings.

VSA instruments, like the computerized voice stress analyzer (CVSA), and its predecessor the psychological stress evaluator (PSE), record subject responses to questions on a chart, which displays the fundamental frequency, a graph of frequency versus / time, and the presence or absence of any modulation to this frequency (Ruiz et al., 1990). The developers of a third voice stress analyzer, the Mark II VSA, chose to use a digital readout to display any differences in the modulation of the fundamental frequency rejecting the use of a chart or graph.

The results of at least three studies (Long, 1988; Long and Krall, 1990; O'Hair and Cody, 1987) suggested that there might be some validity to using the Mark II VSA for measuring voice stress. O'Hair and Cody (1987) used a simulated employment interview to test forty-seven subjects assigned to be either truthful or deceptive. Subjects assigned to the truthful condition simply answered all questions truthfully, while subjects in the deceptive condition were instructed to lie about their last place of employment, a prepared lie. After answering the prepared lie question, deceptive subjects were then asked, "What were your major duties in that position?" requiring the subject to create a spontaneous lie. Analysis showed that the differences in deceptive female subject's stress scores were statistically significant, when the answers to truthful questions were compared to the answers constituting a prepared lie. The differences in stress scores, however, were not statistically significant when the truthful answers were compared to answers given in response to a question requiring a spontaneous lie. Deceptive male subjects had no significantly different stress scores to any question. O'Hair and Cody (1987) concluded that, "[v]oice stress analysis appears to demonstrate some promise as a lie detection technique" (p. 11) when using the Mark II VSA. However, the authors also suggested that future research should examine different types of lies and subjects in other settings.

In another study of VSA, Long (1988) found that under some circumstances state anxiety scores as measured by a written psychological test correlated positively with Mark II stress scores. Following that earlier study, Long and Krall (1990) found that using a Mark II VSA there were significant differences in the stress levels of research subjects who read three words, while they were exposed to a tarantula in a glass terrarium, compared to the stress levels of subjects reading the same three words with no exposure to the spider. Although the authors experienced some operational difficulties using the Mark II VSA, for example, increased volume in a speaker's voice would yield higher digital readings, overall, the results were consistent with the manufacturer's claims that the instrument measured stress in the voice.

Recently, a search of the professional and scientific journals found only three studies examining the reliability and validity of the CVSA. Researchers (Cestaro, 1996 and 1995; Cestaro and Dollins, 1994) at the Department of Defense Polygraph Institute (DoDPI) examined the CVSA to assess, in part, the instrument's technical performance and accuracy both in a setting without jeopardy and then using a mock (staged) crime scenario. Although these studies addressed important questions of interest to scientists and other researchers, the significance of their findings in an applied or field setting were arguably limited for several reasons. For example, some researchers (e.g., Brenner, Branscomb and Schwartz, 1979; Ruiz et al., 1990) suggest that voice stress analysis may not function well in a low stress environment, such as that found in a laboratory setting. The three DoDPI studies were all conducted in a laboratory setting, and used a testing format different than that generally used by practitioners responsible for the conduct of criminal investigations in a real-world field setting. Two of the DoDPI studies (Cestaro and Dollins, 1994; Cestaro, 1995) used peak of tension tests (POT) that are generally used, if at all, only to supplement comparison or control question polygraph testing (CQT). The control question polygraph test is the most common form of lie detection examination used for specific issue testing in criminal investigations.

In the third DoDPI study (Cestaro, 1996), the researchers solicited volunteers from the military or local community as experimental subjects. This practice is a marked improvement over the use of college freshmen, but even drawing participants from this population it is most likely that the range of each subject's life experience was restricted compared to the range of different subjects and personalities normally seen by investigators in the course of "real-world" investigations and other field settings. Although it is possible that some volunteers may have experienced problems with society or the law, it is more probable than not that the people who volunteered to participate in the DoDPI study did not represent to any significant degree the criminal suspects tested daily in many business, corporate, or law enforcement settings. One other point of debate regarding the DoDPI study was that the researchers chose to use one question format for the conduct of the polygraph examinations and a different question format for the conduct of the CVSA examinations. The reasons for using the different question formats are probably more related to the subjective opinions of the polygraph and CVSA "experts" involved in the study rather than any substantive, empirical reason. However, though it was most likely negligible, the effect of using the different question formats has become a contentious point of discussion between polygraph and CVSA advocates whenever this study is cited. Whether the difference in question formats is of any consequence is an issue that debate will not resolve alone.

In the past, there was little information available regarding the validity of voice stress analysis. What was available was found in a few studies conducted to test the PSE in both laboratory and field settings. Several studies (e.g., Barland [experiment 1], 1978; Brenner, et al., 1979; Horvath, 1978 and 1979; Kubis, 1974; Lynch and Henry, 1979; Nachshon and Feldman; 1980) tested the PSE in controlled laboratory settings and found little if any validity supporting the use of voice stress analysis for the detection of deception.

For example, Barland (experiment 1) (1978) told sixteen undergraduate psychology students, one at a time, to pick one number from five possibilities. Each subject was then administered a peak of tension test (Barland and Raskin, 1973) to see if the selected number could be identified. For each trial, subjects were asked if they picked one of nine numbers, including the five earlier choices, and told to answer each question with the one answer "no." There were a total of three trials; the first was a reading of the numbers with each subject responding with an answer of "no." The second trial had the examiner bet each subject $.50 that the number could be identified; fifteen subjects participated in the second trial. Finally, the examiner talked with each subject regarding the morality of telling the truth and then asked the numbers a third time. Across all three trials, the results were equivocal at best.

In two other studies, Horvath (1978, 1979) compared the PSE and the accuracy of the polygraph's GSR used for the detection of deception in a laboratory setting. Subjects were instructed to select one card from five, write the number down and were then instructed to answer "no" when asked if they picked each of the cards. Although the second experiment included a threat component, the possible loss of extra credit related to the subject's participation in the experiment, the researcher found the detection accuracy of the PSE was no different than that in the first study. In both studies the ability to discriminate between truthful and deceptive subjects using the PSE did not exceed chance levels, or that equal to the flip of a coin.

Overall, the results of the available laboratory-based studies strongly suggested that the PSE might have little valve when used for the detection of deception. However, laboratory based studies engender certain weaknesses that PSE and polygraph practitioners alike, cite as reasons why they are skeptical of findings based on such studies (Bell, 1981). For example, those researchers conducting human subject research must of course adhere to ethics that prevent them from creating situations in which subjects will experience a level of stress similar or equal to that found in a criminal investigation, or other real-world setting; the laboratory cannot replicate real life. Additionally, studies were sometimes conducted by persons with little training or practical experience in the use of the instrument or application of the procedures being tested (Barland, 1988).

Continuing to look at the relevant research literature, one finds that there are a few studies (e.g., Barland [Experiment 2], 1978; Brenner, Branscomb and Schwartz, 1979; Nachshon, Elaad and Amsel, 1985) in which the results suggest that voice stress analysis may be valid in some settings for detecting deception. For instance, Barland's (1978) study actually consisted of two experiments. However, it is interesting to note that the references found in the literature, at least by this author, only cite the results of the first experiment, which was conducted in a low stress, laboratory setting. Barland's second experiment, however, compared the PSE's accuracy to the decisions made in fourteen actual polygraph examinations administered to subjects accused of murder, rape, armed robbery, theft, forgery, the selling of illegal drugs, police misconduct, and reckless driving.

Using a numerical scoring technique like that used to score polygraph charts (see Horvath, 1988 for a detailed description), Barland (1978) used a PSE to evaluate the recorded voice responses given by examinees during the polygraph examination. Using a cutoff score of ± 2 (scores greater than +2 were truthful and less than –2 were deceptive, while scores of +2, +1, 0, – 1, – 2, were inconclusive), Barland found six (6) inconclusive decisions relying on the PSE. However, the remaining eight decisions all agreed (100 percent) with the polygraph decisions. Further analysis of the results found that when the different polygraph components, that is the measures of respiration, GSR, and cardiovascular activity, were compared to the voice component for effectiveness, the voice component finished second only to the GSR, while respiration and cardiovascular activity finished third and forth respectively. Concluding, Barland (1978) noted that the voice data was acquired simultaneously with the polygraph data, and that in a situation structured for voice stress analysis, the efficiency of detecting deception may even be much higher.

A study was found that did examine the efficiency of voice stress analysis for the detection of deception in a "real-world" field setting (Nachshon et al., 1985). Earlier, Nachshon and Feldman (1980) had tested the PSE in a laboratory setting and found little support for voice stress analysis using the PSE to detect deception. The results of this study, however, were challenged on technical issues such as those highlighted by Barland (1978). In the first study the researchers used a polygraph-testing format instead of a VSA format, and the use of an unskilled evaluator in scoring the voice stress data. Accordingly, Nachshon invited his critic, Tuvya Amsel, to participate in a comparative field study to test the PSE and the polygraph's detection of deception efficiency in the same field setting (Nachshon et al., 1985).

In the subsequent study, polygraph examinations were administered to forty criminal subjects. The subject's verbal responses to the questions asked were recorded for later voice stress analysis. Subjects were tested for the crimes of murder, rape theft, burglary, false alarm, and fraud. Overall, the PSE and polygraph decisions agreed in twenty-five (74 percent) cases, and failed to agree in seven (21 percent) cases. Two polygraph decisions were inconclusive, and if these were excluded from the results, there was a 78 percent rate of agreement between the polygraph and PSE, which was statistically significant given an *a priori* probability of 67 percent.

The results showed that the ability to detect deception using the PSE by measuring vocal stress was relatively low. Although nine subjects were correctly identified as deceptive using the polygraph, only three (33.33 percent) deceptive persons were correctly identified using the PSE. When used to identify truthful subjects, however, the PSE's accuracy was about equal to that achieved using the polygraph. Twenty-three subjects were identified as telling the truth using the polygraph. At the same time, twenty-two truth tellers (96 percent) were accurately identified using the PSE. In this study, Nachshon et al. (1985) concluded that the use of trained evaluators might account for some of the differences in the results of this and the earlier (Nachshon and Feldman, 1980) research efforts. Concluding, the authors suggested that further research should be conducted before formulating any conclusion regarding the validity of VSA and the PSE for the detection of deception.

Although some research results suggest that voice stress analysis may be valid for the detection of deception, or may provide additional information to better identify truthful subjects, the meager amount of empirical evidence addressing this issue remained problematic. What was clear from the literature was that questions regarding the validity of voice stress analysis in general, and the CVSA in particular, required further scientific evaluation.

In 1995, CVSA advocates first tried to introduce the instrument into some jurisdictions with specific prohibitions against VSA. In the state where I lived, the ensuing debate led state legislatures to ask the state police for guidance regarding the adoption of this technology. At that time I was a state police officer assigned to the Forensic Science Division, and tasked with conducting an extensive review of the literature to find evidence that would provide some direction toward resolving this issue. The literature review I conducted found no substantive evidence on which to base a conclusion regarding either the CVSA or VSA's validity. Recognizing all the limitations of the earlier research, it was suggested that a field validity study be conducted to address these limitations and derive scientific evidence that could be offered to help the responsible legislators to formulate public policy. Permission to conduct the proposed study was given and commenced immediately.

C. The CVSA and voice stress analysis: field validity study results

In a recent decision, the United States Supreme Court held that scientific knowledge is that which can be tested and which has undergone the scrutiny of the scientific community (*Daubert v. Merrill Dow Pharmaceuticals, Inc.*, 1993). Prior to conducting this field validity study, the only other empirical investigations examining the CVSA instrument were conducted by Dr. Victor Cestaro and his colleagues, scientists with the Department of Defense. The studies Dr. Cestaro conducted were set in a laboratory environment and focused primarily on the instruments technical merits (1994). However, many law enforcement practitioners and other CVSA proponents note that the instrument was never subjected to an empirical evaluation in a field setting, a study conducted in the "real world." Those advocating the CVSAs use believe that a fair assessment of the instrument can only be achieved in such an environment.

Charles Humble, the National Institute for Truth Verification's (NITV) founder, had responded to the publication of laboratory-based studies by stating that the CVSA could not be adequately or fairly tested in a simulated setting. And, although Humble had rejected the results of laboratory-based research, he believed that research conducted in a field environment would accurately reflect the CVSA's validity. Humble is reported to have said: "rather than rely on laboratory studies which I do not feel accurately reflect the validity of either the polygraph or the CVSA, I would refer to field studies which, in my opinion, do." (Cestaro, 1995, p. 1)

The absence of a field validity study, the reported number of law enforcement agencies using the CVSA (currently estimated at more than 1,000), and the creator's claimed 98 percent level of accuracy suggest that the instrument may offer some advantages compared to the traditional polygraph process. For example, the NITV claims (C. Humble, personal communication, November 1, 1995) that because a CVSA analysis takes less time than a polygraph examination its use allows more assessments to be made in a given period. If this were true, and the CVSA were demonstrated to be scientifically valid, more law enforcement agencies could employ this instrument to quickly determine whether suspects in criminal investigations, or applicants seeking a career in law enforcement, were truthful or deceptive regarding specific issues. Additionally, many smaller law enforcement agencies that could not afford to employ a polygraph examiner, due to the cost of ten or more weeks of training, may be able to support the CVSA's use, which requires only six days of instruction.

With possible advantages such as these, the NITV's promises regarding the CVSA's use is undoubtedly alluring, especially to law enforcement officials with limited resources who wish only to resolve investigations that before were routinely not investigated or closed due to a lack of investigative polygraph services. Accordingly, given the CVSA's potential value to the law enforcement community, and a plethora of unanswered questions, a field validity study (Palmatier, 1999) was conducted with the primary goal of discovering any scientific evidence that would support the NITV's claims regarding the CVSA's performance.

A total 100 subjects were assigned to one of three groups. Subjects in the first two groups were drawn from a pool of 296 consecutive field CVSA/polygraph examinations conducted over a ten-month period during the course of different criminal investigations conducted by township, city, county, state and federal law enforcement agencies. There were fifty subjects in the first group who were confirmed deceptive by giving a confession in which they outlined details relevant to the offense under investigation. The crimes committed by the subjects in this group included murder, rape, robbery, larceny and fraud. In the second group there were twenty-five subjects who were confirmed truthful after someone else confessed to the crime for which this subject was tested. Finally, there were an additional twenty-five truthful subjects assigned to a third group; these individuals were recruited from criminal justice courses at a local junior college, from a state police Explorer Scout post, and from a state police duty roster to participate in a lie detection experiment.

Both the CVSA and the polygraph data were blind scored by several evaluators. Overall, the five-polygraph evaluators achieved a 72 percent rate of accuracy, 13 percent rate of false negative decisions, that is calling a deceptive person truthful, and a 15 percent rate of false positive decisions, calling a truthful person deceptive. These results were statistically highly significant. The results achieved by the CVSA evaluators however, did not fair as well. Overall, the three CVSA evaluators achieved a 52 percent rate of accuracy, a 20 percent rate of false negative decisions, and a 28 percent rate of false positive decisions. These results were not statistically significant, suggesting that based on this data the results achieved by the CVSA evaluators was no better than the flip of a coin.

These findings strongly suggest that the claims made by CVSA proponents are greatly exaggerated. Law enforcement personnel using the CVSA are overly inclined to highlight or emphasize the number of confessions obtained using the instrument. Unfortunately, law enforcement advocates fail to understand that from a scientific perspective this statistic, the utility of the instrument, is of little interest. CVSA proponents fail to recognize that absent an appropriate methodology, the act of simply tallying the number of confessions obtained using any instrument or devise attests only to its utility and fails to address questions regarding it's scientific validity or reliability.

D. Vericator: detecting deception using voice analysis

In the mid 1990s, due in part to increasing terrorist activities within Israel, Amir Liberman, a young computer programmer, reported becoming increasingly concerned about the difficulty in properly screening people entering his home country. Liberman said (personal conversation, February 3, 2000) he tried to develop software using VSA technology, but was unable to accurately discriminate between truthful and deceptive subjects. Liberman discussed his ideas and the problems he encountered with his father and some other academics from the Hebrew University in Jerusalem. After many discussions, Liberman stated that a basic algorithm evolved looking at different components of the voice. The algorithm focused on several new parameters for the assessment of credibility including the analysis of the entire vocal spectrum, which was divided into high/medium/low frequencies, and a comparative analysis of individual differences in some personal speech characteristics. According to Liberman, he used this primary algorithm as a basis for his first software program, which showed promise in developmental testing. These results were then used to create interest in this new voice analysis (VA) technology in Israel and as a base on which the Trustech organization evolved. After approximately three years of development a professional version of Liberman's software was marketed and has sold in several different countries around the globe (for a more detailed explanation of the software the reader is directed to patent PCT/IL98 /00613, International publication number WO 99/31653). In the United States the software using this technology was first called Vericator, and was marketed by Integritek Systems of Tampa, Florida. Today, Integritek is associated in part with Risk Technologies (www.risktechllc.com) also of Tampa, Florida and the software is marketed under its original name of "TrusterPro."

E. Differences in the technologies

Each of the technologies, polygraph, voice stress analysis and voice analysis, today called advanced digital voice analysis (ADVA), differs in the manner in which credibility is assessed from the data used. The polygraph process uses physical attachments to record an individual's respiration, electrical potential of the skin, and cardiovascular activity. These parameters are continually monitored as a person is asked relevant questions, which address the issue at examination; control or comparison questions, which a subject will have some doubt or will purposely lie to when answering; and irrelevant questions, which are used to establish a baseline for each person examined (Horvath, 1988). The polygraph instrument creates tracings for each channel recorded, which are then analyzed by a trained examiner who must interpret them and render an opinion as to the credibility of the person being tested.

Unlike the polygraph, both the CVSA (VSA technology) and the Vericator or TrusterPro (ADVA technology) software programs do not require any physical attachments to be placed on a person in order to administer an examination. However, in order to create the voice tracings for analysis, the CVSA procedure requires the use of the same types of questions used by polygraph examiners. The manner in which the CVSA is used mirrors the polygraph procedure, with the presentation of irrelevant, relevant and control questions regarding some specific issue. After collecting the voice data, the CVSA voice pattern tracings must also be analyzed and interpreted by a trained examiner who will then render an opinion regarding the examinee's credibility.

The CVSA tracings are a result of the software program filtering out all but the 8 to 14 Hz portion of the frequency spectrum, and then displaying changes in both AM (audio modulated) and FM (frequency modulated) activity. An ADVA software program differs from the CVSA in that it is much more flexible and does not require the use, per se, of relevant, control, and irrelevant questions. The ADVA software can be used as easily to assess free-flowing conversation as it can to examine someone using a structured question format like that used in a polygraph or CVSA examination. The ADVA software differs further from the CVSA program by including in its analysis, the entire vocal spectrum divided into high, medium, and low frequencies. At the same time, the ADVA software uses a comparative analysis of those speech characteristics targeted by the software's algorithms (i.e., mathematical models) to look for significant differences in an individual's speech. The ADVA software first calibrates to a person's voice, accomplishing this in the first 20-40 seconds of monitored speech, by collecting data and defining this period as a normal speech sample. The software program then continually collects data and subjects it to analysis using its algorithms to compare the new speech data with the calibration sample. The Vericator manual (2000) states that (p. 7):

> Vericator™ is an innovative, highly advanced computerized system that is specially designed to provide you [the examiner] with easy access to assessing credibility in a highly professional and discreet manner. Conversations can be analyzed in real-time or offline from recorded files to provide timely and reliable data to assist one in making the right decisions.
>
> It is based on voice analysis technology that gathers data related to several individual speech characteristics and then uses a series of complex, sophisticated algorithms that measure and grade them [the characteristics] accordingly. Vericator technology pinpoints inconsistencies, and reports back with a determination as to whether these may be caused by a lie, excitement, an exaggeration or cognitive conflict.

What ADVA software does is different compared to the polygraph and the CVSA procedures. The polygraph and CVSA were created for the purposes of lie detection, that is regarding a specific issue was the person being examined telling the truth or not, yes or no, black and white. For example, did you steal the money missing from the cash register? August 12th did you rob the gas station on the corner? The polygraph profession teaches practitioners when appropriate, to render inconclusive decisions, or simply state that a decision cannot be made. CVSA practitioners are taught that they must make a yes or no decision and that there is no room for inconclusive decisions; a practice that unfortunately, can only increase the number of errors made. The ADVA software is significantly different from the other two technologies in that it allows one to search out and then assess those issues that lie between the ultimate questions, which are answered "yes" or "no." The ADVA accomplishes this goal by using sixteen common phrases, for instance, "truth," "not sure," "high excitement," "extreme tension," "inaccuracy," "suspected," "probably lie," and "deception," creating a hierarchy that denotes varying degrees of doubt and stress. Unfortunately, this hierarchy is one based on semantics and the subjective interpretation of the user, leaving the difference between terms to individual interpretation and sometimes complicates the bottom line. The Vericator manual (2000) states that (p. 10–11):

Because there are many types of lies, there is no one voice pattern or frequency for deceptive speech. However, there is uniformity to people's speech in truthful situations, where the mainstream thought process flows and is uninterrupted.

This pattern of truth is unique to each person, at any given moment, and will likely change if the situational circumstances change. For example, if a person were sitting in front of you and waiting for the test to begin, he may feel relatively relaxed. However, once the actual testing begins a person's mind will likely focus on factors related to the questions asked. Consequently, he might be more alert, more excited, or confused and so on.

Vericator analyzes any deviation from the more consistent flowing, truthful, thought process and then presents it both graphically and textually. Accordingly, it is the deviations in this pattern, more than the regular and fluent pattern of thought that indicates whether a person is more probably responding to stress, confusion, excitement, etc.

F. Does the ADVA technology work?

The differences in the measures recorded using a polygraph; the CVSA or the ADVA software may or may not contribute to differences in both the validity and the reliability of these technologies. To explore this issue, the comparative accuracy of these three technologies was examined in the same context by using the digital recordings created for the CVSA field validity study, (Palmatier, 2000) reanalyzing them using the ADVA software, and then comparing evaluator decisions with those rendered earlier by trained CVSA and polygraph evaluators. A sample of seventy-seven subjects was drawn from one of two pre-established groups. Subjects in the two groups were drawn from a pool of 296 consecutive field CVSA or polygraph examinations conducted for township, city, county, state and federal law enforcement agencies. Subjects in the first group (n = 36) were confirmed deceptive by giving a confession outlining details relevant to the offense under investigation, while subjects in the second group (n = 41) were confirmed truthful as someone else confessed to the crime for which each subject was tested. The crimes committed by the subjects who were deceptive included murder, rape, robbery, larceny, and fraud.

After the required number of truthful and deceptive cases was verified, copies of the voice recordings were created and sent to trained

ADVA, evaluators in Israel. The evaluators were asked to render opinions regarding each subject's status as truthful or deceptive using only that information gleaned from the copies of the voice recordings they were given. No other information was given to the evaluators regarding the proportion of truthful and deceptive subjects.

The CVSA has been used for several years in the field by practitioners who have developed practices and standards that control the conduct of a VSA (voice stress analysis) examination, and the evaluation practices employed in formulating a decision regarding an examinee's status, that is, truthful or deceptive. The comparison discussed here *was based only on the CVSA evaluator's chart two* decisions regarding each subject's status, that is truthful or deceptive which were then compared to the ADVA evaluator's and the polygraph evaluator's decisions regarding the same subjects. The rationale for doing so was that CVSA examiners are taught to render decisions based only on chart two analyses. The results are presented below. Figure 2.1 shows the relative accuracy of the decisions based on each technology, the CVSA, ADVA, and the polygraph. Analyses found that both the polygraph and the ADVA examiner opinions discriminated between truthful and deceptive subjects at a high statistically significant rate; for both polygraph and for the ADVA D < .000. At the same time, the CVSA results were not statistically significant, D > .169, not exceeding the level of chance.

These results suggest that compared to the polygraph and the CVSA, the ADVA technology may have some advantages. For instance, the ex-

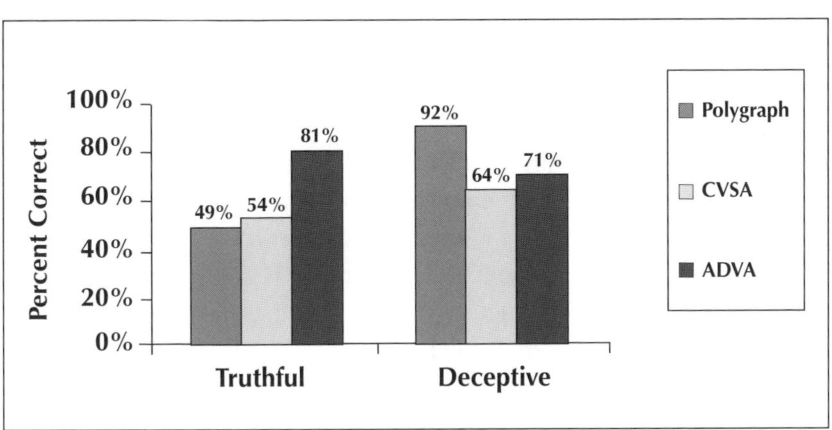

Figure 2.1 *Truthful/deceptive opinions only with no inconclusives allowed*

aminer using the ADVA technology realized a higher rate of accuracy for the classification of both truthful and deceptive subjects compared to the results achieved by the examiners using the CVSA. Although it appeared that the polygraph might be superior for the classification of deceptive subjects, this finding is somewhat misleading as the higher rate of accuracy was achieved only by misclassifying a greater number of truthful (i.e., innocent) subjects as deceptive. False positive errors may be acceptable in some settings, for instance in a security context where even one foreign agent could do grave damage, or in a corporate setting where trade secrets may be lost or even destroyed. However, the vast majority of users would probably be more willing to accept a false negative error that is, allowing a few guilty people to escape rather than accusing an innocent person of being deceptive.

2.3 Conclusions

The results of this study must be interpreted cautiously. It is true that the ADVA software gave a more even balance between accurately classifying innocent and deceptive subjects in a criminal justice context compared to the two other technologies. However, one should keep in mind that the digital tapes used for the CVSA and ADVA analyses were created using professional grade equipment.

More important is the fact that the responses analyzed were monosyllable responses, "Yes" or "No," and the result of a structured lie detection interview in which the pretest portion of the procedure is critical in establishing "psychological set" (Matte and Grove, 2001). Whether the ADVA technology would fare as well in a free flowing conversation has yet to be objectively assessed in an empirical investigation. Minimally, these results call for increased research to explore the limits and contributions to be made by this interesting new technology. The ADVA software is less invasive compared to the polygraph and much more easy to interpret compared to the data created by a CVSA instrument.

The poor showing for the CVSA instrument was surprising as the examination format, the conduct of the examinations, and the use of real world issues should all benefit that procedure. If, on the other hand, the CVSA is not as the NITV claims, an improvement on the older PSE technology, then the results seen here were very similar to those achieved by other researchers who examined the PSE more than fifteen to twenty years ago.

Certainly if nothing else the above findings are provocative and should spark increased debate among researchers interested in the core technologies, and practitioners whose responsibility it is to assess credibility on a daily basis. The importance of searching for new and improved technologies used to assess credibility cannot be over emphasized, especially in the world in which we now live.

References

Barland, G.H. (1978). Use of voice changes in the detection of deception. *Polygraph*, 7(2), 129–140.

Bell, A.D. (1981). The PSE: A decade of controversy. *Security Management*, 25, 63–73.

Bologna, J. and Shaw, P. (1997). *Corporate Crime Investigation*. Boston, MA: Butterworth-Heinemann.

Brenner, M., Branscomb, H.H. and Schwartz, G.E. (1979). Psychological stress evaluator—Two tests of a vocal measure. *Psychophysiology*, 16(4), 351–357.

Bureau of Justice Statistics (2001) *Sourcebook of Criminal Justice Statistics*, 2000, Table 5.5 [On-line]. Available: http://www.albany.edu/sourcebook/1995/pdf/t55.pdf.

Bureau of Justice Statistics (2001) *Sourcebook of Criminal Justice Statistics*, 2000 [On-line]. Available: http://www.albany.edu/sourcebook.

Burgoon, J.K., Buller, D.B., Dillman, L. and Walther, J.B. (1995). Interpersonal deception: IV. Effects of suspicion on perceived communication and nonverbal behavior dynamics. *Human Communication Research*, 2, 163–196.

Cestaro, V.L. (1995). A comparison between decision accuracy rates obtained using the polygraph instrument and the computer voice stress analyzer (CVSA) in the absence of jeopardy (Report No. DoDPI95-R-0002). Fort McClellan, Alabama: Department of Defense Polygraph Institute.

Cestaro, V.L. (1996). A comparison of accuracy rates between detection of deception examinations using the polygraph and the Computer Voice Stress Analyzer in a mock crime scenario (Report No. DoDPI95-R-0004). Fort

McClellan, Alabama: Department of Defense Polygraph Institute.

Cestaro, V.L. (1996). A comparison of accuracy rates between detection of deception examinations using the polygraph and the Computer Voice Stress Analyzer in a mock crime scenario (Report No. DoDPI95-R-0004). Fort McClellan, Alabama: Department of Defense Polygraph Institute.

Cestaro, V.L. and Dollins, A.B. (1994). An analysis of voice responses for the detection of deception (Report No. DoDPI94-R-0001). Fort McClellan, Alabama: Department of Defense Polygraph Institute.

Daubert v. Merrill Dow Pharmaceuticals, Inc., 509 US 579, 125 L Ed 2d 469, 113 S Ct 2786 (1993).

Ekman, P. (1992). *Telling Lies: Clues to Deceit in the Marketplace, Politics, and Marriage*. New York, NY: W. W. Norton and Co.

Ekman, P., O'Sullivan, M., Friesen, W.V. and Scherer, K.R. (1991). Face, voice, and body in detecting deceit. *Journal of Nonverbal Behavior*, 15(2), 125–135.

Horvath, F. (1988). The utility of control questions and the effects of two control question types in field polygraph techniques. *Journal of Police Science and Administration*, 16(1), 1–17.

Horvath, F. (1979). Effect of different motivational instructions on detection of deception with the psychological stress evaluator and the galvanic skin response. *Journal of Applied Psychology*, 64(3), 323–330.

Horvath, F. (1978). An experimental comparison of the psychological stress evaluator and the galvanic skin response in detection of deception. *Journal of Applied Psychology*, 63(3), 338–344.

Kubis, J.F. (1974). Comparison of voice analysis and polygraph as lie detection procedures. *Polygraph*, 3, 1–48.

Lippold, O.C.J. (1970, March). Physiological tremor. *Scientific American*, 224, 65–73.

Long, G.T. (1988). The relationship of voice stress, anxiety, and depression to life events and personal style variables. *Social Behavior and Personality,* 16, 133–145.

Long, G.T. and Krall, V.L. (1990). The measurement of stress by voice analysis. *Journal of Social Behavior and Personality*, 5(6), 723–731.

Lynch, B.E. and Henry, D.R. (1979). A validity study of the psychological stress evaluator. Canadian Journal of Behavioral Science, 11(1), 89–94.

Marx, G.T. (1987). The interweaving of public and private police in undercover work. In C.D. Shearing and P.C. Stenning (Eds.), *Private Policing*. Newbury Park, CA: Sage Publishers.

Matte, J.A. and Grove, R.N. (2001). Psychological set: its origin, theory and application. P*olygraph,* 30(3), 196–202.

Nachshon, I., Elaad, E. and Amsel, T. (1985). Validity of the Psychological Stress Evaluator: A field study. *Journal of Police Science and Administration*, 13(4), 275–282.

Nachshon, I. and Feldman, B. (1980). Vocal indices of psychological stress: A validation study of the Psychological Stress Evaluator. *Journal of Police Science and Administration*, 8(1), 40–53.

O'Hair, D. and Cody, M.J. (1987). Gender and vocal stress differences during truthful and deceptive information sequences. *Human Relations*, 40(1), 11–14.

O'Hair, D., Cody, M.J. and Behnke, R.R. (1985). Communication apprehension and vocal stress as indices of deception. *Western Journal of Speech Communication*. 49(4), 286–300.

O'Hair, D., Cody, M.J., Wang, X.T. and Chao, E.Y. (1990). Vocal stress and deception detection among Chinese. *Communication Quarterly*. 38 (2), 158–169.

Palmatier, J.J. (2000). *The CVSA, Polygraph, and Trustech / Vericator Voice Analysis Technologies*. Unpublished manuscript. Verity Consulting: Tampa, Florida.

Palmatier, J. J. (1999). *The Validity and Comparative Accuracy of Voice Stress Analysis as Measured by the CVSA: A Field Study Conducted in a Psychophysiological Context*. Unpublished manuscript. Michigan Department of State Police: Lansing, Michigan.

Rockwell, P.B., Buller, D.B. and Burgoon, J.K. (1997). Measurement of deceptive voices: comparing acoustic and perceptual data. *Applied Psycholinguistics*. 18(4), 471–484.

Ruiz, R., Legros, C. and Guell, A. (1990). Voice analysis to predict the psychological or physical state of a speaker. A*viation, Space, and Environmental Medicine,* 61(3), 266–271.

Stiff, J.C., Corman, S.K., Krizek, B. and Snider, E. (1994). Individual differences and changes in nonverbal behavior: unmasking the changing faces of deception. *Communication Research.* 21(5), 555–581.

Vericator User Manual V6.30 [Computer Software]. (2000). Tampa, Florida: Integritek Systems Inc.

Vrij, A. (2000). *Detecting Lies and Deceit: The Psychology of Lying and the Implications for Professional Practice.* New York, New York: John Wiley & Sons, LTD.

Chapter 3

Profiling for Corporate Investigators

Raymond M. Pierce

Synopsis

3.1 Criminal Personality Profiling

Because of Hollywood's depiction of criminal personality profiling, most people—and many investigators—think profiling is used in only the most gruesome serial murder cases. While that is one type of investigation assisted by this analytical process, profiling has evolved into a useful method of assisting corporate security in their generally less lethal investigations.

A. Specific uses

The specific areas where profiling has been of most assistance to corporate and private investigators are:

- Evaluating extortion attempts and threats to corporate personnel to determine if there is an immediate potential for violence
- Preparing detailed profiles of anonymous telephone callers and letter writers to prevent harassment from developing into stalking

- Assisting corporate security in identifying employees with an elevated potential to act out violently in the workplace
- Evaluating problem employees, to prevent a violent reaction, prior to termination, and assisting human resource officers with exit interviews
- Identifying current or former employees responsible for leaks of sensitive information or industrial espionage
- Assisting loss prevention investigations with suspect evaluation and developing behaviorally oriented interviews best suited for the identified suspect
- Developing questionnaires and interviewing strategies designed to identify the person actually responsible for corporate crime from a large number of potential suspects
- Providing awareness training in the prevention of violence in the workplace and the identification of employee aberrant behavior
- Developing crisis management skills among designated personnel
- Assisting corporate executives in evaluating clients and potential adversaries during short- and long-term negotiations

B. History and development

The following information provides an overview of how the process of criminal personality profiling developed and explains how it can assist corporate investigators in highly intricate cases. From basic loss prevention to prevention of violence in the workplace to the delicate process of threat analysis, profiling has been very successful in enhancing the protective and investigative skills of corporate security.

Criminal personality profiling began in late eighteenth-century Europe as an informal method of identifying crime patterns within the Austrian criminal justice system. Without a structured, systematic procedure for analyzing these crimes and criminals, interest in profiling decreased over the years. In the twentieth century, the general public first became aware of informal profiling in Sir Arthur Conan Doyle's series of Sherlock Holmes tales.

During World War II, the U.S. Office of Strategic Services (OSS) used a more structured method of profiling. Dr. Walter Langer and several psychiatric colleagues were commissioned to provide a psychological profile of Adolph Hitler. The profile was used to successfully estimate Hitler's vulnerabilities and his fatal response to the allies' effort at the end of the war in Europe.

In the years following the war, law enforcement periodically requested assistance from psychiatrists and psychologists. However, profiling was formally rediscovered by the law enforcement community in the early 1970s at the Federal Bureau of Investigation's National Academy in Quantico, Virginia. As hundreds of local, state and federal investigators were trained each year, certain instructors within the FBI's Behavioral Science Unit began to identify similarities in solved and unsolved cases that investigators brought with them for class discussion. These instructors, with extensive behavioral science and investigative backgrounds, became interested in the similar patterns of offender behavior in crimes from around the country.

The crimes were similar, but the offender descriptions indicated that many different people were responsible for the various crimes. The offenses ranged from the most violent homicides to white-collar and political corruption cases. As the instructors reviewed thousands of cases over a period of several years, they were able to approximate the general personality flaws and characteristics of the offenders, and to categorize the types of criminal personalities that would be more likely to commit certain crimes.

When computer technology improved in the 1980s, the evaluation of unsolved cases became still more sophisticated and systematic. The agent/instructors devoted more of their time to unsolved cases that were sent to the Behavioral Science Unit for what was now called a *psychological profile* of the unknown criminal offender. Investigators from around the country, and throughout the free world, heard of the research and were eager to receive assistance with their open cases.

The formal research program involved interviewing criminals convicted of a variety of crimes and determining not only why they committed the crime, but also what they did before, during and after the initial escape from the scene of the crime. This data, combined with extensive behaviorally oriented background research for each criminal studied, provided a tremendous amount of insight into the criminal mind.

As the research and investigative assistance program expanded, the term *psychological profile* evolved into *criminal personality profile*. As the requests for assistance multiplied, the FBI decided in 1985 to train five investigators from major U.S. metropolitan areas in their analytical approach to criminal investigations. These investigators, after completing a yearlong fellowship with the FBI's Behavioral Science Unit, were certified as Criminal Investigative Analysts. They returned to their jurisdictions and began to provide criminal personality profiles and investigative assistance to the city, state and federal agencies within their geographic areas.

As the demand for investigative assistance with unsolved cases increased over the next few years, the FBI trained fifteen additional investigators from major metropolitan areas in the United States, Australia, Canada and the Netherlands. The FBI has limited the number of certified criminal profilers to maintain a highly trained, and frequently retrained, group of professionals dedicated to assisting investigators with the more difficult behavioral aspects of their unsolved investigations.

C. How criminal personality profiling assists corporate investigations—evaluating threats

Written extortion attempts and threats to executives and personnel often present a challenge for corporate security. When dealing with an unknown person sending life threatening communications, the immediate protection of the recipient of one or a series of harassing letters or telephone calls, and the people surrounding that person, become the major concern of security officers. A primary analytic aspect of profiling is the immediate evaluation of the threats to determine the probability of violence toward the corporation or employee.

While the majority of corporate threats are effectively investigated within the organization, profiling assists in identifying the single or repeated threat that should be cause for serious concern. Based upon extensive training in the study of the precursors of violent behavior, the process of psycholinguistics and numerous years of experience devoted to the systematic assessment of verbal and written threats, the criminal profiler will provide a thorough evaluation of the level of violence which may be anticipated from the individual sending the communication, as well as a detailed description of the offender.

The offender description provided should enable the investigator to narrow the focus of the search for possible suspects from a broad spectrum to a more manageable number of potential suspects. When there is a finite number of possible suspects, an offender profile will often assist in reducing that number to one or two most probable suspects. The profile lists characteristics unique to the individual, which could be easily identified by associates, coworkers or investigators who may have interviewed the suspect in the past. The typical offender characteristics provided in a criminal personality profile are:

- The offender's approximate age
- Sex
- Race
- Marital status and adjustment
- Level of scholastic ability and achievement
- Rearing environment and social adjustment
- Current lifestyle, demeanor and expected personality quirks
- Explanation of mental decompensation (personality disorders) or prior arrest history
- Offender's expected prior contact and knowledge of the victim
- Probable motive for threats

Again, providing these formerly unknown offender characteristics should enable the lead corporate investigator to reduce the vast number of possible suspects, and to focus on a limited number of probable suspects. However, profiling doesn't stop there. Proactive questioning and investigative techniques are then provided to the lead investigators to assist them in bringing the case to a successful conclusion.

While the offender is often identified in these investigations, not every case results in a criminal prosecution. When it is in the best interest of the victim and the corporation, alternatives to arrest have been used to ensure that the offender will stop the threats, and discontinue all contact with the individual and the company.

A recent example of the effective use of threat assessment concerned an East Coast corporation with a newly appointed CEO. The experienced executive, recruited from outside the company, was brought in to turn around a downward trend in sales. Within two months he had orchestrated several innovative systems that began to increase production and sales. With the company pointed in the right direction, the CEO began to receive threatening letters.

As the threats became more serious, local and federal law enforcement agencies were notified by corporate security. After an explosive device was received, (a letter bomb that was designed to intimidate, but not explode), a strong possible suspect was developed from within the company. A lengthy investigation failed to produce witnesses or forensic evidence sufficient for an arrest. This became most frustrating for the victim, and the corporate security officers, because without a probable cause for arrest, they were asked by law enforcement not to confront the employee, and they were unable to fire the suspect.

A threat assessment was requested and that evaluation confirmed the initial suspect as the actual offender. The profiler determined that the offender didn't actually have a need to injure the CEO, but the suspect was in a position within the company where he felt he should have received more recognition for the company's progress. Surveillance techniques suggested by the profiler determined the suspect was purchasing, and probably using, a considerable amount of cocaine each week. The drug use contributed to his aberrant behavior and fueled his perceived need to get even with the CEO.

A well-planned intervention with corporate security, the company's employee assistance program representatives, and concerned members of the offender's family resulted in a successful conclusion to the case. The offender, a long-term employee, resigned without admitting guilt and was provided with a severance package. As part of the agreement, he was voluntarily admitted to a ninety-day drug rehabilitation facility, and has been closely monitored by family members since his release. This is a positive example of an alternative solution, to what should have been a criminal prosecution, provided by the profiler as an experienced evaluator of threatening behavior.

In cases like this, where the evidence is not sufficient for arrest, a profiler can usually provide a number of proactive techniques, and suggest possible alternatives, that will protect the victim and corporation while eliminating the source of the harassment.

3.2 Prevention of Workplace Violence

The intensive investigative training each criminal profiler receives, prior to certification by the FBI, is complemented by a concentrated study of aberrant behavior. Criminal profilers are thoroughly trained in crisis management and hostage negotiations, particularly as they pertain to preventing potentially violent situations in the workplace.

While most corporations have employee assistance programs and human resource experts to help an employee under a great deal of stress and reaching out for assistance, few have programs to identify the potentially violent worker who would never think of seeking help. When these people occasionally act out violently in the workplace, their coworkers and supervisors often describe the employee as quiet, reserved and one of the people they would never have expected to create a disturbance.

However, there are patterns of behavior that can may precede a violent outburst in the workplace, which can be identified by a trained observer. Concerned supervisors can monitor increased stress that may affect employees. Deadlines, interpersonal conflicts, forced overtime or even a sudden reduction in the employees' work hours, can trigger identifiable stress in the workplace. The stress in the personal life of the employee is most difficult to monitor, particularly with individuals uncomfortable with sharing their personal problems with others.

Profilers assist corporations in identifying employees with an elevated potential to act out violently in the workplace by working with human resource personnel to first establish a company wide program of zero tolerance toward workplace violence of any type.

Standardized workplace violence awareness programs can be implemented to inform managers and key personnel about the early warning signs leading to violent behavior. Frequently, coworkers can imply threatening behavior or make veiled threats which many supervisors and employees would not consider serious enough to report. In fact, this type of behavior, combined with other known contributing factors leading to violence in the workplace, could be a strong indicator of an employee about to exhibit extreme aberrant behavior or commit an actual assault.

In addition to providing training about aberrant behavior and violence in the workplace, profilers also assist corporate security and human resource officers with people identified as problem employees. There are proven methods of defusing potentially hostile workers prior to termination. These techniques can be of great value in assisting executives and human resource officers with exit interviews. The specific techniques used depend on the profiler evaluating the employee's potential for violence and the emotional stability at the time of the exit interview.

3.3 Loss Prevention and Leaks of Sensitive Information

When investigations of major losses within a corporation are undertaken, they are often complicated by interoffice policies and restrictions that aren't present in typical criminal investigations. These same problems arise when corporate security officers attempt to identify employees engaged in unethical, but not necessarily criminal, conduct. Leaking sensitive production, merger or new product information can have a devastating effect on morale and profits.

Loss prevention, and investigations into unethical behavior, can often be hampered by the number of individuals who have access to confidential information and products. Once corporate security has narrowed the focus of their investigation to a particular department or group of people, singling out the people responsible becomes a most difficult task. Among the general public, criminal investigations with a number of possible suspects are often successfully assisted by the use of the polygraph. However, labor union agreements and company policies frequently prevent the use of this investigative tool during internal investigations.

Criminal profilers have been trained in identifying truthful, as well as deceptive, behavior and their techniques have been most effective when used in place of the polygraph. The profiler designs a printed questionnaire specific to the investigation, which is presented to a suspect, or a series of potential suspects. Cooperation is usually achieved in the workplace because the subject is aware that coworkers will also be cooperating and completing the questionnaire. It is not as intimidating, or insulting, as being taken to a polygraph machine. The suspect has fewer excuses to decline to assist the investigators. Most offenders, after reviewing the questionnaire, readily complete it because they are more comfortable denying their guilt on paper than verbally to a polygraph examiner.

While the questions are quite different from the limited number typical of the polygraph examination, they are specifically designed to cause the subject a minimal amount of stress (which reduces the likelihood of a person refusing to go on after they have started to complete the questions).

Once the profiler has reviewed the investigation with the corporate security officers, and the questionnaire is prepared, it is generally administered under the supervision of the director of security. The completed questionnaires are then analyzed by the profiler to first eliminate the truthful employees, then to pinpoint the people withholding information and finally, to identify whoever is lying.

The value of distinguishing the people withholding information is that they can be interviewed to find out what they know about the incident before questioning the obvious liar. Frequently coworkers are aware of certain aspects of unethical or criminal behavior, and are in no way involved with the actual incident, but are reluctant to come forward with information during the initial stages of the investigation for any number of reasons.

Once these people withholding information are identified through the in-depth questionnaire analysis, the second step of the process is a detailed interview based upon the subjects' statements in the questionnaire. It becomes very difficult for a person to deny knowledge of the incident when the interviewer can show the person the responses in the questionnaire, in their own handwriting, which indicate they are withholding information. The same approach is used with anyone identified as lying in his or her statement. When shown the areas where they are untruthful, they usually confess.

The psychological impact on the subject is most important in this stage of the process. Imagine someone showing you your own handwritten statement, which you know isn't totally true, and then watching as the interviewer points out to you where you were lying. Wouldn't you be wondering, "If this interviewer knows this, what else does he know?"

The stress and self-doubt created in the subject during the process, which is increased during the follow-up, non-confrontational interview, usually is sufficient to obtain a confession.

The questionnaire prepared for statement analysis has been effectively used by profilers in criminal and corporate investigations around the world, and throughout the United States. An example of this system assisting corporate security in a long-term loss investigation involved repeated thefts of gold from a major jewelry manufacturer. Each time a loss was identified over twenty-five employees, with access to the area where the gold was added to the jewelry, were interviewed. The gold storage room was secure, but the thefts were occurring from within a larger secure work area. After each theft the locks were changed, but the thieves continued to defeat the locks and the video surveillance system.

The assistance of a criminal profiler was requested six months into the investigation. A questionnaire was prepared based on the information from the ongoing investigation and administered to all employees with access to the area of the most recent theft. The profiler's analysis indicated only one employee was withholding information, but it was unlikely he was actually removing the gold. This person consented to a lengthy interview and, when presented with the flaws in his own written statement, he confessed to "slightly" assisting another person with information that may have led to the thefts. The corporate security investigators were then able to determine that this employee, the inside person all along, had been assisting the actual thief—the locksmith who had been changing the company's locks for over fifteen years.

3.4 Evaluating Clients or Adversaries during Negotiations

Profilers have proven to be an asset during confidential, and sometimes hostile, corporate merger and takeover negotiations. While we all evaluate people with whom we deal professionally and privately, profilers are highly trained behavioral analysts and interviewers. The profiler easily identifies minute, nonverbal cues that the average person may miss. These are not broad body language shifts in posture, but simple nondescript movements unique to each individual. Under stress we all, consciously and unconsciously, move our bodies to relieve the tension. Generally, the more intelligent and socially sophisticated the individual the more minute the movements.

In a conference room setting, a profiler assists corporate attorneys and executives by observing the nonverbal behavior of adversaries during business conferences. As discussions become intense it is difficult for an executive to mentally process the competition's statements, weigh the seriousness of the offer, and prepare an articulate response while attempting to determine whether the speaker is honestly presenting the information. Working among the corporate team, the profiler can objectively evaluate the information and the presenter.

During breaks and after the conference, the profiler will discuss the weaknesses in the adversary's presentation. After one or more meetings, the profiler can often identify the areas of discussion where the adversary has attempted to mislead, as well as the likely motive for the misdirection.

A recent example of consulting with a multinational corporation, in the area of evaluating adversaries, involved a profiler and a three-person corporate negotiating/fact finding team traveling to three continents prior to attempting to acquire another major corporation. During several days of meetings, at each corporate headquarters, much information was obtained on the day to day operations of the company. Each corporate director was eager to accompany the team on tours of the corporate offices and plant. However, with information developed by the profiler during the first series of meetings, it became obvious these directors were not comfortable with the company's long-term plans. As the meetings progressed, the team concentrated the questioning on the company's future expectations. Eventually it was determined that the company's Third World ventures were necessary to maintain the current and short term future profits, but their concentration in these areas presented an unstable, long-term projection of profits for the corporation.

The profiler simply assisted the financial experts with his expertise in evaluating human behavior, in this case cross-cultural behavior, to assist the client company in avoiding what would have been a problem acquisition.

In the corporate world that is the true function of profiling: *to assist the company's professionals in enhancing their investigations and negotiations through training and the analysis of human behavior.*

Chapter 4

Surveillance

John S. Belrose

Synopsis

4.1 Introduction

We all need to get on the same page when it comes to the word *surveillance*. The definition in my dictionary is "a watch kept over a person, group, etc." This includes a suspect or prisoner.

I have been involved in stationary surveillances, moving surveillances, and electronic surveillances for most of thirty years. I have performed them in the U.S., the Middle East, Iran, Asia, and several European countries. During those thirty years I learned something very important: *surveillance is not a perfect science*. I learned this the hard way over many cases during the early years,

Before we get into real-case examples, we need to discuss types of surveillances, subjects of surveillances, equipment needed to conduct a proper surveillance and, last but not least, the big word *paranoia*. That word is on the mind of every investigator during a moving surveillance. And let's not kid ourselves, that includes everyone—city, state, federal, and private-sector investigators.

The subjects of the surveillance can be males, females, groups, buildings and so on. After the private-sector agency receives a telephone call from a client or client contact, a case supervisor (or case manager) should personally meet with the client. Field investigators should never be present at any locations where subjects may be present. If for any reason a client insists upon meeting the field investigator, a clandestine location should be arranged.

When a case supervisor meets with a client, he should obtain a complete profile of the subject to be placed under surveillance. *When meeting with a company representative, the case supervisor and company representative must be aware of the Fair Credit Act and its interpretations.* This applies if subject is an individual employed by the company.

Basic information must be obtained from a client regarding the subject of surveillance: name, date of birth, address and vehicle information. Since a vast number of stationary surveillances end up as moving surveillances, it is necessary to obtain in advance as much information as possible about the driving habits of the subject. This will help to control the pursuing investigator's paranoia. The case supervisor should attempt to discover the following:

- Does the subject continuously exceed posted speed limits, drive slower, run red lights and stop signs?
- Does the subject make frequent stops for coffee or at bars, banks, shopping, or restaurants?
- While driving does the subject continuously look into the rear view mirrors or talk on a cell telephone?
- Does the subject consume alcoholic beverages or take drugs?

You will get better information about driving habits in a domestic case. The wife or husband has spent time with the subject and are familiar with the subject's habits.

When all else fails and you cannot get the information regarding driving habits, search the DMV records for the subject's driving history. This can be done in most states. The search should reveal traffic violations such DUI and failure-to-stop. Most records will also give the offense date.

A number of private detective agencies will not take moving surveillance cases if told that the subject of the surveillance consistently disregards traffic laws. In the case of a radar stop, the chances are very good that the pursuing investigator will be stopped as well. Most subjects are not completely stupid. If they consistently violate traffic laws and the vehicle behind them is doing the same, the chances are high the investigator will be spotted.

During a moving surveillance, a well-trained investigator will know immediately if the subject suspects that he or she is being followed. Indications include:

- The subject consistently speeds up then begins to slow down.
- The subject is consistently looking into the rearview mirrors.
- The subject abruptly stops, pulls to the side of the road or into a parking lot.
- The subject runs red lights and or stop signs.
- The subject goes the wrong way on a one-way street.
- The subject continuously goes around the block.

Keep in mind that no two moving surveillances are alike. In some cases the client has suggested to the subject that he or she might be followed, increasing the chance of the surveillance being detected.

With the possible exception of electronic surveillance, the methods used by today's investigators have changed very little over the years. Investigators, however, *have* changed. In years past if a detective agency had five investigators on staff, all of them were expected to be able to conduct a surveillance. Stationary surveillances went well, but most moving surveillances ended with that dreaded call, "I lost him, boss."

Most of today's middle-to-large-sized detective agencies have particular investigators who are proficient at moving surveillances. In recent years, an increased number of women are getting into the investigations business and are performing stationary and moving surveillance.

A well-trained investigator with good common sense is less susceptible to intimidation and paranoia. An example of the necessity of using good common sense occurs when the subject consistently speeds up, slows down, runs red lights, runs stop signs, looks in rearview mirrors, pulls to the side of the road, or makes frequent stops. Basically, the subject is not acting normally. These driving habits may be in complete contrast to those habits furnished by the client.

Since a moving surveillance requires two or more pursuit vehicles, the chances of being caught by the subject diminish considerably. However, things have a way of changing quickly, particularly if the subject of the surveillance has been given advance knowledge that he or she may be under surveillance.

Experienced investigators will know when to terminate a surveillance. The termination should not result from paranoia; the decision should be based on good common sense.

When conducting either a stationary or moving surveillance, the location plays a large part, and will be conducted directly in congested neighborhoods, cul-de-sacs, one-way streets or schools. Generally, inner-city neighborhoods are less of a problem than suburban neighborhoods where everyone knows their neighbor. There, a person sitting in a vehicle for any length of time is assumed to be up to no good, or the police are on a surveillance. Either way the word will spread and eventually reach the subject.

Assuming that the subject's residence or place of business is not across from a donut shop, restaurant, or a shopping mall, maintaining cover will be difficult.

Prior to initiating any surveillance, it is strongly suggested that investigators personally contact local police. Aside from being the courteous thing to do, it helps to prevent a multitude or problems down the road.

When contacting the local police, investigators need not reveal the name of subjects under surveillance nor the type of assignment. The investigators should be prepared to produce proper identification and surveillance vehicle description. Also of interest to police will be the streets or intersections in which the investigators will be stationed. Some police departments might ask about the nature of the investigation, criminal, civil etc. If the surveillance concerns criminal activity, a briefing might be in order.

An initial profile is necessary for all assignments. Field investigators should be thoroughly briefed by a case supervisor before surveillance begins. If the case supervisor has done his job properly, a complete profile of the assignment has been obtained, including whether the assignment concerns individuals, buildings or vacant lots.

Proper equipment is also essential in any type of surveillance, and it should be checked before beginning the assignment. Some field investigators have their own equipment. If a case ends up in court, an opposing attorney might question investigators about the equipment used to expose his client. Also keep in mind that clients expect a high degree of professionalism—which includes proper equipment.

A nondescript motor vehicle is by far the most important piece of surveillance equipment. Such a vehicle is not brightly colored, covered with stickers, with antennas sticking out—it should have nothing that the subject of the surveillance can focus on. This is true for both stationary and moving surveillances because, as previously mentioned, a stationary surveillance can turn into a moving surveillance very quickly.

There are many options open to detective agencies for setting up surveillance vehicles. All that it takes is a little imagination. Some detective agencies customize their own vehicles. For example, they might take a 1995 Chevrolet Cavalier and install headlight and taillight cutoff switches. With these, the driver can immediately cut off one headlight or eliminate all taillights. This is a great tool for night surveillances.

Investigators should be nondescript, but the specifics depend on the type of assignment. If a subject is going to a five star restaurant, hotel, or some other exclusive location, the investigator must be dressed and conduct himself appropriately.

Communication between investigators is vital. Investigators assigned to stationary or moving surveillances must be able to communicate with each other. Hand-held radios (walkie-talkies) with extended range are recommended. Cellular telephones should be used as back up.

Some detective and security agencies have fully equipped surveillance vans, which can make the investigation easier. "Fully equipped" means a roof-mounted turret camera, camera ports, audio listening system, communications system, interchangeable and magnetic signs for exterior use (e.g., Joe's Cleaning Service). The camera system should be state of the art. Investigators must consult state and federal laws regarding audio recording.

For the most part, vans are ideal for stationary surveillances. A properly equipped surveillance van can be left at a surveillance site unattended or contact a surveillance team and alert them that the subject is on the move. However, some thought should be given before the van is used on moving surveillances because some vans may not be nondescript.

4.2 The Case Activity Report

For the most part, surveillance is pointless without a complete and accurate activity report. The client expects a professional report, typewritten and double-spaced. Another reason for a complete and accurate report is the possibility of future litigation regarding the assignment. Attorneys are likely to request all handwritten notes. They should be kept in the case file, but need not accompany the final report to the client.

Always use the word "approximately" when noting times on the activity report. Lawyers have been known to spend hours questioning investigators about the accuracy of their watch or vehicle clock.

4.3 Electronic Surveillance

The most common types of electronic surveillance are covert video, overt video, and GPS tracking (a.k.a. "bumper beepers"). The most common of the three is covert video. Laws in most states prevent the use of audio. Federal law can also prohibit this practice. Placement of a CCTV system should be considered very carefully—no bathrooms, locker rooms, bedrooms and so on. The covert video camera can be disguised as a clock, smoke detector, hat, necktie, pen, pager, cell phone, eyeglasses or the like.

Company-owned vehicles commonly use the GPS tracking systems to record speed, number of stops, frequency of stops, time, location and so forth. The system is also used on cargo containers. The vehicle owner must approve the installation of a tracking system. The best GPS tracking is "real time." This gives the surveillance team immediate feedback that can be received by a laptop computer.

4.4 Case Studies

The following are examples of real surveillance case reports. The names of the client and subject have been changed to protect their privacy. In all of their reports, AM-CO International Investigations identifies their investigators as agents by assigned agent numbers.

Surveillance reports will differ depending upon the type of surveillance, moving, stationary, and electronic. As previously mentioned in this chapter, the use of approximate times is important.

AM-CO International Investigations, Inc
Case Activity Report
Confidential

Operation No: B-01-115

Client: A. P. Jones, Inc
#121 Any Street
Cambridge, MA

Client Contact: Robert Smith

Agent(s) Assigned: M-312 & B-121

Re: Workers' Compensation (Surveillance)

Subject of Surveillance

Name:	William E. Peters
DOB:	21/06/51
SSN:	001-00-0000
Address:	#121 Concord Way Cambridge, MA
Vehicle:	1990 Ford F-100 pickup truck. Color Green. Registration # MA Reg NB-111

A photograph and description of the subject was obtained from the client.

<u>Assignment</u>

The subject (Peters) claimed that he injured his right arm when his arm became wedged between a forklift and concrete wall. The subject claims that he cannot fully use the injured arm and has filed a claim. The injury took place on April 10, 1995.

The client (A. P. Jones) received information on June 22, 1995 that the subject was working for his brother's roofing business.

The subject has been examined by the insurance company doctor. The subject (Peters) was advised by the doctor not to push, pull, or lift using his right arm.

The client has requested a two-day surveillance of subject Peters.

Details

July 01, 1995

At approximately 6:00 A.M. Agents M-312 and B-212 arrived at the Cambridge, MA police dept. Agents advised police that surveillance would be taking place in the vicinity of Concord Way.

At approximately 6:20 A.M. Agents arrived in the vicinity of the subject (Peters) residence. Said residence located at #121 Concord Way, Cambridge.

Upon arrival, agents observed two motor vehicles parked in the driveway of said residence. Vehicle #1: 1990 green Ford truck. MA Reg NB-111. Vehicle registered to subject Peters. Vehicle #2: blue Ford van. MA Reg 1234. Agents ran registration number 1234. Said vehicle registered to Norma Peters, 121 Concord Way.

Agents will initiate surveillance from two locations in the vicinity of the subject's residence.

At approximately 7:10 A.M. A dark blue Dodge pickup truck (MA Reg VVV-345) arrived at the subject's residence and parked in the driveway. Said vehicle was operated by a male subject. The male subject exited the pickup truck and entered the subject's residence. Surveillance vehicle #1 ran Reg # VVV345. The vehicle is registered to Paul Peters. Paul Peters is known to be the brother of the subject, William Peters.

At approximately 7:40 A.M. Subject William Peters exited #121 Concord Way, followed by brother Paul. Subject Peters approached the Dodge truck and opened the passenger side door using his right hand to pull the door open. Subject Peters was video taped opening the door. The subject entered the vehicle. Paul Peters entered the driver's side.

At approximately 8:05 A.M. The Dodge truck containing subject Peters, came to a stop at the donut shop at 345 Mass Ave, Cambridge, MA. The driver Paul Peters exited the vehicle and entered the donut shop.

At approximately 8:10 A.M. Paul Peters exited the donut shop carrying a small bag. He then entered his vehicle and drove off, followed by agents.

At approximately 8:25 A.M. The Dodge truck operated by Paul Peters, and containing subject William Peters came to a stop at #31 Raul Ave, Somerville, MA, a two-story residence. There were no other vehicles at the location. Several bundles of asbestos roof shingles were observed in the driveway. A portion of the roof facing the street was covered with a blue tarp.
Note: Raul Ave is a residential area. Agents will initiate surveillance from a street parallel to Raul Ave.

At approximately 8:28 A.M. Paul Peters and subject William Peters exited the Dodge truck. Paul Peters entered the residence while subject William Peters remained standing in the driveway. A short time later, Paul Peters exited the residence. Agents observed subject William Peters go to the rear of the Dodge truck and remove what appeared to be wire cutters. Subject William Peters then went over to a bundle of shingles and began to cut metal bands that were holding the shingles to the pallet. Paul Peters placed a ladder to the roof. He then went onto the roof and removed the blue tarp. Subject William Peters climbed half way up the ladder and helped remove the tarp. Subject Peters did not appear to have a problem using his right arm. (Video was obtained.) After the tarp was removed from the roof, both subject William Peters and Paul Peters began carrying shingles up the ladder and onto the roof. (Video was obtained.)

At approximately 11:00 A.M. Agents were contacted by case supervisor. Agents were advised to return to the office with video footage of the subject.

The client has requested a second day of surveillance regarding subject William Peters. However, a 6:00 P.M. drive-by on this date July 1, at #31 Raul Ave, will be conducted. This will be done to determine the job status.

At approximately 6:15 P.M. Agent M-312 checked #31 Raul Ave, Somer-ville. This agent observed that the roofing job had not been completed. No vehicles at said location.

Note: Return date will be July 2, 1995.
July 2, 1995

Today's surveillance will begin where subject William Peters was last observed working as a roofer. Location being #31 Raul Ave, Somerville, MA.

An unmanned surveillance van will be stationed on Raul Ave. The van is equipped with two surveillance cameras.

<u>At approximately 6:00 A.M.</u> Agents M-312 and B-121 arrived at Somerville, MA police headquarters. Agents advised the desk sergeant that an unmanned surveillance van would be parked in the vicinity of Raul Ave. Agents furnished police with van description.

<u>At approximately 6:35 A.M.</u> Agent M-312 parked the surveillance van in the vicinity of #31 Raul Ave. After focusing both surveillance cameras on #31, this agent exited said van and walked away. This agent was picked up by agent B-212 two blocks away.

<u>At approximately 8:05 A.M.</u> From an intersection near Raul Ave, agents observed a blue Dodge pickup truck enter Raul Ave. Said truck registered to Paul Peters. The truck contained two males. The driver was identified as Paul Peters. The passenger was identified as subject William Peters. From a parallel street agents observed the blue Dodge truck enter the driveway at #31 Raul Ave.

<u>At approximately 9:00 A.M.</u> Agents left the vicinity of Raul Ave. Agents will return in late afternoon and retrieve the surveillance van.

<u>At approximately 4:30 P.M.</u> Agent M-312 and B-121 returned to Raul Ave. The blue Dodge truck was no longer parked at #31 Raul Ave. Agent M-312 entered the surveillance van and left the area.

<u>At approximately 5:15 P.M.</u> Agents arrived at AM-CO headquarters. Two surveillance tapes were removed form the surveillance van. Both video tapes were examined and showed subject William Peters using his right arm with no apparent problems.

The workers' compensation investigation went well. Confronted with the video evidence, subject William Peters, through his attorney, dropped his claim. The client has advised the subject's attorney that all monies paid to the subject must be returned. If not, the client will proceed with a claim against for subject workers compensation fraud.

A recent operation undertaken by AM-CO International Investigations concerned the backup and surveillance for an undercover agent. The agent was employed by AM-CO, and assigned to a well-known Boston company.

The Boston company contacted AM-CO International Investigations and stated that, based on information from a confidential source, they suspected drug dealing in one of their distribution centers on the 3:00 P.M. to 11:00 P.M. shift.

After the undercover agent had been on assignment for two weeks, he advised the case supervisor that he had learned that two loading dock employees had "stuff for sale." The agent had made it known to an employee he worked with, that he "used a little weed now and then." The agent was told, "You can get anything here."

As time went by, the agent became somewhat friendly with the two loading dock suspects. Eventually the agent was invited to join them and other employees for beers at a bar after work. At the time that he was invited, drugs were not mentioned.

Friday was pay day at the plant. On one particular Friday, the agent observed one of the two suspects remove a small plastic bag containing an off-white powder from his left pants' pocket. The suspect gave the bag to a female employee who then gave the suspect an envelope. This took place on the loading dock next to the boiler door room.

The company's director of loss prevention and the case supervisor decided to conceal a covert camera in the loading dock area on a weekend when no employees would be on site.

When and if the agent made a drug buy, he was instructed to do so under the camera if possible. The covert camera, programmed to record for seventy-two hours on one tape, was wired back to the recorder in the loss prevention office. The integrity of all surveillance tapes were the responsibility of loss prevention department.

After the covert camera system was installed, a meeting with police was arranged. Drug unit detectives were briefed about the operation. Everyone present agreed that the private agent was not an agent of the state. Any drugs purchased by the agent would be turned over to police as soon as possible. All covert videotapes would also be turned over to police.

Both suspects were known to the police. One of the suspects was considered dangerous. However, neither suspect had been arrested on drug-related offenses; most of the charges had been disorderly conduct and alcohol-related.

One week after being invited by the suspects to join them for a beer, the agent was approached by the suspects and told, "A bunch of us are going for beers after work tonight. We are not sure what bar yet—you just follow us." This took place at 4:30 P.M. During a break, the agent reported the bar invitation to AM-CO. He was told to take the suspects up on the invitation, and assured that he would be followed by a surveillance team.

About one hour before the 11:00 P.M. shift change, two surveillance vehicles arrived in the vicinity of company. The agent's vehicle and two vehicles operated by the suspects were noted in the parking lot.

At about 11:00 P.M., the agent was observed walking with the suspects and an unidentified female employee. A prearranged signal from the agent to the surveillance team was given. Everything was still a "go."

The surveillance team followed the suspects and the agent to a neighborhood bar. The suspects and the unidentified female entered the bar, followed by the undercover agent. The surveillance team kept watch on the front and rear doors of the bar.

At about 12:45 A.M. the agent exited the bar and drove off, followed by one member of the surveillance team. The agent was contacted on his cellular phone and was told that he was being followed by a member of the surveillance team. About four miles from the bar, the agent pulled into a shopping mall parking lot. He reported that he arranged to buy a small amount of cocaine from the suspects at the company on pay day. Only one of the suspects had made the offer. However, the second suspect and female (now identified) were present and both agreed that it would be "good stuff." The agent agreed to the purchase on the condition that it be done on the loading dock. The suspects agreed and said, "Where else?"

The company's loss prevention director contacted AM-CO operations and reported that the covert camera had revealed two probable drug transactions in which two small plastic bags were exchanged for money. This took place between the suspects and two front-office employees. In return, the loss prevention director was told about the agent's drug purchase that was expected to take place on the next pay day.

Surveillance tapes to date were turned over to police detectives. The police were told of the pending purchase by the agent; they agreed to let the purchase occur in view of the covert camera. Afterward, the police would meet the agent at a prearranged location and secure the drugs.

Until the day of the pay day drug purchase, the agent would be kept under surveillance after he left work at night. This was to insure his safety, since the agent observed one of the suspects taking a long look at his (agent) vehicle in the company's parking lot. Although the agent had been at the plant for nine weeks, the suspects may not have trusted him completely. A one-vehicle counter-surveillance was kept on the agent from the time he left the plant until he arrived at home.

AM-CO International was contacted by the state drug task force, which had apparently taken over the case from the local police. A task force agent asked to speak with the undercover agent before the pay day purchase. It was learned during the meeting that the bar frequented by the suspects was a task force target. AM-CO's recent surveillance at the bar had been noted by the task force.

Pay day arrived. The agent was given $280.00 in marked bills and was instructed to let the suspects approach him for the drug sale. The transaction needed to be as close to the covert camera as possible.

All parties involved in the operation had reviewed several days of covert video tapes. There were nine suspected drug transactions observed between the two suspect dealers and other company employees. All of the employees were identified through the video surveillance. All covert video tapes to date were in the possession of task force agents.

The company, through the loss prevention director, requested that the suspected dealers be arrested immediately after the purchase by the undercover agent. The drug task force replied that they might have a chance to "bag" a lot more people if the undercover operation continued. The company said that some of the employees who were buying the drugs operated heavy machinery. "Imagine our liability if an employee on drugs injures himself or another employee. The purpose of this undercover and video surveillance is to terminate drug dealers and users."

The drug task force agreed with the company. A task force agent was stationed in the loss prevention director's office to observe the pay day drug deal on the covert camera's monitor. He was instructed to radio a task force surveillance team waiting in the parking lot as soon as the first drug deal was made. Task force agents would then immediately take the two suspects and buyer into custody.

At approximately 5:10 P.M., the first drug deal took place. The undercover agent was not the first sale. However, as luck would have it, the sale went down in plain view of the covert camera. The camera was so well placed that it picked up the buyer sampling cocaine and the suspects counting the money. The sellers (suspects) and the buyer were arrested on the spot.

As result of this operation, those employees (and the undercover agent) who purchased drugs on company property were terminated. During termination, each and every terminated employee was told about the video surveillance system. The employees were further advised that, should they attempt legal action against the company, all surveillance tapes would be presented in court. *Note*: This operation took place before the Fair Credit Reporting Act.

This operation indicated how efficiently the covert video surveillance system can operate. However, it takes very good planning and trained technicians to set the system up. It is also important to be able to back up the private undercover agent with surveillance when he is involved in off-site functions with suspects. If working in a foreign country, a local agency should be contacted.

During 1978, this author worked a nasty undercover operation in Iran. This assignment included moving truck surveillances from the Caspian Sea ports to the city of Isfahan. Not one day went by that I didn't wish that I was going from Boston to New York. Fear overshadowed paranoia—the fear factor being having to stop in small towns and be faced with anti-government and anti-American protesters. During every surveillance, the Iranian truck drivers stopped at every small town along the way. These were so-called rest stops.

My Iranian contact at the time was a former SAVAK agent who I called "Tiny." In reality, he was as big as a house. We had another American undercover agent assigned to the city of Tehran. This agent was young and had no moving surveillance training.

It was sometime after my third surveillance from the port to Isfahan, that Tiny contacted me and told me I was not alone on those long drives.

Tiny asked me if I was aware of the steel mill being built by the Russians, outside of Isfahan. I was. As Tiny put it, it appeared that the Russian agents, posing as steel mill workers, were also following trucks from the port to Isfahan. Now I had something to look forward to during the next surveillance.

It didn't take long for me to pick up the Russians. Although during previous surveillances I had observed vehicles close behind the trucks, those vehicles kept on going when trucks came to a stop in towns with angry protesters. I never saw those vehicles again along the way. It was obvious that the Russian agents didn't want any part of the protesters.

This highlights the importance of contacting a local agency in that country. This does not include all countries, however. Do your homework first.

There are issues to consider when conducting surveillances. This chapter has attempted to cover some of them. A well-trained and well-equipped investigator can successfully complete an assignment and avoid detection.

Chapter 5

Eavesdropping Detection and Counterespionage Programs: Philosophy & Implementation

Kevin D. Murray, CPP, CFE, BCFE

Synopsis

5.1 Introduction

"Eavesdropping" is not your enemy's goal. It is the means to an end—money, power, ideology, or the ultimate capitalist offence...killing the competition. Enemies spy. A spy is an assassin.

Your spy may be anyone—competitors, employees, terrorists, jealous colleagues, activists, journalists, unfriendly governments, etc. They may want what you have or detest who you are. Spies need information to achieve their goals. How to get it? Espionage tactics; like eavesdropping. How to frustrate their hostile actions? Look for the eavesdropping.

Before an attack, there is a relatively long and leisurely period when your enemies quietly collect intelligence. They size you up. Evaluate the cost-effectiveness of an attack. And then steal information to fuel the attack.

Electronic eavesdropping is a key component of this intelligence collection process. It is also the easiest of spy methods to detect. All you have to do is look for it. In today's corporate environment, not having a regular inspection program in place is simply negligence or suicide.

"The information you give your enemy is the dagger you die by." When the attack occurs, it is too late to defend yourself. Look for the eavesdropping. Infostarve the enemy.

5.2 The 9-11 Analogy

To prevent a disaster, you have to look for evidence of trouble brewing, noticing people who want commercial flight training—without the landing instructions—for example. Notice this type of evidence, and you still have time to thwart the disaster—at low loss and low cost. Ignore the evidence, or overlook it entirely, and you have a very expensive clean-up project in the offing.

Terrorism and espionage share three common traits:

1. A protracted period of planning and intelligence collection.
2. The instant when the collected information is used to the detriment of the target.
3. The target's reflex reaction of playing patch-up, catch-up.

Most espionage losses, like terrorism losses, can never be recouped. The instinctive responses, on-guard and stand-at-attention, are expensive, nerve-racking, demoralizing, ultimately desensitizing, and doomed to fail. Waiting for the next attack, even with eyes wide open, still doesn't prevent an attack.

The adage, "An ounce of prevention is worth a pound of cure," is more relevant today than ever before. In counterespionage, the "ounce of prevention" is the electronic-surveillance detection inspection.

Think of eavesdropping detection inspections as the canary in the corporate mine shaft. Inspections sniff out trouble. They sound the alarm. They allow you to defend yourself inexpensively and with the best chance for success. A proactive inspection program is a Pre-Attack Early Warning System.

The value of periodic proactive eavesdropping detection inspections offers:

1. A defense against:

- competitive intelligence
- corporate espionage
- terrorism
- malignant activism
- extortionography
- internal intrigue
- strategy spying
- media snooping
- mysterious leaks
- personal privacy concerns

2. Protection of:

- sensitive communications
- boardroom discussions
- mergers and acquisitions
- delicate negotiations
- lawsuit strategies
- employee safety
- trade secrets
- personal privacy
- vulnerable off-site meetings
- executive residences and home offices

3. Inspections help to satisfy:

- fiduciary responsibilities
- due diligence requirements
- "business secret" requirements for court

5.3 Creating an Eavesdropping Detection Inspection Program

Your boss asks,"What is a TSCM Inspection Program?" You answer, "Electronic eavesdropping inspections—sometimes referred to as Technical Surveillance Countermeasures or TSCM—are a systematic effort to detect intelligence collection efforts against us. They provide us with early warning. Thus, we can thwart an enemy's efforts before we are harmed. Very cheap. Very effective." (Gee, you sound smart.)

Start your program, or upgrade your current efforts, by working with an independent security consultant who specializes in surveillance detection testing and overall counterespionage consulting. Make sure they are not product affiliated. You need to be able to trust their judgement 100 percent. Accepting remuneration from product sales, accepting commissions, or having a menu of "other recommended services" that their company can provide, clouds judgment.

The most visible part of the specialist's work is the search for electronic eavesdropping devices. This is not however the only part. A good counterespionage consultant will also identify and make corrective recommendations for other info-loss vulnerabilities such as inadequate perimeter security or poor security habits.

"What areas should be inspected?"

You continue your conversation with the boss..."We don't need to inspect everything, just our sensitive areas: offices, conference rooms, executive dining areas, off-site meeting locations, executive homes, vehicles, etc." (I am really impressed with your speed learning.)

Work with your specialist to develop this list of sensitive areas. Not all areas of a business or governmental agency are equally sensitive. Not all areas will always be sensitive. The list of areas to be inspected is not rigid. Expect it to change with time and circumstances. The process is very economical if planned properly. It is rarely necessary to "check everything." Creating a hierarchy of areas to inspect increases effectiveness and reduces costs.

Once the sensitive areas are identified, your specialist will help you decide how often to reinspect. Each area will have its own window-of-vulnerability-tolerance (WOVT).

"How often should we inspect?"

Your conversation with your boss is going well... "The generally accepted corporate and government security practice is quarterly inspections; with bi-annual inspections being the next most common schedule." (Couldn't have said it better myself.) "Of course, rooms with different sensitivity levels may be mixed, matched, and juxtaposed for maximum effectiveness. In times of crisis or heightened sensitivity, more frequent inspections will be required. Occasionally, there may be an area where an annual inspection will suffice. I will work all this out with our counterespionage consultant." (Show off.)

"But, why do inspections need to be repeated?"

You rattle off:

- To detect the signs of intelligence gathering—a prelude to the real trouble.
- To allow us time to counterattack before damage can be done.
- To limit our windows of vulnerability.
- To satisfy our on-going legal requirements for due diligence.
- To help satisfy the requirements for attaining "business secret" status in court.
- To identify new methods of privacy invasion and information theft.

"And you know, not re-inspecting periodically may be interpreted (in court) as an admission that previously protected information is no longer important."

"So, what does an inspection program entail?"

"The counterespionage specialist and technical investigators bring their instrumentation to our site," you explain. "This is usually scheduled during off-hours so as not to be disruptive to our work. The actual inspection happens something like this:"

A. Preliminary evaluation

At the outset, the specialist conducts a background interview to obtain an overview of the security climate, concerns, and culture. (This discussion is not held within the areas being inspected.) Just like a doctor, they want to fully understand the symptoms and circumstances that preceded the call for assistance, or the decision to begin a proactive protection program.

B. Survey of current security measures

This includes an inspection of perimeter and interior physical security hardware. Doors, locks, windows, vents, alarm devices, wastepaper disposal methods, etc. It also includes a review of current security policies and procedures. A tour of the facility may be part of the process. Have all the necessary keys available, and if necessary, a copy of the floor plans.

C. Visual examination

The areas in question are visually inspected for eavesdropping devices, and evidence of prior eavesdropping attempts (bits of wire, tape, holes, fresh paint or putty, disturbed dust, etc.). The technical investigators rely heavily on their eyes, knowledge, and experience during this stage of their work—these are the finest detection instruments available. The visual inspection is thorough and includes furniture, fixtures, wiring, ductwork, and small items within the area.

D. Acoustic ducting evaluation

Unexpected sound leakage into adjacent areas has been found to be the cause of many information leaks, especially the in-house type. Open air ceiling plenums, air ducts, common baseboard heater ducts, walls common with storage/rest/coffee rooms, and holes in concrete floors have all aided eavesdroppers at one time or another. The acoustical ducting evaluation takes all of this into consideration.

As you see, electronic eavesdropping detection begins long before the specialized electronic instruments are unpacked.

E. Inspection of telephone instruments

An extensive physical examination of telephone instruments is undertaken. There are many types of attacks involving bugs, taps, and wiring modifications which can compromise a basic telephone instrument. Business telephones have additional vulnerabilities, some of which are legitimate system features that, when abused, become eavesdropper-friendly.

After a telephone instrument is opened for inspection, it is put back together and its screws are sealed with security tape. This provides visual proof that the phone has not been opened since the technical investigator last inspected it.

Security seals should be custom-made and serialized so that they cannot be duplicated. Computer-printed sticky labels, nail polish, or even stock security seals are not adequate in this situation.

You can periodically inspect your consultant's security seals yourself. Broken seals may indicate an intrusion, while missing seals may indicate a switch of telephone sets. Either condition is suspicious and should prompt a call to your specialist (from a safe phone, of course).

F. Inspection of other communications devices

Other communications devices, e.g. faxes, speakerphones, modems, computers, etc., are included because they may carry information the enemy finds interesting. One not-so-obvious reason for inspecting is that their connections to the outside world can be hijacked. Standard audio and video room eavesdropping devices just love fax and modem lines, LANs, and wireless LANs! All are additional sound/video/data-moving conduits that need to be inspected.

G. Inspection of telephone wiring

Wiring associated with the telephones under test is inspected for attachments and damage. Damaged wiring is often the only evidence of a prior wiretap.

H. Inspection of junction blocks

Junction blocks—where telephone wires connect to each other within a building—may also be inspected. These connected wires form a path between the telephone instrument and the on-premises, telephone switching equipment. In some cases (e.g., simple residential phone service and facsimile machines) internal wiring connects directly to outside cables which lead to the phone company central office. Junction blocks are an easy and relatively safe place to attach a wiretap device. Extra wiring paths may also be constructed at junction blocks (using the spare wiring already in place) to route the audio/video/data to a remote relay device or a listening post.

I. Telephone room inspection

The building telephone room houses more junction blocks for the internal phone system; switching equipment for the internal telephone system; and telephone company junction blocks for the incoming lines. This is another area of vulnerability which requires an inspection from both a wiretapping and physical security point of view. In large buildings, this room is usually found in the basement / utility area. Historically, small to medium-sized telephone rooms have received minimal security attention.

J. Phone line electrical measurements

Measurements are taken and compared against telephone industry standards. Readings which deviate from the norm can help reveal certain types of wiretaps.

K. Time domain reflectometry analysis

In this test, a pulse is injected into the telephone line. If the two wires are intact and parallel to one another, the pulse continues its trip smoothly. If the pulse passes a point where there is a change in the wiring (splices to other wires, a wiretap, a wall plug, the end of the wires, etc.) a portion of the pulse is reflected back and alerts the technical investigator to a possible problem.

An instrument called a Time Domain Reflectometer (also known as TDR or cable radar) injects these pulses, reads their reflections, and measures the time difference between the two events. This allows the TDR to calculate the distance to the irregularity. A time-verses-irregularity graph is displayed on the TDR's display. This signature is interpreted. Imperfections in line integrity are calculated to within a few inches of their actual location. An in-person inspection of these points is then made. This allows a thorough examination of the wiring even when hidden from normal view. Time Domain Reflectometry allows reliable testing of phone wiring up to 2,000 feet in length and detection of some wiretap attacks at distances of up to 36,000 feet.

L. Non-linear junction detection (NLJD)

This detection technique—similar to retail shoplifting tag detection—is used to locate the semi-conductor components used in electronic circuits, e.g. diodes, transistors, etc.. Bugging devices which contain these components (transmitters, tape recorders, amplified microphones, miniature TV cameras, etc.) are discovered in this manner. They are detectable even when secreted inside walls and objects by using an NLJD. The NLJD emits a radio signal and listens for the return signal from the electronic parts which make up eavesdropping devices.

Special feature: Discovery of an eavesdropping device using an NLJD is not dependent on the eavesdropping device being active at the time of the search!

M. RF spectrum analysis/radio reconnaissance spectrum analysis® (RRSA)

Eavesdropping devices which transmit a radio signal (over-the-air or on building wiring) may be detected with an instrument called a Spectrum Analyzer. In simple terms, it can be thought of as a radio which has a very long and continuous tuning dial. The received signals are shown on a display screen for visual analysis and are also converted to sound. Radio Reconnaissance Spectrum Analysis is a technique which carries the detection process several steps further.

Each signal the technical investigator receives is evaluated to determine if it is carrying voice, data, or video information from the sensitive areas being inspected. Analysis also includes converting video signals into viewable and documentable television pictures. Capturing eavesdropping evidence on the fly is quite important but may not be available from inexperienced or under-equipped purveyors.

In addition to detecting video bugging devices, the RRSA technique detects computer emissions. These are signals inadvertently emitted by some computers which can be received and reconstructed from a considerable distance away. The technique also detects emissions from computers which have been deliberately bugged.

Due to the sensitivity of an RRSA system, radio transmissions from bugging devices are detectable even if the device is not in the vicinity of the areas being inspected. This means that although only certain rooms may be slated for inspection entire sections of buildings benefit from this particular test.

N. Thermal emissions spectrum analysis® (TESA)

Electronic eavesdropping devices and covert spy cameras are discovered with speed and certainty thanks to a relatively new detection method: Thermal Emissions Spectrum Analysis® (TESA).

TESA allows hidden bugs and spy cameras to be 'seen' on a portable video display by virtue of the minute amounts of heat radiated as electricity flows in their circuitry. Surveillance devices hidden in ceiling tiles, in walls, and in other common objects create slight warm spots.

Detecting eavesdropping devices requires sensitivities in the thousandths-of-a-degree Celsius range—much less than the amount of heat your fingertip leaves on an object after you touch it for a split second.

Currently, thousandths-of-a-degree level of sensitivity is only available in special lab-quality instruments priced in the $50,000 and up range. Lab-quality TESA instrumentation is different from the utility-grade infrared cameras used by police and electrical inspectors—as different as prop planes are from commercial jets. Utility infrared cameras cost $8,000-$30,000, but their sensitivity is only in the tenths of a degree range.

Availability of this very worthwhile test procedure is still limited due to the cost of instrumentation. Try to select a consultant who employs this level of testing. Although it is not the only indicator of professional competence, the ability to deploy the latest detection technologies is a good start.

O. Additional tests

As in the medical profession, counterespionage consultants also have many tests that are selectively applied depending upon a client's specific needs or concerns. Every situation is a bit different.

In addition to the group of inspection procedures already mentioned, there are tests which are used as the situation demands. A good technical investigator will bring quite a bit of additional analysis and thought to the inspection process. The overall goal of your specialist should always be to *solve-the-concern*, not simply dash blindly through a one-size-fits-all checklist. "Checklist Charlies" are a spy's best friend.

Expect to be taken on a guided tour of the whole inspection process, test by test, (in easy to understand terms) the very first time one is conducted for you. The more you know about what the technical investigators are doing, the better it is for all concerned.

In addition to the tests outlined above, the investigative process should also take into consideration infrared, fiber optic, hydrophonic, and new eavesdropping threats which will develop in the months and years to come. New threats always arise with new technology.

P. Final report

When your inspection is complete, you should receive a full verbal debriefing. In this meeting the lead technical investigator highlights all serious problems found and recommends solutions which may need to be implemented promptly. Expect a detailed written report within a week.

A final report should include:

- A statement about why the inspection was undertaken—proactive or active problem.
- A description of all the areas and communications equipment inspected.
- An explanation of all tests conducted.
- The findings.
- Recommendations for security improvements.
- A review of other espionage loopholes found.
- Security improvements since the last inspection.
- Photos, floor maps, inspection history logs, etc., and other useful espionage prevention information.

Final reports are important documents. Safeguard each one. Together they show a continuing effort to provide information security for specific areas within your business or agency. This is proof that you took extraordinary steps to classify your information as proprietary and secret. You have gone above and beyond LAG (locks, alarms, and guards). Courts will now listen, stockholders should be satisfied, and enemies will have to move on to someone else's door for easier pickings.

Important extras:

- A counterespionage consultant would be seriously remiss if only electronic eavesdropping issues were addressed.
- Experience has shown that few information leaks can be blamed solely on electronic eavesdropping. Sure, eavesdropping may be the most devastating form of espionage—that information is the freshest. But this is only one piece of the puzzle. To see the entire picture, a good spy will collect the other puzzle parts as well. Each part may seem innocuous in and of itself, but they are synergistically related.
- Make sure your specialist takes a holistic approach to information security and endeavors to solve your problems or concerns no matter what the actual cause.

"How do I identify the right specialist for my needs?"

You need to find an independent security consultant who specializes in electronic eavesdropping detection and espionage prevention. Recognizing this person may not always be easy. There are too few of them, and too many pretenders.

Contact several corporate security directors. Ask them who they are using. Get first-hand recommendations. You may also seek out industry associations for referrals.

- International Association of Professional Security Consultants
  www.iapsc.org
  515-282-8192
- The Espionage Research Institute
  301-292-6430

Conduct an Internet search using key words like "eavesdropping" or "counterespionage." Carefully evaluate (very carefully) the web sites you come across. Red flags include little, if any information about the people who will have access to your sensitive areas, and self-aggrandizing statements that sound too good to be true. Always ask for references. Always verify. Always.

Before developing a long-term relationship with any specialist, do what you do best—investigate! Ask lots of questions, like these:

- Is electronic eavesdropping detection your company's only business?
- How many years have you been specializing in eavesdropping detection?
- How many years under your current company name?
- What did you do before that?
- How many electronic eavesdropping investigations have you personally handled?
- Are your recommendations independent and unbiased? Do they profit you in any way?
- Is your firm licensed by a state police authority?
- Are resumes available for every technical investigator who will be on my premises?
- Can you provide copies of your Certificates of Insurance for me?
- Do you have any professional certifications? (CPP, CFE, BCFE...)
- Do you teach security or counterespionage on a university level?
- Have you written books, chapters or articles that have been published? May I see them?
- Do you have references? (Be sure to call them.)
- What is the dollar value of the instrumentation you use?
- Do you own all your own instrumentation? (Do you rent or "borrow" from your full-time employer?)
- What is the average age of your instrumentation?
- Will you allow your eavesdropping device 'finds' to be verified via polygraph testing?
- Will you sign a "Confidentiality Agreement?"
- Are you qualified to investigate general corporate espionage too?

- In how many court cases have you been qualified as an expert witness? (List please.)
- Do you use some form of Radio-Reconnaissance Spectrum Analysis (RRSA)?
- Do you use Non-Linear Junction Detection to find dormant bugs?
- Do you use Time Domain Reflectometers to check every inch of phone wiring?
- What is your wireless LAN inspection procedure?
- Is Thermal Imaging Spectrum Analysis® (TESA) part of your procedure? What camera do you use?
- How will you inspect for infrared emissions, fiber optic devices, etc.?
- How will you customize your procedures to meet my needs?
- Do you charge extra for inspecting on nights, weekends, or holidays?

Ask yourself the folloring questions:

- Are they sincere about solving my concerns, or are they money driven?
- Will their presentation, dress, and demeanor reflect well on me in my boss's eyes? Or in court?
- Trusting my instincts, do I really feel they are capable of solving my concerns?

If you are still unsure after all this, keep looking. Success hinges on finding Mr./Ms. Right.

Resist the temptation to bypass Mr./Ms. Right for Mr./Ms. Almostasgood just because there are some travel expenses involved or their fees are not the lowest. This is false economy. Use the very best person you can find. You may only get one chance to "do it right." Remember, fees and expenses are minor compared to the value of what you are protecting.

5.4 Cost of an Inspection Program

"What is the average cost of an inspection?"

"A whole lot less than suffering an attack."

Eavesdropping detection inspection services are usually charged on a per-item basis, or in the case of smaller assignments, an agreed-upon flat rate. All budgets may be accommodated simply by inspecting the most sensitive areas first. Counterespionage consulting is usually billed on a daily basis.

Per-hour fees are no longer used by true countermeasures specialists. The length of time it takes to complete an inspection has little bearing on how effective the search is. You are paying for value, not time. A knowledgeable and well-equipped specialist for example may complete an inspection in half the time required by someone who is ill-equipped and not very knowledgeable. A qualified specialist will also be many times more effective.

Shopping tips:

- Always ask to see a written *Fee & Expense Schedule* before discussing job details.
- Avoid per-hour pricing.
- If you hear "I'll have to stop by your location first." from a specialist—instead of receiving the straightforward pricing you requested—you're probably in for a high pressure sales call.
- Inadequate pricing cheats you of quality expertise and instrumentation. If the prices seem low, suspect that the person has not invested in quality instrumentation, training, and insurance. If the cost is unrealistically high, you can rightfully suspect that this person doesn't have much experience either.

Do your research. Pre-qualifying your eavesdropping detection specialist is important.

Average inspection fees

The following samples reflect the charges required to provide corporate/government level eavesdropping detection services. The average prices shown are current as of the publication date of this book.

1. **Small inspections** include five average size offices, five telephones, associated wiring and switching equipment, and a final written report. The approximate cost: $3,700.
2. **Medium inspections** include eight average size offices, eight secretarial areas, one large board room, sixteen telephones with associated wiring and switching equipment, two fax machines with associated wiring, one speakerphone system, one video teleconferencing unit, and a final written report. The approximate cost: $8,500.
3. **Large inspections** include twenty average size rooms, one large board room, forty telephones with associated wiring and switching equipment, five fax machines with associated wiring, six speakerphone systems, one video teleconferencing unit, and a final written report. the approximate cost is $18,500.

5.5 Espionage Is Preventable

Trust your instincts. When it comes to eavesdropping, the thought would not have occurred to you if a problem did not exist. Tell your specialist; this is a legitimate warning flag. It is not paranoia.

Only failed espionage gets discovered. You never hear about successful eavesdropping or espionage attacks. You're not supposed to. It's a covert act. Frequency of publicity is on par with commercial airline flights: only partially completed (failed) flights make the news. Watergate, for example, was a classic case of espionage incompetence in action.

This apparent quiet is what gives uninformed people the feeling that spying doesn't occur—it is a false sense of security. Not only is information theft invisible and silent, it is also prevalent. Spying is a common activity. Discovery relies heavily on proactive inspections—and the target's intuition.

Due to the covert nature of spying, the exact extent of it is not known. However, we can use the failed espionage attempts as a gauge. They reveal over and over again that the problem does exist. Also, the plethora of electronic surveillance equipment being openly sold in "spy shops," over the Internet, and in "executive toy" catalogs gives us a good indication of the magnitude of electronic eavesdropping.

Documented cases of eavesdropping and espionage appear in the news regularly. They show that left unchecked spies and enemies can desiccate a bottom line, wipe out a competitive advantage, and leave a company a shell of its former self.

Information is like any other corporate asset. Management has a responsibility to protect it. Stockholders can claim negligence and hold company executives responsible if this asset is lost due to improper protection efforts. Simple LAG (locks, alarms and guards) will not appear to be proper protection.

Further, the law only protects those who protect themselves. You can't just wander into the courtroom crying "They stole my business secrets" and expect help. You have to show the extraordinary steps you took (and maintained) to elevate your business information to business secret status. Simple LAG will not appear to be extraordinary. Inspect regularly. Detecting espionage before the effects surface will keep you out of the time/money black-hole of court.

Counterespionage is not a D-I-Y Project.

- Don't buy eavesdropping detection gadgets.
- Don't play detective.
- Don't hire a private detective and let them play debugging expert.

Eavesdropping detection is a serious business. Counterespionage work is a full-time specialty within the security field. Professional help is available. Be proactive, and if you encounter an emergency, remember that you may only have one chance to "do it right."

5.6 Final Word

You are no longer helpless. Congratulations! Your security knowledge is now more complete than ever before. No longer will you be powerless to protect your company's ideas, plans, strategies, hard work, and privacy. No longer will you stand helpless as the opposition tries to pick your pockets, and activists and terrorists try to take you down. No longer will you live in fear that stockholders will revolt, or that judges won't take you seriously.

Even better, you will not have to stand by and wonder if your current electronic eavesdropping sweeps are being conducted properly. You now know the qualities to seek when enlisting the aid of professional counter-espionage counsel.

Chapter 6

Voice Identification: The Aural/ Spectrographic Method

Tom Owen and Michael C. McDermott

Synopsis

6.1 Introduction

The forensic science of voice identification has come a long way from when it was first introduced in the American courts back in the mid-1960s. In those early days, there was little research to support the theory that human voices are unique and could be used as a means for identification. There was also no standardization of how identification was reached, or even training or qualifications necessary to perform the analysis. Voice comparisons were made solely on the pattern analysis of a few commonly used words. Because of the novelty of the technique there were only a few people in the world who performed voice identification analysis and who were capable of explaining it to a court.

Gradually the process became known to other scientists who voiced concerns, not about the validity of the analysis, but about the lack of substantial research demonstrating the reliability of the technique. They felt that the technique should not be used in the courtroom without more documentation. Thus, the battle lines were drawn over the admissibility of voice identification evidence, with proponents claiming a valid, reliable identification process, and opponents claiming that more research must be completed before the process should be used in courtrooms.

Today voice identification analysis has matured into a sophisticated identification technique, using the latest technologies. The research, which is continuing today, demonstrates the validity and reliability of the process when performed by a trained and certified examiner using established standardized procedures. Voice identification experts are found all over the world. No longer limited to the visual comparison of a few words, the comparison of human voices now focuses on every aspect of the words spoken: the words themselves, the way the words flow together, and the pauses between them. Both aural (listening) and spectrographic (visual) analyses are combined to form a conclusion about the identity of the voices in question.

The road to admissibility of voice identification evidence in the courts of the United States has not been without its potholes. Many courts have had to rule on this issue without having access to all the facts. Trial strategies and budgets have resulted in incomplete presentations to the courts. To compound the problem, courts have used different standards of admission, resulting in different opinions about the admissibility of voice identification evidence. Even those courts that have claimed to use the same standard of admissibility have interpreted it in a variety of ways, resulting in a lack of consistency. Although many courts have excluded voice identification evidence, none of them has found the technique unreliable. Exclusion has always been based on the fact that the evidence did not present a clear picture of the technique's acceptance in the scientific community and, as such, the court was reluctant to rely on that evidence. The majority of courts hearing the issue have admitted spectrographic voice identification evidence.

6.2 The Sound Spectrograph

The sound spectrograph, an automatic sound wave analyzer, is a basic research instrument used in many laboratories for research studies of sound, music, and speech. It has been widely used for the analysis and classification of human speech sounds and in the analysis and treatment of speech and hearing disorders. The instrument produces a visual representation of a given set of sounds in the parameters of time, frequency, and amplitude. Sound spectrographs are available in both analog and digital models.

The analog spectrograph is composed of four basic parts: (1) a magnetic tape recorder/playback unit, (2) a tape scanning device with a drum that carries the paper to be marked, (3) an electronic variable filter, and (4) an electronic stylus that transfers the analyzed information to the paper. The analog sound spectrograph samples energy levels in a small frequency range from a magnetic tape recording and marks those energy levels on electrically sensitive paper. This instrument then analyzes the next small frequency range and samples and marks the energy levels at that point. This process is repeated until the entire desired frequency range is analyzed for that portion of the recording. The finished product is called a spectrogram and is a graphic depiction of the patterns, in the form of bars or formants, of the acoustical events during the time frame analyzed. The machine will produce a spectrogram in approximately 80 seconds. The spectrogram is in the form of an X, Y graph with the X axis the time dimension, approximately 2.4 seconds in length, and the Y axis the frequency range, usually 0 to 4,000 or 8,000 Hz. The degree of darkness of the markings indicates the approximate relative amplitude of the energy present for a given frequency and time.

Recent developments in sound spectrography have produced computerized digital sound spectrographs ranging from dedicated digital signal analysis workstations to PC-based systems for acquisition, analysis editing, and playback. These sophisticated computer-based systems provide high fidelity signal acquisition, high-speed digital processing circuitry for quick and flexible analysis, and CD-quality playback. The computer-based systems accomplish the same tasks as the analog systems, but the examiner gains a host of comparison and measurement tools not available with the analog equipment. The computer-based systems are capable of displaying multiple sound spectrograms, adjusting the time alignment and frequency ranges, and taking detailed numeric measurements of the displayed sounds. With these advances in technology, the examiner widens the scope of the analysis to create a more detailed picture of the voice or sound being analyzed.

The accuracy and reliability of the sound spectrograph, analog or digital, has never been questioned in any of the courts and never considered an issue in the admissibility of voice identification evidence. This may be due to the wide use of the instrument in the field of speech and hearing for non-voice identification analysis of the human voice. And it may be because, given the same recording of speech sounds, the sound spectrograph will consistently produce the same spectrogram of that speech.

The contest comes in the interpretation of the spectrograms. Proponents of the aural and spectrographic technique of voice identification base their decisions on the theory that all human voices are different because of the physical uniqueness of the vocal track (throat, teeth, jaws, tongue, and vocal cords), the distinctive environmental influences in the learning process of speech development, and the unique development of neurological faculties that are responsible for the production of speech. Opponents claim that not enough research has been completed to validate the theory that intraspeaker variability is less than interspeaker variability.

6.3 The Method of Voice Identification

The method by which a voice is identified is a multifaceted process requiring the use of both aural and visual senses. In a typical voice identification case, the examiner is asked to compare a voice sample from an unidentified speaker with samples of known origin. He is given several recordings: one or more of the known voice, and one or more unidentified samples to be compared to them. The unidentified voice on these must be at levels significantly higher than the background. The greater the number of obscuring events—such as noise, music and other speakers—the longer the sample of speech must be. Some examiners report that they reject as many as 60 percent of the cases submitted to them, with one of the main reasons being the poor quality of the recording of the unknown voice.

Should the unknown voice sample be suitable for analysis, the examiner then turns to the known voice samples. Here also, the recordings must be of sufficient clarity to allow comparison, although at this stage the recording process is usually so closely controlled that the quality of recording is not a problem.

The examiner can only work with speech samples with text the same as the unknown recording. Under the best of circumstances, the suspected speakers will repeat, several times, the text of the recording of the unknown speaker, and these words will be recorded in a similar manner to the recording of the unknown speaker. For example, if the recording of the unknown speaker were a bomb threat made to a recorded telephone line, then each of the suspects would repeat the threat, word for word, to a recorded telephone line. This will provide the examiner with not only the same speech sounds for comparison but also with valuable information about the way each speech sound completes the transition to the next sound.

There are those times when a voice sample must be obtained without the knowledge of the suspect. It is possible to make an identification from a surreptitious recording, but the amount of speech necessary to do the comparison is usually much greater. If the suspect is being engaged in conversation for the purpose of obtaining a voice sample, the conversation must be manipulated in such a way so as to have the suspect repeat as many of the words and phrases found in the text of the unknown recording as possible.

The worst exemplar recordings with which an examiner must work are those of random speech. It is necessary to obtain a large sample of speech to improve the chances of obtaining a sufficient amount of comparable speech.

As in any other form of identification analysis, as the quality of the evidence with which the examiner has to work declines, the greater the amount of evidence and time necessary to complete the analysis and the less likely the chance for a positive conclusion.

Once the evidence has been determined to be sufficient to perform the analysis, the examiner then begins the two-step process of voice sample comparison, one aural (listening) and the other spectrographic (visual). These are two different but interwoven and equally important analytical methods, which the examiner combines to reach a conclusion.

The first step is an aural comparison of the voice samples.[1] The examiner compares both single speech sounds and series of speech sounds of the known and unknown samples. At this stage, the examiner is conducting a number of tasks: comparing for similarities and differences, screening out less useful portions of the samples, and indexing the samples for further analysis. An example of the initial aural comparison is the screening of the samples for pronunciation similarities or discrepancies, such as that the word "the" may be said with a short "a" sound or a long "e" sound. If the word is not pronounced in the same manner, it loses comparison value.

Once the examiner has isolated those portions to be used for the analysis, a more detailed aural comparison is undertaken. This comparison can be accomplished in many different ways. One of the most commonly used methods of aural comparison is re-recording a speech sound sample of the unknown followed immediately by a re-recording of the same speech sounds of the suspect. This is repeated several times, so the final product is a recording of specific speech sounds, in alternating order, by the unknown speaker followed by the suspect. Such comparisons have been greatly facilitated by the use of audio digital recording equipment, which allows for the digital recording, storage, and repeated playback of only the desired speech sounds to be examined.

During the aural comparison, the examiner studies the psycholinguistic features of the speaker's voice. A large number of qualities and traits are examined: general traits (such as accent and dialect), inflection, syllable grouping, and breath patterns. The examiner also scrutinizes the samples for signs of speech pathologies and peculiar speech habits.

The second step in the voice identification process is the spectrographic analysis of the recorded samples. The sound spectrograph is an automatic sound wave analyzer with a high-quality, fully functional tape recorder. The speech samples to be analyzed are recorded on the sound spectrograph. The recording is then analyzed in 2.5-second segments. The product is a spectrogram, a graphic display of the recorded signal on the basis of time and frequency with a general indication of amplitude.

The spectrograms of the unknown speaker are then visually compared to the spectrograms of the suspects. Only those speech sounds that are the same aurally are compared.[2] The comparisons of the spectrograms are based on the displayed patterns representing the psychoacoustical features of the captured speech. The examiner studies the bandwidths, mean frequencies, and trajectory of vowel formants; vertical striations, distribution of formant energy and nasal resonances; stops, plosives and fricatives; interformant features, the relation of all features present as affected during articulatory changes, and any peculiar acoustic patterning.[3] The examiner looks not only for similarities but also for differences. The differences are closely examined to determine if they are due to pronunciation differences or if they are indicative of different speakers.

When the analysis is complete, the examiner integrates the findings from both the aural and spectrographic analyses into one of five standard conclusions; a positive identification, a probable identification, a positive elimination, a probable elimination, or no decision.

In order to arrive at a *positive identification*, the examiner must find a minimum of twenty speech sounds which possess sufficient aural and spectrographic similarities. There can be no differences, either aural or spectrographic, for which there can be no accounting. The *probable identification* conclusion is reached when there are fewer than twenty similarities and no unexplained differences. This conclusion is usually reached when working with small samples, random speech samples, or recordings of lower quality. The result of *positive elimination* is rendered when twenty differences between the samples are found that cannot be based on any fact other than different voices having produced the samples. A *probable elimination* decision is usually reached when working with limited text or a recording of lower quality. The *no decision* conclusion is used when the quality of the recording is so poor that there is insufficient information with which to work or when there are too few common speech sounds suitable for comparison.

6.4 History

The history of speech sound analysis goes back a little more than 100 years to Alexander Melville Bell who developed a visual representation of the spoken word. This visual display of the spoken word conveyed much more information about the pronunciation of that word than the dictionary spelling could ever suggest. His depiction of speech sounds demonstrated the subtle differences with which different people pronounced the same words. This system of speech sound analysis developed by Bell is the phonetic alphabet, which he called "visible speech."[4] His method of encoding the great variety of speech sounds was by handwritten symbols and was language independent. This code produced a visual representation of speech, which could convey to the eye the subtle differences in which words were spoken. This system was used by Bell and by his son, Alexander Graham Bell in helping deaf people learn to speak.[5]

In the early 1940s, a new method of speech sound analysis was developed. Potter, Kopp, and Green, working for Bell Laboratories in Murray Hill, New Jersey, began work on a project to develop a visual representation of speech using a sound spectrograph. This machine, an automatic sound wave analyzer, produced a visual record of speech portraying three parameters: frequency, intensity, and time. This research was intensified during World War II when acoustic scientists suggested that enemy radio voices could be identified by the spectrograms produced by the sound spectrograph. The war ended before the technique could be perfected.

In 1947 Potter, Kopp and Green published their work in a book, the title of which was borrowed from Alexander Melville Bell, *Visible Speech*. Their work is a comprehensive study of speech spectrograms designed to linguistically interpret visible speech sound patterns. This work was similar to that of Bell's in that speech sounds were encoded into a visual form. The difference is that, instead of a pen, Potter, Kopp, and Green used a sound spectrograph to produce the visual patterns.

Research in the area of speaker identification slowed dramatically with the end of World War II. It was not until the late 1950s and early 1960s that the research began again. It was at this time that the New York City Police Department was receiving and investigating a large number of telephone bomb threats to the airlines.[6] At that time Bell Laboratories was asked by law enforcement officers to provide assistance in the apprehension of the individuals making the telephone calls. The task of developing a reliable method of identification of a speaker's voice was given to Lawrence G. Kersta, a physicist at Bell Laboratories who had worked on the early experiments using the sound spectrograph. In two years, Kersta had developed a method of identification in which he reported results yielding a correct identification in 99.65 percent of all attempts.[7]

In 1966 the Michigan State Police began the practical application of the voice identification method in attempting to solve criminal cases. A voice identification unit was established, and the unit personnel received training from Kersta and other speech scientists. During the first few years, the voice identification method was used only as an investigative aid.

The first court of published opinion to rule on the admissibility of voice identification analysis was in the case of *United States v. Wright*, 17 U.S.C.M.A. 183, 37 C.M.R. 447 (1967). This was a court martial proceeding in which the appellate court affirmed the admission of spectrographic voice identification evidence by the board of review. The lengthy dissent by Judge Ferguson, based on the requirements for acceptance of scientific evidence spelled out in *Frye v. United States*, 54 App. D.C. 46 293 F. 1013 (1923), was the beginning of a controversy which continues today.

The first non-military case to review the admissibility of voice identification evidence was the New Jersey Supreme Court in *State v. Cary*.[8] In this case, the court stated that "the physical properties of a person's voice are identifying characteristics."[9] The court also noted that trial courts in the states of New York and California had admitted voice identification evidence, but that these admissions had not been subject of appellate review.[10]

The court declined to rule on the admissibility issue and remanded the case to determine if the equipment and technique were sufficiently accurate to provide results admissible as evidence. The Superior Court of New Jersey, on appeal from a denial of admission after remand, held that the majority of evidence "indicates, not that the technique is not accurate and reliable, but rather that it is just too early to tell and at this time lacks the required scientific acceptance."[11] The New Jersey Supreme Court reviewed this decision and again remanded for additional fact finding "in light of the far-reaching implications of admission of voiceprint evidence."[12] The State of New Jersey was unable "to furnish any new and significant evidence" by the third time the New Jersey Supreme Court reviewed this issue and as such affirmed the trial court's opinion excluding voice identification evidence.[13] California came to a similar holding when the issue first reached the appellate level in *People v. King*.[14] The state brought in Lawrence Kersta as the voice identification expert to testify as to the reliability of the technique. The defense brought in seven speech scientists and engineers to rebut Kersta's claims.

The court held that "Kersta's claims for the accuracy of the 'voiceprint' process are founded on theories and conclusions which are not yet substantiated by accepted methods of scientific verification."[15] The court cited the *Frye* test as the proper standard for admissibility.[16] The court also left the door open for future admission by saying when voice identification evidence has achieved the necessary degree of acceptance they will welcome its use.[17]

In *State ex rel. Trimble v. Heldman*,[18] the Supreme Court of Minnesota held that "spectrograms ought to be admissible at least for the purpose of corroborating opinions as to identification by means of ear alone."[19] The court was impressed by the testimony of Dr. Oscar Tosi who had previously testified against the use of spectrographic voice identification evidence in courtrooms but after extensive research and experimentation now described the technique as "extremely reliable."[20] The court referred to the *Frye* test and to the scientific community's acceptance of Dr. Tosi's study but did not specifically apply the *Frye* test as the standard for the admissibility of the voice identification evidence.[21] In discussing the issue of admissibility, the court held that it was the job of the fact finder to weigh the credibility of the evidence.

> The opinion of an expert is admissible, if at all, for the purpose of aiding the jury or the fact finder in a field where he has no particular knowledge or training. The weight and credibility to be given to the opinion of an expert lies with the fact finder. It is no different in this field than in any other.[22]

In 1972 the Third and Fourth District Courts of Florida, in separate opinions, held admissible the use of spectrographic voice identification evidence.[23] The court in *Worley* held that the voice identification evidence was admissible to corroborate the defendant's identification by other means. The court stated that the technique had attained the necessary level of scientific reliability required for admission, but since it was only offered as corroborative evidence, the court refused to comment as to whether such evidence alone would be sufficient to sustain the identification and conviction.[24]

The Third District Court of Appeals of Florida did not limit the admission of spectrograph evidence to corroborative status. In the *Alea* opinion, the court did not mention the *Frye* test as the standard to be used for admission but rather stated that "such testimony is admissible to establish the identity of a suspect as direct and positive proof, although its probative value is a question for the jury."[25]

In the case of *State v. Andretta*,[26] the New Jersey Supreme Court stated that there was much more support for the admission of spectrographic voice identification evidence than at the time they decided *Cary*. Yet, they refused to address the issue further since the only issue before them was whether the defendant should be compelled to speak for a spectrographic voice analysis.[27]

The California Court of Appeal affirmed the trial court's admission of voice identification evidence in the case of *Hodo v. Superior Court*.[28] Here the court found the requirements of *Frye* had been met in that there was now general acceptance of spectrographic voice identification by recognized experts in the field. The court cited Dr. Tosi's testimony that "those who really are familiar with spectrography, they are accepting the technique."[29] Tosi also pointed out that the general population of speech scientists were not familiar with this technique and thus could not form an opinion on it.[30]

The court in *United States v. Samples*[31] held that the *Frye* test of general acceptance precludes too much relevant evidence for purposes of the fact determining process at a revocation of probation hearing, and the court allowed the use of spectrographic voice identification evidence to corroborate other identification evidence.[32]

In 1974 the case of *United States v. Addison*[33] rejected the admission of voice identification evidence, saying that such evidence "is not now sufficiently accepted" and as such the requirements of the *Frye* test were not met.[34] At the trial the court heard from two experts endorsing the technique, Dr. Tosi and a recent convert to the reliability of the technique, Dr. Ladefoged. Only one expert, Dr. Stuart, testified that he was still skeptical of the technique and thought that most of the scientific community also was.[35] Although the admission of spectrographic voice identification evidence was held to be error by the trial court, the appellate court refused to overturn the conviction due to overwhelming amount of other evidence supporting the conviction.[36]

Attempted disguise or mimic were the grounds the California Court of Appeal used to reverse a conviction based in part on spectrographic voice identification in the case of *People v. Law*.[37] The court found that "with respect to disguised and mimicked voices in particular, the prosecution did not carry out its burden of proof to demonstrate that the scientific principles pertaining to spectrographic identification were beyond the experimental and into the demonstrable stage or that the procedure was sufficiently established to have gained general acceptance in the particular field in which it belongs."[38] The main concern of the court was that no experimentation had been completed studying the effects of attempts to disguise or mimic on the accuracy of the identification process. Without mentioning the *Frye* test, this court used the standards set in *Frye* as the test of admissibility although the court seemed to be limiting the scope of the opinion to cases involving disguise or mimic.

In *United States v. Franks*,[39] the Sixth Circuit Court of Appeals held spectrographic voice identification evidence to be admissible. The court said it was "mindful of a considerable area of discretion on the part of the trial judge in admitting or refusing to admit evidence based on scientific processes."[40] Quoting from *United States v. Stifel*,[41] the court pointed out that "neither newness nor lack of absolute certainty in a test suffices to render it inadmissible in court." Every useful, new development must have its first day in court. And court records are full of the conflicting opinions of doctors, engineers and accountants . . . ."[42] In *Franks*, the court found that extensive review was given to the qualifications of the experts and opportunity to cross-examine the experts to determine the proper weight to be given such evidence.

The Massachusetts Supreme Court, in *Commonwealth v. Lykus*,[43] allowed the admission of spectrographic voice identification evidence. It said that the opinions of a qualified expert should be received and the considerations similar to those expressed in *Frye* should be for the fact finder as to the weight and value of the opinions. The court gave greater weight to those experts who had direct and empirical experience in the field as opposed to those who had only performed a theoretical review of that work.[44] The court also stated that "neither infallibility nor unanimous acceptance of the principle need be proved to justify its admission into evidence."[45] The Massachusetts Supreme Court again, that same year, found no error in the use of spectrographic voice identification evidence in the case of *Commonwealth v. Vitello*.[46]

The Fourth Circuit Court of Appeals, in the case of *United States v. Baller*,[47] allowed the admission of spectrographic voice identification evidence. It said that unless it is prejudicial or misleading to the jury, it is better to admit relevant scientific evidence in the same manner as other expert testimony and allow its weight to be attacked by cross-examination and refutation.[48] The court listed six reasons supporting admission; the expert need be a qualified practitioner, evidence in voir dire had demonstrated probative value, competent witnesses were available to expose limitations, the defense demonstrated competent cross-examination, the tape recordings were played for the jury, and the jury was told they could disregard the opinion of the voice identification expert.[49]

Voice identification evidence was admitted by the Sixth Circuit Court of Appeals in *United States v. Jenkins*[50] using the same logic as in *Baller*. Here the court said that the issue of admissibility was within the discretion of the trial judge and that once a proper foundation had been laid the trier of fact was able to assign proper weight to the evidence.[51]

In 1976, the New York Supreme Court pointed out, in the case of *People v. Rogers*,[52] that fifty different trial courts had admitted spectrographic voice identification evidence, as had fourteen out of fifteen U.S. District Court judges, and that only two out of thirty-seven states considering the issue had rejected admission.[53] The *Rogers* court stated that this technique, when accompanied by aural examination and conducted by a qualified examiner, had reached the level of general scientific acceptance by those who would be expected to be familiar with its use and, as such, had reached the level of scientific acceptance and reliability necessary for admission.[54] The court also pointed out that other scientific evidence processes were regularly admitted that were as, or less, reliable than spectrographic voice identification: hair and fiber analysis, ballistics, forensic chemistry, and serology, and blood alcohol tests.[55]

The California Supreme Court finally put an end to the seesaw ride of admissibility in that state in *People v. Kelly*[56] by rejecting admission because of insufficient showing of support. "Although voiceprint analysis may indeed constitute a reliable and valuable tool in either identifying or eliminating suspects in criminal cases, that fact was not satisfactorily demonstrated in this case."[57] In this case, the court seemed to have the most trouble with the fact that the only expert provided to lay the foundation for admission was the technician who performed the analysis. It was said that a single witness could not attest to the views of the scientific community on this new technique. And that this witness, who may not have been capable of a fair and impartial evaluation of the technique, because he had built a career on it, lacked the academic credentials to express an opinion as to the acceptance of the technique by the scientific community.[58]

In *United States v. McDaniel*,[59] it appeared that the District of Columbia Circuit Court of Appeals would have liked to admit the spectrographic voice identification evidence but had to reject it because the shadow of the *Addison* decision of two years past "looms over our consideration of this issue."[60] The court held the admission of the voice identification evidence to be harmless error in that the rest of the evidence was overwhelming. The court did recognize the trend toward admissibility and contemplated that it may be time to reexamine the holding of *Addison* ". . . in light of the apparently increased reliability and general acceptance in the scientific community."[61]

The Pennsylvania Supreme Court rejected admission in *Commonwealth v. Topa,*[62] holding that the technician's opinion alone would not suffice to permit the introduction of scientific evidence in a court of law.[63] This was the same situation, in fact the same single expert, which confronted the *Kelly* court.

In *People v. Tobey*[64] the Michigan Supreme Court found, by applying the *Frye* test, that the trial court erred in admitting spectrographic voice identification evidence. The court found that neither of the two experts testifying in favor of the technique could be called disinterested and impartial experts in that both had built their reputations and careers on this type of work.[65] The court pointed out that not all courts require independent and impartial proof of general scientific acceptability. The court was quick to add that this decision was not intended in any way to foreclose the introduction of such evidence in future cases where there is demonstrated solid scientific approval and support of this new method of identification.[66]

In admitting voice identification evidence, the United States District Court for the Southern District of New York, in *United States v. Williams*[67] found that the requirements of the *Frye* test were met when the technique was performed "by aural comparison and spectrographic analysis."[68] The court stated in reference to the concerns of the defendant that this technique had a mystique of scientific precision that may mask the ultimate subjectivity of spectrographic analysis. Although they were valid concerns, they could be alleviated by action other than suppression of the evidence, such as opposing expert opinion and jury instructions allowing the jury to determine the weight, if any, of the evidence.[69]

In *People v. Collins*, the New York Supreme Court rejected admission of spectrographic voice identification evidence, saying that the *Frye* test alone was insufficient to determine admissibility and must be used in conjunction with a test of reliability.[71] The court found that the proponents of the technique were in the minority and that the remainder of the relevant scientific community either expressed opposition or expressed no opinion.[72]

In *Brown v. United States*,[73] the District of Columbia Court of Appeals rejected the use of voice identification evidence but held the error to be harmless and affirmed the conviction in light of overwhelming non-spectrographic identification of the defendant as perpetrator of the crime. One of the main problems in this case was the fact that the exemplar of the defendant's voice was recorded in a defective manner but used anyway after the tape speed malfunction had been corrected in a laboratory. Dr. Tosi, testifying as a proponent of the technique, stated that the technician should not have used the defective recording as a basis of comparison.[74] The court held the technique was not shown to be sufficiently reliable and accepted within the scientific community to permit its use in this criminal case, but that this decision did not foreclose a future decision as to admissibility of the technique.[75]

In the civil case of *D'Arc v. D'Arc*,[76] the court found that the requirements of the *Frye* test had not been met and thus the evidence could not be admitted. The court believed that even with proper instructions to the contrary, this type of evidence "has the potentiality to be assumed by many jurors as being conclusive and dispositive" and thus should be subject to strict standards of admission.[77]

The court, in *State v. Williams*,[78] refused to apply the *Frye* standard, citing instead the Maine Rules of Evidence, Rule 401, which states that "all relevant evidence is admissible," with relevant being described as evidence having any tendency to make the existence of any fact that is of consequence to the determination of the action more probable or less probable than it would be without the evidence.[79]

In *Reed v. State*[80] the court applied the *Frye* standard to determine admissibility with a rather wide definition of the scientific community, which included "those whose scientific background and training are sufficient to allow them to comprehend and understand the process and form a judgment about it."[81] The court said the trial court erred in using the more restricted definition of scientific community as "those who are knowledgeable, directly knowledgeable through work, utilization of the techniques, experimentation and so forth" and did not mean the broad general scientific community of speech and hearing science.[82]

In a fifty-one page dissent to the *Reed* decision,[83] Judge Smith points out that the *Frye* standard is much criticized and has never been adopted in the state of Maryland. It was stated that this decision is out of step with other courts on related issues of fingerprints, ballistics, x-rays and the like, with prior Maryland holdings on expert testimony, the majority of reported opinions have accepted such evidence, and that even if *Frye* were applicable, it is satisfied.

In *United States v. Williams*[84] the court did not apply the *Frye* standard but did note that acceptance of the technique appeared strong among scientists who had worked with spectrograms and weak among those who had not.[85] The court then focused on the reliability of the technique and the tendency to mislead. As to the reliability of the technique, the court noted the small error rate, 2.4 percent false identification, the existence and maintenance of standards of analysis, and the conservative manner in which the technique was applied.[86] As for the tendency to mislead, the court felt that adequate precautions were taken in that the jury could view the spectrograms and listen to the recording and the expert's qualifications. The reliability of the equipment and the technique were subject to scrutiny by the defense, and the jurors were instructed that they were free to disregard the testimony of the experts.[87]

In the case of *People v. Bein*[88] the court based admissibility on a two-pronged test: general acceptance by the relevant scientific community and competent expert testimony establishing reliability of the process. The court found that both tests had been met and allowed the evidence.[89] The court described the relevant scientific community "to be that group of scientists who are concerned with the problems of voice identification for forensic and other purposes."[90] The court also suggested that "it is no different in this field of expertise than in other fields, that where experts disagree, it is for the finder of fact to determine which testimony is the more credible and therefore more acceptable."[91]

The Ohio Supreme Court, in *State v. Williams*,[92] relied on their own state rules of evidence, as did the Maine court in *Williams*, and rejected the use of the *Frye* standard. The court refused "to engage in scientific nose counting for the purpose of whether evidence based on newly ascertained or applied scientific principles is admissible."[93] The court noted with approval the playing of the recordings to the jury and that the jury was free to reject the testimony of the expert.[94]

In that same year, right across the border in Indiana, the court in *Cornett v. State*[95] rejected admission of voice identification evidence, saying the conditions set out in *Frye* had not been met. Here the court used a wide definition of the scientific community, including linguists, psychologists, and engineers who use voice spectrography for identification purposes.[96] Although the court held that the trial court erred in admitting the evidence, the error was found to be harmless and the conviction affirmed.[97]

Likewise, the court in *State v. Gortarez*[98] rejected the admission of voice identification evidence but affirmed the conviction, holding such admission to be harmless error. The court also used a wide definition of the scientific community in applying the *Frye* standard, including experts in the fields of acoustical engineering, acoustics, communication electronics, linguists, phonetics, physics, and speech communications and found that there was not general acceptance among these scientists.[99]

In the case of *United States v. Love*,[100] the admissibility of spectrographic voice identification was not at issue. The Fourth Circuit Court of Appeals was reviewing whether the trial judge's comments about a voice identification expert were error. The trial judge told the jurors that they were to assign whatever weight they wanted to the testimony of the expert and even disregard his testimony if they "should conclude that his opinion was not based on adequate education, training or experience, or that his professed science of voice print identification was not sufficiently reliable, accurate, and dependable."[101] The court found no error in the judge's instruction to the jury.

In admitting spectrographic voice identification evidence, the Supreme Court of Rhode Island in *State v. Wheeler*[102] declined to apply the *Frye* standard, holding instead, that "the law and practice of this state on the use of expert testimony had historically been based on the principle that helpfulness to the trier of fact is the most critical consideration."[103]

The court reviewed the cases around the country, both state and federal, and noted that the majority of circuit courts that have considered admission of spectrographic evidence have decided in favor of its admission.[104] The court pointed out that the defendant had all the proper safeguards such as cross-examination and rebuttal experts and that the jury had the right to reject the evidence for any one of a number of reasons.[105]

In *State v. Free*[106] the Court of Appeals of Louisiana did not rely on the *Frye* test for guidance in determining the admissibility of spectrographic voice identification evidence but instead applied a balancing test set forth in *State v. Catanese.*[107] One individual, accepted as an expert in voice identification, testified about the theoretical and technical aspects of the spectrographic voice analysis method. No other witnesses were called to support or show fault with the admission of the voice identification testimony. The court of appeals found that voice identification evidence, when offered by a competent expert and obtained through proper procedures, "is as reliable as other kinds of scientific evidence accepted routinely by courts" and "can be highly probative."[108] Using the *Catanese* balancing test, the court of appeals found that the trier of fact was likely to give almost conclusive weight to the voice identification expert's opinion, which would mislead the jurors. The court of appeals was also concerned that not enough experts were available who could critically examine the validity of a voice identification determination in a particular case. Nine rules were suggested as a basis for which voice identification evidence could be accepted.[109] The court of appeals held that *Catanese* prohibits admission of the voice identification evidence at this time[110] and found the admission of that evidence to be harmless error.

In 1987, the New Jersey Supreme Court again addressed the issue of admissibility of spectrographic evidence in the civil case of *Windmere v. International Insurance Company*.[111] The trial court admitted spectrographic analysis, and the appellate division affirmed that ruling. The supreme court ruled that the appellate court was incorrect in doing so. The supreme court stated that the admissibility of the spectrographic voice analysis is based on the scientific technique's having sufficient scientific basis to produce uniform and reasonably reliable results and contribute materially to the ascertainment of the truth.[112] The supreme court admitted that this standard bore "a close resemblance to the familiar *Frye* test."[113] The court relied upon the "general acceptance within the professional community" to establish the scientific reliability of the voice identification process. In determining general acceptance, the court applied a three-prong test, which included: (1) the testimony of knowledgeable experts, (2) authoritative scientific literature, and (3) persuasive judicial decisions that acknowledge such general acceptance of expert testimony.[114] The court found that none of the three prongs indicated that there was a general acceptance of spectrographic voice identification in the professional community. The court criticized the proponent experts as being too closely tied to the development of this identification analysis to represent the opinions of the community.[115] The court found that the trial court did not undertake to resolve the issue of conflicting scientific literature, and they would make no effort to resolve the conflict.[116] The court also reviewed the judicial decisions regarding admissibility and found a split among the jurisdictions as to the reliability of the identification process.[117]

The New Jersey Supreme Court specifically limited its decision in *Windmere* excluding spectrographic voice identification evidence to that case. The court stated that the future use of voice identification evidence "as a reasonably reliable scientific method may not be precluded forever if more thorough proofs as to reliability are introduced"[118] and that it would "continue to await the more conclusive evidence of scientific reliability."[119]

The Texas Court of Appeals, in the case of *Pope v. Texas,*[120] refused to address the issue of admissibility of voice identification evidence, stating that "the overwhelming evidence against appellant renders this error, if any, harmless."[121] Justice McClung, in his dissenting opinion states that the trial court did err in admitting the voice identification evidence and that the error was not harmless.[122] He suggests that the *Frye* test is the proper standard for assessing the admissibility issue and that the "relevant scientific community" should be defined broadly.[123] When this aspect of the test is so defined the "general acceptability" criterion is not met.

In February of 1989, the United States Court of Appeals for the Seventh Circuit affirmed the decision of the United States District Court for the Northern District of Illinois admitting spectrographic voice identification evidence in the criminal case of *United States of America v. Tamara Jo Smith.*[124] The Seventh Circuit had joined the Second, Fourth, and Sixth Circuits in affirming the use of spectrographic voice identification evidence.[125] The court used the *Frye* standard to hold expert testimony concerning spectrographic voice analysis admissible in cases where the proponent of the testimony has established a proper foundation.[126] The court noted that this technique was not infallible and that the entire scientific community does not support it; however, neither infallibility nor unanimity is a precondition for general acceptance of scientific evidence.[127] The Seventh Circuit found that a proper foundation had been established in that the expert testified to the theory and the technique, the accuracy of the analysis, and the limitations of the process.[128] The court noted that variations from the norm result in an increase of false eliminations.[129] The jurors were not likely to be misled in that they had the opportunity to hear the recordings, see the spectrograms, hear the limitations of the process, witnessed a rigorous cross-examination of the expert, and could reject the testimony of the expert.[130]

In *United States v. Maivia*,[131] the United States District Court in Hawaii admitted spectrographic evidence after a four-day hearing on the issue. The court examined the various sub-tests of the *Frye* test and found that spectrographic voice identification evidence met these tests. The court also noted that "inasmuch as the admissibility of spectrographic evidence to identify voices has received judicial recognition, it is no longer considered novel within the *Frye* test and consequently the test is inapplicable."[132] The court also looked to the Federal Rules of Evidence, specifically Rule 403, in deciding the admissibility of spectrographic voice identification evidence.

In affirming the order of the appellate division, the New York Supreme Court, in the case of *People v. Jeter*,[133] concluded that the trial court was not properly able to determine that voice identification evidence is generally accepted as reliable based on case law and existing literature. The court stated that the trial court should have held a preliminary inquiry into the reliability of voice spectrographic evidence. In the light of the other evidence, the admission of the voice identification evidence was held to be harmless error in this case.

6.5 Standards of Admissibility

Prior to 1993, there were two main standards of admissibility that had been applied to voice identification evidence, the *Frye* test and the Federal Rules of Evidence (and the rules of evidence of the various states). The *Frye* test originated from the Court of Appeals of the District of Columbia[134] in a decision rejecting admissibility of a systolic blood pressure deception test (a forerunner of the polygraph test). The court stated that admission of this novel technique was dependent on its acceptance by the scientific community.

> Just when a scientific principle or discovery crosses the line between the experimental and demonstrable stages is difficult to define. Somewhere in this twilight zone the evidential force of the principle must be recognized, and while courts will go a long way in admitting expert testimony deduced from a well-recognized scientific principle or discovery, the thing from which the deduction is made must be sufficiently established to have gained general acceptance in the particular field in which it belongs.[135]

Out of forty published opinions prior to 1993 deciding the admissibility of voice identification evidence, twenty-three courts applied the *Frye* standard or a standard very similar to *Frye*. Sixteen of the twenty-three courts rejected the admission of such evidence. Six of these courts held the admission of voice identification evidence by the trial court was harmless error and affirmed the conviction or judgment. Eight of the sixteen stated that although voice identification evidence had not yet met the required standard of scientific acceptability, their decision was not intended to foreclose future admission when such standards were met. Two of these courts denied admission because they felt a single witness could not speak for the entire scientific community regarding the acceptance issue.

Seven courts applied the test and found the requirements of *Frye* had been met. Of the thirteen courts applying a standard of admissibility different from *Frye*, only one, the *Free*[136] court, rejected voice identification evidence.

There are three problems with the *Frye* standard: at what point is the principle of "sufficiently established" determined, at what point is "general acceptance" reached, and what is the proper definition of "the particular field in which it belongs."

These three areas have been major stumbling blocks for the courts in deciding the issue of the admissibility of voice identification evidence due to the small number of voice scientists who have performed research in this field. The trial court in *People v. Siervonti*[137] noted the lack of research in this area, saying "one only wishes that the last twelve years had been spent in research and not in attempting to get the method into the courts."[138]

The *Frye* test has been criticized as not being the appropriate test to use for the admission of voice identification evidence. This standard was established and applied to the admission of a type of evidence that is very different from voice identification. In *Frye* the court was concerned with the admission of a test designed to determine if a person was telling the truth or not. This type of evidence invades the province of the finder of fact. Voice identification evidence belongs in the general classification of identification evidence, which does not impinge on the role of the finder of fact. As such, it shares common traits with the other identification sciences of fingerprinting, ballistics, handwriting, and fiber, serum, and substance identification.

Another criticism of the application of the *Frye* test as the standard for admission of voice identification evidence is that general acceptance by the scientific community is the proper condition for taking of judicial notice of scientific facts. McCormick states that general scientific acceptance is a proper condition for taking judicial notice of scientific facts but is not a criterion for the admissibility of scientific evidence.[139]

The court in *Reed v. State*[140] seemed to note this difference between the standard for the taking of judicial notice and that for the admission of evidence such as voice identification. The court said that validity and reliability may be so broadly accepted in the scientific community that the court may take judicial notice of it. If it cannot be judicially noticed, then the reliability must be demonstrated before it can be admitted.[141] The court then applied the *Frye* test, general acceptance by the scientific community, to determine reliability and thus, admissibility.

Scientific evidence has long been admitted before it was judicially noticed, as with the use of fingerprints. The admission of fingerprint identification evidence was first challenged in 1911, in the case of *People v. Jenning*.[142] The court in *Jennings* allowed the fingerprint evidence, saying, "whatever tends to prove any material fact is relevant and competent."[143] It was not until thirty-three years later that fingerprint evidence was first judicially noticed.[144]

The majority of courts deciding the issue of admissibility in favor of allowing voice identification into the courtroom have used similar standards which permit the finder of fact to hear the evidence and determine the proper weight to be assigned to it. Their logic runs parallel to the Federal Rules of Evidence which state that all relevant evidence is admissible. The word "relevant" being defined as evidence tending to make the existence of any fact that is of consequence to the determination of the action more probable or less probable than it would be without the evidence.[145] A qualified expert may testify to his or her opinion if such opinion will assist the trier of fact in better understanding the evidence.[146]

Many of the courts that have upheld the admission of voice identification evidence have done so because the trial court had set up a number of precautions to insure that the evidence was viewed in its proper light. The precautions included: (1) allowing the jury to see the spectrograms of the voices in question, hear the recordings from which the spectrograms were produced, and hear the expert's qualifications and opinions; (2) evidence on the reliability of the equipment; (3) the techniques are subject to scrutiny by the other side; and (4) the availability of competent witnesses to expose limitations in the process. The jurors were also given instructions that they were free to assign whatever weight, if any, to the evidence they felt it deserved.

The United States Supreme Court in 1993 changed the long-standing law of admissibility of scientific expert evidence by rejecting the *Frye* test as inconsistent with the Federal Rules of Evidence in the case of *Daubert v. Merrell Dow Pharmaceutical*.[147] The Court held that the Federal Rules of Evidence and not *Frye* provided the standard for determining admissibility of expert scientific testimony. *Frye*'s "general acceptance" test was superseded by the adoption of the Federal Rules. Rule 702 is the appropriate standard to assess the admissibility of scientific evidence. The Court derived a reliability test from Rule 702.

> In order to qualify as "scientific knowledge," an inference or assertion must be derived by the scientific method. Proposed testimony must be supported by appropriate validation—*i.e.*, "good grounds," based on what is known. In short, the requirement that an expert's testimony pertain to "scientific knowledge" establishes a standard of evidentiary reliability.[148]

The *Daubert* decision concerns statutory law and not constitutional law. The Court held that the Federal Rules, not *Frye*, govern admissibility. The only federal circuit to reject spectrographic voice analysis has been the District of Columbia. *Daubert* may cause the District of Columbia to change its stance the next time such evidence is introduced.

Since *Daubert* is not binding on the states, it will be difficult to determine just how much impact *Daubert* will have on the admissibility standards of the states. Many states have adopted evidence rules based on the Federal Rules of Evidence and may not be affected by this holding. Other states, which have adopted the *Frye* test, will have to decide to either continue following *Frye* or change their standard to *Daubert*. The Arizona Supreme Court declined to follow *Daubert,* saying that it was "not bound by the United States Supreme Court's non-constitutional construction of the Federal Rules of Evidence when we construe the Arizona Rules of Evidence."[149]

6.6 Research Studies

The studies that have been produced over the years have run the gambit in type, parameter, and result. A quick review of the available published data would leave one with the impression that the spectrographic method of voice identification was only somewhat more accurate than flipping a coin. The diversity of the relatively low number of studies and the range of results have only added to the confusion as to the reliability and validity of this method of identification. When one takes the time and expends the effort to analyze the studies in this field, a very different conclusion becomes evident. When the individual parameters of the studies are taken into account—who was being evaluated, what information was given to the examiner to assess, and what limitations were placed on the examiner's conclusions—a much clearer picture of the accuracy of the spectrographic voice identification method develops. The picture is not one of a marginally accurate technique but rather a picture that clearly shows that a properly trained and experienced examiner, adhering to internationally accepted standards, will produce a highly accurate result. The studies also show that as the level of training diminishes or the conclusions an examiner may reach are artificially limited, the error rate goes up dramatically.

The training for accurately performing the spectrographic voice identification method has been established as requiring completion of (1) a formal course of study in the basics of spectrographic analysis, usually lasting two to four weeks, (2) completing 100 voice comparison cases, usually in a one-to-one relationship with a recognized expert, and (3) examination by a board of experts in the field of spectrographic voice identification analysis.

For the most accurate results from the spectrographic voice identification method, a professional examiner (1) will require the original recordings or the best quality re-recordings if the original is not available; (2) will perform a critical aural review of the suspect and known recordings; (3) will produce sound spectrograms of the comparable words and phrases; (4) will produce a comparison recording juxtaposing the known and unknown speech samples; (5) will evaluate the evidence and classify the results into one of five standard categories [1 = positive identification, 2 = probable identification, 3 = positive elimination, 4 = probable elimination, and 5 = no decision]. The final decision is reached through a combined process of aural and visual examination.

It is important to remember that the spectrographic method of voice identification is a process that interweaves the visual analysis of the sound spectrograms with the critical aural examination of the sounds being viewed. Taking the results from all of the studies produced shows that if the examiner's ability to analyze both the graphic representations of the voice and the aural cues found in the recordings is limited or restricted, accuracy suffers. Likewise, the extent of the examiner's training has a direct bearing on the level of accuracy of the results.

In a survey of eighteen studies of the accuracy of the spectrographic voice identification method, the results fall into two categories.[150] Examiners with proper training, using standard procedures, produce very accurate results, whereas those with inadequate training, using limited analysis methods, produce inaccurate results.

In a 1975 study by Lt. L. Smrkovski of the Voice Identification Unit of the Michigan State police, error rates in voice identification analysis comparisons, based on three levels of training and experience, were evaluated.[151] (Table 6.1 summarizes the results of that study.) Lt. Smrkovski's results show that proper training is essential. The fact that his results show a higher "no decision" rate among the professional examin-

Error type	Novice	Trainee	Professional
False identification	5.0%	0.0%	0.0%
False elimination	25.0%	0.0%	0.0%
No decision	2.5%	2.5%	7.5%

Table 6.1

ers than the trainee examiners may indicate that the professional is a bit more cautious in reaching a conclusion than is the trainee.

Mark Greenwald, in his 1979 thesis for his M.A. degree at Michigan State University, studied the performance of three professional examiners (each with eight years' experience) and five trainees (each with less than two years' experience) using standard spectrographic voice identification methods (visual and aural) and result classifications. Greenwald found that the professional examiners produced no errors when using full-frequency bandwidth recordings. When the frequency bandwidth was restricted, the professional examiners still produced no errors but did increase their percentage of "no decision" classifications. Greenwald also found that the training level was an important factor and that the trainees in this study had an error rate of 6.1 percent for false identifications in the restricted frequency bandwidth trials.[152]

In 1986, the Federal Bureau of Investigation published a survey of 2,000 voice identification comparisons made by FBI examiners. This survey was based on 2,000 forensic comparisons completed over a period of fifteen years, under actual law enforcement conditions, by FBI examiners.[153] Each examiner had a minimum of two years' experience, had completed over 100 actual cases, had completed a basic two-week training course, and had received formal approval by other trained examiners. (The results of the survey[156] are show in Table 6.2.) The FBI results are consistent with the Smrkovski study in that properly trained examiners, utilizing the full range of procedures, produce quite accurate results.

By way of contrast, the 1976 study by Alan Reich used four speech science graduate students who had previous experience with speech spectrograms (but were untrained in spectrographic voice identification analysis) to examine, using visual comparison only, nine excerpted words. This study produced an accuracy rate in the undisguised trials of 56.67 percent.

Decisions	Number	Percent
No or low confidence	1304	65.2
Eliminations	378	18.9
Identifications	318	15.9
Errors		
False eliminations	2	0.53
False identification	1	0.31

Table 6.2

When disguise was introduced into the study paradigm the accuracy rate decreased significantly.[154]

Taken as a whole, the eighteen studies support the conclusion that accurate results will be obtained only through the combined use of the aural and visual components of the spectrographic voice identification method as performed by a properly trained examiner adhering to the established standards. Those studies with poor accuracy results are important in that they demonstrate the weaknesses of improperly performed examinations that do not adhere to the internationally accepted professional standards.

A large part of the debate over the admissibility of spectrographic voice identification analysis in the courts results from the fact that the parameters of these studies have not been adequately demonstrated to the courts in the detail necessary to allow the courts to examine the overall meaning. Many of these studies look at only one or two aspects of the spectrographic voice identification method. Frequently, the results of these restricted scope studies have been misapplied to the entire spectrographic voice identification method, resulting in inaccurate information being used as the basis for deciding the admissibility of spectrographic voice identification analysis. It is important to provide an accurate picture of all the studies so the courts will have the foundational information necessary to make an informed decision regarding the admissibility of spectrographic voice identification analysis.

6.7 Forensic Audio, Video, and Voice Identification

A. 12 step methodology

When security directors are faced with making a decision regarding a video tape, audio tape, threatening voice messages, sexual harassment recordings, and a host of other recorded media questions or issues, more often than not a decision on these matters needs to be handled quickly and efficiently. What is the technology? What is the process? What are the legal issues and whom do we contact?

The following 12 Step Methodology procedures will give you a guideline in these areas as to what the expert should be doing to satisfy the requirements of admissibility and whether the expert can say with scientific certainty that a tape is authentic or whether a certain suspect voice is the same voice on the recording.

The typical lab of a certified expert in these areas is valued at around the $300,000.00 to $500,000.00 area. Most experienced practitioners have been in business more than twenty years, and most have testified numerous times in many states.

The questions related to any forensic examination are addressed in *Frey*, *Daubert*, and the Federal Rules of Civil Procedure Rule 26.

Any forensic recorded media examination must pass muster for admissibility, A *Frey* or *Daubert* hearing is usually held before a trial where recorded media will be introduced.

Questions relating to the chain of evidence, originality, identification of participants, authenticity, and the questions of Rule 26:

1. written report and opinion signed
2. basis and reasons
3. data considered
4. exhibits
5. qualifications
6. last ten years publications
7. compensation
8. testimony list for last four years
9. materials relied upon

B. 12 step methodology – video authenticity

1. Receive evidence. Mark and photograph evidence including tapes, recorders, envelopes, and containers.
2. Physical inspection, tape inspection, record lot numbers, punch tabs, and note condition.
3. Note playback speed and format (Time Lapse, SP, SLP, EP, DV, etc.)
4. Load video uncompressed into computer and make an analog copy. Perform azimuth and zenith correction if necessary.
5. Critical viewing, observing one frame/field at a time. Note scene changes, split fields, motion blur, and other anomalies.
6. Waveform Analysis - Utilize spectrum analyzer to observe head switching. Check horizontal and vertical blanking interval. Check synch, front porch, back porch, etc.
7. Audio and Time Code Track Analysis. RF envelope analysis,
8. Recorder Test - Check for dihedral error, defective pixel, and also check HBI, VBI, mistracking, front porch and back porch.
9. Compare test tape signatures to original tape signatures.
10. Check evidence tape for discontinuities such as deletions, insertions, over-recordings, stops and starts.
11. Video Hum - A.C. Power
12. Analyze results. Offer an opinion based on your conclusions. Write a report. The report should include all Federal Rule 26 requirements. Send the client all original materials and report in a secure manner.

C. 12 step methodology – audio authenticity

1. Receive evidence. Mark and photograph evidence including tapes, recorders, envelopes, and containers.
2. Physical inspection, tape inspection, record lot numbers, punch tabs, and note condition.
3. Track configuration (mono or stereo) one or two, control track, etc.

4. Azimuth and zenith alignment on lab recorder, and adjust for proper playback speed.
5. Critical listening and note taking.
6. Waveform Analysis. (Spectrum Analysis, including FFT).
7. Magnetic development.
8. Testing the recorder - All functions must be tested multiple times. Both waveform analysis and magnetic development of the recorder must be included.
9. List all signal anomalies. Print waveforms.
10. Compare recorder signatures against the evidence tape signatures. Note differences and similarities. Form an opinion as to whether or not the tested recorder made the evidence tape.
11. Answer the question: copy or original? Insertions, deletions, over recordings, omissions, mechanical failures?
12. Analyze results, offer an opinion based on your conclusions. Write report. The report should include all Federal Rule 26 Requirements. Send the client all original materials and report in a secure manner

D. 12 step methodology – voice identification

Voice identification: The aural spectrographic method steps for voice ID case procedure

1. Receive, mark, and photograph evidence tapes, recorders and containers.
2. Physical inspection, tape inspection, lot number, condition.
3. Track configuration mono or stereo, one or two, control track etc.
4. Azimuth and zenith alignment on lab recorder.
5. Playback speed analysis and adjustment.
6. Load into computer for electronic enhancement.
7. Critical listening and notes.
8. Create “unknown” word and phrase list.
9. Take verbatim exemplar and create known “best” word list and phrases.

10. Create an audio unknown or known short-term memory tape for aural comparison.
11. Do the visual comparison of the spectrograms of the unknown/known ST phrases.
12. Analyze the results and form conclusions, offer an opinion. Write report to an archive file, make copies and send report to client with original materials (FedEx or certified mail). Include all Rule 26 requirements.

Voice ID criteria aural cues

1. Perceived pitch (eg: voice sounds high or low)
2. Quality (eg: street talk vs. educated speech)
3. Rate (how fast or slow a person speaks)
4. Mannerisms (eg: Someone who speaks fast and then slows down at the end of a sentence, "Sopranos" guys who end every sentence with "forget-about-it".)
5. Amplitude (how loud someone speaks)
6. Pathologies (eg: a harelip, a lisp or a stutter)
7. Breath patterns
8. Dialect/accent
9. Syllable coupling (the way we put the words together when we speak)

Voice ID criteria visual cues

1. Bandwidth
2. Mean frequency (vibrations of the vocal chords per second - average male has a mean frequency 130 cycles per second, average female is 150-160)
3. Trajectory of formants (on a spectrogram the formants are shapes that represent the vocal energy of the words that we're speaking, and our voices)
4. Inter formant information/ intra formant
5. Fricatives ("ch" sounds)
6. Plosives ("p" sounds)

7. Gaps (refers to syllable couplings, how we put words together when we speak)
8. Consonants (have a distinctive look and shape on a spectrogram)
9. Transitions between consonants and vowels
10. Transition between words
11. Rate (average number of words spoken per minute)
12. Pitch
13. Distribution
14. Nasal patterns distribution
15. Evidence of pathology, i.e. nasality, lisp, etc.
16. Relative intensity
17. Other spectral data

Even if the security director or consultant doesn't understand all the terms listed in the 12 Step Methodology, the expert you hire should.

This article is intended to give you a basis for the questions you need to be asking when you hire an expert in the forensic recorded media field. Tom Owen is the author of these testing procedures, and he and Owl Investigations have been performing these tests using these criteria for twenty-five years.

6.8 Conclusion

The technique of voice identification by means of aural and spectrographic comparison is still an unsettled topic in law. Although the spectrographic voice identification method has progressed greatly since it was first introduced to a court of law back in the mid-1960s, it still faces stiff resistance on the issue of admissibility in the courts today. One of the reasons for such opposition regarding admissibility is that the method has evolved greatly since its initial application. Court decisions based on early methods of voice identification analysis are not applicable to the methods used today. No longer are voices compared on the basis of a limited group of key words. Today's aural/spectrographic voice identification method takes advantage of the latest in technological advancements and interweaves several analyses into one procedure to produce an accurate opinion as to the identity of a voice. This modern technique combines the experience of a trained examiner performing the visual analysis of the spectrograms and aural analysis of the recordings with the use of the latest instruments modern technology has to offer, all in a standardized methodology to assure reliability. Court decisions reviewing the early voice identification cases may not be relevant to present day cases because the older decisions were based on less sophisticated procedures. Most of the courts that have rejected admission have been aware of continuing work in this field and have specifically left the door open as to future admissibility.

Proper presentation and explanation of the research pertaining to spectrographic voice identification analysis will allow the courts to understand the accuracy and reliability of the spectrographic voice identification method. When the research is properly presented, the studies show that properly trained individuals, using standard methodology, produce accurate results.

The current trends in the admissibility issue of voice identification evidence indicate that courts are more willing to allow the evidence into the courtroom when a proper foundation has been established which then allows the trier of fact to determine the weight to be assigned to the evidence.

Endnotes

1. This type of speaker identification has long been accepted in the courts, particularly where such testimony is given by lay witnesses.

2. For example, the word "dollars" spoken by the unknown voice can only be compared to the word "dollars" spoken by the suspects. A comparison of the unknown voice saying "dollars" with the suspect saying "money" is not valid.

3. Smrkovski, Lonnie L., D/Lieutenant, *Forensic Voice Identification*, Michigan Department of State Police, 1984 edition, page 36.

4. Bell, Alexander Melville, *Visible Speech: The Science of Universal Alphetics of Self-Interpreting Philological Letters for the Writing of All Languages in One Alphabet*, 1867.

5. *Voiceprint Identification Instruction Manual*, Voice Identification, Inc., Somerville, N.J., 1978.

6. Smrkovski, *Voice Identification*, Michigan Department of State Police, 1984, p.2.

7. Kersta, L.G., "Voiceprint Infallibility," (A paper presented to the Acoustical Society of America at their annual meeting in Seattle, Washington), May 1962.

8. 49 N.J. 343, 230 A.2d 384 (1967).

9. 230 A.2d 384 at 386.

10. Id. at 388.

11. 99 N.J.Super. 323, 239 A.2d 680 (1968), at 685.

12. 53 N.J. 256, 250 A.2d 15 (1969), at 250 A.2d 16.

13. 56 N.J. 16, 264 A.2d 209 (1970), at 264 A.2d 210.

14. 266 Cal. App. 2d 437, 72 Cal. Rptr. 478 (1968).

15. 266 Cal. App. 2d at 456.

16. Id. at 461.

17. Id. at 461.

18. 192 N.W.2d 432 (1971).

19. Id. at 441.

20. Id. at 439.

21. Id. at 438 and 440

22. Id. at 440.

23. *Worley v. State*, Fla., 263 So. 2d 613 (1972), 4th Dist. Ct. of Appeals, *Alea v. State*, Fla., 265 So. 2d 96 (1972), 3rd Dist. Ct. of Appeals.

24. 263 So. 2d at 614 and 615.

25. 265 So. 2d at 97.

26. 61 N.J. 544, 296 A.2d 644 (1972).

27. 296 A.2d at 648. The court did require the defendant to give a sample of his voice for voice identification testing.

28. 30 Cal. App. 3d 778; 106 Cal. Rptr. 547 (1973).

29. 30 Cal. App. 3d at 787

30. Id. at 788.

31. 378 F.Supp. 44 (E.D. Pa. 1974)

32. Id. at 53.

33. 498 F.2d 741 (D.C. Cir. 1974)

34. Id. at 745. Interestingly enough, this is the same court that decided *Frye*, and the court admitted that the requirements of *Frye* retard somewhat the admission of proof based on new methods of scientific investigation (Id at 743).

35. Id. at 744 and 745.

36. Id. at 745 and 747.

37. 40 Cal. App. 3d 69, 114 Cal. Rptr. 708 (1974).

38. 40 Cal. App. 3d at 84.

39. 511 F.2d 25 (1975), cert. denied, 95 S.Ct. (1975).

40. Id. at 33.

41. 433 F.2d 431.

42. Id. at 438.

43. 327 N.E.2d 671 (Mass. 1975).

44. Id. at 678.

45. Id. at 675.

46. 327 N.E.2d 819 (Mass. 1975).

47. 519 F.2d 463 (1975).

48. Id. at 466.

49. Id. at 466.

50. 525 F.2d 819 (1975).

51. Id. at 827.

52. 385 N.Y.S.2d 228, 86 Misc.2d 868 (1976).

53. 385 N.Y.S.2d at 237.

54. Id. at 237.

55. Id. at 234.

56. 549 P.2d 1240, 129 Cal. Rptr. 144 (1976).

57. 549 P.2d at 1242.

58. Id. at 1248 and 1249.

59. 538 F.2d 408 (1976).

60. Id. at 413.

61. Id. at 413.

62. 369 A.2d 1277 (Pa. 1977).

63. Id. at 1281.

64. 401 Mich. 141, 257 N.W.2d 537 (1977).

65. 257 N.W.2d at 539.

66. Id. at 540.

67. 443 F.Supp. 269 (1977).

68. Id. at 273.

69. Id. at 273.

70. 405 N.Y.S.2d 365, 94 Misc. 704 (1978).

71. 405 N.Y.S.2d at 367.

72. Id. at 370.

73. 384 A.2d 647 (1978).

74. Id. at 649.

75. Id. at 650.

76. 157 N.J.Super. 553 (1978), Chancery Division of the Superior Court of New Jersey.

77. Id. at 565.

78. 388 A.2d 500 (Me. 1978).

79. Id. at 503.

80. 283 Md. 374, 391 A.2d 364 (Md. 1978).

81. 391 A.2d at 368.

82. Id. at 377.

83. Id. at 377.

84. 583 F.2d 1194 (2d Cir. 1978).

85. Id. at 1198.

86. Id. at 1198 and 1199.

87. Id. at 1199 and 1200.

88. 453 N.Y.S.2d 343, 114 Misc. 1021 (Sup.1982).

89. 453 N.Y.S.2d at 346 and 347.

90. Id. at 347.

91. Id. at 347.

92. 4 Ohio St.3rd 53 (1983).

93. Id. at 56.

94. Id. at 56.

95. 450 N.E.2d 498 (Ind. 1983).

96. Id. at 503.

97. Id. at 503.

98. 686 P.2d 1224 (Ariz. 1984).

99. Id. at 1233.

100. 767 F.2d 1052 (S.C. 1985).

101. Id. at 1065, fn.16.

102. 496 A.2d 1382 (R.I. 1985).

103. Id. at 1388.

104. Id. at 1388.

105. Id. at 1389.

106. 493 So. 2d 781 (La. 1986).

107. 368 So. 2d 975 (La. 1979).

108. 493 So. 2d 787.

109. Id. at 788.

110. Id. at 789.

111. 522 A.2d 405 (N.J. 1987).

112. Id. at 412.

113. Id. at 407.

114. Id. at 408.

115. Id. at 409.

116. Id. at 410.

117. Id. at 411.

118. Id. at 412.

119. Id. at 411.

120. 756 S.W.2d 401.

121. Id. at 403.

122. Id. at 404.

123. Id. at 409.

124. United States Court of Appeals for the Seventh Circuit No. 86-2994.

125. Id. at 4, footnote 3 also points out that only District of Columbia Circuit so far has held that testimony on spectrographic voice identification is inadmissible but that it might be time to reexamine the court's position on admissibility in the light of increased reliability and general acceptance.

126. Id. at 4.

127. Id. at 11.

128. Id. at 7 through 11.

129. Id. at 10.

130. Id. at 12.

131. 728 F. Supp 1471 (D. Haw. 1990).

132. Id. at 1478.

133. 80 N.Y.2d 818 (1992).

134. *Frye v. United States*, 293 F. 1013 (1923).

135. Id. at 1014.

136. 493 So. 2d 781 (La. 1986).

137. Unpublished opinion of the Municipal Court of the Chico Judicial District, California (1985) No. CR-21695.

138. Id. at page 43.

139. McCormick, *Handbook of the Law of Evidence*, section 203 at 608 (3rd Ed. Cleary 1984).

140. 391 A.2d 364 (Md. 1978).

141. Id. at 367.

142. 252 Ill. 534, 96 N.E. 1077.

143. 96 N.E. at 1082.

144. Murphy v. State, 184 Md. 70, 40 A.2d 239 (1944).

145. Rules 401 and 402 of the Federal Rules of Evidence.

146. Rule 702 of the Federal Rules of Evidence.

147. 509 U.S. 579 (1993).

148. 509 U.S. at 590.

149. *State v. Bible*, 858 P.2d 1152, 1183 (Ariz. 1993).

150. See Appendix 1 for a summary of the research studies in the field of spectrographic voice identification.

151. Smrkovski, L. L., "Study of Speaker Identification by Aural and Visual Examination of Non-contemporary Speech Samples" J*ournal of the AOAC*, Vol. 59, No. 4, 1975, pp. 927–931.

152. Greenwald, M.H., *The Effect of Decreased Frequency Bandwidth on Speaker Identification by Aural and Spectrographic Examination of Speech Samples*, Master's thesis, Michigan State University, 1979.

153. Koenig, B.E., "Spectrographic Voice Identification: A Forensic Survey," *J. Acoust. Soc. Am.* 79(6), June 1986, p.2088.

154. Reich, Alan R., "Effects of Selected Vocal Disguises Upon Spectrographic Speaker Identification," *J. Acoust. Soc. Am.*, Vol. 60, No. 4, October 1976, pp. 919–925.

List of Cases

Alea v. State, 265 So. 2d 96 (Fla. 1972).
Brown v. United States, 384 A.2d 647 (D.C.Ct. App. 1978).
Commonwealth v. Lykus, 327 N.E.2d 671 (Mass. 1975).
Commonwealth v. Topa, 369 A.2d 1277 (Pa. 1977).
Commonwealth v. Vitello, 327 N.E.2d 819 (Mass. 1975).
Cornett v. State, 450 N.E.2d 498 (Ind. 1983).
Daubert v. Merrell Dow Pharmaceuticals, Inc., 509 U.S. 579 (1993).
D'Arc v. D'Arc, 157 N.J.Super. 553 (1978).
Frye v. United States, 54 App. D.C. 46 293 F. 1013 (1923).
Hodo v. Superior Court, 30 Cal. App. 3d 778 (Cal. 1973).
People v. Bein, 453 N.Y.S.2d 343 (N.Y. 1982).
People v. Chapter, 13 Cr.L. 2479 (Cal. 1973).
People v. Collins, 405 N.Y.S.2d 365 (1978).
People v. Evans, 393 N.Y.S.2d 674 (1977).
People v. Jeter, 80 N.Y. 818 (1992).
People v. Kelly, 549 P.2d 1240 (Cal. 1976).
People v. King, 266 Cal. App. 2d 437 (1968).
People v. Law, 40 Cal. App. 3d 69 (Cal. 1974).
People v. Rogers, 385 N.Y.S.2d 228 (N.Y. 1976).
People v. Siervonti, unpublished, Municipal Court of the Chico Judicial District, State of California (1985).
Reed v. State, 391 A.2d 364 (Md. 1978).
Pope v. State of Texas, 756 S.W.2d 401 (Tex. 1988).
People v. Tobey, 257 N.W.2d 537 (Mich. 1977).
State v. Andretta, 296 A.2d 644 (N.J. 1972).
State v. Cary, 230 A.2d 384 (N.J. 1967).
State v. Cary, 239 A.2d 680 (N.J.Super. 1968).
State v. Cary, 250 A.2d 15 (N.J. 1969).
State v. Cary, 264 A.2d 209 (N.J. 1970).
State v. Free, 493 So. 2d 781 (La. 1986).
State v. Gortarez, 686 P.2d 1224 (Ariz. 1984).
State v. Olderman, 336 N.E.2d 442 (Oh. 1975).
State ex rel. Trimble v. Hedman, 192 N.W.2d 432 (Minn. 1971).
State v. Wheeler, 496 A.2d 1382 (R.I. 1985).
State v. Williams, 388 A.2d 500 (Me. 1978).

State v. Williams, 4 Ohio St.3d 53 (1983).
United States v. Addison, 498 F.2d 741 (D.D.C. 1974).
United States v. Askins, 351 F.Supp. 408 (1972).
United States v. Baller, 519 F.2d 463 (4th Cir. 1975).
United States v. Franks, 511 F.2d 25 (6th Cir. 1975).
United States v. Jenkins, 525 F.2d 819 (6th Cir. 1975).
United States v. Maivia, 728 F. Supp 1471 (D. Haw. 1990).
United States v. McDaniel, 538 F.2d 408 (D.C. Cir 1976).
United States v. Raymond, 337 F.Supp. 641 (D.D.C. 1972).
United States v. Sample, 378 F.Supp. 44 (Pa. 1974).
United States v. Williams, 583 F.2d 1194 (2d Cir. 1978).
United States v. Williams, 443 F.Supp. 269 (S.D.N.Y. 1977).
United States v. Wright, 37 C.M.R. 447 (1967).
Worley v. State, 263 So. 2d 613 (Fla. 1972).

References

Greenwald, M., *The Effects of Decreased Frequency Bandwidth on Speaker Identification by Aural and Spectrographic Examination of Speech Samples*, Master's thesis, Michigan State University, 1979.

Hall, M.C., *Spectrographic Analysis of Interspeaker and Intraspeaker variables of Professional Mimicry*, Master's thesis, Michigan State University, 1975.

Hazen, B., "Effects of Different Phonetic Contexts on Spectrographic Speaker Identification," 54 *J. Acoust. Soc. Am.* 650, 1973.

Hollien, H., and McGlone, R., "The Effect of Disguise on Voiceprint Identification," In the *Proceedings* of the Carnahan Crime Countermeasures Conference, University of Kentucky, University of Kentucky Press, Lexington, KY, 1976.

Kersta, L.G., "Voiceprint Identification," 196 *Nature Magazine* 1253, Dec. 29, 1962.

Reich et al., "Effects of Selected Vocal Disguises Upon Spectrographic Speaker Identification," 60 *J. Acoust. Soc. Am.* 919, 1976.

Reich and Duke, "Effects of Selected Vocal Disguises Upon Speaker Identification by Listening," 66 J. *Acoust. Soc. Am.* 1023, 1979.

Smrkovski, L.L., "Collaborative Study of Speaker Identification by the Voiceprint Method," 58 *J. AOAC* 453, 1975.

Smrkovski, L.L., "Study of Speaker Identification by Aural and Visual Examination of Non-contemporary Speech Samples," 59 *J. AOAC* 927, 1976.

Stevens et al., "Speaker Authentication and Identification: A Comparison of Spectrographic and Auditory Presentations of Speech Material," 44 *J. Acoust. Soc. Am.* 1596, 1968.

Tosi et al., "Experiment on Voice Identification," 15 *J. Acoust. Soc. Am.* 2030, 1972.

Tosi and Greenwald, *Voice Identification by Subjective Methods of Minority Group Voices*, Paper presented at the 6th Meeting of the International Association of Voice Identification, New Orleans, La., 1978.

Young, M.A. and Campbell, R.A., "Effects of Context on Talker Identification," 42 *Acoust. Soc. Am.* 1250, 1967.

Appendix

The following are summaries of studies of spectrographic voice identification and an FBI survey of forensic cases.

Kersta (1962)

Examiners:	8 high school girls	Training duration:	1 week
Method:	visual	Speaker population:	123
Number of words:	10 words excerpted from sentences	Context type:	isolated random context
Temporal sequence:	contemporary	Type of trial:	Closed
Total number of trials:	2000		
Type of decision:	forced decisions limited sample limited time random context no aural examination examiners lacked sufficient experience	Results:	Closed trials range of errors for false ID - 0.35 to 1.0% 10 words excerpted 0.00 to 2.0%

Young and Campbell (1967)

Examiners:	7 Ph.D. candidates in ASC 3 assistant professors in ASC	Training duration:	1 week
Method:	visual	Speaker population:	5 adult males
Number of words:	2 words (you/it) in isolation & excerpted from 4 short sentences	Context type:	1 word in isolation 2 words from random context
Temporal sequence:	contemporary	Type of trial:	closed
Total number of trials:	1046		
Type of decision:	forced decisions limited sample random context no aural examination examiners not trained	Results:	closed trials range of errors for false ID - "you" in isolation: 10.4 to 18.0% 'it' in isolation: 22.7 to 33.0% "you/it" from random context in trial 1 of 15: mean error: 62.7%

Stevens (1968)

Examiners:	college students 6 in the open trials 4 in the closed trials	Training duration:	1 week
Method:	aural vs.visual but not combined	Speaker population:	24 males
Number of words:	catalogue of 11 words in different random order - only 1 word used in most trials	Context type:	1 to 4 words
Temporal sequence:	non-contemporary (1 week)	Type of trial:	closed & open
Total number of trials:	216		
Type of decision:	forced decisions limited sample (1 to 4 words) random context no aural examination examiners not trained	Results:	open trials: range of errors for false ID for 4 examiners/1 word visual trials - 31.0 to 47.0% aural trials - 6.0 to 8.0% closed trials: range of errors for false ID - 1 - 4 discrete words visual trials 20.0 to 30.0% aural trials 5.0 to 18.0%

Tosi et al. (1968–1970)

Examiners:	29 of various backgrounds	Training duration:	1 month
Method:	visual	Speaker population:	250 males randomly selected from a population of 25,000
Number of words:	6 & 9 words	Context type:	isolated, fixed and random context
Temporal sequence:	contemporary & non-contemporary (1 month)	Type of trial:	closed & open
Total number of trials:	34,992		
Type of decision:	Forced decisions, but allowed to rate confidence level Limited sample Limited time no aural examination examiners lacked sufficient experience	Results:	range of errors for all trials false ID - 0.51 to 6.43% when only 'fairly & almost' certain decisions are combined, the error of false ID reduces to 2.4%

Hazen (1972)

Examiners:	College students (7 panels of 2)	Training duration:	5 lectures and 3 practice sessions
Method:	Visual	Speaker population:	60 males
Number of words:	5 words in the same context, 5 words physically excerpted from random conversation	Context type:	fixed and random context
Temporal sequence:	Contemporary	Type of trial:	closed & open
Total number of trials:	280		
Type of decision:	forced decisions limited sample (5 words) no aural examination random & fixed context examiners lacked sufficient experience used the most dissimilar spectrographic utterances compared sounds from totally different words studying changing phonetic context examiners could not evaluate effects of coarticulation due to questionable word boundaries	Results:	closed trials errors for false ID - fixed context range:10.0 to 30.0% mean: 20.0% random context range:50.0 to 90.0% mean: 74.29% open trials errors for false ID - fixed context range:16 to 66% mean: 42.86% random context range:66 to 100% mean: 83%

Smrkovski (1974)

Examiners:	7 police & private	Training duration:	more than 2 years experience/less than 2 years experience
Method:	combined aural and visual	Speaker population:	7 male & female
Number of words:	38 to 54 words	Context type:	fixed context
Temporal sequence:	Noncontemporary (1 week)	Type of trial:	open
Total number of trials:	84		
Type of decision:	no forced decisions allowed 1 to 5 conclusions no limited time aural & visual examination trained and experienced examiners	Results:	open trials trainees w/less than 2 yr experience: false ID - 0.0% false elim. 5.0% no decision 25.0% 0.35 to 1.0% examiners w/more than 2 yr experience: false ID - 0.0% false elim. 0.0% no decision 22.0%

Smrkovski (1975)

Examiners:	12 scientists, police and private	Training duration:	novice: no training trainee: < 2 yr Professional: > 2 yr
Method:	combined visual and visual	Speaker population:	20 male & female
Number of words:	9 words	Context type:	fixed context
Temporal sequence:	noncontemporary	Type of trial:	open
Total number of trials:	120		
Type of decision:	no forced decisions allowed 1 to 5 conclusions no limited time aural & visual examination compared words in context - trainees, novices and experienced examiners	Results:	open trials: errors novices false ID 5.0% false elim 25.0% no decision 2.5% trainee false ID 0.0% false elim 0.0% no decision 2.5% Professional false ID 0.0% false elim 0.0% no decision 7.5%

Hall (1975)

Examiners:	4 professional and 20 college graduates	Training duration:	IAVI certified voice identification examiner
Method:	combined visual and visual / visual only	Speaker population:	professional mimic and 6 celebrity voices
Number of words:	mimic (mean of 25 sec.), celebrities (mean of 35 min.)	Context type:	quasi-fixed and random context
Temporal sequence:	contemporary/ noncontemporary	Type of trial:	open
Total number of trials:	aural (20/examiner) visual (200/examiner)	Type of decision:	same, different or undecided 5 IAVA classifications
Results:	Interspeaker variability does not exist between a mimicked, disguised voice and the nature voice of the subject mimicked. Intraspeaker variabilities are minute and not significant when comparing mimics' voice and the nature voice of the mimic. Aurally: The smaller signal-to-noise ratio within the recording and the more similar the context, the greater the percentage of accuracy in distinguishing between speakers. AURAL EXAMINATION: Grand means: RIGHT WRONG UNDEC. Grad. students 0.74 0.18 0.08 Professional 0.92 0.082 0.0		

Hollien and McGlone (1975–76)

Examiners:	5 faculty 1 graduate student	Training duration:	"the authors were familiar with the 'voiceprint' method of speaker identification"
Method:	visual only (spectrograms were cut & mounted)	Speaker population:	25 faculty and graduate students of the University of Florida
Number of words:	7 words	Context type:	"I do not set the same store"
Temporal sequence:	contemporary	Type of trial:	open
Total number of trials:	25/examiner		
Type of decision:	record a match/ indicate none was possible	Results:	". . . even skilled auditors such as these were unable to match correctly the disguised speech to the reference (normal) samples as much as 25% of the time . . . these groups were able to disguise their voices in such manners that their identification by the 'voiceprint' technique became little more than a matter of chance."

Reich et al. (1976)

Examiners:	2 Ph.D. candidates in speech science 2 Ph.D. candidates in speech pathology	Training duration:	3 courses in speech science plus previous experience with speech spectrograms: 4 weeks at 10-15 hr/wk
Method:	visual only (words excerpted and mounted)	Speaker population:	40 adult males (mean: 27.3 yrs)
Number of words:	9 words	Context type:	fixed context
Temporal sequence:	noncontemporary	Type of trial:	open
Total number of trials:	105 (7 matching tasks w/15 known & 15 unknown)		
Type of decision:	1 to 5 certainty scale	Results:	The examiners were able to match speakers with a moderate degree of accuracy (55.67%) when there was no attempt to vocally disguise. Disguised speech significantly interfered with speaker identification. Further research is needed … in which the examiners may listen to the voice as well as view the spectrograms.

Rothman (1977)

Examiners:	30 listeners 6 visual examiners	Training duration:	none
Method:	Study I: Aural Study II: Visual (0 to 8kHz)	Speaker population:	12
Number of words:	four - 2 second speech segments	Context type:	random context
Temporal sequence:	contemporary/ noncontemporary (1wk)	Type of trial:	open
Total number of trials:	5 visual 38 aural		
Type of decision:	same/different for each contemporary and noncontemporary	Results:	94% correct identifications were obtained for contemporary speech segments. 42% correct identifications were obtained for noncontemporary speech segments. 58.45% correct identifications were obtained when comparing different speakers. All examiners in pretest visual achieved 100% correct matching. Aural method is clearly superior to the spectrographic or 'voiceprint' method

McGlone, Hollien and Hollien (1977)

Examiners:	4 phoneticians	Training duration:	experienced
Method:	visual measurement of format fundamental frequency to obtain fo	Speaker population:	23 adult males
Number of words:	7 words ("I do not set the same store"	Context type:	fixed (normal & disguised) context
Temporal sequence:	contemporary	Type of trial:	
Total number of trials:	46/phonetician		
Type of decision:		Results:	A great amount of variability in the fo was found between normal and disguised speech. The mean bandwidth differences (f1, f2, f3) for the group were large and also demonstrated considerable variability. Phonetic means also differed.

Houlihan – Study 1 (1977)

Examiners:	21 undergraduate students	Training duration:	series of lectures & discussions on phonetics, acoustics, and sound spectrography and speaker identification
Method:	visual only	Speaker population:	9 female, 5 male undergraduates - homogenous age and geographic background
Number of words:	9 words	Context type:	fixed context: 5 voice conditions (normal, lowered, falsetto, whispered and muffled)
Temporal sequence:	contemporary	Type of trial:	open
Total number of trials:	18 matches		
Type of decision:	same/different	Results:	correct identifications: F-voice M-voice normal 100% 95% lowered 85% 95% falsetto 95% 90% whispered 5% 98% muffled 75% 100% range: 39 to 70% correct mean: 58.8% Std.D.: 8.7%

Houlihan – Study 2 (1977)

Examiners:	7 students from Experimental phonetics	Training duration:	completion of Exp. I with feedback
Method:	visual only	Speaker population:	8 female, 8 male (mean age: 25.3 yrs)
Number of words:	8 words	Context type:	fixed context: "There's a bomb in the main post office"
Temporal sequence:	contemporary	Type of trial:	closed
Total number of trials:	16/examiner		
Type of decision:	instructed to consider the sets in a particular order. All examiners considered undisguised before disguised	Results:	correct identifications: F-voice / M-voice normal 71% 100% lowered 85% 100% falsetto 100% 67% whispered 71% 71% muffled 85% 100% The results suggest that minimally trained examiners have little difficulty with spectrographic identification in closed, contemporary, undisguised trials. Results do not suggest that female voices are more difficult to identify than male voices.

Tosi et al. (1979)

Examiners:	professional and students	Training duration:	IAVA certified voice examiners and 2 weeks of training, respectively
Method:	aural only, visual only and aural/visual combined	Speaker population:	Chicano (25 female and 25 male)
Number of words:	four sentences approximately 2.4 seconds in Spanish	Context type:	fixed context
Temporal sequence:	noncontemporary	Type of trial:	open - randomized
Total number of trials:	600/examiner		
Type of decision:	same, different, no opinion. qualified percentage of self-confidence from 51 to 100%	Results:	Student and Professional examiners for errors of elimination and identification had a mean percentile greater for noisy samples than for quiet samples, however, the professional examiner errors were due to aural only examinations whereas spectrographic/aural examinations produced 0.0% errors. The 'no opinion' option was used more by professional examiners.

Reich (1979)

Examiners:	24 undergraduate students, 3 doctoral students, 3 professors of Speech and Hearing Science	Training duration:	brief lecture; 120 discrimination trials identical to the experiment
Method:	aural only	Speaker population:	40 adult males (mean age: 27.3 yrs)
Number of words:	9 words (it, is, on, you, and, the, I, to, me)	Context type:	fixed context
Temporal sequence:	noncontemporary (2 weeks +)	Type of trial:	open
Total number of trials:	18 matches		
Type of decision:	same/different (1 to 5 certainty)	Results:	Both groups were able to discriminate speakers with moderately high degrees of accuracy, 92% correct for undisguised. Disguised trials ranged from 59 to 81% depending on the disguise. Recommended further research to study the combined aural/spectrographic method.

Greenwald (1979)

Examiners:	3 professional, 5 trainees (less than 2 years experience)	Training duration:	professionals: 8 yrs each trainees: < 2 yrs
Method:	aural only, visual only and aural/visual combined	Speaker population:	12 female, 12 male; American midwest dialect
Number of words:	24 words	Context type:	fixed context
Temporal sequence:	Non-contemporary	Type of trial:	open
Total number of trials:	192 discrimination types	Type of decision:	the five IAVI alternatives
Results:	Professional examiners produced no errors of false identification or elimination. 1536 decisions by all eight examiners. Effect of restricted bandwidths (240-2K, 240-2.5K, 240-3K, and 240-4K) does not increase the errors but does increase the percentage of 'no decisions'. Training of the examiner is very important on error rate. Trainees produced errors as follows: 6.1% false identification and 4.1% false elimination for all trials. However, at 240-4khz., 0.0% errors of false identification of elimination.		

Koenig-FBI Survey (1986)

Examiners:	Federal Bureau of Investigation voice identification examiners	Training duration:	minimum of 2 yrs experience, completion of at least 100 actual voice comparison cases, formal approval by other trained examiners
Method:	combined aural/visual method	Speaker population:	actual criminal cases
Number of words:	varied with each case	Context type:	
Temporal sequence:	non-contemporary	Type of trial:	open
Total number of trials:	2000 forensic comparisons		
Type of decision:	very similar very dissimilar no decision (low confidence)	Results:	<u>number</u> <u>percent</u> no/low conf. 1304 65.2 elimination 378 18.9 identification 318 15.9 <u>errors</u> false elim. 2 0.53 false id. 1 0.31

Chapter 7

The Statement as a Crime Scene: Low-Tech Tools for Corporate Investigations

Gerald R. (Gary) Brown

Synopsis

7.1 Introduction

Workplace violence is the number one concern of senior executives of both big and small businesses. On the average day in the U.S. corporate world, 16,400 threats are made, 723 workers are attacked and 43,800 are harassed.[1] Every year more than 1,000 U.S. workers are victims of homicide, and one in four full-time workers are harassed, threatened, or attacked.[2] Most of these threats and statements are made either in a written or recorded format which can be studied for small clues often not readily seen by investigators lacking the appropriate training. Each day there are thousands, if not tens of thousands, of statements taken by corporate security personnel in the conduct of their mission. Most of these threats end up in some executive or security officer's drawer never to be seen again unless, of course, something happens and then everyone wonders how with all the "clues" something wasn't done before the tragedy. Many of statements are perfunctory recording of what the investigator already knows and are rarely treated as having little clues or red flags that could indicate the guilty party.

Every investigator knows an uncontaminated crime scene is invaluable to solving a crime and being able to prove who did it. An uncontaminated crime scene can yield not only the obvious information, such as that from dead bodies, missing supplies, fraudulent contracts, etc., but will yield information that the suspect, victim, and witness had no idea could be exposed for discovery by the investigator. Crime scene processing now requires special training in and awareness of forensics. Large, as well as many small police departments have special teams to do nothing but process crime scenes.

This chapter introduces the relatively new and growing use of a low-tech tool, *statement analysis*, to corporate investigations. The tool, a combination of three tools that cross-validate and support each other, turns the written statement (which many investigators view as required to document information already gathered) into another "crime scene," requiring specially trained personnel to evaluate meticulously it. Although the statement may not have the yellow security area ribbon around it to keep others out and prevent contamination, it should be treated and reviewed just as carefully and expertly as any other crime scene. The investigator must understand that the statement can be contaminated just as any other crime scene. The inappropriate use by a suspect of a one-letter word could indicate who committed the harassment, murder, or other crime and whether a fraud was involved. However, if the use of the word is because of the language the investigator, the attorney, or anyone else to whom the person has spoken has used, then that word cannot be relied upon necessarily to have any specific meaning and must be considered to be "contaminated."

Statement analysis is usually employed in two main areas of concern in a corporation. One is in evaluating the dangerousness and behavioral characteristics of an anonymous writer, and describing that author with the ultimate goal that someone in the corporation recognizes the description. The second main area of use of statement analysis is to evaluate the truthfulness of statements and depositions made by suspects, victims, and key witnesses. These techniques are applicable to almost any type of investigation done by corporate investigators, including investigations from threat letters, arson, robbery or theft, and sexual harassment, to loss of proprietary information and insurance or workers' compensation fraud. Throughout this chapter, the term "statement analysis" will include evaluating everything from anonymous letters and historical documents recounting events of importance, to statements and depositions. The technique can be employed by the corporate investigators or third-party private investigators or by the corporate legal counsel. It can even apply to jury selection in high dollar value civil suits.

Statement analysis developed when it became evident to social scientists and expert interrogators that the unique qualities of an individual's handwriting reveals personality characteristics, especially those not often demonstrated by observable behavior. Personality characteristics can reveal whether or not the anonymous letter writer is likely to act out his or her threats. Evaluation of personality characteristics can also raise the question as to whether the investigator is looking at the right person for a particular type of crime. Certain types of personalities start fires, others commit physically violent crimes.

Investigators and handwriting experts also began noticing that changes in the handwriting in written statements could reveal "guilt anxieties" and that the language each of us chooses and chooses to change or leave out reveals changes in reality. In an alleged date-rape case, if the victim does not change how she referred to her date after the assault began, it is likely that, in "her mind" at least, there was no rape. The famous William Kennedy Smith "Blue Dot" case was a case where the victim continued to refer her actions with Smith after the alleged assault as, "*We* did this" and "We did that." Because the language did not change from one of closeness, as noted by the use of "we," to something else, that lack of change becomes a "red flag" to the investigator that this may not have been a rape at all.

Changes in reality can, and often do, indicate who did it or at least reveal information the writer did not intend to reveal. The investigator, who is familiar with statement analysis, might well be convinced to shift the focus earlier rather than later, even when management points the investigator to someone they think is a troublemaker. The investigator will know the personality of the anonymous author is different from the personality management suspects. The statement, both written and recorded, but especially the handwritten statement, is the tool that reveals to the investigator not only what the writer wants consciously for the investigator to know but also reveals much about the subconscious, including things the writer had no intention of revealing to anyone.

Every written or recorded statement taken during an investigation has the potential under close scrutiny to yield bits of evidence much like the "hairs and fibers" found at a traditional crime scene. The three techniques of statement analysis expose those "hairs and fibers."

7.2 Historical Perspective

Throughout history there have been numerous techniques for learning the true character of people and the detection of deception. From throwing suspects into a volcano to see if they would live and thus prove their innocence, to cattle prods still in use in some countries today, to voice stress analyzers and computerized polygraphs. Only in the last few years have corporate investigators and private investigators hired by corporate security or legal counsel become aware of what benefits statement analysis can bring to an investigation, particularly in the savings of time and manpower needed to solve the investigation.

When this author was an investigator in the field, statements were most often the last thing done in an interview and were primarily for the purpose of recording the key points provided by the interviewee during the oral interview. To be sure, investigators reviewed the statements for glaring and subtle conflicts in the facts and what was in the statement, but it was the rare investigator who looked at the statement with the same discriminating eye that all top investigators give to viewing the crime scene. A comprehensive modern day investigator knows that it may be that one little piece of hair or a clothing fiber under a bed that eventually leads to the identification of the perpetrator. Investigators are now learning the techniques of statement analysis can turn a statement, deposition, or anonymous note into a "crime scene" that can, and often does, yield small detailed "hairs and fibers" evidence pointing the investigators in a specific direction.

For the last couple of decades there has been an extensive training program for federal, state, and local law enforcement officers in the *content analysis* portion of statement analysis. The FBI, Secret Service, various other federal agencies, plus hundreds of police departments, large and small, have been studying content analysis. According to an FBI Academy instructor, the Content Analysis course at the FBI Academy runs forty-four hours and is the most popular Academy course for law enforcement personnel.

There has also been a less intense, but growing movement to train law enforcement in the two other statement analysis techniques, *behavioral profiling* from the handwriting and *Form Variance Analysis.*™

As those who have been trained in statement analysis, particularly the content analysis, have begun to retire from public law enforcement and move into corporate security and investigations, these "new" techniques have become an increasingly valuable tool. The use of personality and character analysis from the handwriting, evaluation of changes in the handwriting that indicate stress or deception, and the evaluation of the words and phrases we employ every day as we go about our daily business discourse with others is improving the efficiency and effectiveness of corporate investigations.

In 1994, a young South Carolina woman, Susan Smith, strapped her two sons, Michael, three years, and Alexander, fourteen months, into their car seats and let her automobile slide into a South Carolina lake and drowned them. The day after the murder, she appeared on the cable news channel, CNN, claiming some person had kidnapped them and tearfully appealing to the nation for her babies. Police detectives, who had just recently completed a course in content analysis, strongly suspected something was amiss in her "performance." The choice of language employed by Susan Smith heightened natural investigator suspicions. During her pleas, they noted she used terms such as "My children wanted me. They needed me. And now I can't help them," while the boys' father, David, was saying, "They're okay. They're going to be home soon." [3]

What was wrong with those terms? Content analysis, one of the three tools that comprise what this author calls "statement analysis," immediately raised suspicions. Susan Smith was already using the past tense to refer to her then only "missing" children, while her husband was using present tense. At that point in time, there was no good reason for Susan Smith to be speaking in the past tense, unless, of course, she knew they were already dead and not kidnap victims as she was claiming in those first few days of the investigation.

Statement analysis, as used by this author, refers to the coordinated employment of the three complementary and cross-validating investigative techniques to help solve some of the problems in today's sometimes violent workplace. This chapter discusses those techniques: behavioral profiling—evaluating the personality characteristics exhibited in the handwriting (particularly on written anonymous threat/exposé letters to personnel or about property); Form Variance Analysis™—an evaluation of changes in the format (slant, size, speed, spelling, pressure, and margins) of documents, both handwritten and mechanically or electronically printed; and content/discourse analysis of the actual words and phrases employed by an interviewee.

7.3 Behavioral Profiling

Behavioral profiling in this chapter has little direct connection to the type of FBI profiling that has come to prominence since approximately 1980. They are similar in that they are both about "crime scenes." The statement as a "crime scene" is discussed in this chapter.

Behavioral profiling from handwriting refers to the identification and evaluation of personality characteristics as reflected in the handwriting of the writer. For example, look at the handwriting of someone you know well. Not just an acquaintance, but someone you have observed in many situations over a relatively long period of time. Does their handwriting have the appearance of being straight up and down vertical writing? Or, does the writing slant significantly to the right? If the former, you will most likely think of that person as poised, one who is asking "What is best?" or "What is the right thing to do?" or something similar. This person will appear unruffled when others may be losing their control or not be able to think clearly in a crisis situation. If, on the other hand, the writing slants 50 or more degrees to the right instead of being perpendicular, you will likely describe that person as one who immediately responds to emotional appeals, someone with spontaneity, who may act before thinking the situation through and say things he or she later regrets.

There are other factors that can inhibit or enhance the writing, but the slant of the writing is called a global trait in that it influences all other traits to some degree and is usually a trait that is demonstrated by observable behavior. Other "global" traits are size of writing, pressure of the writing, spacing between letters, words, rhythm, lines and margins, and the use of space on a page of paper. Although, if any personality trait is strong enough, it may very well affect all other traits. However, for purpose of this discussion the traits mentioned earlier are the most common "global" traits that influence all other traits.

Again, take a look at the writing of someone you know well. Look at the size of the writing. If it is very small, like this printing, most likely the person would be described as an introvert and would be quite comfortable in a job such as an accountant. If, however, the writing is much larger, like this printing, you would likely describe this person as an extrovert, one who is more interested in the "big picture," one who is interested in everything going on around him or her rather than concentrating on the small details. This person would be much more comfortable in an outside sales job (where no one is looking over his shoulder all day) than in an accountant or watch repair type job where focusing all the time on small details is a must.

Interesting point: A majority of successful investigators write from normal to the smallish side of average (one-eighth to three-eighths inch) in height and are described by those who know them best as introverts. There are always exceptions to the rule, but it isn't hard to understand why that is so. Are there many extroverts who like to listen more than talk? Nothing against extroverts, but the majority of successful investigators listen more than they talk, while talking a lot is a natural extrovert trait. Listening to and reading every detail, such as a dot out of place, as a personality trait, is even more important in statement analysis.

Excessively large signatures represent a large ego and are often seen in professional athletes and corporate executives. To be the very best there is at throwing a football or making a triple twisting double pump slam-dunk or to run one of the largest companies in the world, we often see a larger than average ego: one that says "I am the best!"

There is a lot more to handwriting analysis than can be explored in this chapter. What is important to understand is the concept that we all write the way we do because we are "comfortable" with the style or symbolism of our writing, whether it is fully connected cursive writing or totally disconnected ALL CAPITAL printing or something in between. The investigator, who understands the concepts of handwriting analysis, interprets what a writer's particular style tells about that writer's personality. If an investigator knows what to look for, he or she often produces or discovers information about that person that may or may not be able to be verified by other means but will almost surely produce information that can significantly lessen the expenditure of human and financial resources.

All investigators at some time have found that they spent time and resources looking at the wrong suspect or narrowing a large number of potential suspects down to the one or two most likely to have committed the offense.

Anonymous letters are often not intended to be a physical threat to the receiver or anyone else. They can be, and often are, upsetting to management. If they are posted on the company's bulletin board and make disparaging remarks about many employees, it can indeed significantly affect morale and be very damaging to the trust between management and their employees. Supervisors often think they know who is most likely to have written that anonymous letter. And just as often they are wrong.

The vast majority of threat letters are sent by those who are usually introverts, reluctant and afraid to speak out and generally loathe bringing attention on themselves by being a "loudmouth." In this technological age they are also more often than not printed out on a computer printer and not handwritten; the writer thinking it will be hard to prove who wrote the letter if it is printed out and not handwritten. This is often a fatal mistake on the part of the perpetrator as the techniques discussed in this chapter will show. The typical anonymous writer will exhibit behavior that most will look back on and describe as that of an introvert. Looking at the large loopy and rounded writing of the person management suspects, the investigator knows that it is highly unlikely that the anonymous letter came from that person. While not discounting management's prime suspect, and there not being other evidence that would point directly to management's suspect, the investigator will know that someone with writing that is smaller than average and probably more angular than normal will be much more likely to be the unknown perpetrator. This is, however, a tricky area for evaluation as most anonymous letter writers are women (roughly two-thirds) and women tend to have more rounded writing.

Threat or exposé letters will usually show a stronger than average degree of "resentment" in the personality. Obviously, this is quite common in threat letters in particular, since it usually takes the introverted person a long time to become so dissatisfied with a situation that he or she will send a threat letter. The pressure builds and the offenses build, in number and seriousness, until that person cannot stand it any longer and must write that letter. Resentment is one of the "global" factors in most threat letters. It is less of a factor in "exposé" type letters (those accusing an executive of some misconduct) but often still present. In exposé type letters there are other indicators and clues, which help separate the physical threat letters from the boisterous but not physically threatening letters.

Those very few threat letters that truly represent a physical threat to the receiver of the letter, or the company itself, will almost certainly have many other indicators both in the handwriting and the content that the analyst can use to help determine the seriousness of the threat. For example, assume one has two different letters with the exact wording. The handwriting on one has the appearance of the writing pen barely touching the paper. The writing on the second has the appearance of extreme pressure, even to the point of tearing the paper on key threat words, such as kill, knife, and gun. Will the threat be the same? No, of course not. Why? Because there is no force behind the light line writer, while the heavy line writer exerts a great deal of pressure and force, with special emphasis on key words. Pressure equates to strength of emotion. All things being equal, and the content (to be discussed later) not having a lot of contrary indicators, the investigator should take the second letter quite seriously.

Generally in writing, consistency of pressure, slant, and size reflect the existence of controls over one's emotions. One very important exception is the handwriting that has an appearance of being perfect (computer printer generated). That latter personality could be a onetime explosive type person. The person has built pressure from all the years of insuring perfection and with the right stimulus, usually very personal in nature, that person could explode in violent rage. The concept to learn is that extremes whether uncontrolled or controlled can, and usually do, adversely affect the personality and deserve the investigator's attention. The astute investigator will also notice writing where letter formations have the appearance of weapons, especially the appearance of daggers. The appearance of "weapons" in the writing is a more serious threat than writing without weapons.

There is a lot more that goes into a full-fledged analysis. This chapter gives investigators a brief overview of the concepts involved.

When the CEO or other employees receive an anonymous threat letter, or a letter claiming some misdeeds on some employee's part, the investigator who understands some of the basic principles of handwriting analysis will begin immediately to "draw" a mental picture of what the unknown author may be like. When it is believed that the anonymous letter came from inside the company or from someone known to the recipient the profiling is especially helpful in providing observable characteristics leading to identifying the author. When the letter comes from outside the company and there is an unlimited number of suspects, profiling helps determine dangerousness and provides a personality profile but is obviously limited in specifically identifying the unknown author.

Many companies that have problems with anonymous letters from time to time—and almost all do at some time—will often think the anonymous letter is from one of their already identified "troublemakers." Sometimes that opinion by management is accurate. If management is correct, it is a simple matter to have a questioned document examiner compare the unknown writing with writing from the suspect's personnel file to establish if that person did or did not write the anonymous letter. But in those situations where the letter is printed out on a computer printer it is usually not so easy to prove quickly who wrote the letter. Obviously, the content analysis then becomes the primary tool. And it is increasing in importance now that many companies are switching to computer processing of all personnel records, often leaving no handwriting in the file for comparison purposes.

However, it is often the case that the company doesn't strongly suspect or know who the writer is, or the questioned document examiner tells them it isn't the same person they may suspect. Being able to profile the writer can then be a tremendous asset. The profile is most effective when employed in the early stages of the investigations, but as a practical matter many companies wait to employ the profiling until the latter stages of the investigations when the investigators need additional insights. (This increases the time and costs of an investigation and as more investigators learn the power of the techniques discussed in this chapter, profiling and content analysis are being employed earlier in the investigation for maximum effectiveness.)

The profile can identify the type of job one is likely to have, assuming the person is in a job he or she is most suited for, and what type of behavior is most likely observable when the employee interacts with a superior, peers, and subordinates. The handwriting analyst investigator can often describe enough behaviors that co-workers and supervisors will "recognize" the combination of behaviors described as likely being John or Mary Doe, the employee in the personnel division.

Interesting note: The majority of anonymous writers are women who are less likely to be openly confrontational, especially in the work place.

Interesting note: A significant number, approximately 17 percent, of anonymous letter writers are the person(s) who received the obnoxious or threatening note in the first place.

Interesting note: The longer a note which complains about other employees and wrongdoing of others, the more likely the person who wrote the note is named somewhere in that note.

Take, for example, a situation in which it is strongly suspected that internal theft is occurring at a warehouse. There are thirty-five employees in that warehouse and this small company has one investigator. Where does the investigator start? The investigator who knows handwriting analysis can take statements from all employees. From those statements the investigator can identify the employee(s) who have the personality characteristics that would easily allow them to rationalize stealing from their employer. The investigator can then focus from the beginning of the investigation on those most likely to have committed the offense, thus often saving man-hours and associated costs.

Handwriting analysis does not, as yet, have enough validity and reliability studies behind it to use this tool to take administrative or legal action against someone based solely on the handwriting analysis. It is used to focus the investigation on the person(s) most likely to have been involved. It may prove to be that the primary focus is not the actual author. Once the focus is on one, or a few, person(s), through more routine investigative efforts the investigator can exclude or include the person(s) as the author relatively easily. If the case warrants, the focus can be redirected on the next most likely person to have committed the offense.

What about signatures? We often hear people say, "My signature doesn't look at all like the rest of my writing." What does it "tell" about that writer? The signature is what we all use every day to "represent" ourselves to the outside world. We may type on a computer all day, but when we write those checks or sign that report, we are purposely writing for others to see. In this day of computers and micro-recorders to record our thoughts, others may rarely see our "normal" writing, but it is still difficult to live in today's world without ever signing a document others will see. Our signature is our "projection" of ourselves to others—how we wish others to see us. If that signature is considerably different than our normal writing (such as a love letter to our lover), then the investigator who understands the symbolism of writing knows that there is a facade that must be broken down if you want to get to the truth. What is seen when first meeting someone is not necessarily the true self. However, if the signature looks exactly like the rest of the writing, then the investigator can reasonably assume that "what you see is what you get." There will normally be few pretenses when the signature and remaining handwriting are very similar. That doesn't mean they are necessarily telling the truth, but only that the personality you perceive is very likely the true personality. The investigator can then alter the interview techniques accordingly.

In the last two decades handwriting analysis/behavioral profiling has been increasingly used by corporate security, legal, and third-party corporate investigators to help solve matters from A to Z and everything in between. In essence, any time you want to know more about a personality, handwriting analysis/profiling can often provide information that you either can't find or would be considerably time consuming employing other investigative techniques.

7.4 Form Variance Analysis™: "The Common Man's Lie Detector"

The previous section discussed how the investigator understands the writer by identifying personality characteristics from handwriting. This portion of the chapter reveals how the patterns of changes in our handwriting can reveal indicators of problems the writer is having, which, in turn, can often be interpreted as lying or some other form of deception. Those changes include variations in the size, slant, pressure, spacing, margins, and spelling. Those variations are caused by psychological changes, which in turn, cause physiological changes in the muscles when a person is diverging from the absolute truth or editing out information. The patterns of variances in our writing will reveal more "hairs and fibers" to the astute observer than the guilty have any idea they are revealing.

When investigators notice patterns in those variances, clues can be red-flagged. When there are changes in the writing, there is always a reason. Just as some "clues" left at a physical crime scene may have nothing to do with the investigation, some of the "clues" in a written statement may not relate to the investigation. It is the job of the investigator to determine relevance.

When the investigator asks a suspect, victim, or key witness to sit down and write out a statement explaining what happened the truthful writer will be playing back in his or her head what happened, and concentrating on what he or she is writing about, not how he or she is placing pen to paper. As the writer relates what happened, the writing tends to flow without major changes. It is an extremely rare writer who, if he or she is being deceptive in what he is writing about or making up parts of what he or she is saying, can think smoothly and write with a steady and even hand. (The only persons this author has ever seen who can are psychopaths who lie so easily they almost appear they aren't even aware they are lying. These same personalities would most likely pass the polygraph too, even though they were telling a lie.) When there are changes in the slant, size, spacing, spelling, pressure or margins, this is a signal to the investigator to review the content of that particular area quite closely. The investigator may need to go back over that area of the statement with the writer, after the first uncontaminated version is completed, of course. (The uncontaminated statement is one prepared by the suspect, victim or, key witness without the "interference" of having talked with others, including others involved in the investigation, particularly the police and/or the investigator, Once a person has talked with someone else about an offense, there is bound to be contamination. This is especially true if an attorney has already become involved.)

For example, review the following sentence. Most of the writing has a consistent right slant:

"I left my office at my usual time of 6:00 A.M."

The word "usual" and the time "6:00 A.M." have a significant change in slant. What kind of clue does that give to the trained investigator who understands the concepts of handwriting analysis and Form Variance Analysis? What should be immediately suspected? We know the writer's routine writing has a slight right slant, but for some reason the slant changed to a more vertical slant at two key points, which raises the question of when did the writer actually leave the office? From your knowledge of the principles of handwriting analysis you know that the perpendicular vertical writing indicates that the emotions have generally been suppressed, but we already know this writer's routine writing has a right slant. Why would two key points show suppressed emotions? The normal emotions were left out of what he or she was writing because he or she wasn't telling the truth. He or she was making it up. What potential clue would the investigator be alerted to when all the writing was in its normal slant except, instead of the words "usual" and "6 A.M." being vertical, the writing of those two words leans even further to the right? Assuming the interviewee hasn't provided a believable reason to explain becoming even more emotional than normal, the investigator would not necessarily think the writer is lying, but that something very significant happened at that time, hence the increase in emotional responsiveness. Is this something that might be extremely important to the investigation? Who knows; but it is definitely a clue that something is being withheld and that something may very well be important to the investigation.

Assume the investigator has a statement from an early morning robbery when only the warehouse superintendent was present. In his statement he talks about how the robber placed a gun to his head and he was afraid for his life. The problem is that the normal writing of the superintendent is right slant but when talking about the gun placed to his head, the writing changes to perpendicular. If he were telling the truth about the gun, it would be common sense to assume that the writing at that time would not become perpendicular (less emotional), but would at least be his normal *right slant* and, more likely, slant even further to the right (increased emotions). Why? If he is telling the truth, he would become even more emotional as he "replays" what happened and remembers his feelings.

Let's look at a situation where there are significant spacing changes. When writing about what happened, a suspect will usually include an "alibi." As the investigator reviews the statement, he or she notices a change in spacing when the suspect writes about where she was at the time of the crime. For example, look at the following two statements representing handwritten statements, and decide which one is more likely the false alibi that was included in the statement, just by looking at the spacing as she talks about what she was doing during the theft that occurred at approximately 7:00 P.M.:

> "From 6-8 P.M., I was at the Jim   Stanaslowski Special Art Exhibit."
>
> "From 6-8 P.M., I was at the   Jim Stanaslowski Special Art Exhibit."

The investigator should at least be suspicious of the second statement as being a false alibi. Why? In the first statement the person couldn't immediately remember the full name of the exhibit. In the second statement, it appears that she had to stop for a split second and think about what she was going to use as an alibi.

What else does the spacing indicate? In this writer's case her emotions remain the same, but her thinking processes slow down. Whiles he is thinking that extra split second, her hand is still moving slightly across the page making those gaps in the writing appear. Does that mean she is lying? Again, it is hard to tell just from this input, but we can easily see that something has slowed the thinking process. If the person is telling the truth and nothing but the truth, the writing will, more often than not, flow with its normal style, spacing, slant, etc. There could be other reasons for this spacing "problem" and that is why variances are used for investigative clues only and not for prosecution purposes.

Form Variance Analysis is based on the concept that when there are changes in the writing there is a reason, whether it is loud noise that startles the writer, or a psychological reason related to attempting to deceive the investigator. The investigator who can spot and properly identify clues given up by those seemingly inconsequential "changes," will significantly enhance his or her ability to discover efficiently and effectively those bits of "hairs and fibers" type evidence in statements.

If the investigator comes across a list of numbers or names, and one number or name is considerably larger than the others, it may be another of those "hairs and fibers" type clues that alert the investigator to a problem area. For example, an investigator is interviewing a witness and asks the witness to write down the names of all the other witnesses. The witness identifies the following individuals as other witnesses: John, Billy, Big Eddie, Luther, Little Dweeb, and Shirley. The investigator would most likely ask the witness if he knows their last names or if any of them are friends of his. The witness might answer, "No, man, all I knew is their names and I don't do anything with them. I barely know any of them." That may well be a lie. However, if he says, "I barely know any of them other than their first names, except for Luther who I shoot dice with and play some pool. I also dated his sister a couple times." That may well be the truth about that specific detail. Why?

In Form Variance Analysis, when you have a list of things, names, numbers, etc., and one of them is significantly larger or smaller, there is a difference in relationship between the "odd" one and the others. For example, one of the reasons it was opined early on that the anthrax letters to Senator Tom Daschle and to NBC's Tom Brokaw were probably not related to the September 11, 2001, tragic terrorist incidents at the World Trade Center and the Pentagon, was the date "09-11-01." (There were several confirming clues, but "09-11-01" was of particular importance.) The date size variance tends to indicate the most important thing on that page was the date. Not the message, not the "Death to Americans" and "Death to Israel" phrases, but the dates. (One letter was sent on Sep. 18, 2001, and one on Oct. 9, 2001.) The reasoning, again along with several other clues supporting the conclusion, was that if the notes were part of the overall 9-11 terrorist incident, something other than the date would have been the most important and therefore largest item on the page. In the case of one of the letters, the item listed "Death to Israel" was the smallest and thus the least significant item on the note. It doesn't make sense that "Death to Israel" was less important to a 9-11 terrorist than was the phrase "This is next."[4]

Another example: You have a person who is known to be well educated and has demonstrated throughout the statement that he is a good speller, suddenly has problems with the spelling of a simple word(s) and goes back and corrects the spelling. It may mean nothing, but since the words where the spelling problem occurred just happen to be key words that have to be true if the statement is to be evaluated as true, the investigator has a huge clue there may be a problem (lie) there. Here is a verbatim quote of a statement taken by the special investigations unit of a major insurance firm concerning a $22,000+ theft:

> "Mother found House Broken into
> & Called Police. Gaind Entry
> Through Sliding Glass Door
> According to Police. Missig Items
> Include Camera outfit Men's Ring
> Woman's Ring, Computer & Printer.

The claimant in this case was a well-educated world traveler and shouldn't have been making easy spelling mistakes. Investigators will most likely note other clues; especially those who already know something of content analysis, but for this particular paragraph only look at the two originally misspelled words, "gaind" and "missig." The "e" was left out of "gained" and the "n" was left out of "missing," both were inserted later as corrections by the writer. The question was "Are the spelling problems related to an inability to spell or related to the "anxiety of guilt?" In order for it to be a valid claim, someone had to have "gained" entrance and there had to be something "missing." His misspelling of both "gained" and "missing," indicates possible deception. (The result of this was that the writer never admitted that there wasn't a theft, but he immediately withdrew his claim for over $22,000.)

Investigators need to know that a person should not be having spelling problems to come to the conclusion above. When someone who is poorly educated has problems with misspellings of many words, the investigator can't evaluate the clues the same. In fact, in the latter case they would probably not be clues at all.

To show that the subconscious memory in her mind wants to tell the truth, look at the following sentence from a statement of the head cashier regarding what she did during the period that a $25,000 internal theft occurred.

"I also dropped some money (1,800.00) to the bottom safe, so that the book Keeper can buy some money with the $1,800 for the day."

In the actual handwritten statement (Figure 7.1) there is an actual confession as to what she did. She did not actually steal the money, but she carelessly helped the theft along by violating company procedure. In her statement she is trying to cover up that violation of company procedure, which calls for her to count out $1,800 in change for the other clerks, and to drop the money through a slot to the bottom drawer of a two-drawer safe. In her statement she first wrote, instead of "...money" the word "...none," as in "I dropped some none..." Her mind knew the truth and "said" none. Her subconscious mind knew the reality but her conscious mind knew what she had to cover up. In reality she had left the $1,800 change on top of the safe and had gone downstairs leaving the door unlocked. When she came back, not only was the $1,800 gone, another employee (who was identified from their statement as the perpetrator) had opened the safe and taken the rest of the $25,000 and skipped town in the middle of the night.

The most important point to learn about Form Variance Analysis is there is a reason for changes in handwriting. Some are innocent, while some are very clear clues that there is a high likelihood of deception in the statement. Changes in handwriting could occur because somebody suddenly turned on the television, or a car backfired, startling the writer, or because there is a psychological reason perhaps indicating anxiety of guilt or additional unrevealed knowledge. The investigator who can identify the most likely reason for such changes in size, slant, spacing, spelling,

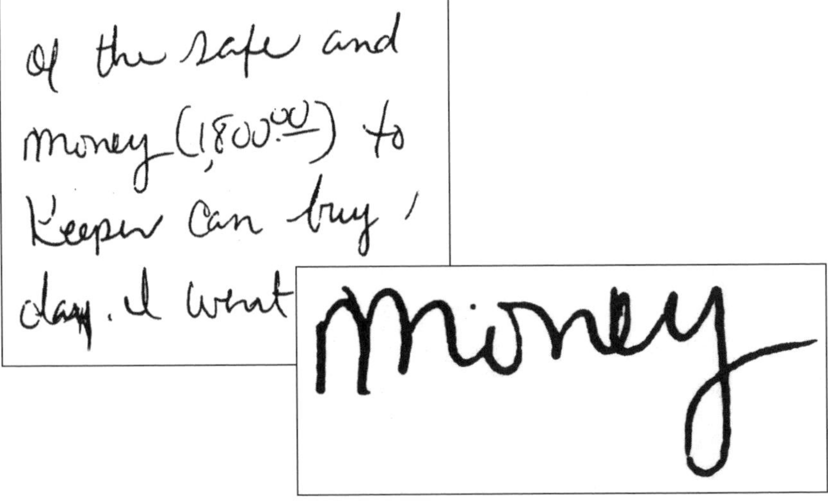

Figure 7.1

pressure, and margins may well save much time and effort as opposed to hunting for those same clues by more conventional means.

The impulses from the brain to the hand are a combination of the writer's innate personality characteristics and experiences in life over all the years with the writer's current emotional make up. What we are looking for in investigations is to identify the truthful from those who may be deceitful in their statements. The changes in the writing result from the anxiety of guilt and at the key point in the statement will betray the writer's anxiety, which alerts the trained analyst who can identify and analyze to understand their true implications. These subconsciously revealed clues can, and often do, give the investigator an edge. It may even appear to the "guilty" that the investigator has mind reading skills, although the truth of the matter is that the concepts, once understood, make simple common sense.

7.5 Content Analysis

A. Introduction

Donald Foster, in his recent book *Author Unknown*, noted that "since no two people use language precisely the same way, our identities are encoded in our own language, a kind of literary DNA." The manuscript dubbed "The Unabomber" can be directly tied through language to a specific person (in real life Ted Kaczynski). Significant amounts of potentially valuable information are included in statements, depositions, and other documents prepared by suspects, victims, and witnesses but are often either unnoticed or discounted in importance by the average investigator Content analysis, the third arrow in our statement analysis quiver, is the most powerful and undoubtedly will be the first of our three investigative "arrows" to be fully accepted in court. Personality analysis from the handwriting has already been accepted by courts in fifteen states but has not yet been fully accepted in courts around the country, while content analysis is the most popular course at the FBI Academy and will no doubt soon be fully tested in court. The latter technique has been accepted in at least two murder cases.

After the mid-1990s book *Primary Colors* by "Anonymous" was published, there was a huge political guessing game to identify the anonymous author of that thinly disguised novel about the administration of

President William Clinton. The book revealed much "inside" information on the personalities and foibles of President Clinton and members of his inner circle. Don Foster, the English professor at Vassar College, performed a content analysis along with known writings of the potential "suspects" for authorship of the book.

Foster eventually identified the news columnist, Joe Klein, as the author. After months of denial with many famous people backing up Klein's denial, he confessed to being "Anonymous."

Interesting Note: Foster first rose to prominence in 1995 when he identified, employing content analysis, two old manuscripts of previously unknown authorship as being authored by William Shakespeare. Most of Don Foster's work in this area has been in these large manuscript-type cases. But today's corporate investigator can and does make rather startling discoveries with much less content to work with than might be available to someone like Don Foster.

B. Content analysis—the nitty gritty

Unlike the large-scale style comparisons a Donald Foster might make in identifying "Anonymous," in most statements taken in corporate security situations the investigator will be looking for those "hairs and fibers" language indicators taken in statements of one to three pages.. Here are some of the clues to look for:

1. Nouns—particularly changes in nouns and those used as subjects and objects
2. Pronouns—especially the "missing" pronouns like the "I" from a sentence represented to reflect what the interviewee did or didn't do. Pronouns that show possession, responsibility, or too many capital "I's" can be important red flags.
3. Verbs—especially changes in tenses and the use of first or third person
4. Narrative time—especially how it is divided between minor or insignificant events and the main event, avoidance or concealment of the main event and items that are chronologically out of order
5. Writing mistakes—a cross out often equals stress and insertions often equal very important information. This latter concept is particularly important if the interviewer doesn't initially see the importance.

If it is important to the interviewee, it should be important to the interviewer until proven otherwise.

6. "No proof" statements—like "No one knows . . . ," "No one saw . . ." and "There's no proof . . ." beg the question "How do they know?"

And sometimes, when all else fails, the analyst is just like the untrained investigator. They think something just doesn't sound like the right answer. For example, in answer to the question "Give us some reasons as to how this could have happened," here are the answers from the person who claimed he had not received his tool reimbursement check. (A second check was sent and then both were cashed.) Here are the first two answers:

- He couldn't be trusted.
- They were in dire need of ready money.

Every reader should have noted the change in pronouns from "He" to "They" which raises red flags for sure. But what else is wrong with that second answer? Had the writer said "They needed the money" or something similar, that would have been "normal" response by most honest people. But this person added the terms "dire" need and "ready" money. In those two sentences we have most of the story. "He" was his feeling about himself. "They" referred to the fact that he and his best friend cashed the checks, and the "dire need of ready money" tells us the motive. This employee was not under suspicion as he was a lottery winner and why would a lottery winner risk so much for $300 tool reimbursement? (Includes both checks) When he confessed, he related that he had invested his annual lottery check, but his twenty-fifth wedding anniversary was coming up, and he didn't have enough money to take his wife out in the style he desired; hence the "dire need for ready money" to take his wife out to dinner and entertainment.

The concept analysts rely upon is that with the exception of compulsive liars and psychotics who have no guilt stress very few will out and out lie to the investigator's face. They will avoid and issue non-denial denials, but the guilty will rarely lie directly, except in answer to a direct question when they might say "No" in answer to the question "Did you do it?" Both truthful and the non-truthful will generally answer that question the same way—"No," but they won't voluntarily directly lie. They will often ask a question in response to the investigator's question. Of course, all investigators are aware of that being a red flag.

In an arson investigation in the mid-1990s, a statement was taken from the owner of a house that had mysteriously burned down one Saturday night. The owner, when asked to describe what he did from the time he woke up that Saturday until he found out about the fire, recounted, in part, the following:

> After breakfast I left my house about 9:30 A.M to do some shopping at the local mall. I returned to my house at 12:15 PM, ate lunch and relaxed for a while before leaving my house again at about 2:30 P.M. I went bowling and returned to my house about 5:30 P.M. My friend, John, came over to my house about 8:00 PM and we left the house about 10:00 P.M. to do some night clubbing. We stopped by his house a little after midnight and had a drink and were discussing mutual interests when at 12:45A.M, we heard the fire engine go by and noted that it stopped in the vicinity of where I had lived. I subsequently found out it was the house that was burning down.

There was more to the statement, but notice the key change of wording and reality that raises a red flag that no investigator can ignore? Note that all references to his house prior to 10:00 P.M. used the term "my house." That language showed a form of "relationship" with his house of many years. When he left at 10:00 P.M. to go night clubbing with this friend, John, the language changed to describe what had formerly been referred to as "my house" as now being "downgraded" to "the" house. When he previously referred to leaving his house that day he used the term "my" house, but not now. Why? Could it be because he knew, psychologically, that this was the last time he was going to see "my" house and that he was already downgrading his "relationship" with that house? Of course, the obvious question is how did he know at 10:00 P.M. that it was no longer "my" house but "the" house? The obvious answer was that he knew it would be the last time because he had arranged for the house to be burned while he was establishing his alibi. And that is exactly what happened. In the last sentence of the statement he also used the term ". . . had lived" when much like the Susan Smith case there was not yet reason to believe his house was past tense.

7.6 The Key Considerations and Questions in Content Analysis

The content analysts must ask themselves the following questions about statements:

1. What did the person say?
2. Why did he or she say it that way?
3. Why did he or she say it that way at that particular place in the statement?
4. What are the time patterns in that statement?

Let's take the last one first. When one is asked to write an uncontaminated statement about what happened, there are usually three distinct parts of the statement. There is the "prologue" where the person tells us what he or she was doing before the incident started. There is the description of the actual incident. The epilogue, where the person tells us what he or she did after the incident, includes comments about how afraid the person was or expresses other emotional type information and what the person did after the main event. Generally speaking, the person takes a certain amount of time for each. Usually, 20 percent of the statement is devoted to the prologue, 50 to 60 percent to the actual incident, and roughly 20 percent to the "aftermath" or prologue. These are not exact percentages, but when you see a significant variance such as no epilogue, this should raise a red flag that this may not be the whole truth and nothing but the truth.

Why might a person take 40 percent of the statement to discuss what he or she was doing prior to the incident, especially when combined with a rather skimpily detailed incident description? The person isn't too anxious to tell you all the details for some reason. Or what about the person who in telling you what happened is writing along at approximately twelve lines per hour of elapsed time (or any unit of time) and all of a sudden slows down to six lines per hour with no reasonable explanation based on the content? Who knows what that person is actually thinking, but something has materially influenced his or her telling the truth about what happened and when. That "something" may well be a major clue as to what really happened and when.

When someone is telling the truth, the handwriting flows smoothly throughout the statement and the language has a flow and consistency to it. There is a reason we all choose the language we do to communicate to others. When we change language, we are also communicating a changed reality at some level.

What is the difference when someone says in answer to the investigator's question about whether or not the interviewee committed the offense, "I wouldn't do such a thing. My mother raised me to be a God fearing honest person," or the person who says "I didn't do it" or "I told the truth" or something along those lines? The first comment is what we call a non-denial denial. The implication is that he or she didn't do it, but did he or she really say that and, more importantly, the person didn't firmly commit to being innocent? If the interviewee will not commit to being innocent, the investigator can't assume the interviewee is innocent. Sometimes there are innocent reasons for changes in language. It is the job of the investigator to notice those changes and determine whether or not the changes are important to determining the truth of what happened.

What is the difference between, a "No" in response to your question, "Did you do it?" and the person who voluntarily says "I didn't do it" or "I told the truth" somewhere in answer to a less direct question about what happened? If a truthful person is asked, "Did you do it?" the response is almost always, "No, I didn't do it." Will the guilty person say anything different to the same question "Did you do it?" Maybe, but probably the guilty person will say the very same thing, "No, I didn't do it." The key point here is to remember that information that is volunteered is usually much more reliable than that which is in response to a direct question.

In 1998 during deposition of President Clinton, in the *Jones v. Clinton* sexual harassment civil law suit, the attorney for Paula Jones often asked President Clinton a specific question to which the President gave a short direct answer. Other times after answering the question that was asked, President Clinton would start to add more information. Most of the time, he was immediately cut off by the Jones' attorney with the next question. One time the President even said "Don't you want to hear more about . . .?" The Jones' attorney said something to the effect they would come back to the matter, which, of course, they never did.[5] Based on other content in the deposition, it appeared that the President wanted to make an additional comment about the Kathleen Willey situation.

Interesting Note: Kathleen Willey was one of the women who alleged the President had sexually harassed her in the White House.

Interesting note: If there were ever a case where one would think there would be so much contamination it would be impossible to accurately evaluate the President's statement, it would be demonstrated in the 1998 *Jones v. Clinton* sexual harassment civil case. Can you imagine the minute scrutiny the President's words received and the coaching he received? It was actually easier to identify those places where the President was telling the truth in that deposition than where he was lying. President Clinton lied so often that when he was telling the truth he wanted to make sure everyone knew that was the truth. Normally in statement analysis the more one stresses something to be the truth, the more the red flags go up as to whom the interviewee is trying to convince of his innocence? In President Clinton's case, all his words about sensitive situations had been very carefully chosen. (How can we forget the comment about "it depends on what the word 'is' is,") but when he was telling the truth (which often could be verified as truthful) there was a change in language and an emphasis that was rarely present in his comments that had some degree of deception. Even in a situation of extreme contamination, the principles of content analysis remained solid.[6]

A strong word of caution is that in the vast majority of cases the more contamination (from attorneys and/or others, or the length of time between the incident and the interview) of the interviewee, the harder it will be to evaluate accurately the words employed by the interviewee. It is the rare case, such as the *Clinton v. Jones* cases, where the personality of the interviewee is such that contamination by others can actually make the statements of the interviewee easier to evaluate accurately.

In cold case homicide matters, the detectives appear to have a listing of the questions they are going to ask. They ask the question and as soon as they have an answer, they often cut the interviewee off in mid-sentence to ask the next question. No one reading this book would make that mistake. Right? Fortunately, newer interview techniques are emphasizing the benefits of the interviewer keeping their questions and comments to a minimum and letting the interviewee talk without contamination from the interviewer. Yet with disturbing regularity, even today and particularly in corporate investigations, violations of that rule abound. It is like some investigators are more interested in hearing themselves talk than in obtaining all possible information.

How many have asked a suspect, victim, or witness questions to which the answers or part of the answers really didn't appear to be important? It is a natural tendency to place something that appears to have no importance on the back of the stove, if an investigator even considers it for checking out later. Content analysis theory in most cases indicates that information that is volunteered is not only more reliable than a response to a direct question, as noted in the previous paragraph, but is often more important to the investigation. True, the investigator may get some superfluous information. Just because it doesn't initially appear to be pertinent to the investigation, the investigator must not reject volunteered information. If it is important enough for the interviewee to include, then it is important enough for the investigator to evaluate it until it is proven superfluous.

Fortunately, the individual giving apparently "unimportant" information will often give a clue "up front" that "Hey, I am about to say something important." When an interviewee uses a term like "Oh, by the way," "I forgot to mention" or something similar, this is a red flag the following information was initially "edited" out, but as the interview progressed the interviewee decided "I'd better include that in my statement." If the interviewee decides it is important, the interviewer must consider it important until proven otherwise. And, important or not, the investigator must also ask if this was what it appeared to be and the interviewee simply "forgot to mention?" Or is the interviewee giving a clue that this may be one of the most important items of information provided and the interviewee consciously "forgot to mention" the information, earlier in the interview, for a reason? Come back to the question an interviewer should be asking about everything in the statement, "Why did the person say what was said and why was it in that particular location of the statement?" I know it can be tempting to cut the interviewee off to move on to "more important" parts of the interview. However, what somebody rambles on about can tell you what's important to the interviewee, or at least what's on his or her mind at the moment, and may give you insight into the interviewee's thought process or the associations he or she makes between one event and another."[7]

7.7 The Statement: The *First* Step, Not the Last

When conducting an interview or interrogation, the investigators of the 1970s and early '80s usually asked an interviewee to "tell me what happened" or "tell me what you saw" or similar phrases. Then as the interview progressed, the interviewer often interrupted with questions. Interruptions and questions, especially those questions not using the interviewee's specific language, contaminate the interviewee. When contamination occurs, it won't be long before the interviewer hears his or her own language coming back. The really good investigators of course waited until the interviewee had related all the way through what had happened. Whichever way the interview was conducted, the last thing that was asked for was often a written statement covering the points already discussed and then the interviewee was asked if there was anything he or she would like to add.

Today's astute investigators have learned that the *first* thing to do in an interview is obtain an uncontaminated version of a statement in the person's own words. The investigator needs to obtain a version of what happened without the person being contaminated by others, especially by the investigator's language or questions. In other words, the first thing to do after the investigator meets the interviewee (whether suspect, witness, or victim) is to obtain in his or her own words a handwritten statement of everything the individual knows about the incident.

A. The virgin statement

Once the interviewee talks with the investigator about the incident, or talks with friends, lawyers, other witnesses or anyone else, that interviewee's version is tainted to some degree. It may be only to a degree that the person is more definite about what did or did not happen because the friend or another witness confirmed what the interviewee "thought" he or she had seen and thus related the story with perhaps a greater than deserved positive emphasis. On the other hand, it could be that the interviewee is contaminated to the extent he or she uses words and phrases that are not in his or her normal vocabulary.

For example, in a sexual assault investigation the interviewer's contamination might lead to the interviewee's recognizing and subsequently employing the interviewer's more sophisticated term "fellatio" when the interviewee's life's experiences and personal vocabulary would normally have her using the equivalent street term or the somewhat more polite term—oral sex. Why is that important? The investigator needs to "recognize" the interviewee's normal vocabulary and life's experiences. The interviewer should recognize she would probably use the street term. In the statement, if she uses or changes to the term "fellatio" the investigator should be immediately alerted to the fact that it is highly likely that someone, perhaps an attorney or someone else more sophisticated or educated, had been talking with the person about her story. That might well prove to be a useful "fact" to know.

B. Benefits of statement analysis

All investigative tools have certain benefits and usually certain disadvantages over other tools. This section of the chapter covers the positive and the negative potentials. Positives include the fact that statement analysis can:

1. *Reveal information not available either at all or at least not as quickly.* One of the most significant benefits of employing statement analysis is to gain knowledge from a behavioral profile of unknown-authored letters. It is obviously difficult to evaluate the personality of the unknown writer of the thousands of anonymous letters large corporations get each year. Companies that generate strong feelings by some, such as the tobacco companies, liquor companies, some software companies, any company that pollutes, many more thousands of companies, large and small, receive unknown thousands of such letters a year. Anonymous letters are not just the bane of senior management, but a significant number (exact figures are not available) of anonymous letters received by corporate employees are from one employee to another and not just directed solely at the company or its executives. Fortunately, most of the writers of anonymous letters are not serious physical threats to any person or company regardless of the vulgarity of the language used. Most of the males who write anonymously are cowards, while most of the female anonymous writers (highest in sheer numbers) may also just want to avoid conflict. However, a number (numbers on this are very inexact) are a threat to someone or some thing.

   The psychologists can give you an inductive-reasoned general profile based on past experiences. (Professional handwriting analysts often either are psychologists or work with psychologists to enhance each other's profiling accuracy.) But, a behavioral profiler employing handwriting analysis can give management additional insight about that specific writer that no one else can provide. At the time writing occurs there is a confluence in the mind of past experiences and current emotional feeling that reveals in the handwriting "demonstrated" behavior.

When an anonymous writer is writing a threatening letter, as he or she plays back whatever injustices triggered the urge to write the letter in the first place, he or she is reliving some of those same feelings. The person is getting angrier as he or she writes. There are changes seen in the writing. For example, let's discuss two threat letters with exactly the same wording. The application of content analysis techniques to only the words will most likely result in the same evaluation of the two letters.

However, one letter is written with fairly consistent spacing, size, slant, and pressure and appears generally rounded. The second letter is written with exactly the same wording, but the slant varies from back-slant to the left to almost laying down to the right with every slant in between. The size of the mid-zone letters (a, e, i, o, u, s, etc.) varies from very small to large. The spacing varies from what appears to be cramped to some words to sentences that have considerably wide spacing. And, as the investigator runs her finger across the back of the letter, the investigator notices that there is no indentation in some places and in others the pen has driven through the paper with such force that it has broken through, ripping the paper. In addition, the writing appears to be much more angular than the first note. Even an untrained person will intuitively know that although the words are exactly the same, the likely threat level is considerably different. The writer who is controlled and consistent may, in fact, be just as angry as the second writer but has controls in the personality that regardless of how threatening the words it is highly unlikely the person will physically act on the anger. The second writer, however, lacks these controls and is much more likely to act on any threats.

2. *In many cases the person being evaluated doesn't even know they are being investigated.* In the beginning stages of an investigation, investigators can use existing company records to obtain sufficient writing to enable a behavioral profile to be completed without interviewing the individual concerned. This advantage is being increasingly reduced as many companies, especially large corporations, are converting their personnel records to computers and have little, if any actual employee handwriting in the files.
3. *The technique acts much like a polygraph without the intrusive nature of the polygraph.* As noted earlier, the Form Variance Analysis part of statement analysis operates on much the same principles as the polygraph. However, asking someone, especially the guilty but as yet uncaught, to prepare a statement is usually met with more receptivity by the interviewee than if you ask if the person is willing to take a polygraph. Both management and the individuals concerned often are uneasy with the polygraph; whereas, the use of the three techniques of statement analysis can and often do reveal the same information as the polygraph and is often much more acceptable to management.
4. *Often in an investigation of the loss of proprietary information or the loss of physical equipment one or more of the possible suspects or potential witnesses will be on vacation.* The person can be sent a letter or a questionnaire (discussed elsewhere) or both, and that resultant response can be evaluated, profiled, etc., all before the employee returns to work. The only problem with "long distance" is that you can't be sure who filled out the statement or questionnaire. It is rare that this is a problem, but it has happened.
5. *Content analysis eliminates the truthful.* The content analysis portion of statement analysis eliminates the truthful during the first cut. One who volunteers a strong, first person past tense denial is rarely untruthful, assuming he or she has not been "contaminated." The key is the word "volunteers." If the

strong denial is in response to a direct question, it means very little. It is only when the person who is asked to prepare a statement or complete a questionnaire voluntarily in the narrative notes that strong, first person past tense denial that a statement analyst takes it seriously as an indicator of truthfulness.

6. *If done as a first step, establishes uncontaminated record of commitment.* The statement and questionnaire is completed at the beginning of the first interview and should be as close as possible to the first time the interviewee is aware of the investigation. An uncontaminated record will reflect the most accurate information you are likely to obtain from that individual. It also commits that person to what is said about the matter under investigation. The most accurate statement is before the individual has discussed the matter with others, including fellow coworkers, attorneys and, perhaps most important, before the investigator can contaminate the interviewee. The only detailed questioning that should take place during the first interview should be after the statement, and with the investigator using only the words and situations discussed by the interviewee. If the interviewee uses a coarse language to describe what happened, the investigator, at least during this initial period of obtaining commitment from the interviewee, should use that same language. Don't change the equivalent street term to fellatio because it sounds better. When the investigator changes wording, at least in the first interview, the investigator is contaminating the interviewee and the resultant statement will be contaminated to some extent.

7.8 Key Questions for Detecting Truth and Deception

A. Introduction

When conducting an interview you may want to consider including the questions noted below. The answers thereto are as below and, while they are not 100 percent guaranteed, will give even the newest investigator some clues to truthfulness or deception by the interviewee. It is almost always better to take a statement as to what happened without any specific questions from you. The writer chooses where to start chronologically and what details to include or edit out. (We all edit when we are giving statements to someone else.) After you have that initial statement and analyzed the "uncontaminated" version by the writer, then the questions below may be asked.

Here are the questions and hints as to what the answer mean:

1. Do you think the situation actually happened? *Yes is truthful. No or evasive is deceptive.*
2. Who would you eliminate as a suspect and why? *Vouching for someone is truthful; vouching for no one is deceptive.*
3. Who would you not eliminate as a suspect and why? *Volunteering names is truthful.*
4. What do you think should happen to the person who did this? *Strong, appropriate punishment is truthful; no opinion is deceptive.*
5. Should someone who would do something like this get a second chance? *No is truthful; yes is deceptive. (Other content will be important to evaluate.)*
6. Have you been completely truthful in all your answers? Why should we believe you? What would you say if we later determined that you lied? *These questions should always be asked in this order. We are attempting to elicit a strong denial from the truthful persons. If none is forthcoming the red flag should go up.*
7. Why would someone do something like this? *Don't know or emotional needs are deceptive.*
8. Did you ever think about doing something like this even though you didn't go through with it? *Yes, is usually truthful; not really, is deceptive.*

Note: The astute investigator will always remember that one deceptive answer alone does not necessarily point to the guilty party. One deceptive answer could be very telling if the accompanying form variance problems, and the personality characteristics both point in the same direction. The key to remember, no one indicator of any kind is absolutely conclusive.

B. Obtaining a statement

Statements can sometimes be accurately evaluated no matter at what point and in what format they are taken or, in essence, how contaminated they may be. For example, no one can doubt that before the deposition of President Clinton in the Paula Jones sexual harassment case the President was about as contaminated by time and the advice from others as one could be. Yet it was relatively easy to identify where he was telling the truth. Unfortunately, that is not normally the case. From the time of an incident and especially from the time the investigator arrives on the scene, suspects, victims, and witnesses are being contaminated, most unintentionally, but nevertheless contaminated, reducing the effectiveness of statement analysis techniques. In fact, the investigator who asks many questions, at least at the beginning of the investigation, is one of the most prolific sources of contamination. When a victim in a sexual assault case says in her statement that she committed fellatio, depending upon background and education of the interviewee, one should suspect that is not the term first used by the victim. When a statement analysis is done, the analyst has to rely on the fact that the language of choice is that of the suspect, victim, or witness. If not, totally erroneous evaluations may be, and are, made.

To obtain the most accurate statement possible the following techniques should be employed:

- Ask the interviewee to tell you everything he or she knows about the situation.
- Obtain the statement in written or recorded form—in the case of transcriptions of recorded statements, the transcriber should include all pauses, and other audible sounds such as ah, mmm, etc.

If the investigator is asked "where should I start" or ". . . end" or any other question about what should be in the content, the *only* answer is "Start at the beginning and end at the end." It is a personal statement and you should not set any parameters. Where the person chooses to start can often trip up the guilty very early on. Sometimes the first sentence of a statement is the key sentence.

The key to identifying deception is the analyst's ability to differentiate between what is called "recall memory" and "constructive memory." The former being truthfulness from the interviewee's perspective and from what is remembered; the latter, constructive memory, is a combination of truth and deception/lies with the deceptive part being what they "made up/constructed" or left out.

C. Cautions when using statement analysis techniques

Statement analysis, like all "soft sciences" (such as sociology, psychology, etc.) that deal with the brain and how the human species acts and reacts has reasons that it is not universally accepted in the scientific community. The techniques of statement analysis individually have their own weaknesses. When behavioral profiling from the handwriting, Form Variance Analysis and content analysis are combined into Statement Analysis, and the strengths of the whole fortify the weaknesses of an individual technique. If one technique points in a different direction, while two techniques point another way, that is an obvious red flag that one of the tools is reflecting false clues. This most often happens in the handwriting because if you don't know under what circumstances a writing was prepared (cramped while riding in a car or with plenty of room while sitting at a desk) the analysis may not be accurate. The other two techniques may alert the expert to that possibility.

D. Reasons for using statement analysis

The primary reasons statement analysis techniques are currently employed by relatively few people, are threefold:

1. Almost all evidence pointing to any of these techniques as successful investigative tools is anecdotal.
2. There are extremely few professionals trained and experienced in all three of the statement analysis techniques. While Form Variance Analysis™ can be learned with relatively little training, behavioral profiling from the handwriting and content analysis both take extended periods, often years, to master, especially in the case of handwriting analysis. Con-

tent analysis has only been taught to police officers since the late 1980s and those officers are just now moving into private investigations and into corporate security work.

3. There is relatively little case law on the admissibility of any of the techniques. Content analysis does have one very significant case where it provided the only evidence used to obtain the search warrant that resulted in the finding of all the proof that led to the capture and imprisonment of Ted Kaczynski, the Unabomber. The defense team quickly challenged the original search warrant for Kaczynski's shack in Montana on the basis of content analysis not having been proven valid and reliable. Donald Foster, a professor of English at Vassar College, reviewed, for the FBI, the famous Unabomber Manifesto. He was able to show, to the judge's satisfaction, many similarities between the writing of the Manifesto and many other papers the suspect had written during his college teaching days. The judge ruled the known documents and the unknown authored Unabomber Manifesto could only have been written by one person and one person only. The style and language of the Manifesto were like fingerprints. The rest is history, and the Unabomber, who had escaped capture for over two decades, was convicted.[8]

There is little doubt that many of those who have employed statement analysis have found the insights it provides to be valuable tools in their investigations. If customer satisfaction was the primary criterion for proving something to be scientifically valid and reliable, statement analysis would be fully accepted by the mainstream of the scientific community. However, since the change in the court criteria for determining "junk science" was changed from the *Frye* criteria to the *Daubert* standards,[9] it is not hard to understand why judges, who have a much greater "gatekeeping" function under *Daubert*, are reluctant to accept what are scientifically unproven tools. Most statement analysis practitioners, whether they use one, two, or all three of the primary techniques individually or combined, recommend that until there are additional validity and reliability studies and additional case law, these tools be used primarily as investigative tools as opposed to tools for prosecution and courtroom presentations.

7.9 E-mails Analyzed

With the exponential increase every year of the use of e-mails, many people are doing their mischief over the Internet. Not only are obnoxious and threatening notes being sent by e-mail, but increasingly online discussion lists (such as those found on Yahoo, AOL, MSN, and several other e-mail providers) are being used to attempt to manipulate stock prices. Some of the most significant cases where statement analysis has been employed have involved Internet chat rooms discussing stocks, where one or more "chatters" either appear to have attempted or have actually attempted to manipulate stock prices. Although it is obviously more difficult to profile accurately a personality from electronically writing, some profiling can be done, as well as Form Variance Analysis (message formatting, etc.) and, of course, content analysis can be fully applied.

7.10 Statement Analysis in Other Languages?

Can statement analysis techniques be applied to all languages? Of course, but with some reservations. If the analyst is not a native speaker of that language and must rely on interpreters, the content analysis portion will have to be a qualified analysis. The analyst will never be sure that the "changes" in language, and thus changes in reality are not the translators and not the original writer or speaker.

However, the Form Variance Analysis and the behavioral profiling can be just as accurate as if the analyst were a native speaker of that language. Although the analyst will have some added difficulty, especially when dealing with Arabic and Chinese writing, the variances in the writing and the personality characteristics can still be evaluated. Assuming a very good interpreter is used, investigative clues should still be discernible.

It is essential that only analysts who are full-time and have been using all three techniques for several years apply them to foreign languages. The difficulty for corporate investigators is that these techniques are relatively new. Only a handful in the U.S. meet those qualifications; however, as the benefits of employing statement analysis techniques are recognized, more analysts with training in all three statement analysis techniques are being trained.

7.11 Using Third-Party Experts

While some corporate security departments have individuals trained in the content analysis portions of statement analysis, most corporations do not have investigators trained in all three statement analysis techniques. Hiring a third party to complete a statement analysis is no different than hiring a private investigator. You will want to consider whether it will be best to hire the expert directly through the corporate security office or through the corporate legal counsel. In the latter case, some if not all the work done by the statement analysis expert will most likely come under the heading of "attorney work product." In any event, the case will more likely be successful with close cooperation between the corporate security director, the corporate legal counsel, the director of human resources, and the statement analysis expert.

In those cases where the questionnaire is employed, close coordination between the legal counsel and the statement analysis expert should preclude any questions arising later about how the employees who were chosen to take the test were identified. For example, in a case involving obnoxious typewriter generated anonymous letters reflecting the names and alleged misdeeds of fifty employees, past experience in similar situations enabled the statement analyst to give the legal counsel justification for the specific employees selected to take the questionnaire. In that particular case, it was reasonable to assume that no one with as much anger and resentment could write a letter of that length and detail without mentioning himself in the letter. As a consequence, all fifty, including the CEO, the legal counsel, the vice-president for operations, the vice-president for human resources, as well as several dozen other employees, were mentioned in the letter and completed the questionnaire. The statements had no names to contaminate the statement analysis person. (This case was solved through more rountine investigative activities once the suspect was identified employing statement analysis.

7.12 Summary

When the corporate investigator obtains an uncontaminated statement, treats the statements of suspects, victims, and witnesses as a "crime scene," and applies behavioral profiling, Form Variance Analysis and content analysis to find the "hairs and fibers" clues, the ability efficiently and effectively to solve investigations can be dramatically enhanced. Matters such as anonymous threat letters, which in the past may have gone unsolved for lack of clues disclosed when employing more "routine" investigative techniques, can often now be solved.

The bottom line is that this relatively new low-tech tool is valuable and will become in future years an even more valuable tool to increase the corporation's bottom line by reducing investigative expenses and solving more investigations.

Endnotes

1. Workplace Violence Research Institute, as reported in June 2001 issue of *Security Magazine*, p.34.

2. Analysis in June 2001 *Security Magazine* based on Pinkerton annual survey of Fortune 1000 and e-mail poll of 800 business executives as conducted by the Midlantic Business Alliance.

3. *The Washington Post*, Nov 5, 1994, A 15.

4. The author of this chapter was asked by the Washington Post/LA Times News Service to analyze the anthrax notes. His opinions are reported in the October 25, 2001, edition of the *Washington Post* article by Peter Slevin.

5. *Jones v. Clinton*, 1998 civil sexual harassment suit, deposition hearing.

6. The author of this article reviewed and analyzed, for the *Washington Post*, 155 pages of the *Jones v. Clinton* deposition, with some of his comments being reported on the front page of the Sunday, April 26, 1998, Opinion Section of the *Washington Post*. Article available through the archives of the *Washington Post*, www.washingtonpost.com.

7. Quote from *Reading People: How to Understand People and Predict Their Behavior-Anytime, Anyplace*, by Jo-Ellan Dimitrius, 1998, p.129. Dimitrius is the internationally famous jury selection expert who was on the O.J. Simpson defense "dream team."

8. See *Author Unknown*, by Donald Foster, Henry Holt & Co., NY. 2001.

9. *Daubert v. Merrell Dow Pharmaceuticals, Inc.*, 509 U.S. 579 (1993), changed the responsibility for allowing or prohibiting evidence in court. Daubert made it the judge's responsibility to make that determination on the evidence being "junk science."

Chapter 8

The Art and Science of Communication During an Investigation

William J. Majeski

Synopsis

8.1 Introduction

In the good old days investigation was a generic term used to describe the efforts of an individual or a group to accomplish a given task, usually getting the answers to questions and solving a mystery. As society evolved, so too did the investigative process. Today, in the investigative field, we find ourselves in a sea of specialists, and rightfully so. The conundrum of crime in modern day society demands the expertise and competence of specialization.

8.2 The Importance of Communication

A. Introduction

The complexities of modern day criminal activity place many demands on investigators. It is the skilled investigator who has developed a solid foundation with sound investigative techniques who ultimately solves the crime. All successful investigators share a common denominator; that is the ability to communicate effectively. Good communication skills are essential to a good interview, and a good interview is essential to a good investigation.

Investigative styles vary as much as the personalities of the investigators, and there is no one best way to conduct a particular investigation. However, the type of investigation, its purpose, and its goals will help to determine the most appropriate techniques that should be used. Yet, regardless of the specific situation, every investigation requires some form of dialogue, and those interviews are most successful when solid communication skills are employed.

The ability of the investigator to convey a message and successfully interact is fundamental to the investigative process. The communicative skill of the investigator has always been an essential ingredient in the formula that will uncover useful information and eventually lead to a successful outcome. There is a direct correlation between investigators communication skills and the successful completion of an investigation.

B. The nature of communication

Communication is an exchange of information between two or more people. That exchange runs the entire spectrum from two people in intimate conversation, to two groups engaged in dialogue, to one speaker addressing an audience of thousands. Communication is cyclical in that the sender and receiver are in a constant verbal and nonverbal action and reaction to each other. They engage in a complex process of idea sharing. By its very nature, this process of sharing is a continuous exchange. The messages sent and received and the responses sent and received are communicated continuously on both the verbal and nonverbal levels. There is a continuous and simultaneous action and reaction that takes place during the communication process. Messages and responses to those messages are interpreted and integrated with one another on a continuous basis.

C. Perception

Perception, when added to the complex mix, can really begin to muddle things. The receiver perceives the messages that are being sent both consciously and unconsciously. Those responses are the result of both a conscious effort and an unconscious reaction, which is manifested at the conscious level.

Picture a man and a woman sitting at a table across from one another in a restaurant. Let's call them Lou and Sue. They are having a conversation (engaging in a dialogue), a quiet intimate conversation. You, the trained investigator with good interviewing skills are sitting one table away. You can barely hear the hush of their imperceptible whispers.

Suddenly, your skills of observation recognize that Lou just said something to Sue that she did not like. You know this because of Sue's facial expression, her gestures, and the rising pitch and volume of her voice.

You also recognize that Lou realizes that he has said something that he wished he had not. You know this because Lou has pushed back from the table, speaking in a hushed whisper, and making conciliatory gestures towards Sue.

Now, did Lou intentionally say the wrong thing? Or did Lou say something that came out wrong? Did Sue not like what Lou said? Or did Sue misinterpret what Lou was trying to say?

Lou's conciliatory gestures morph into gestures of pleading, his hushed whispers rise in pitch and take on a staccotic delivery. To no avail. Sue's gestures increase in intensity, and she wags her finger as she rises from her chair. She throws her napkin and, as she leaves, her final nonverbal message is delivered by a straight finger rather than a wagging one. They are interpreting, evaluating, and responding to and at each other—continuously on both the conscious and unconscious level.

Communication is a complex process which we take for granted. We engage in conversation, which is ongoing, both verbally and nonverbally. This then develops into simultaneous action and reaction, which is delivered and received. Then our individual perception helps or hinders in the process of interpreting and evaluating.

Fundamentally, perception relies on experience more than it does intelligence; although a combination of both would be best. Perception, however, is in the eyes of the beholder.

A case in point would be the following. My wife and I were walking down a street in a metropolitan area. Across the street we saw two men approaching each other at a distance of about thirty to thirty-five feet. One yelled to the other, the other responded. As they came in contact they shook hands, patted each other on the back, and continued on their separate ways.

I turned to my wife and said, "Did you just see that?"

"Yes, I did."

"What did you see?" I asked.

"I saw two people that obviously knew each other, perhaps hadn't seen each other for awhile," she replied. "Obviously, they were both in a hurry; they greeted each other and went on their ways. What did you see?"

I said, "I saw a drug transaction taking place."

My wife's perception of this event relied on her intelligent assessment of the social interaction she witnessed. My perception of the event relied on my twenty-one years of law enforcement experience. During the years when I worked narcotics investigations, I had witnessed that same sequence of events numerous times. I took into account the surrounding area, their physical descriptions, their overly apprehensive demeanor, and their quick departure from one another. Only this time, there was no arrest.

D. Verbal and nonverbal

Although there are two types of human communication, verbal and nonverbal, spoken words often represent only the bare bones of a message. The strength of most messages lies in the delivery.

Sue reacted to what Lou said. Her perception could have been correct or incorrect. On the other hand, based on the delivery, I'm sure that Lou perceived Sue's final message correctly.

Watching people in a restaurant can be entertaining, but the process exhibited by Sue and Lou plays out in similar fashion when an investigator is interviewing a witness, a suspect, or anyone else who can provide information. The anger displayed by Sue can play out in your next interview. Rather than the interviewee jumping up, he or she will go through that process mentally and deliver to you the very same results that Lou received, though not so graphically.

Nonverbal communication or body language is a science called kinetics and is indeed the language of truth. Facial expressions, eye movements, hand and leg movements, gestures, other body movements, and silence are all elements of the nonverbal communication process. The old expression of one picture being worth 1,000 words is an absolute understatement when it comes to interpreting body language. Watching the language of truth in progress is sometimes like looking into a kaleidoscope.

Picture if you will the body movements of an enthusiastic traffic officer orchestrating a symphony of vehicles through a busy six-corner intersection in New York City during rush hour. That's command of silent communication being delivered to scores of drivers simultaneously.

All you're required to do as an investigator is control your own body language and make sure that the subject is receiving the messages you're sending.

E. Characteristics of communication

Communication is all of the following:

- It is action-packed. The process is a series of behaviors occurring simultaneously between the sender and the receiver. The investigator must consciously control both the spoken word and the accompanying body language.

- It is interwoven. The average person selects and amplifies incoming data and responds to it. The investigator can select and deliver a response but could ill afford to listen selectively.
- It is circumstantial. It is in part the result of the situation and in part the result of the context in which the message is being sent and received. The investigator must establish and control the situation and its content.
- It is representative. It is a process of producing symbolic behavior which carries a message. The investigator should send the correct message and confirm same by correlating the response.
- It is interpretative. A meaning is derived from the response. The investigator should control the delivery of messages he or she sends and coordinate them with the messages he or she receives.
- It is sometimes irreversible. First impressions are usually lasting impressions. It is the investigators responsibility not to miss any representations and control the delivery of their concepts. Choose what you say and do carefully.
- It is ethnic. A clear understanding of a person's ethnic and cultural mores is an important ingredient in the communication process.
- It is generational. At times trying to bridge a generational gap is like trying to communicate with a Martian. Know your subject and be prepared.
- It is language-sensitive. Foreign birth, social status, and education all play a role the interpretation of dialogue and body language.

F. Some added complications

There are about 900,000 words in the English language. Most people are acquainted with only a fraction of that number. Indeed the average professional has an active vocabulary of only 30,000 to 50,000 words and a passive vocabulary of 70,000 to 120,000 words. The average person on the street has a vocabulary which is much lower, and there are some people out there who survive the vagaries of life on a few hundred words.

Complicating matters even more, it's disconcerting to consider that the normal attention span of an average person is about twenty seconds. Pay attention to the next TV commercial you watch. Regardless of the length of the commercial, they will be repeating the product name or flashing it on the screen about every fifteen seconds. They do not want the average couch potato to miss the message. As an investigator you may be required to re-enforce your intended message repeatedly.

G. The interview

Communication during the simple, mundane, ordinary investigative interview is much more complex than most care to believe. During an interview the investigator is trying successfully to extract information which will be true, false, or a combination of both. The investigator has to first understand the whole complex process of communication and then use it to his or her benefit. It is necessary to prepare to deal with all kinds of personalities, harboring all kinds of notions, fears, and emotions. Very often the emotions change during this complex process; consequently, the investigator must recognize those changes and adjust accordingly.

H. Looking for hidden messages

The key to finding those hidden messages is consistency versus inconsistency.

Theoretically, the spoken word should complement and be complemented by the body language of the speaker. The verbal and the nonverbal should be synchronized. When this harmony is not present, it is indicative of something wrong, usually some level of deception. However, this inconsistency should be proved by the investigator. The investigator has to identify first the inconsistency and then confirm that it is a constant.

A recent past president usually gestured with his left hand to emphasize a point. However, when that point was less than accurate, the gesturing would be with the right hand. That right hand would consistently reappear with every reemphasis of that less-than-truthful point. That then established the consistency in the inconsistency. The truthful dialogue remained consistent with the left hand gesturing.

From an interviewing prospective, if your query was, "Do you have any knowledge about the incident?" and your subject responds by saying, "No I did not see anything," as he leans back in his chair or looks to the heavens or closes his eyes or brings a hand up toward his face or touches his nose or crosses his legs—or anything else that he was not consistently doing before. (And that could be just sitting still.) That inconsistent gesture, that break in the established norm, is a telltale sign and often a hidden message.

In this situation, you have two inconsistencies. One is a break in the harmonious body language; the other is the choice of words used in the less-than-direct response. If the question is, "Do you have any knowledge about the incident," and the response is, "No, I did not see anything," that answer might be an evasion. Not seeing anything is a far cry from not knowing anything. It is an inconsistency that should be pursued to the next level.

I have often encountered individuals who attempt to evade the question by not answering it directly. In this case, I would then follow up by saying, "I didn't ask if you personally saw anything. I asked if you know what happened." More often than not, he answer would be "yes."

Subtle nuances and dialogues which may seem insignificant are often explosive signals that should alert the investigator to potential deception. All too often the complexities of the communication process are taken for granted. The investigator's sensitivities should be at a heightened state during any interview, especially one conducted as a part of an investigation.

Our individual capacity to detect deception, identify discrepancy, recognize indiscretion, feel hostility, and sense the incongruous has a long history. Each of us endured a long training program beginning at birth. Observe an infant, see how its eyes watch and follow and absorb everything around them. Watch the expressions as it listens to every little sound. As toddlers, the process amplifies, and you can almost hear them absorbing everything around them. By the time they're talking, they begin testing out their sensitivities. Curse in front of them and see how quickly they repeat it. Not because they know the word is bad but because they identified your expression, your body language, the change in the pitch of your voice, or some other inconsistency which they identified as significant. We all had keen sensitivities, but the functions of the brain change as we mature. Those learned sensitivities can be brought back to a conscious level.

8.3 Conducting the Interview

A. Purpose of the interview

For the investigator, an interview is a conversation with a purpose. The interview is both an art and a science. It is also a communication process in which we deal with people, their thoughts, their actions, their reactions, and their emotions, none of which is always predictable.

Ideally, we would all like to think that our interviewing skills are masterful and can be adapted to all interview levels, depending on the subject being interviewed and the circumstances under which the interview is taking place. A good interviewer will secure the most relevant information. The investigator should develop the ability to listen with intensity. Observational skills should also be enhanced.

B. Listening

Listening is hard work. Imagine yourself sitting in a movie theater and this is the scene you are watching:

As the train eased into the station, Claude grew anxious. This was the fourth stop and the messenger hadn't made contact. He wondered if it would be someone familiar or a new face. As the doors opened, about a dozen people got onto the train. He didn't recognize anyone. A woman walked over, sat beside him and opened a magazine. As the train rumbled out of the station and began its ascent, the metal wheels screeched against the tracks and vibrated through the open windows. The woman leaned toward Claude and began to speak softly.

If you were to check yourself at this point in the scene, you would most likely be leaning forward. There would be a slight increase in your flow of blood causing an increased heartbeat. Your eyes would be opened wider, your lips could be slightly parted, and your body temperature slightly higher. You're using energy to listen intently because you want to hear what the woman is going to say.

That's part of the enjoyment of a movie. What we're dealing with is the intensity of real-life listening and trying not to miss anything.

C. Classifying listeners

Investigators fall into a number of categories when we classify listeners.

- Poor listeners—These people would prefer not expending the energy necessary to absorb what is being said. They are those people who go to a movie with a group then spend the rest of the evening asking everyone else what went on. If they are investigators, they always try to get someone else to do the interview.
- Indifferent listeners—They develop a habit of tuning out too much information. They lose the ability to concentrate because it requires too much effort. They are the people who will ask you the same question or listen to your old story as though it were new information. If they are investigators, they shy away from one-on-one's and usually fall short on successful results.
- Good listeners—They are people you like to talk with. Most everyone likes to be paid attention to and people sense when the other person is truly listening. If they are investigators, they are usually very successful in obtaining all of the essential information most of the time.

If you don't concentrate, you will not hear. If you do not hear, you will not know. Without knowledge, you cannot understand, and understanding is essential in helping distinguish between the truth and a lie.

D. Ability and effort

In the author's expert opinion there is a direct correlation between the ability to listen and comprehend and the expenditure of individual effort. A working barometer of your listening ability and capacity to absorb information is how much you remember from the conversation, the interview, or the discussion that you had last week or yesterday or this morning over breakfast. How much do you remember? Naturally, the more intense the conversation, the more you should be able to retain. Think about it.

What category do you fall into? To be a good listener, you should listen effectively. That requires awareness. If someone were to say to you, "Wait a second, pay attention now, what I'm going to say is very important," that command generally heightens your awareness of whatever is to follow. But it's not necessary to wait for that command. You can teach yourself to be more consciously aware of the words that are being spoken. Your goal is not only to remember what you hear but also to understand it more fully. We are all capable of perfecting this with practice.

People who have not been blessed with the gift of sight or who lost it somewhere along life's path have developed a keener sense of hearing and listening. The next time you are on the telephone (preferably when no one else is around) close your eyes for the duration of the conversation. You will find that hearing will become more discerning, your listening will become more absorbing, and you will more easily identify any inconsistencies which may slither into the conversation.

E. Words

Words are the conscious part of a person's message. Words are often chosen for their effect, and they are relatively easy to control. The choices of words, the sequence in which they are expressed, could be significant. How people express themselves can also be important.

Understanding the personality, identifying their mood, and recognizing their intentions are all important. The exact phrase or word can be spoken by the same person and given different meaning each time through tone, inflection, volume, and accent. The phrase, "you look marvelous," can be complimentary, sarcastic, funny, or sincere, depending on how it is delivered.

- Listen to determine if they are truly responding to the message or introducing their own message.
- Are their responses in line with the theme you introduced or are they changing the direction of the conversation?
- If they are staying with the theme, are they responding to your message or circumventing the response you are looking for?
- If they are introducing something different, does it have positive or negative connotations? Be mindful that there are also wide ranges of unconscious sounds that are an integral part of the speaker's communication process.

A sampling of the sounds would be a change in the rhythm, a change in the tone, a change in the pitch, a cracking voice, a sudden stutter or stammer, a slurring, a grunt, a groan, a moan, a gulp, a snort, a sniff, a hum, a whistle, teeth grinding, hesitation, pause, and silence.

F. The observation of body language

Most experts in the field agree that the verbal element of the communication process represents only about 35 to 40 percent of the message being delivered by the person you are interviewing. The other 60 to 65 percent of the communication process is observation; it, too, requires a great deal of effort.

We have to train ourselves to look intently at the person from head to toe looking for those subtle nuances, those subtle changes in body activity which occur while the person is speaking or sitting silently, listening to what the interviewer is saying.

If during the course of what appears to be a truthful interview, your subject adds a sniff or a gulp after responding to a newly introduced issue, well that's an inconsistency. Is it a lie? Not necessarily. Does it have to be further explored? Absolutely. Just as you learn to absorb the words being spoken, you can learn to absorb those sounds. When there is an inconsistency between the words and the accompanying sound, that inconsistency could translate into an identifiable area which must be viewed more closely.

Try listening more carefully on your next interview. Become a good listener by intensifying your conscious level of concentration. The result of that effort will be positive and most assuredly, more tiring. Listening is hard work. As you develop good listening skills, you will see a significant improvement in the information obtained in an interview and during the entire investigation process.

With regard to facial expressions, we are looking at the smiles, the frowns, the laughs and smirks, the sneers, the squints, and the breaking of eye contact—to mention a few. We are looking to recognize the raised eyebrows, the dilating of pupils, closing of eyes, any rapid blinking, a startled look, a worried look, tight lips, sticking lips, biting of the lip, biting the cheek, and a stare.

With gestures we're looking for a hand or fingers, covering the mouth, or covering the eyes, rising of the hand in a defensive or stop sign fashion, ringing of the hands, waving the hand, a shake of the head, a nod, making a fist, pointing a finger, cracking the knuckles, rubbing the face, scratching the head, swatting an imaginary fly, tapping fingers or playing with fingers.

With the body we are looking for a head bowing down or turning away, rapid breathing, deep breathing, dry cough, a nervous tic, shrugging of the shoulders, stretching the arms, folding the arms, crossing the hands or the wrists, slumping, restless sitting, body shrinking away, legs crossing and recrossing, feet pointing away, toes tapping, leaning forward, or leaning back.

Once we've developed the ability to focus in on these subtle nuances or body movements, what we are looking for are inconsistencies between the activity and the spoken word. As previously mentioned, the word and the gesture should work in harmony with each other. If they do not correlate, then that is an area that must be further explored.

What we're looking for is a series of consistent inconsistencies. If the same question were asked in three different ways and each time the person responded to that question the verbal and nonverbal responses were not in harmony then we have a bifurcated message. Using the proper techniques of good listening and the skills of observation allows us to get to the point where the spoken word and the accompanying nonverbal language are not synchronized. When they are inconsistent with each other, they highlight the hidden messages—the truth.

The truth can best be seen by those who pay strict attention to the nonverbal actions of the person being interviewed. The investigator will develop a keen sense of identifying the unspoken words of nonverbal communication. Remember that body language is instinctive and unconscious in nature. The interviewer can generally rely on it to help determine the truth. As noted previously, a substantial portion of most conversations are transmitted on the nonverbal level. It is important to learn to read what a person is not articulating. What we hear and what we see are not always the same. If we just listen, we may hear only what the person wants us to believe. Gestures, body movements, and facial expressions react most dramatically to stimuli. It does not matter if the stimuli are introduced or self-induced. The stimulus in dialogue could be a word, a phrase, a thought, or an action which causes a change in the harmony. Observing these changes in conjunction with what is said helps to identify hidden truths.

G. Understanding your own body language

Generally, people respond to nonverbal communication on both the conscious and unconscious level. By controlling your own body language, you can communicate a full range of messages from forceful to meek on a subliminal level. The person who has a good command of the silent language is viewed as charming; the person who does not is a scoundrel. They can both be delivering the same message, but the scoundrel has less command in controlling the delivery of the nonverbal subliminal message.

H. Communication chess

The rate at which we speak is lesser than the rate at which we think. The rate at which we absorb is greater than the rate at which we listen. That gives us a tremendous amount of spare time that can be used to think as we listen.

Ideally, a good investigator can develop a heightened sense of awareness. As we listen, we can analyze, evaluate, and assess what is being said. That information can then be condensed for temporary or, when appropriate, permanent storage. We can then prepare the next few messages and anticipate their expected responses. Additionally, we should be watching the subject's reactions to our actions and messages and making adjustments to achieve our goals. That is all of what you should be doing with the spare time while you are listening to the subject responding to your questions. That is the game of communication chess.

Now, what to do with that spare time when you, yourself, are speaking. Choose the words and your accompanying actions very carefully. Recognize and adjust to the type of person you are dealing with.

- First establish a specific goal, then direct your efforts toward it. Attaining minor goals and building towards a particular end is an appropriate approach. Watching and responding to the subjects reactions to your verbal and nonverbal delivery while making the necessary adjustments to convey your message and control the environment.

- Preparation is essential in any investigative communication process.
- Knowing your subject matter as well as the person and group you are investigating allows communication with confidence. (This is an information gathering process. The more information the investigator has going into the interview, the better.)
- Self confidence helps to maintain control over the communication process. (This is having a belief in yourself and knowing that you will accomplish your goals.)
- Well-chosen words, delivery, and accompanying nonverbal skills will manipulate the conversation, adding to your control over the process.

I. Structure of the conversation

A loosely structured conversation, when prepared properly, will achieve results in a convoluted way. Tightly structured conversations limit the range and scope of the subject matter but, when used properly, yield quick results. During an investigative interview, recognize that an appearance of weakness on the part of the investigator will foster resistance. Hesitancy will encourage a lack of cooperation, but confidence fosters cooperation.

J. Pre-interview preparation

Prior to embarking on the actual interview we should develop a habit of preparation; that is, our own mental foreplay, which is a process by which we can mentally prepare ourselves to the task at hand. All of these preparations should be done beforehand, preferably on paper, but at the very least, mentally.

- The investigator should gather all available information for the evaluation, then form a basic idea of what he or she wants to accomplish in the interview.
- An attempt should be made to identify any potential weak spots in both the subject being interviewed and the circumstances under which the subject is being interviewed. Recognize the possibility of any potential psychological deficiencies in the subject being interviewed; that is, any weak links

in his or her personality. To control the direction of the interview, the investigator can often use these weak spots or deficiencies.

- Then we have to identify, evaluate, and note specific points for areas of discussion. As we are doing this we should try to identify common bonds that may be able to be established between the interviewer and the interviewee.
- The interviewer should be prepared to use all types of questions, i.e., direct, casual, suggestive. The interviewer should be prepared to make adjustments as the interview progresses.

The preparation is so basic to the interview process that it is at times ignored or forgotten, yet it is the first step in a long and complex journey.

- Identifying and properly categorizing the magnitude of the crime, incident, event, or issue allows for the proper perspectives.
- Establishing the cast of characters and the parts each may be playing as the case unfolds. You will be identifying witnesses, victims, suspects, participants, and informants.
- As you gather your independent information, you assimilate and catalogue data, draw a basic hypothesis, identify psychological deficiencies, recognize potential weak spots, and prepare specific points of discussion. If the homework is done, the test will be easier.
- The questioning process—setting goals, sequential order, logical progression, sizing up the subject, taking control of the set, dealing with outside factors.
- The cyclical nature of communication—your perceptions versus their perceptions, selecting, organizing, interpreting, verbal communication, your control of words and sounds; nonverbal communication—your control of facial expressions, gestures, body language, silence, impressions, symbolic behavior, levels of confusion, context of the situation, creating the proper conditions, knowing yourself, adjusting to circumstances, knowing the person, maintaining control,

the ability to be flexible, structure of conversation, positive adjustments, negative adjustments.

- Implementation—logic versus experience, maintaining objectivity, the do's of an interview, the don'ts of an interview, specific questions, each specific subject, each specific crime; confidence, knowledge and ability communicate themselves to the person being interviewed

K. Creating the proper conditions for an interview

Every good investigator knows that no matter how good he or she is, he or she has limitations. This also applies to the interviewing process. Some investigators are better interviewers than others. It is important for the interviewer to know his or her limitations before embarking upon something that might be a out of his league. This requires a little bit of soul searching. An investigator has to sit back and think about the last four, five, or ten in-depth interviews that she conducted and do a self-analysis as to how successful they were. Keeping that in mind, the interviewer should either begin this new challenge independently and with confidence or seek assistance from another investigator. Another possibility would be having a second investigator present during the interview. Clearly, every poor interviewer can become a good interviewer and every good interviewer can become a better interviewer. It is all about self-confidence, and it's all about making acknowledgments to yourself.

L. Think before you say and do

Your clients and the people you interview will think better of you as an investigator if there is thought and consideration given as to what you say and how you approach an issue. This form of self-regulation (thought police) will also lead to more successful investigations. It is important to acknowledge any limitations that you have and it is equally important to identify your strengths. During an investigative interview, those strengths should be emphasized and any personal limitations should be recognized. This self-examination should be a self-contained analysis but a truthful analysis.

One of the characteristics that makes a great investigator is a high level of confidence. That confidence should be demonstrated without taking on the appearance of arrogance. Over the years I have often witnessed investigators misstep by conducting poor interviews. The results were less than stellar results for the client. Ego will at times interfere with a productive investigation.

M. Know the facts and circumstances

A good investigator can jump into any situation, almost instantaneously, and achieve some level of success. A very good investigator will wade into that same investigation and achieve a much greater level of success. The more information that is made available to you and the more information that you review, the better prepared you are, and that translates into a productive interview. Ask yourself:

- What is the purpose of this interview?
- What are its goals?
- What is expected of me and how can I accomplishing that task?

Once you have established a specific goal for the interview, formulate a plan to achieve that goal. This is done by thinking it through forward, from inception to goal, and then backward from goal to the inception of the interview. In complex situations, you should put pen to paper. It is always better to have notes. If that is not possible, then rely on a mental process.

N. Know the person that you're speaking with

Here an investigator tries to identify the type of personality that he or she is going to be dealing with. Personnel files are of great assistance, although they are not always available. This task can be accomplished sometimes by preliminary discussions with people who are familiar with the person you will be interviewing. Very often in investigations that require a number of interviews, you can find out a great deal about all of the other perspective interviewees from each person you are currently interviewing.

No good interviewer will conduct every interview in exactly the same fashion. Adjustments must be made to accommodate the personality you are dealing with. Compounding that, during the course of an interview, a person's psychology or emotion can very easily change; there too, adjustments must be made by the interviewer. You must also identify any outside considerations regarding the person being interviewed. Is this person being influenced in any way by someone outside of the realm of the reason for the original investigation (e.g., is he in the middle of a nasty divorce, does she owe a loan-shark money, is there an illness in the family).

Let's look at two specific interview situations. The first one involves a woman, a mid-level manager, who is claiming sexual harassment by her immediate supervisor. Her name is Cynthia Johnson; she is a thirty-seven-year-old single female who has been with the company for the past eleven years. She aggressively handles distribution for the company product on the East Coast of the United States. She is highly respected by other people in the company and her allegation came as a complete surprise to upper management. The person accused of sexual harassment is Robert Jones, a fifty-six-year-old managing partner who has been with the company twenty-five years. No previous allegations of any kind have been made against him. He, too, has an aggressive personality and is very well respected in the company.

The second case is a twenty-one-year-old male, Dennis Smith, working in the mail room. He is suspected of intercepting and sabotaging mail coming into the company—specifically, mail addressed to George First, one of the company's senior VP's. On a number of occasions, Mr. First never received packages that he knows were sent to him. Additionally, a number of letters he wrote were never delivered.

Now we have the challenge. You are assigned to interview these four distinctively different people. The circumstances for each individual is independent, yet there exists a coupling in each set of alleged facts. You should be interviewing each one differently. Give it a moment of thought and establish how you think you would best proceed in interviewing each of these four people.

In the sexual harassment case you will be interviewing the alleged victim, Cynthia Johnson, and you will also be interviewing the person she is accusing. How different should these interviews be? Then you have the mail room person, Dennis Smith, and George First, the senior vice-president. How different should these interviews be? Keep those four interviews in mind as we move forward.

O. Psychological deficiencies or weaknesses

During an interview with an individual, we will be looking to identify any weaknesses in his or her personality. We are also looking to identify vulnerabilities. Everyone does, indeed, have vulnerabilities. We are not necessarily going to use this information; however, it is better to have it in hand in case it becomes necessary than to not be aware of it at all.

Hypothetically, Cynthia's weakness may be frustration over a series of failed personal relationships. Additionally, she is angry about not having been promoted as quickly as she believes she should have been. The accused in her situation, Robert Jones, may be going through an emotional mid-life crisis. He is not happy with his station in life. In addition to that his wife is philandering, and he has just become aware of it.

In the other situation, Dennis Smith from the mail room is finding it very difficult to maintain any kind of relationship with anyone. In addition to that Dennis thinks he is much smarter than he actually is and believes that he is woefully underpaid. George First, the executive vice-president, whose mail is being lost, has problems with two of his children who are into drugs. In addition to that he is a recovered alcoholic, and he's dealing with the emotional situation of having perhaps set the tone for his children's behavior.

Now do any of these weaknesses in any of these people have anything to do with the interview? Well, we don't know, but it's better to understand these things about them than not. Weaknesses or deficiencies can become extremely useful tools used by the interviewer in achieving the goals of the investigation.

Remember that the good qualities of an individual in everyday life can easily become a weakness during an investigative interview. For example let us look at Charles, who has very strong religious beliefs. Charles feels strongly about protecting a long-time friend and coworker. Charles will not volunteer information crucial to the successful results of the investigation because it will implicate his friend. When Charles is confronted with choosing between a long-time friend and his own strong personal religious beliefs, he will eventually choose the latter.

P. Initial impressions

The initial impression you give to the person you are interviewing and that person's perception of you are extremely important. Your initial posture and approach are the opening signals to the person you are interviewing. It is essential for the interviewer to be self-assured. These initial impressions will very often predict the interviewer's level of success. The interviewer should be mentally establishing goals and expectations and conveying them on a nonverbal level to the subject of the interview.

Earlier on we talked about preparation. There is a direct correlation between the level of preparation and the level of success for the investigator. As you would not go into combat without ammunition, so you should not go into an investigative interview without information. Your level of confidence is conveyed to the person being interviewed. That image of confidence gives some level of comfort to the cooperative and uninvolved. It also caused great consternation to those hiding information.

Q. Maintaining control

It is absolutely essential that the interviewer maintain control of the interview at all times.

Maintaining control with Dennis Smith from the mail room would be significantly different than maintaining control with Cynthia. Here we talk about the interviewer portraying an image of stability yet having the capacity to identify situations or conditions that would require some flexibility in the approach being used. Dennis comes into the interview somewhat docile. Somewhere along the line he realizes that his job may be in jeopardy, and he becomes very defensive and perhaps a little bit aggressive. Then he sees that he may be overreacting and reverts back to his original posture. How would you, as the interviewer, handle those changes if they took place over a ten or fifteen minute period of time?

The investigator should have the flexibility in his or her approach as the interview progresses. Initially Dennis Smith is docile. The investigator's demeanor would be soft-spoken, but the choice of words would be firm. Ten minutes into the interview, Dennis begins to show expressions of agitation, he takes on a defensive posture, and he begins to verbalize a defensively aggressive attitude. The investigator should have seen this coming and prevented Dennis from escalating to this point, but he or she didn't. So now the investigator has to make adjustments to maintain control. At times, all that is necessary to prevent further escalation by Dennis are a few nonverbal gestures. The investigator should raise an open hand in stop-like fashion. It should be close to his or her own face and could be accompanied with some inexplicable utterance like, “woo.” If Dennis does not respond, other gestures can be added. In sequential order, they could be: breaking eye contact, moving head and body at an angle away from Dennis, raising the other hand, then finally, if all of that fails, which would be rare, the investigator should speak in a firm tone saying, “Stop—Let’s keep this civil.” When Dennis reverts back to his original demeanor, so too should the investigator.

Cynthia comes in as an aggressive, successful woman who suddenly becomes hostile because she thinks that you do not believe her. After a while she recognizes that you are, indeed, there to find the truth and settles back down. How would you handle those emotional changes, which take place over a ten or fifteen minute period of time?

Whenever a subject comes into an interview the investigator must immediately assess how to best approach that person. Cynthia Johnson initially portrayed aggression in her nonverbal language and hostility with her spoken words. One of the best approaches is for the investigator to respond to her with conciliatory gestures, a stoic calm and silence. If only one person is arguing, there cannot be any disagreement. Usually, the subject will soon recognize that she is behaving poorly and nothing will be accomplished by her actions. Clearly, there are other approaches for the investigator, based on his or her assessment, but that is a judgment call. Once the investigator recognizes that the subject is running out of steam, he or she should adjust to the next posture. Still using less conspicuous conciliatory gestures firmly state, “I’m here to help you. Please sit down and let me help you.” This type of statement creates an interest or at least a curiosity on the part of the subject. Usually, the subject will display a demeanor which is more passive than her norm, and eventually she will settle into her normal behavior. Simultaneously, the investigator will eliminate any hint of conciliation, take on a nonverbal air of being in charge and speak gently, yet firmly. As the subject retreats to her normal level of behavior, so too should the investigator, maintaining a level of control.

It is absolutely essential to control the process of the interview and clearly one of the best ways to prepare for that is, just that, preparation. Preparation becomes absolutely essential not only with the information that you are gathering but also with your preliminary assessment of the individual you are going to be interviewing.

As the investigator you are in change of the interview and effectively you are setting the guidelines on how it is going to proceed. You are creating an image in that person's mind. The words that you choose become very important; your actions become even more important. The way you deliver those words is equally important. It is essential for a good interviewer to have good nonverbal skills. Remember that most communication is on a nonverbal level and most people interpret nonverbal communication on the unconscious level. You, as the interviewer, should be very much aware of your nonverbal communication and it should be brought up to a conscious level. Through a conscious effort you will be able to control not only your spoken word but also your unspoken word. In effect, a good interviewer will be manipulating to some degree the person being interviewed; and equally as important, the interviewer has to guard against being manipulated by that person.

R. Structure of conversation

The structure of the conversation is extremely important. This goes back to the early preparation. Whether you are using prepared notes or just a mental process, your hypothesis should have long ago been drawn and the structure of your conversation, whether it be loosely constructed or tightly constructed, should follow along a specific path. In a loosely structured conversation, it may be a convoluted path where you use a cause-and-effect concept. You're giving the person being interviewed an opportunity to elaborate on specific issues. In a tightly structured approach, you're being more narrowly defined and limiting the range of the dialogue.

Regardless of the investigation, the investigator deals most of the cards. You can stack the deck against yourself or you can win almost every hand.

8.4 Understanding the Use of Polygraph in the Corporate Culture

A. History

As early as 1895 a medical instrument known as the Hydrosphygmograph was being used for the purposes of measuring blood pressure changes and pulse rate. These changes were being documented in an effort to detect deception.

By 1915, William Marston was the first American to become involved with the so-called lie detector. His technique used an ordinary sphygmometer by which he obtained period discontinuous blood pressure readings during the course of a test. This method was based on the premise that there is an increase in blood pressure during deception. By 1921 John Larson built an instrument capable of continuously recording three parameters—blood pressure, pulse, and respiration. He was the first person to use more than one parameter in an attempt to detect deception. A few years later Leonard Keeler constructed an instrument that incorporated a galvanometer which recorded the galvanic skin reflex. He also devised a chart roll paper and the foundation of the method of questioning the subject.

B. Modern polygraph tests

Today's modern day polygraph is either a computerized instrument or an electronically enhanced pneumatic instrument. They are both capable of simultaneously recording at least three physiological indicators of arousal.

- The cardiovascular measurement utilizes a standard blood pressure cuff by which it measures increases in the blood pressure and changes in the heart rate.
- The respiration component utilizes two pneumonic tubes, which are placed on the upper chest or thoracic region and the other on the abdominal region. These low-pressure tubes measure the depth and rate of the inhalation/exhalation cycles.
- The third essential form of measurement is the GSR or galvanic skin reflex. This component uses two metal plates, which are placed on two fingers of the subject's hand, and they measure the conductivity of electricity across the surface of the skin.

C. The examination

The polygraph examination procedure is generally divided into three segments:

- The interview process
- The actual testing
- The post-test interrogation

D. Is it appropriate?

Prior to scheduling any polygraph examination procedure, the polygraph examiner should confer with the corporate client. After ascertaining the facts surrounding the specific issue event or crime, an assessment of the information should be made and a determination should be reached as to whether a polygraph examination is appropriate.

There are many issues that have to be taken into consideration in determining whether a polygraph test is appropriate for a given set of circumstances. Clearly, the laws vary not only from state to state but from county to county and sometimes from town to town. Additionally, there is overriding federal legislation, the Employee Polygraph Protection Act of 1988. This prohibits certain types of polygraph testing and establishes the guidelines under which an employee can be asked to take a polygraph examination. Any examiner who deals with a corporation should be well acquainted with the laws, rules, and regulations pertaining to polygraph in that particular jurisdiction. Understand that a polygraph test cannot be administered without the written consent of the person being tested.

If it is determined that a polygraph examination is appropriate and necessary, then the examiner should gather all of the information relating to the incident. The information obtained from the client is then used by the polygraph examiner as a basis from which to go forward. Before the examiner meets with the first subject to be tested, the examiner will have already evaluated the case facts as they are known to the client.

E. Pre-test interview

The pre-test interview phase of the polygraph examination procedure is divided into three segments:

- The first segment will consist of queries made by the examiner of the subject about his or her personal background. Standard background forms are generally used for this purpose. There are many underlying reasons for this background portion which make it absolutely essential.
- The second phase is a discussion relating to the issue, event, or crime, which caused the need for the polygraph test. They should discuss at length as many details about the event as possible, initiating the dialogue with events leading up to the incident, circumstances surrounding the incident, and the results of the incident. This phase is giving the examiner the other side of the story. It is also giving the examiner the criteria by which the questions for the testing will be established.
- The third phase is the question formulation and the question review with the subject. Ideally, the examiner will have previously determined specific questions that will be asked on the test. Semantics of the examinee are usually a consideration in the question formulation. After the questions are established they will then be reviewed by allowing the subject to respond to each question the way he or she will be responding to them during the actual testing. That is, with a simple yes or a simple no response.

This first phase should take at least one hour and, more often than not, it will last quite a bit longer. During this phase the conversation is usually open and free flowing.

F. The test

The second phase of the polygraph procedure is the testing phase.

Before the actual tests are conducted, the examiner explains to the subject the polygraph instrument and how it functions. The examiner will then place the various attachments onto the subject, explaining the purpose of each component. The examiner will then review each question with the subject and the subject's response to that question. Once complete, the testing phase will begin.

Test formats may vary depending on the education, discipline, and background of the examiner. However, any valid test will have some form of the CTF, which is the comparison test format. In this type of test, comparisons are made between relevant questions, control questions, and irrelevant questions. The relevant questions are directly related to the issue, event, or crime being tested. There is a limit of three or four specific relevant questions, which are intermingled among other questions on the test. A series of tests are run during this phase.

After the completion of all test charts, the examiner independently interprets the chart tracings. After an analysis and evaluation the examiner will render an opinion that will be no deception indicated, deception indicated, or inconclusive.

Most examiners participate in some form of a quality control review. Depending on the test results the examiner will then move to phase three of the procedure, that is, the post-test interview or interrogation depending on the results of the tests. In tests where deception is indicated, the examiner will engage in a follow-up interview with the subject.

This is only a summary of how the procedure is conducted. The polygraph is based on the hypothesis that conscious deception can be deduced from certain involuntary physiological responses. This is all predicated on questions which are answered with a simple yes or no. The examiner asks the subject the question, the subject thinks about the answer to that question and responds to it. That psycho-physiological response is then measured and recorded onto a chart.

8.5 Conclusion

Over the years, millions of polygraph tests have been conducted. Today, law enforcement agencies on the federal, state, and local levels use polygraph extensively. In 1988, when the Congress, in its infinite wisdom, was prohibiting the use of most polygraph testing in the private sector, they chose to preclude the federal government from those very same restrictions. The federal government uses the polygraph quite extensively today.

Over the last ten years or so, the amount of polygraph examinations conducted has grown dramatically. Does polygraph work? As an investigative tool, absolutely. Should it be used by corporations? Absolutely, given the proper circumstances and conditions. The polygraph is an effective investigative tool. When used properly, the polygraph can complement the investigative process and be an asset to an investigation.

Chapter 9

Doing Business with Your Experts

Reginald J. Montgomery, CPP, PSP, CLI, CFE, CP, CST

Synopsis

9.1 Introduction

Businesses do not operate in a vacuum. The global economy has necessitated partnering with a variety of specialists to ensure that fiduciary responsibilities are met, production can be maximized, and intellectual property preserved. A natural outgrowth of this expanding marketplace is the need to employ specialists. Security personnel may well become the most significant specialized subdivision of corporate America. Threat to the workplace may rear its head in many forms. Workplace safety and security are needed for the protection of employees. Defense against theft of ideas is vital in a competitive society. Property and lives must be safeguarded against harm and insulated from terrorism. The security expert, SIU director, or investigator hired by a company or corporation provides the knowledge to facilitate this process. Investigators use experts as tools to document evidence and provide consulting for direction and advice with regard to given situations.

Investigators and security specialists have an obligation to themselves and to their clients to understand the limits of their ability.

There is a value to the team approach to investigating. Using the services of a variety of individuals with expertise in many specific areas increases the credibility of the private investigator or in-house security person. That same investigator or security specialist might be called upon for the value of his or her experience as an expert to another professional in need. We are a small community of interdependent professionals.

Learning the proper way to use the expert enhances the overall productivity and integrity of the industry.

9.2 What Is an Expert?

An expert is "a person with special or superior skill or knowledge in a particular area."[1]

This indicates that the expert is an individual to be respected for his or her abilities that far surpass the average person. Having someone with the proper credentials, experience, or knowledge as a part of any team is a positive addition. The adjunct assistance of an expert in an investigative or security-related case may prove the difference between success and failure.

All expert witnesses are experts in their field. Not all experts are expert witnesses. An expert witness must be qualified by a court that acknowledges his or her credentials. Once confirmed as rising to that court's standard, the individual has established proper authority for future occasions to testify as an expert witness.

It is a fact that experts are called upon to do the one thing that all other individuals are precluded from doing in the law: *offer an opinion.* The opinion is based upon that person's ability to apply knowledge, experience, and observation to situations that are merely hypothetical. The expert is not an eyewitness. In fact, the expert gleans all of his or her knowledge from information and evidence of events long since transpired. This is the unique quality of the expert witness. The expert is a valuable resource to the events of a situation the expert has only read or heard about from third parties. Experts are nonparticipants whose judgment is considered before decisions are made regarding guilt, innocence, or the awarding of punitive or compensatory damages.

How does one handle this particular species of person? How does one identify the proper expert for a situation? Is the individual truly qualified to render an opinion? Can the expert witness be discredited easily? These are all questions that will be addressed as this chapter unfolds. An expert can be a problem or a blessing for the investigator or security person who has reached the limits of his or her own ability.

9.3 Need

When does one need an expert? This, of course, is a decision to be made based upon the severity of the matter. If a court-related case has been initiated, the resulting litigation can be costly to the company. The presence of an expert witness could mean the difference between winning and losing. The financial outcome of litigation is frequently enhanced by retaining the proper expert witness for the job. The expert then becomes a primary necessity as either a foundation upon which to build or a support upon whom to rely. Within companies and corporations requiring the services of a security expert to evaluate the safety of personnel, equipment, or proprietary data the expert becomes a valuable resource to supplement the knowledge of the investigator or security specialist.

Before anyone can determine if the specialized services of an expert should be included in a program, the entire problem must be understood. This begins by having all known information made available to the investigator. The objective of the security problem should be identified and a budget clarified by the client. The investigator then has the duty to perform a preliminary review of all data, physical evidence, and personnel involved before determining the possibility of bringing in one or more persons to serve as a team to solve the problems of the client.

9.4 The Expert's Credentials

Credentials are not always awarded from major universities or schools of education. Sometimes they are learned from the proverbial school of hard knocks.

Experience and ability are the two major criteria for identifying the appropriate expert. Before working with anyone who claims to qualify as an authority it is valuable to have a complete knowledge of his or her qualifications. A curriculum vitae (CV) will help to provide the requisite information. Note that an expert needs to have a CV and not just a resume.

A resume generally only touches on the highlights of one's career. A CV is more appropriately a full "life" (*vitae*) that details accomplishments, experience, and education.

In a case that may involve litigation you must assume that the opposition will attempt to "debunk" your expert. It is highly recommended that prior to engaging an individual an investigation be conducted to determine what, if anything, might be available to any party seeking information on your expert witness. This precludes any surprises at a later time that might invalidate the ability of your chosen expert to participate in a case. Confirm the credentials; research the educational qualifications, confirm that this individual did attend the schools and receive the degrees alleged, find out if the writings are real and in actual journals, and thoroughly evaluate the information.

Do not disregard experience as a great teacher. A worker without formal education whose years on the job with a particularly intricate piece of machinery may have far more knowledge than a graduate of a technical school with no experience. "Hands on" experience often qualifies one for expert status.

9.5 Retaining the Expert

At times the expert is an individual or firm hired by the investigator to assist in properly assessing a problem and documenting the facts and evidence of those facts.

You cannot be proactive or reactive to a problem or situation until you have the full information available.

Examples of how to use experts in this book would have to include the *voice print* (by Tom Owen). Recordings can possibly identify a particular subject or suspect in an investigation; i.e., sexual harassment, threatening phone calls, kickbacks, extortion, and so forth.

Audio and video tape enhancement (by Tom Owen). The questionable tape can be used to provide evidence or facts to a situation.

Electronic countermeasures (by Kevin Murray) are sweeping a questionable area for eavesdropping devices. This expert service would be useful in many situations. Intellectual property investigations, stockholder information, competitive intelligence, terrorist activity, and so on.

Statement content analysis (by Gary Brown) may be useful in murder, violent crime, theft, and terrorist threats. The limitations are only confined by the known facts.

Computer analysis (by Harry Coyne). Document files, accounts, businesses, any kind of Internet communication, timeline pornography, and so on.

These are only a few examples of the experts covered in chapters in this book. Your use of these resources is only limited by your imagination and your knowledge of the capabilities and limitations of your expert. Read the book.

The investigator himself or herself might well be the expert retained directly by a company or corporation. Expertise in a specific area of threat or danger to a business will necessitate that a specialized individual or company be retained to ensure the safety and well being of that entity.

One designated party or team should be charged with the responsibility of providing information to the expert. In large corporations the mere number of partners, team leaders, or workers may make communication difficult. Assigning the task of communication to one individual or a small group of people will facilitate the job of the expert. The expert will need access to information in order to assess the needs of the client. This access might be in the form of company records, entrance to facility property, or merely discussion regarding various individuals of concern to the problem at hand.

The expert will be remunerated for his or her work. Establish in advance from whom the expert will receive this remuneration. Determine the value of obfuscating payment versus paying the expert directly. It might be necessary to hide the fact that an expert has been hired so as to protect the delicate nature of the security detail. Be sure that remunerative measures are in place so that the expert has the confidence that his or her work product is properly compensated.

When working on a matter involving what appears to be a theft of product, it might behoove the investigator to retain the services of a CFE[2] or a CPA.[3] The very fact that such a person has achieved either certificate is indicative of specialized knowledge. In fact, certification and education specific to the needs of the client should be understood and researched. While it is not necessary that certification exist, it is vital that it is understood. The testing authority and certificate granting association should be proven to be a viable entity with the proper credentials or the expert's ability might be invalidated.

A decision should be made as to whether the expert is a member of the investigator's team or an independent contractor working directly for the client. Concerns such as "work product privilege" or confidentiality might affect this decision. It might also be advantageous to protect all knowledge of the expert's existence by hiding him or her under the investigator's umbrella. Obfuscating the presence of an expert may well protect the integrity of an investigation by limiting the time frame in which suspects can concoct cover stories or destroy documents.

Understand that experts are generally highly paid for their time and efforts. However, seen in the light of the ultimate value to the outcome of the matter, this may be an insignificant amount. Be prepared to pay for the service that is rendered. The knowledge and information provided will be well worth the financial outlay.

At the time of initial client contact, the professional expert has the responsibility for identifying to the client what services are to be provided and practices to be conducted. This should include the identification, as well as clarification, of services that are available. Special services and instructions should be acknowledged in accordance with proper business practice.

9.6 Selecting the Appropriate Expert

The volume within which this chapter appears contains the work of approximately thirty different authors. Each is an expert in his or her field; that is the reason they were selected. Each has a credential or experience that equates with the ability to perform the work they discuss and provide guidance to others in need.

Experts can be found in many different venues. Investigators and security specialists who belong to associations have the added benefit of Internet list-servs where they can post the need for an expert in a particular field or venue. The wealth of knowledge from these sources is invaluable.

When one is working on a specialized field and needs an expert to assist, one might consider going to a particular professional association and requesting the name of an authority in their vicinity. Professional magazines generally maintain advertising sections for experts. In fact, professional magazines often archive articles that might pertain to a specific problem. These articles would have the name of the author, who is generally exceptionally experienced or knowledgeable about the subject.

It is also important that the expert be compatible with the needs of the client. In an extreme example, one would not send a Caucasian, Anglo-Saxon Celtic Irish maiden into a Chinese laundry as an undercover operative. Note that sometimes experts are needed for work involving racial or sexual discrimination. A specialist in interviewing victims of rape might well be a female. Although this does not preclude the use of a very effective male investigator, the male may not necessarily be the best "man" for the job. Many issues should be considered before hiring a person merely by credentials. A personal interview, at least, would be a prerequisite to determine his or her appropriateness for the job.

Experts can be found in all parts of the country for a wide variety of professional tasks. Railroad trains, for example, are no longer the number one means of transportation in our country. They do, however, travel throughout the United States, providing a means of conveying people, produce, and materials. The greatest number of experts on railroad safety seem to congregate where the offices of the major railroad companies are headquartered. It might be best for the investigator to retain a Texas-based specialist for a job in Vermont. Consider the costs and expenses. Weigh them against the benefit to the client. Geographic proximity is not always the most important factor in retaining the best person for the job.

9.7 Professional Conduct

It is incumbent upon the professional to provide the highest quality of service available. The security or investigative specialist is obliged to maintain technical confidences. Often this individual will be dealing with proprietary data that requires excessive levels of secrecy. Under any circumstances, the expert should uphold the tenets of excellent work sufficient to the needs of the client with reports of a thorough nature provided in a timely manner.

Many associations and organizations provide codes of professional conduct for their members.[4] They are generally similar in that they dictate an approved method of behavior for their members. These ideals are logical, good business practices. They include:

- professional demeanor
- fairness in billing
- maintaining client confidentiality
- avoiding controversy with other investigators
- honesty in reporting of information obtained

Nothing less is expected of the expert.

9.8 Legal Considerations

The exception to the general principle of providing a contract for each work effort is the professional handshake. Although having a written document will ensure that there are no questions about work product or remuneration, there are "gentlemen's agreements" still in effect in this profession. When one has an excellent working relationship with former clients, a written contract is not normally required. Many experts whose reputations are well-valued still work on the concept of a professional word of honor. This is, of course, a decision to be made by and between the parties engaged. There is both a benefit and a detriment to each party in working without a contract. However, the value of trust may far outweigh the legal hassle of contract negotiations. Sometimes the old-fashioned way is, indeed, the best way.

9.9 Reports

The type of report expected by the client must be determined during the initial client contact. The method of transmission of reports is equally important. If a case is in the stages of "discovery"[5] it may behoove the expert to provide verbal reports to the client. Generally, experts provide an "expert report" which is replete with opinions based upon information observed, reviewed, or discovered. The report usually includes such wording as "it is my expert opinion to a reasonable degree of certainty that . . ."[6] As this report may find itself as the basis of a court-related matter, the expert may wish to hold off on a final draft until all information has been revealed. Opinions may change as a result of new information. It should also be remembered that, while the expert is retained for the purposes of assisting the client, the final opinion may not coincide with that of the client. It is the client's decision as to the form and method of a report, if any.

If the matter is not being reviewed for court testimony, the expert may well have a standardized reporting form that is followed. This, too, should be discussed with the client prior to work being performed.

Often the expert is called upon to work in a foreign venue. If such necessity arises it would be important for the expert to have a clause in the employment contract outlining the language in which the report is to be submitted. As differences and nuances in language might cause misunderstanding, it may be necessary for the expert to provide his or her own interpreter. The interpreter would be someone with whom the expert could communicate to ensure the proper understanding of all information.

9.10 Maintaining a Professional Reputation

Within any industry, the value of a good professional reputation cannot be over estimated. Within the security and investigative professions a reputation is of extreme importance because an investigator is only as good as his or her work product. Results are not always the measure of the professional. The effort, ingenuity, integrity, and perseverance of an investigator or security specialist are as important as the final artwork is to the craftsperson. The essence of work ethic is the product of the professional in these cases. Obviously a positive product that enhances a client's point of perspective is a desired result. However, even without providing such results, the true professional can satisfy a client that his or her problem was thoroughly investigated, evaluated, and executed.

Working with the client's ultimate objectives in mind, the professional should do all that is humanly and ethically possible to achieve closure on a case. This may involve hiring another individual or several persons to carry on the work of the client. It might mean work above and beyond the normal course of action. Ours is a service industry and as such makes demands upon the practitioner that are not necessarily a requirement in other industries.

Maintaining client communication and providing informative and timely reports make the individual practitioner a true professional. It is this reputation that ensures continued work. The old adage "we are only as good as our last job" is more telling in this field than in any other.

9.11 Testimony

In general, an expert will not appear to testify either at a deposition or during trial unless the expert has first rendered a professional report. The report is an expert opinion based upon the facts as known and commented upon by the expert.

Initial stages of testimony include "voir dire,"[7] when questions will be asked by opposing counsel and possibly by a judge as to the qualifications of the individual to be recognized an expert. If both sides approve the qualifications offered, the judge has the ability to accept that individual as an expert witness. At this time questioning may commence. This individual now has the ability to offer opinions, based upon his or her experience that affect the facts of a case.

Testimony should always be truthful. It should not exceed the limits of the expert's knowledge or authority. The expert has been recognized within a specific field of expertise and cannot possibly know everything about everything. Credibility is established in the expert's ability to recognize when the bounds of knowledge have been exceeded.

The professional expert witness is well advised to be neutral, judging each issue on the merits of the facts. Having a reputation as a hired gun for either defense or plaintiff cases diminishes the value of the expert. A good investigator will research the history of decisions by the expert under consideration. Having a good balance of ideas and being seen as working toward truth, not directed results, enhances the reputation of the expert.

Obviously, as with all professions, the expert should dress and sound the part. That does not mean that a degree in English (or French, or Russian or whatever the appropriate language is for the venue) is a requisite. It does, however, mean that the individual should be able to clearly and logically answer all questions without obfuscation or exaggeration. Making a point clearly and succinctly is of great value. Whenever possible, inquire of the expert if he or she is due to testify in the immediate future. Make arrangements to observe the deportment of this individual in action. It will assist in the decision making process—to hire or not to hire.

9.12 Summary

The expert or expert witness is an individual highly suited to a particular task for which he or she has the qualification, background, and credentials. Selecting the best individual for the job will enhance the role of the investigator or security specialist. It will also confirm that the very best service is provided to a client in need. Searching for the appropriate expert should include considerations of ability, cost, proximity, and work product. The expert's ability to testify well, and to the point, is of grave importance.

An expert should be respected for his or her ideas and opinions. The expert should, however, be properly directed so that he or she is completely aware of the problem at hand and can address it accordingly. The investigator or security specialist has the benefit of being enhanced by the expertise and commitment of a good expert. Reputation is most important to all professionals. Maintaining integrity and a good work ethic while dealing with both the client and the hired adjunct expert will ensure a continued, positive reputation for the investigator or security specialist.

We, as professionals, are only as good as the network of knowledge that we have assembled through our experience. We are only able to afford our clients a professional service if we have constantly increased our abilities, finely honed our expertise, and practiced our craft to the benefit of the industry.

Endnotes

1. *Merriam-Webster's Dictionary of Law*, Merriam-Webster, Inc. (1996)

2. CFE: Certified fraud examiner. One who has achieved certification for ability in the field of forensic investigation with specialized knowledge of accounting procedures and financial investigations. Certification is through the Association of Certified Fraud Examiners.

3. CPA: Certified public accountant. One who has established superior expertise in the field of accounting and who is licensed and qualified through state board examination.

4. Author's note: Professional associations such as the Council of International Investigators, American Society for Industrial Security, World Association of Detectives, Association of Certified Fraud Examiners, National Association of Legal Investigators and many state associations have a section within their by-laws prescribing the manner in which business should be conducted with the public and with fellow members of the association. They can be found by visiting the web sites of each of these organizations.

5. NOLO.COM, internet plain English.com: discovery A formal investigation—governed by court rules—that is conducted before trial. Discovery allows one party to question other parties, and sometimes witnesses.

6. Author's note: This wording has been extrapolated from a variety of expert reports read and reviewed for the purpose of this chapter. It has been found that the language is accepted by the court system as a standard in the writing of reports by experts whose opinions are to be considered in light of other evidence in rendering a decision.

7. *Merriam Webster's Dictionary of Law*, Merriam-Webster, Inc (1996) defines'"voir dire" as "a formal examination esp. to determine qualification (as of a proposed witness)."

Chapter 10

The Changing Role of Law Enforcement in Private Security

Robyn R. Mace, Ph.D.

Synopsis

10.1 Introduction

Complexity and change are constants. Accordingly, a great deal of human activity is directed toward minimizing uncertainty and reducing risk. Since the mid-nineteenth century, the private security industry in the United States has developed to address and manage uncertainties and necessities related to changing economic, industrial, and social conditions. As a result of identified security and safety needs within the public and private sectors, and perceived shortcomings in law enforcement response to corporate concerns, there has been enormous growth in the private security industry, and a tremendous recent proliferation of private security services and products. This industrial growth has coincided with a sustained reconsideration of how what security responsibilities are approached and managed, and by whom.[1]

Attacks on the World Trade Center in Manhattan and the Pentagon in Washington, D.C., on September 11, 2001, were a searing national tragedy. They simultaneously redefined individual citizens' perceptions and expectations of order and safety, redirected the national security agenda, and reaffirmed the necessity for a serious, comprehensive approach and response to modern safety and security threats by both law enforcement and private security. The aftermath will shape the foci, scope, and tenor of relationships between law enforcement and private security professionals for decades.

10.2 Historical Overview

In the United States, the histories of private and corporate security and law enforcement run a similar and interwoven course. The basic responsibilities of these major constituents of the security sector[2] remain unchanged from their respective, original mission and functions: protection of life and property.

Law enforcement agencies and the private security industry emerged in the United States in the nineteenth century, as a response to concerns about social unrest and disorder in the emerging political and economic order. Subsequently, the definitions, scope, and application of both private security and public safety have expanded significantly, as the nation's population and economy have grown larger and more complex. Awareness of actual and potential business losses combined with prevailing concerns and fear of crime have stimulated widespread interest in the increasingly complicated tasks of providing security in modern workplaces and society.

This chapter will briefly examine the elements of the increasingly dynamic security sector, offer observations about the changing role of law enforcement in the private security realm, and present several important issues for consideration by private security and law enforcement managers and personnel.

A. A brief history of private security

Western expansion, immigration, and the industrial revolution rapidly changed the American economic and social landscape throughout the nineteenth century. The private security industry in the industrial United States developed mid-century, almost concurrently with the public police, with the expressed purpose of protecting private persons and property beyond the capacity and obligation of the owners and the local police. A century and a half later, "security executives perceive their industry's role as a supplementary one, protecting property and assets in ways that exceed the resources of public law enforcement."[3]

Much of the early period of formal private security industry in the United States is associated with the exploits of reknown contract-investigation agency founders Pinkerton and Burns. As industrialism progressed along with the railroad and telegraph, worker management became a significant concern of private security functionaries that provided riot control, strike breaking, and other services related to labor unrest. As the private security industry developed, larger security firms eschewed "family" cases, a demand that generated the sometimes notorious private investigation industry. The rise of factory-based mechanical production in the twentieth century brought a changing role for private security, first exploited by Henry Ford's defining in-house security program. This model adopted many militaristic organizational features and prominently included discipline and force as measures of control. Until the early 1970s, private security was generally categorized as follows: security guard services, security professionals (in-house and consultants), alarm services, security equipment, armed couriers, and private investigation agencies.[4]

In recent decades, the private sector has grown considerably. Global economies and indiscriminate, wide-ranging security threats (e.g., a virus that targets the computer e-mail, order processing, or financial operations of an international company) have required private security practitioners to take a more active, problem-solving approach to managing security. Multi-site facilities and digital information and communication networks have expanded both the domains of corporations the and potential threats to corporate assets. While much of the industry is still composed of in-house or contract guard services, corporate security professionals are responding to growing demands for facility, personnel, and information security. Another recent trend involves high-profile national and international mergers and acquisitions that have created a new breed of international security conglomerates and consultants.

Security professionals of the twenty-first century are moving into the era of enterprise security. Enterprise security marks a philosophical shift toward understanding security as a core part of an organization's operations rather than as an afterthought to its primary functions. Enterprise security involves recognizing the fundamental elements of value in an organization (chiefly, employees, proprietary information, and technologies), and formulating security activities to fit the needs generated by the system's members and their activities.

In the most basic terms, modern corporate security functions encompass facility, employee, information, and communication security.[5] A corresponding shift in law enforcement orientation is not occurring as quickly, although there is a strong movement toward preventive activities in addition to traditional, reactive enforcement services.

Modern security professionals are cultivating unprecedented cooperation with internal corporate divisions and are working with law enforcement. In part, this cooperation is result of "civilianization" and privatization of traditionally public policing functions.[6]

B. A brief history of public policing

There are five generally defined historical eras in the development of public policing in the United States: the watchman/vigilante (pre-1830s); the political (1830s-1890s); reform (1890s-1930s); the professional (1930s-80s); and the community policing or problem-solving era (1980s-present).

Policing services were initially supplied as a continuation of the watchman custom. Early public police forces initially were charged with maintaining order and often used brutish methods to control their watches. Early formal policing organizations and efforts were dominated by the tactics and vagaries of local politics. The ensuing reform era was largely a reaction against political influences in policing and was characterized by reorganization within the paramilitary and civil service models that transformed American social institutions in the early twentieth century.

The professional era began in the early 1930s with a reorientation to impersonal ("just the facts, ma'am") crime fighting. It was during this time that federal police agencies began to exert national influence, and the FBI began to track and to publish Uniform Crime Reports as a matter of public information and a measure of police efficacy.

The current era, the community policing or problem-oriented policing era, is characterized by enhanced personnel education and training standards, a growing understanding of the dynamics of criminal behavior, and cooperation between researchers and police practitioners in evaluating police activities. This era features a philosophical reorientation toward community oriented problem-solving that includes the active participation of individuals, neighborhoods, and businesses to improve the quality of public safety in communities and the quality of worklife and management in law enforcement agencies.

C. The security sector: law enforcement and private security

Until the last couple of decades, the historical relationship between law enforcement and private security might have best been described as "adversarial codependence," an uneasy reliance necessitated by the reciprocal exchange of certain, and often selective, information and services. The two elements cooperated only when they had to and operated on very different levels conceptually and administratively. They drew from separate labor pools and followed substantially different selection and training procedures and, in some cases, operational, practices. Although security directors often had prior law enforcement experience, and there were tendencies to hire retired law enforcement officers, there seems to have been little constructive interaction with public law enforcement. Part of the standoffishness was (and remains) directly related to the conflict between their respective roles, protecting public versus private interests. At that time, few could have predicted that the future, extensive demand for private security and public safety services would necessitate their willing cooperation, much less blur the distinctions between the type and scope of services provided by these traditionally distinct sectors.

Security and safety issues had emerged as broad public concerns well before September 11, 2001. By the 1990s, law enforcement and private security had acted on recommendations by the Law Enforcement Assistance Administration's (LEAA) Task Force on Private Security (1976). As indicated by the report, educational, accreditation, and professional standards should (and did) rise in both law enforcement and private security. This was, in part, due to the availability of funding, orientation, and support provided by LEAA, and, in part, due to the emergence and influence of professional organizations.

Professional organizations provide training, technical assistance networks, and opportunities for private security and law enforcement personnel to intereact informally. These organizations establish standards and certify practitioners and enhance the availability of resources and expertise for specific types of problems or investigations. Now they exert tremendous influence over where and how public and private security agencies do business together.

The first professional organization to involve the major security sector elements was the American Society for Industrial Security (ASIS), established in 1955 to bridge the considerable animosity and mistrust between the government and industrial security sectors. Today, there is no shortage of membership and professional organizations devoted to various aspects of preventing, controlling, and correcting crime and wrongdoing in the public and private spheres, from fraud to information security to competitive intelligence and beyond. Professional organizations will continue to play a leading role in developing security solutions to problems created by our society's complex and changing economic and social activities. For example, automated teller machines (ATMs) have introduced convenience for consumers and reduced labor costs for banks; however, they have also introduced new, attractive (crime) targets into urban and rural environments. As law enforcement and private security share more and better information and cooperate more, they will become more effective in resolving, preventing potential offenses, and reducing harm.

As the security sectors continue to enhance professional standards and improve performance, private citizens remained uninformed about the duties, functions, and operations of police and private security organizations. Even fewer are aware of the scope of the industries and the important, often unknown, roles they play in creating safe environments. While exceptional public scrutiny and media attention may be directed to specific incidents involving public police (e.g., Rodney King, Abner Louima, Amadou Diallo), the public knows very little about the recruiting, hiring, training, and promotional practices that create police departments and even less about the private security industry.

Although there is a growing literature on crime, law enforcement agencies, and public safety activities, similar information from the private security side is less available. Security-related data is considered proprietary, competitive, and potentially litigious in character. Public and market perception of the value of an investment is directly related to how functional and solvent a company appears to be. Reports of unsavory or criminal activity within the corporation are, at a minimum, distasteful, and, at worst, disastrous. There is little motivation to publicize these events; prevention of future acts may not be compelling enough reason. Publicity may create consumer panic and a lack of confidence in the company or its products. The recent, and as yet unresolved, Enron and Arthur Anderson debacle demonstates clearly how perception generates its own, often uncontrollable, momentum and points to some possibly serious problems with the ways in which some industries and firms are self-regulating.

The absence of systematically collected data about corporate and private security activities limits the ability of the security industry to respond to potentially serious, yet hidden, security or safety concerns or to develop and promote consistent professional standards and procedures. Criminal acts may go unreported for many reasons: the act may not be discovered, as when a trusted, long-time bookkeeper embezzles from the family doctor. In some instances, victims may not want to become involved with law enforcement for a variety of reasons, including the potential for "second victimization," expected time spent and results from official action, and distrust of government. As with reporting for other types of offenses and in other contexts, some combination of victim awareness, severity of loss, victim willingness to report, and the response capacity of law enforcement agencies affect official reporting and prosecution of wrongdoing.

A great deal remains to be learned about how private security mitigates and prevents wrongdoing and which techniques might be productive in other situations. Law enforcement agencies have become much more open to research, data collection, and information sharing than have private security concerns. In response to their constituents' demands and to indicate relevant and emerging trends, professional organizations and networks have begun regularly to conduct and publish surveys and estimates of incidents and damages within specific industries. The annual Computer Security Institute/Federal Bureau of Investigation Computer Crime and Security survey is among the best of these estimates. These reports generally focus on industry segments or proprietary concerns of the private, client-driven and nonprofit organizations that serve them.

The necessity of protecting corporate assets in a global environment exerts considerable pressure on private security managers to consider and make fundamental changes in the way they conceptualize and to execute required tasks as need demands. With the relatively recent exceptions of public interest groups, victims' advocates, and due process advocates, there are few analogous historical performance pressures on law enforcement organizations. The importance of security in both the public and private realms continues to escalate, and private security seems to be outgrowing law enforcement. The influential Hallcrest report also identified a growing interdependence between the public and private sectors in terms of privatization of services and better management of limited resources.

10.3 Strengthening the Security Sector

Communication is among the most important and fundamental of human endeavors. It is how we indicate and get (or not) what we want. Ironically, despite the importance of interpersonal communications, there are few established formal communication training programs in the security sector designed to address the continual need for improved communications in an ongoing manner. Effective communication can improve the quality of working relationships and increase favorable incident and case outcomes across the security sector.

Both sector elements, their clients, and their constituents clearly stand to benefit from better communication. The ability of private and public safety organizations to define clearly their roles and goals, separately and together, can only improve their interactions and outcomes. Professional organizations facilitate this formal and informal communication and the development and transfer of the knowledge base, through regular meetings, newsletters, conferences and training, and special and social events.

Tensions in working relationships between law enforcement and private security may stem from any of a number of factors and should be expected. Most relate to the goals, roles, authority, jurisdiction, and reporting requirements of the organizations and their personnel. Anticipating areas of potential conflict allows the security sector as a whole to consider alternatives and to establish methods to resolve differences before an emergency arises.

Expectations of cooperation are frequently met with disappointment as hapless investigators discover during the course of an investigation that agencies may be working at cross-purposes. The goals, motivations, and actions of those involved may not, in fact, be compatible. Such difficulties can shift the focus from the criminal act or perpetrator to dynamics of power and control between agencies. Poor communication makes bad situations worse; it undermines the common stated interests of the organizations and individuals involved.

10.4 The Security Sector in the Twenty-first Century

The events of September 11, 2001, have significantly raised interest and concern over both public and corporate security. Over the past several decades there has been a shift from public to private ownership and management of many elements of the economic infrastructure. Combined with growing public expectations that business must provide additional security to complement governmental efforts, this indicates the importance of a more strategic and structured approach to interactions between the private and public security sectors around several focal issues: (1) national, civic, and worklife; (2) threat assessment and mitigation; (3) disaster management and recovery; and (4) design and prevention issues.

A. National, civic, and worklife issues

National, civic, and worklife issues are of exceptional importance to the security sector and society more generally. The economy and extended social lives enjoyed by Americans will cease to function if citizens are too fearful to participate in them. The current consensus is that law enforcement and government officials must lead the national discussion and direct activities related to national and industrial security, such as recent changes in airport security management. In terms of civic and worklife issues, the security sector has crucial roles to play by setting and maintaining standards of safety and security in a huge variety of communities throughout the country, in an apparently increasingly insecure world.

B. Threat assessment and mitigation

Law enforcement and private security specialize in responding to discrete, immediate threats, as well as in addressing nonemergency issues at the discretion of the organization and its capabilities. Threats may emanate from any number of sources: disgruntled employees, disenfranchised high school students, abusive or jilted spouses, and opportunistic or serial offenders. Threats and issues can range from incipient to ongoing criminal activity, to incidents of workplace violence and victimization, to more general public safety threats, such as natural or manmade disasters. While each sector may respond to different threats with distinct procedures and little to no interaction or reliance on the other sector, certain types of threats will involve both sectors. By creating a forum for discussion and review on a regular basis, security professionals have the opportunity to consider near-term and long-term security concerns and to address them in a non-crisis resolution mode. The knowledge and trust that develop from ongoing relationships make both threat protection planning and response (mitigation) easier and more successful. The agency that is aware of a credible threat must be responsible for general notification—especially if it does not have the capacity to respond. In this way, knowledge and potential resources are shared among all participating organizations.

C. Disaster management and recovery

The crucial importance of disaster management and recovery became obvious on September 11th to those who did not recognize it before. The scale of destruction from man-made or natural disasters has not been lost on Americans in recent years. Wildfires, flooding, hurricanes, bacterial attacks, school and workplace shootings, and computer viruses have created an unprecedented national awareness of utility, social, and service disruptions. Only in concert can law enforcement and private security undertake the massive organizational and operational efforts necessary to reconstruct limited or extensive geographic devastation. The primary responsibility for life safety and rescue rests with law enforcement, although increasingly recovery efforts have become conjoint efforts, owing to the private ownership and management of infrastructure features, as well as (readily) available private support personnel and equipment. Each segment of the security sector must continue to work diligently to improve the process of disaster management and speed recovery and resumption of regular activities and services (utilities, phones, roads): they will continue to rely heavily upon each other to do so successfully.

D. Design and prevention efforts

The importance of design and prevention efforts is frequently overlooked by non-security professionals. Crime prevention through environmental design (CPTED) is a concept widely used within corporate and private security, particularly the ability to design out many problems with access control architecture and technology. In order to have the greatest advances in design-related safety and prevention, private security practitioners must continue to take the lead to promote safe designs, to educate, and to support the efforts of their law enforcement counterparts in this regard. In the redesign of public venues and civic spaces, law enforcement should generally assume the lead role, with private security providing technical assistance, training, experience, and frequently, additional resources to realize improvements to the physical and social environment that prevent crime and violence. Business and special improvement districts in Manhattan (34th Street Partnership, Grand Central Partnership), Philadelphia (Center City District), and many other cities have created excellent opportunities for public-private partnerships in redesigning urban and entertainment areas. In Santa Barbara, California, the police department uses movable traffic barricades combined with traffic enforcement to manage entertainment district crowds. In Washington, D.C., the Metro system uses access control fare cards, monitored closed-circuit television, and its own employees to maintain a safe transportation system.

10.5 Toward an Enterprise Security Sector

Inter-jurisdictional crimes and the technological complexities of modern crime necessitate comprehensive security: comprehensive security requires the full cooperation of the public and private security sectors. Enterprise security is a comprehensive safety and risk management approach, distinguishable by philosophy and strategy, not by functions. Enterprise security encompasses personnel, facility, information, and communication security and will naturally include regular communication and cooperation between law enforcement agencies and private security concerns.

Today, many private and corporate security professions practice comprehensive security management techniques, blending functional and operational security activities into an integrated, planned system of security extending from disaster and crisis management to investigations, from safety awareness and injury prevention programs to daily facility and personnel security. Similarly, many progressive law enforcement agencies are engaged in a variety of management and operational activities related to comprehensive, strategic public safety planning.

The obvious challenges to the security sector in the twenty-first century are tremendous and perplexing: to be successful, efforts to manage these challenges must simultaneously address instant concerns while maintaining the ability to redirect resources needed to manage emergent threats. The role of professional organizations in the development of an enterprise security sector cannot be overemphasized. Training and task force participation encourage professional and personal interactions essential to the effective management of current and future operational and criminal threats. Law enforcement and private security and must endeavor to establish, to maintain, and to expand the good working relationships in place and revisit those relationships that are not constructive. National, economic, and personnel security depend on it.

Endnotes

1. For an excellent discussion on modern policing and security, see *The New Structure of Policing: Description, Conceptualization, and Research Agenda*, David H. Bayley, and Clifford D. Shearing. July 2001. Washington, D.C.: National Institute of Justice, NCJ #187083.

2. Throughout this chapter, the term "security sector" indicates the universe of organizations involved in safety and security services. In addition to the two major components, the traditionally distinct law enforcement (public safety) and private security (the industry of corporate security, manufacturing and equipment, solution and service providers), the security sector includes non-governmental organizations and community groups.

3. *Private Security Trends: 1970 to 2000—The Hallcrest Report II*. 1990. William C. Cunningham, John J. Strauchs, and Clifford W. Van Meter. Stoneham, Mass.: ButterworthHeinemann, 1990.

4. *A Primer in Private Security*. Mahesh Nalla and Graeme Newman. 1990. N.Y.: Harrow & Heston.

5. Diane Levine and Robyn Mace. Spring 1999. Security Management Training Curricula. Jersey City, NJ: Intellitech Security Group.

6. For an excellent discussion of these issues, see *The Privatization and Civilianization of Policing*. Brian Forst. 2002. Boundary Changes in Criminal Justice Organizations, Volume 2:19-79. http://www.ncjrs.org/criminal_justice2000/vol_2/02c2.pdf.

Part II

Due Diligence and Forensic Accounting

Chapter 11

The Due Diligence Investigation

Don C. Johnson, CLI, CII

11.1 Introduction

A. Definition

"Such a measure of prudence, activity, or assiduity, as is properly to be expected from, and ordinarily exercised by, a reasonable and prudent man under the particular circumstances; not measured by any absolute standard, but depending on the relative facts of the special case."[1]

B. A historical perspective

Due diligence as we know it in the United States evolved from our securities laws and defined a standard of care required under law when conducting regulated financial activities. Modern due diligence has moved beyond the realm of these proceedings and now includes many day-to-day management operations and decisions in national and international commercial transactions, including mergers and acquisitions.

Although the term due diligence entered our lexicon in modern times, its practice has been with us throughout history, whenever anyone trading or bartering with another sought to protect his or her interest or welfare. After all, it was the ancient Romans who gave us *caveat emptor*, buyer beware. Today, conscientious consumers perform due diligence routinely in the decisions they make about which product to buy or which tradesman or service professional to engage. What is less clear is how well business people and government regulators perform this duty.

11.2 Business and Investment Losses

For decades, studies have illustrated that the U.S. economy loses billions of dollars annually to various frauds and economic crimes. Although the estimates of the cost of fraud vary greatly, occupational fraud and abuse costs organizations over $600 billion annually, when applied to the U.S. Gross Domestic Product.[2] In the larger arena of economic crime, the annual losses are astronomical, one to two trillion dollars.[3] Economic crime is in itself a growth industry, especially since the early 1990s and the convergence of the dual influences of global marketization and information technology. The rapid rise of business diversifications has proven a fertile ground for the enterprising and sophisticated criminal, of which there are plenty.

In one segment of the financial services market, mortgage banking, fraud is estimated to cost $120 billion annually. Real estate is by and large an undisciplined sector of our economy that attracts the white collar criminal, and real estate fraud and real estate loan frauds are the intemperate children of mortgage fraud. White collar criminals have discovered they can easily transfer their skill sets from the less lucrative area of credit card fraud to mortgage fraud. The average credit card criminal shares in an average pool of $15,000 in ill gotten gains, while an average mortgage fraud can result in a $59,000 profit, which is the average FHA loan loss, one of the few figures available in a under-reported area of economic crime.[4] Inadequate and fraudulent real estate appraisals played a large part in the savings and loan failures of the 1980s. The S&L scandals resulted in $300 billion in losses. The U.S. House of Representatives' Committee on Governmental Operations, investigating the scandals, attributed as much as $1 billion of the losses to appraisal problems, criminal and otherwise.[5] According to statistics provided by the Federal Bureau of Investigation in 1995, mortgage fraud accounted for $30 billion in losses, and one in nine loan applications contain inaccurate or falsified information.[6] Due diligence played a large part in these losses, in that it was often absent or wholly inadequate.

In the world of big business and high finance, it seems the lessons of history are frequently ignored, and the sins and crimes of the past are regularly visited upon the incautious.

11.3 Case Studies

Stock market investors in the Sunbeam Corporation and numerous business partners lost millions in the late 1990s as the company's stock plummeted when it was revealed they had been reporting fraudulent profits for a number of years. By the time the corporation collapsed in 2001, it was in bankruptcy and its CEO and other executives were charged with accounting fraud by the Securities and Exchange Commission (SEC). Also charged was the company's accounting firm, Arthur Andersen, which had agreed to certify fraudulent financial statements after uncovering the false sales figures in an audit. The auditors' position was not unheard of in a profession that is by and large self-regulated. They determined that Sunbeam's "sham profits," in the millions of dollars, were immaterial to the company's financial viability and that their audit conformed to accounting standards within the industry. At the time, an Andersen spokesman shrugged off the charges as "professional disagreements about the application of sophisticated accounting standards." A due diligence investigation would have established that Sunbeam's exaggerated profits came from some creative shams. Once such deception centered on the company's huge spare-parts inventory. Sunbeam and the company that stored its spare parts, EPI Printers, agreed to a scheme where Sunbeam sold all its spare parts to EPI for $11 million, a figure that exaggerated the true value by $9 million. EPI balked at the arrangement and the deal was never closed. That did not stop Sunbeam from posting the profits in an earnings report.[7]

As 2001 came to a close, it was alleged that the Arthur Andersen accounting conglomerate applied these "sophisticated" accounting techniques when it audited the Enron Corporation, the Texas-based energy trading firm whose tentacles reached around the world, wrapping around countless investors, employees, and business partners who lost millions as the artificial empire collapsed. Lawmakers accused the Enron executives of creating the world's largest pyramid scheme. The harsh words of Congress have wrung true as criminal indictments and convictions have subsequently been handed down and against former Enron executives.

There were a few lone voices in the wilderness, business writers and others, warning about suspected false profits reporting schemes at Enron, schemes that went on for years. Of special interest to the due diligence investigator are the complicated business partnerships that enhanced Enron's balance sheet but which were never reported on its financial statements.[8] These partnerships were created by Enron executives to appear as independent business ventures, and Enron reported profits received from their investments in the partnerships before one single dollar had actually been earned. Burned in the deals were investment bankers, outside investors, and business contractors. One question remains to be answered: Where was the due diligence?

And where were the lessons learned from times gone by? Due diligence was absent over two decades ago when a scandal similar to the Enron and Sunbeam affairs engulfed Penn Square Bank. Penn Square was a small Oklahoma City bank in a shopping center that amassed a portfolio of illusionary profits before going bust in the early 1980s. As in the Sunbeam and Enron debacles, accounting firms were accused of participating in shady schemes that resulted in fraudulent earnings reports.[9] As the Penn Square Bank disappeared like a cheap magic trick, so did the fortunes of several businessmen who had entered into investment ventures promoted by Penn Square but who had failed to ask the most basic questions that a due diligence program would have solicited. At the time, outrage was free and frequent, Congressional hearings were conducted, but, in the end, no changes in regulatory law resulted and the business world moved on to the next venue of hocus pocus and fast fortunes.

After the collapse of Enron and Arthur Andersen, other accounting frauds materialized in publicly held companies. As it turned out, many chief financial officers, their bosses, and their accountants were regularly reporting false profits in order to manipulate stock market results. This time Congress, under intense public pressure, decided to take a stand against marketplace fraud by passing the Sarbanes-Oxley Act, which was signed into law on July 30, 2002.

Sarbanes-Oxley introduced stringent new rules on how companies are governed in the financial markets, "...to protect investors by improving the accuracy and reliability of corporate disclosures made pursuant to the securities laws." The act went further than previous legislation to fight corporate fraud, in order to "...deter and punish corporate and accounting fraud and corruption, ensure justice for wrongdoers, and protect the interests of workers and shareholders," as President George W. Bush noted when he signed the bill into law.

History tells us these changes will do little to modify the behavior of individuals intent on fraud and other economic crimes. And the will of Congress and the public for greater oversight and enforcement may already be waning. A little over two years after Sarbanes-Oxley went into effect, U.S. businesses were already complaining about the costs and legal penalties for non-compliance to the act and the tough stand taken by the SEC. A lot of the criticism comes from the SEC rule designed to fight financial fraud, known as "SOX 404," which requires companies to improve their internal controls. SOX 404 compliance is imposing significant costs on companies in technology upgrades and legal and accounting fees.

However, there is no will in Congress to challenge the intent of Sarbanes-Oxley to protect the investor and the integrity of the financial markets, especially in light of new corporate scandals coming to light on a regular basis. New York State Attorney General Eliot Spitzer has led the fight against Wall Street's corrupt practices, and nationwide others are following his lead, as shareholder lawsuits are emerging alongside states' enforcement actions.

One thing is sure: With the implementation of Sarbanes-Oxley and a greater emphasis on corporate accountability, the need for due diligence was never greater.

11.4 Standards of Care

A lack of due diligence by a buyer in a failed business transaction does not necessarily mean that a fraud will be perpetrated by the seller. However, due diligence by a buyer is the best way to avoid becoming the victim of a fraud or making a bad business decision, and, in many instances, due diligence by a seller is required to avoid abetting the criminal intent of another or making a bad business decision. Perhaps the easiest element of fraud to prove in a civil or criminal proceeding is misrepresentation or concealment of a material fact. Anyone who unwittingly aides in a misrepresentation could find himself or herself charged with the fraudster. Although the specific act might not be criminal, it could easily be determined to be negligent and subject the person to civil liability.

In the legal aftermath that accompanies a failed business or investment venture, charges of criminal fraud or civil wrong may result. As in other areas of the law, the courts are not always consistent in determining the appropriate degree of due diligence, but they will consider a multitude of factors in establishing negligence through a reckless disregard of duty.[10]

- *Business acumen.* What was the level of expertise of the buyer or investor (the plaintiff)? How knowledgeable or understanding was he or she about the financial aspects of the enterprise?
- *Access.* Did the plaintiff (or defendant) have access to all relevant information about the business, real estate, or investment opportunity which was under consideration?
- *Relationships.* Did the plaintiff (or defendant) have any standing relationship to the enterprise, or to anyone associated with the business? Was the relationship business, fiduciary, or personal? Was there a conflict of interest, at any point, by anyone who contributed to the eventual outcome of the transaction?
- *Elements of fraud.* Did the plaintiff (or defendant) have any opportunity to detect the fraud, and, if so, did he or she intentionally or otherwise, perpetuate its concealment or further a misrepresentation?

- *Degree of misrepresentations.* How specific were the misrepresentations that were made? Were they easily detectable, or too general in nature?
- *Culpability.* Did the plaintiff initiate the contact that lead to the transaction or move to speed up the closing of the deal? Throughout the due diligence process, the investigator should look for any conflicts of interest, directly or indirectly. The appearance or impression of a conflict is sufficient to investigate further.

11.5 The Due Diligence Program

The goal of any due diligence investigation is to avoid a bad business or investment decision, or if conducted after the fact, to assess responsibility for a business failure. Unfortunately, due diligence is not always part of standard operating procedures, and, even if its value is begrudgingly recognized, its performance is often perfunctory. A cursory due diligence investigation is arguably barely better than no due diligence. A due diligence program should be carefully defined, in terms of its goals and the team that is responsible for achieving those goals.

The goals of a due diligence can be broken down into units of exploration, general areas of concern that the investigation should focus on. At various times during the process, different team members may be assigned to a unit of the investigation.

- *Dig deep.* The investigative due diligence should develop complete profiles on all the individuals involved in the pending transaction. Are there any ancillary associations or influences that could adversely affect the merger or acquisition?
- *Look for masquerades.* Financial problems and sales figures can be disguised. Product or sales diversions may have occurred. Unusual sales projections and growth figures should be independently verified through industry sources.
- *Read between the lines.* A company's books, annual report, board minutes, in-house newsletters, and marketing materials are usually designed to put the company in the best possible light. What do the materials leave unsaid, or unprovable?

- *Look for industry covenants and caveats.* What industry or trade influences could have an effect on the merged company's future? Are there any undisclosed agreements that could limit a company's ability to increase prices in a market, or prevent entering into pricing agreements with vendors and suppliers?
- *Beware of free agents.* Does the company have a high turnover of management and executive teams? Will the team that led a company to prominence stay with the company if it is purchased in an unpopular merger? Will the departure of any or all of the managers affect the income potential or projections that were critical to the purchase agreement?
- *Look for skeletons in the closets.* Businesses that suffer from employee fraud and theft or sexual harassment or discrimination problems will often settle these matters quietly and no records will be generated. Law enforcement or other legal authorities may never have been involved. What is the potential for future risks in these areas?

11.6 Terminology

Like many disciplines and areas of interest, due diligence will require familiarity with a new lexicon. Here is a sampling of terms that may be encountered at various stages in a due diligence investigation.

Benford's Law. A fraud examination technique designed to find a pattern in the frequency of digits in a list of figures that may indicate fraud.

Channel Stuffing. Moving inventory onto the books of distributors and recording the move as sales.

Chop Stocks. The difference in what a broker pays for a stock and what they sell it to the public for is known as a chop. It becomes a crime when the sell price is artificially inflated through fraudulent means.

Cookie Jar Reserves. A catchy term to describe fake profits. For example, expenses in one calendar year or financial reporting periods are applied to a previous year.

DASH. Deal Approval Sheets. Internal documents that show the names of those who authorized various activities and business arrangements and summarize those arrangements.

Earnings Management. A catchy term for creating artificial sales and earnings figures in a financial report, often utilizing questionable accounting techniques to validate the figures.

Flipping. A mortgage loan fraud that involves buying a property at real value and quickly reselling it in a fraudulent transaction that inflates the sale price substantially, creating an artificial market value on the property. One property can be flipped numerous times before the scheme will be discovered, enabling the fraudster to generate extraordinary profits before dumping the property on an unsuspecting buyer.

Lapping. An accounts receivable fraud that involves an employee diverting payments from one customer to another, and on and on, in an attempt to conceal embezzled revenue.

Product Fronts. Fake financial instruments, such as stock or borrower certificates or exchange rates, used by a grifter to perpetuate a fraud. Product fronts are often seen in pyramid investment schemes, which the Better Business Bureau has labeled "the biggest single fraud threat confronting American investors."[11]

Pump and Dump. The Internet has given us a new popularity for this term. Swindlers, or their unwitting accomplices, "pump" a stock on a popular online newsgroup or message board. When the stock's value has reached a new high, the fraudsters will suddenly "dump" their shares, by quickly selling them at the falsely inflated value. The buzz just as suddenly dies down, and the value of the stock plummets, leaving the new investors with virtually worthless paper.

Round-trip Trades. Seen in the energy business, these are trades where energy is bought and sold simultaneously and at the same price. The transaction has provided no profit to the seller, yet revenue or trading volumes are inflated. In late 2002, Dynegy, a Houston energy firm, paid a $3 million fine to the SEC when they were accused of using these sham trades to boost profit projections and cash flow.

11.7 The Due Diligence Team

The goals surrounding a particular due diligence assignment will be dictated by a variety of factors, including the scope of the business or financial transactions, the various entities and individuals that are part of the enterprise, the time frame allowed for the due diligence, and the monies available to fund the operation. The due diligence team can be broken down into three principal players, each of which offers a unique skill set to the process.

A. The lawyer

The due diligence program should be established and maintained by competent legal authority. Depending on the nature of the venture or investment under consideration, a variety of local, state, and federal laws may effect the transaction. For example, the Sarbanes-Oxley Act, mentioned above, has very specific provisions that require financial due diligence. Furthermore, the Foreign Corrupt Practices Act of 1977 (FCPA) imposes a due diligence obligation on any U.S. business that is considering expanding into overseas markets.

The FCPA came about after the Watergate scandal in the 1970s and the disclosure of the widespread bribery and corruption practiced by U.S. corporations in their dealings in foreign countries. Although the act's enforcement has been spotty historically, anti-bribery enforcement has increased during the 1990s. Such practices can give a business liability issues not clearly defined on a financial spread sheet, and prosecution can result in stiff civil and criminal penalties. A due diligence investigation is essential before any business person engages a foreign consultant or representative or enters into any business relationship or joint venture.[12]

Any business merger or acquisition that involves moving employees from the seller's payroll to the new or merged company's roster of employees could subject the buyer to the provisions of the Fair Credit Reporting Act (FCRA) and its reporting and disclosure provisions. Pre-employment screening and background investigations conducted on the new employees must comply with the FCRA and the comparable state statute.

The securities laws have to be factored into the equation, especially when investigating public companies or offerings. The Securities Act of 1933 (the Securities Act) imposes liability on individuals who make material misrepresentations in these transactions, no matter the level or extent of their participation. Section 11 of the Securities Act addresses the due diligence defenses that are acceptable under law, and the burden of proof is on the defendant.[13]

The Comprehensive Environmental Response, Compensation and Liability Act of 1980 (CERCLA) and its related statutes, including the Superfund Act and the Clean Water Act, impose strict liabilities on real property owners and "operators."[14] Investigations into the history of property ownership and related assets should proceed under the authority of competent legal authority and other experts familiar with the risks and dangers involved in environmental hazards, such as asbestos, polychlorinated biphenyls (PCBs), and other leeching pollutants. Any buyer who acquires real estate in a business merger or acquisition cannot claim the "innocent landowner defense" against violations of environmental law if he or she failed to conduct due diligence.[15]

B. The accountant

The overwhelming majority of accountants, auditors, and fraud examiners practicing today would neither condone nor align themselves with the controversial practices of their peers involved in the scandals illustrated earlier in this chapter. Certified public accountants and forensic auditors are trained to identify fraud risk factors and other irregularities among a corporation's financial statements and accounting practices. The American Institute of Certified Public Accountants (AICPA) developed a code of professional standards, known as the Statements on Auditing Standards (SAS), which put auditors and accountants in a proactive posture in seeking out and reporting on fraud.[16]

Forensic auditors should be in charge of examining and evaluating all financial documents relating to a merger, acquisition, or investment portfolio. Examining a business' accounting practices and financial records is a key component in a due diligence program in support of a merger, acquisition, or other business or investment venture. The accountant may require follow-up from the investigator, in conducting background investigations on individuals or other companies found in a forensic audit that revealed indicators of fraud or material misrepresentations.

C. The investigator

A due diligence investigation encompasses the legal, accounting, and investigative processes and should be distinguished from investigative due diligence. Investigative due diligence is the specific process of information gathering and is the natural province of the professional investigator.

In the public sector, federal and state laws, if not common sense, dictate that a securities or investment firm exercise due diligence in structuring the portfolios it offers its clients. In the private sector and the high dollar world of mergers, acquisitions, and joint ventures, where extraordinary profits are common, extraordinary due diligence should be demanded.[17] When a cursory approach to due diligence is accepted, the siren call of greed may be too deafening for the corporate soldiers seeking fast fortune. Any narrow measure of danger may go unheeded, and far greater risks will go undefined. In order to discover or unmask these deceptions or inadequate representations, a carefully planned and executed due diligence program must include the professional investigator.

11.8 The Investigation

A. Definition

"The process of inquiring into or tracking down through inquiry." *Mason v. Peaslee*, 173 C.A.2d 587, 343 P.2d 805, 808.[18]

The disciplinary process surrounding investigative due diligence contains many of the elements of traditional business intelligence gathering. Business intelligence is a broad category of information gathering, whether that business is a competitor or not, and it can include competitive intelligence gathering. Business intelligence gathering is essential not only for a company with designs on a national or international market, but for any small market competitor interested in establishing or maintaining a viable business. Business intelligence gathering is not a dishonorable calling, although there are purveyors of the practice who often step over the line of what is legal, ethical, and moral. Crossing such boundaries is the province of unimaginative minds.

The twin disciplines of business intelligence gathering and investigative due diligence are honorable undertakings that require the skills of investigative professionals who operate within the relevant laws and codes of ethics and conduct.

Investigative due diligence should be conducted by *investigators*. It should accompany the traditional legal and accounting components of a due diligence program, but it should be recognized as a distinct function performed by professional investigators. Professional investigators bring a unique array of skills and experiences that are essential when applying the following elements of investigative due diligence.

B. Business and media database research

Extensive research and investigation should be applied in developing a broad profile of the targeted businesses and individuals. There are numerous resources available to the investigator to make this task practical. The Internet offers valuable media and business research sources. The following is not intended to be an exhaustive resource list, as new databases and compendiums are appearing regularly. Let us start with the "Big Three."[19]

- The Dow Jones Publications Library is available online at http://djinteractive.com. The Dow Jones Publications Library contains the full texts of the major newspapers, *The New York Times, The Los Angeles Times, The Washington Post, Forbes, Fortune, Business Week, Barron's*, and, of course, the Dow Jones flagship publication, *The Wall Street Journal*. This database is considered by many to be the most intuitive of the large database services. Dow Jones Interactive is a subscription service, but many of these publications offer their own online databases which can be searched at little or no cost.
- LEXIS-NEXIS, it can be argued, has no match in its legal database. It also offers news, business, and special interest resource files. In addition to the print resource files, the Big Three offer a broadcast media resource file. Many business managers and executives make television or radio appearances, and any thorough investigative due diligence will search out these utterances.
- DIALOG has science and technology resource files you will not find on Dow Jones Interactive or LEXIS-NEXIS. DIALOG also offers the *Encyclopedia of Associations*, the standard reference source for researching and identifying nonprofit corporations and trade and professional associations.

Published by Gale Research, the *Encyclopedia* is available in hard copy at many libraries.

- Dun & Bradstreet's business reporting products are available through Dow Jones Interactive, DIALOG and other online reporting services, or directly by going to the D&B web site (dnb.com). D&B reports are valuable when researching privately held companies and should be among the first business research reports obtained. Among other things, these reports contain payment histories and financial reporting by the company, a history of people associated with the company's management, business credit histories, and its net worth. The key to relying on business credit reports and other company-reported filings is verification. Caution and a critical eye are always advised in scrutinizing a company's own published information. However, a company's self-reporting may become evidence in a subsequent investigation into fraudulent business practices.
- BizAdvantage (formerly BrainWave) is, according to its web site (bizadvantage.com), "... a pay-as-you-go resource for business information such as company profiles, credit reports, market research, and more." It includes links to the D&B and LEXIS-NEXIS and other online resource databases. BizAdvantage's *Exporters' Encyclopaedia* offers guides to worldwide markets and export information on close to 200 companies. It includes information on trade regulations and import and export procedures that are valuable in determining if a target company of the investigation is in compliance.
- Experian (formerly TRW), one of the three major credit reporting bureaus, publishes its own business credits reports. These reports are not subject to the individual consumer controls of the Fair Credit Reporting Act and are available online through Experian's web site at www.experian.com. Business credit reports can also be purchased at www.businesscreditusa.com, the web site of Credit.Net, a division of the large market research firm, InfoUSA. The advantage

here is information on hard-to-find, small, privately held companies.

- The American Society of Association Executives (ASAE) has its own web site (asaenet.org), in case you don't have immediate access to DIALOG for an associations search. ASAE is a gateway source for determining exactly what associations exist within a specific trade category or profession.
- *The Thomas Register of American Manufacturers* and *Thomas Register Catalog File* is now available online. This is a multiple volume resource directory for identifying individuals within a company or industry who can be contacted during an investigative due diligence. Thomas also includes a brand names index, company catalogs, and a portal to company websites.
- *Standard and Poor's Register of Corporations, Directors and Executives*. This is a standard reference source in conducting business research. Published in three volumes each year, it offers timely information on approximately 46,000 U.S. and Canadian companies. The directories include biographies on executives, as well as obituaries for the previous year. Many business schools and college libraries carry these volumes.
- *American Reference Books Annual* covers up to 1,800 new titles each year, in about 300 categories of reference books. This is a good resource to identify recent publications in a discipline or field of endeavor.
- *The Readers Guide to Periodical Literature*, published by H.W. Wilson, is a well-known series that indexes articles in a variety of general interest magazines. It is readily available in public libraries.
- Information Today, Inc., publishes *Information Today* (www.infotoday), an online resource for publishers and users of electronic information. *Information Today* provides access to commercial database locations or web links to news wire services, newsletters, newspapers and magazines, and television and radio transcripts. This source is a primary resource tool of information and library professionals.

- *Net.Journal Directory 10*, released in January 2002, is published by Hermograph Press and can be found in interactive form at their web site, hermograph.com. This catalog indexes full text periodicals available on the web, including scholarly journals, U.S. and world newspapers, and various periodicals and magazines. It also contains a web directory of resource databases.
- *The Investigator's Little Black Book 3*. This handy one-stop resource directory is not to be overlooked. This unique compendium contains thousands of phone numbers and web sites where information can be found on people, businesses, and organizations. These hard-to-find sources have been tested and utilized by thousands of investigators, law enforcement agencies, and media organizations. It can be purchased through Crime Time Publishing Company at www.crimetime.com.

Facts On Demand Press is an imprint of BRB Publications, Inc. (www.brbpub.com), the leader in resource directories for the research and investigation professions. Four of their more popular titles are valuable reference works for the due diligence investigator.

- *Find It Online*. This award-winning reference by journalist Alan M. Schlein is definitely an "insider" guide to researching on the web. Whether you're new at surfing on the Internet or a seasoned professional looking for the latest and best resource tool, this book is a necessary addition to your library. It contains web addresses for thousands of sites and includes "tricks of the trade" for online research.
- *Online Competitive Intelligence* by Helen P. Burwell is just what the title implies; a resource book for gathering online information on public and private companies. "Cyber-intelligence" is a fast-growing area of corporate competitive information gathering in a world that is quickly becoming a global marketplace. This book tells not only how to find the information, but how to analyze it.

- *Public Records Online*. This is BRB's master guide to public records online. It includes almost 8,500 direct government online sources and over 200 national and regional database providers. Jimmie Mesis, the publisher of *PI Magazine, the Journal of Professional Investigators*, noted in a review: "This book bridges the gap between wasting time on the web and finding what you need... quickly and easily."
- *The Sourcebook to Public Record Information* has information on over 20,000 government agencies; including the U.S. district courts, state agencies, county courts, and local recording and assessors offices. The sixth edition includes new sections on Canadian driver and criminal information. Also included are handy U.S. county and city cross references and state maps. Not to be overlooked is the Sourcebook's chapter on "Guidelines for Public Records Searching," which is more than a primer on the methods and myths of public record research.

C. Public record research

No inexperienced investigator should be in charge of an investigative due diligence, and no experienced investigative professional would conduct an investigative due diligence without checking all applicable public records. Experienced investigative professionals are familiar with public record sources at the various levels of local, state, and federal government. Checks of criminal and civil records are essential in profiling a potential business partner, whether individual or corporate. A complete history of litigation and other civil proceedings and filings must be developed. Information derived from public record searches can be used to develop additional leads and for other verifications.

There is an axiom often heard in regards to online public record or other database research: Nothing in, nothing out (or garbage in, garbage out, depending on your point of view). Online public record files are often limited in the time span of their database and contain data entry errors. Furthermore, many local and state public record databases are not yet available online. Central repository sources of criminal history and arrest records are notoriously unreliable. Many states require that the county courts and local police agencies report conviction and arrest data to the state's central repository, often maintained by the state police. However, many of these state repositories do not contain all the criminal histories found in the local public record repositories at the city and county levels.

Some of these state reporting laws were never funded when enacted by the legislature, and the local governments have neither the budget or staff resources to comply. Even among those counties that do report, their reportage is often several months late, leaving a further shortfall in the state's repository. In some states, not all court records are centralized in one county court. Indices and files are maintained at a variety of different courts and offices. Criminal and civil history checks on an individual should be conducted at the local level, by a hands-on researcher or investigator familiar with the local court structure wherever an individual has resided for a period of time and where criminal indictments and civil lawsuits would have most likely originated.

Many states now have their corporation records online, but once again, the online information is often cursory and incomplete. The best evidence will be found in the hard copy files maintained by the appropriate state agency, such as the secretary of state. However, in the real world of investigative due diligence, exhaustive field investigations are not always feasible, especially over a wide area of the country, and online resources have to be relied upon, while recognizing their limitations. The following is an overview of public record resources at the local, state, and federal levels.

- *City and town government.* City clerks often maintain records on building code violators, for example, as well as those who have applied for variances and other considerations. Police departments will have records of incident logs, although the information found in these records will vary depending on the state's public access laws and the department's willingness to comply with those laws. An investigator must be prepared to invoke access laws and other Freedom of Information rights when denied access to public information.
- *County government.* Here, the local court(s) clerk's records should be checked for criminal and civil histories. Although personal information on voters in voter registration records has been redacted in many jurisdictions, these records should

still be checked. Address and time line discrepancies might be identified. The county's recorder, auditor, and assessor maintain their own files. Recorders will have deed and mortgage documents on file, as well as Uniform Commercial Code (UCC) filings and search requests. Tax records and property valuations and assessments will be available through the auditor and the assessors, respectively.

- *State government.* Corporation records, state UCC filings, and professional licensing information will be maintained by the appropriate state agency. States have their own securities laws and requirements for registration. Other regulatory agencies have databases, such as insurance departments, land management agencies where hunting and fishing licenses are often found, environmental management bureaus, and utility commissions and agencies. Many states now maintain sex and violent offender databases on their web site.
- *Federal government.* The majority of the U.S. District Courts now offer an online search option on their criminal, civil and bankruptcy indices. Complete files are not available online, and that is unlikely to change in the future, because of the perceived privacy dangers in posting public records online. To find the appropriate federal court, go to the PACER system, online at http://pacer.psc.uscourts.gov. The quickest way to determine if an individual has ever been incarcerated in a federal prison is to go to the Bureau of Prisons web site at bop.gov.
- All *public companies filing* with the Securities and Exchange Commission can be found by searching the Edgar database, on the web at sec.gov/edgarhp.com. Edgar will show financial reporting, including the earnings of corporate executives over a period of time, which are valuable in creating time lines and in comparing to other, non-public disclosures.
- The *Excluded Parties Index* provides a list compiled from about sixty government agencies of individuals and firms that have been excluded from federal procurement and non-procurement programs. The index is maintained by the U.S. General Services Administration and is available on the

Internet at http://epls.arnet.gov. The list of excluded parties includes "...individuals, entities, and contractors..." who have been barred from doing business with the federal government for a number of reasons, including misrepresentations, fraud, or failure to perform. Exclusions may brought by executive action or by statutory or regulatory authority.

- A link to the Excluded Parties Index and a many other U.S. government public record sources can be found on the web at publicrecordfinder.com/usgovt.html. This is a one stop resource for finding a specific federal database during a public record research phase.

These additional online resources are valuable for developing information on an individual, a business, or an area of interest to the investigation.[20]

- *Library of Congress* (www.loc.gov or http://thomas.loc.gov). The full *Congressional Record* can be found here, including profiles of members and staff. You will also find here multiple links to international, federal, state, and local government sites.
- *National Technical Information Service* (www.ntis.gov). This is the site for the government's "clearinghouse" on unclassified technical reports where government funding was involved. NTIS collects not only science and technology research from the U.S., but from other countries as well.
- *Defense Technical Information Center* (www.dtic.mil). This is a good resource site for an investigation involving subjects with a history of dealings with the Department of Defense or other defense related entities.
- *National Archives & Records Administration* (www.nara.gov). This is an exhaustive database of documents, photographs, film and video archives, including the complete government file on the assassination of President Kennedy.

The major Internet and World Wide Web search engines should be employed when conducting a background investigation of an individual or developing information on a corporation or business enterprise. The best known and perhaps most powerful is Google, but Yahoo is once again becoming a strong player on the search engine field. Microsoft now offers its own search engine on the MSN web sites. One powerhouse search engine is available through www.copernic.com. It scans several search engines at once and can perform e-mail searches as well, looking for Internet chat rooms and other sites where an individual may have left an e-mail "calling card." The Copernic browser will maintain a folder of searches for later retrieval and further research. The investigator must practice his or her own brand of due diligence when conducting online research: If you have used as many search engines as possible, don't assume that you have found all the information there is available about a company or person. Be sure to identify and use local resources as well.

D. Direct contact with industry, government, and confidential sources

When developing a profile on an individual or business, contact should be established with sources within the relevant professional or industrial sector. If part of the investigative due diligence requires research into an esoteric area of science or technology, the investigator should not hesitate to contact an expert in the field for additional research or source assistance. For example, many of the database services available online do not include all the writings or documentation available in a special field of endeavor. In these instances, the research should include traditional information sources, such as the hard copy indices of professional and trade journals or interviews with people who work in that industry or profession. Experts should be contacted at any time in an investigative due diligence when the value of a piece of information is difficult to determine or further or more extensive resources become hard to define.

E. Personal disclosures and authorizations

In many situations involving a merger, acquisition, or pending business arrangement, a personal history statement or other personal history document such as a curriculum vitae may have been provided by a potential business partner. Furthermore, a separate authorization to release information should be obtained from the potential partner. When the appropriate authority has been granted, an individual's credit report should be obtained and examined. If a release is not available, such as in a sub-rosa investigation conducted early in a venture, the investigator will have to rely on traditional public and non-public records sources that can be accessed without a release. In an ideal scenario, a public history statement will be available. The importance lies in not only what an individual will reveal about himself or herself, but in what he or she will not reveal. The personal history document should be designed by the due diligence investigation team and should solicit at least the following information, or more, depending on the parameters of the investigation.[21]

- Personal identifying information; date of birth and Social Security number
- Marital status and history; name(s) and identifying information on spouse(s)
- Family history; include children and living parents and siblings
- Residential addresses; go back to the subject's birth
- Educational credentials and history
- Employment history; include honors and awards
- Hobbies, habits, social and fraternal affiliations
- Driver's history and other motor vehicle information
- Medical history; ask for past histories of drug use and alcoholism
- Military history; include dates and branch of service, and any extraordinary circumstances, such as dishonorable discharge, medical disability, or commendations and medals
- Criminal and civil histories
- Business and civic organizations and associations memberships

In the absence of a personal history statement, the above areas should be investigated anyway, with the investigator being responsible for "filling in" the form. A section of the statement can be devoted to a list of character and business references, with possible contact information on each one listed. The personal history statement should be the subject's autobiography in digest form, and the basic investigative resource tool for verification or impeachment of information on the subject, as well as developing additional sources and information.

F. Premises inspections and site surveys

In some instances, the investigative due diligence may involve either an overt or covert inspection of a business and its assets, such as property and inventory. Exaggerated inventories are a common misrepresentation and can usually be verified by an unannounced inspection at the primary business site or other facilities. Many frauds over the years have involved dummy corporations and bogus business addresses for shell companies that could have been discovered in a simple due diligence "visit." A sub-rosa surveillance may be required where questionable activities surrounding the day-to-day operations of a company are discovered. Surveillance and other sub-rosa investigative activity may be required in a due diligence assignment involving inventory diversions or trademark and counterfeit product issues. Intellectual property assets can involve complex legal issues, and both buyers and sellers in such business transactions would be advised to conduct investigative audits of product inventories and other non-financial assets.

11.9 Caveat Actor

A. Definition

"Let the doer, or actor, beware."[22]

B. Investigator beware

To paraphrase a colleague, due diligence is one of those catchy terms, like "paradigm shift," that people use too freely, in a brochure or other marketing material, without giving careful thought to the fact it can mean different things to different people.[23] As mentioned previously, inexperienced investigators should avoid complex due diligence assignments, unless under the supervision of a colleague who is experienced or has specialized in the area. In all instances of investigative due diligence, exacting steps should be taken by the investigator, both to avoid any missteps or oversights in understanding the assignment and to create an audit trail of the investigation.

The investigator will most likely be retained by an attorney representing a buyer, seller, or corporation involved in a pending transaction or by in-house corporate counsel. Working directly for a businessman or company executive can create problems with work product privileges, something an investigator cannot offer when contracted directly by anyone other than an attorney.

Due diligence can be "...a fluid concept that varies from situation to situation."[24] The investigator in a due diligence assignment should qualify the parameters of the investigation, in concert with the client, and this qualification should be documented in writing by the due diligence team. The investigator must maintain a careful chain of custody of engagement agreements and all correspondence relating to the assignment, including interim reports and memoranda, logs of phone calls and faxes, and the final investigative report.

Time and money often limit the scope of investigative due diligence, an unfortunate reality we have to recognize. When these restraints are present, the investigator should advise his or her client, in writing, of the risks inherent in a shortcut to investigative results. There is no handy formula for determining how much money should be reserved or dedicated to an investigative due diligence. However, losses that result from an inadequate due diligence will be easily measured in hard dollars and a possible business failure.

C. Investigator's audit trail checklist

1. The engagement agreement, or other appropriate legal document, should be signed before the investigation commences. It should outline the investigative target(s), the fee and expense reimbursement structure, reporting format(s) and schedules, and deadlines for completion and final reporting. The investigator should consult private legal counsel in the development of this agreement. During the reporting periods, the investigator should call to the client's attention adverse, suspicious, or unverified information that needs to be investigated further. The investigator's correspondence should be documented, as should the client's response to the investigator's recommendations and suggestions about how to proceed.

2. Each report should contain the appropriate disclaimers about the sources utilized by the investigator. For example, in reporting on public record searches, an investigator might include the following disclaimer at the end of his report:

   This investigation is being conducted within the parameters defined in our original phone conversation and the subsequent memorandum of understanding which we signed. The primary sources of information as detailed in this report and its attachments were various public records as defined herein. Both electronic public record databases and actual state, court and county offices' indices and files were checked. These records are compiled, maintained and indexed by the government agency(s) which were searched. Our firm conducted this research using the record indexes and books, and/or the public access computer terminal provided by the government agency(s). We cannot independently verify the completeness or accuracy of the underlying government records. The client has the final decision making authority as to the relevance of the information revealed herein.
3. Secondary sources of information, such as proprietary database searches and direct contact with individuals and confidential informants should be documented as well as reported on. Obviously, confidential sources must be protected, but if the information provided by a confidential source is critical to the furtherance of the investigation, that information must be relayed in the appropriate format and in such a manner to protect the investigator's vested legal interest in the final work product. In reporting information derived from secondary record sources and personal interviews, a disclaimer should be appended to the report. Where appropriate, signed statements and audio or video recordings of statements should be accompanied by a chain of custody document. Once again, it should be detailed that the client has the final decision making authority as to the relevance of the information being reported.

11.10 Conclusion

"If you pay peanuts, you get monkeys."[25]

An investigative due diligence operation may be subjected to time and budget constraints, but these limitations can be recognized and dealt with by the investigator who is cautious, thorough, and professional in business relationships. The investigator is obligated to exercise good faith, sound judgment, and his or her own due diligence in the performance of his or her duty; and, furthermore, to protect and guard, in accordance with applicable laws and circumstance, the client's right to confidentiality. However, investigative services often involve a search for the unknown or the nonexistent, or the discovery of information unfavorable to the client's interest. Therefore, investigative results cannot be guaranteed.

We live in a litigious society. The investigator in a due diligence action cannot protect himself or herself from every vexatious litigant but can ensure that defenses are in order, that professional liability insurance premiums are paid, and that the work product is the best possible one in the instant matter.

Nothing in this chapter should be considered a substitute for professional advice from a competent legal authority familiar with due diligence and other relevant areas of law.

Endnotes

1. Henry Campbell Black, M.A., *Black's Law Dictionary*, West Publishing Company, Sixth Edition 1990, page 457.

2. *Report to the Nation on Occupational Fraud and Abuse*, Association of Certified Fraud Examiners, 2003 (available at www.cfenet.com). A 2003 fraud study by accounting giant KPMG found that business organizations are reporting more fraud activity than in previous years. The most costly type of fraud is now medical and insurance related crimes, although employee theft remains the most prevalent. The KPMG survey also found that businesses are learning to fight fraud by incorporating a new focus on due diligence and legal compliance.

3. James Kerins, "Avoiding Credit Fraud with Due Diligence," *Business Credit*, National Association of Credit Management, September 1998, Volume 100, No. 8, pp. 17, 19.

4. Steven R. Smith, "Mortgage Fraud: A White Collar Crime Story," FDN Fraud Report, April 3, 2001, retrieved online via a subscription account, at www.fraudreport.com. A division of the Fraud Defense Network, this service may no longer be found at this web site. The Fraud Defense Network was merged into the ChoicePoint company of data services.

5. Gordon Bing, *Due Diligence Techniques and Analysis: Critical Questions for Business Decisions*, Quorum Books, 1996, page 48.

6. John R. Saltzman, CLI, "Investigating Real Estate and Mortgage Fraud," *Advanced Forensic Civil Investigations*, Lawyers & Judges Publishing Co., 1997.

7. *The New York Times*, "SEC Accuses Former Sunbeam Official of Fraud," Wednesday, May 16, 2001, page A1; "They Noticed the Fraud but Figured It Was Not Important," Friday, May 18, 2001, page C1.

8. *The New York Times*, "Fuzzy Rules of Accounting and Enron," Wednesday, January 30, 2002, page C1.

9. *The New York Times*, "Learning Old Lessons from a New Scandal," Saturday, January 2, 2002, page A29.

10. Bing, pp. 53-54.

11. *How to Prevent Small Business Fraud*, Association of Certified Fraud Examiners, Copyright 2004.

12. Wendy C. Schmidt and Jonny J. Frank, "FCPA Demands Due Diligence in Global Dealings," *The National Law Journal*, March 3, 1997, page B16.

13. Bing, pp. 37-38.

14. Ibid., page 32.

15. Ibid., page 50.

16. Michael J. Ramos, CPA, *Considering Fraud in a Financial Statement Audit: Practical Guidance for Applying SAS No. 82*, American Institute of Certified Public Accountants, Inc., 1997, pp. 3-60.

17. Extraordinary due diligence is not to be confused with "extraordinary diligence," a specific legal term. The reference here is for emphasis in defining a degree of due diligence. Black defines extraordinary diligence as an "...ex-

treme measure of care and caution..." applied by an individual "...in securing and preserving their own property or rights" (Black's Sixth Edition, page 457).

18. Black, page 825.

19. Helen P. Burwell, *Online Competitive Intelligence: Increase Your Profits Using Cyber-Intelligence*, Facts on Demand Press, Tempe, AZ, 1999. Page 36.

20. John M. Carroll, *Confidential Information Sources: Public and Private*, Butterworth-Heinemann, Second Edition 1991, page 283.

21. Alan M. Schlein, *Find It Online: The Complete Guide to Online Research*, Facts on Demand Press, 1999, page 109.

22. Black, page 222.

23. Bill E. Branscum, *The SFIA Journal*, newsletter of the South Florida Investigators Association, July 1999, page 1.

24. Ibid.

25. James Goldsmith (1933-), British businessman, quoted in *The MacMillian Dictionary of Quotations*, Chartwell Books, Inc., 1989.

Chapter 12

Forensic Accounting, Financial Fraud and Financial Statement Fraud

Robert J. DiPasquale, CPA, CFE

Synopsis

Financial crimes are commonly referred to as "robbery without a gun." In fact, the magnitude of financial fraud (i.e., occupational fraud and abuse) has been estimated by the Association of Certified Fraud Examiners (CFE) to be $400 billion annually.

12.1 The CFE Study

The Association of CFE, headquartered in Austin, Texas, is presently the largest private organization in the world dedicated solely to the education of fraud detection and deterrence. The Association's study of occupational fraud and abuse estimated the losses incurred by employers resulting from employee theft and abuse to be $660 billion annually. The Association's Report to the Nation addresses the following areas:[1]

- Cost of occupational fraud and abuse
- Methods Detection
- Victims
- Perpetrators
- Legal outcome

A. Scope of the CFE study

The study entailed a review of 1,508 actual cases where frauds occurred. The frauds studied totaled $761 million dollars and involved sixteen major industries.

B. Summary of the Association's report

1. Cost of fraud

Organizations lose an estimated 6 percent of annual revenue to fraud and abuse. It costs U.S. organizations $660 billion annually.

2. The perpetrators

- 67.8 percent of frauds were committed by employees.
- 12.4 percent were committed by owners/executive.
- 34 percent were committed by managers.

3. Losses

- Losses caused by perpetrators sixty years old and over were twenty-nine times those caused by the youngest perpetrators.
- Men committed nearly 52.9 percent of the offenses. Median losses caused by men were $160,000 in comparison to females, which were $60,000.

Median losses by category are shown in Table 12.1 and median losses sustained by various financial accounts are shown in Table 12.2.

C. Victims

Companies with 100 or fewer employees were the most vulnerable, amounting to approximately 46 percent of the 90 percent of the cases reviewed.

D. Methods

Asset misappropriations accounted for cash was the most frequently targeted of the 472 cases reviewed, 93 percent involved the misappropriation of cash.

Category of Loss	Amount
By sex	
Males	$160,000
Females	$60,000
By age	
< 26	$18,000
26-30	$25,000
31-35	$75,000
36-40	$80,000
41-50	$173,000
51-60	$250,000
≥61	$527,000
By industry	
Manufacturing	$125,000
Banking	$101,000
Service	$139,000
Government	$45,000
Other	$145,000
Insurance	$172,500
Retail	$35,500
Health Care	$172,500
Education	$35,500
Construction	$145,000
Transportation	$225,000
Oil and Gas	$145,000
Communication	$150,000
Utility	$30,000
Real Estate	$385,000
Agriculture	$1,080,000

Table 12.1 *Median Losses Reported by the CFE Study, by Category*

Cash	$100,000
Wages	$135.000
Travel and entertainment	$160,000
Supplies	$175,000
Sales revenue	$250,000
Other expense	$250,000
Accounts payable	$250,000
Inventory	$285,000
Services	$300,000
Accounts receivable	$300,000

Table 12.2 *Median Losses Reported by Account*

Corruption constituted 10 percent of the offenses (bribery, illegal gratuities, conflicts of interest, and economic extortion). Fraudulent statements accounted for about 5 percent of fraud cases.

E. Recapitulation

The CFE's study clearly indicates the magnitude of financial fraud caused by occupational fraud and abuse. Financial fraud encompasses many different types of scams using many creative techniques that are limited only by one's imagination. Therefore, where does one begin in a financial investigation when allegations of fraud exist? A proper investigation entails interviews with appropriate parties and a thorough review and analysis of an entity's "books and records."

The following will be discussed:

- Reconstructing financial records
- Common scams perpetuated against companies
- Fictitious employees
- Fictitious vendor scams
- Front company scams
- Kickbacks
- Checklist to identify potential financial motives to commit arson

12.2 Reconstructing Financial Records

A. Types of records involved

Although businesses differ as to the form of various books and records, the following are typical books that are maintained, either manually or computerized:

- General ledgers
- Cash disbursement journals
- Cash receipt journals
- Purchase journals
- Sales journals
- Payroll journals
- Inventory (if applicable)
- Accounts receivable journals
- Accounts payable journals

Many perpetrators, to frustrate and potentially prevent financial discovery, destroy or attempt to destroy financial records. This is not unusual in frauds such as arson for profit (later discussed at length), bankruptcy fraud, and in situations where high level management have control over the books and records.

B. The investigation

1. Lost or destroyed records

When records are destroyed or cannot be located, where should one begin the reconstruction process? The investigation should seek to identify parties who could be instrumental in developing clues and information to reconstruct the records, such as current or former employee, and outside third parties.

2. Interviews

Interviews with the following categories of employees may be helpful in obtaining information because they generally have some knowledge as to what records may have been maintained, as well as other financial information such as the company's customers, vendors, banks, and so on.

- Vice-president for finance or controller and assistants
- Bookkeeper and assistants
- Receiving and shipping clerks
- Payroll employees
- Purchasing agents
- Sales department personnel
- Secretaries
- Receptionists
- Inventory personnel
- Shipping department personnel
- Personnel department
- Computer programmers and key punch operators

However, situations will arise where employees cannot be located. In such situations, where does the investigator begin? The following illustrates some techniques for finding a starting point.

Case Study 1: The Swindled Investor

A wealthy investor was approached by various business people and asked to invest funds in a manufacturing company. The company, in business for several years and apparently showing good potential, needed these funds for working capital purposes. After reviewing internal financial statements, the investor agreed to invest the sum of $1,000,000.

As the investor was not involved in the day-to-day management of the company, he relied on the representations of management regarding the growth and profitability of the company. Although the investor was being paid some interest on his investment, in those months when he was not he rationalized that the company was short of funds and it was instead funding working capital and growth. Approximately one year after the investment was made, the investor was notified that the company filed for bankruptcy under Chapter 7 (liquidation). To say that the investor was surprised is an understatement. He was under the impression that although the company still required working capital, it was profitable and showed great potential. The investor, being a substantial creditor, organized a creditors' committee to examine the books and records of the newly defunct company in order to determine if there

> were any assets recoverable from the bankruptcy estate. When the creditors' committee attempted to review the books and records with the assistance of their forensic accountants, it was quite apparent that a substantial portion of the company books and records were either discarded or destroyed. The creditors' committee had two options: (1) discontinue discovery of the books and records, or (2) attempt to reconstruct the books and records. It was the creditors' committee decision to proceed in an attempt to reconstruct the records. Where do they begin?
>
> The initial starting point was an attempt to reconstruct the company's cash transactions, i.e., deposits and checks written. However, to accomplish this it was necessary to find the financial institutions in which the company had bank accounts. By interviewing other trade creditors disclosed in the bankruptcy petition, various bank accounts were identified. After obtaining complete copies of the bank statements, accountants were able to proceed in their investigation, and a detailed analysis of the disbursements was prepared. At first glance, nothing appeared suspicious. However, upon analysis of the deposits some concerns were raised. It was noted that the deposits from a major customer were consistently decreasing from month to month. This decrease in sales spurred additional discovery attempts. The investigation proceeded to determine why the sales were decreasing. What the investigation revealed was startling. Upon interviewing the customer, the reason the sales were decreasing was that sales were being made to another entity formed by management rather than to the investor company. The sales were made to this new entity and when paid, the funds were then disbursed to the business owner. The diversion of sales to the new entity was certainly one reason contributing to the cash flow problem. Further contributing to the company's demise was the fact that it, not the new entity, was paying for the product.

The foregoing case study illustrates a number of important facts. First, the importance of identifying an entity's financial institutions in the initial reconstruction process. Second, the transactions must be analyzed to make sure they make sense. In this case, the accountants' initial review of the cancelled checks did not reveal anything suspicious, such as payment for personal expenses, i.e., country clubs, colleges, vacation resorts, etc. If a forensic analysis of the deposits had not been done, the diversion of sales may never have been discovered.

3. Additional procedures

The following are additional forensic procedures that also can be employed in the reconstruction process:

a. Interview the company's officers and directors. Interviewing a company's officers and directors is an excellent start to gathering information. The names of officers and directors can be obtained from public records such as annual reports filed with the secretary of state. This information can be obtained by contacting the secretary of state or by utilizing on-line data base companies.

b. Third-party sources. Third-party sources that can be helpful in obtaining information or records concerning a target company are:

- Landlords
- Tenants
- USPS/UPS/Federal Express
- Security company
- Landscapers
- Maintenance companies
- Cleaning service companies
- Other service companies
- Customer vendors (further discussed later)
- Telephone company

c. Lenders and lien holders. Lending institutions and other types of secured parties can potentially provide important information. To perfect their security position, outside lending institutions generally will file a lien with the respective secretary of state. This information can be obtained from public filings as well as from database companies. The lien search generally would disclose the secured party and the nature of the security interest.

Once the outside lien holders are identified, which normally would include financial institutions, consideration should be give to subpoena these parties for additional information which may indicate the target company's banks. Important documents in the reconstruction process can be obtained through subpoena such as bank statements, cancelled checks, and deposit slips.

The information from the lien holders may also include certificates of insurance, which typically are required by secured parties in the event property or equipment is held as collateral. Subpoenas can be sent to the insurance company or insurance brokers to obtain the insurance policy and addenda. The insurance policies will supply you with the assets insured, such as transportation equipment, buildings, inventory, artwork, and other types of tangible assets.

d. Business tax returns and financial statements. It is not unusual that the financial institution who lent the target company funds will have tax returns and financial statements in their possession, possibly both personal as well as business. These documents contain an abundance of financial information, as the following explains.

Federal, and sometimes state business tax returns, are filed for business entities. The forms will vary depending on the type of tax paying entity. For example, corporate returns for taxpaying corporations, commonly referred to as C corporations, file returns using Form 1120. Chapter S corporations, which are not tax paying entities (as the tax is generally paid by the stockholders) use Form 1120S. Partnership entities file the return using an information Form 1065. Regardless of the type of business entity, the tax forms used are a type of financial statement that discloses an entity's taxable income or loss, as well as a balance sheet, which reflects a company's assets and liabilities, consistent with the accounting method used by the company. For example, an accrual basis company's tax return will include accounts receivable and accounts payable amounts, whereas a cash basis return will not. Determining the tax method used by the company is necessary when analyzing returns. If not, the analysis will not only be incomplete but may also be misleading.

The tax return may identify the name of the tax preparer (i.e., the accountant). The accountant's work papers, not normally protected by the attorney-client privilege, can be obtained by subpoena. The accountant's work papers may include key records, such as:

- Books of original entry such as general ledger, cash disbursements, cash receipts, payroll

- Copies of contracts
- Lists of other business entities the target may be involved with
- Names of other partners
- Previous business interests owned
- Names of relatives
- Business correspondence
- Names of financial planners, attorneys, and other professionals
- Other guarantors of obligations (i.e., related parties, relatives, etc.)

A forensic review of business tax returns can offer a wealth of information to reconstruct financial data as well as obtaining information pertaining to a target company, such as the following:

- Method of accounting
- Other business affiliations and related companies
- Ownership changes in businesses
- Social Security numbers
- Loans to stockholders
- Unusual trends in income and expenses
- Business real estate
- Life insurance
- Reduction in business assets
- Possible royalty agreements
- Redemptions of capital stock
- Retirement plans
- Percentage of time devoted to business

A forensic review of individual tax returns also offers valuable financial information such as:

- Bank accounts (domestic and foreign)
- Certificates of deposit
- Stock
- Bonds
- Self-employment interests
- Existence of outside storage facilities

- Tax-free investments
- Prior marriages
- Brokerage accounts
- Individual retirement accounts (IRA)
- Pension plans
- Real estate
- Business interests
- Income from estates and trusts
- Mortgages
- Accountants (tax preparer)
- Safe deposit boxes
- Lifestyle analysis (assists in proving unreported income)
- Previous addresses
- Potential diversion of assets
- Asset purchases with unreported income

e. Personal financial statements. Personal financial statements disclose a person's net worth (deficit). Net worth represents how much a person is worth (i.e., assets at market value less liabilities). The following financial information is generally reported in personal financial statements:

- Bank accounts
- Businesses owned and percentages owned
- Securities owned (i.e., number of shares, name of the security, and the current market value)
- Mortgages owned
- Real estate owned
- Motor vehicles owned
- Notes payable to banks
- Mortgages payable to mortgagees, by property
- Brokers margin accounts
- Contingent liabilities (i.e., lawsuits)
- Pledged or hypothecated assets
- Insurance coverage
- Current annual income and living expenses

Typically, the statement would include the names of the financial institutions, brokers, and lenders that can be subpoenaed for information. Once a personal bank is known, it provides the ability to obtain by subpoena complete bank statements, including cancelled checks and the checks deposited. The checks deposited would generally consist of deposits from the target company such as payroll, loans, etc. as well as other sources of income.

C. Analysis of the records

As seen in Case Study 1, once the target company's bank has been located and the records obtained, a thorough analysis will provide a wealth of information.

A review of the bank statements will reflect the activity in the account for deposits and withdrawals. An analysis of the monthly receipts and disbursements will indicate trends in activity, daily bank balances, and positive or overdraft positions. Unusual reductions in the activity may be an indication of diverting the deposit's activities to other bank accounts or entities.

Review of the deposit slips and the related checks will indicate the source of the deposits, such as payments from customers' loans, transfers from other bank accounts, or wire transfers from other entities. The customers' checks will usually indicate the address of the customers which allows you to obtain additional information to reconstruct the records, such as:

- Sales to this customer which normally includes specifics as to what was sold
- Payment history of products sold
- Freight companies used

Customers can also offer additional information that can be used in the reconstruction process, such as:

- Other banks the company may have used
- Employees of the target company (i.e., accounts payable personnel, bookkeepers, controllers)

- Related companies of the target company
- Other business locations

Both incoming and outgoing wire transfers should be analyzed to determine the source of the transfer. The investigation can be expanded to obtain the documentation pertaining to the transfer to further analyze it as to its nature and propriety (i.e., are funds being wired to other entities under the control of the target company or its management).

Analyze the bank statements for excessive purchase of travelers' checks, cashiers' checks, and so forth which may be an indication of diverting funds from the company. The deposit slips and perhaps the bank statements will differentiate between cash deposits and checks. If the cash deposits are either below or in excess of what is expected in the industry, it may warrant further analysis.

Cancelled checks can offer a wealth of information. Cancelled checks may indicate transfers to other bank accounts which, once found, can also be requested by subpoena. The review of cancelled checks can indicate payments to outside third parties that also may be able to supply you information, such as payments to:

- Attorneys
- Accountants
- Utility companies
- Vendors
- Lessors
- Financial institutions
- Leasing companies
- Insurance companies
- Telephone companies
- Freight companies
- Brokers

Information contained on a cancelled check is often overlooked. For example, a cancelled check made payable to a telephone company will contain the telephone number of the customer on the back of the check. (For security reasons, additional numbers typically are included to break up the sequence of the telephone number.) Similarly, a customer's account number will appear on the back of the cancelled check. This is relevant because payments may be made for telephone numbers and utilities for premises unknown to you at the time. Discovering previously unknown premises can expand an investigation to question such areas as:

- Possible diversion of inventory to this premise
- Possible other companies owned or under the control of the target
- Other third parties that can be interviewed, such as landlords, employees, etc.

An investigation and review of telephone bills will indicate telephone numbers to third parties that may also be a source of information, such as to:

- Vendors
- Customers
- Accountants
- Lawyers
- Financial institutions
- Insurance brokers
- Employees

The names of these parties can be obtained from numerous Internet search engines that cross link telephone numbers and names.

Records are not always destroyed or stolen. Although the books and records and other forms of business documents that will be necessary to review depend on the specific investigation, the following serves as a guide to the records you may likely request in a financial investigation.

D. Checklists of records

1. Books of original entry—business records

- General ledgers
- General journals
- Cash disbursements journals
- Cash receipts journals
- Purchase journals

- Payroll journals—including Social Security numbers and addresses of all employees (both current and former)
- Sales journals
- Inventory records (perpetual and otherwise)
- Schedule of fixed assets and depreciation
- Payroll records, including W-2s and quarterly reports
- Returned W-2s
- Checkbook stubs
- Subsidiary ledgers
- Payroll cards
- Any other books of original entry which may be maintained
- All financial records and documentation supporting the entries in the above mentioned books of account
- All diaries
- List and explanation of all records maintained in archives or other storage facilities

2. Other business records

- Copies of all financial statements (both internally generated and those prepared by independent accountants) for both interim and annual periods
- Copies of all forecasts, projections, budgets, proposals, business plans, or business strategies
- Opinions and reports, whether issued final or draft form of all consultants, financial advisors, or other professionals
- Copies of all business plans
- Complete bank statements (including canceled checks, deposit slips, bank memos, and wire transfers) for the period
- All savings accounts, money market accounts, and certificates of deposit
- Petty cash vouchers and receipts
- Schedules of aged accounts receivable schedules and ledgers
- Listing of all major accounts receivable write-offs
- Customer addresses and names
- Credit granting files
- Shipping records

- Sales invoices, including purchase orders and bills of lading
- Documents showing receipt of goods, etc.
- Log and copy of all telex, telegrams, or facsimile transactions
- Original and amended federal and state tax returns; including all schedules and attachments thereto; copies of any revenue agent's reports issued in connection therewith and all Internal Revenue Service and state and city tax correspondence
- Schedules of investments in marketable securities and brokerage statements in support thereof
- Original paid and unpaid bills
- Schedule of credit cards held and copies of all credit card invoices and charges in connection therewith
- Cellular phone bills
- Telephone records (including long-distance)
- Memos, outlines, summaries, abstracts, reports, and records of personal or telephone conversations
- Schedules of aged accounts payable schedules and ledgers
- Approved vendor list
- Details concerning business borrowings and lines of credit, including loan agreements and submissions to obtain credit
- Lawsuits for or against the company
- List of all related or affiliated companies, joint ventures, or other forms of entity
- All 1099s and back-up for payment of services
- Copies of any Current Transaction Reports (Form 4789)
- Detail on all patents, copyrights, and trademarks owned or pending
- Detail on all intellectual property owned
- Detail on all other intangibles owned or pending
- Business correspondence, interoffice memos or notes
- Copies of all work papers, correspondence, notes, memos, or other form of communication made with consultants or other professionals
- Reports and other writings given to any financial institution
- Listing and copies of all appraisals
- Copies of all valuations of the company or any division or profit center of the company

- Personnel files (current and former)
- Schedule of insurance and all insurance policies (including cash surrender value of officers' life insurance and loans payable thereon)
- Stock registers
- Corporate minutes
- Board of directors' minutes
- Copies of all accountants' work papers including, but not limited to, working trial balances, adjusting journal entries and account analyses in support of all financial statements and tax returns, permanent files correspondence, notes, memos, or other form of communication made between the parties
- Listing of all safe deposit boxes and any record as to entry
- History and copy of all press releases
- Copies of all marketing plans
- Brochures and pamphlets
- Market studies
- Sales and marketing reports

3. Agreements

- Partnership agreements, shareholder agreements, and amendments
- Buy-sell agreements and amendments
- All guarantee/cross guarantee arrangements
- Employment contracts
- Consulting agreements
- Management fee agreements
- License agreements
- Commission agreements
- Royalty agreements
- Deferred compensation arrangements and detail on all unpaid or deferred wages
- Retirement plan documents and retirement and benefit plan financial records
- Leases (as lessor and lessee)
- Bonus agreements

- Severance pay agreements
- Detail on all agreements and matters in which the company is contingently liable
- Any contractual obligation whereby the company is committed to purchase assets other than in the normal course of business
- Any memo, letter, note, contract, or other form of documentation concerning the sale of the assets of the company other than in the normal course of business
- All contracts with customers, vendors, or subcontractors

4. Computer and electronic files

- E-mail, voice mail, electronically created or recorded documents
- Machine-sensible data, data set names of all files (DSNs) (tapes and disks)
- Electronically stored listing of documents stored such as microfiche, microfilm, optical disks, laser disks, computer output microfilm (COM), computer output laser disk (COLD) documents
- System documentation (flowcharts, manuals, narratives)
- Program documentation (flowcharts, manuals, narratives)
- Archival copies of machine-sensible data or electronically stored documents
- Documents logically deleted, but not physically erased
- Actual hardware and software (i.e., DBMS software—original version, and all updates) that have been used to recall or store documents if current system cannot process and retrieve
- Inventory and explanation of system program, operations and user manuals of all computer applications (records management documentation and internal control documentation of off-site locations)
- Computer hard drives, software, and passwords
- Other data including, but not limited to, voice mail, dictation, transcripts, e-mail or telephone records or any information contained in any computer, electronic, digital or diskette al-

though not yet printed or delivered in tangible form in your possession, custody, or control of any employee, officer, director, agent, partner, stockholder, or any other person purporting to act on behalf of the plaintiff or defendant, or any entity controlled, directly or indirectly, or common ownership or control with the plaintiff or defendant.

5. Personal books and records

- Original and amended federal and state tax returns, including all schedules and attachments; copies of any revenue agent's reports issued in connection therewith and all documents used in preparation of the returns and all Internal Revenue Service correspondence
- Checking and savings accounts statements
- Cancelled checks, deposit slips
- Brokerage statements and schedule of securities owned
- Partnership tax returns and Forms K-1
- Subchapter S returns and K-1s
- Insurance policies (including home owners) and cash surrender value thereon
- Personal financial statements and all documentation used to prepare statement
- Checkbook registers
- Copies of any financial statements submitted to any bank or lending institution
- Details of real estate and other assets (e.g., automobiles) owned and closing statements (invoices, registrations, etc.) in support thereof; current fair market appraisals
- Detail as to all leases as either a lessor or lessee
- Schedule of tax-free securities held at any time during the defined period
- Schedule of personal credit cards held and copies of invoices received from issuer of card and documents reflecting payment on account
- History of all safe deposit boxes and any record as to entry
- Credit and loan applications

- Regarding any matrimonial actions, copies of all case information statements, filed
- Diaries
- Copy of all employment and consulting contracts
- Detail on all bonus agreements
- Detail on all severance pay agreements
- Access to all legal bills
- Access to wills and all codicils
- All estate and gift tax returns in which the subject is donor or donee
- Names and addresses of all financial planners retained
- Names and addresses of all insurance brokers and companies retained
- Names and addresses of all attorneys retained
- Names and addresses of all accountants retained
- Names and addresses of all travel agents used
- Access to all computer hard drives, software and passwords
- All documentation relating to all IRAs (past and present)
- All documentation relating to all Keoghs (past and present)
- All documentation relating to all savings plans, profit sharing plans and pension plans (qualified and unqualified)
- All documentation relating to all deferred compensation agreements
- All documentation relating to any stock option or bonus plans
- Detail on all pending lawsuits
- Detail on all lawsuits in which the subject was plaintiff or defendant
- Documentation on all agreements in which the subject is a guarantor
- Documentation on all agreements in which the subject was continently liable
- Information as to all business entities either owned directly or indirectly
- Access to all business agreements and amendments
- Access to all stockholder agreements and amendments
- All telephone and cellular phone bills

12.3 Common Scams Perpetrated Against Companies

The difficulty in detecting certain fraudulent scams perpetrated against a company, such as on-book schemes,[2] is that fraudulent transactions are recorded in the books and records in a similar manner as normal business transactions. The books and records are not color coded to signify fraudulent transactions. To prevent detection, perpetrators will disguise fraudulent transactions in the books and records by recording the transactions as if they were conducted in the normal course of business.

The following are examples of various scams wherein the perpetrator attempts to legitimize the theft in the books and records by recording them as if they were paid in the normal course of business.

A. Fictitious employees

1. Overview

Payments to fictitious employees are scams whereby funds are paid by a company under the pretense that the payments represent legitimate payroll to employees. However, the payments made are not to legitimate employees but to fictitious employees for services never rendered. Fictitious employees are also commonly referred to as "ghost" or "phantom" employees. This scam can be very difficult to investigate, as it may not become suspected until years after it has been perpetrated. Also, the investigation may be restricted to only the review of available records, as the company may no longer be in business and the location of legitimate employees to interview may not be known.

An effective investigative procedure employed to detect this scam includes identifying atypical transactions associated with payroll payments. Since fictitious employees do not exist, the payments normally have predictable identifying characteristics that differ from legitimate payroll payments.

Case Study 2: The Case of the "Terminated Employee"

John Jones, CPA, was controller for a substantial subsidiary of a multinational company. The subsidiary could at any time have between 350 and 500 employees. Although this company was a publicly traded company, the subsidiary was not considered material to the overall financial activity of the parent company and its other subsidiaries. It was not normally audited by the company's outside certified public accountants, so the company's internal audit department was likewise rather lax since this subsidiary was not considered material.

The scam started quite by accident. The normal procedure regarding the issuance of payroll checks employed by the company was that all payroll checks would be delivered to the controller who would then distribute the checks to the appropriate department head for delivery to the employees. On sorting the checks by department, the controller recognized a check that was issued to an employee who was terminated the prior payroll period. After some thought, the controller, who felt he had been underpaid for quite some time, took the check of the terminated employee and cashed it at the company's bank. This was a common practice and the bank typically accommodated this service.

The controller did not notify the payroll department of this oversight and continued to cash the checks of this "terminated employee" for several months until the controller accepted another job offer.

The controller felt confident that the theft of this employee's payroll checks could never be found. His rationale was that the amount was insignificant and, upon his departure from the company, he corrected the payroll department's oversight so no additional checks would be issued to this former employee. However, as fate would have it, the fraud was in fact discovered. How?

The terminated employee, upon receipt of his annual W-2 form (which discloses gross payroll), realized that the total W-2 wages were in excess of the total shown on his last payroll stub from the company. (The payroll stub also disclosed gross wages to date in addition to the weekly salary.) As the terminated employee did not want to file an incorrect tax return and pay more taxes than he owed, he contacted the payroll department and was informed that they would review their records. The review showed that there was a dual endorsement with the controller's name on these checks. Once confronted, the former controller admitted to the theft.

Fictitious employee scams can be even more complex and can involve employees who, in fact, do not exist—as the following will show.

Case Study 3: The Employee Who Never Existed

Louie Lunk, a controller for a midsize company, thought he could commit the perfect crime. After all, he was a controller of a company where he exercised significant management control, generally without supervision and oversight. The owners were far removed from the financial aspects of the company and were more concerned with sales. Louie Lunk had authority to hire and fire employees as he deemed necessary and was also in charge of payroll and disbursement of checks. Realizing that there was no separation of duties and that internal control was weak, Louie devised a scheme wherein he would create a "fictitious employee" and take the funds for himself. Everything was in place. Louie made sure the required W-4 forms (indicating the amount of withholding per paycheck) as well as an employee application, etc. were in the file. This was so easy Louie created a second "phantom employee." Again, he crossed his i's and dotted his t's and made sure all appropriate payroll and internal forms were completed. In the event that the outside accounting firm requested to look at the W-4s, etc., they were on file. However, Louie's luck was short-lived and the scam was uncovered quite by accident. How was the scam detected?

Although the internal controls were weak, the owners did routinely open the mail and then ultimately distributed the mail to the appropriate employees in the company. However, they always placed great importance on any correspondence from any taxing authority. The mistake Louie Lunk made was simple. When he created the "phantom employees," he assigned the employees Social Security numbers that were never issued. Because Social Security numbers are required to be reported on most payroll tax forms, the invalid numbers were questioned by the Internal Revenue Service, and the matter was investigated by an outside accounting firm at the direction of the owners. Upon review of the documents, and discussions with Louie Lunk, it became obvious what had happened. Louie Lunk could not explain why the fictitious employee checks were endorsed by him and deposited in his personal bank account.

Social Security numbers are not random numbers issued by the Social Security Administration (SSA), but are issued in a manner to identify the state of issuance and approximate time of issuance.

The first three digits of a social security number are referred to as the area number. For example, the digits 316 to 361 are Social Security numbers issued from the State of Illinois, the digits 135 to 158 represent the Social Security numbers issued from the State of New Jersey and so on. Generally, the Social Security numbers begin with the digits 1-6 and in some rare circumstances, with a 7. It is anticipated the 800 numbers will not begin until sometime in the twenty-first century. The 700 digits were reserved for railroad employees and were discontinued in 1963.[3]

The fourth and fifth digits are referred to as the group numbers and are not assigned by the SSA in consecutive order. The SSA does publish a list indicating the highest group issued for the fourth and fifth digits.

To combat and minimize the effectiveness of fraudulent Social Security cards, those issued subsequent to October 31, 1983, contain primary anti-counterfeiting measures.[4] The cards contain three kinds of printing, microprinting, offset printing, and intaglio. The microprinting is so small that it is not possible to reproduce it on copying machines or even computer printers. Microprinting is used on the signature line on the card that reads "Social Security Administration." The offset printing leaves a slightly raised impression of the card in the word signature. Intaglio printing causes a slight emboss effect on the card which can be distinguished by sight and feel.

Also, the front side of the social security card uses a security font similar to those used by safety checks. The word "void" appears repeatedly and it is obscured by the marbling effect of the document.

2. Other characteristics of fictitious employee scams

a. Incorrect tax withholding. In typical fictitious employee scams, the fictitious employees do not file income tax returns. As such, the income tax withholdings, such as the federal withholding tax and state income taxes will be a minimal amount or zero. The withholding taxes should be reviewed and compared to what would be withheld by a legitimate employee based on the tax status and number of exemptions. Significant differences should then be investigated further.

b. Review optional withholdings. Also common in fictitious employee scams is the fact that since the employees do not exist, there is no reason for optional withholdings to be withheld from payroll, such as withholdings for:

- Savings plans
- 401K plans
- Profit sharing plans

- Pension plans, etc.
- Health care insurance

Similar to the above, employees with no such withholdings should be identified for further investigation.

c. Other procedures. Other investigative procedures that should be considered are as follows:

- Identify employees who did not take vacations. Generally, employees take vacations at some time during the year. Obviously there is no need for a fictitious employee to do so.
- Identify employees with either a post office or mail-drop address. Some perpetrators may not use a residence address.
- Identify and investigate employees with the same addresses as other employees, past and present.
- Identify and investigate employees with the same telephone numbers as other employees.
- Review cancelled payroll checks to determine whether they were cashed or deposited. If the checks are cashed, then how does the employee pay for expenses normally paid by check, such as telephone, insurance, and utilities? Although some people do not have checking accounts and pay such expenses by money order, most do not.
- Request and investigate all returned W-2 forms. As discussed previously, although fictitious employees do not file tax returns, they are reported in the books and records as if they were legitimate employees. As such, they would appear in the tax filings, which would include a Form W-2 that indicates their address. If the address is bogus, then the W-2 will be returned by the postal service to the employer.
- Review cancelled checks for unusual endorsements (i.e., second endorsements by other employees or other unknown persons).

d. Pertinent records. In investigating this scam, the following records should be obtained:

- Payroll journals
- Time records
- Payroll tax returns including W-2s
- Returned W-2s
- Personnel folders
- W-4s
- Cancelled payroll checks
- List of employees (former and current) indicating names, Social Security numbers, addresses and telephone numbers

B. Fictitious vendor scams

1. Overview

Fictitious vendor scams generally involve the payment to a nonexistent vendor for goods never received or services never rendered. Fictitious vendor scams are commonly perpetrated in bankruptcy fraud, employee embezzlements, against companies with high a concentration of absentee management, and by those with the ability to override existing internal controls such as partners, controllers, bookkeepers, and other financial employees. This scam attempts to legitimize transactions conducted in the ordinary course of business and with the proper fraudulent documentation and offers the "appearance of legitimacy" to the transaction.

The following illustrates a typical fictitious vendor scam.

A company in the ordinary course of business may purchase inventory product used in its operations. An employee in a position of control and trust, such as a controller, may independently or in collusion with other employees submit fictitious invoices for payment to the company. The invoice is approved internally for payment by the employee perpetrating the fraud. The fraudulent disbursement is classified in the books and records as a "legitimate expense." This is a simple example, yet not uncommon.

Some of the forensic techniques used to identify fictitious vendor scams are:

- Identify new suppliers used by the company. The investigation should involve inquiries to determine the following:
- Who authorized the vendor?
- When was the vendor authorized?
- Specifically, what types of goods or services were purchased from this vendor?
- Were the goods and services typically used in the business?
- Were they of the same quality as other vendors goods and services?
- Were the goods or services required at the time of purchase?
- Who authorized payment?
- Was the employee who authorized the payment in the position to override existing internal controls, or possibly in collusion with other employees?
- Were payments made to the vendor in the normal course of business (i.e., were the payments made faster than the company's normal payment terms)?
- Are there vendors with similar names such as Ajax Company, Inc., and Ajax, Incorporated? (It is not unusual that fictitious vendor names are similar to existing vendors utilizing similar invoices and logos so they cannot be differentiated.) The investigation should also inquire into companies with alphabet company names such as ABC, Inc., or the XYZ Corporation or other similar nebulous names that are unusual in the ordinary course of business.

2. Techniques for identifying fictitious invoices

The invoice used by the perpetrators in fictitious vendor scams is critical to the scam's success and, to avoid detection, must be indistinguishable from legitimate invoices. Perpetrators usually will take extreme care to make sure that the invoices, on their face, look legitimate. If the invoice that has been used to perpetrate the scam is indistinguishable from a legitimate invoice, the following investigative techniques can be used in an attempt to identify fictitious vendors.

Investigate vendors who use a post office or mail-drop address. A mail-drop address is nothing more than a fancy word for a P.O. box, the main distinction being that the mailing address is labeled as a "suite."

Various databases are available to determine if such addresses are in fact mail-drop addresses. P.O. and mail-drop addresses are used when no legitimate business exists with a legitimate address.

Compare the addresses on the invoice with those of former and present employees. The obvious question is why would they be the same. To control the illicit funds, perpetrators may be inclined to direct the funds to their addresses.

Compare the telephone numbers that appear on the invoice to those of both former and present employees. Similar to the common addresses, it is highly unlikely that companies will transact business with vendors owned by employees. Many companies prohibit this, and some companies require conflict of interest forms to be prepared by the employees so the company has full knowledge of an employee's involvement in such a company.

Investigate a vendor's change of address. Did the company actually relocate or is the perpetrator using a different address (i.e., their personal address or a P.O. box) and minimizing, if not eliminating, business transactions with the legitimate vendor?

Is the invoice sequentially numbered? Most companies use sequentially numbered invoices, not only for internal control purpose, but also as a referencing mechanism for the transaction.

If the invoices are sequentially numbered, are the numbers appearing on the invoice too close in proximity to each other in comparison to the date of the transaction? By way of example, if invoice 0001 was issued in January of a particular year, is it reasonable that the invoice number 0002 or 0003 is the invoice number for a transaction conducted two, three, or four months later?

Do the invoices include charges such as sales tax, freight, handling charges, typically charged by other vendors in the normal course of business? If the invoices lack such charges, or appear abnormally high or low in comparison to normal transactions, investigate the reason why. Many perpetrators will not charge sales tax to avoid possible tax fraud charges that might result if the sales tax was paid to them and not remitted to the respective taxing authority.

Another investigative technique commonly overlooked in these types of scams is examining the invoice to see if it was folded. This is not to say that unfolded invoices are fraudulent, but typically invoices are folded and then placed in an envelope and mailed. If the invoice was not mailed, then how did it arrive at the company? Was it placed in the file by the perpetrator?

Compare the unit prices for the vendor being investigated with similar products purchased from other, unrelated vendors. If the unit prices varied too much from other vendors for the same product, why is this? When fictitious invoices are prepared, the arm's length competitive price for the product or service may be overlooked. Database software can offer the ability to sort transactions by product and vendor. That done, differences in unit prices can be identified and further investigated.

Are vendors on the approved vendor list? Many companies who have effective internal control policies and procedures and quality control policy procedures only authorize transactions with approved vendors. If this vendor is not on the approved vendor list, why not? Has there been a follow-up about who authorized the transaction and why wasn't it included in the approved vendor list?

Is the company registered with the secretary of state in the state in which it is allegedly conducting business? If not, why? If the company is not registered within the state to do business, then perhaps it is not a legitimate business. If it is registered, consider requesting the annual report, which typically indicates the names of the officers, directors, and registered agents. Are the officers and directors of the corporations, as listed on the annual report, company employees? Or, perhaps relatives of employees, using a wife's maiden name?

If possible, obtain the original cancelled checks and investigate the following. Was the check cashed? The obvious question is why would a vendor cash the check rather than depositing it in its bank account. A cashed check can be identified by a recognizable "cash code" used by the bank. Banks utilize a "cash code" which typically is a stamp that identifies a cashed check. Some banks will stamp the front of a check and others will stamp the back of the check. Cash codes may note "cashed check" or "foreign check cashed," or use another form of stamp so that a cashed check can be differentiated from a deposited one. If the cash code cannot be determined by examining the check, the bank's operations manager can interpret it. All cashed checks should be examined, but particular attention should be paid to any cashed at a local bank for an out-of-state vendor.

Review unusual endorsements, such as personal endorsements, as opposed to a check deposited in a business account.

Are the vendors listed in related trade publications? If not, why?

Consider calling the vendor using the telephone number as indicated on the invoice. It may be obvious it is not a business telephone number if, for example, a child answers or the voice mail box is personal.

Is the address used on the invoice on its face unusual, such as a manufacturing company located in a rural community versus an address in an industrial area? This can be determined by reviewing the zip codes appearing on the invoices.[5]

3. Review of accounting records

If a fictitious vendor scam is suspected, consideration should be given to reviewing the books and records to analyze the following.

Are perpetual inventory records updated for the items appearing on the invoice? Companies with good internal controls typically segregate receiving and shipping functions from the payment cycle. As such, in a fictitious vendor scheme, the inventory records would most likely not be updated.

If the perpetrator is able, either through collusion or the ability to override internal controls, to update inventory records for fictitious purchases, investigate unusually high differences between the actual inventory quantities from those appearing in the perpetual inventory records. When a scam is suspected, inventory observation counts should be conducted on a surprise basis rather than a predictable, routine basis (i.e., quarterly, semiannually, annually).

When records permit, investigate product lines with lower than expected turnover (the number of times inventory is sold during a defined period). If a fictitious purchase is entered in the perpetual inventory records, the recorded turnover could be substantially less than expected.

Does the amount of the inventory on hand per the inventory records appear to be excessive for this product? Inquire about the software the company uses, as it is possible the software can identify inventory quantities on hand in excess of normal amounts.

Analyze unusual swings in gross profit percentages (sales minus cost of sales = gross profit), which would identify excessive costs resulting in lower gross profits.

Many of these procedures can be accomplished using database software that allows the sorting and historical comparison of information. Such software can save a substantial amount of time.

Case Study 4: The Company That Never Existed

Bob Price, the owner of a very successful manufacturing company, in addition to being a successful business owner, was also a "people person" and, with reason, rewarded his employees for a job well done. Nothing came easy to Bob; he had worked since he was fifteen years old. Being in his early sixties, he felt now was a good time to relax, travel, and see the world. He felt comfortable, having built a very good organization with solid management support. Being a trustworthy person, Bob announced that he intended to become semiretired and placed his trust to run his company with his CFO, Jim Turner. Jim was an employee of the company for over twenty years. Although Jim was making a six-digit salary he was required to support his ex-wife and to pay for his two children's college education. Jim came up with what he felt was a great idea to ease the financial pressure on him. Since he ran the show, he was able to bypass internal controls. He incorporated and registered a company similar in name to a vendor the company actually did business with. He had invoices prepared and billed the company for fictitious goods. The company would then pay these bills and remit the payment to a P.O. box that he controlled.

As history tells us, when frauds are perpetrated, they generally increase over time as perpetrators feel safe and the "greed factor" takes over. How did Jim get caught? Jim made a very simple mistake, he took Bob Price for granted. Although Bob Price was a trusting employer, he was not a fool. He realized that, being an absentee owner, he needed additional assurance that his company would be operating efficiently and properly. He instructed his accountants who were experienced in fraud investigations to keep "an eye on the shop." In performing their agreed-upon task, the accountant noticed that the invoices from Jim's company were not folded. The logical question was, how did these invoices arrive at the company if they were not placed in an envelope and mailed? The accountant reviewed the cancelled checks in support of the payment of these invoices and found that they had been endorsed by the CFO. Once confronted with these facts, Jim had no alternative but to confess.

12.4 Investigating Front Company Scams

Front companies are established for a multitude of fraudulent reasons. They can be organized in order to divert funds from one company to another, to camouflage and disguise the ownership of a company, to avoid judgments or to circumvent covenants not to compete, as well as for concealing the existence of silent partners.

Although not limited to the following, the following front company scams will be discussed:

- The establishment of a front company to divert assets and funds from one entity to another.[6]
- The establishment of a front company to act as a successor to a predecessor company.[6]

A. Front companies organized to divert assets and funds

These types of front company scams are perpetrated to divert assets and income from one entity to another, to embezzle funds, as a mechanism to divert profits to silent partners, to steal from partners, and in bankruptcy frauds.[7] The following will illustrate the mechanics in these types of "front company" scams.

Payments will be made to the front companies designed to appear in the ordinary course of business, such as payments for services, purchases of inventory, or the rental or lease of premises or equipment. In such scams, the services may not be rendered nor the merchandise received; further, the rental and lease payments generally are either excessive or paid for nonexistent assets or premises.

It is not unusual that a multi-tier structure of other front companies will be organized. This is done to frustrate discovery and to camouflage the illicit transactions. The other front companies may be organized out of state or even off shore to further impede the discovery process, as the Figure 12.1 illustrates.

B. Front companies used to disguise a successor company

These types of front-company scams occur in situations where a "secondary company" is formed to conceal the continuation of a predecessor company. This may occur to avoid levies or to camouflage the continuation of

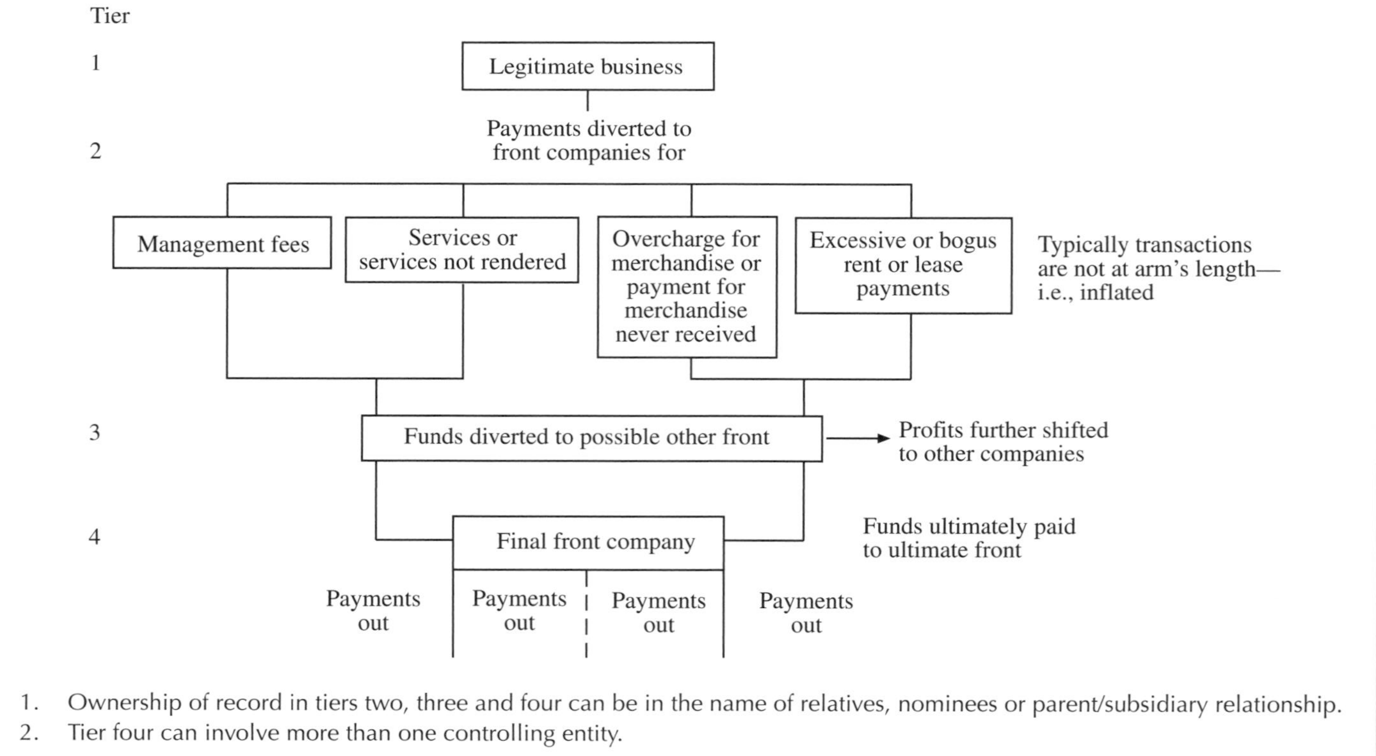

1. Ownership of record in tiers two, three and four can be in the name of relatives, nominees or parent/subsidiary relationship.
2. Tier four can involve more than one controlling entity.

Figure 12.1 *Typical front-company structure*

a company previously believed to be discontinued. The following, although not intended to be all-inclusive, are questions to consider in investigating whether a secondary company was formed, in effect, to be an alter ego; they attempt to identify a "link" to the predecessor company.

1. Organizational considerations

- Was the secondary company organized at or about the time the predecessor company was in financial trouble?
- How was the secondary company capitalized (i.e., funds directly from predecessor company or its stockholders)?
- Were the operations of the secondary company funded from the predecessors company's line of credit?
- Did the predecessor company indirectly fund the secondary company (e.g., guarantees, etc.)?
- Did the secondary company depend on the cash flow of the predecessor company for working capital?
- Is there common ownership of the entities?
- Are there common officers and directors?
- Was the secondary company formed at or about the time levies or liens were placed against the predecessor company?
- Were assets transferred from the predecessor company to the secondary company without observance of legal formalities?
- Were consolidated or combined financial statements prepared?
- Was the secondary company ever presented as a division or subsidiary or branch of the predecessor company?
- Is ownership of the secondary company questionable (i.e., owned by spouses, relatives, and other known business partners)?
- Did the companies maintain the appearance of separate companies in the public eye?
- Was the secondary company formed to avoid legal obligations?

2. Operational considerations

- Is the operation of the secondary company substantially identical to the predecessor company?
- Do the companies have business contacts that are substantially identical?
- Are there joint insurance policies (i.e., multi peril liability)?
- Are the companies required to use similar worker's compensation rates?
- Are the companies required to use similar rates for other types of insurance, such as liability insurance?
- Are there common characteristics between the companies that would not exist if they were not related companies, such as common:
  - Product lines
  - Price lists
  - Customers
  - Chart of accounts
  - Premises
  - Keys to premises
  - Computers
  - Computer software
  - Computer passwords
  - Employees
  - Policy manual
  - Vendors
  - Logos
  - Brochures
  - Catalogs
  - Telephone numbers
  - P.O. boxes
  - Registered agents
  - Banks
  - Lawyers
  - Accountants
  - Insurance agencies
  - Other professionals

  - Organizational chart
  - Advertising
  - Utilities
  - Leases
  - Dress standards of employees
- Were similar company policy manuals used?
- Were the employees of both companies compensated similarly, such as:
  - Bonus arrangements
  - Overtime policy
  - Employee review process
  - Vacation and holiday policies
  - Employee fringe benefits (i.e., profit sharing, pension, etc.)
  - Severance pay
  - Work day
  - Other perks (i.e., health care, auto allowances)
- Did unused vacation, sick pay and so on.(earned while employed by the predecessor company) carry over to the secondary company?
- Were common employees required to turn over automobiles supplied by predecessor company when employed by the secondary company?
- Did the secondary company use the predecessor company's equipment or vice versa?
- Was any rent charged?
  - Was rent charged at fair value?
  - Were contemporaneous records maintained indicating use of equipment?
- Was there intermingling of funds between the companies?
- Did the predecessor company pay debts or expenses of the secondary company (i.e., loans, vendors, payroll, utilities, rent, etc.)?
- Were customer payments of the predecessor company deposited in the secondary company's bank accounts?
- Was a common bank account used between the companies?

- If different bank accounts were used, are there similar signatories?
- Is there a common payroll paymaster?
- Did the predecessor company guarantee debt or cross guarantee any loans of the secondary company (or vice versa)?
- Was there any commingling of business functions and assets (pointing to substantive consolidation)?
- Does the level of commingling approach the level of "hopeless obscurity?"
- What is the degree of difficulty in segregating and ascertaining separate assets and liabilities of the companies? (Are the businesses so commingled that separating them would be virtually impossible or extremely costly?)
- Did the companies assume contracts or obligations for each other?
- Were nebulous (not logically calculated) expenses incurred between the companies such as:
  - Management fees
  - Consulting fees
  - Commissions
  - Sharing of common area expenses

3. Related-party transactions

Analyze related-party transactions to determine if the nature and amount of the transactions are critical to their operations, such as:

- Magnitude of intercompany loans and advances
- Were borrowings from the primary company repaid?
- Did the predecessor company have to borrow funds to fund intercompany borrowings?
- Were the loans interest bearing?
- Was interest charged at a fair rate?
- Were formal notes drafted?
- Was there collateral?
- Was a Uniform Commercial Code filed?
- What was purpose of intercompany loans (i.e., to fund payroll, working capital, etc.)?

- Quantify the extent of intercompany sales and purchases between the primary company and the secondary company. Why would these transactions be necessary?
- Were they at arm's length?
- In the absence of intercompany sales and other intercompany transactions, would the secondary company survive?
- Is there a legitimate business reason to have both companies, other than to siphon off profits?
- Are the companies named as either plaintiffs or codefendants in lawsuits?
- Were sales of assets between the companies consummated at fair market value (i.e., were sales made at amounts above or below fair market value)?
- Were transactions between the entities created by accounting "journal entries" rather than actual arm's length transactions (i.e., checks and deposits)?
- Were there leases between the predecessor company and the secondary company?
- What were the leases for?
- When were they entered into?
- Are terms typical to leases transacted between unrelated parties (i.e., were terms at arm's length)?
- Do the assets actually exist?

12.5 General Procedures

Analyze the following key ratios for several years and investigate major variations:

- Gross profit percentage (= sales minus cost of sales)
- Accounts receivable turnover (number of times accounts receivable collected during the years)
- Inventory turnover (number of times inventory sold during the year)
- Major fluctuations of income and expenses

Analyze significant changes in customer sales activity (develop a time line). Were the customers transferred to the secondary company?

Consider interviewing former and current employees to determine their knowledge and understanding of the "entities."

- Management
- Bookkeepers
- Controllers and assistant controllers
- Credit manager and assistants
- Billing clerks
- Secretaries and support staff
- Human resource departments
- Sales managers and.assistants
- Purchasing manager and assistants
- Inventory control personnel
- Shipping personnel
- Warehouse personnel
- Shop stewards
- Receptionist

Did these employees consider the two companies, in essence, to be the same? (Obtain details.)

12.6 Tax-Related Issues

Did the secondary company use the predecessor company's unemployment experience rate? (By state law, such as in New Jersey, a secondary company may be required to use the unemployment experience rate of the predecessor company.)

Are the companies considered related parties for federal and state income tax purposes?

Are the companies considered related, requiring all the employees to be included in employee benefit programs (e.g., pensions, profit sharing plans, etc.)?

Case Study 5: Alter Egos Used to Perpetuate a Bankruptcy Fraud?
In a case in which we were retained by the plaintiff's counsel, a bankruptcy fraud was perpetrated and the company's bank became the unsuspecting victim.

Company A, a successful manufacturing business, borrowed a substantial amount from their bank in order to expand their business into Canada using a newly created company. The expansion was not as successful as planned, partly due to the economy, but principally due to their incompetence. Company A reported substantial losses and, as a result, the bank's collateral base dissipated to virtually nothing. Company A claimed that the losses were incurred as a result of the economy and eventually closed the Canadian operation.

The bottom line was that the bank had no collateral to satisfy the loan obligation. Although incurring losses was not uncommon for companies during this time frame, the bank was not convinced that the losses were incurred for economic reasons rather than improprieties of management. The bank was also suspicious of the fact that Company A had established two new companies, B and C.

Based on the limited financial data supplied to the bank, it was clear that some financial relationship existed between Company A and Companies B and C. As a result, we were retained by the bank to investigate the financial transactions of the companies to determine whether the losses were due to valid economic reasons or actually due to a management scheme to dissipate the bank's collateral.

Our discovery was hampered because Company A did not submit to us the books and records we requested. Management claimed that the records either did not exist or were unavailable. This is not unusual in these situations. Accordingly, at least in the preliminary stages of discovery, we had to make use of the few records supplied. Requests for records not received need to be aggressively pursued as delays can be a telltale sign of fraud and mismanagement.

During depositions of the defendants, a number of interesting facts and conflicting accounts came to light. We discovered that Company A had used three different accounting firms during the last three years and was currently not using the services of an outside accounting firm at all. This was highly unusual. We also learned that a portion of one of the defendant's 50 percent interest in Company A was pledged to his mother as collateral for a loan, which was never repaid. In fact, the stockholder could not supply us with any proof that a loan was made by his mother.

In addition, we later discovered that Company A's other stockholder had been divorced for approximately three years, and that substantially all of his previously owned assets were now in the name of his ex-wife. It appeared that this could have been a divorce for convenience, since he had continued living with his ex-wife.

Also, according to the divorce agreement, which was obtained by our attorneys, he was obligated to pay substantial child support and alimony, which is not dischargeable in bankruptcy. In addition, his divorce agreement contained a stipulation providing for additional equitable distribution to his wife if it was subsequently determined the value of his interest in the companies was greater than stipulated in the divorce agreement. Based on the facts in this case, there was a basis to conclude this stockholder in effect planned to make himself "judgment proof."

Perhaps the most crucial aspect of the depositions was the two stockholders' conflicting accounts of how Company B was initially capitalized. One stockholder asserted that inventory from the Canadian operation was liquidated and, together with cash from this entity, was used to capitalize Company B. The second stockholder stated that half of the initial capitalization came from cash which he had kept in a safe in his home. While this was inconsistent with his earlier deposition, it also did not make sense from the standpoint of basic finance (i.e., leaving over $300,000 in a safe at home earning no interest at all).

Whichever version of the capitalization, if either, was accurate, it further did not agree with the initial bank statements of Company B which we obtained through third-party subpoena. According to the depositions and the tax returns, Company B was capitalized with approximately $600,000. The bank statements for their first three months of existence showed deposits substantially less than that amount.

Other matters which surfaced during the depositions and discovery included:

- The stockholders testified that no income or cash receipts belonging to Company A were ever deposited into Company B. Upon receipt of relevant bank statements and documentation, we proved that this statement was false.
- One of the stockholders claimed to have no recollection of a large tax refund check belonging to Company A, that was received and deposited into Company C.
- The stockholders claimed that they never personally guaranteed the bank loan, while bank documentation clearly indicated that they did.
- The stockholders had no reasonable explanation for the drastic decrease in Company A's gross profit percentages during its last

months of operation. Such a decrease was obviously caused by the diversion of cash and inventory to Companies B and C.

These inconsistencies and false statements certainly gave us and the bank feelings of uneasiness. Based on these depositions and evidence provided, including Company B's initial tax return, it appeared that Company B was capitalized solely with the assets of Company A. With the successful motions filed by the attorney in procuring other records of Company A or as the result of third-party subpoenas we were able to prove the following:

- Company C's ownership was identical to Company A's, and Company B was owned by Company C (parent-subsidiary). Company B's business operations were identical to Company A's, as were its customers, vendors, product catalogs, locations, telephone numbers and employees.
- Accounts receivable of Company A were collected and deposited into Company B's bank account, in effect diverting cash. The amount of cash diverted approximated the loan principal due the bank.
- A tax refund check belonging to Company A in the amount of $250,000 was received and deposited into Company C's bank account.
- Company A paid management fees to Company C. There was no written agreement between the two companies and no apparent business purpose for the fees. Inventory owned by Company A was transferred to Company B for no consideration. In fact, it appears that these assets were used partially to capitalize Company B.
- Company A finally filed a petition for bankruptcy protection, claiming that there were no assets available to satisfy the bank loan or other creditors' claims.

As a result of proving the diversion of assets, we were successful in horizontally "piercing the corporate veil" of Companies B and C. The companies were the alter egos of each other. Proving this is easier said than done and requires a pattern of occurrences and traits that clearly demonstrate the companies were organized and structured to be, in effect, the same company.

12.7 Kickbacks

Kickbacks are crimes against companies involving outside third parties in collusion with an inside employee (e.g., purchasing agents). Kickbacks are payments to influence a business decision, without the employer's knowledge and consent. They are considered by many to be the most pervasive commercial scam perpetrated against companies.

The following sections describe types of kickbacks perpetrated by employees against their employer

A. Inflated purchase price kickback

In this scheme, the purchasing agent in collusion with an outside vendor agrees to have its customers pay higher than competitive prices for products or services. The difference in price represents the illegal payment that is subsequently split between the purchasing agent and the outside vendor. These types of kickbacks occur generally when the approval process in the purchasing department is inadequate or absent, duties are not properly segregated, and competitive bids are not required. Figure 12.2 shows how this works.

- Purchasing agent normally has complete control over purchasing function
- Purchasing agent works in collusion with vendor and orders goods at an inflated price
- Purchasing agent and vendor split the "excess purchase price"

B. Deflated sales price kickback

In this situation, a salesperson that has discretion in establishing the sales price for a particular product or service to a customer is in collusion with the customer. The salesperson sells the products or services at a deflated sales price, and the difference between the reduced selling price and the normal selling price is split in an agreed percentage as a kickback between the salesperson and the customer. Figure 12.3 illustrates this.

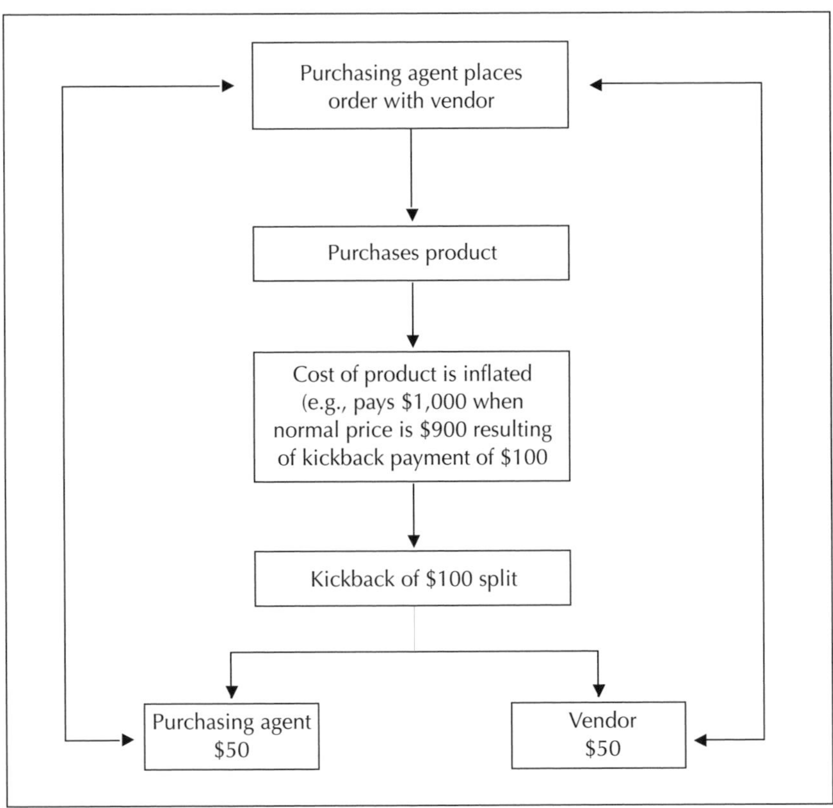

***Figure 12.2** Inflated purchase price kickback*

C. Bad debt write-off kickback

In this scheme, the salesperson generally has credit functions in addition to sales responsibilities, which is a major flaw in internal control structure. In his sales capacity, the employee makes a sale to the customer, who, in collusion with the employee, does not pay the amount due the company. Then in his or her credit and collection capacity, the employee allows the accounts receivable to be written off as a bad debt. The sales/credit representative receives a percentage of the write-off as a kickback payment, as shown in Figure 12.4.

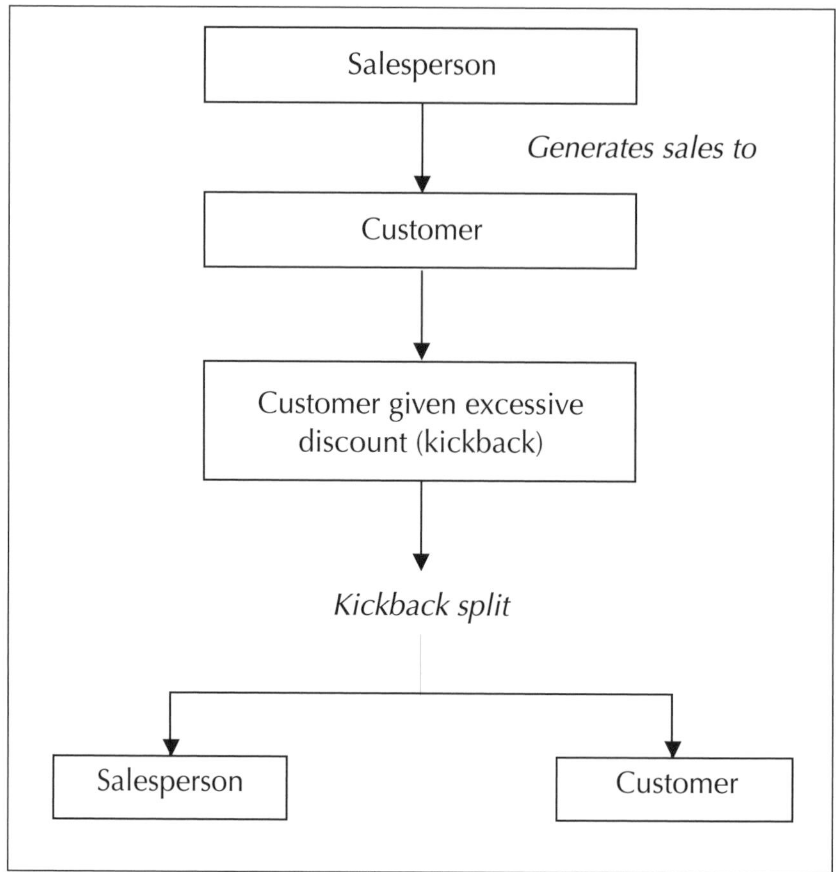

Figure 12.3 *Deflated sales price kickback*

D. "Red flags" for kickbacks

Because they are off-book schemes,[2] and the illegal payments do not directly appear on the company's books and records, kickbacks are often difficult to detect. The following are red flags associated with kickback scams:

- The company is experiencing lower gross profits after employing a new purchasing agent.
- The company is experiencing a lower gross profit and a higher bad debt write-off after employing a new credit manager.
- A new customer requires significantly higher write-offs.
- A new vendor produces significantly lower gross profits.

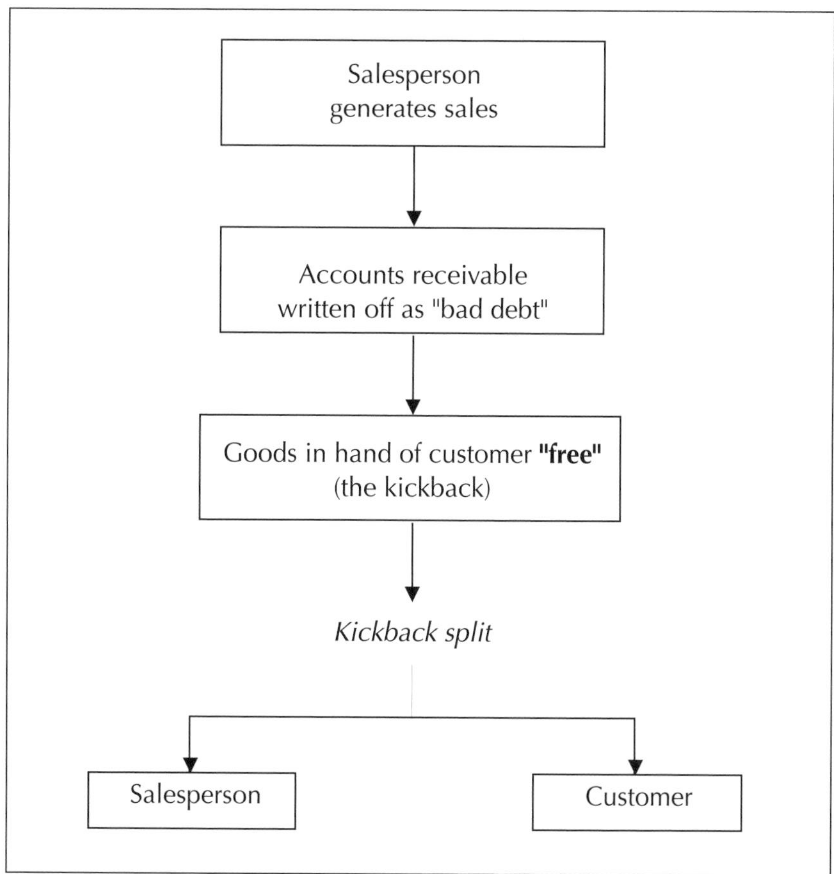

***Figure 12.4** Bad debt write-off kickback*

- The purchasing agent's personal spending habits have increased dramatically.
- Products are purchased at above market prices (e.g., pens cost the company $1.50 that retail for $0.89).
- The vendor is not on the employer's approved vendor list.
- Competitive bids are not received by the employee.
- Lower quality of goods received
- Bad service
- High rate of rejects
- Items purchased when not needed
- Excessive inventory of product

12.8 Checklists to Identify Potential Financial Motives to Commit Arson

Many people who commit financial crimes do so not only out of greed but also as the result of financial pressures such as a failing business, a drug or alcohol problem, and so forth. When funds are not readily available to them from their company, financial institution, or other creditors, they may commit arson to obtain funds from an insurance company. The following are investigative inquiries to consider in identifying potential financial motives to commit arson.[9]

A. Personal issues

Investigate the financial condition of the owner or owners to determine:

- Was the owner overextended financially? Was there a reduction in his or her asset position (i.e., forced to use cash or sell securities)?
- Did the owner guarantee debt of any other entities?
- Was the owner having marital difficulties or other personal problems (e.g., drugs or gambling)?
- Was the owner involved in any lawsuits in which the potential existed for financial damages being assessed?
- Did the business require the owner to inject additional funds to support working capital and cash flow?
- Did the owner have any past experiences with other failing business interests or ventures?
- Did the financial worth of the owner deteriorate over the last several years?
- As shown on financial statements and tax returns, were there unusual changed in net worth or the income stream?
- Is the owner a target of any criminal investigation such as tax fraud, money laundering, and so on?
- Is there any indication that the fire was used to camouflage a diversion of assets to other entities directly or indirectly controlled by the owner?
- Were there any anticipated or substantial uninsured medical costs?

Forms of documentation that can be reviewed to determine the above include:

- Personal income tax returns
- Business tax returns
- Business financial statements
- Personal financial statements
- Business books and records
- Personal bank statements (savings and checking)
- Credit card bills
- Loan applications and agreements
- Diaries
- Passports
- Partnership agreements
- Stockholder agreements
- Life insurance policies
- Medical records

B. Business issues to review

Did the company's financial condition deteriorate over the last several years as a result of:

- Poor profitability
- Poor cash flow
- Inability to obtain financing
- Excess inventory write-downs for obsolescencent or slow-moving stock
- Excessive bad debts from customers
- Lawsuits

Other questions to ask include:

- Was the fire a way to camouflage any fiduciary violations potentially facing the owner such as embezzlements, trust violations, unpaid payroll taxes, and unpaid sales taxes?

- Was there any loss of substantial customers over the last several years that significantly impaired the profitability of the company?
- Was the company's equipment adequate to fulfill production orders?
- If not, was the company unable to acquire the necessary equipment?
- In terms of the company's inventory, was a substantial part of the inventory unsalable? Indicators of unsalable inventory would be as follows:
  - Reduction in a company's inventory turnover (i.e., number of times inventory sold in a year)
  - Reduction in a company's gross profit percentage (sales minus cost of sales)
  - Excessive write downs of inventory values (i.e., to reduce to realizable value)
- Did the owner(s) personally guarantee any long-term leases or other long-term commitments?
- Did the owner(s) personally guarantee any company obligations such as:
  - Loan guarantees
  - Trade payables
  - Debt of others
  - Employment contracts
  - Buy/sell agreements
- Was there any substantial increase in insurance coverage immediately preceding the fire (i.e., one year or less)?
- Were there any other known entities in which the owner directly or indirectly had control of or maintained a financial interest in? If so, determine:
  - Were funds needed for these entities?
  - Were customer accounts diverted to this other entity?
  - Were customer accounts receivable payments diverted to this other entity?
  - Were transactions between entities at "arm's length" (i.e., did the company pay "premiums" for purchases to overinflate its value)?
  - Was there any recent change in ownership of known entities?
- Were any substantial levies or liens filed against the company?

C. Investigate diversions of substantial assets to the other entities

- Obtain complete history of all other known affiliations including:
  - Owners
  - Percentage of stock ownership
  - Changes in ownership and when change took place
  - Nature of business
  - Nature of customers
  - Taxable years of all entities
  - Tax status of all entities
  - Nature and amounts of any intercompany transactions between entities (i.e., sales, purchases, loans, guarantees, etc.)
- If property is owned by the company or the owner(s), is there significant cash flow to operate the property (i.e., did the owner(s) have to fund any cash flow short fall)?
- Were there any significant intercompany transactions that manipulated the bottom line to give the false impression that the company was profitable?
- Did the company acquire any substantial assets at or about the time of the fire? Determine if these acquisitions were at arm's length.
- Were there unfunded pension costs (i.e., pension or multi-employee pension plan)?
- Was there a threat of a strike that would have financially impaired the company?
- Was there any pending legislation that would cause the company to expend significant dollars (i.e., environmental issues)?

D. Other

- What books and records were maintained?
- Were the books and records manually prepared or computerized?
- Is there a backup to the computer hard drive (off site)?
- Who maintained the accounting records and where were they stored?
- Were physical inventories taken? When? By whom?
- Is there a detail accounting?

- Was it observed by an outside party, such as the accountant, outside inventory companies, etc.?
- Consider interviewing:
  - The bookkeeper and or controller
  - Former employees such as bookkeepers/controllers or other key employees (disgruntled employee are useful sources of information)
  - Bankers
  - External accountants
  - Attorneys
  - Insurance brokers
  - Financial advisors
- Is there a board of directors; if so obtain details.
- Who are the officers?
- Who was the registered agent?
- Was the company bonded; if so, by whom?
  - Was the bond revoked?
  - Was there a loss of bonding limits?
- Identify major suppliers and major customers to determine other possible related entities.
- Were budgets or projections ever prepared? If so, was a loss anticipated?
- Was the company in consistent non-sufficient funds positions?
- Was there any substantial decrease in the pattern of deposits at or about the time of the fire?
- Were there delinquent or no tax payments being made; if so, develop a time line.
- Were any substantial checks made payable to cash; if so, develop a time line.
- Were there frequent purchases of cashier's checks; if so, develop a time line.
- Were there credit difficulties with vendors and financial institutions?
- Were there any unusual events that occurred to the owner or the business at the approximate time of the fire (i.e., excessive purchases potentially moved off-site)?

- Were there any unusual dealings with suppliers or customers at or about the time of the fire (i.e., excessive purchases potentially moved off-site)?
- Was the business recently offered for sale and negotiations fell through?
- Were there any substantial withdrawals of funds or assets at or about the time of the fire?

The above are guides that can be used in an investigation that may lead to clues and evidence if the fire was, in fact, arson for profit.

12.9 Financial Statement Fraud

Financial statement fraud is the intentional misrepresentation of a company's financial position, results of operations, or disclosures in its financial statement. Financial statement fraud can either cause an overstatement or an understatement of the financial position or profits, depending on the reason the financial statements are fraudulently prepared.[10]

Similar to other frauds, financial statement frauds are perpetrated depending on the need of the perpetrator. For example, a public company needing to "meet street expectations" may inflate its income so as not to affect negatively the stock price and Wall Street's expectations. Other companies, in order to obtain financing, may overstate profits or face the risk of not obtaining the financing. Another reason to inflate earnings and net worth is to enable a company to comply with bank loan covenants. An often overlooked reason is to inflate assets and profits is to camouflage an embezzlement (i.e., diverted assets are replaced in the books and records with "fictitious assets").[10]

Alternatively, financial statement fraud may also result in an understatement of the financial position and profits. This may occur when a business partner understates profits to lower the buy-out of a partner or, as a result of a personal divorce action, a business owner wants to keep the value "low" so the spouse receives less in an equitable distribution of marital assets.

Financial statements take different forms. The common financial statements are a balance sheet, an income statement, and a statement of cash flows. When the financial statements are prepared under the accepted standard referred to as "Generally Accepted Accounting Principles" (GAAP), they also include explanatory or additional notes to the financial statements. In ordinary language, a balance sheet represents a financial snapshot of a company's assets, liabilities, and net worth at a point in time. For example, a balance sheet prepared as of December 31 would include the asset amounts, such as cash, accounts receivable, inventory, and liabilities, like accounts payable and bank debt, as of that date. The profit and loss statement reports the company's profits or loss for a specific period of time, such as three months, six months or an annual period. The statement of cash flows, similar to the profit and loss statement, is also prepared for specific periods of time. The cash flow statement reports a company's cash transactions pertaining to its operating, investing, and financing activities. All these statement are generally used by investors, investment bankers, and stockholders to analyze and interpret a company's financial strength and performance. Certainly, if the financial statements are materially misstated, incorrect conclusions will occur when they are relied upon.[11]

The manipulation of financial statements occurs when the amount of a company's assets, liabilities, and income are improperly reported on the financial statements. This can occur in many ways, such as by overstating or understating assets and by recording fictitious assets and liabilities. In a sense, fraudulent financial statements are "trick photography." That is, what you perceive you see is not necessarily reality.[11]

Similar to other financial frauds, there are also roadblocks in detecting financial statement fraud. As upper management typically perpetrates financial statement fraud, they are in a position to override existing internal controls and manipulate the accounting records.

There are six common techniques used to manipulate financial statements:[12]

1. Transactions with related parties
2. Fictitious revenues
3. Improper asset valuations
4. Timing differences
5. Concealed liabilities and expenses
6. Improper disclosures

A. Transactions with related parties

Related parties are defined under Statement of Financial Accounting Standards (SFAS) 57 as people with a relationship that offers the potential for transactions to be at less than arm's length, favorable treatment, or the ability to influence the outcome of events differently from that which might result in the absence of that relationship. SFAS 57 further states that related party transactions cannot be presumed to be at "arms length," as the requisite conditions of competitive, free market dealings may not exist. The importance of understanding the effect of related party transactions on financial statements is paramount. First, let's discuss the disclosure as mandated by SFAS 57. SFAS 57 requires that disclosures of material related party transactions include (1) the nature of the relationship, (2) a description of the transactions, (3) the dollar amounts of the transactions, and (4) amounts due from or to the related parties. This is necessary so third-party users of financial statements can determine the extent the related parties transactions have affected the financial statements. Without such disclosures, the ability to analyze a company's financial picture in comparison to similar companies and industries can be impaired.

Transactions with related parties can, and typically do, occur in the normal course of business. Typical transactions with related parties may include a landlord/tenant relationship, one company buying a product from another, or one performing a service for another. The question is, if they are typical and ordinary business transactions, why is it so important when analyzing the financial statements to identify them? The following example will illustrate:

To obtain additional financing, a company must report an increase in revenues and profits to the bank. The reality of the situation is that the company only had a mediocre year, far less than they projected. The officers know full well the bank will not be receptive to lend more funds with these results. So what do they do? Simple. A bogus sale is recorded to a related party, thereby increasing revenues and the bottom line. The financial statements now reflect the company's projected goals and everyone is happy. The company receives the additional funding and the bank increases its loan portfolio. Unfortunately, unbeknownst to them, the bank relied on financial statements that were materially misleading. What will happen next year? How will the financial statements be "fixed?" Predictably, bogus revenues have to be recorded again, and more than likely for a larger amount. Why? Similar to other type frauds (i.e., embezzlements), in the beginning the fraudster misappropriates a small amount in order to "test the system." If questioned, there is a chance they can "bluff their way through." If successful, misappropriations will, over time, increase as the greed factor takes control. This is also true in financial statement frauds, especially when a company must report continued growth and profits.

Typical fraudulent techniques used to "manipulate the bottom line" can include the following:

- Purchases and sales transactions between related parties to shift income and/or expenses.
- Purchases and sales between undisclosed related entities.
- Purchasing/selling assets between related entities at inflated values or vice versa.
- Bogus inter-company charges and allocation of expenses between entities.
- Overstating amounts due from affiliated or understating amounts due from affiliates.
- Other techniques used to confuse and cloud related party transactions include creating affiliates with different fiscal years and different accounting methods.

B. Fictitious revenues

Recording fictitious revenues is a common technique used to manipulate financial statements and can take different forms. It is estimated that over 50 percent of financial statement frauds result from fictitious revenues. For example, revenues can be inflated by recording fictitious sales to existing customers or to non-existent customers. Revenues can also be manipulated by the misapplication of accounting methods. For example, a company may prematurely record a sale before the earning process is complete. This will inflate not only sales but also the bottom line and net worth.

The following are various scams involving fictitious revenues:

- Sales being recorded to phantom or legitimate customers
- Swap transactions (i.e., round trip, circular). Two or more companies conspire to enhance payments/services for the purpose of inflating revenues (collusive).

- Parked inventory sales. Recording sales for ground shipment to a location controlled by seller to give appearance of a valid sale. Goods ultimately returned to warehouse.
- Falsification of documents.
- Channel stuffing. Overselling products with a hidden understanding that the customers will receive significant discounts at a later date or ability to return the product (collusive).
- Improper accounting method.
- Undisclosed side deals.
- Backdated contracts (i.e., deals—ability to cancel sale).

The following are some procedures that can be used to determine if fictitious revenues were recorded:

- Know the industry, why is the target company "outperforming the industry?"
- The documents requested for investigation are important. For example, accounts receivable aging schedules throughout a year should be examined, not just "year-end schedules." When reviewing these schedules:
  - Scrutinize old accounts. Are they legitimate? *Remember fictitious accounts will not be collected.*
  - Scrutinize accounts located overseas or other obscure locations.Are they legitimate?
  - Scrutinize unusual and larger items.
  - Analyze non-cash reductions to accounts receivable. Were adjustments posted to cover up the diversion of accounts receivable payments? Were credits issued to eliminate the "bogus receivables?"
- Review larger sales transactions at or around time of a reporting period (i.e., year end). Investigate their legitimacy. Were they "reversed" in a subsequent period?
- Were any sales to customers at or about time of a reporting period made with more favorable terms than previous sales? Why?
- Is there supporting documentation for sales? Are they originals or photocopies?

- Are there significant sales with new customers? Are the companies "real companies?"
- Are they related? Are the sales "real sales"?

C. Improper asset valuations

Improper asset valuations occur when assets are valued at either greater or less than their cost or net realizable value. This commonly occurs in valuations involving inventory, fixed assets, accounts receivable and business combinations. This is important to understand because if assets are overvalued or undervalued, there will generally be a corresponding overstatement or understatement to net income and net worth. For example, if a company's inventory or accounts receivable is overstated, its working capital, net income, and net worth will also be overstated.

The following are various methods used to manipulate the values for inventory and accounts receivable.

1. Inventory

Inventory values can be manipulated by falsifying actual quantities on hand, improper provisions for obsolete or slow moving inventory, and recording fictitious inventory.

Various questions that can be raised to assist in determining if inventory is properly valued are as follows:

- Does the Company actually own the inventory?
- Were the inventories physically counted? Who took the counts? When? Was it observed by an outside party (i.e., outside accountant)?
- Were costing policies consistent with prior periods?
- Do inventory quantities include consigned inventory or "bill and hold" items (as these are not owned by the Company)?
- Was there a proper cutoff in recording the purchase of inventory and the corresponding liabilities?
- Were adequate adjustments made properly to value inventory at its net realizable value?
- Were inventory values reduced to factor obsolescence and slow moving items?
- Were inventory values artificially overvalued by non-arms length transactions with related parties?

2. Accounts receivable

Accounts receivable represents trade credit granted to customers. If the accounts receivable are inflated so will the net income and net worth.

Some questions that can be raised concerning accounts receivable balances are as follows:[12]

- Was the earning process complete (i.e., was the accounts receivable and related income recorded prematurely)?
- Are there any major contingencies surrounding the sale such as acceptance of the product and return provisions?
- Are the accounts receivable amounts collectible and was a proper provision for bad debts made?
- Were the sales recorded in the proper period (i.e., were the books "kept open")?
- Are there any non-arms length receivables with related parties?

D. Timing differences

When financial statements are prepared it is essential that transactions are recorded in the proper period. This is referred to in accounting jargon as the "matching principle," i.e.," to properly match revenues in a period with the expenses in the same period." If the matching principle is not adhered to, an improper matching of revenues and expenses would occur, causing what is commonly referred to as an "improper cutoff." This could result in a material misrepresentation of the financial statements.

Examples of timing differences include prematurely recording future revenues in the current accounting period or recording expenses in the wrong period, (i.e., failure to record current costs and postpone recording to a subsequent reporting period).

The following would be the effect on financial statements when timing differences occur:

Manipulation	Income	Net Worth
Overstate Assets	Overstated	Overstated
Understate Assets	Understated	Understated
Overstate Liabilities	Understated	Understated
Understate Liabilities	Overstated	Overstated
Overstate Expenses	Understated	Understated

Understate Expenses	Overstated	Overstated
Premature Recognition of Income	Overstated	Overstated

E. Concealing liabilities and expenses

Another method used to manipulate financial statements is the failure to record liabilities and expenses. Concealing liabilities and expenses would cause both the balance sheet and income statement to be incorrect. General techniques used can result in fraudulently omitting liabilities and expenses, as follows:[14]

a. Failing to record liabilities and expenses, such as:
   - Inventory purchases
   - Settlement of lawsuits
   - Liabilities with related parties
   - Other material amount of expense
b. Reporting revenue rather than a liability when cash is received
c. Failing to record contingencies

F. Improper disclosures

Generally Accepted Accounting Principles require that when financial statements are prepared, material and relevant information regarding the economic affairs of a company be disclosed.In the opinion of many third party users of financial statements, disclosures are the most important element of financial statements.

Generally, improper disclosures result in the following areas:[15]

a. Liability omissions
b. Significant events
c. Management fraud
d. Related party transactions
e. Changes in accounting policy

Examples of improper disclosures would be the failure to disclose the following:[16]

a. Application of a non-GAAP accounting method

b. Failure to disclose potentially material items such as:
c. Related party transactions
d. Contingent liabilities
e. Commitments
f. Debt guarantees
g. Debt terms
h. Failure to disclose non-compliance with loans covenants
i. Departures in Generally Accepted Accounting Principles
j. Inconsistent treatments of accounting
k. policies and principles
l. Failure to disclose risk concentrations between customers, vendors, employees, and economic dependency

G. Conclusion

The detection of financial statement fraud can be very difficult and generally would not be detected by just reading the financial statements. The following are some suggestions when reading financial statements:

1. Ask the right questions. Do the financial statements make sense? Are the statements and notes confusing and difficult to understand and follow? Are the statements always historically late? Why? Are there frequent changes of accounting firms? Why?
2. Question what's happening in the industry in the same geographic area? Is the company you are reviewing outperforming the industry and the economy? Why?
3. What are the trends in this particular company? Does it make sense?

Endnotes

1. Association of Certified Fraud Examiners, *Report to the Nation on Occupational Fraud and Abuse.*

2. Association of Certified Fraud Examiners, *Fraud Examiners Manual.*

3. Kim, Leslie. The John Cook Financial Report, August/September 1996.

4. Special report: Detecting Counterfeit Social Security Cards Print Advising. Vindico, Inc. 1998.

5. Cramer, Michael. *The White Paper*.

6. DiPasquale, Robert. "Investigating Alter Egos." *Financial Fraud*, Warren Gorham & Lamont, 1998.

7. DiPasquale, Robert and Michael Cohenson. "The Many Faces of Bankruptcy Fraud." The White Paper, 1995.

8. DiPasquale, Robert. "Frauds Perpetrated against Companies by Third Parties." *Financial Fraud*. Warren Gorham & Lamont, 1998.

9. DiPasquale, Robert. "Financial Motives to Commit Arson." *Financial Fraud*. Warren Gorham & Lamont, 1998.

10 DiPasquale, Robert. "Financial Statement Fraud: Frequently Asked Questions," *Commerce*, January 2002.

11. DiPasquale, Robert. "Creative Accounting at Its Worst," 2003.

12. Certified Fraud Examiners, "Financial Statement Fraud."

13. See note 11.

14. See note 10.

15. Ibid.

16. See note 11.

Chapter 13

Net Worth Applications in Corporate Investigations

Al Ristuccia

Synopsis

13.1 Introduction

The use of net worth calculations in determining income by the Internal Revenue Service has long been used when sources of income earned by taxpayers under investigation have not been easily identified and quantified. The greatest example of the application of the net worth theory of proving income was the investigation and successful prosecution of Al Capone. Capone had long been suspected of being the overlord of the Chicago crime family during the prohibition years but no one could legally prove his involvement in criminal activity. He was insulated from the day-to-day criminal activity perpetrated by members of his gang. He did however reap the vast profits generated by the various illegal enterprises such as selling bootleg liquor, prostitution, illegal gambling, labor racketeering, etc.

The Internal Revenue Service was finally able successfully to investigate and cause Capone to be prosecuted and convicted of federal income tax violations for failing to file federal income tax returns. To prevail in these charges, the Internal Revenue Service had to prove that Capone had a duty to file income tax returns for the years that he did not file returns. The Internal Revenue Service had to show that Capone earned sufficient income to require him to file returns. Because all of Capone's income was generate by illegal activities and, by the very nature of this activity, was received in the form of cash, the Internal Revenue Service had to employ an "indirect method of proof" to document with legal sufficiency that Capone earned sufficient income in the years under investigation to require him to file income tax returns. The Internal Revenue Service employed the net worth method to document Capone's income. The Internal Revenue Service also bolstered the results of the net worth method of proof by also using the expenditures method of proof. The net worth method of proof involves documenting assets owned and subtracting from the value of these assets liabilities owed. The expenditure method involves tracing and documenting monies spent for everything including clothing, vacations, gambling, entertaining, etc. These expenditures usually include money spent for items that do not necessarily result in accumulated assets.

Mr. Capone had accumulated vast wealth, represented by business ownership, real property ownership, etc. The Internal Revenue Service went about to prove his interests in these assets, including a network of bank accounts that were vested in names of "straw men" and other "nominees". The difference between the value of the assets held by Capone and the money owed by Capone (if any) was his net worth. The increase in Capone's net worth from one year to the next is legally considered income. Non taxable items that could increase net worth had to be investigated and considered in the net worth calculation. These items could include insurance payouts, court settlements, inheritances, etc. However, I don't believe that the Internal Revenue investigators had these issues to contend with when they investigated Al Capone. When all was said and done, Al Capone was charged with and convicted of tax evasion for a six-year period. It was proved that he earned approximately $1,038,654 during those years. He was sentenced to serve eleven years in prison and assessed court costs and fines totaling $80,000.

The Internal Revenue Service has more recently used the net worth and expenditures method of proving income in connection with investigations of high-level drug traffickers. We know that drug transactions are not accomplished with the use of checks or credit cards. Cash is the medium of exchange, and this cash is then laundered and turned into assets for the drug lords. By virtue of the nature of the illicit drug business, it's very difficult to establish income using the direct method of proof; that is, having a witness or a group of witnesses testify to payments made to drug traffickers and to introduce into evidence checks issued to the drug traffickers in payment of the "product" supplied by the trafficker. Therefore, the only viable method to determine income for tax purposes is the net worth method, supported by the expenditures method.

You are probably wondering how all this relates to conducting corporate investigations. Very often those involved in corporate crimes such as vendor fraud (receiving kickbacks/bribes, employing phantom vendors, etc.), theft of corporate assets, sales of proprietary information (trade secrets) and products to competitors and others receive money for these deeds in a manner that cannot be easily traced, thus making it difficult to prove who committed the illicit acts. A net worth calculation can determine if these individuals are accumulating assets at a rate that is not consistent with their known income and therefore indicative of receiving income from other sources; possibly from illicit activities. As an example, a company can suspect that a key member of its management staff is receiving kickbacks from vendors to insure that the company continues to use those vendors despite higher costs and shoddy service. A standard overt investigation, including contacts with the vendors suspected of paying these kickbacks, fails to develop the relevant facts. If it can be proved that the suspected employee has increased his or her net worth over a period of time in amounts that cannot be supported by the reported income from the employer and that all other acceptable reasons (outside employment, inheritances, insurance payouts, court settlements, etc.) for this increase have been considered, you may be able to draw a nexus between the value of the above reflected illegal activities and the increase in the net worth of the suspected employee. This information can also form the basis for determining economic loss to the corporation as a result of the illegal activities from which judgment amounts can be calculated if civil litigation is undertaken by the corporation against the employee.

The net worth calculation can also be used in corporate espionage cases when investigating the company that is sponsoring the espionage activity. The net worth exercise will be much more involved and complicated because business assets and liabilities will be examined but the basic calculation is the same. Again, the results can also be used in calculating economic loss to the victim business and this could be used in the causes of action in a lawsuit and form the basis for judgment amounts to be calculated.

Several internal corporate investigations have been worked since the first edition of this book was published. The net worth calculation was applied in a couple of these cases to determine if there was potential for unaccounted income derived by the targets of these investigations. The theory used was that the likely source of the unaccounted income could be the bribes and kickbacks that the targets were alleged to have received. One of these matters will be detailed in section 13.7 of this chapter.

13.2 What Is Net Worth?

Simply put, net worth is the difference between what is owned and what is owed. If a person's only asset is a home, the net worth of this person can be determine by establishing the value of the home (usually reflected as the purchase price)[1] and subtracting from that value what this person owes on the home. As an example, Mr. Smith works as a purchasing agent for ABC Company. He is paid a yearly salary by ABC of $30,000. Mr. Smith buys a home for a purchase price of $100,000 and obtains a loan in the amount of $75,000 to facilitate the purchase of this home. If Mr. Smith has no other assets and no other liabilities, Mr. Smith has a net worth of $25,000. This example is overly simplistic because most people have more than one asset and they also have other liabilities. However, the basic equation, assets minus liabilities, is how net worth is calculated. Most individuals own homes and vehicles and have bank accounts and insurance policies with cash values. Most individuals also obtain loans to buy homes, vehicles, and other items. All assets and all liabilities must be considered in establishing the net worth of an individual.

Getting back to Mr. Smith, lets add to his list of assets by including a vehicle for which he paid $20,000; stocks for which he paid $10,000; a vacation home for which he paid $45,000. In addition, Mr. Smith owes $7,500 on his car and $20,000 on his vacation home. The net worth summary for Mr. Smith would look like Table 13.1.

Assets	Home	$100,000	
	Vehicle	20,000	
	Stocks	10,000	
	Vacation Home	45,000	
	Total Assets		$175,000
Liabilities	Home Mortgage	$ 75,000	
	Vehicle Loan	7,500	
	Vacation Home Loan	20,000	
	Total Liabilities		$102,500
Net Worth	Net worth is assets minus liabilities. Net worth is expressed on a given date.		$ 72,500

Table 13.1

13.3 What Are Assets?

Assets are items of value. Assets can include cash, real property, vehicles, boats, airplanes, jewelry, art, furniture, stocks, bonds, loans receivable, intellectual property (patents, trademarks, etc.). When considering the value of an asset for computing net worth to determine income, the asset is usually valued at cost; that is, what the owner paid for the asset. As an example, Mr. Smith purchased his home for $100,000 in 1995. The home may have a market value of $125,000 in 1999. When computing the net worth of Mr. Smith as of December 31, 1999 to determine income, the value of this home would be reflected as $100,000.

13.4 What Are Liabilities?

Liabilities, for net worth purposes, are financial obligations or debts. The mortgage on real property is a liability. The loan on a vehicle is a liability. Any debt owed is a liability. When valuing a liability for net worth computations, the value given the liability is what is owed at the time the net worth computation is done. As an example, if the net worth computation is for the period ending December 31, 1999, the values assigned to liabilities are as of December 31, 1999.

13.5 Net Worth versus Income

As previously stated, net worth is established as of a given date, usually at the end of a certain period of time such as the end of a calendar year (December 31) or the end of an established fiscal year (June 30). An increase in net worth from one year to the next is usually indicative of income earned. A decrease in net worth from one year to the next is usually indicative of negative income; that is, spending more than what is earned. There are exceptions to this and adjustments are made to the net worth computation to consider the exceptions.

Generally, an increase in net worth from one year to the next is reflective of income earned. If Mr. Smith had a net worth of $25,000 as of December 31, 1995, and a net worth of $72,500 as of December 31, 1996, Mr. Smith's net worth increased $47,500 during the one-year period. If there were no adjustments to be made to the net worth computations, it could be established that Mr. Smith had income in the amount of $47,500 in 1996.

One of the fundamental requirements in determining income through net worth computations is establishing a "starting point." A starting point is a moment in time when net worth can be established with certainty. The starting point must be a period prior to the first year that you are attempting to establish income. In the case of Mr. Smith, if 1999 is the first year for which income must be established, December 31, 1998, could be the starting point for net worth purposes; but it does not have to be. If you can only establish a starting point with certainty on December 31, 1996, you must compute net worth for all the years subsequent to 1996 so that an accurate base year can be established as a "starting point." In the case of Mr. Smith, perhaps he did not begin his illegal activities until 1999. Mr. Smith's net worth would have to be determined for 12/31/96, 12/31/97, and 12/31/98 so that an accurate increase in net worth can be computed from 12/31/98 (base year) to the year ending December 31, 1999.

13.6 Adjustments to the Net Worth Computation

After the basic net worth equation is computed (assets minus liabilities) certain adjustments must be made to the net worth computations to arrive at an accurate amount that could be considered unreported or unaccountable income. Keep in mind that the net worth method of proving unreported or unaccountable income is used because a direct method of proving unreported or unaccountable income could not be used for some reason. Therefore, adjustments to the net worth computations must be made to take into consideration such things as inheritances and large amounts of cash expenditures not made to accumulate assets. These adjustments to the net worth computation are called "below the line adjustment."

In order to make the net worth computation credible for the purpose of identifying unreported or unaccountable income the investigator must back out items that add to net worth but do not reflect unaccountable income. Those items can include inheritances, insurance and/or court settlements, gifts, cash hordes, etc. The investigator must also attempt to identify and add to the net worth computation expenditures that do not stick to the target, such as identifiable assets do. These expenditures could include expensive vacations, gambling expenditures, expenditures to maintain girlfriends or boyfriends, expensive gifts given to others, etc.

Let's assume that Mr. Smith has a girlfriend he helps support. The investigator documents that Mr. Smith pays the rent for his girlfriend's apartment. The rent is $750 per month. The investigator also discovers that Mr. Smith purchased an automobile for his girlfriend and the purchase price of this vehicle was $12,500. For the sake of our example, let's assume that these expenditures were made during 1999, the year that Mr. Smith is suspected of receiving approximately $33,000 cash from kickbacks from vendors. Let's also assume that during 1999 Mr. Smith received a $5,000 inheritance. Our net worth computation to identify kickback income for that year would look like Table 13.2.

We can assume that the "likely source" of the unaccountable income is kickbacks from vendors.

Net worth.12/31/99 (taken from the computation previously cited)			$72,500
Net worth.12/31/98 (Assumed base year)			22,500
Net worth increase during 1999			$50,000
1999 Adjustments to Net Worth			
Additions			
Girlfriends Apartment $750 x 12	$ 9,000		
Vehicle Purchase for Girlfriend	12,500	$21,500	
Reduction			
Inheritance		(5,000)	
Adjustment to 1999 Net Worth			16,500
1999 Income			$66,500
Accountable Income for 1999			(30,000)
Unaccountable Income for 1999			$ 33,500

Table 13.2

13.7 How to Apply to Corporate Investigations

The net worth method of proving unreported or unaccountable income is extremely complicated and therefore should only be used as a last resort in attempting to prove that a target of an investigation personally profited from his or her wrongdoings. This may be necessary to compute damages for civil judgment or restitution purposes. This method also should only be used when a target of an investigation receives cash as a result of his or her misdeeds. In our example of Mr. Smith receiving cash kickbacks from vendors, the net worth computation would be appropriate if we were unable to obtain cooperation from any or most of the vendors that were suspected of paying kickbacks to Mr. Smith and it was necessary to quantify what Mr. Smith earned from his unethical activities. This method of proving income can also be used when one company believes that a competitor has misappropriated trade secrets or other proprietary information. The basic computation is the same but determining the appropriate amounts would be much more involved and complicated when dealing with company assets, liabilities, and other financial information. Computing net worth increases to prove income for business entities would probably require the engagement of an accounting firm in addition to an investigator. The investigator can gather the facts and the accounting firm can make the computations and provide testimony as to the methods used to determine the values placed on the assets and liabilities.

In 2004 we completed an internal corporate investigation on behalf of a very large international retailer. Our investigation related to allegations that a high-ranking management official was receiving bribes and/or kickbacks to direct business to certain vendors. We discovered that the manager had extensive remodeling work done on his residence. This manager had the responsibility of retaining services of contractors on behalf of our client to make repairs to company stores. We were able to establish the value of the remodeling project on the target's residence by obtaining copies of building permits that reflected the estimated value of the remodeling. We also were able to determine the increase in the assessed value for property tax purposes of the residence due to the remodeling. When computing all of this information and preparing a net worth analysis, we were able to show that this individual somehow generated several hundred thousand dollars of unaccounted income. When confronted with this information, in addition to other information that we gathered through interviews, the target admitted to receiving money from certain vendors. The target also admitted that the remodeling project on this residence was accomplished, at no charge to him, by a contractor that also is retained to provide contracting services to our client. This target subsequently resigned from our client company and the contract for services with the offending contractor was not renewed.

In another investigation that did not relate to an internal corporate matter, we conducted a net worth exercise to show that an individual could not have acquired the assets that he acquired on his own. We were attempting to show that the funds to buy large commercial office buildings and other real property actually came from this target's brother. The brother was an international fraudster who swindled literally thousands of elderly Americans out of an estimated \$300 to \$400 million. Although this investigation is not on point with the subject of corporate investigations, the procedures used to calculate income were the same. We needed to prove that the fraudster used his brother to hide assets (real property) that were purchased with the proceeds of his fraudulent activities. This was rather easy to the extent that we were able to establish the "starting point" for our net worth calculation on the brother when the brother filed for bankruptcy about four years prior to when he began accumulating very expensive commercial buildings. We were able to show that the target of our net worth calculation was able to increase his net worth from approximately $0 to several million dollars in two years. Also, since the net worth target could not have accumulated the required funds to purchase the commercial buildings, we were able to show that the likely source of the funds to purchase the buildings was the fraudster brother. The fraudster used his brother's name to vest ownership interests in real property in an effort to hide the assets and thus avoid the satisfaction of inevitable judgments against him.

13.8 Summary

Net worth is assets minus liabilities. A very simple equation to state but very complicated to compute. Why use it? The net worth method of proving income may be the only way to show that an individual or business entity profited from misdeeds. This method of proving income has been upheld by the United States Supreme Court when contested by defendants in criminal income tax cases. The use of the net worth method can also point out to the court and juries that the target entity took extraordinary measures to hide misdeeds and the proceeds received as a result of the misdeeds.

The net worth method of proving income is a very powerful tool but also very expensive to use. It takes many investigative hours to identify and quantify assets, liabilities, expenditures, and other components to the net worth equation. The investigation must be significant enough and the client must be financially capable and willing to employ this investigative technique.

Endnotes

1. Assets are generally valued at cost when computing net worth for determining income. When computing net worth for other purposes, assets are valued at market value.

Part III

Types of Corporate Risks

Chapter 14

Environmental Business Risks: A Legal Investigator's Consultant Role

Larry R. Troxel, CLI, REA

Synopsis

14.1 Introduction

A company with a proactive environmental management program, or well-thought-out preventive measures, can wind up spending little compared to the bankruptable fortunes that can be levied to clean up its contaminated mess and force compliance with environmental law.

The purpose of this chapter is twofold: (1) to encourage the professional investigator to become an informed consultant to his or her corporate client, and (2) to offer some common sense that the investigator/consultant can share with the valued client.

14.2 The Usefulness of an Environmental Consultant: Four Examples

A dictionary reference defines a consultant as *1: one who consults with another, 2: one who gives professional advice or services: EXPERT.* Given this definition, what astute legal investigator has not served at some time as a consultant for a client? The investigator may have never considered being called a consultant, but in essence, he or she often is. In being so, the investigator shares expertise on how best to deal with, or overcome, an issue with the client, or perhaps, provide expert testimony. That expertise comes in many fields of study, which in this case is the knowledge of environmental management and regulatory compliance. The application of the indispensable commodity of common sense is always required.

Four typical situations in which the environmental consultant can assist the corporate client include the following:

1. Three employees of a chemical plant have complained several times to a foreman and a manager that they were concerned about having to breathe chemical fumes and have developed skin rashes. The employees ask that they be given better personal protection equipment or be reassigned to other jobs where they would not be exposed to the chemicals. The forty-year old plant has never changed its manufacturing processes and the employees are told to quit their "bellyachin'," go back to work or be fired. After all, the managers reason, no one else had ever complained or gotten sick.
2. A manufacturing facility is continually inspected by a tenacious regulatory inspector and is often levied fines for noncompliance of its hazardous materials and hazardous waste management program. The company is unknowingly and

rapidly creating what is referred to as an "environmental rap sheet" that can later be used against it in enforcement actions and criminal prosecution.

3. Corporate managers of an industrial plant are surprised early one morning by a multi-agency task force serving an inspection or search warrant on the facility. Throughout the day, the managers and officers stand by while enforcement investigators and regulatory inspectors go freely about the facility searching for files and seizing documents, obtaining soil and chemical samples throughout the facility, freely photographing plant operations, and interviewing many employees.
4. Company A became one of Corporation B's many subsidiaries when it was purchased in 1960. Corporation B, the parent company, soon selected all of A's board of directors and populated A's executive ranks with B officials. One of B's officials played a significant role in shaping A's environmental compliance policies. In the early 1970s B sold A, but not before it created substantial contamination at the site where it operated. In 1998, government prosecutors attempted to pierce B's corporate veil and to sue the company and its shareholders for the pollution created by Company A *thirty-five* years earlier.

14.3 Due Diligence

A. Introduction

Each of the above examples have actually occurred, and more than once. Presented below are ten guidelines for increasing corporate due diligence and minimizing the corporate clients' compliance risks. They can also help reduce civil and criminal liability as set forth in CERCLA (Comprehensive Environmental Response, Compensation and Liability Act, 42 U.S.C. Sec. 9601 et seq.) and RCRA (Resource Conservation and Recovery Act, 42 U.S.C. Sec. 6928 et seq.).

Due diligence is a nebulous legal standard that, in part, can be defined as that conduct, care, or attention that a reasonable person will exercise in a particular situation which is sufficient to avoid a claim of negligence. As consultants, we should convince the client that due diligence will significantly reduce the company's environmental business risks while increasing its reputation as being a good *environmental neighbor*. At the same time, the company will enjoy capital that it would otherwise spend defending itself.

B. Taking the necessary steps

1. Set up a due diligence file

Any conduct on the part of the company which demonstrates a sincere effort to maintain its facility in regulatory compliance should be well documented. Set up a personal file entitled *Due Diligence* in which all documentation is kept and preserved. This file is maintained by the environmental compliance or other corporate officers and will serve as a reference for all past due diligence, all compliance corrections and efforts, and all identified areas of potential concern.

2. Develop a policy statement

Develop a corporate environmental policy statement. It should set forth a well thought out statement of the company's policy concerning its environmental due diligence and compliance practices. Every employee of the company should have a copy, or access to one. Such a well-published and widely distributed policy will help demonstrate the company's concern and attention to being environmentally responsible, and to employee health and safety.

3. Conduct random inspections

Conduct random in-house inspections to ensure the enforcement of company policies. Such inspections, directed by the environmental manager or health and safety supervisor should be unannounced and performed in such a way as to simulate a regulatory inspection. Note in the due diligence file the time and place the inspection was performed and what was observed. A follow-up inspection should note improvements and changes, and it is important to always keep the inspection forms and notes together. Another benefit is that on-the-spot, in-house inspections will remind employees to be constantly aware of health and safety compliance.

4. Know your company's waste

Know the company's waste stream and where it goes. This includes knowing waste type, quantity, storage, transportation and disposal requirements. It is essential to identify all hazardous waste vendors, service companies, hazardous waste haulers and subcontractors, as well as knowing that each is in full compliance, with all required permits and certifications. Consideration should be given to alternative processing methods that can reduce the total amount of waste. This may lessen potential CERCLA liability or liability of subcontractors. Waste minimization equals risk minimization.

5. Conduct audits

Conduct independent annual environmental audits and make corrections wherever appropriate. The auditor should provide the company with recommendations and detailed correction notices. During the audit, surprise interviews of employees should be conducted to evaluate the type of information routinely given to regulatory inspectors. Also, auditing should include a review of the company's commercial general liability insurance policies for coverage of environmental issues. It is important to save hard copies of policies in which proof of past coverage can be demonstrated. Proof of well-timed and well-documented audits will impress regulatory inspectors.

6. Establish a hotline

Establish a hotline phone system between employees and the chief executive officer or plant manager. This should be readily accessible to plant personnel and available to disgruntled or concerned employees to anonymously vent concerns, problems and complaints. Use of the hotline phone system should be encouraged so that each complaint can receive attention and corrections where needed. The price and consequence of not having an open and problem-solving corporate attitude will be costly if the employee voices his concerns to regulatory and enforcement agencies instead.

7. Train your employees

Periodic training seminars for employees should include instruction on OSHA (Occupational Safety and Health Administration) guidelines, a reemphasis of the company's environmental statement policy, management training on how to conduct an in-house inspection, and what to do in the event of an execution of a regulatory inspection or search warrant at the facility. A thorough, detailed *Employee Training File* should always be updated and maintained next to the *Due Diligence File* as a ready reference.

14.4 Protective Measures

Determine in advance what company documents are privileged as attorney-client documents. These documents should be kept in a clearly labeled folder and maintained in a confidential file marked "Privileged and Confidential, Attorney-Client Communication." The client should rely on counsel's direction and suggestions as to what documents are privileged communications. Often, documents such as investigator and consultants' correspondence and reports can enjoy that privilege, depending on their content.

The company should join and remain active in an industry trade association. While an association can be a source of networking and social activity, more importantly it can often have an imposing presence and exert influence on critical legislation that is constantly evolving on environmental issues. By remaining active and supportive, individual members can encourage the association, and perhaps its lobbyist, to take a position that can greatly affect the regulations that impact the industry and perhaps save cost.

14.5 The Agency Visit or Inspection

A component of corporate training needs to include the appropriate responses in the event of an agency visit to the facility. Typically, most states have given environmental regulatory agencies the authority to enter and inspect the premises for compliance. However, training should be structured to identify regulatory authority, cover the ramifications of denying admittance to inspectors, develope procedures to respond to enforcement actions and search warrants, and guidelines about how only designated personnel should talk to inspectors and investigators.

Know the local, state, and federal agencies. It is often helpful to invite agency personnel to view the client's facility so they become familiar with the environmental compliance manager, and to understand the plant layout before a scheduled inspection or in case of an accident or emergency.

Having a professional and accommodating relationship with inspectors who regularly visit the plant will assist in passing the "attitude test" to which agencies are sensitive. A trained, designated corporate contact as a regulatory escort will help minimize the time that inspectors are on site by providing them with required documentation, access, and information necessary for them to complete their site visit. The in-house designee can sometimes mean the difference between regulatory headaches and an Excedrin® #10 relief. Usually, he or she is familiar with the inspector and conveys to the agency that the client's facility is a good and responsive industrial citizen.

14.6 Corporate Response Plan

On a few occasions, the corporation and its designee may be confronted with adversarial incidents, such as when enforcement investigators enter the premises and announce a surprise regulatory inspection or serve search warrants. Most often, the front office or gate guard notifies management that the agents have just entered the client's facility for an unannounced audit or inspection of the plant's manufacturing processes and waste management practices. In such an event, the client should activate its *corporate response plan*. With any number of variations, the plan should implement the following steps.

A. Agency meeting or screening

The company's gate guard or receptionist should initially confirm the identity of the agency investigators or inspectors and request that they sign the visitor's log with name, title, and time of arrival. Concurrently, the employee greeting the officials should alert the corporate representatives and the company's *agency response team* (ART), and then advise regulatory personnel that plant officials will meet with them shortly.

B. Agency conferencing

The ART, which should include the environmental compliance manager, a corporate officer and other key personnel knowledgeable in production processes and waste management, should meet and query the agency personnel before the plant area is entered. The ART members should have with them a note pad, a camera, a tape recorder, and a sampling kit capable of securing liquid and solid material samples. Questions the ART should ask and tape record include:

1. Request business cards or identity from each agency official
2. What is the purpose of the inspection or search warrant? (Be sure to obtain a copy of the warrant.)
3. What is the authority for the inspection?
4. What are the company's rights?
5. Whether the company or employee should have counsel present.
6. What parts of the plant do they intend to visit?
7. If they intend to collect samples, take photographs, copy documents, or conduct employee interviews (request split samples of any collected by the agency).
8. If the inspection or search warrant could be delayed until corporate counsel responds.

C. Notify corporate counsel

As soon as possible, corporate counsel should be notified, advised of the circumstances, and requested to respond. It is important that the counsel, after identifying himself to agency personnel, declares whom he represents, makes appropriate inquiries, counsels and advises the client, and observes the overall agency actions.

D. Media access

The ART should decline any request from members of the media to accompany the agency inspection or investigation team. The company's public relations representative, who should be informed as soon as possible of the circumstances, should address any response to the media.

E. Monitoring the inspection or search warrant process

If it is an inspection, ART members should attempt to accompany the inspectors wherever they may go in the facility.

If a search warrant is being levied, then ART members should stay close by, monitoring and documenting all that occurs. In either case, ART is not to interfere or impede agency personnel in performance of their duties.

Members of ART should record all conversations involving the inspectors or investigators, or at least should take extensive notes. General or innocuous questions can be answered, however all other questions should be deferred until the agency visit is concluded so that pending answers can be discussed and reviewed with counsel.

ART members should photograph all that the agency officials are photographing and copy each document that the agency copies. Further, duplicate or split samples should be obtained from all that the inspectors sample.

It is important that ART members take careful and thorough notes of those objects and areas that investigators inspect and visit and in which they may show particular interest.

If an apparent violation of environmental regulation or law is discovered by inspectors, ART members should not attempt to offer an explanation until they have had time to investigate and discuss the matter with corporate counsel.

F. Confidential and privileged documents

Where necessary, ART members should refuse to produce any arguably privileged document to inspectors until counsel has first reviewed that document. Certainly, attorney-client-privileged documents and correspondence should never be reproduced or seized by agency personnel.

Proprietary or trade secret documents also should never be produced unless counsel has a negotiated protective agreement with the inspectors. Whenever law enforcement is carrying out a court order (search warrant), they should know that attorney-client materials are normally prohibited from seizure.

G. Agency personnel-employee contacts

Whenever inspectors attempt to interview facility employees, every effort should be made by ART members to be present during those contacts and note all that is asked and answered. Whenever that is not possible, ART should debrief the employee(s) immediately following the completion of the inspection.

In almost every instance, investigators with a search warrant will attempt to interview as many plant employees as possible. No company personnel are under any obligation to submit to interviews other than to identify themselves. It is important that they understand that. Company officials, however, should not tell the employees not to talk to the inspectors or investigators.

Employees should not be subjected to unreasonable detention by agency personnel. Employees should know not to interfere with the search warrant process. ART members, or corporate counsel, are then to inquire if anyone at the facility will be arrested.

H. Closing conference

At the conclusion of the agency site visit, the ART should accompany the officials to the front gate or lobby.

In the case of the surprise inspection, ART members should ask agency personnel what they found, the significance of their findings, and what plan of action, if any, they intend to take.

Also, they should attempt to identify the laboratory the agency will use for sample analysis and request that a copy of the lab report be made available to the client.

Finally, officials should be asked to sign out on the visitor's log.

In the event the company just suffered a service of a search warrant, it is unlikely that investigators will be forthcoming with information about their intent, findings, and laboratory reports. However, they should provide a receipt or inventory of all that was seized pursuant to the warrant. ART members should query the investigators to whatever degree they will answer questions.

I. Agency visit in-house review

Following the agency visit, ART should immediately confer with corporate counsel and officers, reviewing all that has just occurred for corrective actions and "damage control."

At the direction of corporate counsel, ART members are to preserve and store all notes, reports, photographs, and tape recordings generated during the agency's visit. A decision must be made concerning the disposition of the split samples, the need for their analysis, and so forth.

A plan should be developed for company personnel or counsel to conduct frequent follow up contacts with the regulatory or enforcement agency, and perhaps the prosecutor's office, to determine the intent for administrative or enforcement actions, if any.

J. Importance of an effective compliance program

To a great extent, environmental business risks can be averted or minimized if a corporate client, by utilizing its environmental consultant or compliance manager, adopts a due diligence program by employing these steps. Having an effective compliance program prevents, monitors, detects and corrects violations. With anything less than full commitment to compliance, the corporation and its officers may be liable civilly, criminally, and personally to the stockholders and to the government.

14.7 Corporate Liability

Many corporations today have systems that may fail to adequately shield its officers, board members and owners, particularly when there are subsidiaries involved.

Under the responsible corporate officer doctrine, a corporate official can be held liable for the actions of a subordinate who violates a public welfare statute. There were some interesting rulings made in the litigation that followed the *Exxon Valdez* incident when aground in Prince William Sound on March 24, 1989, resulting in one of history's worst man-made environmental disasters *(U.S. v. Exxon Corporation and Exxon Shipping Company)*. The court made it clear that in an environmental criminal case, the corporate veil did not shield the parent company from liability for the actions of its subsidiary. This, and other case law, has paved the way for vicarious liability of the parent company's subsidiary when it (the subsidiary) engages in a crime while acting as the parent's agent.

Thus, in the matter of Example #4 (when Corporation B began to exercise tremendous control of Company A by selecting its board of directors, by staffing A's executive ranks with B officials, and by B significantly influencing A's environmental compliance policies), A, in effect, became a part of B's business and so the corporate veil was pierced, thereby reducing the shield of liability protection for its owners, officers and stockholders. It did not matter that the contamination was created more that thirty years earlier by A. The government successfully prosecuted B as a vicariously liable parent.

The investigator-consultant can play a significant and cost-saving role by informing the client about how to manage its environmental risks. Like any other investigator with developed, recognized, and accepted expertise, the consultant can provide information and direction as to the best way the client can avoid undue enforcement and regulatory attention.

It makes good "envirosense" to keep your corporate client informed. May all your clients' environmental risks be *de minimis*.

Chapter 15

Intellectual Property Theft

Julius Bombet, CLI, CFE, Matthew Buchert, and Steven Cooper, JD

Synopsis

15.1 Introduction

An area of growing concern in worldwide culture is the theft of intellectual property. It is such a concern that the United States has developed the Intellectual Law Enforcement Coordination Council to begin combating the billions of dollars lost each year through intellectual property violations and the Economic Espionage Act of 1996 which makes the theft of trade secrets a federal criminal offense. A majority of the largest American corporations have full-time staffs whose only purpose is to gather intelligence information about their employer's competitors. As of now, copyright industries alone account for almost six percent of the Gross Domestic Product (House of Representatives, 1999). With the boom in civil litigation related to intellectual property and the increasing need for protection of citizen's rights, this pressure extends to the investigative front. It is therefore commensurate with this lack of protection of citizen's and corporate rights that private investigators have knowledge and an understanding of both the laws pertaining to intellectual property and, more importantly, the skills and tactics necessary to properly investigate such violations. This will require than an investigator be educated with the basics of intellectual property. It is a fair statement that this is a highly specialized area of law, which has unique rules and processes that may be foreign to other civil litigation investigations. A basic understanding of concepts and terms is imperative for the investigator to be able to supply a client with the information that can be used to protect the client's interest. With this premise in mind, the following discussion should serve as a guide.

15.2 The Law

The notion that information should be protected from the unauthorized use of others has been traced to the Roman Empire. (Merges citing Suchman, 2003) By the time of the Renaissance, many European states had enacted laws that protected the use of secret processes and ideas without the permission of the owner. (Merges, 2003)

The source of current protection of intellectual property in the United States is rooted in Article 1 Section 8, Clause 8 of the United States Constitution. The clause provides the Congress shall have the power "to promote the progress of science and useful arts by securing for limited times to authors and inventors the exclusive right to their respective writings and discoveries." From this broad proposition, intangible property and ideas, which are collectively known as the abstract term "intellectual property," are afforded protection.

Black's Law Dictionary (1990), surprisingly, has historically contained no definition for intellectual property. It has previously, however, defined property as: "That which is peculiar or proper to any person; that which belongs exclusively to one" (1990). *Black's* also stated that property is "an aggregate of rights which are guaranteed and protected by the government" (1990). As such, investigations into this area have always been warranted, and the property of persons, intellectual as well as other, was similarly protected. With this understanding, the mental concoctions of a person, if unique, are as guaranteed as the home in which they own. In its definition of property, *Black's* also included subsections, one of which is intangible property. Intangible property is defined as "Property which cannot be touched because it has no physical existence such as claims, interests, and rights" (1990). This definition would certainly apply to areas of intellectual property and give a basis for its protection under the law. As the preceding has shown, defining intellectual property can be a daunting task. It was not until the recent edition published in 1999 that *Black's* included the definition for intellectual property. It states that intellectual property is "A category of intangible rights protecting commercially valuable products of the human intellect...A commercially valuable product of the human intellect, in a concrete or abstract form, such as a copyrightable work, a protectable trademark, a patentable invention, or a trade secret" (Black, 1990). For our purposes here, let us simply define intellectual property as any product of human intellect that has value in its uniqueness. With this definition in mind, it is easy to see that intellectual property is as diverse and complex as any other area of law. Historically, intellectual property falls into three categories: patents; copyrights; and trademarks. This discussion will also add trade secrets and the obligatory category of "other" which will be discussed later. These two categories, "other" in particular, are added to give full attention to the paradigm that our definition of intellectual property encompasses.

15.3 Patents

A patent is "a document issued by the U.S. Patent and Trademark Office (PTO) that grants a monopoly for a limited period of time on the use and development of an invention which the PTO finds to qualify for patent protection" (Elias, 1996). The PTO ensures that each application for a patent meets the five requirements needed to record a valid patent. The five requirements include (1) the application falls under one of the general categories of patentable subject matter, (2) it is not identical in form to prior art which has preceded the application, (3) it is useful, (4) it is not a nontrivial extension of what is known, and (5) it is sufficiently described that allows other to make use of the invention through ordinary skill in the art. (Merges, 2003). Patents are found in everyday products such as tools, phones, pagers, and virtually every other product we constantly use in our lives. Typically, these patents last for twenty years commencing from the date of the application and prevent anyone from using the product commercially without the patent holder's permission. Patents are granted for products that contain new ideas in their inception. Patents therefore, are wonderful protections for a creator of a new product, and wonderful tools for the investigator to use in establishing violation.

15.4 Patent Investigations

Usually a patent investigation will ensue upon a potential infringement of a valid patent. A patent may be infringed in three general ways. The first is direct infringement, which occurs when someone other than the patent holder makes, sells, or uses a patented product. The second is indirect infringement, which occurs when someone is vicariously liable by inducing another to infringe upon a patent. The final method is contributory infringement which occurs when someone sells or offers to sell or imports a material component of a patented invention when no other valid use is available and he knows that component sold is specifically adapted to the patented invention and the buyer's use that leads to a direct infringement of the patent.

Patent investigations are quite simple. A legal battle will rarely ensue unless there is evident patent violation or serious suspicion thereof. In such a case, a creator holds a valid patent on his or her creation and has a belief that another person is using this product commercially without contract or payment of satisfactory royalties. The investigator could then conduct a surveillance to document the accused doing such. With legal and codified proof of ownership of an idea, there is little gray area to be disputed. A recent investigation in China documents how lucrative this violation can be. An industrial company developed and patented a new way of extracting natural gas that decreased cost and therefore improved efficiency. A smaller company wishing to become more financially stable took the invention, which was brought by a former employee of the original company, and built similar units. These new units worked so well, the smaller company began construction on several new sites. Before long, the smaller company was large enough to compete with and be noticed by the company holding the patent. An investigator was hired to find out about the operations. Upon securing a job with the smaller company, he obtained pictures of the operating units and was able to find copies of schematics as well. These units were exact replicas of the ones under patent. Overall, the smaller company had gained over sixty million dollars in profit from use of the unit, without payment to the true owners of the invention.

15.5 Copyrights

A copyright is "a bundle of rights held by the author or developer of an original work of authorship" (Elias, 1996). Copyright protection exists in accordance with 17 U.S.C. § 102, which protects "original works of authorship fixed in any tangible medium of expression, now known or later developed, from which they can be perceived, reproduced, or otherwise communicated, either directly or with the aid of a machine or device." Copyrights are a more complex area than patents. Copyrights apply to particular expressions. These expressions extend to literary works, audio-visual works, software for computers, music, sound recordings, paintings, sculptures, etc. As such, the realm of copyrights is far reaching, and yet it must be discriminate by nature. Most importantly, a work must be tangible in some way in order to qualify for this protection. As compared to patents, the U.S. Copyright office ensures that the work only contains some original content and it does not issue copyrights, instead the copyright is protected from its inception. Finally the range of protective subject matter is broader than that of patent law. (Merges, 2003). In addition, copyrights have a much longer life. Usually, a copyright lasts for the life of the author plus fifty years. In the case that the author is a business, copyrights last for 75 to 100 years, depending on the date of publication versus the date of creation.

As such, the commercial value of copyrights is a serious issue to the holder, and investigations of copyright violations are equally as serious to the client.

15.6 Copyright Investigations

Investigations into copyright infringement are commonplace in society. A traditional profession, which has protected their copyrighted material and conducted investigation of infringement of their work, is photographers. Photographers frequently use investigators to pose as customers who take copyrighted material to photo reproduction labs to obtain additional copies. Upon the occurrence of the infringement the holder of the copyright sues for damages.

However, due to the increase in technology, copyright investigations have focused on other sources of copyrighted material. Over the past few years, copyright infringement had gained nationwide attention. With the advent of the Internet and web sites such as NAPSTER, large record labels and movie studios have stepped up their investigations against copyright infringement. In the past, movie studios have used investigators to investigate the unauthorized reproduction of copyrighted material on videocassettes. The Motion Picture Association of America, MPAA, has employed investigators to pose as customers who rent or buy videocassettes from retail outlets and then examine these items for indicia of originality that are placed on the legal copies of the material. Some video stores have infringed on the copyrighted material by purchasing a legal copy then reproducing multiple illegal copies which they then rent or sell to the public. Investigators posing as customer can lawfully obtain the fraudulent copies, which can be used as evidence in subsequent criminal and civil proceedings against the person who infringed. See *Columbia Pictures Industry, Inc v. Landa*, 974 F. Supp. 1, (D.D.C. 1997).

The federal appellate courts have upheld this type of undercover investigation. In *RCA/Ariol International, Inc. v. Thomas and Grayston, Co.* 845 F. 2d. 773, which involved the duplication of musical tapes where the owner of the copyright employed investigators to "shop" various retail stores where unauthorized copies of the protected material were being distributed. The investigators visited these stores and requested certain audiotapes be copied. The court determined that the copies made at the investigator request were an infringement of the owner's copyright. Another appellate court has gone as far as stating that a copyright holder's inducement of the person to infringe by giving money to that person in order to obtain unauthorized copies of the material was not sufficiently serious to preclude recovery. (Ray, 493 and 494).

Recently, Bombet, Cashio and Associates has been employed to investigate the theft of computer software associated with telecommunication automation systems. Investigators have applied for credit cards, cell phones, and various banking accounts that employ an automation system. Once the investigator has gained access to the system through their own account, the investigator can use their access to test the automation system and determine if the software being used is authorized or a registered copy of the protected material. Without these covert investigations owners of copyrighted material would suffer and economic loss due to the rampant infringement of their copyrighted work.

Not all copyright investigation will be complex. Every college student writing a research paper is subject to such an investigation. Every time the student fails to cite properly a quote or paraphrase, he or she is committing a copyright violation. Investigation into this area is also rather simple. If an author holds a valid copyright, then an unauthorized expression on some tangible medium is necessary for a violation to occur. Therefore, the investigator must obtain the unauthorized expression and prove it was authored by the accused to prove the violation. In today's computer age, copyrights are violated on a daily basis on the Internet. A news story was recently heard detailing how a person on the Internet was marketing downloads of a book to which they claimed ownership. The true author was checking the Internet for possible reviews when he stumbled on his own book available for download. Upon seeing this, he quickly contacted his attorney and put a stop to the violation. With the volume of data available on the ever-growing Internet, it is easy to see how copyright infringement is of pressing concern to authors. Much debate has been raised, and sites such as Napster are finding new ways to skirt the law, remaining just to the side of legal while the courts struggle to define this new area. As time presses on, this legal refinement will be an important area for the entire legal community to remain aware of and stay current on all developments.

15.7 Trademarks

"A trademark is a distinctive word, phrase, logo, graphic symbol or other device that is used to distinguish a manufacturer's or merchant's products from anyone else's" (Elias, 1996). A trademark is different from copyrights and patents in that novelty, invention, or any work of discovery does not play a role in determing whether the work is protected. Instead it is simply based on the first to use the distinctive mark in commerce. A trademark is then protected against the use by subsequent users in order to avoid the likelihood of confusion by consumers between products. (Merges, 2003) Trademarks are seen in every aspect of life. Anytime a person turns on a television set, they are saturated with trademarks of every possible denomination. Fast food, cars, computers, radios, clothes, and every other arena in the marketplace are subject to trademark protection. At base, trademarks are the means by which manufacturers distinguish their products from others. It is therefore easy to see how capitalizing on the success of someone else's trademark is too lucrative for some to pass up.

15.8 Trademark Investigations

Trademark infringement is one of the most prolific forms of intellectual property theft practiced. Virtually every form of trademark infringement has occurred and has therefore been investigated. One recent investigation by Bombet, Cashio, and Associates in Baton Rouge, Louisiana, involved an example of simple trademark infringement. A local wholesale company was using a mark that was similar in appearance to the trademark of a national company. The investigation of this matter involved pretexting the company with a visit. Under the guise of being a local contractor, the investigator toured the warehouse in order to view the company's trucks and production facility. Brochures and cards were obtained from the owner, and the visit went so well, the investigator was offered a large discount. From there, pictures of the facility and its signs were taken, and the case was closed. Investigations also range to highly complex and time consuming. Another example investigation conducted by Bombet, Cashio, and Associates involved teams of investigators monitoring unlicensed apparel for sale during a major sporting event. Since festivities can last for days for these events and entire cities can be transformed into marketplaces, it is easy to see how only a small number of infringements can be expected to be detected. It is important that the client and the investigator be aware of this fact. It is also important for investigators, especially in this instance, to work closely with law enforcement personnel to assure the success of the investigation. In this case, the sports league had the foresight to equip all of their merchandise with holograms to ensure authenticity. Licensed investigators accompanied by police officers simply walked up to the vendors posing as potential customers and checked the merchandise for the requisite hologram. In this case, several thousand items were confiscated from multiple vendors.

15.9 Trade Secrets

Trade secrets are a tricky yet valuable area of legal concern. Trade secrets are information which yield some economic value to a person or company yet is not patented. A trade secret claim can be broken into three basic elements. The first element is the subject matter must qualify for protection, meaning it must be a secret and not generally known to the public. The second element is the holder of the secret has taken reasonable precautions under the circumstances to prevent disclosure. The final element is the holder must prove that the person who infringed acquired the information by wrongful misappropriation. (Merges, 2003) As such, the holder takes precautions to safeguard the information by having persons privy to the information sign agreements wherein they promise not to disclose the information or use it on their own for profit. An item such as the recipe for Coca-cola is a trade secret. This is important because patents have lives whereas trade secrets do not. At the expiration of a patent the information becomes public domain. By utilizing a trade secret agreement, the holder maintains rights to the information indefinitely. As such, trade secrets do not have the codified legal protections of patents, a point which makes them riskier, yet more lucrative.

15.10 Trade Secret Investigations

Trade secret investigations most typically involve a lengthy surveillance and undercover work in order to establish use of the protected information by an unauthorized party. Upon conclusion, this surveillance should yield documented proof that the person who agreed to confidentiality has divulged the information in some restricted way. These investigations can be difficult, and the proof can be even more difficult. Typically the information is highly valuable which therefore makes the offender all the more protective of his or her activities. The difficulty in proof also arises in the establishment of ownership. If a third party independently invents the same product, he or she may patent it. The original inventor, working under trade secret, would then lose the right to profit and sale of the item. The risk involved in trade secrets is thereby quite high. For the investigator, a relationship must be developed between the original developer and the person using the invention for commercial gain. A relationship must be found in order to prove there was not independent invention by a third party. Bombet, Cashio, and Associates has also handled this type of investigation. In a recent case, a large Colorado-based company developed new machinery, which would increase their profitability by a sizeable margin. A high-level employee, who signed a confidentiality and non-disclosure agreement and was bound by trade secret agreements with the company, subsequently acquired the blueprints for the machine. After shopping around for investors, he finally sold the blueprints for a considerable profit. After three years of investigation, spanning several countries and countless individuals and businesses, a legal battle to claim ownership of the intellectual property involved in the machinery ensued. An extensive network involving both a money trail and a line of witnesses was unearthed to lead back to the employee who originally stole the information. After this enormous undertaking, the employee was caught in actual possession of the original blueprints. The Colorado company was awarded not only close to $1.7 million in damages but was also given all technology and machinery from the dissolution of the at-fault business. This corrupt company was then bound to a twelve-year agreement to refrain from competition in the business and the employee who stole the information was barred under the same constraints for life. According to the executives involved in this investigation, private investigators were more important than the lawyers. The key to the entire suit was the statements and interviews conducted. If investigators had not been thorough and extensive in their search, several main witnesses would never have been found.

15.11 Other Intellectual Property

Since our definition of intellectual property extends to include any product of human intellect that has value, our discussion must also go so far. Copyrights, patents, and trademarks are easily definable due to their longstanding legal tradition. As such, their investigation can be categorized and simplified. But what of other areas that are not covered by these three? There are cases that exist where the ideas of a person were too new in inception to be covered by patents, trademarks, or copyrights. These cases must also be extended the same guarantees of protection and proper investigation that would be had otherwise. Suppose a person had an idea for a new breathing apparatus that would revolutionize the world of undersea diving. That person discussed the idea with a close friend who then thought it was a good enough idea to look into. That friend, realizing the commercial value for such an invention develops it into reality. He stands to makes millions and the true inventor is quickly being left by the wayside. Obviously this is morally wrong. But how does the true inventor prove his or her right to ownership? The first thing that must be proved is that he or she thought the idea up. A good thing to have is dated scribblings, drawings, blueprints, or notes giving a date to the idea. Another good thing to have is a witness. The person should be able to find another "friend" to whom he or she told the idea. An investigator should conduct as many interviews as possible to find another "friend" who was told the idea. As much credibility as possible should be developed for ownership of the idea, particularly showing inception at an earlier date than the so-called friend. From there it is up to a good attorney and some degree of luck to recover from such an egregious breach of trust.

15.12 Targeting

Intelligence gathering routinely targets areas of a company such as research and development, marketing, manufacturing, production, and the human resources department. Researchers routinely publish in industry journals, inadvertently revealing confidential information. Test marketing, promotions, and advanced notice of production dates can all lead to the unintentional interception of valuable information. Pretext calls to manufacturing and production personnel can result in the release of intellectual property. Furthermore, help wanted ads and job announcements can lead to interviews arranged by clever individuals to deprive a company of sensitive data revealed to a job applicant either by an interviewer or by the applicants own observations while on the premises.

Vulnerable areas include the company's offices, documents, maintenance workers, visitors, meeting rooms, computers and computer networks, and communications equipment including voice mail and paging. Specific plans to prevent the unauthorized acquisition of proprietary information should be developed with specific attention given to each of the areas detailed above.

Preventing employee theft is challenging. Education and awareness, coupled with non-disclosure and non-compete agreements, are helpful but do not solve the problem. Aggressive internal measures are essential and must be developed with clear and concise goals and objectives in mind.

15.13 Conclusion

As the previous discussion has shown, intellectual property is an area of serious interest for the citizen, the corporation, and thusly the investigator. Armed with an understanding of the law, each investigator can turn to personal skill, individual tactics, and an ever-present breadth of knowledge to complete successfully an intellectual property investigation. The four main areas: patents, trademarks, copyrights, and trade secrets; together with an understanding that some intellectual property is not covered by these yet still holds the same protections, are necessary items of interest for investigators of every denomination. As the economic boom of recent years yields more and more attention to this area, it is certainly to become more of a hotbed for investigative protection than it has ever been.

Glossary

Copyright. "a bundle of rights held by the author or developer of an original work of authorship" (Elias, 1996).

Patent. "a document issued by the U.S. Patent and Trademark Office (PTO) that grants a monopoly for a limited period of time on the use and development of an invention which the PTO finds to qualify for patent protection" (Elias, 1996).

Property. "[t]hat which is peculiar or proper to any person; that which belongs to one" (Black, 1990).

Intangible property. "[p]roperty which cannot be touched because it has no physical existence such as claims, interests and rights" (Black, 1990).

Trademarks. "a distinctive word, phrase, logo, graphic symbol or other device that is used to distinguish a manufacturer's or merchant's products from anyone else's" (Elias, 1996).

Intellectual property. any product of human intellect that has value in its uniqueness.

Trade secrets. information which yields some economic value to a person or company yet is not patented.

References

Black, Henry C. *Black's Law Dictionary*. West Publishing Co., 1990.

Black, Henry C. *Black's Law Dictionary*. West Publishing Co., 1990.

House of Representatives. "Violations of Intellectual Property Right: How Do We Protect American Ingenuity?" U.S. Government Printing Office, 2000.

Elias, Stephen. *Patent, Copyright and Trademark*. Nolo Press, 1996.

West, Michael J., CFE, "The Brain Drain – Theft of Intellectual Property." *The White Paper*, Vol 15 No 1, Jan/Feb, 2001.

Suchman, Mark C., "Invention and Ritual: Notes on the interrelation of Magic and Intellectual Property in Preliterate Societies, 89 Colum. L. Rev. 1264.

Merges, Robert et al. "Intellectual Property in the New Technological age" Aspen Publishers, New York, NY, 2003

Ray, Susan J., "Copyright Law – the Protection of Photograph Copyright owners under the Copyright Act-Olan Mills, Inc. V. Linn Photo Co. 23 F. 3d. 1345 (8th Cir. 1994) 68 Temp. L. Rev. 491.

Chapter 16

Investigating the Sexual Harassment Case

Grace Elting Castle, CLI

Synopsis

16.1 Introduction

Investigating the claim of sexual harassment can easily be the greatest challenge ever experienced by the professional investigator. From the initial acceptance of a case until it is submitted to the jury, the investigator will be faced with preconceived opinions of what constitutes sexual harassment in the workplace.[1]

Beginning with the 1964 passage of the Civil Rights Act (CRA)[2] which made sexual harassment a civil rights violation, this accusation has been the most difficult to prove and the most difficult to defend against. Then the 1998 decisions of the United States Supreme Court increased the difficulty in determining what is, and is not, a valid sexual harassment complaint.[3]

In May 1999, a letter written by a Federal Trade Commission attorney complicated the manner in which such an allegation can be investigated, and by whom.[4]

Prior to these decisions, and opinions, business owners could feel relatively assured that they had complied with the government regulations if employees had signed a form stating that they were aware of the company's non-sexual harassment policy and if the employees had been informed on how to file a complaint alleging sexual harassment. If such a complaint were filed, the business owners could feel comfortable that the allegations could be investigated by an in-house personnel manager or by an independent investigator hired specifically for that purpose.

Employers are now not only held responsible for maintaining a workplace free of sexual harassment, they may be liable for the unlawful conduct of their agents, supervisory employees, employees, and even non-employees who sexually harass at work.[5] In addition, the "letter" has identified previously unrecognized responsibilities and liabilities regarding the actual investigation of the allegations.

The professional investigator who accepts a sexual harassment assignment without complete and current knowledge of these decisions and issues is a fool at best. Relying on outdated information and techniques in a sexual harassment investigation will not only put the corporate client in jeopardy of a lawsuit but may also put the professional investigator in the position of having to defend his or her professional license.

The information in this chapter should be viewed only as the beginning of preparation for such an investigation. Laws and administrative rulings are in a constant state of flux. The investigator must be responsible for doing the research necessary to find the most current court decisions, or agency rulings, and the resulting laws and regulations.

16.2 The Civil Rights Act of 1964 (CRA)

With the historic passage of the 1964 CRA (commonly referred to as Title VII), employers were suddenly held accountable for the sexual harassment behavior of their employees. The Civil Rights Act of 1991[6] provided amendments to several sections of the 1964 Act, including authorization of punitive and compensatory damages.

Following the passage of the 1964 Act, the courts began to recognize two specific types of sexual harassment: *quid pro quo* and *hostile work environment*.

To qualify as a quid pro quo case, the supervisor on a job had to have conditioned the job, or some part of it, on the employee's cooperation in a sexual activity. For instance, if a female employee was denied a promotion when she failed to acquiesce to her male supervisor's request for sexual favors, it was a quid pro quo example of workplace sexual harassment. This type of case gained automatic judicial approval.

A hostile work environment could result from coworkers and supervisors making life uncomfortable for the complainant through posting of objectionable posters or making remarks unacceptable to the complainant. The Supreme Court defined this type of complaint as *"conduct that has the purpose or effect of unreasonably interfering with an individual's work performance or creating an intimidating hostile or offensive work environment."*[7] These cases were more difficult to prove and were more likely to result in hearings or trials.

An example of the kind of "good old boys" behavior that should have been eliminated in the workplace following the CRA is the posting of sexually explicit materials such as magazine centerfolds and "girlie" calendars in employee areas of mills, factories, auto repair shops, and other traditionally male-dominated sites. Unfortunately, some of these employers have not yet received the message and an investigator may still, occasionally, encounter allegations of workplace hostility and sexual harassment involving visually offensive materials. Additionally, it is not unusual to find other violations of the CRA in workplaces where these items are still allowed.

In determining whether or not the conduct was sufficiently severe and pervasive, the courts considered how frequently the conduct occurred, its severity, whether or not the conduct was physically threatening or humiliating or just offensive and whether it unreasonably interfered with the work performance.[8]

16.3 The Supreme Court Decisions of 1998

The three opinions issued in 1998 by the United States Supreme Court "recognized same-sex harassment, expanded employer liability for the sexually harassing acts of its supervisory employees, and detailed an affirmative defense against the expanded liability."[9] The Court decided that employers are "always responsible for sexual harassment of (by) their supervisors, regardless of whether the harassment is hostile environment harassment or quid pro quo harassment. The fact that an employer does not know, or reasonably should not know, about the conduct is irrelevant to a determination of liability."[10]

Oncale provided the case law for determining whether or not Title VII protected against same-sex harassment. The Court found in the affirmative, saying that the prohibition of sex discrimination protects men as well as women. In this case, the plaintiff had alleged that he was subjected to humiliating sexual acts in front of the rest of the crew on an offshore oil platform, physically assaulted in a sex-related manner, and threatened with rape. When no action was taken on his complaints, he quit.[11]

> In *Faragher v City of Boca Raton*, and *Burlington Industries, Inc. v Ellerth*, the Court considered the liability of employers when their supervisors sexually harass employees. Faragher worked as a lifeguard for Boca Raton, Florida, using her earnings for her college education. Two male supervisors repeatedly touched her and other female lifeguards in impermissible ways, and made sexual gestures and comments to them. She, like many women who find themselves harassed by their bosses, did not complain to city management because she thought she would lose her job. In the *Burlington* case, the plaintiff, Kimberly Ellerth, quit because of the sexual advances of a supervisor.[12]

In these three cases, the Court determined that the unsuspecting employer is liable for harassment if the supervisor's actions result in adverse employment consequences, such as firing or demotion. And, even in the hostile environment situation where no adverse employment actions occur, the employer is liable unless (1) "the employer has exercised reasonable care to prevent and correct promptly any sexually harassing behaviors; and (2) the plaintiff has unreasonably failed to take advantage of any preventative or corrective opportunities provided by the employer or avoid harm otherwise." [13]

16.4 "The Letter"

In the spring of 1999, employers, law firms, and professional investigators were shocked to learn that the people they investigate in a sexual harassment case might sue them. In an advisory letter issued by an attorney for the Federal Trade Commission (FTC), it was opined that the federal Fair Credit Reporting Act (FCRA) contains notice and disclosure requirements previously unrecognized by the legal community, and especially by investigators.

According to the letter, which, though not binding authority, has been accepted as the "new rule," employers may be required to obtain permission from the accused employee before conducting the investigation. In addition, the employers may need to provide a copy of the report to the employee if an adverse employment action is taken, and also to give that employee the opportunity to dispute the findings.[14]

The requirements, as defined in this letter, sounded an alarm for investigators. The manner in which sexual harassment investigations must be conducted, and the preparation of investigative reports, became extremely important. There was no doubt that the FTC, responsible for oversight and enforcement of the FCRA, considered independent investigators to be *consumer reporting agencies*. That distinction subjected investigators to all the requirements of a "consumer report" described as a "communication . . . bearing on a consumer's creditworthiness . . . character, general reputation, personal characteristics, or mode of living, which is used or expected to be used as a factor in establishing the consumer's eligibility for . . . employment purposes."[15] The letter advises that employers will have to get permission from an accused harasser if it hires an outside investigator. The letter's author suggested that this can be done at any time, including when a person is hired, but the consent must be written, and must be in a separate document, not included in the employment application or buried in an employee handbook.[16] Included in the requirements is that if an investigation involves interviews, then the employee must be notified that a report is being created and that he or she has a right to a copy of it. In addition, if the investigation reveals information on the character or general reputation of other employees, those employees will then fall under the same notice and disclosure requirements.

Understandably, the opinions expressed in this letter sent an alarm throughout the legal and investigative communities. Committees were formed, legislators were contacted. Obviously, investigators cannot effectively work under such restrictions. The battle continues, and the matter is still far from settled. So, once again a reminder to the reader, do not neglect to research the current laws and regulations, paying particular attention to the FCRA.

Caveat: The investigator may receive a request from a client that all reports be given *orally*, in an attempt to avoid the requirements of the FCRA, as outlined in "the letter." Beware—the FCRA lists "oral communications" as part of the consumer report.

Caveat: There may also be a request from the client for the investigator to sign an indemnification agreement in case all the requirements of the FCRA aren't met. Discuss such requests with your own attorney. The investigator should insist upon a written contract/agreement. Get specific agreements as to what type of report the client is requesting, who will be responsible for providing prior notice to the appropriate employees, who will be responsible for providing copies of the reports to the appropriate persons, and specify exactly what (and who) is being investigated. Most investigators will want the employer to assume responsibility for notice and disclosure to the employees, but don't make the mistake of *assuming* that will happen. Spell it out in your contract.

Caveat: Do not attempt to use pretext, or "ruses," in these investigations without knowing the current pertinent laws and regulations. Be certain also that your client has agreed, preferably in writing, to this form of investigation. It is the author's personal opinion that few, if any, investigations are ever worth taking a chance with a pretext; but other professional investigators consider it to be appropriate and important. If you're planning to use this tool, use it wisely and with knowledge of the law.

16.5 What Is Sexual Harassment?

Sexual harassment is defined by the Equal Employment Opportunity Commission (EEOC) as a form of unlawful sex discrimination, including unwelcome sexual advances, requests for sexual favors, and other verbal or physical conduct of a sexual nature that are made a condition of employment, that unreasonably interfere with work performance, or that create an intimidating, hostile, or offensive work environment.[17]

The person who brings a sexual harassment claim must be able to prove that he or she was harassed *because* of his or her sex, but the harassment itself does not have to be sexual. The two kinds of sexual harassment include harassment motivated by hostility to men or women and harassment motivated by pathological sexual desire. The categories may overlap.[18]

Examples of harassment motivated by hostility would be discrimination in assignments, refusing to assist or train the person, saying or demonstrating to the person that they are unwelcome, and acts of vandalism or assault.

Examples of harassment with sexual overtones, or pathological sexual desire, would include such behavior as exposing oneself to the person or public, spreading rumors or publicly joking about the person's sexual activities, talking or joking about sex in an unwelcome or demeaning fashion, talking about the person's body to him or her or to other people, displaying sexually vulgar pictures, or inviting the person to engage in sexual activity, or retaliating against her (or him) if the offer is not accepted.[19]

It is important to understand that the CRA does not distinguish between sexes—the victim and the harasser may be either a woman or a man. Allegations of harassment have been approved against the victim's supervisor, agents of the employer, coworkers, non-employees, and supervisors from an entirely different area than the victim's regular work site.

Economic injury is not a necessary component of a successful harassment complaint, nor does the victim's employment have to have been terminated. *The harasser simply must have been displaying conduct that was not welcomed by the victim.* The plaintiff's legal team will be attempting to prove that the case is about the alleged misconduct of the employer. They will want to prove that the employer recklessly ignored its responsibilities.[20]

16.6 What Is a Hostile Work Environment?

Often overlooked due to the heavy emphasis on eradicating sexual harassment, hostile work environment is very difficult to determine and to investigate.

In her groundbreaking study, Professor Vicki Schultz explained that much sex-based hostility and abuse that is experienced in the workplace is neither driven by the desire for sex nor even sexual in content. Many of the most prevalent forms of this kind of harassment are actions that are designed to maintain work as bastions of masculine competence and authority.[21] Response to Schultz's 1998 published work regarding definitions of a hostile work environment has led to a new discussion of the original intent of Title VII.

Though, to date, most cases have been centered around sexual harassment and other issues alleged to have been based on sexual intent, an improved understanding of Title VII is leading to other types of cases being brought against employers for sex-based hostile work environment. Schultz's study shows that such harassment is "designed to undermine women as workers and preserve a gendered hierarchy in the workplace."[22]

Schultz cited the following as examples of ways that females have been harassed in the workplace: ". . . denigrating women's performance or ability to master the job; providing patronizing forms of help in performing the job, withholding the training, information, or opportunity to learn to do the job well; engaging in deliberate work sabotage; providing sexist evaluations of women's performance or denying them deserved promotions; isolating women from the social networks that confer a sense of belonging . . . assigning women sexstereotyped service tasks that lie outside their job descriptions (such as cleaning or serving coffee) . . . "[23]

Investigators working in this field should become aware of this emerging trend toward seeking a non-hostile work environment. Keep in mind that although the examples given used female models, hostile environments exist for men, as well. The author has found this to be especially true in the case of homosexual males. In some workplace environments, the homosexual male (and, in one case I investigated, a man who was only "perceived" by his coworkers to be homosexual) is a consistent target for men who seem to have an overwhelming need to prove their own masculinity through the use of degrading language, persistent bullying, and job task sabotaging.

Case research is often the best training an investigator can get. Reading the opinions of federal and state courts can provide the latest thinking on a subject such as sexual harassment and hostile work environment. If you do not have legal research expertise, don't despair. Ask your attorney or paralegal friends for assistance or hire someone to do the research. And don't forget about the Internet where one can often find not only the opinions, but also interpretations and articles based on the new case law.

The issue of males being subjected to a hostile work environment is a good example of the research material available to the investigator. As an example, in *Nichols v. Azteca Restaurant*[24] the court pointed out that sexual harassment is actionable under Title VII to the extent it occurs "because of" the plaintiff's sex. This protects both men and women.

Azteca included allegations from the employee that coworkers hurled verbal abuse at him, called him vulgar names, accused him of acting "like a woman," and ridiculed him for not having sex with a female coworker. These allegations were determined by the court to be sex-related abuse that created a hostile work environment. Further, one of the court's several decisions in this matter was to hold that the employer did not exercise reasonable care to correct promptly the behavior. As a result, the employer was held liable for the hostile environment.[25]

Though you may not soon encounter an actual sex-based hostile work environment complaint, you may well hear allegations of such behavior in your investigation of the sexual harassment complaints. Always be cognizant of the importance of what you are hearing and make certain that your corporate client is informed of the problem so that appropriate action and safeguards can be implemented.

16.7 Who Has to Comply?

It is not easy to escape the discrimination laws established by Congress and the Supreme Court. All private employers, state and local government employers, and education institutions that employ fifteen or more individuals *must* comply with the sexual harassment component. In addition, private and public employment agencies, labor organizations, and joint labor management committees controlling apprenticeship and training must also comply.[26]

Keep in mind, however, that it is not likely that *any* employer, even those with *less* than fifteen employees, will escape the wrath of the courts if an employee can prove sexual harassment. This type of behavior is recognized as unacceptable in all work environments, from blue-collar work sites to penthouse office suites. Also, state or local laws could expand the scope of liability to employers of even *one* employee.

16.8 Who Enforces these Laws and Rules?

The EEOC enforces Title VII of the CRA. Persons who believe they have suffered sexual harassment have 180 days from the last alleged act to file a complaint with the EEOC in order to pursue a federal claim. State or local laws may differ as to procedure and time limits. For example, the complainant may or may not have to first file with the appropriate state agency in order to pursue a claim based on state laws. Relevant deadlines may extend to allow a plaintiff additional time to pursue the claim in court. Because of these sometimes complex rules, it is always advisable to check with the EEOC, or the state enforcement agency, to determine current requirements if a complaint is being filed.

Investigators should always check the deadlines to ascertain if the current complaint was in compliance.

The EEOC is required to accept the filing of a complaint. An EEOC preliminary investigation is then conducted to determine the merits, and a decision is made on whether to pursue a full investigation or to dismiss the charges. Employers have an opportunity to mediate the charges before referral to investigation. It is important to remember that even if the EEOC dismisses the charge, or even before the EEOC's investigation is complete, the complainant has the right to file a lawsuit in federal court. In the event the EEOC finds that harassment may have occurred, conciliation discussions are conducted. If those fail, the EEOC may sue the private employer or give the complainant the right to file in federal court. *There are deadlines associated with all stages of these procedures. The investigator should review them for relevancy to the current matter.*

If the complaint is upheld, the employer may be liable for the full amount of lost wages and attorney's fees, as well as damages ranging from $50,000 to $300,000, depending on the number of persons employed by the firm.

16.9 Accepting the Assignment

If you've decided to accept a sexual harassment assignment, you should first review your own "protections." You must enter into this work knowing that you may very well be the target of a complaint for violation of one or more of the "rules" related to investigating sexual harassment allegations—if not by the alleged victim, or by the alleged perpetrator, then perhaps by your own corporate client.

The potential for retaliatory action against an investigator is always present. At the very least, an investigator should anticipate that his or her reports will be highly scrutinized by everyone involved at several levels of review. Anticipate, also, that the potential for receiving a subpoena duces tecum, or deposition summons, is equally high.

Review the following and make sure your own house is in order before you have that first meeting with the potential corporate client:

A. Your business preparation

Are you, and your firm, in compliance with all licensing requirements in your area?

Do you (your firm) have non-sexual harassment policies in place?

If you (your firm) have ever been accused of sexual harassment are you prepared to show how that was defended and what, if any, changes were made in your policies to avoid future complaints?

Do you have adequate insurance coverage should you be named in a complaint as a result of this sexual harassment investigation project?

B. Your personal preparation

Are you prepared to demonstrate knowledge of the sexual harassment laws and regulations?

Are you familiar with the vocabulary regarding sexual harassment claims and investigations?

Have you conducted a preliminary background on the potential client's firm so that you can demonstrate an understanding of the allegations and suggest an investigation plan? An investigator should arrive at the initial meeting with knowledge of the potential client's type of business, as well as the names of key people.)

Have you prepared a preliminary "To Do" list that will help you work through the various stages of the investigation? (See the Appendix.)

Do you have a written contract for this client to sign? *If you don't do written contracts for any other type of investigation, this is the one that should be the exception!*

16.10 The Preliminary "To Do" List

(Refer to the Appendix.)

The complexity of a sexual harassment case necessitates the preparation of a work sheet, a "to do" list, that can be referred to as you work through the case.

Be certain that this list contains not only information and tasks to ensure compliance with the CRA, and other government regulations, case law, and special rules, but information and tasks specific to the allegations in the current complaint. This list may actually grow to be quite lengthy, so be prepared to divide it into specific topics, including, but not limited to, CRA Title VII requirements, EEOC regulations, federal and state law, history of prior complaints filed against the company, and, of course, the case at hand. The last two will be added after your initial meeting with the client.

16.11 Discussion of the Appendix

The Appendix is an example of how this list may be formatted. The following brief review of it will provide some guidance as you create your own work sheet.

A. The FTC letter

Research the current status of the FTC's "letter." Have any recent decisions been made or opinions handed down that clarify (or further confuse) the responsibilities of the investigator and accused firm? *An investigator should have one or more trusted attorney-advisors who can provide current legal advice. If you don't have one, now is the time to establish that relationship! Don't rely on your corporate client to know the law.*

B. EEOC requirements

Review the requirements, deadlines, and other materials that are readily available on the Internet.

C. Laws of the state (of the incident)

Research your own state laws regarding sexual harassment to see if there are additional requirements that must be followed when a complaint is filed or an investigation is conducted. If there are, add them to this area on the Appendix,.

Be sure to review these with your client, or your client's legal advisor, so that you are in complete agreement as to the actions required by all the pertinent laws and regulations. You may want to have this part of the work sheet become an addendum to the contract with all reviewers signing it.

16.12 History of Prior Claims against the Corporation

Review complete case files of all prior claims against this client, make note of names, allegations, date filed, date of determination, determination, civil action filed, civil action completed, damages awarded, damage paid, action taken by employer, current employment status of each complainant, and the names and information of any witnesses.

Determine whether any changes were made in written company policy following any of the prior cases.

Determine what non-tolerance policies were in effect at the time of the prior alleged incident(s). *Were they in writing and signed by the employees?*

Determine what grievance/complaint policies were in effect at the time of the alleged incident(s). *Were they in writing and signed by the employees?*

16.13 The Current Case

Once you've decided to take the assignment, never lose sight of the fact that recent court decisions have penalized employers for failing to investigate, promptly and appropriately, an employee's harassment complaint.[27]

Immediately begin constructing a chronological timeline of all occurrences in this case. Include everything known about the accusing plaintiff, as well as the defendant company and employees. Include deadline dates, filing dates, original and subsequent complaints by the plaintiff, and the dates any action was taken by the defendant(s). Eventually, you may discover a pattern within the dates and activities that will provide useful information for the legal team. Or, you may discover that the plaintiff was involved in another life stressor when she (or he) made the initial complaint against the defendant(s). That wouldn't excuse illegal behavior by the defendant(s), but it might point to a plaintiff's lie.

Compare current company policy with requirements of the FCRA, CRA, EEOC requirements, and state law. If not in compliance, determine how that happened, when changes should have occurred, and whether that led to the current allegations in any way.

Remember that your job as an investigator is not just to try to prove that the harassment didn't happen. You will provide a great service to the client if you can identify what went wrong, what changes can and should be made, what matters should be discussed promptly with the corporate attorney, and what the complainant's attorney is apt to discover in an investigation.

Review training records to determine if all employees have received reminders of the policies on a consistent basis, and whether all supervisors have been trained to respond seriously to complaints of sexual harassment.

Is the company keeping accurate and complete records of all complaints and subsequent actions?

Make a list of the allegations, including the dates and times.

Compare names and allegations of the current case with prior cases. *Is this a repeat occurrence? Are the same witnesses involved?*

Add to that list the response action taken each time by the victim

Did the alleged victim use the employer's established reporting policies?

Did the alleged victim inform the harasser that the conduct was unwelcome?

Did the alleged victim take advantage of established reporting procedures?

Add to the list the action(s) taken by the employer in response to any notification or complaint.

16.14 Investigation Tips

Remember that it is imperative that employers (managers, supervisors, etc.) take sexual harassment complaints seriously, no matter what their own personal evaluation of the alleged activity may be. They are also obliged to take their own written policies seriously. Watch for remarks such as "They were just kidding," or "It was just a joke," or my favorite,

"She has no sense of humor." These are early warning signs that the appropriate attention may not have been given to the complaint.

There should be no distinction between the way male and female employees are treated. It is no more appropriate to ridicule a male employee, or make physical gestures to him, than it would be to treat a female employee in that manner. Be alert to comments by the client that may show lack of knowledge of these requirements. A "boys will be boys" attitude is outdated and may lead to lack of attention to legitimate complaints. An August 2000 EEOC $500,000 settlement with a Colorado auto chain has further enforced the fact that male-on-male harassment is an expensive violation.[28]

The EEOC points out that an employer is liable if it knew or should have known of the misconduct, unless it can show that it took immediate and appropriate corrective action. The standard is the same for non-employees, except that the employer's control of the misconduct of such individuals will be considered.

The EEOC describes a *supervisor* as one who (1) has authority to undertake or recommend tangible employment decisions affecting the employee (such as hiring, firing, promoting), and (2) the individual has authority to direct the employee's daily work activities. This is true, even if the supervisor does not have the *final* say. The person responsible for the employee's *daily* work activities also qualifies under EEOC guidelines as a "supervisor."

Caveat: There is a tricky EEOC guideline that says that even if a harasser had no actual supervisory power over the complainant, if the complainant *believed* that the harasser had such authority, the employer can be held liable.

Remember, to avoid liability the employer has to show that it discharged its duty of reasonable care *and* that the employee unreasonably failed to avoid the harm. The standard set by the Supreme Court decisions in *Ellerth* and *Faragher* is more stringent than the minimum standard of negligence.

A harassment complaint must be investigated whether or not that complaint was in any particular format or was made in writing. In addition, the complaint procedure must provide a way for the employee to bypass his or her immediate supervisor.

16.15 Cultural Differences

One of the most shocking sexual harassment and hostile work environment cases that the author was ever retained to investigate involved such blatant sexual groping and public ridicule of female employees that I found it difficult to believe my attorney client had correctly understood the alleged victim!

My interview of the plaintiff, an older female who had a long tenure with her employer, convinced me that not only was the attorney's memory accurate, but that the facts were actually worse than she had told him. Her witnesses, who were also victims, not only confirmed her reports but had horror stories of their own.

All of the victims were longtime employees of the company. The problem was the president, the new owner, who was having a wonderfully good time with all his recently acquired female employees. He seemed oblivious to laws and regulations that should have prevented him from groping female employees as they passed him the hallways. It should also have prevented him from suddenly turning to a female employee, who he had just introduced at a large industry conference, and firmly grabbing her by both breasts—and then just standing there with a stupid grin on his face!

The problem was that this happy new president was not from the United States. He was from Japan, where women's issues were not as far advanced as in the United States. Even his Japanese wife, also an officer of the new company, was bewildered by the employee's complaints. She carefully explained to one employee that her husband was "happy to have so many women," and that in Japan it was considered his right to touch the women that he paid.

Investigators must be certain to bring enough information to the client to allow appropriate action to be taken. The fact that the company's owner, in the previously mentioned case, was a foreign national with insufficient knowledge of "American ways" didn't stop the victims from filing a lawsuit. Having background information on the president, as well as cultural information on the treatment of female employees in Japan that had been developed by the investigator, was helpful to the attorney as the case progressed.

Had this same president hired an investigator when the complaints were made, he might well have better understood the problem, and been able to change his behavior before it became a crisis.

Always be aware of significant differences, such as the cultural example, that may be the root cause of the problems being experienced by your corporate client or the employee client. It won't always be something this obvious.

16.16 Conducting the Interviews

Prior to conducting the interviews, the investigator should:

- Analyze the written complaints and all accompanying documents thoroughly. *The investigator should know the contents of the complaint so well that there is little need to look at it during interviews.*
- Determine who should be interviewed (and why)
- Prepare a list of vital questions.

An investigator should carefully consider the questions to be asked in each interview. The following suggested, basic, questions are based on EEOC investigation guidelines and the author's personal investigation experience:

1. Who committed the alleged harassment?
2. What occurred or was said?
3. When did it occur, and is it ongoing?
4. How did it affect you?
5. How did you react?
6. What response did you make when the incident(s) occurred or afterward?
7. Did you seek medical attention as a result of this incident(s)?
8. Did you seek counseling, psychological or other attention, as a result of this incident(s)?
9. Has your job been affected in any way?
10. Has your ability to perform your job been affected in any way?
11. Are there any persons who have relevant information?

12. Was anyone present when the alleged harassment occurred?
13. Did you tell anyone about it?
14. Did anyone see you immediately after the episodes of alleged harassment?
15. Did you notify anyone, file any written reports, or have any meetings regarding this incident(s)?
16. Did the person(s) who harassed you harass anyone else?
17. Do you know whether anyone made a complaint about harassment by that person?
18. Do you have any notes, physical evidence, personal journals, or other documentation regarding the incident(s)?
19. Do you have any opinion as to why this person(s) may have behaved in this manner towards you?
20. How would you like to see the situation resolved?
21. Do you know of any other relevant information?

The defense investigator may never have an opportunity to ask these questions, but if the attorney conducts a deposition, the investigator should try to be present. If that is not possible, at least provide the list of questions to the attorney and then read the answers in the transcript.

If you have the opportunity to interview the alleged victim, be sure that your mannerisms are above reproach. Be gentle, understanding, compassionate, without asking leading questions. You must remain forthright without appearing to be judgmental or accusatory. You are gathering facts. Listen attentively to the answers but also "listen" to the interviewee's body language and tone of voice. Listen carefully for what may be alluded to or for signs of animosity that suggest this accusation may be a means of retaliation for a real or perceived slight, rather than on a factual sexual harassment or hostile environment occurrence.

An allegation of sexual harassment or hostile environment is often frustrating to investigate because of the "he said, she said" situations. Seldom are there witnesses whose recollections help to clarify the events. Honing your listening and observation skills prior to accepting one of these cases can be very beneficial.

The EEOC also suggests the following:

1. The accused harasser(s) might be asked for his or her response to the allegations, why the complainant might lie, names of other persons who have relevant information, and whether any documents or physical evidence exist regarding the allegations.
2. Third parties might be asked what they saw, heard, read. They should be asked to describe the alleged harasser's behavior toward the complainant, and toward others in the workplace, what the complainant may have told them, and when, and for the names of anyone else with relevant information.

The author has found that often the most useful tool in interviewing the alleged harasser is to make sure that the interview does not take place in his or her home or in the presence of any family members. A husband and father who has been inappropriately touching a female employee or a wife or mother who has demanded that her male assistant perform sexual favors is not apt to admit to that in the presence of a family member.

Interviewed alone, in the bosses' office, with you behind that great big desk that is a symbol of power in the company, may not do it either. That office and that desk are very vivid reminders of the very real possibility that this person's job is on the line.

However, a "casual conversation" type interview, (a real interview nonetheless, with no promises of "off the record") will often bring out the truth from a very frightened and repentant employee. Even if the alleged perpetrator continues to deny the allegations, this type of interview will often let you see the real person and hear the real comments, sufficient to make a judgment on whether or not he or she is being truthful. Too many comments about "She just leads guys on," or "He does have a cute little butt," tend to make me realize that Mr. or Mrs. "I would NEVER do such a thing" has some hidden agendas or, at the very least, an insufficient understanding of the laws, rules, and policies that should be guiding him or her.

The old "She asked for it" attitude is still too prevalent in our society. An investigator has to be careful not to get sucked in to believing that the accuser is in the wrong simply because she may not have been dressing appropriately for the workplace. Inappropriate dress does not equate to inappropriate groping or demeaning or suggestive language.

Determine whether or not the interviews will be videotaped. Videotaping an interview may save you and your client a lot of grief. There can be no question of what was asked, or what the response was with this tool. However, there may be reasons for not videotaping, so thoroughly discuss this option with your investigation team and your client. Always review the videotape at your office. It's easy to miss vital points while doing the videotaped interview so take the time to watch and listen again from a different perspective. Often, it is useful to the team to have a written transcription of the videotape. You may want to consider having a court reporter present for the interview so that a certified record will be available.

16.17 Additional Tips

Constantly review the information throughout your investigation.Reread the complaint, your notes, your reports, and any discovery acquired by the attorney to avoid missing vital points. Do this out of the sight of the accuser and the witnesses, of course.

Remember that the plaintiff's investigators and lawyers are going to be doing a complete investigation of the accused company and employees. They'll be demanding lists of prior employees, the policies and procedures, training manuals and materials, employment files, payroll records, calendars, and datebooks.[29] Make sure that you know what is in everything that your client turns over to the plaintiff. You must know what "they" know!

Don't forget to do a complete background not only on the accusing plaintiff but also on any expert witnesses they present, as well as on your own expert witnesses.[30]

16.18 Preparing the Report

As discussed previously, the type of report to be prepared in a sexual harassment investigation should be discussed, decided upon, and included in the written contract with the investigator's client. *This cannot be stressed too strongly.*

If you are to prepare written reports, first be certain that you are familiar with the *current* requirements of the FCRA, and that you adhere strictly to them.

Keep each report focused on one individual interview.

Do not talk to six people in one day and then lump them all into one lengthy report. Do individual, concise reports. Although it is not clear in the requirements if *every* report has to be provided to *every* interviewed employee, reporting each interview separately will allow the employer's attorney more easily to make that determination.

Always prepare a cover letter when transferring reports to the client so that you have a record of when and to whom the information was provided. Attach a copy of all transferred reports to the copy of the cover letter and place them in your case file.

Caveat: If your file retention policies are not in order—get them in order immediately. You cannot afford to have sloppy files in a sexual harassment case. You *must* keep complete and accurate copies of your reports to protect yourself if a lawsuit or complaint is filed as a result of the investigation. The FCRA requires that *nothing be redacted* from a report when it is copied to an employee. You may need your file to prove that the report was complete when you presented it to the client.

16.19 Conclusion

The intense scrutiny of a sexual harassment investigation may cause an independent investigator to decline the assignment. However, if the investigator is thoroughly prepared, having researched the laws, acts, requirements, opinions, and other pertinent information, it can be a welcome respite from less challenging assignments. The reader is advised to also read Investigator Bruce Hulme's chapter on the FCRA in this book.

This type of investigation assignment must be conducted with the utmost respect for, and knowledge of, the federal, state, and local laws, regulations, and court opinions.

Endnotes

1. Christensen, Laura. "A Case Study of Sexual Harassment." *The Legal Investigator,* August 1992.

2. Title VII of the Civil Rights Act of 1964 (Pub. L. 88-352) (Title VII) 42 USC § 2000e.

3. *Faragher v. City of Boca Raton*, 118 S Ct 2275 (1998); *Burlington Industries v. Ellerth*, 118 S Ct 2257 (1998); *Oncale v. Sundowner Offshore Services, Inc.*

118 S Ct 998 (1998).

4. Hsieh, Sylvia. "Employers, Lawyers Who Investigate Harassment Liable Under Credit Act." 99 *LWUSA* 481.

5. For information on the EEOC and small business, see http://www.eeoc.gov/.

6. The Civil Rights Act of 1991 Pub. L. 102-166 (CRA).

7. *Meritor Savings Bank v. Vinson*, 477 US 57 (1986).

8. Despard, Allison. "The New Legal Landscape for Workplace Sexual Harassment." *Illinois Bar Journal*, August 1999 Vol. 87 p. 422.

9. Despard.

10. Schroder, Ginger D. "Supreme Court Lowers the Bar on Sexual Harassment." *Woman Attorney Magazine,* April–May 1999

11. Despard.

12. Goldberg, Jan. "New Rules for Sexual Harassment Defense." Hershner Hunter Andrews Neill & Smith, LLP Memorandum, March 3, 2000, Eugene, OR.

13. Ibid.

14. Hsieh.

15. 15 U.S.C §1681a(d).

16. Hsieh.

17. http://www.eeoc.gov/

18. Strauss, Paul. "Handling a Plaintiff's Sexual Harassment Case." *Litigation Magazine* Summer 2000 Vol. 26 No.4

19. Ibid.

20. Ibid.

21. Schultz, Vicki. "Reconceptualizing Sexual Harassment." *Yale Law Journal* April 1998, Yale Law Journal Company, Inc.

22. Ibid.

23. Ibid.

24. *Nichols v. Azteca Restaurant*, Case #99-35579 July 16, 2001, Ninth Circuit.

25. Ibid.

26. http://www.eeoc.gov/

27. *Smith v. First Union National Bank*, 2000 U.S. App. LEXIS 683 (4th Cir. 2000). Also, Shaw Pittman "Alert" newsletter. May 2000 Number 1. www.shawpittman.com.

28. http://www.eeoc.gov/

29. Christensen.

30. Ciolino, Paul J. *Advanced Forensic Civil Investigations,* Lawyers & Judges Publishing 1997 Tucson, AZ. Ch. 22 "Investigating the Experts," p. 481.

Appendix
Sample Investigation Checklist for Sexual Harassment Case

Case Name ____

"The Letter" FTC

_____ Research the current status of "The Letter." Have any recent decisions been made, or opinions handed down, that clarify (or further confuse) the responsibilities of the investigator and accused firm?

Title VII EEOC Requirements

_____ Review all requirements, deadlines, and other materials. Make a list of tasks to be completed.

Laws of State of (state of incident)

_____ Are there any additional, special, laws or regulations in your state?

_____ Review with your client and your client's legal advisor.

History of Prior Claims Against the Corporation

_____ Review complete case files, make note of names, allegations, date filed, date of determination, determination, civil action filed, civil action completed, damages awarded, damage paid, action taken by employer, current employment, status of each complainant.

_____ Determine whether any changes were made in written company policy following any of the prior cases.

_____ Compare current company policy with requirements of the Civil Rights Act,EEOC requirements and state law. If not in compliance, determine how that happened, when changes should have occurred, and whether that led to the current allegations in any way.

_____ Determine what non-tolerance policies were in effect at the time of the alleged incident(s).

_____ Determine what grievance/complaint policies were in effect at the time of the alleged incident(s).

_____ Compare names and allegations of current case with prior cases.

The Current Case

_____ Start a chronological timeline of all events relative to the charges, and to the persons involved.

_____ Make a list of the allegations, including the dates and times alleged.

_____ Add to that list the response action taken each time by the victim.

(Did the alleged victim use the employer's established reporting policies?)

(Did the alleged victim inform the harasser that the conduct was unwelcome?)

_____ Add to the list the action(s) taken by the employer in response to any notification or complaint.

_____ Analyze the written complaints and all accompanying complaints.

_____ Determine who should be interviewed and why.

_____ Determine if interviews will be videotaped.

Chapter 17

Computer Forensics

Harold F. Coyne, Jr., PPS

Synopsis

17.1 Introduction

Computer forensics has fast become the topic of conversation among security professionals and corporate officers. Never before has such a vast array of information and evidence been readily available to anyone who wants and knows how to obtain it. With the wide spread of computers, a new profession has emerged, the computer forensic investigator. These investigators need to be able to obtain, analyze, and report their findings of information on suspect data to a wide range of professionals.

Criminal prosecutors, civil attorneys, insurance companies, accounting firms, corporations, law enforcement and private citizens use computer forensic professionals. Each and every day a new professional acquires the need for a computer forensic investigator.

Years ago, investigators wore the leather of their shoes tracking down leads; in today's climate, the investigator turns on his or her personal computer. During investigations and evidence collection one of the first items seized and investigated is now the personal computer. Individuals use computers for every part of their lives; they write their communications and record their calendars as well as communicate with the outside world. Everything an individual does on a personal computer is recorded. Even when the information is deleted from the hard drive, it is still possible to retrieve the deleted information. By examining a computer hard drive the forensic professional can view e-mails, web site visits, schedules, and so on. It is virtually impossible to remove information from a hard drive. Just as one company is creating software to erase information, another company, many times the same company, is creating software to restore the information. If an individual wants to completely remove information so that no one can review it, the simplest way is to destroy the hard drive itself. Other than that, the individual takes the risk of having his or her information retrieved and examined.

17.2 Hiring Process

Computer forensic investigations must be planned and executed with great precision. Every act must be intentional and recorded. No mistakes can be made; if a mistake is made the entire investigation could be in jeopardy. When hiring a forensic professional, make sure of her reputation, check her previous cases in court, did she follow proper evidence-collection techniques? Does she have recommendations? Does she have the experience she needs to conduct the investigation and to testify effectively?

Choose the professional carefully; a simple keystroke at the incorrect time, a simple report error, or any deviation from accepted procedure can and will impair the credibility of the investigation. When choosing a forensic investigator make sure not only that he can analyze the subject computer, but can also explain his investigation and conclusions in plain English. Many times a computer professional will not be able to explain or report in layman's terms. Without clear reporting and testimony, a forensic case can become convoluted. The attorney or corporate representative should ask to see a copy of a sanitized forensic report. Can you understand it without making a list of questions to the investigator? Is it written in nontechnical language? It is expected that some technical terms will be necessary; after all this is a technical topic and investigation, but it should be kept to a minimum. Remember, judges and juries are regular people—they are not computer forensics professionals; if you don't understand the report, they certainly won't either.

The number one rule of performing computer forensic investigations is that the subject's computer cannot be altered or damaged in any way. If the original information on the subject's computer is altered or damaged, the credibility of the case is seriously jeopardized.

At no time should the forensic investigator perform any investigation on the original hard drive of the subject's computer. A forensic professional should copy the information to a separate storage device to be examined later. At every step in the investigation, as previously stated, complete and detailed notes must be taken. Every observation must be recorded: Where is the subject's computer located? Is the computer on or off? Is the monitor on or off? Are there multiple storage devices connected to the subject's machine, such as CD-ROM burners or stand-alone storage devices? Is the computer connected to a network? All of these possible occurrences need to be recorded. Once the investigation is complete and the notes become a report, it may be necessary to re-examine other locations for possible needs of the investigation. If the report states that a computer network or a stand alone storage device is involved, did the client expand the scope of investigation to cover the other computer systems and storage devices. Every observation recorded in notes can and will help to preserve the evidence.

Once the forensics professional arrives at the site, she should chronicle every observation and action she takes. It is imperative that a timeline be setup and achieved. This needs to be done to ensure the integrity of the case. Every action needs to be recorded, both in writing and with digital photographs and video.

A video should be made of the entire workspace where the computer is located. This will not only help to ensure everything is put back where it was when the investigation started, but it also can be used later to identify anything that may have been overlooked. A video recording of the copying process can show that the forensic copying of data was done correctly, which will help with report writing, as well as the investigator's testimony in the event the case enters legal proceedings. The video camera should be set up on a tripod so that it is stationary and still. The camera should be positioned so that every action that is performed is in view of the camera. In addition to the video camera, pictures should be taken with either a digital camera or a 35-mm camera.

Up-to-the minute notes should be taken throughout the filming and photographing. An example would be:

> 9:03 A.M. approximately
> Investigator entered office of subject.
>
> 9:11 A.M. approximately
> Investigator started recording surroundings and workspace with video camera.

If time and procedure were constantly recorded in this manner, it would be very difficult to attack the procedures in a court of law.

Once the workspace is recorded and photographed it is then time for the investigator to inspect the subject's computer itself. He or she will check to see if the computer is on or off, what type of computer it is, what type of keyboard or mouse is plugged into the computer, and if there is a scanner, printer or PDA cradle. This must all be observed and recorded. Pictures should also be taken at this point of the connections at the rear of the computer. Small labels should be placed temporarily on each cable or attachment so that when the investigation is complete, the investigator can then be sure of each cable's location.

If the subject's computer is running when the investigator arrives at the location he or she should unplug the computer immediately. Doing this will stop all information from being recorded and prevent information on the hard drive from being overwritten by new information being stored there.

For the purpose of this chapter an example of how an investigator conducts forensic copy of the subject's hard drive at the subject's location is given. As stated before, this is a common procedure during a civil investigation. If law enforcement was involved, the computer would most likely be impounded, labeled as evidence, and transported to the police station or another location to be examined.

17.6 Forensic Copying

When all labeling and recording of the procedures are complete, the investigator should open the subject's computer, and remove its hard drive. Again, each step in the procedure should be video recorded and photographed. Power and data cables of the hard drive should be labeled. The investigator should also record the hard drive's serial number, make, model and jumper settings before performing any forensic activity on it.

After recording all the pertinent information about the hard drive, the hard drive is installed into the forensic computer. The forensic computer is used to access the subject's hard drive without disturbing the startup files and so on. By using this method of copying, it is possible to copy all files on the hard drive without altering any of them. Once the hard drive is installed the forensic computer should be turned on. A number of different operating systems can be used on a forensic machine. The operating system of choice should be flexible and easy to use. Once the forensic machine is turned on, it is possible to access the subject's hard drive.

The data from the subject's machine can be stored on a separate hard drive located in the forensic machine or it can be copied through a local area network to a separate storage device. The separate storage device is used for a number of reasons. If the information is stored in a separate location, it can be stored easily to keep the chain of evidence with greater safety to the data enclosed on it. One such storage device is called a SnapServer.™ These devices have enough space to hold the contents of an entire machine or even a small office network. This avoids the use of multiple storage devices.

If the subject's hard drive is to be returned to the subject's machine, two separate copies of the data should be made. This is done so that an original copy will be available for comparison to the copy that the forensic investigation was performed on. The copy is also created to give the investigator a copy of the hard drive as it was presented the day of the investigation. This pristine copy of the subject's hard drive must never be changed or altered in any way. If alteration takes place, the investigation may be compromised.

When copying the data from the subject's hard drive to the storage device a complete sector copy must be made. A sector copy is made by copying all information from the hard drive to the storage device, even the deleted files on the hard drive. This is not done by simply copying files. Rather, the investigator copies each area, or sector, of the hard drive. Thus, it copies all files, even hidden files, system files, boot files, deleted files, and so on. If a sector copy is not made, only the easily accessed files are copied. That is not acceptable because files that are needed for the investigation could be missed.

17.7 Examining the Data

Once the data has been copied and the subject hard drive has been returned to either storage or the subject machine, the meat of the investigation starts. Analyzing the data can be long and arduous. The investigator must return to his or her notes.

The inspection of the data also needs to be meticulously recorded in the investigation notes. The investigator can use any number of special tools to search for files and data needed for the investigation. Different types of files can be searched for different cases. For example, if the case was about accounting practices, spreadsheet files may be the first and most frequently accessed source of information. If the case involves the search for pornography, image files may be listed for search. In addition, files can be searched for words that may be pertinent to the investigation. For example, typing the name "Coyne" in the search criteria would search all documents for that name, and any documents with the word "Coyne" would become apparent.

17.8 Conclusion

In any investigation, the procedures and investigative techniques can make the difference between winning or losing the case in court. A computer forensic case is no different. The same rules apply: do your homework, get qualified investigators, maintain the chain and integrity of evidence, and write a clear and concise report. If the forensic investigation is done correctly, there is no room for the subject individual to contest information taken from his or her computer. After all, computers do not lie, they simply tell the truth of the data that was entered into the system.

17.9 Addendum

Since the last printing of this chapter, a number of different approaches have come to the forensic world, mostly in data storage.

With the advent of newer technologies data storage can make the forensic professional's life truly easier. In addition, it can also make it harder for the forensic professional to find the data needed to be investigated.

One such example is the newer storage capabilities of compact flash cards. These cards are used mainly in digital cameras, but can be connected directly through a cradle to the computer. These cards can hold as much as eight gigabytes of information on one disk. That information can be in the form of files, pictures, movies or any other type of data. To think of the storage space, imagine that over eleven CD-ROMs of information can now reside on one compact flash card no larger that a book of matches.

We have found that with these new removable storage devices, the search for the questioned data needs to move into other areas or devices beyond the normal computer.

For instance, someone can now connect the data storage device to the computer and write directly to this media.

For example, in a case that we had worked on recently, a number of files were stored on such a storage device. Even though a search of the computer system was performed, the files could not be found. In fact the subject had written the files directly to the compact flash storage device via a cradle connected to the computer. The individual then removed the storage card and inserted it inside of a digital camera to hide it form investigators.

When a civil search warrant or law enforcement warrant is made out for search of files, the investigator must now think of all storage devices that are possible to hold such files, such as digital cameras. Without this approach, the files and evidence can easily be overlooked.

In an advantageous way, this new storage medium can now be used by forensic professionals to copy information to examine. With these devices developing each and every day, soon the amount of equipment the forensic professional will need to perform the audit on could possibly fit in their coat pockets.

The devices can hold computer software needed to complete the audit as well as hold copes of files in question. Thus, a skilled investigator can now remove a suspect hard drive, connect to their forensic machine and through a USB cable copy the information to the card.

We have started using this approach; to copy the files needed for investigations. No longer are there large areas of our office to hold removable hard drives, Snap Servers, CD-ROMs, and so on. Now our storage area consists of a small shelf inside a safe. The files are both safe and no longer taking up huge amounts of storage.

In addition, once a copy of the information is made to another CF card, the investigator just simply needs to carry a laptop and the cradle to present evidence. The entire case can be carried to the court proceedings, instead of a larger hard drive or many CD-ROMs.

In conclusion, it is important for the investigator to remember to not only do an investigation of just the computer system, but of all disks, even ones that look as if they only belong to cameras or other devices.

Chapter 18

Investigating Internal Theft in a Small Business

Paul J. Ciolino, CFE, CII, BCFE

Synopsis

18.1 Introduction

"Outraged," "shocked," and "stunned" are the words most commonly heard from an owner or comptroller of a small business who has just discovered that their company has been victimized by a loyal employee(s). The initial steps taken in gaining control of the theft problem will determine the successful or catastrophic outcome of the investigation.

Every day, in every city, there is an employee in a company or service organization either planning the theft of goods, or involved in a continuing criminal enterprise that is victimizing the small or medium-sized business. In a world where profit margins are slim, and the competition cutthroat, an enterprising thief can bankrupt a business. The private investigator's role in stopping the theft is critical to that business remaining viable.

Literally billions of dollars are stolen every year in every imaginable industry that produces, ships, or brokers goods of any kind. The vast majority of the people who commit these crimes go undetected and unpunished. Most of them, when caught, or detected, are simply terminated, and let go without punishment. The merits of whether or not to seek retribution or criminal punishment of the perpetrators are the basis of this chapter.

The author would recommend that prosecution be sought, to the fullest extent allowed by law, in all but the most unusual circumstances. The way the investigator builds the criminal case will determine whether that is possible.

Recently a business owner in an urban area who had just completed the first computerized product inventory contacted our firm. What the owners of this family-run, third-generation company discovered was that they were one fiscal quarter away from bankruptcy, and personal ruin. This company specialized in brokering and transporting food products, in a specialized industry.

What began as a simple theft investigation turned into a three-month marathon that saw eleven employees arrested for felony theft. All eventually plead guilty in separate trials. In addition, the company's insurance carrier was eventually sued, and the company recovered over $450,000 and $50,000 that had been written off as a loss. This enabled the small business owner to at least recover investigative and legal fees in this matter.

18.2 The Initial Conference with the Client

One of the most critical aspects of the internal theft investigation is the initial meeting with the client. It is in this meeting that all of the critical details need to be worked out. Very seldom will the business owner, security director or comptroller realize the depth of the problem. The investigator's role in this meeting is to lay out a basic investigative plan that will stop the hemorrhaging and identify the thieves. As with most clients, they will want a quick and painless (cheap) solution—but problems of this type are neither simple, nor inexpensive.

So, in addition to being a brilliant investigator, one has to be able to articulate the complex nature of this type of investigation. The best way to accomplish this is to be brutally honest about costs.

Costs will vary from region to region; they are very seldom the same. The single biggest obstacle that occurs in investigator/client relations is usually related to money or, even more importantly, the *shock bill.* The shock bill is the one that is presented to clients at the end of a case, and the clients are so shocked by the amount that they generally refuse to pay it or they insist upon a substantial discount. The way to avoid this very problematic issue is to establish parameters in the initial conference.

Ask the clients exactly what they want done. If they don't know, then it is up to the manager of the investigation to propose a budget that is in line with the job's requirements. In the case on which this chapter is based, the following was the initial investigative plan:

Type of Service	Hours Required	Estimated Cost
Body guard for Ex. V.P.	60	$6,000.00
Undercover employee	120	7,500.00
Undercover employee	120	7,500.00
Bkgrnd. inv. on 26 employees	–	5,000.00
Surveillance team	100	10,000.00
Hidden cameras & assc. costs	–	6,500.00
General investigative & supervisory	250	30,000.00
Polygraph examination fees	–	3,000.00
Preliminary initial costs		$75,500.00

By having a frank discussion about the preliminary costs, and being as honest as you can about what the investigation is going to entail, you will have eliminated many of the problems that seem to crop up as a result of poor communication. Of course, any discussions regarding billing should be spelled out in the initial engagement letter or contract so that, in the event of any dispute that occurs at a later date, this part of the conversation will have been adequately documented without the usual "he said/ she said" rhetoric.

18.3 Initial Investigative Steps

All too frequently you will come into a situation of this type and discover that the firm has never done a background investigation on its employees. In this particular case, the employees were largely hired on the recommendation of other employees. This led to a situation where many of the employees were, in fact, related to each other, or from the same neighborhood and, in this instance, members of the same street gang.

We immediately pulled all of the employees' personnel files and started verifying information. We also started running local criminal and civil background investigation checks. What we discovered was that at least one-third of the employees were convicted felons. Almost all of them had numerous civil suits filed against them, in some cases going back ten years. Civil cases are important because they show how financially desperate one might be. All of the civil suits dealt exclusively with employees who were clearly living beyond their means, thus giving them a motive for "going into business for themselves." The clients were incredulous. How could this happen? They felt as if they were running a halfway house for convicted felons, not a viable business.

Simple and inexpensive background investigations would likely have prevented any major theft problems. However, as security and investigative professionals from around the world are aware, most employers forego the basic cost of employee background checks in the foolish hope of cutting costs and saving money. This employer found out that failure to conduct these minimum efforts cost the business hundreds of thousands of dollars.

The initial paper investigation will help you to obtain a list of potential and often well-motivated thieves. As in any investigation undertaken, history is our best teacher. This review also will show you "who's who in the zoo." In other words, who is related to whom, who referred the employee for the job? These are all excellent investigative tools for figuring out who may be conspiring with whom.

In addition, you will want to do database searches on your more likely suspects. This will show property records, vehicles, and luxury items such as boats, motorcycles, and jet skis. When you have an employee making $40,000 a year, and his lifestyle looks like something out of the *Rich and Famous*, you may assume that he is not a lottery winner, but a potential unknown silent partner of the business.

18.4 Undercover Operations

In this particular investigation, we recommended that we place an undercover operative (UC) on the afternoon and midnight shifts. As there were many supervisors about during the day shift, we felt that we could forego an undercover investigator during the day shift. Generally, you will want your uncover operatives to possess the minimum basic qualifications:

- Age: appropriate to the employees with whom he or she will be working. Do not put a forty-five year old accountant type in with twenty-year-old dock workers.
- *Race, sex, and ethnic issues should always be considered.*
- Must be well versed about the potential targets. Do not waste time and effort by targeting the secretarial pool, when the truck drivers are the main suspects.
- Must have a clear and concise idea as to what he or she may do, and what not to become involved in. Communication between the UC and the handlers are imperative. Daily debriefings are a must.

The single biggest potential problem for a UC is being discovered or "burned." The only personnel who should be involved in the undercover process are the investigative supervisor, the company owner and, occasionally, the personnel manager. Remember that the more people involved in this process, the higher the likelihood that the UD will be discovered and the entire investigation short-circuited.

The main role of the UC is to discover how the thefts are occurring, when they are occurring, and who is involved. Just by listening and observing, these issues are usually quickly discovered. At some point the UC may be asked to participate in these deeds. The UC will also be a big asset in helping the employer discover what supervisors are doing their jobs, and which ones are turning their back on any potential problems.

No matter what the case, the UC's work must be documented in explicit detail on a daily basis. The key to any successful UC operation is close supervision.

18.5 Electronic Surveillance

After you have done the preliminary work and have your undercover operatives in place, it is time to start thinking about how to prove these thefts to the satisfaction of a court of law. The quickest and most effective way is, without question, hidden cameras and recording equipment—but the problems are numerous. Placement, installation, monitoring, retrieving and changing tapes are all land-mine problems, which can jeopardize the entire investigation at any phase.

The first issue is cost. None of this is inexpensive. The smaller the device, the more sophisticated the lens, the higher the costs. Placing a camera in a forty-foot warehouse ceiling that will overlook the loading dock area is great, but will it be able to identify personnel who all wear the same uniform and are from the same ethnic group? Will the picture be clear enough to see serial numbers and identify particular brands that are all shipped in the same packaging, and same shape box? These issues need to be worked out in advance. It does not help the investigation if this evidence is ruled inadmissible due to clarity issues.

When dealing with the electronic issues, be creative. Utilize Global Positioning System (GPS) monitors on delivery trucks. Put hidden cameras in the back of semi's. Place cameras on the exterior of the buildings, near unguarded or loosely watched alleys or exits. Hire specialists. Do not attempt to be the expert on everything. You will come out ahead, in the long run, if you subcontract other experts in matters in which you are not experienced. So long as you plan ahead, and don't surprise the client with that "shock bill," everyone should be happy.

18.6 Surveillance

Once you have identified the key suspects, catching them stealing is nice—but finding out who they are selling the stolen goods to is better. In this particular instance, surveillance of the company truck drivers showed who was making unauthorized deliveries, and who was helping themselves to produce off the back of the truck. One truck driver who had been employed for twenty-three years was caught delivering product to his home on a daily basis. After work he would return home and start delivering stolen product to local convenience stores where he would be paid cash for the product. Search warrants were obtained for his residence and over $25,000 worth of product were recovered. In addition to being arrested and convicted, he lost his pension.

Surveillance was also maintained on the loading dock every night. Employees were filmed dumping product into the dumpsters. When their shift was over, they were filmed recovering the dumped product and placing it into their personal vehicles.

The undercover operatives were also able to notify the surveillance teams of what was occurring inside the facility and out of their line of sight, thus enabling them to be ready to film or follow the more likely suspects.

18.7 Interviews and Interrogations

Once your firm has documented and identified the ringleaders and thieves through the use of human and electronic surveillance, there should be enough evidence to confront the suspects. Hopefully, the thieves are unaware of your efforts to date, and you still have the element of surprise. However, in all likelihood, "rumors" have begun to spread, and the suspect employees realize that "something is in the air."

How the confrontations with the suspect employees are handled will often determine the success of the entire operation. In this particular case, all of the employees were members of the Teamsters union and, as members of a union, they had certain rights. One of the most important rights was that the union steward had a right to be present when an employee was being accused of any misconduct. In this instance the union steward was a suspect, so management asked a senior union representative to represent the employees.

By now, the investigator should have very carefully thought out how to reach the established goals. This only can be accomplished by involving members of management, their lawyers, the insurance adjuster and any internal security personnel. The goals in this case were to terminate and prosecute the suspect employees, ensure the safety and security of the plant operation and non-involved employees, remove the undercover personnel, and coordinate the arrest and any subsequent search warrants with the local police department and prosecutor's office. Management also had to have replacement personnel standing by and ready to work. Sometimes management personnel can fill in for the terminated employees, but in this case the theft was so rampant and far-ranging that replacements had to be hired, trained and ready to replace the suspect employees on the day of the confrontations.

Many hours and days were required to coordinate all of these efforts. As the investigation progressed, more of management had to be made aware of what was occurring within the company. Maintaining secrecy during this phase is difficult. Secretaries start getting numerous telephone calls from strangers who refuse to say why they are calling, You and your staff are spending an inordinate amount of time with the client's management, and the daily activity of the operation is suddenly charged with electricity. Employees do and will talk. Office gossip is unavoidable. A plausible cover story must be in place—an IRS audit, an EPA inspection—whatever the reason given for the influx of new people and the increased activity, the story needs to be credible.

Careful planning can help avoid alerting the suspects prior to the investigator wanting them to know that the game is over. However, detailed planning is a must. You have to insist upon complete control at this point in the investigation.

The day arrives when all of these plans are to be implemented. The first order of business is to make sure adequate security is in place. Generally, a substantial show of armed and uniform security is required. This accomplishes a number of goals. Number one this is no time for a workplace violence incident. Remember, employees who are about to lose their jobs, pensions, and potentially their freedom, may feel that they have nothing to lose.

In addition to armed and uniform security, the interrogation personnel must have private rooms in which to work. Also required are one or two court reporters to take sworn statements and confessions. The interrogation personnel must be extremely competent and professional in both appearance and demeanor. This is no time for training new or inexperienced people. This is where the case is made or lost.

All potential suspects must be separated from one another during this phase. Coordinate this with the client's personnel manager. Get them separated and out of the building, but available for interviews as soon as you need them. A plan must be in place as to who will be interviewing whom. Photographs, videos and physical evidence gathered during the investigation must be ready so that the suspects can be confronted with the apparently overwhelming amount of evidence you have gathered.

Often you will want to use props such as a large four-inch binder with the suspect's name and "Theft Investigation Report" plainly visible in large bold lettering on the front. The book may contain empty paper, but the suspect doesn't know that. Surveillance photos can be blown up and taped to the wall. The more props, the more intimidated the suspect—and the union rep—will be. Remember that this is more a psychological battle than a physical one.

The order in which you start interviewing is critical. Remember that the goal is to learn how long the theft problem has existed, who has been involved (both past and current employees), who has witnessed what, and who may be involved that you have not identified.

Employees who are not involved in the thefts should be interviewed first. Honest employees want to help. They want to work in a safe and drug-free environment. Although they may at first be reluctant, they will normally become more comfortable and wind up supplying much-needed intelligence. Never fail to ask every person interviewed *whom he or she believes is responsible for the thefts*. This question is perhaps the most critical one you will ask. They will almost always supply an answer. In addition, they will also help you learn a number of things that were not picked up in your previous endeavors.

After speaking with the non-involved parties, it is now time to turn the spotlight onto the real thieves. Remember that you are operating from a position of the moral superior. The suspects know it, and you should never relinquish that position. The goal is to get the guilty employee to confess, confirm previous bad acts, implicate other guilty employees and lead you to the stolen product. All of this must be done with the guilty party believing that the more he or she cooperates the less severe the penalties—but never guarantee anything to the guilty party. The only guarantee you will ever make is that, if he or she cooperates fully, you will attempt to minimize the damage to them.

After you have gotten all you are going to get, it is time to bring in the court reporter and take a formal statement. This is essential, because it will be used later at union hearings, court proceedings and the like.

After you have secured the confession in a formal setting, it is time to decide if a criminal arrest and prosecution are necessary. We would almost always say "yes" because it sends a message to all future employees that dishonest acts will not be tolerated. It also helps shield the employer from potential costly civil litigation brought on by the discharged employees' legal counsel and union. A government-led prosecution helps insulate the employer from all kinds of potential legal mine fields.

We would suggest that the police and the local prosecutor *not be brought in* until the investigation is almost completely finished. Our experience is that although the police are helpful, they are not necessarily very experienced in running these types of operations. They are also not usually too concerned about the potential civil liabilities that the employer could face if these matters are civilly litigated at a later date. As the investigative firm that is primarily responsible, you must be very concerned because the employer's attorneys will not hesitate to "third party" you in any litigation that comes down on his or her client.

18.8 Summary

The mark of a qualified, professional firm is not only the results it obtains, but also how well its investigators document their work. Reports and all subsequent attachments must be laid out in a formal, well thought out, and planned manner. All of your firm's hard work will fall by the wayside if this most critical aspect is ignored, or is done improperly. Personal opinions, theories and "I think, I believe" have no place in your final report.

Your final report will reflect the professionalism of your company. It may be reviewed by dozens of individuals in the years to come. Always be conscious of the fact that at some point your investigation will be reviewed and critiqued. Remember what Dirty Harry said: "A man has to know his limitations."

Chapter 19

Product Diversion

Reginald J. Montgomery, CPP, PSP, CLI, CFE, CP, CST

Synopsis

19.1 Introduction

Product diversion, by definition, refers to products sold by the manufacturer, that are distributed into markets other than originally intended by contract, law, or regulation. This enables third parties to undercut the intended price of the product to the public and reap huge profits. This international scheme hinges on an industry practice in which manufacturers set up different prices for the same product. It is a way to break into new markets and expand name recognition outside the United States. Because of tax incentives and other cost savings, American businesses can sell their products to overseas distributors at dramatically lower prices than those paid by distributors based in the United States. When products are diverted, those goods are illegally rerouted by a third party back to American markets.

The hierarchy of the pricing of products is generally familiar to most Americans. It is apparent in everyday life. One store will have a pair of designer jeans for $65.00. That same pair of jeans can be purchased at a discount store for $30.00 and at a flea market for $15.00. Sometimes this reflects nothing more than a legal pricing of merchandise that has been bought from the manufacturer at a wholesale price and sold at various discounts depending on the necessary overhead.

However, there are several tiers of wholesale. That same product might be purchased as a promotional or institutional item at a special rate, lower than the wholesale price available to the regular retail market. This allows special rates to large purchasers of merchandise who are promoting a particular product.

19.2 Diversion Is Not Theft

Most investigators have had exposure to theft of product and tend to confuse the two situations. When is it diversion and when is it theft? The answer is simple. *Theft* is the unauthorized taking and *diversion* is the unauthorized distribution achieved by misrepresentation. An example of theft can be seen in an investigation conducted several years ago.

A large manufacturer of designer leather handbags was known for its exclusive and costly product. The company did not sell to discounters. They maintained the quality and exclusivity of their bags because of this limited but highly priced market. Someone happened to purchase a bag with the designer label from a street vender. To all appearances it was an identical bag. In fact, when compared with a sample from Bloomingdales' showroom floor, it was exactly the same. Upon this discovery, the manufacturer initiated an investigation. It involved the placing of an undercover operative inside the workroom of a company that was subcontracted to assemble and finish the handbags. The operative discovered that the theft was actually an internal problem being perpetrated by one of the senior management personnel in collusion with a subcontractor. Records indicated that only three bags could be cut from a piece of leather. The remainder was written off as scrap. In reality, if the patterns were laid out carefully, an extra two bags could be cut from each piece of leather. This allowed thousands of additional bags to be made, right in the subcontractor's own workroom. The overage was shipped to wholesalers who undercut the product and sold it through venders on city street corners. In fact, it was the same bag and of the same quality. This is theft.

19.3 How Diversion Occurs

Diversion will most likely occur in the areas of:

- export sales
- promotional offers
- regional promotions
- samples, trial, and travel packs
- hotel amenities
- charitable donations
- U.S. (and foreign) government sales
- destruction of excess merchandise

A classic example is an investigation that was successfully conducted on a dental supply company. For purposes of anonymity and client confidentiality it shall be referred to here as PC Dental Supply. This is a company that sells products to dentists and institutions where dental work is performed. In May, PC Dental negotiated a special promotional package with ABC Hygiene Company to distribute small bottles (3 oz.) of ABC's most popular mouthwash. The promotion stated that for every $500 in mouthwash sales, the institution would be given a free case of mouthwash to be provided to patients at the time of their yearly checkup. Everything looked legitimate until the records began to indicate that PC Dental had purchased in excess of 100,000 cases of mouthwash in a four-month period. That's over a million small bottles. The original contract allowed ABC's representatives (in this instance, the investigators) to review the distribution records of PC Dental.

This is a key factor in the ability of an investigator to be effective for the client. When products are purchased according to these specific discount schedules, there is a contract negotiated between the manufacturer and the purchaser. This contract gives the specific right for the manufacturer, or his representative, to review all records related to the purchase and distribution of the discounted product.

The investigators were, therefore, able to review and compare shipping, receiving, and payment records. A large portion of the mouthwash order had allegedly been shipped to a hospital distributor in California. With the help of a local investigator, the distributor's receiving clerk and warehouse workers were interviewed. They swore that they never saw, received, or unloaded this product. There were no records of buying the product and no one had ever heard of PC Dental. Ultimately, admissions were obtained from the parties involved in the diversion. Armed with the documents provided by the diverter in the paper trail, information was uncovered proving that the intended party never received the merchandise.

The culprits "rolled over" when interviewed, and their statements were verified by polygraph. The product was actually sold to a wholesaler in Brooklyn and then to a large distributor in Maryland. The Brooklyn wholesaler originated and financed the scheme.

This was a diversion case. It was a contractual matter because PC Dental misrepresented the stated and intended use of the product from its contractual agreement, and it was also a fraud. In addition, because it involved more than one party, it was a conspiracy to commit fraud. Because PC Dental was located in New Jersey, the institution in California, the wholesaler in Brooklyn, and the distributor who ultimately received the product in Maryland, it became an interstate situation and thus a RICO charge. The corporate client was interested only in recouping the money they had lost because of product underselling. By invoking the contractual agreement, which allowed for treble damages and the payment of the difference between the very low wholesale price and the actual retail price to the consumer, they were able to recover their lost profit. A negotiated settlement was agreed upon. This case exemplifies the difference in theft and diversion. It also is indicative of the various consequences of diversion in the legal world.

19.4 Diversion versus Other Forms of Product Abuse

It can be said that diversion is unauthorized distribution achieved by misrepresentation. Diversion is a result of established contractual relationships between the manufacturer and the distributor. When that product is purchased at one price but diverted for a separate and unintended use, it falls within the scope of the product diversion case. Since the concept of diversion is so specific and generally not understood by the public, it is often confused with several other areas of product abuse:

Counterfeiting is the making of an item to *look like* the original. Generally it is of lesser quality.

Pirating is the theft of product, such as the bootlegging of HBO or pay-per-view cable programs that are normally sold (such as boxing matches and soccer matches that sell exclusively through television vendors).

Trademark infringement involves the use of a name or label which closely approximates that of the original, authorized manufacturer. We have all seen Cucci instead of Gucci and initialed designer clothing with a similar logo but slightly different initials.

Gray market also deals with the sale of American branded products which are manufactured for less in foreign countries and sold in the United States for lower than retail prices. It is not uncommon for items such as shampoo, which is made in Mexico (where the peso is grossly devalued), to be purchased from that source and brought into the U.S. to be sold in Spanish-speaking neighborhoods. The item is purchased for less, sold for less, and has the added value of being labeled in Spanish.

These non-diversion forms of product abuse need to be understood so that the investigator learning about the intricacies of diversion will not confuse them.

19.5 The Four Areas of Diversion

Concentration in the remainder of this chapter will be on four specific areas where product intended for one market is diverted to another: (1) charity, (2) closeout or counterfeit dating, (3) market diversion, and (4) dated product.

A. Charity

Charity diversions are not only unethical but illegal as well. A prime example of this type of diversion can be seen in the area of consumables. Food packages are coded uniquely by manufacturers, and each item has a "shelf life" (a date after which the product should not be sold; frequently product safety is an issue, but it is also used to insure product flow and turnover). When its shelf life has expired, the product is not necessarily unfit for consumption (in fact, it is generally good for a year or more after that date—except, of course, for milk and dairy products). Therefore, when a product has come within a month or so of its shelf life, the retail store (supermarket) will remove it from the shelves. The store receives credit for this unsold product from the manufacturer, so there is no loss to them. In the name of goodwill these products are often shipped to local food banks where they can be purchased at minimal prices by homeless shelters and state-subsidized nursing facilities.

The author was once retained in a case where an individual was purchasing great amounts of grocery products from the food bank, alleging to be supplying a daycare center. In fact, what he was doing was storing the product in two rooms of the center (limiting the space for the children) and selling the product on weekends at local flea markets for his own profit. This is a classic charity case of diversion.

B. Closeout or counterfeit dating

Closeout or counterfeit dating involves these same "shelf life" dates. Often items are packaged in cases and the expiration date for use is stamped all over the outside of the carton. There are highly sophisticated syndicates that specialize in "repackaging" product and stamping new, later expiration dates on the outside. Therefore, they are *selling outdated products* which appear to be timely. When the closeout dates are replaced by new dates on original packaging by innovative diverters, this is the diversion of product from its intended use. In most cases, this product would be destined for destruction.

C. Market diversion

Market diversion is common. It can be observed simply by walking through the ever-growing weekend flea market or observing products sold by street venders.

A recent case involved the exposure of a large diverter who was purchasing merchandise by the truckload at institutional promotional prices and selling that same product through regular retail stores. The item was cough syrup. The stated, contractual use of this product was to place a packet of cough syrup in college kits to be given to new students as promotional merchandise. (Similar "kits" are given to hospital patients and generally include a miniature toothbrush, toothpaste, hand cream, and talcum powder.) Because of the stated use, the buyer/diverter was given a large discount from the normal wholesale cost for these items. The buyer/diverter ordered forty tractor-trailer loads of this cough syrup. Simple arithmetic would dictate that there was enough cough syrup for every man, woman, and child in the United States to stem a sore throat for a year! The quantity raised corporate eyebrows, and an investigation ensued. Surveillance and investigation revealed that the cough syrup was being repackaged and sold directly to retail channels, tripling the normal profit for the buyer/diverter.

D. Dated product

Dated product, as previously explained, does not necessarily become unusable after the expiration date has passed. One has but to walk through a flea market to note a large variety of items generally seen on supermarket shelves for sale at extraordinarily low prices. A closer inspection of items such as over-the-counter pharmaceutical products (Tylenol®, aspirin, Neosporin® cream, etc.) will reveal that the bottles have dates that have expired. The products were most likely taken off the shelves with intent to be either returned to the manufacturer or sent to another venue by the manufacturer for sale at a lesser price.

While the traditional methods of surveillance (undercover operatives, taking witness statements and interviews) are often useful, the diverter maintains the real evidence himself—the paper trail of his own records. Comparing original contracts and "use" statements (in which the intended end use of the product is clearly spelled out) of the diverter against those of the manufacturer is the starting point. Next, the bills of sale from the manufacturer generally provide the dates and quantities purchased and the responsible parties. Shipping orders and bills of lading should be examined and compared to warehouse receipts from receiving clerks. Checks paid for the transportation of merchandise are also compared. Invoices reflecting to whom merchandise is sold and method of shipment are scrutinized. It becomes a numbers game, and the numbers sometimes just don't match up.

On Wednesday, July 26, 1995, a news release was issued by First Assistant U.S. Attorney Robert J. Cleary: "Three Charged for Roles in Alleged 'False Export' Diversion Schemes That Cost Four American Manufacturers Millions in Losses." The article provided information on three individuals (Kotbey Mohamed Kotbey, Mary Ellen Kitler, and Urs Brunschweiler) charged in a 122-count indictment by a Newark, N.J., federal grand jury. The counts included conspiracy, wire fraud, mail fraud, interstate transportation of goods obtained by fraud, issuing false bills of lading, and money laundering.

It continued, stating that:

> U.S. manufacturers of branded consumer products often export their products to foreign customers for sale overseas, and commonly grant the export customer a discount of up to 50 percent below U.S. prices. Manufacturers are willing to grant such steep discounts in order to open new markets and expand worldwide sales. The great disparity between domestic and export wholesale prices for finished U.S. products creates the opportunity for the fraud known as "product diversion," according to court documents in a related case . . . In all four schemes Kotbey was able to obtain lower prices by falsely claiming the products would be distributed in Eastern Europe or the Middle East. Instead, Kotbey sold the products for distribution in the United States and did not distribute them in foreign countries. In two of the four schemes, Kotbey claimed the goods would be donated to the poor. In one of the four schemes, Kotbey claimed the goods would be distributed to military organizations for humanitarian purposes, the Indictment alleges. Through these schemes (he) obtained blood sugar monitoring devices used by diabetics, popular Nestle products such as Taster's Choice Coffee and Nestle's Quick, and prescription drugs. During the sentencing of an alleged co-conspirator, it was established that Nestle alone lost millions of dollars as a result of this scheme.

Additional charges were explained:

> According to the indictment, Brunschweiler supplied bogus export documents to Johnson & Johnson, making it appear that the goods purchased were shipped overseas. Brunschweiler was arrested in France on July 12, upon a warrant issued by U.S. Magistrate Judge Dennis M. Cavanaugh, also in Newark. Brunschweiler is being detained in a French jail pending extradition proceedings to the United States. The

> U.S. Department of State is expected to present a formal extradition request to French authorities sometime in the next several weeks . . .

The news release makes many valid points, echoing the experiences I have encountered while investigating product diversion cases for the private sector:

> Goods sold for export (which) never actually leave the United States, cause two distinct harms.
>
> - First, there is a monetary loss to the Government through the payment of export incentives on goods destined for foreign countries. For example, in the Indictment returned yesterday, Nestle relied on false shipping documents allegedly provided by Kotbey to purchase refined sugar through a U.S. Agriculture Department (USDA) program that allows U.S. manufacturers to purchase sugar below U.S. market prices.
> - Second, essential regulatory procedures are compromised. For example, medical devices and prescription drugs sold for export, but distributed in the United States, cause regulatory problems for the Food and Drug Administration (FDA). Because the FDA requires U.S. pharmaceutical companies to maintain accurate records of drug distributions to aid recall in the event of defective, adulterated, or tampered products, it is particularly concerned about the public health implications of schemes involving diverted prescription drugs. . . .
>
> Although the pharmaceutical products involved in this case are not known to have been mishandled, the diversion of these products violates the strict FDA record keeping requirements regarding sales of prescription drugs, which brings into question the ability of pharmaceutical manufacturers to recall specific lots of drugs, and subjects the drug products to undocumented and potentially unsafe storage and distribution methods. . . .

19.6 Indicators of Diversion

Word-of-mouth. Frequently, salespersons or even consumers provide information about merchandise being sold for cheaper prices.

The numbers. Figures indicate that sales are down, yet there is an increasing volume of the company product available in a given demographic area.

Complaints. Customers call with the irritating news that they have competitors within their sales area undercutting their price structure.

Physical evidence. Stores, which are not known to carry the product line, are seen to stock and advertise the merchandise at ridiculously low prices. New markets are opened which did not carry the product line previously.

Ineffective marketing. Promotional sales do not result in increased profits.

Profits decline. Merchandise is "on the street" in volume, but the bottom line is not indicative of its sale.

19.7 The Role of the Investigator

A. Identify the diversion

This is generally the role of the company. Once the indicators have been observed, management should start pooling its resources to determine the extent of the problem. However, the investigator can become involved at this early stage to organize the proper investigation and obtain information from various sources known to management. Look for unusual shipping requests, excessively large volumes of merchandise going to geographic locations that could not handle the market glut, and so forth. Examining the company's own sales records is perhaps the most logical and effective starting place.

B. Tracking suspicious sales

Internal security can secretly mark product in a particular manner which will allow them to determine if merchandise allegedly destined for overseas finds its way to store shelves in the United States. Import databases maintained for cargo vessels, airplane exports, etc., are a source of information, that can be used to verify that materials earmarked for foreign markets are actually shipped to those locations.

C. Using informants

Inside information is perhaps the most reliable source of data. Persons within the industry (drivers, warehouse workers, etc.) are often cooperative as informants. In lieu of these aides, investigators can place infiltrators or undercover operatives within suspected warehouses to observe activity first hand.

Informants can be developed as part of a negotiated settlement that could have resulted in their prosecution. The investigator is instrumental in identifying these individuals and soliciting their cooperation.

D. Investigating through the sales force

Diversion cannot happen without the cooperation of someone within the corporation's own sales force, either by conscious collusion or inattention to obviously suspicious circumstances. When a company (such as PC Dental) places an order which is highly unusual, exceeds the normally placed order by hundreds or thousands of dollars, and commits itself to spending money it could not possibly afford to invest, then there is something amiss. The investigator can pull a D&B on the firm, check its assets, and determine its normal functioning ability. These are indicators of a possible diversion scheme in the works. If this is done prior to completing the sale, the potential for fraud is reduced or eliminated.

19.8 Countermeasures

A. Positive action

Strong company policy, ironclad contractual agreements, and stiff penalties for dealing with diverters are all steps for preventing diversion problems. Written policy regarding dealing with diverters should be issued. Prohibitions against changing established price categories for purchasers should be enforced, unless justification can be offered. Contracts which prohibit purchasers from ever dealing with the company again and financial penalties for misuse of the product will hinder the potential diverter. Removing the commission from the salesperson who authorizes the sale to a diverter should quickly put an end to collusion.

B. Regular check-ups

Just like going to the doctor, large purchasers of merchandise should receive regular check-ups. A periodic review of records, shipping documents, bills of lading, and the like can and should be performed. The investigator is perhaps the best person to act as the auditor in such a circumstance. Armed with knowledge of the potential for fraud, he or she can determine if purchase orders, bills of lading, transportation invoices, and accounts receivable checks are indicative of dealing with diverters.

19.9 Examples

There is a reality to be recognized and understood. The profits gained by product diversion are astronomical. The possibilities are only limited by the imagination of the diverter. In order to combat the problem, the penalties must be great. The investigation must be conclusive and undeniable. The evidence is in the paper trail, and it must be uncovered by methodical attention to detail. Inconsistencies must be uncovered, discrepancies noted, unusual activity recognized, and the possibility for fraud thoroughly investigated.

There has been a resurgence of interest in product diversion by manufacturers and legitimate distributors because of the growing number of diverters. The United States Department of Justice, U.S. Attorney's Office, has been bearing down on the diverters. Charges ranging from wire fraud to defrauding the United States Customs Service have been levied against a wide variety of persons involved in the trade of diversion.

The following are excerpts from a classic case which might prove useful to investigators pursuing this line of endeavor. This is, at the very least, interesting reading for any investigator whose trade revolves around the uncovering of criminal activity. Conspiracy, wire fraud, mail fraud, false statements on a matter within the jurisdiction of a federal agency, the interstate transportation of goods taken by fraud, and the issuing of false bills of lading constitute a large number of the charges you will read about in the following citations.

> News Release
> U.S Department of Justice
> Office of Robert J. Cleary
> First Assistant U.S. Attorney
> Newark, New Jersey
>
> A 42-year-old food broker from Saddle River was given a four-month federal prison sentence . . . for his role in false export diversion schemes that cost nearly 40 American pharmaceuticals, health and beauty aids, and food products manufacturers as much as $20 million.

. . .

Steven LaSala of Saddle River, NJ was ordered to pay $1.9 million in fines, forfeitures, and restitution from a Swiss bank account. Additionally he received a four-month home detention as a result of pleading guilty to wire fraud, customs fraud, and causing a pharmaceutical company to maintain false records of drug distributions.

U.S. manufacturers of branded consumer products often export their products to foreign customers for sale overseas, and commonly grant the export customer a discount of up to 50 percent below U.S. prices. Manufacturers are willing to grant such steep discounts in order to open new markets and expand worldwide sales. . . .

There is a large difference between the wholesale prices charged to domestic consumers and the cost to the export wholesaler. Steven LaSala participated in at least 39 schemes by purchasing products, which he alleged would be sold overseas. However, LaSala did not have any export customers. Instead he resold the product right here in the United States. His profits from these schemes were enormous because his purchase price was significantly lower than the price offered to other domestic distributors.

LaSala's devious diversion schemes included shipping goods overseas to an intermediate port (such as Belgium or Holland) but immediately returning the goods to the United States as "American Goods Returned." This title allowed the goods to enter duty-free. He accomplished his scheme by false invoicing and fraudulent documents giving the impression that the goods were destined for overseas sales, but were not successfully sold in that market. Therefore, Customs officials saw the returning goods as "returns." In fact, they were heading directly to the originally intended destination on the shelves of American Retail stores.

LaSala's scheme in which goods were never shipped overseas caused direct harm to the U.S. Government . . . because defrauded food manufacturers often used shipping documents (which in this case they did not know were false) to obtain monetary and subsidy benefits from U.S. Customs and Department of Agriculture programs designed to promote exports of U.S. finished goods.

For example, the First Brands Corporation, in Stamford, Conn., used false bills of lading obtained from LaSala's group to obtain rebates, called 'drawback,' from the U.S. Customs service, of duty that was paid on imported raw materials used to make exported finished goods.

> First Brands manufactures 'Glad Bag' brand plastic bags, importing petroleum-based resins to manufacture the bags and paying an import duty to Customs when it brings those resins into the U.S. Under the 'drawback' program, First Brands submitted the false bills of lading in order to obtain a refund of the duties that it had previously paid to import the resins. Since the goods were never exported, First Brands was not entitled to the drawback. . . .
>
> Additional charges against LaSala included the "causing (of) Bock Pharmacals Company of St. Louis, MO, to maintain false records of drug distributions by falsely representing that goods bought by LaSala would be sold in Nigeria." These drugs never reached Africa, but found their way to shelves in the United States. Thus the FDA regulations on accurate recording keeping for drug distributors was rendered inadequate. It allowed for defective, adulterated and tampered product to enter the marketplace and caused the possibility of a public health problem.
>
> Of the 39 admitted false representations, the following companies were subject to LaSala's fraud: First Brands; Nestle; Duracell; Eveready; Cadbury/Mott's; American Cyanamid/Lederle; Tedmond; General Mills; Ralston Purina; Alpo Pet Foods; VanCamp/Hormel; White Laboratories; American Dermal; Bock Pharmacal; Forest Pharmaceuticals: Cetylite Industries; Research Industries; ICN Pharmaceuticals; Fissons Pharmaceuticals;Schwarz Pharmacal; Polythress Labs; Baker Cummings; Elder Pharmaceuticals; CIBA Pharmaceuticals; Ferndale Laboratories; CB Fleet; Fleming & Company; Fujisawa Pharmaceuticals; CCA Industries; DeWitt Corp.; John O. Butler Col; BIC; Golden Grains Company (Rice-A-Roni); Quaker; R.T. French; Tsumora Medical; Pro-Line; Hunt/Wesson and Proctor and Gamble.

This scheme, involving Steven LaSala and John Trimarchi in the United States and Adamu Ahmed Abdulkadir in Nigeria, came to a conclusion in January of 1995. From approximately 1987 until 1992, these men and others wove their uncanny and complex web of deception. Posing as exporters, but hardly ever removing product from this country, they purchased everything from chocolate to over-the-counter drugs at the enticingly low prices offered to overseas purchasers. They artfully placed these products in the hands of retailers, most of whom had no idea that they were purchasing wrongfully obtained merchandise. Their profits were phenomenal. They literally tripled, and in some cases quadrupled, the profit margin of the normal wholesale purchaser, causing havoc with the U.S. Customs Service, special government purchasing programs, and pharmaceutical accountability standards.

Abdulkadir was the owner/operator of "Elstow Nigeria, Ltd" which co-conspired with LaSala and his U.S.-based company "Kally United." Health and beauty aids were shipped to his country and immediately turned back to the United States. All three men were charged and sentenced in this matter.

> News Release
> U.S Department of Justice
> Newark, New Jersey
>
> On August 7, 1995 another scheme was uncovered and a 55-year-old American doctor of pharmacology was arraigned on charges that she and two others conspired "to commit 'false export' diversion schemes that cost four American manufacturers of consumer goods, medical devices and prescription drugs millions of dollars in losses.
>
> Mary Ellen Kitler . . . of Norristown, PA . . . was charged in an indictment returned by a federal grand jury on July 25th with conspiracy, wire fraud, mail fraud, false statements on a matter within the jurisdiction of a federal agency, the interstate transportation of goods taken by fraud, and issuing false bills of lading. Named as victims in the Indictment are Johnson & Johnson of New Brunswick, New Jersey; Bayer Corporation's Miles Diagnostics Division ("Bayer") of Tarrytown, New York; ICN Pharmaceuticals, Inc. ("ICN") of Costa Mesa, California; and Nestle U.S.A. ("Nestle") of Glendale, California.

These two examples represent only the tip of the iceberg. There are thousands of diversion schemes ongoing regularly across the United States. This author has investigated cased that have crossed the country in pursuit of misdirected merchandise. Diversion schemes have been investigated in Colombia, Gambia, Belgium, Mexico, Canada, Thailand, and Japan.

19.10 Prevention

Diversion is a totally preventable abuse of product distribution. A well-versed product diversion investigator accompanied by a motivated management team could bring diversion activity to a standstill. Strong corporate policy accompanied by strict controls and harsh contractual penalties would be the first step.

Prophylactic measures can be conducted to avoid the possibility of diversion. Tracking can be done of all large wholesale cash purchases. This is especially important where wholesalers are requesting tier discount pricing for such specialties as closeouts, charity, or international sales.

Product coding (lot numbers, including dating, intended distributor, factory designation and special packaging) should all be employed as part of the manufacturing process. Contracts should be backed by performance bonds to ensure that distributors maintain the intended lines of distribution. Product and price integrity could be maintained if the proper programs and contracts were put in place. Enforcement of controls and policy must be maintained in order to provide notice to diverters that distribution abuse will not be tolerated. These measures, and their maintenance, are only cost effective for Class A companies.

While the East Coast seems to be the home of an abundance of diverters, diversion can and does occur almost everywhere. The investigative work is exacting and the hours of thrashing through documents seem endless. However, there is nothing quite like the satisfaction comes from successfully putting the pieces together.

Aggressive corporate policy and security departments that have committed the proper resources, own use agreements, strong distribution contracts, and experienced diversion investigators have recovered millions and millions of dollars of lost profits for many companies. This specialized investigative arena is the home of some of the country's most capable investigators.

References

Humphries, S. "Preventing Product Sales Scams" *Security Management Magazine*, July 1995.

NEWS, United States Department of Justice U.S. Attorney, District of New Jersey (Robert J. Cleary, First Assistant U.S. Attorney) Distributed on Wednesday, July 26, 1995.

Chapter 20

Investigating Embezzlement and Other Employee Crimes

Jonathan Turner, CFE, CII

Synopsis

20.1 Emerging Trends in Fraud Prevention

A. The new environment

The current economic climate presents a unique opportunity to discuss organizational attitudes towards fraud. The economic downturn of the last few years created strong pressures within companies to reduce costs by cutting budgets and reducing employees through layoffs and other means. At the same time, the attacks of September 11, 2001, raised security awareness in general, and the ensuing corporate scandals created increased scrutiny of fraud matters in particular. Finally the legal environment has changed; with the passage of Sarbanes-Oxley public companies are now required to tackle fraud and their programs are held accountable in ways they have not been before.

Based, at least in part, on these legal and regulatory changes, there has been new research conducted into both fraud prevention and fraud perpetrators. Significant studies by the Association of Certified Fraud Examiners, leading accounting and consulting frims, and academics have helped to flesh out an understanding of the current status of fraud attacks and corporate fraud postures. While there are still some companies who pay only lip service to fraud prevention, their numbers are shrinking.

B. What are the challenges ahead?

Fraudsters are slowly but steadily getting ahead. Too many companies still lack basic fraud policies. And even among those that have fraud prevention functions, many are understaffing fraud departments, underfunding them, or both. Yet consistently, in surveys, the vast majority of people believe that fraud is under control at their company. This inability to see the problem close at hand is one reason that fraudsters are successful.

Academic research and empirical evidence suggest that the fraudsters are continuing to innovate and that they are being successful. Every recent survey has documented increasing numbers of fraud attacks and increasing loss amounts per attack.

20.2 Employee Crime

A. Overview

There is a saying in the security profession: locks keep honest people honest. And it is an unfortunate reality that a disturbingly large percentage of people will, if given the chance, steal with little to no hesitation. Companies can mitigate this risk through the creation of an honest corporate culture, installation of effective policies and procedures, and maintenance of an effective internal control environment. Even with these efforts, they cannot eliminate it. Locks may work for honest people, but they will not stand in the way of determined thieves.

While employee dishonesty is certainly nothing new, today's companies face greater challenges; there are more business risks and more elements to successfully resolve in employee fraud issues. The wave of consolidation in many industries and the increase in international and multinational businesses place more access in the hands of fewer employees while, at the same time, reducing the effectiveness of the control structure. As a result, companies have been assaulted by increasingly sophisticated employee fraud schemes and have suffered millions of dollars in losses.

Many organizations purchase crime policies, or package insurance programs, to cover this type of risk. But what else can be done? What are the benefits of doing more? And, are there any risks in taking action? This article will explore the reasons, trends, and solutions to mitigate employee theft risks. By understanding the core risk areas, and the strengths and weaknesses of a company's environment, its management can properly assess ongoing risks and actively work to reduce them.

But, why worry about employee dishonesty—after all, isn't that the reason for a crime insurance package? Too many companies fall victim to this mentality and thus fail to see the corollary effect of allowing or even empowering a corrupt corporate culture. How does relying on insurance nurture corruption? Because employees are watching everything an organization does and, possibly more importantly, everything it is not doing.

In the early 1990s New York City embarked on a novel crime reduction program. When Americans were demanding safer streets, most governments were responding by building bigger jails and focusing on the most heinous of crimes. What the NYPD did, very controversially, was to focus on all crime. By demonstrating that *all* crimes, from littering to loitering and solicitation, all the way through the most violent felonies, would be targeted and responded to, they sent a message—we will not tolerate crime. While the specifics of the implementation can be debated, the effect it had on crime in New York City cannot.

Similarly, many organizations fail to act in the face of smaller employee crimes. A review of litigation, from racial discrimination to embezzlement cases, reveals that in most of the cases information was brought to the company's attention yet no action was taken. When employees see that some graft is tolerated or that reports of violations are ignored they may stop looking out for the company.

Protecting an organization from employee crime is really about protecting its honest employees, their jobs, and their livelihoods from the actions of dishonest employees. It involves more than simply purchasing an insurance policy or putting a lock on a door. It involves looking at the policies and procedures necessary to ensure protection and making sure they are in place and functioning. Whether an organization is like New York City, requiring sophisticated solutions, or small town America, requiring a simpler structure, today's companies have the information and tools to make those decisions actively, managing the risk instead of simply administering it.

While prudent businesses carry crime insurance, it is rarely invoked, leaving the company inexperienced in the intricacies of the coverage and the special claim requirements. This coverage is often not thought of until catastrophic losses occur. However, the ensuing fallout can distract management from the claims issues, diluting focus and initiative while the clock is ticking.

In the face of traumatic fraud, the company must establish corporate objectives to bring about a successful resolution. Public relations, investor issues, criminal prosecution, financial redress, and employee morale are all elements that must be balanced and managed as part of the recovery process. The employee issues are the most critical, with the message sent back to the employees having the greatest effect on other potential fraudsters.

In most situations, the only practical means of financial recovery is the fidelity portion of the company's crime insurance program. Filing a successful multimillion dollar claim requires careful attention to detail throughout the process. Investigation, documentation, and claims management must be carefully coordinated from the front end.

B. Why are employees dishonest?

A company's employees are no more, or less, likely to be dishonest than society at large. The bad news is that society at large is quite willing to be dishonest. Studies have calculated that a full 25 percent of the United States' work force will steal, given the opportunity. While that seems high to some, it probably underestimates the total. While different groups have explained this in different ways, the core elements remain the same. Take a motivated person, provide him or her with opportunity, allow him or her to justify it, and the crime is done. To consider how easy it is for people to make the leap, take a look at the number of cars that you see speeding on your way home today. Each one of those drivers, consciously or unconsciously, has made the decision that his or her personal agenda is more important than the law; each knows it is wrong, and each has justified the decision. And, most probably gave it no thought.

C. Motivation

People are motivated by an incredibly wide variety of things. For some it is laziness; for others it is greed; still others seek revenge for wrongdoing (real or imagined); and others see it as "their due." The key to understanding motivation is appreciating its personal nature. The question is not whether you would be tempted by something but, rather, would that thing tempt anyone.

In my career investigating and resolving employee dishonesty cases, I have seen people destroy thirty-year careers over small change, public employees wash out of politics over inconsequential gifts, and low-level employees embark on multimillion dollar schemes. For some it is payback against a boss or organization that has passed them over for advancement. For others it is the need to support a lifestyle, possibly including alcohol, drugs, gambling, or other vices. Whatever the cause, internal or external, the temptation exists.

It is not possible to identify or even predict what will motivate an employee to steal. The range of choices is simply too extensive. Knowing that the temptations are out there, and that this is a variable that cannot be controlled, or even recognized in advance in most cases, illustrates the potential risk that each employee represents.

D. Opportunity

The next ingredient is opportunity. By watching what the company does and does not do, the dishonest employee identifies a potential for abuse. All organizations have them, and you have probably seen numerous examples over the course of your career. Some are easy to recognize, like bank tellers or retail clerks stealing from the cash drawer. Others are subtler, like steering business through a particular vendor in return for a kickback. Each opportunity for theft is closely linked to the employee's job or function, otherwise the possibility for discovery is too great. By the same token, senior employees, by virtue of experience with the organization, position, and often-greater responsibility, steal considerably more than junior employees and are often much less carefully controlled.

Every organization knows to audit the petty cash box, but what about less obvious exposures? For example, a national bank recently suffered a long running embezzlement when a senior bank officer was found to have been stealing customer funds. There was nothing novel in the scheme, but it succeeded because the officer was in personnel and thought to have no access to accounts—so he was controlled as an administrator would be. In a manufacturing facility, the accounting records were closely controlled and petty cash was double-counted daily. However, only a single employee counted the delivery trucks that were contracted by the load. While the petty cash box never had more than $200, a contract delivery fraud cost them over $6 million in three years. If it were obvious, it would not be an opportunity to steal.

Opportunities exist in the cracks between controls or in the spaces between what is supposed to happen and what actually happens. Many organizations fail to look actively for possible failure points, creating embarrassing incidents when somebody exploits one.

E. Justification

Unfortunately, when a motivated employee finds an opportunity, the justification is often simple. While there are people who will never steal, no matter what, far more people will look you straight in the eyes and say, "I didn't consider it stealing." This is where the most convoluted stories will emerge—elaborate constructions involving undocumented, interest-free loans are not theft because "everybody does it," "they owed it to me," and "I deserved it."

It is this key step, a personal choice made by the employee, which divides the work force into those who will steal and those who won't. Similarly, it is this justification that allows the employee to come to work each day and continue with 99 percent of their activities, outwardly unchanged, because they have convinced themselves that what they are doing is not wrong. It is precisely this justification step that makes it vital that companies visibly address incidences of employee crime. If employees see no response to employee theft, it lowers the bar, making it easier for successive employees to justify their schemes. The employees are watching to see what message management sends out. Will the organization tolerate theft or not?

Why focus on motivation, opportunity, and justification? If they exist for each employee, why is this important? Because understanding how and why it happened are often the keys to unraveling the scheme. Most fraud cases are found by accident, in spite of management controls and internal and external audits. Fraud and employee theft are carefully concealed, masked among the perfectly legitimate business acts of the company. When indications of employee theft are found, the organization typically knows it is a small part of the puzzle.

20.3 What Can Be Done?

Given that such a significant proportion of its employees will steal, if given the chance, what should a company do to mitigate its risk? A successful fraud and employee theft prevention program is based on a foundation of policies, procedures and internal controls. However, to keep the control environment functioning effectively the organization has to audit for compliance and test for abuse. Each of these builds upon the next, and all are required to identify potential abuse and resolve active fraud schemes.

A. Policies and procedures

Corporate policies and procedures should be structured to promote transparency and accountability. Fraud schemes hide in the details. Irreconcilable processes, obtuse reporting standards, oversimplification of results, use of slush accounts and similar techniques promote a fraud-friendly environment. Similarly, organizations whose policies clearly differentiate between different types, or levels of employees, will also find themselves at an increased risk for employee theft.

Some organizations find themselves challenged by the "speeding" principle: unpopular policies and procedures are simply ignored. These organizations are setting themselves up for significant fraud losses. Employees pay close attention to compliance and senior management's attitude towards policy enforcement. Inconsistencies generate resentment and form the foundation for both the motivation and justification.

The appearance of impropriety at a management level can quickly lead to perceptions of unfairness among employees. More importantly, if employees lose faith in the uniform application of policies and procedures they will quickly disregard them. This can lead to a rash of new attacks against the company.

One multinational found this out the hard way. After missing its internal goals, the company suspended its profit-sharing payment. Simultaneously, the company's senior management team took a week-long retreat at an expensive resort, spending millions on lavish entertainment. The news spread rapidly through the largely professional organization, and employee dissatisfaction grew. Over the next year the company discovered four large fraud schemes, all initiated after the news. Interviews with the involved employees revealed that they were deeply affected by the perception that management had "spent the profit-sharing money on a party."

B. Internal controls

Similarly, the effectiveness and follow-though of the internal control environment has a measurable effect on the incidence and size of employee dishonesty losses. Objectively measuring the status of internal controls is a much more elusive goal. Certain components are readily measurable: size of internal audit staff, cycle rate for facility reviews, presence/absence of a fraud/abuse/compliance hotline, and establishment of an internal theft response policy. Other aspects are notoriously difficult to assess, like employee confidence, corporate culture, industry-sector competitiveness, and related areas.

The most typical failure in internal controls is an off-balance concentration of priorities. A manufacturing company provides a good example of how this can happen. Faced with decreasing resources and growing demand, the company focused on automated reviews of employee expense reports and put great efforts into devising a profile of acceptable activities. The resulting system provided consolidated reporting and complete management reporting on types, styles, and trends in reimbursed expenses. At the same time, the company quickly discovered that most of its traveling employees fell outside of the parameters established and thus required manual approval. The high volume of manual approvals masked any fraud trends that might have otherwise been visible.

By concentrating so heavily on one area, the company lost sight of other internal control aspects. Complying with expense reporting systems encouraged managers to suggest to employees that they artificially "fudge" expense items in order to bring them within the systems parameters. The result? Several significant internal fraud schemes by managers under pressure to meet goals who believed that it was more important to report things the way the company wanted than to report them honestly.

C. Auditing and testing

The final aspect to making the policies, procedures, and internal controls effective is regular and routine auditing and testing. The information gained by probing what should be and determining what is can be invaluable in identifying potential weaknesses and putting solutions in place before a scheme gets started.

Audits are well understood by most organizations, and between internal and external audit roles a picture of compliance is provided. But auditing alone, without proactive testing, is insufficient. Just as many organizations have brought in outside hackers and IT professionals to test their computer systems, companies must actively test their internal systems for abuse. It is not enough to know what appears to be; a company must go further and find out what *can* be. The disaffected employee will be actively exploring that side and working even harder to make sure that it stays hidden.

Traditional audit testing is not designed to find internal theft. Occasionally it does but only in a very small percentage of identified schemes. This is not to disparage auditors, but given the scope of their activities and the ingenuity of creative criminals companies cannot afford to place all their eggs in one basket.

Since every organization has dishonest employees, management will know its program works when it regularly detects abuse. Failure to find abuse is a sure sign that the program needs reviewing. But the purpose of the program is only to deter, detect, and identify abuse. Discovery leads to the next aspect, recovery.

D. Crime insurance

Even the most effective program will only keep honest people honest. Every organization will have its share of dishonest people; at least some will find a way to act on their impulses. To mitigate this risk, most organizations purchase crime insurance or other forms of fidelity bonding. Many readers might consider this obvious, but a growing number of organizations are considering limiting or even eliminating this protection. That is a significant mistake. (Disclaimer: the author neither sells, markets, nor benefits from the sale of crime insurance policies.)

Crime insurance, in providing an effective means for financial recovery, does more than reimburse the company for covered losses. It also provides a significant motivation to search out and identify potentially covered losses and fully explore the extent of the scheme. This financial incentive is important, as many people are more inclined to simply write off an investment or make a correcting entry *and leave the cancer in place*. Fortunately, using insurance to ensure financial performance and encourage certain behavior is a solidly established concept. So if these policies are going to serve as the primary recovery method, it is important to understand them.

1. Limits and applicability

Crime policies, like all insurance, are designed to protect against specific types of risks. Since crime claims are much less common than other types of insurance claims, many organizations misunderstand exactly what the policy provides. As with all insurance contracts, read the specific policy. Further, make sure that the people who might be involved in a crime claim are also aware of the policy and its particular conditions and restrictions. Because of time limits, many perfectly viable crime claims have been damaged, or even lost, because the security department never notified risk management that the loss occurred.

Without concentrating on specific dollar limits, it is important to know and understand the limitations of the policy. The most important limitation is that the policy covers t*he company's* loss not a third-party loss or damages awarded against the company. While specific policy language varies, the standard form covers losses due to a variety of employee crimes. Make sure that the policy covers all types of employee crime that could occur in the business.

The largest problem that many companies discover is that the policy limits are too low. Since most organizations believe that it cannot happen to them, they set limits that fail to adequately protect them against the size of modern fraud schemes. One bank learned this lesson after a typical lending officer scheme caused over $5 million in losses. Unfortunately, the bank only maintained $2 million in coverage. Upon reviewing why the coverage was set at $2 million, the bank discovered that the amount had not changed in almost ten years, despite record growth.

Another organization discovered that a dishonest employee and some outside purchasing agents had defrauded it and its customers over a period of years. The company promptly repaid its customers and then filed a claim for the full amount in both loss categories. The insurance company promptly paid the covered losses and disallowed the customer loss segments. Since the outside purchasing agents were employees of the customers, a better strategy would have been to cooperate with them and encourage the customers to file crime claims of their own. But having reimbursed the customers they no longer had a loss, and when the company's claim was denied it was left in the unenviable position of having either to sue its own customers or to let the matter go.

While coverage issues can be complicated legal questions, most are straightforward. By educating itself about the specifics of the policy, and making sure that all of the potentially involved people are at least aware that there is a policy, management in a much better position to assess the scope of its coverage and ensure that the limits are set properly.

2. Deductibles

Setting the deductible amount is another area where companies can inadvertently decrease the benefits of these policies. Crime insurance provides not only a means of financial recovery (every dollar recovered goes directly to the bottom line) but is the mechanism to ensure that the company is looking for potential problems and exploring them for possible coverage.

For economic reasons companies consider a range of deductible options. Some companies even drop the coverage altogether, justifying the move as self-insurance. But installing an overly high deductible can be just like dropping the policy in that it removes the incentive for companies to root out fraud and abuse.

What should the deductible limit be? At what point is a company large enough to self-insure this type of loss? Each organization will have to find the proper point based on its own risk and tolerance, but there are some rules to consider in finding that point. Some companies have deductibles of $10,000 or $20,000 while similar organizations are at $100,000 or $250,000. The difference, in addition to premium, is attitude. The company with the lower deductible is willing to pursue aggressively any potentially claimable loss—because they know that the hurdle rate is low enough to justify the exercise. The company with the higher deductible is more willing simply to write off losses or let them go uninvestigated rather than "throw good money after bad."

But what if the company is a worldwide super-conglomerate? How much risk should it self-insure? The same logic applies. Every dollar it raises its deductible raises the hurdle that internal managers have to jump before they are willing to investigate complex schemes. While trading premium for risk makes sense in a lot of areas, in this case the corresponding decrease in responsiveness is a hidden cost that must also be considered.

3. Riders

As with all policies, a variety of riders is available to customize the standard form. There are some standard riders that should be carefully considered for the extra benefits they provide, particularly riders to limit the definition of discovery and cover investigative costs associated with the claim investigation.

The insurance company must be notified within a period of time from the discovery of the crime. This immediately raises the issue of "discovery by whom?" Large organizations use a rider to define it as discovery by the risk manager or select members of senior management. In organizations with hundreds of corporate officers, the limitation of who must discover the event and start the clock is important. But what about smaller organizations? Do the same benefits apply? They do. No matter the size of the organization, attaching discovery to a specific person, position, or level, supports the organization's ability to respond.

Similarly, adding coverage for investigative costs makes solid business sense. Uncovering and documenting repetitious, large scale, or long-term fraud cases takes time, and that is always in short supply. The natural tendency is to outsource this role—and investigative costs coverage makes it a nearly no-risk proposition. But what level is sufficient? The decision-makers should contact some outside fraud examiners and take a survey. Find out what kind of costs can be expected and then make the decision.

Understanding policy and coverage, including its deductible amounts and any riders, will provide the information needed to make this tool effective.

20.4 Making the Process Work

Effective company policies, coupled with a balanced crime insurance program to provide incentive, provide a company with the foundation to foster, support, and develop an honest workplace environment. Perhaps more importantly, they provide the tools needed to demonstrate the value of proactive theft prevention measures.

A. Putting the right systems in place

Where does one begin?

1. Hiring

It starts with the first contact a potential applicant has with an organization. Does the application ask for complete details? If details are missing, do the recruiters require the applicant to provide them? The hiring decision is one of the most important any organization can make, and it serves as the front gate of defense against employee crime. If applicants learn that they can provide incomplete or false information to be hired, what message does that send about the likelihood that the company has an effective crime prevention program in place?

2. Review the hiring process

Does it include a background investigation? Verification of application data? What is done to applications that contain false or misleading information? While these questions may look like an intrusion into the human resources department, they are not. Their role is to manage people, not to assess risk. Testing for flaws should start at the beginning for accurate results.

3. Apply the process beyond hiring

This same process should continue with all aspects of employees' involvement with the company. Times, places, and opportunities where disinformation or misinformation could enter the process should be identified, and specific steps to catch these problems should be tested. Since internal controls and audits find fraud so rarely, attention should be focused on the areas where employees can report problems. How accessible is senior management? How receptive? Is there an internal security department? How accessible and receptive are they? Is there an anonymous reporting process? Is it well known and publicized in the company? Do the employees use it? Questions like these will allow one to gauge a company's current posture towards employee crime. *The key here is in regularly and repeatedly reviewing these areas, assessing their effectiveness, and measuring the gap between the actual and the ideal.*

B. Testing the organization

It is not enough simply to assess; the systems must be periodically tested to see that they work. Systems testing should be approached the same way the IT systems are tested and the company prepares for fire alarms or other disaster drills. These tests can be conducted by the company or an outside vendor. Either way, the whole process must be tested. Submit incomplete applications and see how far an applicant gets. Incomplete invoices can be submitted to see if they are approved for payments. Employees can be questioned about their observations and perceptions of management knowledge, response, and attentiveness to internal and external fraud issues.

In fact, suggesting such a test can often be an effective gauge of where a company stands. Organizations that disdain testing or consider it too unimportant or unnecessary to bother with probably need to boost their crime policy limits. It is also a strong indicator of management attention across the board. An honest corporate culture requires senior leadership to lead the team not just call in plays from the sidelines. Another potential indicator of an organization's trouble is when management agrees verbally but refuses to participate. Again, the work force is watching. What do they see?

C. Responding to dishonesty

The final and most important test is the organization's response to allegations or indications of employee dishonesty. Some companies quietly allow the employee to resign. While tempting, this option only encourages employee theft.

A manufacturing company in the Midwest discovered this lesson too late. To hide their warts they never fired anyone for theft. When confronted with enough evidence, they simply called the person in, confronted him or her, and allowed the employee to resign. While not publicized, the practice was widely known. In the mid-1990s a senior manager initiated a series of frayed schemes, embezzling several million dollars over several years.

The company initially discovered only $300,000 of the theft and, true to form, allowed the manager to resign. As his replacement sorted through the records, the full scope of the fraud was uncovered. Indignant, the president of the company called the former manager in for a meeting and confronted him with the multimillion dollar total. The manager admitted his role, apologized for letting the company down, and prepared to leave. Only then did it sink in to the senior leadership team in the room—the manager had no idea that they might prosecute. They had so successfully spread the message, unintentionally, that he thought he could just walk away.

Allegations of employee dishonesty require prompt action. If proved, management must be willing to take corrective action, both in removing the employee (no matter what level), fixing the control failure that allowed the scheme, and referring the matter for possible civil and criminal prosecution. Companies that are willing to allow a person to resign and are not willing to file a criminal complaint are telling the other employees that stealing from the company is not serious.

There is no gray area in employee dishonesty. If an employee is willing to lie, submit false documents, and so on, the company cannot afford to keep him or her. Even if that person "never took much," it is the message that this type of tolerance sends to the rest of the employees that is dangerous.

D. Coordinating the response

To coordinate its response, the company should assemble a small, balanced team early. This team should include fraud examiners as well as representatives from senior management, legal, and risk management. Ideally, the investigator should know in advance who would be on the team. If not, getting those people up to speed on the special requirements of a crime claim is the first priority.

Fraud is usually discovered by accident, via a tip from the company fraud line, anonymous sources, or even involved employees. Sometimes the tipster has private motivations, and that possibility that will also have to be explored. But the important issue is the allegation itself. Is it credible? Questions as to possibility, probability, and testability of the potential fraud must be answered. The answers to those questions are vital. When the allegation is deemed credible and possible, whether or not it seems probable, it must be approached as if it is an active fraud. After all, it is better to find nothing than to leave a scheme in place.

In taking these steps, a company begins to manage the fraud rather than be abused by it. All of the actions that follow from this discovery must support corporate objectives and recovery goals. With a potential fraud scheme identified, there is the opportunity to investigate fully the scheme, its participants, and related matters. A premature response can allow some participants to mask their involvement, destroy evidence, or otherwise hinder the full documentation of the scheme.

Upon discovery (a formal term defined in a specific policy), the company will be required to notify its insurance carrier. This is the first of a series of formal and informal communications between the company and the carrier. These form the foundation of the claims process. While some carriers take a hands-off approach during the company's formal investigation, most will appreciate being regularly updated. Some carrier's adjusters will take a more active role in the process, which can greatly expedite a successful settlement.

E. Identifying fraud losses

Investigators should begin with the basic issues of what, where, how, when, and why? Take the example of a small retail business that serviced a metropolitan community through three retail outlets and a warehouse. It provided regular customers with house charge accounts. Customer complaints following the busy Christmas holiday season were the first indications of a problem. In January several customers called to complain that payments had not been posted to their accounts. The bookkeeper was out sick, so the complaints were directed to the company's owner. The owner became concerned when he heard that this was a regular problem. He was more concerned when the bookkeeper was unable to explain why the accounts were not properly credited and did not know how long this had been going on.

The owner examined the accounts receivable records. He quickly identified several irregularities in recording customer payments and was unable to reconcile the payment entries with the deposit records. Finally, he came across records that indicated that rather than credit payments the bookkeeper had made over $15,000 in miscellaneous credit adjustments to customer accounts. That information, coupled with the missing deposit items, convinced the owner that his bookkeeper was stealing. He notified the police department and made a formal criminal complaint.

In this case the owner acted prematurely. His complaint to the police was well founded, but he did not yet know the extent of the scheme or what had happened to the missing deposits. When the police interviewed the bookkeeper, they were unable to confront her properly because they had only a small piece of the puzzle. As a result, she provided a seemingly rational explanation for the credit entries. Without further proof, the police dropped the investigation. By introducing the police department before documenting the scheme, the owner lost the support of law enforcement.

In contrast, a small community bank was faced with similar circumstances. This time, the owner of the bank became aware of irregularities when a standard FDIC audit revealed problems in the bank's loan department. He reassigned the loans and began investigating the cited problems. Aware that this might lead to an employee fraud case, he took great pains to state publicly that the problems were merely technical issues and nothing more, setting the fraudsters at ease. Working with external fraud investigators, the bank owner unraveled the scheme before confronting the involved employees. In the subsequent referral to law enforcement, the bank owner laid out the frame of the well-hidden scheme and provided substantial assistance in documenting the criminal case.

While the core circumstances in both cases were similar, it was management's actions that led to failure in the first case, and success in the second. Addressing these situations, the investigator must identify the scope of the scheme. Bearing in mind that the scheme is designed to be concealed, it is like the iceberg that sunk the Titanic, only aimed at the company. The investigator should assume that the true scope is far larger than the piece that can be seen.

Having now defined the "what," and to help in narrowing this scope, we move on to the remaining questions, which should bring the scheme into focus.

The next key piece is "where." Every position at the company allows employee access to certain information that could be abused. The purpose of internal controls is to limit that abuse or at least make it readily detectable. Despite these controls, all organizations have loopholes that can be exploited. The fraud will begin to take shape when motivated insiders act on this information.

With the potential attack in mind, the next issue is "how." Just having access is not enough. There must be a mechanism that provides a benefit to the fraudster or the scheme will not succeed. Identify and analyze any loopholes from this perspective and opportunities will appear. Successful fraud schemes take advantage of these precisely because they are so often overlooked.

Now that the picture is coming into view, depth is the next area to address. How long has the scheme been going on? Successful frauds rely on small, unnoticeable losses which consistently accrue over time. By setting up a system of very small thefts hidden among the volumes of legitimate transactions the fraudster can cause a substantial loss to the company. If this goes on over a period of years, as many successful scams do, even comparison to historical data will not reveal the scheme. In the previous examples, both schemes ran over several years, obscuring the effects of the scam in the changing cost of doing business.

The final component is, of course, "why." This is the motivation that justifies the fraudster. This may be personal, such as greed, jealousy, or revenge. It may also be behavioral, such as gambling, drugs, or lifestyle choices. Whatever the cause, understanding what motivates the fraudster will clarify two important components and complete the picture of the scheme. How will the person(s) committing the fraud be caught and who else could be involved in the scheme? Identifying all of the involved parties is vital to a complete understanding of the scheme. Identifying one does little good if three are left behind to continue the scheme. In the second example above, the meticulous approach taken by the bank owner allowed him to identify two customers who were involved in the lending scheme. These customers provided a source of financial recovery and records that substantiated the owner's allegations when they were seized by law enforcement.

F. Assembling the team

With the initial identification of the scheme and associated losses the company is ready to assemble a team to deal with the situation. There are numerous sometimes contradictory objectives to be accomplished. Skillful team selection can be essential to the smooth and efficient handling of what could turn into a very disruptive process.

Any team should include fraud examiners as well as risk management and legal personal. In addition, the group should be supplemented as necessary with other departments or areas affected by the scheme. Finally, add outside specialists if and when they can add value to the process. Principal outside specialists would include: outside counsel, external fraud examiners, and technical experts such as document examiners and other forensic experts. The assembled team should be no larger than necessary and have a single person in command. Most importantly, the team needs to have the time, resources, and management support to accomplish its objectives.

In one recent case, a senior accounting controller orchestrated a complex vendor scheme. Using an outside accomplice, he manipulated the purchasing process to set up a series of fictitious vendors, authorizing and approving payment for the invoices from these vendors. Due to the elaborate nature of the scheme, the company had to balance its vendor relationships against its need to root out the fraud. From the initial assessment, the company had concluded that as many as fifteen vendor companies were involved but was unable to confirm that these were the only vendors in the scheme. Operations personnel, who used the vendors' products in production, had the knowledge to help resolve this issue. Hence, one individual was temporarily assigned to the team.

His involvement netted the recovery team several unanticipated benefits. With his understanding of the actual products involved, the team quickly identified several other companies whose deliveries were outside normal standards. Further analysis of the invoice and delivery detail for these companies revealed that the numbers were inconsistent with industry practices. Using this information, the team discovered that the ghost vendor scheme had only two participants rather that the fifteen that initially appeared to be involved.

From the beginning, the team included a member of the internal audit staff. This person was involved in accounting for the loss as well as running audit tests on the entire payable and vendor processes. Her detailed knowledge of the controls and procedures available in the accounting software yielded one of the first keys to uncovering the scheme. She identified the first series of vendors who were receiving multiple checks for a single invoice. Coding the invoices for partial payments, the controller ensured that the fraudulent payments were under his approval authority.

A secondary search revealed that 95 percent of the payments that he authorized were within 10 percent of his approval authority. A detailed review of those invoices revealed that all of them were for deliveries from the suspect vendors. Further analysis of the internal audit records revealed a recent audit that noted some of the questionable transactions. While it is unfortunate that the audit did not detect the fraud, it was very helpful that the notes included a memo from the controller explaining the process and linking the suspect vendors to several other vendors. When these additional vendors were placed under scrutiny, they too had questionable activity.

In contrast to an audit, risk management is often not brought into the situation until late in the process. This is a mistake. The special requirements of employee dishonesty claims are often unknown outside of risk management circles, with the exception of some specialists. As a result, the team is dependent on the risk manager to educate them as to the pros and cons of these claims as they consider recovery avenues. Further, by interacting with the insurance carrier throughout the process, the risk manager can help prepare the carrier for the claim and reduce any obstacles encountered in resolving the claim.

In this case, the company did not even know it had a crime insurance policy until the risk manager was notified of the loss in a management meeting. He quickly became involved with the team, educating them about the requirements of a successful fidelity claim and guiding the team through the unfamiliar territory of carrier notice requirements and filing deadlines. Later, well into the investigation, it became apparent that the fraudster's assets were not sufficient to cover the loss and that the fidelity claim was the only viable economic recovery.

Integrating corporate counsel into the team also provides a variety of benefits to the process. By shielding the investigation under legal counsel, the company can ensure that its notes and drafts are protected by the various privileges, including the doctrine of self critical examination, and the more common attorney/client communications, attorney work product, and, in some instances, attorney/investigator privileges.

Many fidelity claims involve litigation at some stage, usually against the perpetrators. The discovery aspects of litigation are especially useful, including subpoenaing information from banks, casinos, mortgage companies, and other records sources whose documents are protected by privacy statutes.

Finally, the legal representative can ensure that the team does not inadvertently expose the company to liability as it documents the scheme, investigates the involved parties, and assesses the damages caused by the fraud. In the previous case, the scheme first appeared to center around a small group of vendors. Then it appeared to cover most of the vendors for a specific type of product. By working with counsel to identify legal options, the team developed a strategy that allowed them to question potentially involved parties, increasing the pressure if they received unsatisfactory answers. In this manner, they successfully approached all of the potentially involved vendors. Only those vendors who were actually involved required more drastic measures.

To supplement these insiders, the team may need specialists. These people can come from inside the company, when specialized product or industry knowledge is required, or outside the company. External consultants include: forensic, document, and information technology specialists, claims consultants, fraud experts, and outside legal counsel. All consultants should be retained and managed through the legal representative to ensure that the privilege covers their activities as well. The most common reason to add external consultants is time. The team members may have limited time because of their other duties, and filing a successful claim requires hitting scheduled deadlines.

In this case, the company supplemented the internal team with fraud experts and outside counsel. They maximized the time value of the investigation by dividing the various responsibilities among the team members and the consultants to complete the investigation and simultaneously sent a detailed criminal referral to law enforcement, filed a civil suit for damages, and a claim against the crime insurance carrier. They were successful in that the fraudsters received criminal conviction and jail sentences, and the company received a civil judgment for damages, which they subrogated to the carrier, who paid the seven-figure claim in full.

Not all companies achieve this synergy. In another case, the company put responsibility for recovery solely on in-house counsel, who was also responsible for a number of active litigation matters. The corporate counsel had little background in insurance law and quickly filed a series of suits against all of the potentially involved parties. The resulting litigation has mired the company in complicated court battles, essentially fighting a multi-front war. Further, the pre-emptive strike caused all of the witnesses to seek legal counsel and effectively ended the company's investigation. The delay also caused the company to miss the deadlines required for filing a bond claim. While this is not typical, the situation can easily escalate to this level without full integration of the legal and risk management aspects of the team.

G. Identifying the objectives

1. Overview

Another recent case illustrated how even a balanced team can go astray. Working from several divisions of a multinational company, the team was composed of fraud examiners, representatives from the operations, audit, and legal departments, with input from risk managers. They identified a fraud scheme and initially made rapid progress only to get bogged down trying to process the volume of material their inquiries were generating. The first challenge is identifying and prioritizing the corporate objectives. Without clear leadership, the team differed on these objectives, wasting valuable effort clashing and going in different directions.

The first reaction to fraud is often anger, and rightfully so. These are not only attacks on the company, they are betrayals of trust. Despite this honest reaction, it is important to move past retribution and identify the goals. For many companies these come in three primary categories: punishment of the fraudsters, recovery for the company, and process improvement to lessen the chance that the scheme could reoccur.

Punishment of the wrongdoer(s) is a legitimate corporate goal, but one that can be complicated to execute. It may involve filing a criminal complaint or dealing with the matter in civil courts with its press, publicity, and employee morale issues. These factors must be explored and balanced early in the process to ensure that they are fully thought out and developed. With the corporate objectives identified, the team can begin assembling the elements necessary to accomplish the goals.

2. Criminal prosecution

Criminal prosecution of the wrongdoer(s) is a process that many companies pursue. Under a criminal complaint to the appropriate law enforcement agency, the fraudster faces potential incarceration or probation, publicly branding him for his involvement. While some companies shy away from the resulting publicity, a criminal conviction or guilty plea can be a very strong factor in presenting a fidelity claim or litigating a civil lawsuit for damages. If criminal prosecution is one of the corporate objectives, the team needs to have a member familiar with criminal procedures oversee this area.

Filing a criminal referral is required for some industries. This process involves educating the law enforcement agency as to the specific facts in the case and presenting them with evidence that a crime has been committed. Unfortunately white-collar crime is not a high priority for many jurisdictions, requiring the company to assemble all of the necessary evidence in advance. Once the criminal referral is made, the company changes from advocate to victim, and the decision-making shifts to the prosecutor. From this point forward the company has no control over the prosecution and sentencing. Therefore, it is essential that the information given to law enforcement include all of the relevant details of the scheme, a detailed presentation of the facts, the key players, the key documents, and a list of relevant witnesses.

In a recent case, the company notified law enforcement too early in the process. This led to unintended consequences. Having law enforcement involved in some team meetings and interviews created tensions that limited the effectiveness of the internal investigation. Further, after a strong start, the law enforcement investigator was reassigned to a more pressing priority, effectively dropping the criminal investigation. A more effective strategy would have been to conduct the internal investigation and present the completed facts and information to the prosecutor or law enforcement agency.

3. Civil remedies

The elements necessary to prepare the civil case are less complicated and more commonly understood. Once the internal investigation has progressed to the point where the primary players are identified, civil litigation becomes an option. The discovery procedures can give the company access to third-party records, depositions, formal "on the record" answers, and other tools to complete the documentation of the fraud. In preparing the civil claims, local counsel will be invaluable in providing information about local rules and practices. In some jurisdictions, discovery is automatic, while in others it is delayed. It also can be problematic to introduce new parties to the suit in some jurisdictions. Finally, the investigator will need to work closely with the risk manager to coordinate the claim preparation. The risk manager already has a relationship with the insurance carrier and is in the best position to manage the deadlines required under the policy.

With the criminal, civil, and claims elements being managed effectively, the investigator can proceed on a balanced front. Weighting any one section over the others will cause difficulties. For example, there are several well-known companies that have lost viable financial recoveries by leaving the risk manager out of the loop until after the claim window had closed.

H. Managing the investigation

One of the most challenging aspects for the project team is determining its size and involvement. Organizational dynamics differ, and the team will require management support to be effective. At the same time, a camel is a horse built by committee (as the joke goes), and the smaller the team can be, the more effective and efficient it will be. An ideal project team would include no more than three people, with each focusing on a primary objective. Outside of that core group, be ready to bring in internal and external specialists when appropriate.

In many organizations, several layers of management and control will want to be involved. This is usually not helpful, both in the drain on management time and the potential to fall into inefficient large group meetings. One strategy that several companies have used successfully uses legal counsel to provide a restricted management briefing to selected people so that they are kept in the loop, while leaving the working team small enough to respond to changing conditions.

The final key to success is managing the process like any other project. Assemble the right team, empower them to respond as the situation warrants, structure a clear reporting chain, and let them do their job. In the above case, the team divided the various tasks, enabling them to deal with the complicated issues. This allowed them to identify quickly and implement a successful recovery strategy. Following this process, the company can prepare detailed statements for use in the criminal referral and civil litigation. If an insurance claim is part of the recovery plan, there are several other nuances that come into play.

I. Preparing a claim

As with all insurance matters, begin with a thorough reading of the policy and any special riders. While some people are familiar with the terms of fidelity policies, most have never made claims under them. These policies differ in several important ways from other types of policies. In disability and health insurance policies, insurance carriers partner with the insured. In workers' compensation, there is often a close relationship and interaction between the two. Claims under fidelity policies place the two parties on opposite sides of the table. They are rarely in partnership and can easily fall into adversarial positions.

Interaction with the carrier begins when the company notifies them of discovery. For standard policies, this often means knowledge on the part of an officer or director. Others have customized the policies to trigger notice requirements upon knowledge by the risk management department, or even personal knowledge of the corporate risk manager position itself.

From that point, the company has a specific period of time to file documentation of the loss. Notice is to be given when the carrier is contacted and is best confirmed in writing. While not common, lack of timely notice can be grounds to disallow a claim, leaving the company with no effective means of recovery.

While minimal information is all that is required at this point, this is the company's opportunity to lay the groundwork for the claim. The more educated the carrier, the better. From this point forward, the information provided will allow the carrier to receive and adjust the forthcoming claim. These claims usually concern custom schemes involving a specialized industry or company. As such, the company will benefit by providing regular information to its carrier.

Despite the differences from other policies, this is also an opportunity to establish and develop a good working rapport with the claims personnel. If the company utilizes a broker in the process, it needs to keep the broker informed to encourage a united approach with the carrier.

During the ensuing investigation, the carrier is officially waiting for the company to present its proof of loss. However, many carriers would prefer advance indication and information so that they can properly position themselves to adjust the claim. Given that many of these types of claims will involve substantial sums, this approach will aid the carrier in setting proper reserve amounts and can substantially ease settlement negotiations. Regular conversations and updates can accomplish this goal while helping to develop rapport. There is one significant caveat. The company is trying to overcome the inherent adversarial posture in these claims. But it cannot forget that this underlying posture stems from the duty of the company to prove its claim and the possibility that the carrier might not accept the proof.

To protect the company against this risk, a single contact should handle all direct communications with the carrier. Information relayed by telephone should be summarized and confirmed in writing, along with anticipated schedules, time lines, and outstanding document requests. The key to preparing the file for potential litigation is a foundation of reasonable action, accurate information, and timely responses, all documented in writing.

Another recent case involved a complicated management fraud issue. The company aggressively managed the case, investigated the related facts, and prepared a detailed proof of loss. To maintain control over the process, this company elected to limit information to teh carrier in the notice letter until the proof of loss was filed. The proof of loss and associated exhibits was almost two feet tall. It detailed a complex scheme structured by senior managers and outside conspirators that had successfully defrauded the company of over $7,000,000 before being revealed by chance.

Following the submission of the proof, the carrier sent a detailed request for additional information. The risk manager took over four months to respond. Several subsequent requests were treated similarly. Almost a year passed with no further communication between the parties.

When the matter again became a priority for the company, the carrier developed a complicated list of unresolved issues with the claim. The company responded by sending the claim to litigation. This outcome could have been avoided. The risk manager had sufficient time to manage the claim, and his inaction damaged any relationship with the carrier. Finally, the lack of response by the company provided the carrier with strong arguments that proved difficult to rebut in litigation.

The opportunity to avoid these issues was early in the process. Every company has more in common with the claims representatives than might appear at first. With a common objective and regular interaction, the company and the carrier can discuss and analyze complex issues as they arise. This is also a great opportunity to evaluate potential arguments and refine them before the official presentation.

J. Filing the claim

Having laid the groundwork with the carrier, the company is positioned to make a claim under the policy. Due to deductible issues, the specific facts, or specific policy provisions, some companies elect not to file a claim. For those that will file a claim, the key to success lies in documenting the facts accurately, drafting the proof of loss, and gathering the attachments. These three elements will form the argument that the carrier should issue payment under the policy.

During the course of the investigation, the team will uncover and process a large volume of data. This will include witness interviews, management reports, physical documents, analysis, and custom work product by the legal department and fraud examiners. The largest issue is managing the flow of data to distinguish the relative importance of each and scheduling them to provide a coherent explanation of the scheme.

Most white-collar crime cases are very document intensive. For example, one team was faced with recreating an entire year of accounting data deleted by the fraudster. Taking advantage of the opportunity the challenge presented, they rescheduled all of the base documentation and allocated the charges to the proper accounts. While the task was larger than they would have liked, the end result was a clear illustration of the effect that cooking the books had on the company.

In one of the earlier examples, the project team reconstructed a fairly simple scheme involving forged documents. The fraudster had inserted his own documents into the normal flow to initiate fraudulent payments. After the reconstruction, over 2,000 forged documents were identified out of a pool of more than 300,000.

Since the intent is for the scheme to go unnoticed, witness cooperation is another essential element. In some cases, the fraudster confesses or provides adequate information to reconstruct the scheme. In others cases, anonymous tipsters provide the first indication. Whatever the source, identifying and documenting those personal statements will strongly support the claim.

Most of these cases involve the work of specialists in the identification, accounting, and valuation aspects of the assembly process. These reports, and the methodology and support that accompany them, form a compelling argument in the body of the insurance claim.

K. Proof of loss

The proof of loss and its associated exhibits are often the result of a joint collaboration among team members. It must be clear, concise, and effective in transmitting its message to the carrier. The proof of loss itself is a story document. It is designed to explain the scheme to the readers and position them to be receptive to the company's arguments regarding coverage and damages.

In most cases, this should be a short, detailed document that explains the facts of the case in a clear, logical format. While some carriers have a specified form for submitting the proof, most understand the diversity of these claims and initially request a narrative format. Either way, it is usually beneficial to make sure that the company get the chance to tell its story its way rather than simply submitting raw facts and allowing for misinterpretation.

The proof of loss submitted by the above company provided a summary of the scheme, followed by a chronological explanation of the scheme as it was later discovered to have occurred. This provided the carrier with a time-oriented approach to the accompanying documents and enabled the adjusters to understand the claim easily. The proof concluded with a recitation of the composite losses cited throughout the proof and a summary of the criminal and civil actions against the fraudster. Following a basic analysis and verification of the information claimed, the carrier paid the seven figure claim without delay.

To help expedite the process, cite the relevant support documentation throughout the claim. With all of the supporting affidavits, documents, analysis, and worksheets the carrier can readily trace the verbal arguments to the financial results of the scheme.

These exhibits of the proof of loss can run into thousands of pages, and the volume must be examined for necessity, clarity, and relevance to the claim. Since somebody will actually be sitting down to read the claim and trying to follow the company's steps through the documents, careful consideration should be made to include all documents that are material to the claim.

The need for brevity, on the other hand, must be balanced against the company's obligation to present all of the facts to the carrier. As a rule of thumb, if the carrier is going to need the document to make its decision, it should be attached and submitted with the proof of loss. In the worst case scenario, where the company and the carrier enter into litigation, a complete and thorough proof of loss can make a conclusive difference in the eyes of a jury.

20.5 Conclusion

All companies deal with employee dishonesty. It is how they deal with it that separates the leading companies, with happy secure employees, from the rest. Employees recognize and respect corporate cultures that value honesty and trustworthiness. They know that there will be some bad apples and expect the company to identify them and get the bad apples out.

To do that, companies must recognize the damage that a dishonest employee can do. They must prioritize systems and processes to detect improper activities. Most importantly, they must take internal theft seriously. A district manager for a multinational company received an anonymous letter one day. It contained allegations of a purchasing agent taking kickbacks. He considered the claims in the letter and discounted them based on his knowledge of the person and his tenure with the company. Fortunately for the company, the writer sent a second letter to another manager. When that manager acted, he discovered that the purchasing agent had indeed taken almost $1 million in kickbacks from a group of suppliers.

Successful resolution depends on a number of factors that are at least partially outside of the company's control. However, skillful planning and coordination of the factors within that control can dramatically affect the outcome of the investigation, litigation, and insurance claim process.

By establishing a detailed and flexible action plan to address employee fraud matters, the company can position itself to maximize any potential recovery. The question is not whether there will be an employee fraud, but when and how large? Faced with this unfortunate reality, companies are changing to a proactive approach, empowering active fraud identification and deterrence procedures.

The key lies in the early identification of potential employee fraud and the response the company makes to the indications of fraud. By empowering a specified team to address and resolve the allegation, and then providing the necessary time and support for their actions, the company can produce substantial financial recoveries. Furthermore, this strategy for early intervention and active management positions the company to reduce collateral damage in the areas of morale, employee efficiency, and public relations.

Chapter 21

Retail Loss Prevention

Jeffery Richardson, Sr.

Synopsis

21.1 Introduction

Whether your business is a mass discounter, clothing, electronics, fast food, or a supermarket, if there are customers, vendors and employees, a sound retail loss prevention program is essential for your business to maximize profitability.

Unless you are the owner who handles every aspect of your business, you must have written policies and procedures that create audit trails in order to control your business. When there is a lack of compliance in policy or procedures that creates a loss, those established policies and procedures will help to identify the weak links in your system thereby giving you the opportunity to make corrections.

In this chapter, we concentrate on one segment of the retail industry that has all of the exposures that all retailers experience: back and front door deliveries from outside vendors, customers from all walks of life, and employees from baggers to general store managers, from age fourteen to seventy.

21.2 Shrinkage in the Supermarket Industry

The average chain supermarket in 2000 is slightly over 50,000 square feet with sales from $200,000 to $1,000,000 per week, with very low overall profit margin. Every dollar loss comes directly off the bottom line and should be the concern of everyone in the company. But are they concerned?

In 1999, the National Supermarket Research Group's Shrink Survey mailed questionnaires to over 7,000 retail grocers. Completed questionnaires were received from 250 companies representing 10,608 supermarkets, making the survey the most comprehensive and industry representative survey reporting exclusively on supermarket shrink. The National Supermarket Research Group's 1999 survey was the tenth annual survey and showed a steady increase in shrink and the causes of shrink in supermarkets.

Table 21.1 shows shrinkage, by category, from 1994 through 1998.

Let us examine a chain with 100 stores that average $500,000 in sales per week or $26 million per year with a 2.48 percent of sales shrink, year ending December 31, 1998. Just look at the total dollars that this company has lost due to all the causes of shrink in 1998.

	1994	**1995**	**1996**	**1997**	**1998**
Employee theft	51%	51%	55%	54%	56%
Shoplifting	25%	24%	27%	26%	25%
Back door receiving	9%	9%	8%	9%	9%
Accounting	4%	5%	2%	3%	3%
Damage	5%	7%	5%	5%	4%
Retail pricing	6%	4%	3%	3%	3%
Number of stores reporting	4,174	3,419	4,301	7,359	10,608
Avg. retail shrink as a % of sales	1.99%	2.09%	2.01%	2.24%	2.48%

Table 21.1 *Shrinkage as a percent of the store's total shrink, or loss of profit*

$26,000,000 yearly sales per store
2.48 percent yearly shrink per store
$644,800 yearly shrink per store
100 store chain—$64,480,000 total chain shrink 1998

Setting a goal to reduce this chain's shrink from 2.48 percent in 1998 to 2.0 percent in 1999 will reduce shrink by $12,480,000 and increase the profitability of the chain.

How would one direct their efforts to accomplish this shrink reduction for this supermarket chain? Let's look at the causes again and direct our assets and effort into those things that cause shrink. An audit plan must be developed to monitor each cause of shrink which will help to identify causes so that a plan of action can be developed to reduce the stores' shrink.

1. Retail pricing (3 percent)
   - Are pre-priced vendor items coming in at the correct price?
   - Are all coupons authorized?
   - Are price changes being made weekly, up or down?
   - Are all price overrides at the point of sale (POS) authorized?
   - Are electronic coupons ringing properly?
   - Are all items credited to proper departments?
   - Are you using the proper price book?
   - Are prices per pound correct for random weight items?
2. Damages (4 percent)
   - Are markdown procedures used within company guidelines?
   - Are throwaway logs being maintained for all departments?
   - Are throwaways in perishable departments (meat, seafood, produce, bakery) logged properly?
   - If employees are allowed to purchase damaged markdowns, are they damaging product to create markdowns?
   - Are packout clerks damaging product to avoid packing it out?
   - Are outside vendors issuing proper credit on damages?
   - Are customers creating damages to create markdowns?
3. Accounting department (3 percent)
   - Have you checked for improper credits?
   - Have you checked for wrong-store billing?
   - Have you checked for going-in gross profit errors?
   - Have you checked for posting errors?
   - Have you reviewed your purchase register?
   - Have you checked for hand-listed items?
4. Back door receiving (9 percent)
   - Are all vendor deliveries being checked in according to policy?
   - Are all vendor over and shorts being logged for proper credit?
   - Are vendor credit items compared to credit slip?
   - Are proper credit dollars being issued?
   - Are warehouse deliveries handled properly?

- Are receiving doors locked when not in use?
- Are vendor spot checks being performed by the store management team?

5. Shoplifting (25 percent)
   - Are unopened front end lanes blocked?
   - Are circulars removed from carts before a transaction is completed?
   - Are bags available only on open lanes?
   - Have you reviewed low-shelf allocation for high-ticketed items?
   - Are high valued items displayed by the exit door?
   - Are large items under the cart being rung up?
   - Are fire exit doors controlled?
   - Should electronic article surveillance (EAS) be considered?
   - Are storage areas secured?
6. Employee theft (56 percent)
   - Unauthorized discounts
   - Sweethearting (unauthorized discounts)
   - Shoplifting
   - Theft of time
   - Theft of money
   - Wrong pricing
   - Improper mark down
   - Eating unpurchased merchandise
   - Use of shelf product for supply items
   - Giving customers free merchandise
   - Unauthorized void or refunds

The store management team must look at all issues daily to control shrink issues and report any dishonest to the loss prevention team for proper follow-up action. The areas that cause shrink have been identified by the National Supermarket Research Group as important and must be controlled. Two shrink causing categories have caused more than 75 percent of store shrink in all of the surveys from 1994 to 1998: employee theft (in excess of 50 percent of total store shrink) and customer shoplifting (averaging about 25 percent of store shrink). Even though all causes of shrink must be addressed, the largest percentage of your efforts and loss-prevention budget must be concentrated on those two major contributors to shrink.

Customer shoplifting on the average is 25 percent of total store shrink. Using the 100 store chain that we developed earlier in this chapter, 25 percent of the total store shrink equals $161,200 in customer shoplifting. One very effective method of reducing customer shoplifting with very little capital investment is to create an employee awareness program that includes offering assistance to all customers all the time. The customer who plans to steal from your store does not want to be identified and, as employees offer assistance, this type of customer gets uncomfortable and change his plan of action.

Other methods used to deter shoplifting include EAS (electronic article surveillance), where high-ticket and highly pilfered merchandise is tagged with targets that set off an alarm at the entrance and exit doors if store associates have not deactivated them at the point of sale (POS). This will allow you a chance to retrieve unpaid merchandise at the entrance and exit door and act as a deterrent for all other customers. This method does require a capital investment and ongoing labor to control the entrance and exit doors. An additional cost is incurred if the merchandise requiring the targets is not source tagged by the manufacturer. Then, store associates must tag the items.

The use of CCTV in combination with loss-prevention agents to make apprehensions is a very effective method of controlling customer shoplifting, but does require capital investment and generally a larger labor cost (for the loss prevention agents based on the number of hours covered per store). This method is generally more effective in high crime areas (urban stores in large cities).

In 1998, 56 percent of total store shrink was reported as due to dishonest employees and, based on the NRSRG shrink survey, 29 percent of employee theft was created at the point of sale by cashiers. Using the supermarket chain with 100 stores and 2.48 percent total store shrink, cashier shrink would have meant a loss of $104,716 per store in 1998. This makes cashier shrink the second largest contributor to shrink in the supermarket. There are several different methods that can be used to reduce and deter cashier shrink. The POS exception report is a software package developed by the POS supplier that will identify cashier exception that could create cashier shrink. For example, a cashier with more voids than the other cashiers for the same time period would be an exception to the norm.

CCTV observations by loss prevention personnel at the POS, using the same CCTV capital investment for customer shoplifting and using the same loss prevention monitoring budget as used for customer shoplifting, helps to maximize productivity.

Cashier-awareness programs, educating newly hired cashiers during orientation about the POS exception reporting, loss prevention capability with the use of CCTV, automated front-end monitoring systems, and automated front-end systems combined with CCTV systems make it easier to detect dishonest acts.

Mystery shoppers are often used to observe during shopping trips and report their findings to loss prevention and store management teams.

Customer service supervision being highly visible on the front end is a great deterrent in the reduction of cashier shrink. Addressing the smallest issues with each cashier makes him or her understand that what they do is important to the business and, at the same time, reminds them that they are being monitored.

21.3 Conclusion

Our goal was to reduce company shrink from 2.48 percent to 2.00 percent producing a shrink savings of $12,480,000 for the year. By reducing shrink by 0.48 percent, profitability increased by $12,480,000 without increasing sales. Where did the $12,480,000 shrink reduction come from?

	2.48% shrink	**2.00% shrink**	**reduction**
employee theft	1.40	1.10	.30
shoplifting	.62	.53	.09
back door	.22	.20	.02
accounting	.07	.06	.01
damage	.10	.07	.03
pricing	.70	.04	.03
total %	2.48	2.00	.48
dollars	$64,480,000	$52,000,000	412,480,000

Table 21.2 *Shrink reduction according to plan*

Developing policies and procedures, and sticking to them, will help reduce shrink in all areas.

Identifying the causes of retail shrink and developing policies and procedures to reduce and control those causes is the only proven method to reduce retail shrink and increase profitability.

Chapter 22

Corporate Conferences—Asset Protection, Loss Prevention, Access Control

Herbert Simon, CPP

Synopsis

22.1 Introduction

Loss prevention (LP) is asset protection. The most important asset to protect is personnel; however, proprietary information and physical assets must also be secured. Asset protection begins at the workplace and it must travel with your employees. Off-site events such as seminars, conferences, and training and awards programs expose a corporation's personnel and proprietary information to threats that are effectively deterred at the office. Vulnerability increases greatly when a corporation's employees leave the home base's protection. Extensive pre-planning and competent implementation are critical with regard to ensuring that the corporation's assets are protected and personnel safeguarded when both are transported from normal to detached venues.

Corporate LP professionals can secure their buildings, operating seamlessly with proper protective measures, but do the venues to which your employees travel use the same or even similar measures? Convention centers, conference locations, and major hotels have security departments and loss prevention procedures, but are never specific to a corporation's needs. Additionally, these venues are by nature accessible to the public. This unrestricted access creates exposure and risk. It is within these venues that a protected environment must be established. Through cooperation with a subcontracted loss prevention professional, the meeting planner and the off-site facility's security professionals, the corporation's loss prevention can coordinate appropriate access control, deny unauthorized individuals and make an event secure.

Ensuring employee safety is always the primary assignment. Nothing is more significant than providing a risk-free working environment for conference attendees and employees. Protection of all assets, i.e. personnel, proprietary information, property, etc., is the ultimate goal. For a successful conference loss prevention program, cooperation, coordination, and communication are essential. While there always exists the need for budgetary constraints, protection must not suffer as a result.

It is understandable that conference attendees expect to enjoy themselves and most every opportunity to do so is provided; yet, employees must remember their loss prevention responsibilities, with increased awareness while traveling. Only a minority of conference attendees perceive that loss prevention is a nuisance. The vast majority, however, view loss prevention as validation that their company takes their safety and proprietary information's protection seriously. Loss prevention gives employees pride, knowing that what they are doing is important. Following an event, conference attendees, supervisors, and corporate officers repeatedly express gratitude for the protection afforded. In fact, once experienced, most corporate officers insist that loss prevention become an integral conference component.

Corporate espionage is a genuine threat. As technology advances, so too do the tools used for espionage. Corporate America's competitive nature has made information protection a priority. Laptops, promotional literature, training manuals, and product specifications must be secured at all times. Research and development programs cost millions of dollars, and the resulting information and products must be kept confidential. Allowing such information to be taken and used by others can be financially disastrous. Such intellectual and proprietary information is greatly exposed during corporate conferences.

At virtually every corporate conference, meeting planners create an event-specific program, usually a binder with schedules and support documents. Every program should include a page addressing attendees' security responsibilities, written by the corporation's loss prevention department. It may be generic; however, each location differs and the document should reflect any changes to the basic information. The document must have emergency contact numbers such as police, conference LP supervisor, and meeting planner, as well as information relating to attendees' security and confidentiality responsibilities. For example: conference attendees, wishing to experience the location's local flavor may intend to go on a'walk-about.' The attendees should be cautioned regarding certain areas that might not be safe and directed to the ones which are. Attendees should be reminded to speak with the facility's concierge, the LP professional, or the establishment's security *prior* to any unaccompanied excursions.

As conferences may occur throughout the United States and abroad, it is critical to find and hire LP professionals who are familiar with local law enforcement agencies and who have the ability to call for support during serious situations. Most corporations do not have enough LP staff to cover all conferences. Thus, a sub-contracted LP professional who will work the event must be carefully selected. The professional must have conference protection experience. When possible, the on-site conference lead LP professional should be current or retired local, state or federal law enforcement, military intelligence, licensed private investigator (with tested, functional corporate comprehension), or a professional referred by trusted contacts. Such persons will receive a better response from local law enforcement if there is trouble.

By definition, loss prevention must be proactive, not reactive. Qualified LP professionals must handle any incidents of demonstrations or threats of violence.

While many convention centers and hotels have solid and effective in-house security forces, using a LP professional is still strongly recommended. If the conference center does not have its own 'in-house' officers and their sub-contracted security is a private organization, then other arrangements must be made. It is NEVER recommended to use private, subcontracted physical security guards for such assignments.

Suggestions made by LP professionals before and during each event should be carefully considered. The LP professionals will always work with the meeting planner to accommodate requests, unless a request jeopardizes the attendees' safety. If a conflict arises, regarding the LP professional's suggestions and a meeting planner's requests, the corporate office should have a contact available to resolve the dispute.

22.2 Coordination

Planning and coordination are the cornerstones of every successful loss prevention program. Constant communication is necessary in order for a conference's protection detail to proceed smoothly and incidents responded to efficiently.

When possible, it is best to coordinate loss prevention coverage at least one month prior to an event. There are qualified LP professionals in every major city in the United States, as well as internationally. The earlier contact is made, the better.

Have the LP professional contact the conference's meeting planner.

Prior to the conference, best case scenario, one to two weeks, the lead LP professional, whose staff will work the conference, should visit the facility's security director as a courtesy and to discuss needs and concerns such as visiting dignitaries, equipment shipments, special events, VIP's, etc.

Having a meeting agenda greatly increases the ability to coordinate LP staffing requirements. The meeting planner should provide a draft meeting agenda to the LP professional. It should note meeting times, in which rooms the meetings will be held, which off-site venues will be visited, how many attendees, etc. It is understood that the agenda may change, but a general idea of how the conference will proceed always helps.

The LP professional should obtain the facility's schematic floor plan. The LP professional will review this information during the on-site visit with the facility's security director. Some establishments have websites, which provide this information.

Some corporations request greater loss prevention presence than others. In many cases, the meeting planner can offer staff to supplement the loss prevention team in order to avoid the billing the LP staff would charge. The meeting planner's staff, when supplementing LP, should not be given any critical loss prevention responsibilities.

Regarding attendance numbers, as a general guideline, pertaining to access control:

- 100–200 attendees can be handled by two LP professionals.
- 200–400 attendees can be handled by two to five LP professionals.
- 400–600 attendees can be handled by four to seven LP professionals.
- 600–800 attendees can be handled by six to nine LP professionals.
- 800+ requires a careful examination of traffic control in order to ensure sufficient loss prevention presence.

A hotel room should be reserved for the LP professionals. Check-in should be the night before the conference's first day, if the general session has an early start. Checkout will be the last day of the conference. Room charges should be included in the corporation's master bill. Providing the LP professionals with rooms enables them to get a fresh start without having traffic concerns or delays. It also provides an added response if something happens as, even when the LP professionals are not on-duty, they will be in the area.

Loss prevention should be given radios that are on the same frequency as that of the meeting planners. There should never be a time, during the conference when the meeting planner is unable to contact a LP professional.

The lead LP professional should be included in the pre-conference meeting. This lets the meeting planners as well as all facility and convention staff to become acquainted with the LP professional. It is suggested the lead LP professional speak, briefly, at the conference's first general session. What the attendees' loss prevention responsibilities are and what the LP professionals will be doing during the conference can be communicated. It can be reiterated that attendees should not discuss the conference with anyone they do not know and be wary of people trying to extract information. The attendees should be reminded, when receiving their badges, that identification badges will be worn at all time and no recording devices will be allowed. The attendees' supervisors or corporate loss prevention can also send a memo ahead of time regarding loss prevention responsibilities.

The lead LP professional should make contact with local law enforcement. A short visit to introduce oneself goes a long way towards garnering expeditious response. Exchanging contact information and discussing the conference's purpose as well as what aspects might attract trouble, i.e. a birth-control product's training seminar could be protested by right-to-life activists; a corporation that sells fur coats could be picketed by animal rights groups, etc., will better prepare all parties.

22.3 Identification Badges (ID)

In order to keep unauthorized persons out, it must first be determined who belongs. When all authorized attendees are wearing badges, the attendees themselves become aware of and alert for persons who are not wearing ID. Every supervisor, meeting planner, and LP professional can firmly enforce the ID requirement. ID badges are an access control program's most fundamental and important component. The loss prevention staff must wear badges that clearly identify themselves as such to the conference attendees.

ALL attendees must clearly display their ID badges at *ALL* times: General sessions, breakout rooms and during on-site social functions, breakfasts, lunches, and dinners. It is strongly recommended that the event's ID not identify the corporation's name, any product, or conference topic (see Figure 22.1).

The meeting planners should also ensure that conference signage not have the corporation name or the product and purpose for the conference displayed. The conference theme or slogan should be chosen carefully in order to maintain confidentiality. The conference attendees know why they are there; others, the public, hotel patrons, and visitors, do not need to know.

Photographic IDs should be used whenever possible. Some meeting planners have purchased digital ID systems that can create photo-ID at the conference, with little disruption. The LP professional's job can be performed much more effectively when able to match a face on an ID to the

Attendee Photograph	**PHILIP HEALD** **DIRECTOR SPORTING EVENTS**

EXCELLENCE AWARDS
HORSESHOE CONVENTION CENTER
NOVEMBER 16-21, 2004

Figure 22.1 *Sample Identification Badge (no corporate identifiers)*

bearer. If such hardware and software are not available, it is recommended that some be purchased.

All ID badges must be protected! ID badges, when pre-made, must not ever be placed on an unattended table. Lines leading to registration should not pass near the ID badges, and attendees must never be allowed to 'find' their own ID badges. It is strongly recommended that the LP professionals assist in the registration process. If desired, LP professionals can be stationed as 'first contact.' The LP professional will ask the attendee for photographic ID to confirm identity. If the attendee has no photographic ID, an inspection of identification documents can be made in order to confirm the person is who he or she claims to be. Once the identification is confirmed, the attendee proceeds to regular registration to obtain the conference program and the event-specific ID badge.

22.4 General Sessions

General sessions draw the highest volume of attendees. Sessions can reach several thousands of attendees. General sessions' access control is critical! More often than not, general sessions are held in 'ballrooms' with many entrances and exit doors, backstage passages, and serving corridors. This fact makes it vital to meet with the facility's security director prior to the event in order to determine what must be secured and from which direction trouble might come.

Egress doors cannot be locked because of safety regulations. Entrances, however, can be limited if desired (see Figure 22.2). Considering general sessions' volume, two LP professionals per entrance will help ensure a smooth attendee flow. Poor planning or inadequate personnel and entrances can create 'logjams,' aggravate attendees, and create a negative LP experience.

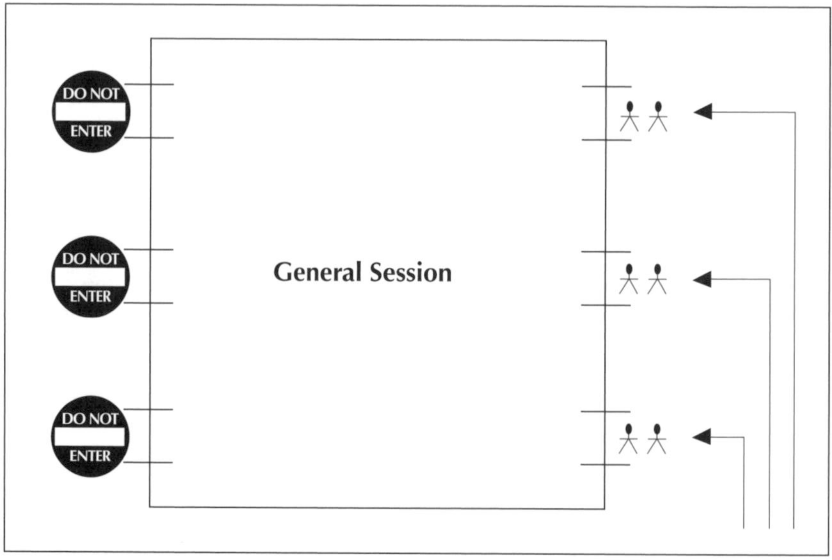

***Figure 22.2** General sessions and social events traffic control (minimize access points, ID verification at entrances)*

As general sessions are held in large rooms, audio amplification is usually strong. The speaker's words can be heard through closed doors, and therefore, the LP professionals should be alert for unauthorized persons. The area should be restricted if possible. Any persons' 'loitering' should be questioned and asked to move.

If the material being presented within the general session is very sensitive, such as intellectual property, an electronic sweep using a qualified counter-measures expert should be considered immediately prior to the first session. Monitoring activity within the room and securing it when vacant should eliminate the need to conduct the sweep more than once.

These technical counter-measures should be considered for any room where such proprietary information is being discussed.

It is suggested that a 'visual inspection' be conducted of any bag being brought into the general session. A visual inspection is non-invasive, and attendees should not feel violated if the LP professional does not touch belongings. Looking into a bag should not slow entrance. Physical searches should always be discussed with the corporation's general counsel. In many cases, it is advisable to have a female LP professional conduct such inspections for the female attendees. If a recording device is discovered, the attendee should be asked to step aside. The LP professional should question the attendee. If the attendee offers satisfactory reason for the device's existence, then have the attendee temporarily surrender the device to the LP professional and allow entrance. The LP professional should give the device to a meeting planner until the attendee recovers it subsequent to the session. Clearly visible signage indicating "No Recording Devices Allowed" will deter most attendees from bringing such devices.

If a weapon is discovered, the lead LP professional must be notified immediately. The attendee carrying a weapon should be taken aside immediately and questioned by the lead LP professional. Local law enforcement can be contacted when necessary.

Regarding mobile phones with photographic capability, the LP professionals who observes an attendee wearing a photographic mobile phone should tell the attendee that absolutely no pictures are to be taken.

If a LP professional observes an attendee violating this directive, the attendee should be asked to step aside, or be taken aside and brought to the meeting planner. As the corporation's representative, the meeting planner, NOT the LP professional, can make the appropriate determination.

22.5 Breakout Rooms

At many conferences, early morning general sessions are followed by the attendees segregating to breakout rooms or smaller training or roll-playing venues. Even then there is need for loss prevention. Breakout rooms might be located on the same floor as the general session, and this is greatly preferred, or they can be scattered throughout the facility, making access control much more difficult.

Two LP professionals should be onsite whenever attendance, even if it is breakout rooms only, is over 100 persons. When attendance is less than 100 persons, one should be sufficient.

Every breakout room does not need to have its own LP professional. It is the responsibility of the breakout rooms' supervisors to ensure that all breakout rooms' attendees are wearing their ID Badges and belong in the room. The LP professional should remain in the area to address problems. The LP professional can conduct a 'walk-through' to ensure only authorized attendees are present, by badge verification. This badge confirmation procedure should be conducted at the breakout session's beginning.

Breakout rooms, even when on separate floors, should be located in as small an area as possible. This should be discussed with the meeting planner in the earliest conference coordination stages. The rooms should, if possible, be accessed by one main entrance route so the LP professionals can ensure persons entering the areas belong. If the breakout rooms are on a common corridor, the LP professionals can create a 'choke point' and more easily control traffic (see Figure 22.3).

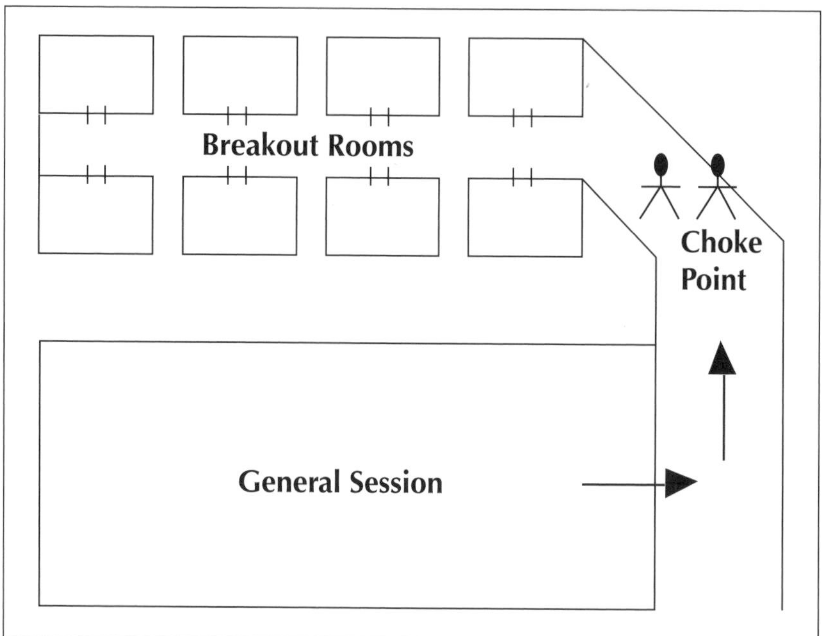

Figure 22.3 *Breakout rooms, ID verification at choke point*

The breakout rooms should be locked when vacant. The breakout room's supervisor, who is the person conducting the breakout session, should be the last person out and ensure the room is secured. Loss prevention should followup to ensure the breakout rooms are secured. Loss prevention and, if coordinated, the meeting planners' staff will physically ensure these rooms are secured during breaks, lunches, and at the end of the day. In situations where there are many breakout rooms, this process can take a substantial amount of time, depending on the amount of rooms and number of LP professionals conducting the task. Even when meeting planners and their staffs are setting up the breakout rooms i.e. putting pads and pens on desks, each time the rooms are left, they should be secured. If proprietary information or equipment, such as laptops, are left in breakout rooms and the hotel is 'refreshing,' i.e., cleaning and replenishing sodas or bottled water for the next day, then the LP professionals should be at hand to ensure the task is completed without any corporate property being disturbed.

An example: a meeting planner is 'setting up' a breakout room in a hotel venue. The meeting planner has to go in and out ten to twenty times to complete the task and leaves the breakout room's door propped open. While going to another floor to get more supplies, a drunken teenager who is another hotel guest, enters the breakout room and writes on a desk's pad that was set up by the meeting planner, "I'M GOING TO KILL YOU!" The teenager walks out, laughing hysterically at the joke. No joke—the next day, an attendee sits at the desk, reads the note and becomes extremely upset. A true story, with a lesson—lock the door.

It is strongly recommended that when possible the locks on the breakout rooms be changed immediately prior to the conference's commencement. The meeting planners, loss prevention and the establishment's security director or staff should be the only persons with keys.

If AV personnel require breakout room access, they should see and communicate with the meeting planner and/or loss prevention. The meeting planner should notify loss prevention that AV personnel will be in a room, at what time, and the equipment being taken in and out. As it may be impossible to monitor all rooms, coordination is critical.

Either the meeting planner or loss prevention will conduct sweeps of the breakout rooms during breaks, lunches, and at the conclusion of breakout sessions. Proprietary information and electronic equipment left behind, if the room is not absolutely secured, will be removed and brought to the meeting planner's office. The rooms will, of course, be secured upon the sweeps' completion.

22.6 Special and Social Events

Special events are held at many conferences e.g., a concert, VIP speaker, celebrity, etc. Occasionally, the' 'special' event is a 'secret' kept from the attendees.

The lead LP professional must be informed of any and all 'special' events. This enables the LP force's supervisor to coordinate appropriately event protection. You can be confident the LP professional and staff will not share any 'secret.'

An example: Dover Lot Six Productions is throwing their annual awards banquet and as a secret surprise has arranged for the hottest band in the world, "The Monkey Boys" to entertain 1,100+ attendees. Fearing the 'secret' will get out, the LP professional is only told "there will be a concert." The LP professional assigns staff appropriately to control the conference's attendees. Inevitably, word gets out, and the hotel where the conference is being held is 'buzzing' with excitement. Many hotel guests hear "The Monkey Boys are playing!" and assume the concert is open to all hotel guests, or they understand access is restricted and intend to 'crash' the event. The hotel guests are getting prepped for the big night. Often, alcohol is consumed, and sometimes drugs. As doors open, non-conference hotel guests gain access through doors that conference attendees know are not to be used, human traffic volume increases beyond loss prevention's manageability, and uninvited people fill the room. The LP professionals enter the room, after 'controlling' what traffic they could, and confront unauthorized attendees. None of the unauthorized persons leave without confrontation, mostly verbal, although some become physical. An efficient access control task turns into the LP professional's nightmare. The lesson? Meeting planners must trust the LP professionals and share information in a timely manner.

When 'special' events are held, access points to it should be minimized. When extra doors are opened at such events, it has been demonstrated, several times, that access cannot be properly controlled. Loss prevention will conduct the same access control functions as would be done during a general session.

ID badges must be worn while at 'special' and social functions inside the conference facility. Social functions can present good opportunities for infiltrators to obtain confidential information. Attendees are less 'guarded' with their conversation during such events. When traveling away from the facility e.g., 'dine-arounds,' sightseeing tours, etc., it is not necessary to wear ID badges or to have loss prevention. An LP professional can attend the off-site event if circumstances suggest it is appropriate.

22.7 Visiting Dignitaries

Whether it is an *outside* dignitary or one of the corporation's high-ranking officers who is present, the lead LP professional must be notified of who is coming

Often a corporate officer will request protection, or the corporation's LP department insists upon it, when the officer is traveling to off-site functions. Some corporate officers are very uncomfortable with such attention and are resolute there be none. This is when a corporation should ensure its succession policy is firmly in place. Advanced notice to the lead LP professional regarding dignitary protection is necessary.

If a VIP is arriving, the lead security professional should advise the facility's security director of the impending visit. The security director can coordinate alternate entrances and exits to maintain a' 'surprise' and ensure the VIP's safety.

As some VIP's have their own security details, it is critical for the LP professional's staff to coordinate and communicate with them.

22.8 Laptops

All employees are responsible for their own laptops. For some reason, however, responsibility is not taken seriously at conferences. In the 'field', an employee would never leave a laptop unattended, but at a conference the laptops are too often found left on tables during breaks or lunches and in unsecured rooms. This is a serious matter. The laptop's purchase cost is inconsequential compared to the associated costs when a laptop goes missing, i.e., reloading software, lost productivity, re-training, etc. The proprietary information on an employee's laptop, in the wrong hands, can cripple a corporation. Everyone involved in a conference must understand the gravity of protecting these computers. A warning to this effect should be included on a separate page in the conference program.

Laptops must NOT be left in any unsecured room. A room is considered secured if there are security personnel assigned to it or if the room is locked immediately following its vacancy and access is controlled.

Laptops that are left in unsecured rooms will be removed by the LP professional and given to the meeting planner to be held until the owner comes to report its' 'disappearance' or 'theft.'

The meeting planner should notify the laptop user's supervisor of the 'incident.' Loss prevention should log the date, time, and location at which the laptop was found and to whom and when it was delivered.

If laptops are being delivered to the conference location, other than being hand carried by attendees, it is critical that the laptops be secured when they arrive. Loss prevention and, if they wish, the meeting planners, must coordinate with the conference facility's security director and receiving managers to secure the laptops. Loss prevention must control this laptop intake and transfer process from receiving dock to final destination.

The locks for the rooms where laptops will be stored should be changed immediately prior to the conference commencement, and keys as well as access, controlled.

Some establishments have 'cables' and other devices that can secure laptops to tables. If these are available, they should be used.

22.9 Audio Visual (AV)

The corporation will, more than likely, use an audio visual subcontractor. The AV supervisor and the AV staff should comply with all loss prevention regulations.

The AV subcontractors are responsible for protecting their own equipment. Equipment should be stored in as few locations as possible. In most cases, the AV subcontractor will employ the facility's in-house security or subcontracted private security to protect equipment overnight.

AV personnel, all, must wear their ID badges at all times. AV personnel usually have access to all rooms and will be allowed to remove equipment. AV personnel must not leave their ID where someone can take them. To non-authorized persons, these AV badges are good as gold, even more valuable than employee and attendee badges.

AV personnel sometimes take their loss prevention responsibilities lightly. Special scrutiny is therefore required with these and other subcontractors. Loss prevention, if given the responsibility, or the facility's in-house security should log what equipment is moved or taken and when. If this type of recording is prohibitive, loss prevention must ensure that persons moving equipment are the persons allowed to do so.

The AV supervisor should provide names and photographs, if possible, of their personnel to the meeting planner and loss prevention supervisor prior to the conference's commencement.

AV personnel must often be in and out of certain rooms in order to set up and test equipment. If laptops and/or proprietary information are kept in these rooms, the rooms must be secured when the AV personnel leave, even for a short amount of time. An LP professional can, if necessary, be used to watch these rooms during this period. If security is *augmented* to protect AV equipment, these services should be billed to the AV company.

When choosing an AV subcontractor, the corporation should ensure that 'protected' equipment is used. Concerning wireless microphones, the potential AV subcontractor must be told, "If you want our business, you will use digitally encrypted wireless microphones." This is necessary to prevent the signal from being intercepted by people outside or near the room where the device is being used. All videotapes and digital recordings must be accounted for to ensure the conference's contents are not shared, compromised, or sold. The AV subcontractor must understand compliance with the corporation's proprietary information protection program is not an option. The corporation's general counsel should draft and insist the AV subcontractor sign a binding contract that specifies penalties for improper use or dissemination of the corporation's confidential and intellectual property.

22.10 Alcohol

Many conferences have events at which alcohol is served. Alcoholic consumption can generate trouble.

It has already been mentioned that competitor's agents may attempt to infiltrate venues where alcohol is served and attendees talk more freely. Keeping unauthorized individuals out of venues where alcohol is consumed is the first, best step to minimizing the risk of an alcohol-related incident.

An example: A hospitality function is arranged at a bar or restaurant near the conference location. Some 850+ attendees enjoy themselves for two to three hours, eating and drinking. All is well until the return walk, which crosses a major intersection, when an attendee steps off the curb and is struck by a passing vehicle. Worst case scenario? Yes. Avoidable? Also, yes. Have one or two LP professionals present to help the people safely across the intersection. Therefore, the LP professional must know to which venues the attendees will travel and prepare accordingly. Meeting planners are concerned about employee safety; in an attempt to entertain the troops, however, good intentions may have poor results. Working together and constantly communicating gives the LP professional a better opportunity to anticipate and prevent incidents.

22.11 Miscellaneous

There may be times when an LP professional chosen to work a conference is certified as an EMT (emergency medical technician). This can prove to be incredibly beneficial but is by no means, mandatory. In emergency situations, the LP/EMT can respond, and fortunately so. However, the LP/EMT is not to be asked for medical advice and under no circumstances is to give any. The LP/EMT can address emergency needs and then advise an attendee to consult a medical doctor and even arrange for such contact and transport. The LP's *first duty* is protection and not ongoing medical attention. In fact, an alleged medical situation could be used as a diversion in order to pull an LP/EMT off post. Additionally, the issue of liability arises. If the LP/EMT administered treatment in an emergency, the recipient could in a worst case scenario die. This could generate undesirable legal action. The LP/EMT should always have a witness when administering emergency medical attention. The witness could be used to refute allegations of inappropriate touching or even sexual assault. As there are many potentially negative ramifications regarding providing medical attention of any kind to an attendee, many corporate LP professionals, following conversation with and direction from the corporation's general counsel, have decided their own as well as subcontracted staff should not provide such response. This issue, attendees receiving and LP professionals providing medical attention, should be discussed and determinations made prior to any conference and can be forged into existing corporate policy.

If an LP/EMT responds to an emergency, that LP/EMT's position must be immediately backfilled with another LP professional. Any incident or diversion that might create a vacant post must be anticipated and appropriately addressed prior to the conference's commencement.

In some cases, the corporate LP director might use an LP professional and become totally comfortable with that professional. Based upon this comfort zone, the corporate director might request the LP professional to travel to different locations or states than the one in which the LP professional is licensed. It is important to know that in some states, the traveling LP professional will have to comply with the state's appropriate licensing requirements prior to commencing the assignment.

Professional certifications are always solid indicators the LP professional is proven and recognized by peers for outstanding knowledge, experience, and functional ability. It is advisable that the LP professional chosen have a CPP. The CPP stands for Certified Protection Professional and is awarded by ASIS International. ASIS International is the world's largest security organization, primarily composed of LP professionals. The certification is only earned by validated experience and written testing.

22.12 Conclusion

Corporate conferences celebrate successes, conduct training, continue education, and bond employee attendees in fraternal comradeship. Cost for travel, housing, food, and entertainment can be huge, and while a loss prevention presence will increase the conference's budget, it is essential. As with most protection programs, the corporation's financial professionals will wonder why, following the uneventful conference, so much money had to be spent for loss prevention? The answer is, the conference was uneventful because the loss prevention program worked! Achieving loss prevention's objective is hard work; however, when attendees leave, having enjoyed a comfortable, safe, and secure conference, the effort and protection afforded is priceless.

Over the years, corporate conference loss prevention and access control procedures have developed. Many improvements have resulted, unfortunately, when learning from mistakes. A seamless program, designed for thorough and efficient loss prevention, providing attendees a safe, secure, and comfortable atmosphere can be realized with proper planning, communication, and implementation. The corporate and subcontracted LP professionals can coordinate protection for the largest (or smallest) events competently when working together with program directors and meeting planners, the conference locations' security directors, and local law enforcement.

Chapter 23

Investigating "Bust-Out" Fraud

Todd Sheffer, CFE

Synopsis

23.1 "Bust-Out" Defined

Convicted fraudster, Alan, said that a "bust-out" is an upside down pyramid. The bust-out, or sometimes called a "break-out," starts small and grows to proportions limited only by the bust-out operator. Alan should know, he was indicted for the insolvencies of Spero Trading Co., Spero Ltd., and Blue Ribbon Foods and charged with using fake references and misrepresentation to obtain millions in merchandise as well as a $1.2 million bank loan.

Alan said that all you need for a bust-out is to start a business and then get three suppliers to extend you credit. Once you have three suppliers ship you products on credit, you have is sell the inventory under cost, and use the money to stagger the payments to the creditors. While you are making payments to the initial suppliers, you must also place new orders with the suppliers and apply for credit with additional suppliers.

All this activity may seem like a lot of work but, according to Alan, "What other job can you make a million dollars a month and not pay taxes?" Alan may have made a million dollars per month, but that all ended when he was convicted of wire fraud and sentenced to approximately nine years in prison. One of the reasons Alan received such a long prison sentence was because the court had learned that while Alan was out on bond awaiting his trial for the fraud charges, he was involved with another business insolvency.

A bust-out is a planned business insolvency. The plan is to run the business' credit to its highest limits and then close, stiffing unpaid creditors. The bust-out's upside-down pyramid starts with small orders with a few suppliers in the beginning and over time the pyramid can grow to large orders with hundreds of suppliers.

Alan said that he started his bust-out by opening two bank accounts, one that the suppliers knew about and one that they did not know about. He also needed a facility (any rented warehouse), a crew (people to help receive and ship the merchandise) and trade references. Alan knew that suppliers would not normally extend credit to a new business, so he lied about his start date and arranged for some phony references to say that they had been doing business with Alan for years.

Phony trade references are sometimes called *singers* because they sing the praises of the bust-out business. A supplier would call the phony trade reference, which would have been Alan's friends, relatives, or other businesses that were outlets for the bust-out product. The phony trade reference would tell the supplier that it had sold to Alan for years, with multi-figure high credits, and prompt payments on thirty- or sixty-day selling terms. When the supplier called the bank the bank would say that Alan had a substantial balance; whether or not the bank told of the newness of Alan's bank account depended on the individual asking the questions.

Alan said that he did not have to be smarter than the suppliers he duped, he only had to be smarter than they thought he was. Like many con men, Alan simply told his victims what they wanted to hear. Alan would initially apply for credit for a small order with the promise of future larger orders. Alan also said that when a sales representative from a supplier called on him, he never placed an order on the first visit. He would make the sales representative come back so the salesperson would be a little hungrier, and then Alan would place the order. Alan said that with the salesmen pushing for his order to be approved and his made-up trade references singing his praises, the suppliers could not wait to ship the product. And ship they did.

Once Alan started paying his initial suppliers, he replaced the singers he had used as initial trade references with the legitimate suppliers that he had paid. Using real companies as trade references gave Alan additional credibility with the industry in which he was operating. Alan said that he started his bust-out career in the electronics industry and then he gravitated to doing bust-outs in the meat industry. Why meat? Alan explained that, at the time, a truckload of meat was worth several hundred thousand dollars more than a truckload of electronics. It's lucky for the computer distribution industry that Alan was already in jail before that industry grew to prominence.

Alan ran his business ordering product on credit, selling the product "out the back door," paying the creditors within terms, and ordering more product from more and more suppliers. If suppliers questioned Alan's increased ordering pattern he would tell the supplier that he was expanding, or pioneering new markets for the product. Alan said that since the suppliers were getting paid, they really did not ask too many questions.

Alan did pay his suppliers for a while, but then payments slowed; however he continued placing orders to the suppliers. Excuses like "we had checks stolen," "we had a break in," and "we can't pay because the principal is away or sick" were used to lull the creditors into to giving additional time for payment on the past due balances. If Alan used the suppliers as legitimate trade references, at the end of the bust-out the suppliers' would typically start getting several reference calls for Alan's business every day. When the suppliers were pushed to the point of placing Alan for collection or forcing him into bankruptcy for nonpayment, Alan would simply skip from his premises and started a new business under a new name.

For an investigator, a bust-out presents some unique challenges and, as in any white-collar crime investigation, the key word is frustration. The investigation is frustrating because most victims do not know that they have been victimized until after the bust-out operator skips, and sometimes never. So conducting a post-mortem investigation of someone like Alan who created a real-looking business is difficult. In addition, most professional bust-out operators have little tangible assets to attach in civil remedies and most law enforcement will look at business-to-business disputes as a civil matter. Law enforcement as a whole does not receive the proper white-collar fraud training and does not have the resources to handle a bust-out investigation. Even if you are lucky enough to find a law enforcement official who will take the case, if the bust-out is in a major metropolitan area, the dollar amount must be substantial in order for law enforcement to proceed.

Investigating bust-outs may be discouraging; however, a bust-out investigation is the type of crime that poses the type of intellectual challenge that made many individuals become investigators in the first place.

Because the bust-out investigation is so difficult and resource-consuming, and with little hope of financial recuperation, it is best for your employer to stop the bust-out operator before he gets in the door. The investigator should educate the credit and sales departments of his employer about the warning signs of a bust-out operator; they can serve as the first line of defense against the bust-out operator. Like any con man, if the bust-out operator encounters resistance at the beginning he will simply go to another victim.

The example of Alan's bust-out has many of the warning signs:

- Unverifiable length of time in business
- Phony reference
- Increased ordering pattern
- Numerous trade reference calls

23.2 The Investigation

If you are faced with the task of investigating a bust-out, gather as much information as possible. Information is the key to success, and start gathering information from the beginning of the bust-out.

Make sure you obtain all the documentation from your client or your employer. The documentation should include any credit applications, financial statements and correspondence with the bust-out, including copies of checks.

Use the checks to trace bank accounts. Remember, Alan always used multiple bank accounts. Typically a bust-out operator will deposit checks into a different bank account different from that he lists on credit applications. Check all the accounts from the returned checks and you may find some attachable assets.

Try to find as much information as possible about the bust-out when it started. Public information is a great place to start. Obtain corporate information from the secretary of state. Many states' corporate information will list the date the business incorporated, the business' registered agent and address, the listed officers and addresses, any fictitious names for the business, and the corporation's mailing address. Many times the bust-out's registered agent can be a source of information.

Next, check out local business licensing information. Most municipalities require businesses to register with the its business licensing department, which is usually located in the county or city clerk's office. That department can tell you the date that the business started (or the date of the first taxable sale), and who are the business' listed principals. Compare the start date from the business licensing department with the length of time in business listed by the bust-out on a credit application.

Why do you need to learn about the bust-out's early history? Because, just as in the movie *Silence of the Lambs* when Agent Starling found the killer by going back to the initial crime scene, the bust-out operator will also make mistakes in the beginning of the bust-out when he knows that no one is watching. The bust-out is most likely to use phony references in the beginning. *Proof of phony trade references is a great way to prove intent for both legal and criminal remedies.*

This is a good time to mention the front man. *A front man is someone who is paid by the bust-out operator to pose as the owner of the business.* Many times he will be an individual with a clean credit history. If Alan ran two or three bust-outs per year hitting the same suppliers over and over, sooner or later, the suppliers are going to identify him. So Alan, like most other bust-out operators employs a front to pose as the businesses principal. This is another reason why gathering the initial business licensing information is so important. Alan may have tripped up and listed his name as the incorporator of the business or signed the lease on the facility or for the utilities.

All are great sources of information as to the real players in the bust-out. I will bet you that the real individuals behind the bust-out are not who is listed on the credit application.

Next you want to identify the references used by the bust-out. Credit applications from your victim company and the credit files of other creditors are where this information is found. You can identify other creditors from a bankruptcy schedule if the bust-out filed bankruptcy and submitted the information to the court. However, in my experience most bust-outs do not file bankruptcy. The credit department of your client, or employer, should be in an industry group or at least they should know others in the industry, which is a good place to look for other victims. Mail left after a bust-out skips is also a great source of creditor identification. Most likely the majority of mail consists of letters demanding payment.

Communication between the victims is very important to painting the entire picture of the bust-out case. Victims should combine their resources to seek legal remedies and to approach law enforcement. Law enforcement will be more likely to initiate a case if it is approached by numerous victims combining for a larger dollar loss than if it is approached by a single victim complaining about a bad debt.

Once you have identified the references used by the bust-out, you should verify their authenticity. Verify the references with the same public information as you used to verify the bust-out business. Check state corporate information, local businesses licensing, and see if the references are listed with directory assistance. Address databases can be used to check the addresses of both the bust-out and its trade references. Many times bust-outs will use mail receiving services or answering services for phony references.

Address databases are also a great source for neighbor information. Neighbors to both the bust-out and any suspected trade or bank references can be great sources of information.

All of this verification will tell you if the reference is a real or phony business and may also produce some links with bust-out. For example, try to obtain the names of the individuals found on the mail receiving services that were rented for the bust-out's phony reference and you may find links back to the individuals at the bust-out. Using these types of links and showing misrepresentations will make the case in both civil and criminal litigation.

If the references you investigate are real businesses, then the next step is to call the references and talk to them. You should assume that the trade references are in on the bust-out, so it is a good idea not to identify yourself as an investigator looking into a suspicious insolvency. Simply call the reference and ask for the credit department, then ask for a reference on the target. Even though you know that the bust-out has already skipped, do not initially volunteer this information. Simply ask the standard questions like "How long have you been doing business with the subject?" "What is the subject's high credit?" and "How does the subject pay its bills?"

Take note of the responses to the questions and compare the information with the information your credit department received when the bust-out first applied for credit. Once the basic information is received ask the reference if they have a current mailing address for the subject. Believe it or not, but I have had references linked to a bust-out give me the bust-out operator's new business address just by asking for the new mailing address.

The key to a successful bust-out is the outlet to the product. Because the bust-out operator is stealing the product it is difficult for the bust-out operator to find an outlet that they can trust. This is the reason that most bust-out operators stay in the same industry. If you are a bust-out operator in the apparel industry and you have an outlet who will pay you for the apparel you get, it makes sense that you will hit the apparel industry in future bust-outs and go back to that same outlet for payment. I am sorry to say that long-standing, seemingly legitimate businesses have served as an outlet for bust-out "stolen" product. So trust no one.

Many times an outlet determines which product the bust-out orders. As previously noted, sometimes the outlet for the product is listed as a trade reference—because it is in the outlet's best interest to get the product shipped to the bust-out, the outlet will give a glowing trade reference. This is another reason to identify the bust-out's trade references. Of course, shipping information and checks deposited into the bust-out's bank account are great sources of clues as to the outlets for the product. Unfortunately, outlets for bust-out product have rarely been prosecuted because it is difficult to prove that the outlet knew the product it had purchased was stolen.

I have seen a case in which a law enforcement official lost his job for seizing bust-out product from an outlet's facilities, so be very cautious when approaching the outlets. I have seen some successful legal cases when it was shown that the outlet paid for the product with cash, which was not its normal course of business. In these cases, product was not seized; however, civil judgments were assessed.

When gathering documentation on the bust-out, don't overlook financial statements. Almost as important as the financial information is the identity of the accountant who prepared the information. Showing that a nonexistent accountant was listed on a financial statement is a good way to prove the bust-out operator's intent. If a real accountant was used, the he or she may be a good source of intelligence, especially if the accountant had not been paid by the bust-out operator, or if the accountant's information had been altered. The real individuals behind a bust-out, not the front man, will probably deal with the accountant. Most of the time, the accountant's contact with the bust-out will lead you to the individuals whom you should be targeting.

Alan said that once a credit manager asked him for his financial statements. When asked why, the credit manager told him that, without them, he could only extend credit up to 10 percent of Alan's total equity from his balance sheet. Alan went home that night and made up a balance sheet listing $250,000 in equity, and the next day the credit manager granted him $25,000 in credit.

Financial statements paint a picture of a business at a certain point in time. The majority of financial reports from the bust-outs that I have seen paint a very good picture of the business. The bust-out operator wants his suppliers to think he has lots of money so they will extend him more credit. By gathering as much financial information from the bust-out as possible an investigator can use the comparative information to contradict the contentions made by the bust-out operator at the end of the bust-out when he most certainly will claim poverty.

Another good trick is to use questions about the bust-out's pro-forma financial information to ask the bust-out operator questions he probably does not know how to answer. In one case I investigated, the pro-forma balance sheet of the business showed a six-figure opening inventory and no liabilities. When questioned, the principal claimed to be a cab driver prior to starting the business. I asked him where he obtained the money to purchase the businesses' opening inventory; from his savings, he said, and a loan from his brother-in-law. The next question was whether he had to repay the loan; he answered in the affirmative. When I asked him why this business loan was not reflected on his opening balance sheet, he said that he did not know and terminated the conversation. *In most states, using false financial information to obtain credit is a crime.*

When referring a bust-out case to law enforcement the investigator should have the case organized and neatly packaged if he expects to get any action. A clear and well-documented case, listing the misrepresentations of the bust-out, the victims, and the dollar amount of loss is the most successful way to get law enforcement into action. Federal and state laws covering white-collar crime such as mail fraud, wire fraud, and interstate transportation of stolen property are the traditional statutes covering the activities of the bust-out.

23.3 Conclusion

Investigating a bust-out is not rocket science; it is simply a matter of tediously gathering as much information as possible. The facts of the case will reveal themselves, However, it is impossible to tell which fact will be the most important until they are looked at as a whole. By using the facts to highlight the bust-out operator's misrepresentations, the bust-out investigator can be successful.

Chapter 24

Parking Lot Investigations

Ben Scaglione, MA, CPP

Synopsis

Violent crime is more likely to occur in parking lots than in any other commercial property location. According to the National Institute of Justice, 80 percent of criminal acts at shopping centers, strip malls, and business offices occurs in their parking lots. Approximately 20 percent of all negligence lawsuits arise out of parking lot or garage incidents, and 10 percent of all awards in parking lot liability cases exceed one million dollars.

Liability Consultants, Inc., of Sudbury, Massachusetts, conducted a study on parking lot liability from 1992 to 2001. They reviewed over 1,000 premise liability lawsuits. The study revealed that about 42 percent of all crimes occurring in parking lots lead to an inadequate security lawsuit, with assault and battery being the most common type of crime resulting in a lawsuits. In almost one-third of reported cases the basis for a lawsuit was murder, rape, robbery, or assault. Jury awards and settlements averaged between one million dollars for assaults and two to three million dollars for homicides.

Lawsuits associated with violent crimes like rapes and muggings, in addition to liability claims from falls and accidents, make investigations a necessary part of parking lot management. Complete and thorough investigations limit liability claims by accurately documenting details on specific events. These events include reported incidents by individuals, accidents to persons and vehicles, or audits on inventory and revenue.

24.1 Key Components to a Successful Investigation

The key to a successful parking lot investigation, and the best defense against a liability claim, is the accurate and timely collection of information. An investigator's job is to ensure that information is collected in detail and that all details are corroborated so information is accurate and complete. The investigator must collect information in an unbiased manner without offering or pursuing an opinion and if possible use secondary sources of information to confirm data. An investigator must possess basic skills in interviewing and interrogation, collecting evidence, taking photos, using secondary-source information, and writing reports.

Collection of information on an incident or accident must be timely because, in general, persons using parking lots are transient and may not use the lot again or for a very long time. Investigations may have difficulty contacting ex-patrons because of incorrect contact information or ex-patrons may become uncooperative because of pending litigation. That is why it is so important to respond to an incident promptly and gather all of the necessary information as quickly as possible. Once a person leaves the parking lot or garage, the chances of getting additional information is greatly reduced.

A. Interviewing and interrogation

Fundamental to a parking lot investigation is the interview of those persons involved with the event. Correct questioning techniques lead to the discovery of pertinent information. Using the six questions listed below, when conducting a parking lot investigation, provides the investigator with detailed information necessary for a complete and thorough report.

- What occurred?
- Who was involved in the incident?
- When did the incident occur?
- Where did the incident occur?
- How did the incident occur?

- Why did the incident occur?

Example 1:

A parking lot patron returning to his car finds his window smashed and his car radio missing. When the investigator interviews the car owner, he should ask him to describe in detail what happened, making sure the patron answers the six questions listed above. The investigator, if necessary, should then ask more detailed questions in order to obtain a clearer picture of what occurred: Exactly where did the incident occur? Where was the radio before the incident? Who had access to the car? Who does the patron think took the radio, and exactly how was the radio taken? And of course, why do you think the radio was taken? Questions should be continuously asked obtaining more detail until a complete and thorough picture of what occurred is established. For example, if the patron indicated that certain persons had access to the car, ask the patron who they are and why they had access. Did they have access immediately before the theft? Is there any reason those person(s) might steal the radio?

It is important for an investigator to understand that when interviewing an individual, he or she is more likely to remember an event and be able to describe it in detail, if they are asked to recall and describe the event in chronological order.

Interrogation is a necessary part of the parking lot investigation process. *Investigators should know when to interview and when to interrogate.* While interviewing is casual questioning to gather facts and information, interrogation is pointed questioning to make a reluctant subject or witness provide information. During an interrogation, questioning is conducted under duress. Using the previous example, if you are speaking to a witness who in your opinion could have stolen the radio, you may want to change the tone of questioning from that of an interview to an interrogation. During the interrogation the investigator would ask in a condescending voice," Where were you during the time the car was parked in the lot? Why did you take the radio? In an interrogation, the investigator wants to create a stressful environment. He or she would require quick answers and may ask the same question several times and in several different ways to determine the validity of the individual's statement.

B. Collecting evidence

The collection and maintenance of evidence are vital to the parking lot investigative process. Evidence must be collected correctly if it is going to be used as information to reduce liability. The person who collects the evidence should bag it, mark it, and secure it (to maintain a proper chain of evidence), then place the bag(s) in a secure location.

When collecting evidence during an investigation, an investigator should always carry latex or rubber gloves, self-sealing plastic bags, tape, and a permanent marker.

All evidence should be placed in self-sealing plastic bags. Once a bag is closed it must be marked and sealed. Place tape over the bag's seal so evidence tampering can be detected. Mark the bag with the date, the time, the investigator's name, a description of the item, the location where the item was found, and any case or investigation number.

In the case of the stolen radio, for example, if a screwdriver was found on the seat of the car, the screwdriver may have been used to break the window or pry the radio out of the dashboard. Pry marks found around the area where the radio was housed, which are similar to the screwdriver, would confirm its use in the theft of the radio. The screwdriver may provide fingerprint evidence necessary to identify the perpetrator of the crime. The investigator should put on latex gloves, pick up the screwdriver in the middle of the shaft, and place it into a self-sealing plastic bag. Wearing gloves and handling the screwdriver in the middle of the shaft is done so as not to smudge possible fingerprints on the handle or shaft.

C. Photographs

Pictures are of the utmost importance to a parking lot investigation. They provide accurate documentation of the incident and provide evidence for the investigation.

On average, an investigation requires a minimum of three photos. A picture of the general scene (distance shot of the entire event area) should be taken first. This photo should depict the overall area in which the event occurred. Next, the scope of the photos should be narrowed, and a photo should be taken of the specific event area, followed by a close-up photo depicting the specific cause or result of the event. Last, photo(s) should be included of any evidence found. Additional photos of any injuries sustained should be recorded. Photos showing the injuries sustained by the victim(s) and perpetrator(s) should be in the form of a close-up of the injury along with a picture of the individual's full body. The full body picture should include the individual's face and the injury site.

In Example 1, the investigator should take an initial photo of the vehicle showing its position in the parking lot, with the broken window included in the shot. Then a photo should be taken showing the area where the radio was in the dash. This photo should focus on any tool marks or other evidence demonstrating how the radio was taken out of the car. An additional photo can be taken of the screwdriver lying on the car seat showing exactly where it was found.

Example 2:

A patron reports falling and injuring himself on a raised corner of sidewalk on the path into the parking garage. Photos taken for the investigation of the accident should be completed as follows.

The first photo should show the entire area in which the fall took place. The exact spot of the fall should be in the middle of the photo, taken at a distance. If the picture is taken correctly a neutral party should be able to view the photo and tell you the location in which the accident occurred.

The next photo should be a closer shot of the reported spot where the person fell. The "fall spot" should be in the middle of the picture. Two or three blocks of sidewalk surrounding the "fall spot" should be recorded on the photo. Then a close-up shot of the exact spot should be photographed. This photo should be a close-up of the "fall spot," showing the height of the raised corner in comparison to the block next to the raised block.

Pictures of the injured party should be taken as well. In this case, the victim skinned his knee. A close-up shot of the injured knee should be taken. Then a full body shot of the victim should be taken, showing the skinned knee and the victim's face.

D. Report writing

This aspect of the investigation is the most important to liability reduction. Lawsuits can drag on for years, and memories can fade. The documentation of an investigation can be the determining factor in the outcome of a lawsuit.

Written incident reports need to provide detailed accounts of what occurred, the evidence collected, and the investigator's evaluation. A typical report should include:

- The time and date the report was taken.
- The time and date the event occurred.
- The location the incident occurred.
- The type of incident which occurred.
- The names and contact information of all parties involved.
- The investigator's name.
- A report number or classification demarcation.

In addition to this information, the report should include a brief summary outlining what occurred. This short paragraph should contain the answers to the six questions outlined earlier in this chapter.

Investigative reports must always be documented in chronological order. Reading reports in chronological order helps individuals recall details forgotten years prior.

Reports should be written clearly and neatly, be detailed, and be written in a concise manner. Reports should state the facts of the incident in clear, short sentences.

E. Secondary information sources

In the course of an investigation it may be necessary to collect background or corroborative information on events, individuals, or vehicles. This information may include address, finances, credit and criminal history. Some sources commonly used to obtain this information are:

- The company's human resource department
- The company's parking services department
- Local, state or federal law enforcement
- The state motor vehicle agency
- Local insurance companies
- Local credit agencies

24.2 The Incident Investigation

In parking lot investigations, property crimes are the most common incident type encountered. They include larceny, burglary, vandalism, lost property, auto hijacking, trespassing, fire or arson, and the sale or use of illegal drugs. Larceny and burglary are the two most frequently encountered types of property crime. Violent crimes are encountered less frequently but have a higher liability risk. They include rape, assault, robbery, muggings, and homicides.

Because parking lot users are transient, an incident investigation should start immediately after an incident occurs.

The first task for the investigator is to make a list of all participants involved in the incident. The list should include names, addresses, phone numbers, and their status as victim, witnesses, or perpetrator. This list is generated first so that all individuals involved in the incident are identified and can be reached in the event they leave the parking lot before being interviewed. *Remember that the investigator's goal is to obtain statements from everyone immediately after the incident, before they leave.* Contacting witnesses and victims by phone at a later date can be problematic, especially if the incident results in a lawsuit.

Once the list is completed, the investigator should obtain statements from all those involved. Statements should be obtained from the witnesses first because they are most likely to leave the area first. Make sure anyone in the area of the incident is contacted and asked to make a statement, even if he or she claims to have seen nothing. The victim should be questioned next, followed by the perpetrator, if one is apprehended.

Photos of the incident scene should be taken after statements are obtained. Make sure photos are taken of the incident area, and then injury photos of the victim.

Physical evidence should be collected and processed last. All of the information collected should be placed in a folder, and a formal report should be completed. The report, statements, photos, and evidence should be filed together for future use.

The police should be notified on all complaint investigations. They are best equipped to locate and followup with witnesses, victims, and perpetrator once they have left the parking facility. The names and badge numbers of the responding police officers should be included in the written report in the event they need to be contacted in the future.

In Example 1, the investigation would begin with the identification of all witnesses. The investigator and/or security staff should survey the incident area and question all persons in the vicinity. Detailed information should be obtained from all of the witnesses. The investigator should ask each witness, "What time were you in the lot? Did you see anything unusual? Can you describe what you saw? Did you see any strangers? Describe the strangers. What were the strangers wearing? What did the strangers do? Did you see the victim in the lot? What was he or she doing?

Make sure all witness contact information is included and correct before concluding the interview. A witness may need to be contacted if followup is necessary.

The car's owner will be questioned next. Have the victim describe in chronological order his or her stay in the parking lot from the time entered until the time he or she noticed the radio missing. Remember to obtain detailed information on the victim's story. The investigator should ask the victim:

- Exactly what time did you leave your car?
- Was the car locked? Who knew you had a radio in the car?
- Did you see anyone in the area when you left and returned to your car?
- If you saw someone, what did he or she look like?
- When did you notice your radio was stolen?

Next, photos of the incident should be taken. A photo should be taken of the entire car and its location in the parking lot, showing the broken window and the vehicle's license plate number. Then a close-up photo should be taken of the car, centering on the broken window. Last, a photo should be taken of the area on the dashboard where the radio was removed. In this example, additional photos should be taken of any glass found on the ground outside of the car and on the floor inside the car. The area where the largest collection of glass exists indicates the direction the window was broken.

Collect any evidence at the site of the incident. In this case, a screwdriver was found on the front seat of the car and blood was found on some glass fragments lying on the ground.

The report concerning this incident should be written in chronological order, based on the victim's statement. The victim would be the complainant. The witnesses' statements should be included in the report along with all evidence and photographs.

24.3 The Accident Investigation

An accident may be defined as a mishap occurring to a person, a vehicle, or both. Liability resulting from accidents can be costly to parking lot owners, depending on the circumstances of the event. Falls are the prominent type of accident encountered in parking lots. They include falls caused by damaged sidewalks or streets, slips on snow and ice, or trips up and down stairs. Other accidents involving people include being struck by a vehicle or being injured by faulty equipment (e.g., elevator doors or parking gates).

Accidents involving vehicles are most often collisions (e.g., a moving vehicle hitting a parked vehicle). Vehicle accidents also include two or more moving vehicles colliding, hit and runs, and equipment failures (e.g., vehicles being struck by a faulty entry or exit gate).

As with incident investigations, an accident investigation must start immediately after the accident occurs. It is important to obtain statements from all parties involved and take pictures of the accident before the witnesses, victims, perpetrators, and vehicles leave the parking lot.

As in an incident investigation, a list should be made of the all those involved: witnesses, victims, and perpetrators. Next, the investigator should obtain statements from all persons involved, staring with persons who could have witnessed the accident.

In a vehicle accident investigation it is important to obtain the driver's license, the vehicle's registration, and insurance information on all drivers and vehicles involved.

A detailed drawing of the accident should be completed. This drawing should outline:

- The demographics of the accident area, noting north, east, south, and west.
- All landmarks, traffic signs, or traffic lights.
- The direction of traffic flow.
- The exact location of the vehicle(s) involved.

- The direction the involved vehicle(s) were traveling.
- The exact location of all damage to the vehicle(s).

Photos should be taken of the accident. Like an incident investigation, pictures should be taken of the accident area, damage inflicted on the vehicles, and the victim's injuries.

In both cases, make sure close-up photos are taken of injuries and the damage to vehicles. Pictures should include evidence indicating the cause of the accident, e.g., skid marks, paint marks on the vehicles or posts, etc.

Drawings, photos, statements, and a formal report should be filed together and stored for future reference.

In all accident cases the police should be notified. As in an incident investigation, the police are in a better position to follow up with victims, witnesses, and perpetrators after all parties leave the parking lot. In addition, the persons involved in the accident may need a police report for any insurance claim.

Example 3:

A car backing out of its parking space hits the car parked directly behind it. Upon notification of the accident, the investigator should respond immediately and should identify all parties involved in the accident and any possible witnesses.

The witnesses should be interviewed first and statements obtained from them. Next, the driver of the moving vehicle and the owner of the parked car should be interviewed. The driver of each vehicle needs to provide a driver's license, the vehicle registration, and proof of vehicle insurance.

The accident is sketched, indicating the location of each vehicle and the direction the moving vehicle traveled. The sketch will include the location of the damage to each vehicle.

The photos should show the damage to each vehicle, the location of the incident, and the position of each vehicle at the time of the accident if possible.

Photos would include pictures of the rear passenger side of the moving vehicle and the rear of the parked vehicle. The local police should be called, so that an official accident report can be prepared and filed.

In Example 2 (a patron tripping and falling on the sidewalk), it is important to move quickly to gather information on the event. When it comes to "fall" investigations, it is especially important to locate witnesses to the event. Falls represent the highest frequency of claims against property owners. A parking lot owner's liability for a fall could depend on the statement of one or more witnesses.

The injured patron should be quickly interviewed to determine if he or she can identify any witnesses. Then, the witnesses should be interviewed, and statements should be obtained. A more detailed interview of the victim should then be conducted.

Photographs should be taken of the fall area and the injury. Make sure photos are taken of the exact location of the fall and document the exact cause(s) of the fall.

Arrangements should be made to provide the patron with medical attention if necessary. Depending on the seriousness of the injury there may be a limited amount of time to speak to the victim before he or she is transported to a hospital or medical facility. Make sure the interview with the patron is complete before he or she leaves. And again, the police should be notified and should take an accident report.

24.4 The Cash or Asset Audit

Investigators may be required to conduct audits on revenue produced by the parking lot or on assets held by the parking lot. An audit is a detailed accounting of income and inventory to determine if improper practices were used in the collection or expenditure of monies. Audits are conducted to determine if fraud, extortion, or theft of company property has occurred. Audits in parking lots are most commonly conducted on the collection of parking revenues by comparing the vehicle payment amount (including all cash, checks, and credit card transactions) against the specific number of vehicles parked in the parking lot and the time the vehicle was parked in the lot/garage. Parking lot revenue audits are usually conducted for a specific time period.

For example, an audit might look at the revenue collected for the use of a parking lot during a particular calendar month. In this example revenue is collected from lot users based on an hourly time rate. The audit would determine if the total amount of money collected by the parking lot workers for an entire month equals the total number of hours cars parked in the lot during the same month. *If the total number of hours that vehicles parked does not reflect the total amount of cash collected, either the parking staff is making errors or they are committing fraud.*

Example 4:

The total cash collected for all cars parked in the lot for the month of February equaled $25,000. If the parking lot charged $1.50 an hour to park a car, then parking receipts should total 16,666 hours. An audit would check every parking payment collected through the cash register for the calendar month of February and compare it to the tickets issued to each vehicle parked for the same calendar month. If a ticket recorded two hours of parking, and two hours cost $3.00, then the amount entered into the cash register for that ticket should be $3.00. When all of the tickets collected for the month of February are added there should be a total of 16,666 hours that vehicles parked in the lot and the total sum of money collected by the cashiers should equal $25,000. A revenue audit could also include contacting a random sampling of patrons to verify the amount of money they paid for their parking. This amount should be verified with the ticket collected from the patron and the amount of money recorded in the cash register. Another way to audit parking fees is by comparing copies of receipts issued to parking patrons against the parking tickets issued to them and the amount of money registered in the cash register.

An audit may be conducted to determine if parking revenue is being spent appropriately. In this case, an auditor looks at specific dollar amounts spent on supplies, salaries, repairs, etc., and matches all receipts for expenditures to the funds allocated for payment of the particular items purchased. *If the receipts and funds spent do not match up, either an error has occurred or fraud has taken place.*

In addition, the auditor can verify that a piece of equipment onsite is the same make and model number as the one listed on the purchase receipt.

Example 5:

If the parking lot purchased a snow blower for $1,200, the auditor would verify the cost of the snow blower with the store it was purchased from, check the receipt to see if the two match, and then see what amount of funds were recorded and issued to pay for the snow blower.

24.5 Conclusion

Parking lot investigations are different from other types of investigations because of the transient nature of the population using them and the high level of incidents which result in the filing of lawsuits. *When conducting parking lot investigations it is important to remember to act immediately to collect information.* Be thorough in the collection of information: collect statements, take photos, and collect all evidence available at the incident or accident scene. Take the time to be complete, accurate, and thorough in the recording of information for a report. Finally, make sure to keep all information on an incident together and file it in a secure location.

Report records should be kept in storage for at least five years, unless a lawsuit has been filed, then records need to be available until the lawsuit has been terminated. These key components can limit liability claims by accurately documenting details and assuring that all information concerning an investigation is readily accessible.

References

Bates, Norman J., "Major Developments in Premise Security Liability III," Framingham, MA: Liability Consultants.

Bates, Norman and Jon Groussman, "More Wins for Defendants in Premise Liability Cases," *Security Management*, February 2000, pp. 94.

Gorman, Dave, "Lose Prevention Racks Up Success," *Security Management*, March, 1996.

Healy, Richard and timothy Walsh, *Protection of Assets*, POA Publishing, LA, California, 1999, Chapter 16, Investigations.

Parking Facilities: "Is Your Highest Risk of Liability Going Unchecked?" *Security Director's Report*, January 2000, Issue 00-01, pp.3-6.

Chapter 25

Security Liability

James P. Carino, CPP, VSM

Synopsis

25.1 Introduction

To the security professional, the words "You have been sued" are offensive.

You have a history of training, education, and experience that has equipped you well to do your job. Then an incident occurs on property for which you are responsible, and an attorney—who may not have a clue about physical security—sets forth in a complaint a litany of negligence charges.

Your first reaction may well be that all are erroneous; but then reality sets in. Can you convince your superiors that your security program is defensible? Can you convince the insurance company that the incident happened despite your best efforts? It does not matter what the incident was—you need to answer the allegations of negligence and pursue your defense with the same rigor. The only difference between, say, a serious crime against persons and a theft or damage of personal property is the number of zeroes that follow the first number on the cost of the settlement, whether it be an out-of-court arrangement or jury verdict.

There are many factors that bear on a finding of negligence or no negligence in those rare instances where a security negligence claim goes to court. Simply stated, tort law says that the owner of the premises is responsible for the property, that the onus of the foreseeability of crime is on the owner, and that the owner must provide a reasonably safe and secure environment for the business invitee. Obviously, then, the question to be asked is: what is "reasonable security"? If your case goes to trial, the jury will tell you, and if negligence is found, in many states that same jury will tell you how much your "negligence" is going to cost.

The security director is not concerned with how the company constructs its legal defense. That is decided by the legal counsel. Further, once the civil suit has been filed it is already too late to improve your security posture. Your company either wins or loses based on the security in place at the date and time of the incident and how well that security posture is presented in defense. Toward that end, the written word is much easier to present than is the oral word.

There is general agreement among security professionals that a security program or system should be based on some type of security model. One early approach was suggested by Walsh and Healy in their *Protection of Assets Manual.*[1] For example, an early edition (I use 1988 as a benchmark) sets forth a three-component model—security officers, procedures, and hardware (defined as inclusive of physical barriers and electronics). This writer prefers to use the four-component system, splitting the "hardware" into two separate components. This does have value in expert witnessing since not all civil cases will require analysis and evaluation of all four components. For example, physical barriers may not be relevant to a mugging in a parking lot of a supermarket where easy ingress and egress is the norm. However, CCTV might be.

To the knowledge of this writer, there are no standards that dictate how a security department should be organized or where it should be situated on the corporation's organizational chart. There is also nothing that requires a security department to prepare a security plan, or that a formalized security or loss prevention survey must have been conducted in order to avoid negligence allegations, as is frequently "opinionated" (I choose this word intentionally) by a number of security experts who specialize in serving plaintiffs. While security planning and "surveying" the threat on a continuous basis are prudent, the competent security professional is evaluating the security posture on a daily basis in the performance of his or her duties. I am of the opinion that any plaintiff's expert who declares that negligence results from the lack of a security survey is self serving and engaging in a not so subtle attempt to promote billable time.

As of this writing, the prevailing rules are: the foreseeability and prior similar incidents rule and the totality of circumstances rules. The former basically states that a property owner could be held liable for failing to take reasonable steps to prevent a crime that was foreseeable. Early cases developed the notion that a crime was not foreseeable unless it had occurred at the premises before. This became known as the prior similar incident rule. The totality of circumstance rule is unpopular with property owners because they believe that it sets an impossible standard, implying that anytime a crime occurs, it can be argued that security was necessarily inadequate.[2]

The interpretation of this legal jargon is the function of lawyers. It is sufficient only that security professionals are aware of the existence of these legal rules in a general way. Guard security planning and a balanced security program that a "reasonable person" would feel comfortable with should meet the foreseeability or totality of circumstance rules.

This chapter will primarily address premises liability. It is the one category of many civil suits that falls exclusively in the domain of the security department.

25.2 Keys to Successful Litigation Defense

Following are some of preventive steps that can reduce the risk of adverse decisions in civil suits. It is not intended to be all-inclusive. It is intended to stimulate discussion within the security department and generate additional techniques to create a more litigation proof posture. These are many, but not all, of the areas a plaintiff's experts will consider in formulating an opinion. The expert for the defense will also closely evaluate these areas to see if there is evidence of good security policies, procedure, and practices with which to counter the charges.

A. Organization and responsibility

Where is the security or loss prevention office positioned within the organization? To whom does the security director report, and to whom does the director's boss report? The positioning is important if we accept the premise that a department head can direct only those under him or her but can only suggest security policy to others. Obviously, the answer for a large corporation is the same as for many smaller and medium sized companies: don't bury security under the human resources manager or the chief of maintenance. Positioning on the second or third line in the organizational structure is a plus. Also, the position title can be an indicator: security director, security manager, and security supervisor each denote different images to different jury members. The important words in the title are directing, managing, or supervising; the implication is that a supervisor has less authority and responsibility than a director.

Other factors to consider include: preparation of a security mission statement; a functional statement outlining the duties of the security officer; job descriptions of staff; guard post orders; a comprehensive incident reporting system; detailed security procedures; and a system to ensure compliance with these established protocols.

B. Security guard force

How were the number and locations of security officer posts determined? Were they cost driven, or arrived at by a risk or threat assessment? It is important to keep in mind that a plaintiff's attorney will always allege that no matter how many security officers you have posted it was not enough to protect the client. Is your facility amenable to flexible scheduling (very common at shopping centers and hospitals)? I have always professionally felt that a flexible schedule that varies the number of security officers at a given time was a good indicator of planning and forethought.

It has always been a basic tenet of mine that if a security post has been established it must be manned—but, if its presence is not justified, then eliminate it and save or use the funds elsewhere. If scheduling calls for five security officers and only four are on duty, you will be at a disadvantage if an incident occurs unless you compensate for the lesser presence (e.g., by closing down a parking lot). Compensating measures—a Nuclear Regulatory Commission (NRC) concept—is discussed later.

C. Guard force suitability and supervision

From the civil litigation perspective, whether the security officers are in-house or contract usually has no bearing, per se, on an opinion.

However, the recruitment, selection, training and supervision process are vital. You can expect a plaintiff's attorney to check on the suitability of any security officer involved in the event. If a contract security officer is used (in those states with private detectives acts—PDAs), was a background check run according to the provisions of the act? While a case can be made for negligence on the part of the contract guard agency that hired a security officer with a checkered past or criminal record, a case can also be made that in the final analysis security is the responsibility of a corporation's top management. Negligent hiring cases have increased substantially in recent years. A background investigation should also be conducted if your security force is in-house, even though this type of force may not fall under a PDA. A company using a contract agency must be certain that the contract clearly establishes training and qualification standards and that a system will be in place to check that these specifications are being met. It only takes seconds to ask a security officer, "Was a background check conducted on you?" "Have you ever seen an office supervisor on the premises?" "What type of pre-site training did you receive?" If the answers are all in the negative, it can lead to a nondefensible position in a civil suit.

D. Contract

Another very common mistake is the scope, depth, and breadth of contractual agreements between clients and guard agencies. A boilerplate agreement with no site specific requirements can make it extremely difficult, if not impossible, to place culpability on your security guard provider. Of course, a worse scenario is no written agreement at all. This is not as uncommon as one might think. At one place where I conducted a security survey, there had never been a written agreement in the seventeen years the contract guard agency provided service. In fact, the only written documentation from the provider were copies of the biweekly invoices. No one at the company was able to identify any commitments of the contract guard agency other than to provide security officers during certain hours. All too often, clients sign contracts prepared by the contract guard agency without a proper review by the appropriate, knowledgeable people. That can increase apparent corporate negligence to the point where the contract guard agency is dropped as a codefendant in a lawsuit.

E. Security training

Do you, or does your contract guard agency, document the training given to the security officers?

With a three-tiered training program (basic or pre-assignment; on-job or site specific; and refresher or in-service) set forth in a training procedure, it is extremely difficult for a plaintiff to show negligence in training. It is virtually impossible to prove negligence if all training is documented in both a general training file and a training record for each security officer. In a recent case, there was evidence indicating that the key security officer on duty—the one who responded to the incident—had not been trained and that his record had been "doctored" to falsely show successful completion of training. Normally a major hurdle to overcome, this charge was dispelled by showing that the performance of the security officer was exactly as required by all rules, regulations, and procedures (the company's, the client's, and government's).

Documenting training can provide important evidence. In one case, the security officers were asked in depositions whether their training in a long list of subjects was completed. Many security officers responded in the negative (i.e., in specific recall of a particular subject), but the individual training records, backed up by the security officer's initials after each entry, showed training had been received. Thus, the impact of the charge of negligence—that appropriate training had not been completed—was minimized as a result of an evidentiary paper trail. It could have been totally negated had tests been given, scored, documented, and retained.

The training and qualifications of the security staff also frequently come into play. Maintaining proficiency and currency in the career field —through involvement with relevant associations to include seminars, conferences, and workshops—may or may not have a positive benefit, but the absence of such involvement and commitment can render suspect your credibility with regard to professional standing. Also, acting as presenters in seminars can further enhance the credibility of a security director and department; records of these make for a better defense than simple memory.

F. Incidents and crime history

Whether the foreseeability or totality of circumstance rule is used, criminal incidents will play a major role in any plaintiff's case. Frequently the premises liability case will involve a serious incident—from a Part I, UCR Crimes Against Persons (i.e., homicide, rape, robbery, aggravated assault), through the range of lesser felonies and misdemeanors to the lesser "crimes" which result in serious injury (e.g., a slip and fall, vehicle accidents, or equipment malfunction).

Crime statistics can be obtained from the federal or state UCR, local police departments, or other methods such as a CAP index. Incidents documented by the facility's own security department are another source. Of all possible sources of criminal incident information, and one which—in my professional judgment—is the least reliable (to the point of almost no reliability) is that from witnesses as recounted in depositions. These could have value, but only as indicators of when and where to search for validation or verification.

One point of view maintains that offering documentation about criminal incidents is counterproductive in a civil suit because the plaintiff could use it to show prior history. However, it is my position that the documenting of incidents can be considered a defensive tool. First, it offers evidence that a negligence charge is unfounded since—by documenting and analyzing events and establishing a retrieval system—the company is meeting its obligation to provide a safe and secure environment. The collection, collation, and analysis of crime statistics also give companies empirical data to use when making security budget decisions.

All incidents should be documented, including lesser-grade incidents (confrontations, purse snatches) and vulnerabilities (open door, lost keys, illegal parking, accidents, etc.). They can assist measurably in a defense against a very serious incident or Part I crime against a person, for example, by showing how unusual the occurrence was. It is a given that the plaintiff will allege poor, and perhaps imply intentional, non-documenting of serious incidents. However, it is a persuasive argument to state that you document *all* incidents reported—and then cite the number of propped doors, lost keys, lost employee access cards, and the like. In short, it serves as excellent proof that the security department is efficient and effective.

In one case, the plaintiff's expert claimed that the police department, for reasons perhaps based on inefficiency or ineffectiveness, failed to document all serious incidents; in his judgment, the location could not have been devoid of Part I crimes. However, the police did document incidents such as a stolen license plate, two cut tires on a car, a stolen car battery, a broken car window, and theft. I testified that the police department was extremely competent in their documentation of these lesser crimes. It gave evidence that there were no previous serious incidents, and the jury returned a non-negligence verdict.

A comprehensive incident reporting and recording system allows analysis of patterns and trends. It is one of the most powerful defensive tools in the arsenal available to establish the effectiveness of security.

G. Written security policies and procedures

Security procedures are one of the four components of a security system. Virtually cost free to develop and implement, these require only the time for preparation, someone to prepare them, and a system to ensure adherence. For companies using contract security officers, the security agency may prepare these procedures for the client. This is a generally acceptable method in smaller and midsize companies without a full-time security director. However, all such procedures should be approved by company management prior to implementation. In a civil case, some procedures are better than none; it is easier for the plaintiff's expert to testify to negligence when there were no policies and procedures than it is for the expert to convince a jury of the deficiency of policies and procedures that were in place.

In the final analysis, however, no matter how detailed and comprehensive, if the security officer fails to act properly, not act at all when a situation so dictates, or acts improperly, negligence is easier to demonstrate. A well-trained security officer, fully versed in its procedures and policies, is a great asset to any company.

H. Guard post orders

Orders and instructions posted at every station should be standard for the security industry. In a negligence case, their absence can serve as an indicator that security planning was deficient. A strong case can be made that the lack of clearly written instructions was the proximate cause of the adverse incident. A plaintiff's attorney can be expected to cite specific tasks that would convince a jury.

The author knows of one company that, in its request for proposal (RFP) for contract guard services, specifically required preparation of guard post orders as a condition for awarding the contract. After the term of the initial contract was completed without guard post orders, the guard company was put on a month-to-month extension. After six months and there were still no guard post orders, the contract with the guard company was terminated and a new contractor was brought in. Risk exposure to civil suit was, thus, lessened.

Unfortunately, too many sites operate without this important tool. As with many other written security procedures, the preparation of guard post orders does not require an outlay of funds or purchase of equipment, merely a small amount of time to write them down. Failure to do so could contribute to a costly settlement. As a corporate security director or company designee, one could be very uncomfortable on the witness stand, in a civil trial, trying to explain why the department could not take the time write down what a security officer was supposed to at a specific location.

Guard post orders or instructions should be sufficiently detailed to permit a substitute security officer to perform at least all essential duties without diminution of quality of service.

I. Security awareness training

This is one of the most frequently overlooked avenues for a company to project both the appearance and the reality of its security. Some companies, moreover, are directing their entire security program under the *security awareness model*. There are several useful tools under this "umbrella" term. I note, however, that I have never used when retained by a plaintiff the absence of a security awareness program as an example of negligence. It is not a standard and it is not required or mandated by any law, rule, regulation, or prior court decision to my knowledge. It can be a powerful tool in the hands of the defense, however, as an example of a balanced and integrated security program to protect assets and personnel.

Many companies use in-house receptionists at public entrances or access-control points, while others have security officers there. Security officer training will include appropriate public relations skills, as the office is usually the first person a visitor will meet. At those locations using receptionists, security training will include access control procedures, the handling of difficult people, and other training usually given to portal security officers. By receiving documented training, a receptionist becomes a "security officer asset." It is important to keep in mind that it is not the uniform that makes a person a security officer but the level of training given to the person. With this little tool, it can be argued that the security force (in terms of number and deployment) is actually greater than the "uniformed" force because a security-trained receptionist is indeed a security resource.

Other workers who can be trained in appropriate security subjects are maintenance, landscape, and custodial personnel—if they are in-house employees. Such training, if properly done, will also extend the "eyes and ears" of security and contribute toward a safer and more secure environment, thereby enhancing the defensive security posture.

J. Signs and signage

Most facilities effectively use signs for access control (e.g., "authorized access only"); fewer use "no trespassing" signs and, outside of high-rise office buildings and shopping malls, fewer still will post temporary weather related interior signs (e.g., "caution—wet floors"). These types of signs serve to give notice and, in the case of some signs, warnings to be alert for danger. Parking garages (both commercial and corporate) and parking lots should contain signs to direct vehicles and pedestrians to follow paths that maximize personal safety. Equipment malfunctions normally require signs (or a person) to provide pertinent information to include directions, identification warnings, and other information. Elevator and escalator malfunctions are certainly appropriate instances for signs.

Signs should be plain, concise, easy to understand, and effectively accomplish their stated objectives. To post signs at any natural hazard on the premises is a strength; to ignore it can be a weakness and fertile ground for negligence allegations.

K. Lighting

When an incident occurs at night, plaintiffs' attorneys like to include deficient lighting in their litany of negligent acts. One case I worked on cited negligent lighting for a parking lot assault at 2:45 in the afternoon on a cloudless day.

Police rarely note lighting conditions in their initial complaint or incident report or follow-up investigation. In my judgment, it is virtually impossible to assess the efficiency of lighting months or years after the fact. Simply, plaintiff oriented depositions will cite deficient lighting at the time, while defense depositions will highlight its adequacy.

Court cases have cited poor lighting as the proximate cause or contributory factor in crimes against persons. However, if lighting prevented crime, then there would never have been a criminal act committed at high noon on a full sun, cloudless day.

A few preventive measures are appropriate, however, to counter lighting deficiencies. For example, a lighting plan or policy, per se, is a defense because it shows that the issue has been considered—and the more detailed the plan, the better the issue has been addressed. If city lighting is a factor in providing perimeter or interior parking lot lighting, notify the city of any outages. It will not speed up repair or replacement, but that is beyond your authority or responsibility. This situation might require measures such as increased frequency of patrol, temporary lights in the darkened area, and so on.

The numbering of parking lot light poles is also popular in the more progressive security programs. It better pinpoints incident location and facilitates replacement of inoperative lighting.

Challenge anyone who claims deficiency in lighting to cite an authority setting lighting standards for security. As noted previously, there are court cases, but a colleague of the author conducted an exhaustive search and found no prior security study. If one is claimed, demand a copy of it. There is currently an effort to establish security lighting standards but as of this writing nothing has been published. Keep in mind, however, that there are *safety* lighting standards, so this defense will not work for a trip and fall or similar accidents.

L. Security equipment and electronic devices

In any security operation, it is imperative that all security equipment be in place and working. This does not specifically, for purposes of this comment, mean radios, flashlights, note pads, or vehicles. These are areas that, by and large, are not critical and can easily be handled by compensating measures.

The most critical piece of equipment is the closed-circuit television (CCTV). The plaintiff will view it as negligence if it was important enough to install but was not functioning at the time of the incident. In my professional judgment, most exterior cameras, even if being monitored, have little or no deterrent value: a security officer viewing the incident in progress is already too late to prevent it. Exterior CCTV can, and frequently does, provide investigative leads to assist police in the identification of perpetrators, but this is after the fact.

The key point regarding equipment—especially CCTV, alarms, and devices—is this: if it is nonfunctional, repair it or remove it. But keep in mind that if it is removed a comparable system or program must be installed. That way, you will not expose yourself to a degradation in security protection. As a preventive measure, prepare an analysis showing why the device was no longer necessary.

These areas are pretty much standard fare in many lawsuits. It is impossible to address every possible aspect of negligence that attorneys can conjure up—they are only limited by their imagination and ingenuity (or lack thereof). In one defense case I worked (c. 1983), I commented to the lawyer who retained me that the complaint had many blatant, false, and outlandish deficiencies. His remark at the time surprised me. He said that when you throw a lot of garbage against the wall, no matter how hard you scrub, you cannot remove all the stain.

M. Other factors

There are, of course, other factors that bear on security requirements and need to be considered in the overall security program and, as a result, can become targets of negligence.

1. Consider the geographical location of the facility

Is it in an urban, suburban, or rural area? You may need wire grates over windows in any downtown area, but to push for that as a security measure to reduce breakage or break-ins at a rural facility will probably result in a need to update your resume. High crime statistics are not necessarily a negative; they may be valuable for plaintiffs but can be invaluable to security departments looking to upgrade or supplement their systems.

2. The building design can be a factor

- How vulnerable is it to unobserved break-ins?
- Does the structure provide easy hiding places?
- Was the building constructed decades ago—before security became critical for product and personal protection?
- Is the building an architectural, award-winning marvel for its aesthetic appeal but a nightmare for security (e.g., from overuse of non-shatterproof glass)?
- Is the property perimeter walled or fenced? Does it need to be?
- Are all fences and walls in good repair?
- Is the property well maintained or untidy and messy-looking, with overgrown shrubbery and debris?

3. The products or services of your company are a factor

- Does it pollute and is it a target for criminal or terrorist elements?
- Is its product a potential target for theft and resale (including at flea markets)?
- Does its waste material have sufficient value to make it worth stealing?

4. What is the company's image and reputation?

- Does it rape the land of natural resources, exploit the workers, or is it a good neighbor?
- Is it a large employer of locals?
- Does it provide good leadership to, and support for, community affairs?

- Do the residents and the local news media embrace and extol or protest against and harangue the company?

5. The philosophy and view of top management with regard to security is also a critical factor

One indication of good support is the position of the security director in the company, as well as access by the security director to the top echelon of company management.

Several of these are intertwined. Any or all can become major issues you must defend against when the lawsuit comes. The security director's job is to implement a defensible security posture.

N. Written directives

Security departments are accountable for all written security directives, policies, procedures, rules, and regulations. This includes either internal survey and audit reports or written security surveys conducted by outside security consultants. In any case, everything that is written is discoverable and must be provided upon request. The author suggests that the recommendations of any internal or external audit have a written response either documenting implementation or explanation as to why implementation was rejected.

Alternative solutions, as long as the deficiency or need is addressed, are always an option. The Nuclear Regulatory Commission (NRC), in setting forth its standards for licensed nuclear facilities, used the term *compensating measures* to address those safeguards, countermeasures, or protective devices that could not be implemented because of the physical limitations of the facility. An example would be to install a camera at a location instead of a manned security post.

25.3 The Impossibility of Absolute Security

I have made several references to high crime and high risk areas. There are some security professionals, serving as expert witnesses, who put forth the notion that a high crime area automatically translates into culpable negligence. But another—and more rational—school of thought says that if it is indeed a high crime area, then at least some security measures may be necessary. The higher the crime statistics, more may be needed. However, an effective security measure may be no more than having the normal work day as the only shift during which the facility is open—if the crime pattern indicates that this "high crime" occurs after dark.

No business can be the insurer of absolute security, nor should any company be held responsible because it has failed to anticipate a catastrophic event. In a major city (best left unidentified), a news reporter asked a building owner if he had a security plan to preclude an airplane from crashing into his high-rise. The stunned building spokesperson was speechless.

In a totally crime free society, there would be no need for security. However, there is no such thing. Having some security, even a little, helps address the issue of "foreseeability." Where companies get into trouble is if they take inadequate or no measures (such as those described earlier in this chapter) to reduce exposure.

Companies are in business to provide a product or a service and—if not a nonprofit—a return on investment. This could require operating in a so-called high crime area. The alternative is to set up the operation in a remote, isolated location—not a satisfactory option. Military bases, especially those with aircraft operations, used that approach in decades gone by. Many of these bases are now industrial parks, college campuses, or housing areas because businesses followed and residential developments appeared; low-flying aircraft became noise polluters and a safety threat Now, even if a remote location was selected, there is the recently developed use of the airplane as a bomb, so even a remote location is no guarantee.

Often, there is no logic in a plaintiff's charges. Further, plaintiffs (i.e., their lawyers) will focus on the specific event and attempt to bar testimony about the totality of security. A case in point: a number of years ago, a switchboard operator, located on the top floor of a hospital, was found stabbed to death shortly after midnight. She had just received a call from her sister who had seen the operator's estranged boyfriend outside the hospital. The switchboard could only be reached by a stairwell which was not adjacent to the top-floor elevator access level. Security procedures routinely called for the doors to the switchboard operation to be bolted shut from 6:00 P.M. to 6:00 A.M. There was also a red phone (literally) on a little table that could send an alarm to the security command post if the cradle became separated from the phone. Security had twelve officers on duty until midnight, then eleven from midnight to 6:00 A.M. The "weakness" in the security posture, according to the plaintiffs (relatives of the deceased), as noted by the lawyer, was a renovation project which had an opening to the street for a short period of time. The possibility therefore existed that anyone could have entered the building through it unobserved, if the security guard posted there had his back to the renovations. Anyone could have entered through the front door, as well. The case settled early, with safeguards to preclude the estranged boyfriend from sharing in the financial settlement. Had the victim followed security procedures and not left the door unsecured or opened it for the assailant, or had she alerted security about the warning phone call from her sister, the assailant might not have been able to get at her.

25.4 The Security Plan and Civil Case Examples

I have been retained by both plaintiffs and defendants in these civil litigation cases. Part of my decision to accept a case is based on whether there was a security program in place and, if so, if it was reasonable.

Some examples from the plaintiffs' side include:

> "This was an avoidable and foreseeable incident. There is no doubt that had the police been called at the first indication [a patron had so requested] . . . the stabbings would not have taken place."

> "Despite testimony by _____ to the effect that the . . . security force was to provide public relations and customer service, the *Security Department Procedures Manual* quite clearly in its opening sentence states that the job of the security department is to protect people and property from injury, damages and loss. Plaintiff was injured and suffered a loss of jewelry and cash—the security department failed in its primary job."

> "Exacerbating the problem was the apparent but sloppy cover up attempt on the part of [the defendant] to first deny the assault and then to conceal evidence and to give untrue testimony. . . ." (The assault became a homicide within hours.)

> "The indicated absence of [any security or police officer—both posted] during the period . . . is a clear-cut case of negligent planning." (Other testimony indicated that the security director was receiving kickbacks

and allowing security personnel to leave early without clocking out. This was a stabbing at a high school.)

"Had the security department ensured that all established security posts been manned on the 4:00 P.M. to 12 midnight shift, and manned by adequately trained security officers, the likelihood of occurrence of this incident would have been greatly diminished if not totally eliminated."

"If [the perpetrator] was a suspect, then he was detained, restrained or taken into custody without proper authority. If not a suspect, [the plaintiffs] violated their own policy and his rights by placing him in the van against his stated desires." (This individual was left alone in the back seat, keys in ignition and engine running. He stole the van and smashed head-on into another vehicle, killing one person and seriously injuring another.)

"[Defendants] did nothing for almost a several-year period of known instances of vandalism to its rooftop equipment, despite requests from [the plaintiff, a tenant] and also suggestions from the police department." (This case involved severe fire damage to multi-tenant commercial building caused by vandals.)

"Had the defendant implemented any type of security program, the likelihood of the plaintiff [a police officer] to have to chase a suspected drug dealer would have been reduced if not negated." (The police officer was severely injured falling into a hole unseen as a result of light fixtures not functioning because of destruction by vandals months before.)

25.5 Conclusion

It can be argued that the more precautions a company takes, the better their defensible position in a civil suit. It also follows that few, or no, precautions can leave a company extremely vulnerable for an adverse outcome. In a trial, it is a jury that decides whether the defensible posture met reasonableness at the time of the incident or event.

A successful security program will be able to dissuade an individual from filing a lawsuit or, if filed, will be significantly persuasive to render a jury verdict of non-negligence. The following elements should be included in such a program:

- A security mission statement
- Strong, documented evidence of good security planning
- Capability to define the risks and threats and institution of a security program or system to meet the reasonableness requirement

Endnotes

1. Walsh, T. and Healy, R.J. *Protection Assets Manual.* The Merritt Company, Santa Monica, CA. 90406 (1985 edition).

2. Bates, N.D. and Groussman, J. *Major Developments in Premises Liability II* (1999). Liability Consultants, Inc., 39 Union Avenue, Sudbury, MA. 01776 for a more full discussion on the "Totality of Circumstances Test."

Chapter 26

Corporate Responsibilities and Identity Theft

Robert A. Dudash

Synopsis

26.1 Introduction

While the topic of "identity theft" seems to have been around forever, the actual reporting on "identity theft" goes back less than a decade. Identity theft has become a significant issue and it continues to grow, not only with regard to individuals but also to the responsibilities of corporations. According to a Federal Trade Commission survey conducted between March 17 and April 23, 2003, an estimated 3.25 million Americans discovered that their personal information has been misused to open new credit accounts, take out new loans, or engage in other types of fraud such as misuse of the victim's name and identifying information when someone is charged with a crime, when renting an apartment, or when obtaining medical care.

A good starting point is to define what identity theft is and how it can affect those whose identity has been "stolen."

The Identity Theft and Assumption Deterrence Act of 1998, which made identity theft a crime, prohibits "knowingly transfer(ring) or use(ing), without lawful authority, a means of identification of another person with the intent to commit, or to aid or abet, any unlawful activity that constitutes a violation of federal law, or that constitutes a felony under any applicable state or local law." There is a note that under this act, a name or Social Security number (SSN) is considered a "means of identification."

Identity theft and identity fraud are terms that are used interchangeably. According to the Department of Justice, identity theft and identity fraud are terms used to refer to all types of crime in which someone wrongfully obtains and uses another person's personal data in some way that involves fraud or deception, typically for economic gain.

Identity theft occurs when an individual or a group of individuals obtains and uses the personal data of someone else such as their name, address, telephone number, credit card number(s), mother's maiden name, and/or Social Security number without the knowledge of that individual for the purpose of committing a criminal act, specifically, use the information of the individual(s) to commit some form of financial fraud or deception.

The most unique aspect of identity theft is that the victim, be it an individual or a corporation, must on their own take the time to sort out what damage has been done and then pursue the credit card issuers and credit reporting agencies to correct their records. If the perpetrator of the crime is identified during this process, then the victim has the added responsibility to notify the appropriate law enforcement agency. There is no guarantee an investigation will follow. There is no other crime in the United States where the victim must first determine the extent of the crime, make the crime known to the credit card issuer or credit reporting agency and insure that their credit status is corrected, and at the same time report it to the police with the knowledge that there may not be a comprehensive police investigation.

26.2 Corporate Responsibility

Corporations, large and small, and their security/information technology directors, have a responsibility to guard against the theft of identities of their personnel and, if applicable, their clients and/or customers whose identity has been entrusted to them for safekeeping for legitimate business uses. Where a corporation has both a security director and an information technology director, it is good practice for these two entities to work closely together to ensure the two offices do what they can to protect employees' personal data. Corporations have a direct responsibility to ensure that intrusions into their databases or other repositories of information regarding the specific "points of identification" of employees and clients/customers are prohibited. Specific points of identification are defined as name, date of birth, Social Security number (SSN), address, and any other information that could provide information for a "thief" to collect and use this personal information to either initiate new credit accounts or gain access to established accounts. Unfortunately, there are many individuals who devote their skills to "stealing the identities" of hard working individuals and in turn, using these skills to cause considerable hardships to unsuspecting individuals.

The disclosure of personal data by individuals or groups within an organization represents a growing percentage of data thefts, in both the raw numbers of actual thefts and the amount of personal data compromised. There are two primary internal types of thefts: actual physical theft of data files at an organization by employees and those caused by employee access to systems that have information on customers/clients or other consumers. Investigations into the theft of personal data have resulted in determining the personal data were compromised by some of the following means:

- An insurance company with a legitimate reason and with permission was accessing a state's Department of Motor Vehicles records. It was subsequently determined that employees of the insurance company were caught improperly accessing and distributing confidential information from the state's records.
- A former employee of a large insurance company was determined to have accessed and obtained personal information on former co-workers from the company's database that contained over 60,000 names. This former employee was subsequently identified as advertising the sale of thousands of Social Security numbers to others.
- A help desk operator at a large telecommunications company was selling the company passwords to a ring of identity

thieves, allowing them access to the company's records to obtain credit reports on thousands of individuals.

- In Canada, a hard drive containing information on an estimated one million people was stolen from the company. Authorities eventually found the hard drive, which had been taken by a company employee.
- Posing as a reputable company on the Internet, identity thieves had a web page that looked authentic as they copied "their corporate information" from legitimate corporations. This phony company was very successful in duping inquiring customers into sharing their credit card numbers and other personal information.
- Identity thieves set up a booth at an advertised job fair and unsuspecting job seekers unknowingly provided considerable personal data on job application forms. The completion of this personal data provided these thieves with information which permitted them to initiate numerous banking and credit accounts in the names of the job seekers.

These are only a few examples of how sensitive, personal information may be compromised. Fortunately, law enforcement personnel were able to identify these identity thieves which resulted in prosecution of the individuals. There are many other scenarios where the thieves have not been identified or caught. The need to remain vigilant and to protect the identities of everyone is a significant challenge to not only the individuals but to corporations as well.

The responsibility of the corporation to protect proprietary information entrusted to them is paramount. While corporation management can delegate these responsibilities internally, the corporation is ultimately responsible if the system is compromised. Corporations may delegate these responsibilities to the security director and information technology director, along with all other responsible corporate officers, to include support personnel, to ensure their individual systems maintain the best possible safeguards against intrusion. These same professionals also have a responsibility to inform and educate their employees and customers/clients on ways to protect their individual identity and to guard against identity theft.

26.3 Methods of Obtaining Personal Information

Despite the best efforts to maintain the integrity of protecting personal data, skilled identity thieves can use a variety of methods to gain access to the personal data of individuals; these methods can be both low and high tech means. Following are some of the ways thieves can obtain the personal information of individuals and as a result, take over identities.

Here are just several ways thieves collect personal information:

- They steal wallets and purses containing identification on the individual, along with other identification such as a driver's license, credit and bank cards, a checkbook, and any other information that may be contained in the wallet or purse.
- Your mail is stolen, which may include your banking and credit card statements, pre-approved credit offers, telephone calling cards, and even tax information.
- These thieves can complete a "Change of Address Form" to divert your mail to another location.
- They obtain your personal or the corporation's trash, thieves search for personal data which would then be used to compromise the identity of those individual's whose personal data may have been discarded and not destroyed.
- They fraudulently obtain your credit report by posing as a landlord, employer, or someone else who may have a legitimate need for, and a legal right to, the information.
- Thieves capture and use personal information you share on the Internet.
- They obtain your business and personal records from the corporate repository (corporation vested with the responsibility of protecting this information).
- These thieves buy personal information from "inside" sources. Here, the thieves can pay an employee for information about you that appears in the corporation's records.

26.4 Uses of Personal Information

Here are some of the ways thieves use the personal information they have stolen:

- While pretending to be you, they call your credit card issuer and ask to change the mailing address on your credit card account. The thief then uses the credit card for multiple charges on "your" account. Because the credit card statement is now being sent to a new address, it may take some time before it becomes obvious that there is a problem.
- They open new credit card account(s) using your name, date of birth and SSN. When they use this credit card and do not pay the bill, the account becomes delinquent and is subsequently reported on your credit account.
- Thieves establish telephone or wireless service in your name using your personal data.
- The theif opens a bank account in your name and then writes checks on that account which obviously has insufficient funds. While the thief may have to make an initial deposit to activate the account, by the time checks stop clearing, numerous checks for varying amounts may have been written.
- These thieves may produce counterfeit checks or debit cards which are subsequently used to drain your personal account(s).

26.5 Methods to Thwart Identity Theft

Security and information technology directors must be vigilant and maintain a constant communication between their offices and with their employees and customers/clients. While the following is provided as an aid to thwart intrusion into the personal data they maintain, this list is not intended to be all-inclusive. The thieves spend many hours devising ways to penetrate and obtain information from corporate files and individuals. These steps are merely a general guide, and if you, as a responsible person, identify other vulnerabilities share or coordinate your finding with the appropriate director.

1. Encourage the cooperation of your customers/clients to provide any early warnings they may detect that something is ramiss. Implement a program that makes it easy for employees and customers to report any suspicious spam e-mails or websites that they encounter. Employees, suppliers, distribu-

tors, and even customers or investors can help a company monitor the Internet-based corporate identity attacks by sounding the alert in time to mitigate the damage.

2. Encourage customers to NEVER "click" on links in e-mail. Instead, customers should directly type or "bookmark" trusted Internet sites. Spam e-mail can be easily altered so that it appears to have originated from a legitimate source and can be practically indistinguishable from a legitimate site. Although many companies and organizations have tried to educate consumers on how to detect fraudulent e-mail, even experts can sometimes find it difficult to detect.
3. Adopt a policy never to contact your customers/clients via e-mail for any reason that would require them to share personal or account information. Communicate this policy to your customers/clients and ensure they understand the policy. Educating customers that responding to e-mail notifications, even those which appear to be legitimate, makes them vulnerable to future identity theft attacks.
4. Make sure the company is easy to find online. Promote your website address and keep it simple to avoid typographical errors and misspellings. Exert as much control over the customers' online experience as possible by trying not to rely on others to deliver your customers to your site. When customers attempt to locate your website through other means such as search engines, partners, or spam, it provides an opportunity for others to intercept them before they arrive at your site.
5. Carefully manage your domain registrations and consider monitoring for new registrations that include your company name or trademark(s). You should also register common typographical errors and misspellings of your website address before someone else does. You can then automatically redirect wayward customers to the correct address.
6. Determine your response to an attack BEFORE it happens. There are numerous resources to help you with your action plan. Many trade associations have formed committees and working groups to share best practices. It is also advisable to seek advice and establish relationships in advance with law

enforcement and appropriate Internet service provider(s) (ISP) who can investigate and possibly "neutralize" fraudulent sites if an attack occurs.

A security director is responsible to provide the utmost possible protection to the information entrusted to that entity, be it a corporation, company, or individual. It should be noted that you may never be able to prevent theft entirely, however, by managing the personal data cautiously and making individuals aware of the ways an identity may be stolen, you can help guard against identity theft.

Security directors and individuals in positions of trust and responsibility have an obligation to continue to educate their employees and customers/clients on how to protect themselves by using some of the following steps:

1. Make them aware that before revealing any personal identifying information they should determine how that information will be used and whether it will be shared with others. Ensure they are aware to ask if they have a choice about the use of their information and whether they choose to have it kept confidential.
2. Tell the individuals to pay attention to their billing cycles. They should be aware when these cycles occur, and they should follow up with creditors if they do not receive their statements on time: each credit entity has a specific billing time. Not all credit statements are processed at the same time. Individuals should know when they should be receiving a statement. A missing credit card statement could mean an identity theft has occurred and that credit card account may have been taken over by an identity thief who has changed your billing address to ensure you are not aware of the thief of your identity.
3. Brief personnel to guard their mail from theft. If an individual has outgoing mail, it is best to deposit this mail in a post office collection box or to go directly to the post office and deposit the mail there. They should be told to remove promptly mail from their mailbox after it has been delivered. If the in-

dividual is planning to be away from home for any length of time and cannot pick up the mail, arrangements should be made with the post office to request the mail be held at the post office for pickup upon return. Some individuals have their neighbor pick up the mail while away. Doing this is a personal decision, but the best practice is to have the post office put a hold on their mail.

4. Ensure they put passwords on their credit cards, bank, and phone cards. They should also be instructed to avoid using easily available information as passwords such as mother's maiden name, date of birth, the last four digits of the Social security number or telephone number, or a series of consecutive numbers. Thieves are aware that individuals may not be too creative and want to use passwords that they can easily remember. They should also be told to avoid, if possible, using the same password on all their accounts.
5. Make sure they minimize the identification information and the number of credit cards they carry to what they actually need.
6. Tell them not to give out personal information on the telephone, through the mail, or over the Internet unless they have initiated the contact or know with whom they are dealing. Identity thieves have been known to pose as representatives of banks, Internet service providers, and even government agencies to get individuals to reveal Social Security numbers, mother's maiden name, financial account numbers, and other identifying information. Legitimate organizations with whom they conduct business have the information they need and will not ask the individual for it. As a matter of practice, these organizations will ask the individual to verify certain types of information that is already on file.
7. Have them keep items with personal information in a safe place. To thwart the efforts of an identity thief who may pick through an individual's trash or recycling bins to collect personal information, instruct the individuals to tear up or shred all charge receipts, credit applications, insurance forms, bank checks, and statements that the individual is discarding. They

should also obliterate expired credit cards and credit offers that are received in the mail. While it may be recommended that the individuals should tear up items they intend to discard, shredding is a much better method of destroying the information. Shredding items makes it much more difficult to attempt to reconstruct these items; individuals who tear up receipts, statements, and the like normally tear the items once or twice which would enable someone to reconstruct the document with relative ease.

8. Ensure personnel are cautious about where they leave personal information in their homes, especially if they have roommates, employ outside help, or are having service work done in their home.
9. Have the individuals determine who has access to their personal information at work and have the employer verify that their records are kept in a secure location.
10. Tell them to provide their Social Security number only when absolutely necessary. Have the individual ask to use other types of identifiers when possible. Instruct the individuals that if they must provide their SSN, it should only be provided in a discrete manner and not where others may overhear the number, as many identity thieves have excellent memories and are capable of memorizing all personal data they overhear.
11. Make sure they *do not* to carry their Social Security number card; leave it in a secure place.
12. Tell them to order a copy of their credit report from each of the three major credit reporting agencies every year. Make sure the information in their credit report is accurate and includes only those activities they have authorized.

A person's credit report contains information on where the individual works and lives, the credit accounts that have been opened in his or her name, how the person pays their bills, and whether the person has been sued, suffered tax liens, or filed for bankruptcy. Checking a credit report on a regular basis can help identify mistakes and fraud before they wreck havoc on an individual's personal finances.

Security directors may assist employees or others by providing the following information for the three major credit bureaus.

1. **Equifax**—www.equifax.com
   To order your report, call: 800.685.1111 or write:
   P.O. Box 740241, Atlanta, GA 30374-0241
   To report fraud, call: 800.525.6285/TDD: 800.255.0056
2. **Experian**—www.experian.com
   To order your report, call: 800.397.3742 or write:
   P.O. Box 2104, Allen, TX 75013
   To report fraud, call: 888.397.3742/TDD: 800.972.0322
3. **TransUnion**—www.transunion.com
   To order your report, call: 800.916.8800 or write:
   P.O. Box 1000, Chester, PA 19022
   To report fraud, call: 800.680.7289/TDD: 877.553.7803

26.6 After Theft Is Discovered

Security directors should insist employees immediately report any case of suspected theft. If an individual suspects his or her personal information has been stolen or misappropriated to commit fraud or theft, instruct the individual to keep a record of conversations and correspondence. They should keep a detailed record of the date, time, telephone number called, and the identity of the individual to whom they talked. The Federal Trade Commission has prepared a form which may be used in the event a person feels his or her identity has been stolen. A copy of this form is provided for possible use in a suspected identity theft (see FTC Form). If someone suspects his or her identity has been stolen, there are steps that must be taken as soon as possible. The exact steps necessary to protect one's identity depend on the circumstances and how the identity may have been misused. There are three basic actions that are appropriate for an individual to take:

First, *contact the fraud department of each of the three major credit bureaus.*

Tell the person to inform the credit bureau that he or she is a victim of identity theft. The person should request a "fraud alert" be placed in the file, as well as a victim's statement asking that creditors call the individual before opening any new accounts or changing any existing accounts. This action can help prevent an identity thief from opening additional accounts in the person's name.

At the same time, order copies of credit reports from the three major credit bureaus. The credit bureau must provide the individual with a free copy of the report if the report is inaccurate because of fraud and the request is in writing. Individuals should be instructed to review the credit reports very carefully to make sure no additional fraudulent accounts have been opened in his or her name or unauthorized changes were made to existing accounts. Check the section of the credit report that lists "inquiries," which is listed at the end of the credit report. Where "inquiries" appear from the company(ies) that opened the fraudulent account(s), request that these "inquiries" be removed from the credit report. Then order new copies of the credit report in several months to verify that the corrections and changes were made to the credit report and to ensure that no new fraudulent activity has occurred. Obviously, the person should retain the old credit reports as a means of cross-checking.

Second, *contact the creditors for any accounts that have been tampered with or opened fraudulently.*

Creditors can include credit card companies, telephone companies and other utilities, and banks and other lenders. Instruct the individual to speak to the security or fraud department of each creditor and *follow up with a certified letter*. It is particularly important to notify credit card companies in writing because this is the consumer protection procedure the law spells out for resolving errors on credit card billing statements. Immediately close accounts that have been tampered with and open new ones with new personal identification numbers (PINs) and passwords. Again, avoid using easily available information such as mother's maiden name, date of birth, the last four digits of your SSN or your telephone number or a series of consecutive numbers.

Third, *have the individual file a report with the police department that has jurisdiction where the theft occurred or if this is not possible, the police agency in the community of residence.*

Make sure to obtain a copy of the police report in case the bank, credit card company, or others need proof of the crime. Even if the police do not catch the identity thief in this individual's case, having a copy of the police report can help the individual when dealing with creditors.

Security and information technology directors can assist an individual whose identity has been stolen as a possible result of vulnerability in their system. The theft of anyone's identity can be very traumatic and can have a devastating effect on financial stability. Following are some additional ways managers can help the individual regain control of his or her personal situation:

- **Stolen mail.** If someone has stolen mail to get new credit cards, bank, and credit statements, or if the thief has falsified a change-of-address form, that is a crime. Report this to the local postal inspector. Contact the local post office for the telephone number of the nearest postal inspector service office.
- **Change of address on credit card accounts.** If someone has changed the billing address on existing credit card account(s), close the account(s). When the individual opens a new account, ensure that he or she asks for a password to be used before any inquiries or changes can be made to the account.
- **Bank accounts.** If there is reason to believe that someone has tampered with bank account(s), checks, or ATM card, close these accounts immediately. Insist on'"password only access" on new accounts to minimize the chance that an identity thief can violate the accounts. If checks have been stolen or misused, stop payment immediately. If an ATM card has been lost, stolen, or otherwise compromised, cancel the card as soon as possible and get another card with a new PIN.
- **Investments.** If the person has reason to believe someone has tampered with securities investments or a brokerage account, have the individual immediately report it to the broker or account manager and contact the Securities and Exchange Commission. The individual can file a complaint with the SEC.
- **Telephone service.** If a thief has established new telephone service and is making unauthorized calls that seem to come from, and are billed to, a cellular telephone or is using a telephone calling card and PIN, contact the service provider im-

mediately to cancel the account and/or calling card. Open new accounts with new PINs.

- **Employment.** If someone is using the stolen SSN to apply for a job or to work, that is a crime. Report this to the Social Security Administration's Fraud Hotline at 1.800.269.0271.
- **Driver's license.** If the individual suspects that his or her name and SSN is being used by anyone to get a driver's ID card, contact the Department of Motor Vehicles.

26.7 Wi-Fi

One of the newer threats to a corporation's internal workings is the use of Wi-Fi or wireless connectivity to the Internet. While wireless connectivity is one of today's newest technologies, no portable device, whether a laptop, PDA, or smart phone is complete without it, and the workplace without walls is now a reality. But that is precisely the problem. Wireless communications relies on radio waves, and radio waves do not respect conventional boundaries. Anyone with a laptop, wireless Ethernet card, and an antenna can tap into a wireless local area network (WLAN) for either fun or nefarious reasons.

There is now a cult of WLAN "crackers," and the problem is widespread. "War driving," which is locating Wi-Fi networks while driving around and freeloading broadband access, is the latest techno-geek game. War drivers even leave each other signposts, in the form of special symbols chalked on walls and pavements, pinpointing the whereabouts of vulnerable networks.

Educating people about this vulnerability is essential. Unprotected wireless networks are now a very high-risk problem. It is important for desktop users and mobile workers to understand that security precautions need to be taken when installing Wi-Fi technology on computers. This technology has also become the biggest security headache because of the systems' vulnerability. While wireless networks offer significant business advantages when deployed in the work environment, there are risks involved with this technology, and managers must be ever vigilant to the possibility of increasing the potential of penetrations of their systems because of this technology.

26.8 Phishing

In addition to the Wi-Fi issue, there is another way that thieves collect personal information on individuals. This is by a method referred to as "**phishing**." Phishing is a term used to describe fraudulent e-mails designed to steal a person's identity. These imposter e-mails may appear to come from a reputable company but are actually from thieves masquerading as legitimate businesses. The e-mail will ask you to disclose, on a phony Web site or in a phony dialog box, personal information such as your account data or Social Security number. The thieves then steal that personal information. Depending on the information you may have provided, they can access your accounts, open new ones, steal your funds, and even commit crimes—all in your name.

How the thieves steal your personal information.

Phishing e-mails typically suggest that if you do not update your personal information, your account will be closed. The e-mail instructs you to click on a link that redirects you to a fake Web site. These "spoofed" sites look official and include logos and fonts used by the companies they imitate.

Here are some indicators or warning signs that someone is "phishing" for information:

- **Urgent tone.** The message urges you to "act quickly" or your account will be closed.
- **Spelling and grammatical errors.** The wording may be sloppy and contain typographical errors and misspellings.
- **Request for financial information.** They often ask for your e-mail address and password, first and last names, credit card numbers, bank account numbers, account PIN numbers and Social Security number(s).
- **Fake Web addresses.** An "@" symbol in a Web site may indicate that the source might be imitating a company or person (For example: www.microsoft@billing.com is fake). Or, if the address includes any words between Microsoft and com or msn and com, the Web site is fraudulent. (For example, msn.billing.com and microsoftbilling.com are not Microsoft Web sites.)

- **Non-secure Web pages.** Their sites and URL may look like official company sites, but they are not. Be alert for non-secure Web pages that ask for sensitive information. Secure sites use encryption technology to protect your information. They display a locked padlock at the bottom of your browser and add an "s" after http in the address bar (for example, https://signup.msn.com).
- **If it sounds too good to be true, it probably is.** Scam artists can paint attractive pictures of "valuable offers" and "great deals." Odds are they are just looking for other ways to access your valuable personal information.

What can you do to help individuals to protect themselves?

- **Be suspicious.** Messages threatening to terminate or suspend your account without your quick response should be treated as suspicious. Also, be wary of clicking on links in e-mail addresses.
- **Always type in the URL of the Web page you want.** Phishing scam e-mails include a link that takes you to a fake Web site.
- **Scroll over the URL**. If you move your mouse over the URL and numbers and a different URL appears, it is probably fraudulent.

26.9 Conclusion

In closing, whether the threat is external or internal, a data thief cannot steal information that is not collected or stored. The amount of information that may be collected depends on the specifics of the organization. The protection of personal data is paramount and the education of both employees and customers/clients on the importance of maintaining the integrity of the data is never ending.

Chapter 27

Investigation of Breach of Contract Cases

Kitty Hailey, CLI

Synopsis

"Failure, without legal excuse, to perform any promise which forms the whole or part of a contract."[1]

27.1 Introduction

Contracts are legal documents defining agreements between two or more parties to perform or not to perform certain specified activities. A contract is either a written or an oral delineation of the bounds of a particular relationship. Within the business world, corporations and business entities use contracts as vehicles by which they delimit the role of employees, partners, vendors, sub-contractors, and others with whom they have working associations. Business contracts detail the limits of working relationships during their tenure and after separation. Confidentiality agreements and non-compete clauses further refine the scope of employee contracts.

Contracts take many forms. Outside of the corporate world, a marriage contract is an agreement between two parties who intend to spend their life in wedded unity sharing life, home, and related obligations. A marriage contract, however, may be accompanied by a pre-nuptial agreement. This is an additional contract spelling out the distribution of assets and responsibilities during the marriage and in the event of death or divorce. There are contracts for sale/purchase, performance/non-performance, service agreements, insurance, rental/lease, entertainment, and surrogate parenting. Almost every area of contemporary life is replete with contractual relationships of one sort or another.

Entire courses are dedicated to the subject of contracts in law schools and at business institutes. This chapter discusses one aspect of the contractual agreement that most affects the legal investigator: *dealing with a contract that has been broken.*

Investigating the broken contract is a task often assigned to an investigator. Knowing how to deal with the client, obtain information, and initiate investigative steps is of primary importance. To prove that a contract has been breached, one must first understand some of the rudimentary basics of the law of contracts. Then, having an organized plan will provide the investigator with the ability to initiate the job at hand.

27.2 A Short Course in Contracts[2]

A contract is a document or verbal understanding of the parameters of a specific relationship. It has value as a guide of agreed to roles and conduct dictating how business is to be conducted. Each contract is a promise unto itself with uniquely defined duties, responsibilities, and obligations for each party. Enforceable under the law, a contract is a vehicle by which current relationships are formed and future relationships are ensured. When either party does not adhere to the stated provisions of a contract that party is in breach of that agreement.

There are criteria necessary to the proper components of a contract. They include:

A. Offer and acceptance

Each party to the contract must offer a specific obligation (duty, responsibility, financial consideration, product or action) which must be accepted by the other party in order for the contract to be valid. This is a "willingness to enter into a bargain."[3] (Example: XYZ Corporation promises to provide widgets in consideration of adequate financial remuneration from Vendor ABC. XYZ Corp offers the product in return for money from ABC. Each party will be giving and getting something to the mutual benefit of them both.) This is called "consideration."[4] The signing of the contract is the acceptance. "Acceptance is a voluntary act by which the offeree exercises the power conferred upon him by the offer to create a contract."[5]

B. Oral or written

Contracts are generally, but not always, written agreements. It is proper and acceptable for a contract to be an oral agreement. Both are legally enforceable. The written contract has the added value of being a drafted, signed, and dated agreement that has been memorialized. It cannot be altered or changed unilaterally. Oral contracts are enforceable, although the specific understandings of each party may be more difficult to discern than those of a memorialized and documented writing.[6] Either the investigator or legal counsel to the case is advised to consult local statutes under which the investigation is being conducted to insure that evidence is being properly obtained according to venue.

C. Express or implied

All contracts need not be documents in written form. They may be either express (actually written) or implied (inferred from the conduct of the participants.) Working relationships do occur from a history established between parties whereby one party is in the habit of performing certain duties (work, service, etc.) and the other party habitually accepts that performance and compensates it in a similar and regularly accepted manner to them both. "Implied-in-fact conditions are those inherent in the promises given and necessary to the performance of the contract."[7]

D. Legality

The law does not recognize illegal contracts. Under the doctrine of "unclean hands," an illegal contract cannot be enforced.[8] It will not be considered legal or binding and thus has no value.

A contract that has been breached is one that has first met the criteria of a valid working contract. If it has been properly prepared, stating the obligations of all parties, and then signed or accepted showing agreement of all concerned, it is a legal document. The designated responsibilities of each party must be carried out or there is said to be a breach of contract. In the event of such a default or failure to perform, the aggrieved party has several remedies under the law for collecting damages. The remedies are generally not punitive[9] in nature but may find resolution in compensatory[10] form. Restitution is a possibility where the benefits the injured party has conferred upon the breaching party may be ultimately returned. Equity may be an appropriate remedy in the form of specific enforcement (specific performance) of the contract.[11] "Nominal damages are available for any breach of contract, no matter how slight."[12]

When there is a breach or default in a contract the aggrieved party suffers and the broken promise may result in grave consequences for the defaulting party. Frequently a breach will arise because there is an expectation of the contract's viability or there is a detrimental reliance on the fulfillment of a contract that has not come to fruition.

- **Expectation.** If there was an expectation of gain from a contract, and the breach of contract has eliminated the possibility of that gain coming to fruition, there is reason to expect recovery of damages.
- **Reliance.** If a party has relied to their detriment upon the contract and that contract has been breached, then the injured party may be entitled to be restored to the position he or she would have been in had that contract not been made.

27.3 The Investigation

A. Investigator's role

The investigator's role is to provide evidence that will assist the injured party to a contract in proving the actual breach. Understanding the consequences of the breach on the adversely affected party's business will assist the investigator in valuing the job to be performed.

B. The UCC

The Uniform Commercial Code[13] was initially formulated for the purposes of simplifying, clarifying, and modernizing the law governing business transactions. It provides both definitions and remedies for agreements between parties in the world of competitive commerce. The code also clarifies definitions of terms and phrases for the better understanding of the parties concerned. Applicable terms to this chapter are:

> *Contract* means the total legal obligation that results from the parties' agreement as affected by this Act and any other applicable rules of law.
>
> *Fault* means wrongful act, omission, or breach.
>
> *Organization* includes a corporation, government or governmental subdivision or agency, business trust, estate, trust, partnership or association, two or more persons having a joint or common interest, or any other legal or commercial entity.[14]

C. Initial steps in the investigative procedure

1. Establish a contractual agreement with the client

Before agreeing to investigate the contractual dispute it would be intelligent for the investigator to have an agreement in place outlining the parameters of the work to be done. Sometimes contract cases are somewhat ambiguous. It is necessary to establish the role of the investigator. To whom will the investigator report? From whom will the investigator receive direction? Since a contract is a legal document, it is of great importance that an attorney be available as an advisor in such matters. An investigator must not make the mistake of playing attorney. While a great deal of knowledge might have been amassed, the actual evidence needed to prove that a contract has been breached should be done under the advice of counsel.

2. Authorization

Obtain a signed authorization and agreement allowing the investigator to represent the party to the contract for whom he or she is working. This allows the investigator to speak with others and obtain documentation that might otherwise not be available. A signed agreement opens doors. It makes information available and provides data that might have previously been considered privileged.

3. Clearance to communicate

Check with legal counsel to determine the investigator's ability to communicate ex-parte[15] with the individual alleged to have breached the contract. If it is possible to speak with the party at fault, then it might be conceivable that an interview may take place at some time during the investigation. While ruse work is not necessarily the best method of obtaining information, it is sometimes the most appropriate tool. Surveillance, record searches, database research, and third-party interviews might not provide the necessary information that proves an individual has broken a promise. It might behoove the investigator to place an undercover operative in a position to witness the activity of the offending party. In that case, contact might be necessary or unavoidable. If that is a possibility it is necessary to have a written confirmation from legal counsel advising the investigator of the acceptability of such action.

All questions of a legal nature should be confirmed prior to initiating any work. This allows the investigator to plan and fully understand the scope of the work to be done.

4. Understand the parameters of the original contract

All contracts have some similarities in that there must be an agreement between two or more parties. Further, there should be an offer, acceptance of that offer, and consideration. The investigator must understand the extent of the offer in order to comprehend what part of the contract has actually been breached. Evidence will consist of information that proves or substantiates the fact that the offer has not been adhered to fully.

The investigator cannot find evidence of fault if he or she does not understand the duties and responsibilities of each party to the action.

If possible, obtain an original or a true copy of the contract under discussion. Too often clients and attorneys only provide limited information to the investigator, revealing only that which they, the client, believes to be of value. The investigator should understand the entire situation so that all information, including pitfalls and problems, is totally comprehended. It should be remembered that just because the client claims an action is a breach of the contract does not necessarily mean it is so. *Investigators are often found lacking in their ability to provide information because they are not totally informed at the beginning of a case.*

Make a list of each item of responsibility for each party. This will help to clarify the actual limits of the contract. It will enumerate the items that have been invalidated. These will be detailed in the body of the contract itself. They might, however, be written in "legaleeze"[16] or be otherwise ambiguous to the investigator's own sphere of knowledge. Have the attorney or client explain the specifics of each tenet so that the obligations are clear to the investigator.

If a suit has already been filed alleging a contractual breach the investigator should obtain a copy of the complaint with all of its attachments. This will provide another useful tool for the investigator in understanding the particular manner in which the contract was allegedly breached. The complaint will direct the investigator in his or her work.

5. Understand the scope of the breach

Each contract is unique in that it deals with a particular issue, product, or relationship. In situations where the contract deals with a product, all data involving the product, its manufacturing process, intricacies of design, uniqueness of service, and related specifications should be known by the investigator. This extends to food products where specific ingredients, recipe procedures, methods of preparation, and equipment are used to create the final comestible. When a contract deals with a service the scope of activity expected of each party must be known. *The investigator must understand each step of a process to determine if there has been a violation of an agreement to perform, or not to perform, in a particular way.*

6. Non-compete clauses

Non-compete[17] clauses are often breached when a partnership or an employment relationship has been terminated. A non-compete clause serves the purpose of ensuring that there will be no adverse financial status of the original organization because of competition from a severed relationship. Therefore the geographic parameters of sales districts, mileage limitations, or particular groups of clients should all be known to the investigator if he or she is to determine that a former employee or business partner is now working in violation of a previously signed agreement.

7. Confidentiality agreements

Confidentiality agreements are contracts between employee and employer vowing fidelity to the organization. Usually this refers to a prohibition against discussion of work related information with others not employed at the same firm. A confidentiality agreement might extend to the sharing of or revelation about products under development, client lists, or problems, services performed by the company, or trademark and copyrighted materials. Exposure of such proprietary information could prove detrimental to the business of the employer. It could jeopardize future income. If the case at hand is germane to such a matter, the investigator must be aware of the secrets stolen or exposed and to whom the information was provided.

The bottom line is simple. Understand the details of the contracted subject, object, or service before beginning the investigative process.

8. Background work

Let the client do the background work. It is not uncommon for an investigator to spend unnecessary hours obtaining information that is already known to the client. There is nothing worse than investing innumerable hours on case preparation only to be told by the client "I knew that already." Find out what the client does and does not know. Neither the investigator's time nor that of the client should be wasted reinventing the wheel. Have the client provide the particular formula, instructional manual, recipe, client list, telephone numbers, addresses, and names of those persons or items which are "out of bounds" to the offending party. This saves valuable time and money.

9. Discovery

If the case is well into the legal process, obtain all available discovery. There might be telephone bills, client lists, or subpoenaed material in the possession of the client's attorney that is valuable to the investigation.

10. Client interview

Most of all be sure to conduct a thorough client interview. This individual has more information in his or her head than all of the documents. If the client is an organization, at least one or more of the principals has a thorough understanding of the breaches being alleged and their financial effects. The client is a valuable resource. A good investigator must learn how to speak to the client appropriately to elicit all relevant information. This might be the most difficult part of the entire investigation as clients are not always forthcoming and not always truthful. Reasons for this would fill an entire volume, perhaps two.

D. The investigation begins

Investigators know how to investigate—that is the job of a licensed private investigator or detective. Even if an investigator has never handled a matter dealing with contractual issues it is possible for good service and diligent work to have successful results. Many different types of investigations share common methods of approach. There are shared resources and tools that are the lifeblood of all investigators. Thus, when an investigation begins, the practitioner is calling upon all of his or her historic education and experience, applying them to the current case at hand. First and foremost an investigator must understand the matter, identify the objectives, and then begin the search for supportive evidence. With this in mind, it never hurts to review tried and true methods that might be overlooked. Sometimes the obvious is not so obvious until it has been stated. Therefore, a review of the "how to" of the actual investigation follows. It starts, as all investigations should:

1. Organize the data

Do the simple "in house" work to prepare before going out into the field. This includes:

- Running databases to determine the various names of companies and individuals associated with the "other party" in this matter. Sometimes simple on-line research might prove that the individual alleged to have breached a contract is brazen enough to have filed a fictitious name registration, obtained a tax I.D. number, or to have been named as a corporate officer in a rival's business enterprise. A thorough search of all Internet and database resources should include the name and all known addresses of the subject. Businesses might appear at the address of a suspect, but under the name of a different incorporator.
- Check for possible websites under the name of the party in question. Run a LexisNexis, or newspaper search, to see if the name of the alleged offender is mentioned in an article in a local newspaper.
- Review all documentation.
- Cross-reference all compiled data.
- In the event that telephone numbers have already been subpoenaed and obtained, check these with reverse directories (on line services, CD-ROM or city directories). Obtain the names of those individuals most frequently communicated with and compare these names to those provided by the client.

2. Field investigation

Now begin the legwork (field investigation).

Witness interviews are sometimes the most direct and appropriate route. The investigator must be cautious that such communication is sanctioned by law. In many cases it is inappropriate for an investigator or an agent of an attorney/client to speak with the subject or an investigation, a current employee, or a former employee if he or she served in a supervisory capacity. Such contact has to be conducted under the rules governing discovery. Even if permission is granted for such communication, it may only serve to alert the alleged offender that he or she is under investigation.

Often people are not aware that they are abetting others in the breaking of a contractual agreement. Therefore, a former client who is now using a former employee with a non-compete clause, might be the perfect interview subject. A simple question such as, "Who do you use as your service provider?" might bring the desired response. Asking for a referral is often the key to opening the door for additional information. "Whom would you recommend?" is a question that would allow follow up, opinion, discussion, and further enlightenment.

If counsel has given permission, it is appropriate to speak to the subject of this investigation. This would have to be done directly, or while perpetuating a pretext or ruse. A simple conversation with the individual at a restaurant or after-work tavern might bring about interesting results. Subterfuge that allows the subject to brag or boast of his or her work can be creatively conceived. Caution must be exercised to ensure that all work performed by the investigator is within the realm of that which is legal. No exparte contact may be made if the attorney responsible for the matter has not provided expressed approval.

Consider dumpster diving as an initial step. Check with local laws to determine the legality of this process. Some states allow pick up of trash placed out for removal. Others only allow trash pick ups if it is in transparent or translucent bags, using the logic that it was not being hidden, and therefore was not private in nature (while opaque bags are considered *verboten*). Remember to beware of trespassing. This is an activity not ethically allowed under any circumstances. The possibility of finding unshredded duplicate receipts, envelopes from invoices, or paid checks, copies of information or business records is great. In fact, when searching through trash, one is sometimes more interested in return envelopes than in their actual contents. Bank names, brokerage firms, clients, business correspondence, and the like are generally sent in envelopes. People regularly shred the contents of such correspondence. Frequently envelopes are just tossed, unmutilated, into the trash.

Surveillance (following) is sometimes a simple method of determining the activity of the individual believed to have violated the tenets of a contract. Watching the person for a complete work week might show a pattern of visiting locations that are in violation of a non-compete clause. Observations may be made of a former partner meeting with people who have been named as those disallowed by contractual agreement. This can be an expensive source of information, as investigators should be charging an hourly and per-investigator fee. Such surveillance might be money exceptionally well spent. The client should be apprised of all methods and costs prior to initiating work. Ultimately, the choice to do a particular investigative activity falls upon the shoulders of the individual or organization paying for that service.

3. Organize all data

Establish a "cast of characters" and document the results of each interview. This will provide the date, time, and circumstances of the meeting, in addition to outlining the knowledge and importance of each person. It is a truism that one cannot remember everything. If an investigator is active and busy, then the multitude of interviews in a particular case might become blurred and less accurate over time. Some form of "control" sheet should be available for the investigator to check off that which has been done and that which needs to be performed. This is a flexible and constantly enlarging checklist. Information gleaned during the course of one interview may prompt the addition of a name or names of others to be interviewed. Searching for documents may reveal the existence of still other documents that need to be obtained from different sources.

4. Review-review-review

As with all investigations, one must re-organize, review, and re-think every so often. New information may only have meaning if it is compared with, and analyzed in light of, the data already amassed. And, of course, document, document, document. Not only does this justify the investigator's hours for billing, but it memorializes activity and evidence.

E. Other considerations

These simple steps are applicable to investigating all manner of contractual agreements. Obviously the thoroughness, tenacity, and creativeness of the investigator are the greatest tools available. Each case is different, but similar approaches are applicable to the various contractual disputes being investigated. It is vital for the investigator to be ever cognizant of changing legislation that affects the industry.[18] The investigator is cautioned to examine carefully the ever changing statutes that govern his or her ability to obtain information in a legal and ethical manner.

Frequently an investigator can maximize the service provided to a client by incorporating the work of specialists in a particular field. Much of the work involving corporations is financial in nature. Many investigators have the skills and knowledge to review bank statements, financing information, and tax returns. It is sometimes advisable, however, to use the services of a Certified Fraud Examiner (CFE) or other individual expert, in the areas of such forensic financial investigation. It is also sometimes advisable to use the services of a professional document examiner. This individual is capable of determining if the contract in question is actually the original agreement to which the parties both assented. It is not uncommon for fraud to have been perpetrated in the substitution of documents or forgery of signatures. Working in concert with other professionals in the field reveals the investigator to be a thorough individual concerned with the quality of service being performed. A good investigator knows what he or she doesn't know. Admitting the limits of an investigator's ability is an asset, not a detriment. If a particular task is outside the scope of knowledge of the practitioner then he or she does a service to the client by bringing in others with specific expertise. The client should respect such action. A team approach can then be instituted to the benefit of all.

27.4 Summary

As with all investigations, the practitioner is charged with the duties of understanding the job at hand. Communication with the client is a necessary first step in this process. Establishing a financial agreement, time limits, and expectations of the client are all to be completed before the investigator begins the actual work. Once the scope of the work has been delineated, the investigator must obtain and review all supportive documents that are already in existence. Next, obtain those documents that are necessary which have not been obtained to date. It is necessary to ensure all verifiable information is known the investigator. Prior to initiating field work, the investigator should prepare a file and obtain all necessary background data. Appropriate and legally acceptable field work constitutes the final phase of investigation. Continual review and analysis of information helps to keep the work in perspective. Legal counsel should be sought to assure that the investigator has a total understanding of the matter and is legally obtaining the relevant information and evidence.

The breach of contract investigation holds a great similarity to many other investigative endeavors. It is, however, unique in its basis because of the singular characteristics of each contract. Comprehending the general concept of contracts is a helpful adjunct for the investigative professional. Understanding the evidence necessary to prove a particular case is a requirement before embarking on an investigation. A rule of thumb to remember is that a contract is a promise made between two or more parties with specific duties and responsibilities of each. If one or more of the parties has not performed their portion of the agreement it may be cause for a contract to fail. Obtaining evidence of that non-performance, or violation of the agreement, is the job of the investigator. Professional, diligent work with the element of excellent client communication can prove the keys to a successful investigation of broken promises.

27.5 Examples of Various Contractual Investigations

Example 1

Sell-It, Inc., is a distributor of sophisticated communications equipment. Sell-It, Inc., has a contract with a Make-It, Inc., to build and supply global satellite imaging cameras. Make-It, Inc., is being paid a considerable amount of money as a part of a contractual agreement. The cameras are being sold by Sell-It, Inc., to Green Vision, a third party multi-national corporation for use in their environmental studies program. Make-It, Inc., also has the responsibility to service and repair the units and thus has knowledge of the end user of the product. There is a non-compete clause in the contract between Sell-It, Inc., and Make-It, Inc. Make-It, Inc., however, has decided that Sell-It, Inc., is nothing more than a middleman reducing its potential financial gain. Make-It, Inc., realizes that it is their expertise that fuels this relationship. Make-It, Inc., therefore establishes a separate company, which is actually owned through a "straw-man" to obfuscate involvement. This new company, Straw-man, Inc., soon replaces Sell-It, Inc., as the distributor of cameras to Green Vision. Sell-It, Inc., is rightly upset that a new company has stolen their largest account. However, business is business, and they initially take it in stride. Make-It, Inc., has stepped on several toes during its tenure, and a disgruntled ex-employee spills the beans to Sell-It, Inc., informing them that Straw-man, Inc., is really a creation of Make-It, Inc. An investigator is called into the case.

Investigator's Responsibilities: The investigator is charged with the duty of proving that Make-It, Inc., and Straw-man, Inc., are actually one and the same. Each company has its own incorporators and officers, and each has its own address. The investigator must establish a relationship between the parties and prove that the ultimate financial remuneration for Straw-man, Inc., trickles down to Make-It, Inc. This is done through methodical document research and interviews with individuals at Green View, former employees of Make-It, Inc., and a former boyfriend of a Make-It, Inc., supervisor. A physical visit to the offices of Straw-Man, Inc., reveals that there is minimal activity at this location. However, a bookkeeper/secretary does occupy the office. This individual is followed on several occasions and found to visit only two locations during the course of her daily rounds. She first visits the offices of Make-It, Inc., and then is seen to make deposits at a local bank. With this information the client, Sell-It, Inc., is able to initiate a suit. A forensic evaluation of the records of Green View, Make-It, Inc., and Straw-Man, Inc., ultimately provide the proof necessary to verify the allegations and information gathered by the investigator.

Example 2

Thea, Inc., has contracted to perform the job of security for Sweetheart Designs. Sweetheart has a large manufacturing and warehouse facility in Southern California. Thea's contract does not require that a security specialist be on site twenty-four hours a day, seven days a week. The contract does require that sufficient guarding be provided by security gates, surveillance cameras, employee identification badges, or other such devices that would take the place of the presence of a real live person. A Thea representative is required to do regular inspections of all equipment and spot check personal identification reviews of all employees at least seven times each month. Sweetheart has suffered four break-ins during the last two months, consequently suffering the loss of over $27,000 in merchandise. The perpetrator was not caught on any of the cameras. It appeared that the hurricane fencing had been compromised when a wire cutter was used for access along the rear fence line. Sweetheart deems the contract null and void as the specific performance guaranteed by Thea has not been properly fulfilled.

Investigator's Responsibilities: The investigator was initially provided with a walk-through of the Sweetheart facility. Posing as a vendor, the investigator was given a tour of the plant with full knowledge that hidden cameras would record his presence. After identifying the weak areas of the security system, the investigator determined that surveillance might be a good tool in this case. Initially a background was performed on Thea employees assigned to the Sweetheart plant. It was found that two of the three security persons had criminal records for drug sale or possession. Surveillance eventually resulted in proof that several individuals were using not only the severed fencing as an entrance, but the front door as well. The perpetrators of at least one observed theft were found to be Thea employees. In fact, one of the owners of Thea was noted to be present when merchandise was removed from the Sweetheart plant. Further investigation was conducted whereby other Thea clients were interviewed. It was determined that in each and every facility there had been a loss of revenue because of theft of product. These thefts had all occurred during the tenure of Thea as their security team. In this instance, not only were contracts deemed breached and void, but criminal charges were brought as well.

Example 3

James Employee was hired as a sales manager for a lighting fixtures company. His contract dictated that he would exclusively represent the product of Sun-Lite in exchange for a handsome commission. Sun-Lite management is concerned that James Employee might be moonlighting and representing more than one lighting fixture company. To prove this, an investigator is hired. The job is not as easy as it might appear as James Employee works from his home, which is a condominium apartment in a high-rise building. James Employee had already established a sound client base and did not have to visit these locations physically. It was possible for him merely to make telephone calls from his home-office. It is not possible to check paper trash that might contain envelopes, invoices, or other clues to the activities of James Employee, as the trash is mixed with that of twenty-five other apartments on the same floor at a common incinerator room. Sun-Lite has no desire to pursue legal action, but they do not wish to continue to employ James Employee if he is breaching the contract.

Investigator's Responsibilities: The investigator was advised by counsel that as long as no legal action was being taken it would be appropriate to speak ex-parte[19] with James Employee. Surveillance was performed. James Employee was followed one afternoon to a local grocery store where he was observed slowly perusing the aisles. Investigator took a shopping cart and did the same, making sure to criss-cross the path of James Employee at every opportunity. After several "chance encounters" investigator initiated conversation with James Employee which took the form of light banter. She noted that this was an excellent time to shop because the store was not crowded. She mentioned her own ability to do her shopping at this hour because of her flexible work schedule. Soon, the two were in conversation about their mutual work-from-home jobs. During this interlude James Employee admitted to representing not only Sun-Lite but three other lighting fixture companies as well. Armed with the revealing information, the investigator was able to cross reference and verify the admissions of Mr. Employee with the named fixture manufacturers.

Endnotes

1. Henry Campbell Black, M.A., *Black's Law Dictionary*, Fifth Edition (St Paul Minn), 1979

2. Authors note: The law of contracts is a very complex, refined and definitive set of rules involving explanations, definitions, interpretations and application to specific circumstances engendered by contractual agreements. The author has taken great liberty in providing a very simplistic overview of these laws for the purpose of providing a very basic and primitive understanding upon which the rest of this chapter is based. One should understand the primary tenets of a legal contract if one is to understand how such a contract has been breached. It is recommended that an investigator seek legal counsel to fully understand the complexities of the particular contract that has been alleged to be breached, prior to initiating work on such a case.

3. Gilbert, *Paralegal Summaries: Contracts*, Harcourt Brace Jovanovich Legal and Professional Publications, Inc, (NY) pg iv.

4. Consideration: "Any act or forbearance which is of benefit to the promissory or detriment to the promisee. (Rest.2dX71; CA Civil Code X1605).

5. Gilbert, *Paralegal Summaries: Contracts*, Harcourt Brace Jovanovich Legal and Professional Publications, Inc, (NY) p. vi.

6. Author's note: Both written and oral agreements are enforceable. The statute of frauds provides that certain agreements are void able unless it, or some note or memorandum expressing the consideration, is in writing and subscribed to by the party to be charged. For example, an agreement that by its terms is not to be performed within one year from the making; an agreement to answer for the debt of another; an agreement by an executor or administrator to pay debts of the testator; an agreement made upon the consideration of marriage; an agreement authorizing or employing an agent to sell or purchase real property are all covered by the statute of frauds.

7. Gilbert, *Paralegal Summaries: Contracts*, Harcourt Brace Jovanovich Legal and Professional Publications, Inc, (NY) p.xix.

8. Unclean Hands: The court will not enforce contracts that are illegal or made in an unethical manner. A contract made in such a manner is said to have been done with unclean hands and is not valid.

9. Punitive: damages awarded in a lawsuit as a punishment and example to others for malicious, evil or particularly fraudulent acts. *Law.com Dictionary*, www.dictionary.law.com.

10. Compensatory: financial or material compensation or remuneration. Author's definition.

11. Gilbert, *Paralegal Summaries: Contracts*, Harcourt Brace Jovanovich Legal and Professional Publications, Inc, (NY) p. 183.

12. Gilbert, *Paralegal Summaries: Contracts*, Harcourt Brace Jovanovich Legal and Professional Publications, Inc, (NY) p. xxiii.

13. Uniform Commercial Code (UCC): A body of law governing commercial transactions and business conduct intended to make uniform the law among the various jurisdictions which has been adopted by almost all of the states as of this writing.

14. Uniform Commercial Code § 1-201 – General Definitions.

15. Ex parte-a legal term meaning a communication of only one party to an action. This is contrary to the generally accepted court procedure of having both parties present during a matter involving an instant case. Author's definition.

16. Legaleeze-a term referring to the formal manner in which many legal documents are written. Based upon old English terminology, these words are sometimes difficult for the layman to comprehend. Author's definition.

17. Non-compete: a legal term referring to a contractual agreement whereby either a partner or employee agrees that during the life of the contract or after termination of a relationship, he or she shall not establish a business entity that will conceivably threaten the business or financial status of the former relationship. Author's definition.

18. As of this writing there are heated debates in Washington regarding privacy issues. Advocates for and against the availability of information are constantly influencing the manner in which laws are interpreted by the courts and the legal system. The Fair Credit Reporting Act (FCRA) has been interpreted by the Federal Trade Commission that regulates its enforcement. As these interpretations are ever changing it might be necessary for some form of notice to be issued to the individual who is under investigation as a result of a particular assignment.

19. Authors note: It is extremely important for the investigator to obtain written permission from the attorney or legal counsel responsible for the case before making contact with any individual either covertly or overtly. Ex- parte rules of conduct might impact upon the legal ability for such communication. The investigator is often viewed as an arm, or extension, of the attorney. Communication under the Attorney's Rules of Professional Conduct precludes such communication if the individual is also represented by counsel. It should also be remembered that changing legislation might affect the investigator's ability to perform work that is done sub-rosa. Currently the Gramm-Leach-Bliley interpretation of the Fair Credit Reporting Act precludes a third party investigator from performing an investigation against an employee without first providing notice to that employee that such an investigation is pending.

Part IV

Dealing with Threats and Violence

Chapter 28

Corporate Executive Protection

David Roberts, FIPI

Synopsis

28.1 Introduction

The topic of executive protection in general, perhaps contrary to modern perceptions and concepts, is vast and deserving of significantly more application than is being illustrated in this brief missive.

Suffice to say, and in honing specifics to the still-broad term of corporate executive protection, one is achieving little in terms of minimizing a subsection of the whole, that in itself, could occupy encyclopedic dimensions and takes months of training combined with operational experience to perfect.

The popular public conception of a gun-totting, muscle bound, monosyllabic Neanderthal bodyguard is, in reality, as far removed from fact as the difference between two cans joined by a string as a means of communicating and advanced satellite GPS global communications systems; the former hypothesis being the popular perception, the latter being the reality in terms of the sophistication and skill required by professional exponents of the science to fulfill the objectives successfully.

Regrettably perhaps, this misconception is no more prevalent than in those who would consider themselves qualified to be bodyguards. Naturally, there is a catalog of failures and general negativity to be associated with those who are otherwise underqualified for the role—events surrounding the death of Princess Diana and the Bill Gates pie-throwing incident are two that immediately spring to mind. By the same token, if the task is accomplished properly, one will never know of the successes attributable to the real professionals.

When was the last time one heard of a commercial executive protection team shooting their way down Fifth Avenue in Manhattan protecting the life of their principal? Never! Yet, one would be surprised, not only at the insistence of commercial clients who demand their protection team be armed, but of those so-called protection officers who feel naked when asked to deploy without their phallic comforter attached to their waists!

Outside the sphere of governmental agencies, there are very few countries in the world that will allow the carriage of concealed weapons in public and even fewer to a visiting non-national. Yet, the bodyguard of a certain ilk—and regrettably, far too many in the United States—appears unable to think or function without the ability to carry a firearm when performing in such a capacity.

Indeed, many commercial training establishments purposely direct marketing strategies to firearms training as a priority, rather than treat it as an important, but nevertheless by-product of the greater picture! The result of this anomaly is indeed the attraction of a certain element of individuals into the industry who identify with the glamour and glory to be associated with the fictional characterization of the television bodyguard.

There are numerous manuals in existence that provide the basic theory but, in one of the foremost such publications—*The Executive Protection Bible* by Martha J. Braunig, published by Executive Security International in Colorado—the content section alone, combined with the subsection headings attributed to each of the twenty-seven chapter topics, would be sufficient to create a chapter in its own right and without further qualification!

Thus, and in requesting that the reader appreciate that one can but only scratch the surface in this publication, the topics here have been selected with a view to encouraging all to delve further and deeper than the presented façade.

The development of the techniques of threat assessment and that discipline's application to the commercial world in the form of the planning of an operation are developed more as a thought engendering illustration rather than an all-encompassing and definitive set of instructions.

As with all such disciplines, and especially those formulated from set rules, one must bear in mind the adage: *Rules are made for the blind obedience of fools and the guidance of wise men!*

28.2 Threat Assessment Techniques

A. Introduction

Those who may justly consider themselves as personal protection officers and practicing security professionals will be only too familiar with the fact that it is generally accepted that absolute protection against a determined professional attack is technically impossible.

However, it must be the aim of the corporate protection officer and all others involved in the field of commercial executive protection to minimize the chances of success of any real or contemplated attack by the application of the ever present principles of sound common sense.

Couple this essential attribute with an ongoing and insatiable search for site specific knowledge and self-improvement, with a constant upgrading of skill in respect of every conceivable facet of the security and intelligence gathering industries that exist and evolve, and we now have the formula for identifying the ideal profile for the professional exponent of the science of close personal protection.

It is perhaps disturbing to note, in those who seek to portray an image of knowledgeable professionalism, that in more cases than is circumspect, the provision of specialist security services and like professional facilities succeeds more by default than by design!

The essence of this chapter is to alert the professional protection officer to those elements that are considered essential in conducting a viable threat assessment before the implementation or adoption of personal security measures in the form of planning for such an operation.

No two cases are identical. There is no hard and fast rule that must be adopted in such matters; it is purely the application of flexibility to the following definition of personal security principles.

B. Definition

The provision of executive protection can be defined as *the application of scientifically calculated security principles and procedures to daily life, in order to reduce the chance of assassination, kidnapping, or any other illegal act.*

C. Threat assessment techniques

It is rare for those outside governmental agencies, who are tasked with such a responsibility, to be in a position to produce a comprehensive threat assessment. Often, there is insufficient intelligence commercially available to support an accurate prediction of a potential enemy's course of action.

It therefore falls to designated commercial professionals to make their own assessment of the likely or potential threats applicable to their clients and to the given situation to be encountered. "Living within a sphere of controlled paranoia" should be the mantra by which every personal protection officer should guide and dedicate his or her daily working life.

D. Principles

When making an assessment of any given threat, (real or imagined), the following principles should be applied.

1. The assessment must be clear

In all too many instances it is easy (and effectively, a disservice to the client) to formulate an assessment based on hysteria as opposed to controlled paranoia. It is the protection officer (and the team) who is being rewarded to discuss, contemplate, and implement the appropriate course of action for a principal. To instill, or seek to instill, such paranoia in a commercial client (at the unprofessional risk of substituting commercialism for professionalism) is a self-defeating, self-deprecating, unethical, and unnecessary practice, the effects of which will, sooner rather than later, be identified by the client, who will lose confidence accordingly.

2. The assessment must be logical

If one must advise a principal not to proceed along a given course, the protection officer must be able to quantify and justify the recommendations in a logical fashion. Those professionals responsible for addressing board members and executives of organizations on matters relative to any aspect of security can be sure to be challenged by those individuals seeking to make their own impression on the chairman. It is essential therefore that any such personal and gratuitous advances to be gained by those in commercial competition are not secured at the expense of an ill-prepared security specialist presenting illogical facts.

3. The assessment must be accurate

If the facts as presented cannot be backed up by accurate equations giving rise to the content and context of the assessment, the security specialist will lose credibility and respect.

4. The assessment must be relevant to the individual

When presenting such an assessment, there is little merit in expounding one's knowledge in respect of Middle Eastern terrorist groups when the principal is scheduled to visit South America (unless there is relevance between the Middle East, South America, and the principal concerned.) The principal will be concerned only with the itinerary at that time and generally not welcome a lecture on global terrorist tactics!

E. Methodology

The method of assessing threats encompasses, but is not otherwise restricted to, the following elements.

1. Aim

The most likely form of attack. This factor will rely on both the professional and personal terms of reference of the principal concerned.

- A female who wears fur coats would be ill-advised to proceed dressed as such to a demonstration by the Animal Liberation Front. The example is perhaps ridiculously extreme, but the point is nevertheless quite relevant. In such an instance, and having convinced the female concerned not to wear such a garment, the fact that she may be known—by reputation or profile—to wear such a garment on occasions places her at danger of being the subject of a targeted assault in any event.
- A diplomat who in consequence of political affiliations, has received a number of threats and has tightened security accordingly is more likely to be the subject of a rifle, car bomb, or mail-bomb attack.
- A financial magnate's threat may emanate from competitors and relate to industrial or commercial espionage in the form of electronic eavesdropping, as well as any direct physical threat.

In such an instance, an intellectual or proprietary attack may take many forms and it is the responsibility of the protection officer to contemplate and counter them.

The office or boardroom areas in which a principal operates are wide open to electronic exploitation and compromise and like breaches of security of information. Electronic and manual sweeps should be adopted as an intrinsic and vital part of the general standard operation.

2. Procedures

Where industrial espionage is determined to be a major threat, the corporate security professionals should extend their threat assessment considerations to encompass the disposal of any form of printed materials emanating from the principal's office or home. Indeed, it will not come as any particular revelation to acknowledge that valuable (and potentially compromising) materials are simply recovered from the discarded waste of a targeted individual.

- Who is responsible for the disposal of such in the organization, not just at business premises level, but throughout the chain of disposal, from office to eventual destruction?
- Is the principal concerned with green/recycling tendencies?
- Who sends all waste for disposal intact?
- How many shredders are there in use in the office environment? Are they used properly?

Technically this style of evaluation thinking can only be exhausted by the limits of the imagination and in a like format can be adopted and applied to every potential threat assessment.

It is the definitive responsibility of the commercial protection officer to anticipate the entire gambit of relevant threats to the principal, not only in terms of what may occur in the future but also on a constant time sensitive, minute-by-minute basis. *Practicing the disciplines of executive protection is not a job—it is a way of life!*

3. The most likely place for an attack

- Where and when is the principal most exposed?
- At home?
- At work?
- On route to and from either place?
- On holiday?
- When with family?
- When entertaining guests at public functions?
- Through the weak link of family members?

Again, the list is endless, but in all instances by adopting the adage and practice of controlled paranoia, the professional protection officer will by taking every process through and along a logical plane consider all such potential environmental threats—current, imminent, and logically anticipated—and take the necessary precautions, without reducing the principal to a state of nervous exhaustion! That is the skill to be developed and adhered to at all costs.

4. The most likely time for an attack

Exposure to threat of attack depends on the personal and professional terms of reference of the principal concerned and, as has been tentatively examined above, such timing could relate to the attendance at business meetings, public functions, relaxing with the family, jogging (even with the presence of Secret Service protection officers), opening the mail or indeed, anything that contrary to the very principles of the science of close personal protection has been allowed to become routine!

Anyone who still feels and thinks that a black belt in origami is sufficient training to become a personal protection officer at the level being discussed here—and regrettably, they are in the majority—is asked to appreciate the true intellectual disciplines that form the basic profile of the true professional.

5. The target: the personal protection officer

Discounting, for one moment, the fact that one's principal is the obvious target, consider why the protection officers themselves may also be considered so.

a. Their appointment. The fact that they have been appointed to protect a high profile, high risk principal logically means that the protection officer becomes a legitimate target.

b. Their nationality. Wherever one travels globally, one may be certain of one relevant factor—there will always be someone who, for reasons that stretch the bounds of delusionary mental incapacity (extending through the ideals of sheer fanaticism to political extremism) will associate national origins with their own terroristic or criminally maligned motivations to justify selecting the principal's protection officer as a viable target in the furtherance of their delusions or cause.

c. Their host nation associations. Again, this not only relates to the fact that the protection officer, as a U.S. or European national for instance, may be severely testing the sensitivities of the nationals in the country visited. The principal's own affiliations will automatically be transferred to and leveled at the protection officer, with little or no concern for the fact that the officer's own feelings may (discreetly of course) be at total variance with that of the person they are tasked to protect.

d. Their routine. A veritable killer for protectee and protection officer alike is a routine. There is no merit whatsoever in educating one's principal not to adhere to a routine if once the principal is safely deposited in a secure environment the protection officer falls straight into his or her own system of routine, i.e., always going to the same restaurant at the same time on the same day, always collecting the mail at the same time, always polishing the car on the same day. As disciplinarians (on a self-disciplined basis generally), protection officers are invariably the greatest advocates of adhering to routine. This natural failing must be appreciated and actively contemplated and countered by all protection officers, as much in their own regards as in respect of their clients.

6. Enemy identification

A full understanding and knowledge of the nature and scope of the physical threat is essential. Anyone who is deployed with a principal of global disposition and terms of reference, who for political, economic, or religious reasons is considered a viable terrorist target is recommended to the serious study of this topic.

The following items should be researched at length, particularly for those tasked with protecting a principal of diplomatic status:

- Characteristics of terrorism
- Definition of terrorism
- Acts of terrorism
- Terrorist operating procedures
- Terrorist weaponry

The various aspects of the threat elements need to be understood in context to their relationship to:

- Terrorists
- Criminals
- Insane persons
- Mobs and dissidents

Suffice to say at this juncture that by possessing sufficient knowledge pertaining to the known threat and the number and nature of the terrorist groups active in the country to be visited it is possible to deduce which group, groups, or individuals pose the greatest threat, both to the principal and protection officer alike.

7. Study the enemy

It necessarily follows that having identified the origin of the enemy a detailed study should be conducted. Such a study should incorporate the following topics:

a. Identification of potential attackers. By reference to a variety of sources, in the form of government publications, general research, and through the media of the Internet and a host of applicable databases, it is possible to identify named individuals of a particular group of terrorists, criminals, or dissidents, their aliases, descriptions, the history of their cause, etc.

b. The preferred modus operandi. Terrorist and dissident groups have a tendency to prefer specific methods of attack to develop their cause. Such attacks could range from assassination attempts, kidnapping for ransom, hostage taking for political advancement (as in the case of seeking to achieve the release of incarcerated colleagues etc.), car bombing, mail bombing, inciting mobs to riot etc. Again, the list is capable of exhaustion only by the limits of one's imagination, with due deference to the particular realm of terrorist or criminal activities and capabilities as they relate to the principal.

c. The present capability of the group in relation to a proposed itinerary. By dedicated research and study, relying on established and prescribed sources, it is possible to determine the nature and extent of the threat to oneself and one's principal. One must first understand the nature of the beast, inasmuch as it applies to the dissident group, as well as how that group relates to the principal being provided with protective services. Such research should culminate in the protection officer being able to assess, with cautious and controlled paranoia, precisely when the principal is at greatest risk of exposure to compromise. In other words, contemplate and understand what factors have combined to cause the principal to become a legitimate target.

d. Details of the last activity of the group under review. Clearly, one's researches will conclude with the last known, or latest attack reported by the group under review. From a qualified evaluation of the relevant facts, one can generally determine whether the threat to one's principal is currently relevant and topical and the degree of likelihood of an attack being directed to coincide with the intended visit to the region in question.

e. Territorial research. All advance assessments should incorporate the following combined considerations:

- Geography
- Demographics
- Terrain
- Vehicular selection and mobility
- Condition of roads and the transport systems
- Communication facilities
- Available weaponry in the region
- Regional terrorist, criminal, or dissident modus operandi
- Structural strengths and weaknesses in buildings
- Perimeter and temporary residence security
- Vehicle security and travel arrangements

The list is technically inexhaustible—and should be considered so by all professional practitioners. The moment one discards a train of thought, without following that thought through to conclusion, the first exploitable weak link in the threat assessment chain becomes exposed.

When traveling abroad, identifying and securing the assistance of indigenous professionals whose local knowledge skills should never be overlooked and whose knowledge of cultural nuances and customs may prove invaluable in terms of avoiding any potential for embarrassment or failing in issues pertaining to protocol, should be a priority consideration in the early planning stages.

8. Advance party work and timings

Once an itinerary has been established in the region to be visited, it is always recommended that an advance party should proceed to prepare the way for the visit of the principal. During such initial planning processes, routes, times, and alternatives can be prepared and consolidated into briefing notes for the benefit of the principal's staff in general and the security personnel in particular. Once developed, the principal's protection officer will be in the best possible position to advise the principal and team members on all relevant security matters. It is also the ideal opportunity to relate to and with in-house security personnel at the venues to be visited and to seek supplemental assistance based on their unique local knowledge, for which there is no real substitute.

9. Conclusions

By relying upon an all encompassing evaluation and assessment process, conducted along the lines suggested above, the protection officer (and the protection team) should be in the best possible position to reach a reasoned conclusion regarding the most likely form, time, and location of exposure to compromise for a principal and be able to plan a protection operation designed to obviate or minimize any such potential.

It should now be self-evident that the threat assessment process is not a one-off project at commercial or corporate level. It is not something that can be simply evolved and dismissed—it is a form of mental perpetual motion and in many of today's corporate environments may have to be extended to cater for any number of corporate executives traveling in different directions at the same time, each being exposed to any number of different threats.

Again, I pose the rhetorical question: Does the reader still think that a black-belt in any form of martial art is sufficient to qualify the holder to operate in such a professionally involved and intellectually responsible capacity as a commercial executive protection officer, tasked with the awesome responsibility of protecting the life of another with his or her own?

By the same token, is this truly the natural stomping ground for those who appear to operate by relying upon the size of the weapon strapped to their waist, like some form of misplaced phallus? Emphatically—No! This is the age of the intellectual, the theorist with the application and training to apply such disciplines and skills physically—the professional who is as much at home accessing, acquiring, and thereafter applying specific research and intelligence data from qualified resources through the ever present lap top computer and access to the world wide web, as they are on the shooting-range.

This is a professional who also appreciates that all such items are simply tools to accomplish their tasks, all of which attributes and skills come to naught in the absence of a profound understanding of the profession, an overabundance of common sense, and the skill, expertise, and ability to apply it.

28.3 Planning a Protection Operation

In this section, we seek to develop a case-study scenario to illustrate how the disciplines under review can be put into practice.

A. Close personal protection operations

A close personal protection operation usually relates to an operation contemplated in support of a royalty or diplomatic scenario and invariably is geared to a situation where there is a known or particular threat.

Contending with some justification that the general import of this topic and the principles and disciplines it expounds are of equal value to commercial protection specialists charged with the responsibility of protecting their commercial principal, the content of this section has been designed with such appropriately modified criteria in mind and relates to the planning of a protection operation for the benefit of a corporate executive who has a requirement to be away from his or her normal safe-house environment for a few hours.

In many countries if the visitor is sufficiently important, various governmental and law enforcement agencies will automatically deploy to plan and operate a full protection detail.

There is no logical reason heads of commerce, high profile personalities, or any other deserving and discerning commercial client should not enjoy the same level of protective consideration afforded to those entitled to governmental agency protection should they desire it. Accepting that the commercial protection specialist cannot necessarily rely on the identical resources available to the law enforcement, State Department, or Secret Service agencies, it has been shown and is acknowledged that the commercial specialist can indeed emulate the official capabilities to only a slightly lesser degree of perfection.

Unlike military, police, or other governmental security agency operations, it is rare that the specialist in charge of a commercial team of security protection personnel will be afforded the benefit of a full and definitive threat assessment or evaluation at the commencement of the project.

Invariably, the person responsible for arranging the logistics of such a program for a corporate head is initially more likely to be an administrative executive, whose terms of reference encompass different statistical and geographical requirements, the emphasis being on itinerary, protocol, and timing of meetings and schedules rather than applying any great consideration for security applications.

It is therefore the responsibility of the protection team leader to undertake a full and accurate threat assessment based around the schedule of events prepared by others who may not be specifically security oriented in their planning procedures.

In fairness, it is probably impractical to expect an individual with little appreciation of security needs and dictates to contemplate and provide an effective shield against every eventuality.

B. Planning a close personal protection operation

1. Introduction

The essential considerations when planning a close personal protection operation relate to evolving the criteria necessary to the given circumstances of the project in hand relevant to the principal concerned.

Any plan thus evolved must be formulated to satisfy the predetermined criteria, thereby ensuring that when the plan is incepted all relevant factors have been taken into consideration.

It is suggested that in all planning operations the protection team leader should not rely on mental calculations alone but, in the alternative, should prepare a full and written appreciation document designed to garner the best possible results, all aspects having been evaluated and considered for implementation.

What follows in the section can be utilized as an *aide memoir* for those team leaders whose primary function is to prepare and develop protection programs for their principals.

2. Essential considerations

Any protection team program document must consider and include the following items, all of which form individual and conjoint essential constituent parts. These are listed as follows:

- The aim
- The relevant or distinguishing factors
- The best and most appropriate courses of action available
- The plan

a. The aim. The aim, or what one is tasked to achieve, is the crux of the consideration in the preparation of any appropriate planing program. It must be clear, concise, positive and ideally should include an appreciation of any limitations that appear relevant. Such limitations may refer to the following criteria:

- The protection cover must be discreet.
- Protection cover is only to be provided at given locations or nominated environments.
- The size of the protection team must be kept to a minimum.
- Suitable personnel will not be immediately available and will have to be integrated into the system after initial inception.

b. Relevant or distinguishing factors. Anything that may conceivably affect the smooth running of a personal protection operation is a relevant or distinguishing factor that must be considered. A team leader tasked with such preparation and pre-planning should be sufficiently experienced so as not to deviate into consideration of irrelevant tangents not associated with the project at hand. Every relevant factor contemplated must be so designed to evolve a definitive deduction or a series of deductions and each should be inspired by asking oneself, "What could happen next?"

The majority of operations (even accepting that each operation will by definition be very different in its own nature and scope) follow and incorporate certain relevant features. For example:

- The threat
- The location
    1. Local area
    2. Principal's residence—location
    3. Residence—grounds

4. Principal's office—location
5. Routes to and from the residence and office environment
6. The itinerary or schedule of the designated principal
7. Time and distance
8. Staffing—manpower
9. Liaison with law enforcement and other specialized agencies
10. The principal in question:
    a. Likes and dislikes
    b. Physical condition

- Medical condition
    1. Habits
    2. Marital status and family members and constitution
    3. Leisure time activities
- Logistical considerations:
    1. Principal's temperament
    2. Protection team members' temperament
    3. Refreshment, subsistence and feeding requirements
    4. Selection and implementation of dress codes
    5. Accommodation needs of all team members
    6. Equipment—weapons, bomb detection, and so on
- Weather conditions
- Areas of potential compromise to principal—possible modus operandi:
    1. Nighttime
    2. Day time
    3. Method of attack—weapons, physical, and other
    4. Exposure to incendiary devices
    5. Kidnap potential
    6. Embarrassment factors
- Full assessment and evaluation of tasks to be undertaken
- Conclusions to be deduced from the above essential factor considerations

c. The best and most appropriate course of action available. Having thus considered major essential and relevant factors, and the conclusions to be drawn therefrom, it is now necessary to evaluate the effect that they have on available options.

It will be unlikely in the extreme that an experienced team leader will ever be satisfied with a single course of action. There is seldom an occasion when the deduction processes outlined above will induce the team leader to dismiss wholly any potential option.

An appreciation of the difficulties involved in each option is essential, and prioritizing available options on that evaluation basis is equally intrinsic.

At this juncture, the advantages and disadvantages associated with each option *must* be considered in the following suggested format:

- Stage 1—Single phase operation
- Stage 2—Three phase operation
- Stage 3—Small covert operation

Following the prioritization of the above options, considering and discounting the advantages and disadvantages, the team leader must now select the best course of action to adopt.

It is at this stage that any amplification or enhancement of the selected option should be injected, e.g., route "C" by night in a vehicle would appear to be the most efficient and likely to succeed on the basis that any potential for physical and/or other compromise to the principal will be minimal and the greatest areas of vulnerability are identified.

d. The plan. Having undertaken the above exercise thoroughly, the best course of action will have been evolved and the appreciation of essential consideration involved in the planning of a close personal protection operation will be complete from the perspective of the relevant phase but will continue to be considered and developed on a constant review basis.

It therefore remains to convert the evaluation process into briefing notes for the benefit of conveying to the protection team members.

In such a briefing, the following items must be incorporated:

1. The tasks at hand—i.e., the purpose of the protection assignment
2. The general outline of its proper execution

3. The allocation of specific tasks to designated team members
4. Expansion of those tasks for the respective team members
5. Logistical and timing considerations in general terms
6. Details of the administrative layout and functioning

28.4 Sample Report

What now follows relates to a typical planning and appreciation exercise conducted by a close protection team leader charged with that responsibility on behalf of a principal. This stage can be classified as the pre-advance stage to the implementation of the final advance stage and the preparation of operational orders.

CLOSE PERSONAL PROTECTION OPERATION
PRE-ADVANCE SYNOPSIS
TIME SCALE UTILIZED THROUGHOUT OPERATIONAL PLANNING: 24-Hour Clock.

OBJECTIVE:
1. To protect executive / head of international chemical organization, on the occasion of a short stay / visit to a designated location, with the following limitations:
   a. Security protection team must be low profile

RELEVANT FACTORS:
THREAT:
1. Recent suspected attempt at kidnap of Executive under similar conditions
2. Animal Liberation Front has threatened life
3. No known A.L.F. members in area to be visited
   Deductions:
   a. Due to recent events, the team leader must have the immediate ability to escalate the level of protection if necessary.
   b. Constant collation of intelligence required from Law Enforcement Agencies and local knowledge support personnel as appropriate.

LOCATION:
1. The Executive concerned is staying at a private residence overnight on the 10/11th and the assignment commences and terminates at that venue.

2. The residence sits on its own grounds off the main road with a long uphill carriageway drive leading thereto and therefrom.
3. The perimeter of the grounds are fenced but; any intended infiltrator would have little or no problem in breaching the fence and gaining access.
4. The Residence is a solid brick built construction of Victorian design containing three floors and a basement area.
5. There are situated, at the four corners of the residence, security lights which have passive infrared detectors and will illuminate on any approach during the hours of darkness.
6. There is ample protection for a would-be intruder within the grounds courtesy of the shrubbery and general landscaping.

Deductions:

a. All controls affecting access and egress should be sited at the entrance to the driveway.
b. Perimeter patrols may be required to patrol and protect perimeter fencing.
c. Consider the placement of temporary RF motion detectors at vulnerable perimeter points to supplement personnel deployment.
d. Maximum use should be made of all external lighting facilities.
e. The interior of the residence is conducive to implementation of normal close protection measures, should such prove necessary.

ITINERARY:
1. Executive arrives at 19.00 hrs on the 10th and departs 09.30 hrs on the 11th.
2. The Executive will not be leaving the residence during the hours of darkness.
3. There are seven days available to plan and implement the security of the residence.

Deductions:

a. Any security measure adopted MUST be in place prior to dusk.
b. Advance survey and sweep of the Residence can be affected during the daylight hours on the 10th.

PRINCIPAL-CONSIDERATIONS:

1. The Executive dislikes being escorted by security personnel whilst within a building but requires eye contact with security team leader.

2. The Executive does not smoke and does not like those within his proximity to smoke.

Deductions:

a. Selections of suitable positions within property to ensure Executive's movements are covered.
b. Ensure all rooms in respect of which he will require access are covered externally and covered at all times whilst the Executive is within.
c. No security protection team member is to smoke in the view and/or vicinity of the Executive.

OTHER GUESTS & STAFF:

1. There are four members of live-in residential personnel.

2. The Executive will be entertained for dinner by his host and the host's wife and his Secretary will be present.

Deductions:

a. The residential staff will have to be vetted and briefed.
b. The residential staff will be utilized as added protection for the occupants within.
c. Need to establish the time of arrival of the secretary and the vehicle/vehicle driver allocated for the purpose.

LOGISTICS:

1. The entire operation must be considered as a self-contained operation for a minimum period of 24 hours.

Deductions:

a. Brief administrative department on requirements as soon as possible. All essentials to be moved into place prior to the arrival of the Executive. Advance party to deploy 48 hours ahead of Principal, all advance research and contact resources concluded in the four day period prior.

POTENTIAL FOR COMPROMISE:

1. A.L.F. activities unknown in location. Threat—low category. Likely potential compromise to be during the hours of darkness.

2. Probable route to access building by A.L.F. relies of rear approach, but landscaping will defeat their potential for rapid withdrawal.

3. Road approach to Residence best for rapid departure but will not assist any covert operational intentions of the A.L.F.

Deductions:

a. Physical attack and compromise—unlikely but possible.
b. Likeliest method of attack relates to criminal damage and/ or arson attempt.
c. Details of emergency response agencies required.
d. Grounds require sufficient manpower to provide sterile zoning around residence.
e. Consider alerting the local Law Enforcement agencies to provide additional external security presence/patrols.

ASSESSMENT OF ASSIGNMENTS:

TASK: PERSONNEL REQUIREMENTS:

1. Secure Residence:—Four plus team leader.
2. Secure Grounds:—Four team members.
3. Outer Cordon:—Two local Law Enforcement.

Deductions:

a. The personnel based externally will have to be rotated frequently. Utilizing all security team Personnel, rotation should be accompanied with relative ease—internally and externally.
b. Local Law Enforcement may not have sufficient personnel to assist. Must consider utilizing additional security personnel or private and trusted security company.

CONCLUSIONS:

1. There is no evidence to suggest that any threat is current and/or real. However, preparedness for any emergency *must* be the order of the day.

2. Minimum personnel requirement—Eight security team officers and team leader.

TEAM LEADER—AVAILABLE COURSES OF ACTION:

COURSE #1:

To employ the entire security team within the Residence and Grounds.

Advantages:

a. Entire team immediately available to respond to emergency.
b. Administration of personnel and shift rotation easier to control.

Disadvantages:

a. Executive requires low-level protection—it will be difficult to accommodate full security team in situ.
b. No garaging facilities for all vehicles.

COURSE #2:

To employ working teams only in situ, accommodating other personnel in nearby Hotel.

Advantages:

a. Low Level protection stipulation easier to achieve.

Disadvantages:

a. Division of operational and administrative functioning.

SELECTION OF BEST PLAN OF ACTION:

The adoption of COURSE #2 is preferred as it achieves the objectives with due consideration for limitations imposed.

PLAN OBJECTIVE:

To provide Executive Principal with low-level protection during the scheduled visit to the designated residence.

EXECUTION:

a. General outline of threat assessment

Detailing of protection team members

- Team Allocation
- Assignments
- Rotations etc.

28.5 Conclusions

The above evaluation report should be prepared by an experienced security consultant or designated protection team leader. The format has been incredibly simplified for ease of comprehension and to illustrate the basic points sought to be conveyed. The technicalities and requirements will increase many times over with the introduction of any additional facets. This format can be enhanced, decreased, and/or manipulated to cater for all protection detail projects, regardless of their size or complexity. The absence of such pre-planning techniques will introduce elements of difficulty into any given project, weakening the strategy and professional effects of the desired achievement, which will ultimately reflect detrimentally on the person designated as the security team leader. Adhering to the suggested format eliminates the potential for failure at the initial planning stage and bodes extremely well to ensure the success of any close personal protection operation.

Chapter 29

Intelligence and the Risk Assessment Process

Sal Lifrieri

Synopsis

29.1 Introduction

Over the past few years we have heard the terms "contingency planning" and "crisis and consequence management" used more frequently. Today, many companies are actively developing strategies to prepare for unplanned events that are both natural and man-made. Security managers need to ensure that planning efforts include intelligence planning and operations components. Further, they must ensure that their input includes a global perspective. Areas that need to be examined when applying intelligence principles to crisis management are:

- Terrorists and terrorist activity
- The effect of natural disasters
- Methods for intelligence gathering
- Identification of trends and "patters"
- Risk assessments

29.2 Defining Terrorists and Terrorist Activity

People working in intelligence operations and emergency management have all seen international terrorist attacks and are well aware of the stereotypical international terrorist, such as Saddam Hussein and Osama Bin Laden. The areas that need closer examination are domestic terrorism and domestic attacks. State sponsored, organized terrorism has the same effect on your organization as a disgruntled employee who, in some cases, has a better capability, opportunity, and motive to harm your organization.

A. Who is a terrorist?

Terrorism does not have to be state sponsored or international in nature. Regrettably, this how the media often portrays it. It could very well be a small group or even one man or one woman. Let's examine terrorist groups more closely.

Today we see small tightly knit organized domestic groups evolving into terrorist cells. Small group of friends, typically from four to six people, conspire and collaborate to perform terrorist acts. It is nearly impossible to identify these groups. Traditional investigative methods are ineffective. Infiltrating the group with an undercover agent is virtually impossible. It is virtually impossible to intercept telephone calls and develop audio intelligence because it is so difficult to identify the target. Examination of backing record (what is this?) falls into the same category as telephone and audio intelligence. If no one in the group is identified, then how can we monitor and ultimately disband these units? A recent example of this occurred in the New York City area. A small group of men decided to arm themselves with explosive devices and detonate the bombs and themselves at different train stations during the morning rush hour. This group was willing to die for their cause, taking with them many innocent victims. Fortunately one of the participants decided that he was not going to perform this act and left the group. He then went to the local police and reported the planned attack. After securing search warrants, the police were able to foil the attack. This is a perfect example of a terrorist group that could have caused great damage if not for one of its members alerting the police department. Traditional methods of investigation would not have identified this group or shown it to be operational. What methods can we use to identify this type of group, effectively investigate them, and eliminate them as a potential threat? As of today, the answer is none. We must rely on individuals to become driven by conscience or fear, a highly unsettling fact for security managers.

By contrast, patriot and militia groups operate in a truly covert fashion. They are small, well organized, with limited membership and a simple but effective organization structure. While this is true for the vast majority of such organizations, it does not apply to all. Knowledge of their operational strategies is highly valuable. As noted before, they typically operate covertly. They have repeatedly demonstrated the ability to infiltrate organizations, often gaining employment at an identified target. They are incredibly patient, often willing to wait years, if necessary, to complete their mission. Finally, they have the determination and ability to conduct extensive surveillance operations. It is well known that Timothy McVeigh spent months conducting surveillance of the Murrah Federal Office Building in Oklahoma City. What this demonstrates is that all these groups are mission driven and far better organized than most domestic security operations.

B. Natural disasters

When analyzing potential crisis situations, we must keep in mind that not only criminal events and terrorism can be costly. Natural disasters are just as important a consideration in crisis management and regrettably are overlooked when we examine potential threats. We must realize that certain events can be just as devastating as a terrorist attack. A perfect example of this is a water main break that occurs in front of your building. The cause of the break is insignificant at this point, whether it was blown up by a terrorist group or damaged from age. The inability to get water into your building can have a domino effect, causing other systems to fail. Events in a natural disaster could very well occur like this. The water main breaks in front of your building. The first possible impact is that access to your facility needs to be rerouted to another door. This could necessitate a bypass of your access control systems, package handling and screening, and even parking control. Once inside the facility, fire suppression systems may be compromised. Next, air-handling systems, especially those that need chilled water, could fail. This results in a loss of air conditioning. The lack of air conditioning then causes critical computer systems such as servers and routers to overheat. Overheating of computer systems causes disruptions to LAN/WAN operations, telephone systems, and voice mail. While the above example is a true worst case scenario, fortunately many organizations have basic redundancies built into their operations. But the point is clear: natural disasters can be as costly as terrorist events to an organization.

29.3 Approaches to Intelligence Gathering

The first rule to follow in intelligence gathering is simple: Apply the "box" rule. Almost all approaches are derived from "inside the box." How does the box rule apply? Here is an example. When we assess the security of a facility, we tend to look from the *inside* of the building. We train ourselves to look at the six sides surrounding us: the four walls, the ceiling, and the floor. We secure windows and doors, add drop ceilings, and install detectors, alarms, cameras, and so on. We develop a sense of security from inside. Rarely, if ever, do we look *outside* the box.

Yet how many of us have gone outside our building and observed it from across the street? Our entire perspective changes when we view it from that perspective. It is possible that while walking around outside their facilities people notice things that probably were not seen previously or discover conditions they didn't know existed.

How many building owners or tenants use a checklist to ensure that security personnel are examining building perimeters? When are these examinations conducted? Ideally they should be conducted at different hours of the day, during both daylight and evening hours. Examples of issues to be observed are:

- What lights are broken, missing or burned out?
- Are trash receptacles located in areas that could conceal someone?
- What doors that are opened during the day remain open at night?
- Is the parking area well lit? Is it secured? Are gates locked?
- What patterns become obvious from these examinations?

Rarely do we have enough resources to identify facilities threats. Budget constraints make it difficult, if not impossible, to perform covert, undercover operations. These types of investigations are better left to the FBI or local law enforcement. As with most security operations a cost-benefit analysis should be done to see if the proposed expenditures are justified. We are already fighting an uphill battle trying to get management to understand that security operations do not cost companies but rather save money. It becomes nearly impossible to justify the need for security and protection resources when an anticipated threat was never discovered.

When a threat is identified, however, the second part of the problem becomes how to use manpower effectively to evaluate the threat. Many corporate managers feel that this activity is better left to law enforcement, which presumably has sufficient resources to deal with these issues. In reality, this is not always the case. Many law enforcement departments have neither the resources nor the capability to effectively examine threats as thoroughly as you may feel is needed. It is therefore important for building owners and tenants to become self-sufficient through proper training.

Training options available for this purpose include narrative analysis, voice stress analysis, psychological profiling, and behavioral analysis. Unless your firm is located in a large city, existing local law enforcement organizations will probably not have personnel trained in these disciplines.

Restraints on the dissemination of information can also present a problem. Comical, and most often stressing, are the reactions encountered when reviewing information. Frequently we are told that certain information cannot be discussed with us. The reasons are many, the validity always measurable. Sometimes we are told that "Due to national security reasons we cannot divulge that information" or "Due to corporate security policy we cannot release those details." While many times this is true and accurate, most often the real meaning needs to be translated into English. "I can't tell you" translates into two definitive answers. The first is, "I have no clue or don't understand, so in order not to look uninformed, I can't tell you for security reasons." When we break down this answer, we realize that it is based on a half-truth. First, the person does not actually know or possess the desired information. Second, the response translates into power for the speaker: "I have the answer but want to tell the boss the secret first, so I look intelligent." It becomes that person's secret—giving him or her the presumption of power.

Fortunately the trend is gradually changing, with the establishment of working groups for this purpose. Law enforcement organizations are now actively working with private sector business and community groups for the analysis and dissemination of information relating to security.

Three specific approaches to intelligence gathering are available: the crystal ball approach, proactive approach, and reactive approach. Let's examine each in detail.

A. The crystal ball approach

This approach for intelligence gathering involves becoming more aware of your surroundings and events going on around the world. What type of information should you be seeking? The methodology is a critical element.

- Determine how the event, bombing or shooting occurred; this is more important that who carried out the action.
- Determine if a remote control activation device may have been used.
- Determine if the materials were mailed or shipped.
- Determine if tampering was performed on any motor vehicles.
- Determine if any hoax phone calls were made.
- Determine if the company or target of the act had a plan to deal with the event.
- Determine what the effect would be to you or your organization if such a event occurred.
- Determine if you are properly prepared for such an occurrence.
- Review emergency plans, determine if they are up to date, and fix them if needed.

As for resources to perform this intelligence gathering function, it is not necessary to have an organized intelligence operation; for example, articles can be clipped from newspapers and the information organized into a database.

- Be aware of the surroundings.

- Be open and receptive to the information gathered from various sources.
- Encourage staff to read newspapers, if possible from other areas in addition to local papers.
- Encourage staff to analyze the information, develop potential scenarios, and discuss their potential impact to the organization.
- Consider discussing potential threats with technical professionals, such as engineers; these people understand systems and processes and could be an excellent resource. Ask them what they would do if they were to planning attack the building.

Another aspect of the crystal ball approach is to understand how certain world events might effect the organization.

- Does the company manufacture, serve as a middleman, or use products or services that are involved in conflicts elsewhere in the world?
- Is the CEO of your organization a member of a certain ethnic group whose homeland regularly has to deal with major fighting or international conflict?

Answers to the preceding questions are a great starting point for intelligence operations.

B. The proactive approach

To be proactive, security and intelligence professionals must be willing to "get out in front of it." This term supports the crystal ball approach process very nicely, since information obtained at this level encourages a proactive stance. Once a problem area has been identified, prepare a detailed plan to address it. Ensure that the plan is in place before the event occurs, as this will alleviate panic. Not having a plan, and trying to deal with a major situation as it occurs, is the modern definition of panic.

Is it possible to over-prepare and subsequently have too many plans? The answer is no! By instituting a planning process, it is possible to identify business and operational needs and the critical personnel necessary to deal with defined emergencies. It is during these planning sessions that meetings can be scheduled with representatives from law enforcement, fire and emergency medical services, and critical infrastructure operations personnel from utility companies. The time to meet these professionals for the first time is *not* at the scene of an emergency, when you need assistance. Personal relationships are essential and go a long way in crisis management.

A key factor in the proactive approach is remembering to get "out of the box" with respect to planning. Use what you've learned and be aware of your surroundings. Your plan should not be limited to what can happen to your facility. Consider also what can happen next door or in the neighborhood. In military parlance this is known as *collateral damage*. If a company or facility next door to you is a target, you are also at risk. Recent examples include abortion clinic bombings and chemical plant fires. A fire or a bomb affecting an adjacent building could cause structural damage to your facility. Suppose a major chemical plant down the street from your facility becomes engulfed in fire. Because of the chemicals emitted a large area including your building could be forced to evacuate. The problem could grow exponentially if the affected site is closed for a prolonged period of time. In either situation you would probably not have received notice of a real or perceived threat and probably would not have gathered any intelligence suggesting a possible problem.

Planning that involves getting "outside the box" would have revealed the potential for this occurrence. A tested and documented contingency plan would make maintaining operations easier. It is important to recognize that bombings and similar acts like this can and do occur. So plan for the ability to manage your operations either at your local site or at an offsite facility.

When examining the potential situations that can occur, the key point to remember is *"What effect does this have on my company?"*

Being proactive raises the collective consciousness of your staff and, more importantly, your organization. The process by its very nature identifies shortfalls and needs. In addition, and probably most importantly, it identifies potential liabilities that are often never realized or addressed.

The following outlines the process for effective crisis management planning:

1. Identify the crisis or contingency for which a strategy must be devised.

2. Convene small group planning sessions to identify who and what needs to be included in the plan.
3. Invite all identified parties to a planning meeting. Ask each individual the following questions.
   - What can each person provide?
   - What functions can each person perform?
   - What actions have they been asked to perform in the past that were unrealistic?
   - What functions have team members never been asked to do?
   - What suggestions can they offer?
4. Compile and analyze the information for use in developing a draft plan.
5. Conduct subsequent meetings to review the plan documentation.
6. Test the plan, initially using a tabletop format.
7. Critique the exercise results and identify the lessons learned.
8. Rewrite plan documentation that needs to be updated.
9. Conduct a follow-up exercise (full-scale exercise if possible).
10. Perform a follow-up critique and analyze lessons learned.
11. Update plan documentation and issue a final version of the plan.
12. Publish and distribute the plan and have key personal initial the document. If plans are to remain effective, they must not be left on the shelf. Periodic updates are essential; be sure to update relevant resources, phone contact lists, etc., to reflect new information. All too often plans are activated but are virtually useless because critical data, such as contact names or locations, are no longer valid. This often occurs during changes in a company's administration.

Another key ingredient in the proactive approach is the identification of "critical personnel." This activity is probably one of the most challenging and important you will face in the planning process. Those of us who have attempted to issue credentials for a special event are aware of the potential security issues. Everyone is a "special person" who needs unlimited access. Egos are usually quite inflated when attempting to control access to an event. How many of us have been involved with security at events where we were forced to issue as many VIP passes as regular passes? When developing emergency plans, credentials are a critical and often overlooked step in the planning process. When credentials are properly assigned and the staff is trained in their responsibilities the emergency response will run much smoother, largely because the correct people have responded to the incident and are functioning in their assigned roles.

When identifying critical emergency response personnel it is important to ensure that the correct people needed to deal with specific issues are represented on site. While CEOs feels they are critical to their organization's survival—and quite often they are—it is just as important that experts in specific activities, such as communications systems and networks, are available. If your CEO can't operate a VCR, for example, it would not be advisable for that person to assume responsibility for managing the network or other critical assets in a crisis.

Don't overlook other company staff, who are just as important, but may be overlooked, such as the housekeeping staff. For example, suppose the company is faced with an extended disruption or outage and has limited staff available. Who is going to empty the trashcans? Who will clean the restrooms and replenish toilet paper?

Another issue to address when identifying critical personnel is the availability of staff. Often, during the selection process, we incorrectly assume that a large number of staff will be available to work following a crisis. While most employees are probably loyal, certain instances may cause them to think twice about coming to work. During natural events like severe weather and snowstorms, it is possible that many will choose to remain at home and not brave the elements. This is especially true during times of great personal danger. For example, suppose your organization receives a letter allegedly containing anthrax or some biological agent. Faced with that kind of situation, can you be certain that all of your employees will show up for work? *The key point here is that proper planning needs to include a heavy dose of reality.*

Finally, make sure that contact lists of critical staff are regularly updated. It is also good policy to have copies of the list stored in off-site locations for easy reference. If contact information is maintained on devices such as Palm Pilots, Blackberrys, or other similar devices, be sure to use the security features and password protect the data. Other options can include copying the information to a CD and storing it in a safe location. When attempting to contact emergency team members in a crisis, it may be appropriate to use an automated emergency notification system. Most of these are Web-based and can be implemented either on company premises or at an alternate location, thus creating a "virtual" emergency notification capability.

C. The reactive approach

As the name implies, the reactive approach process entails responding to the scene or the crisis after it has occurred. Many of these situations could involve your facility, and a well-planned and orchestrated response there is needed.

1. Off-site response

Off-site emergencies can affect your operation; recall the chemical plant example. It is critical that you or your designee report to the command post at the disaster scene and attempt to gain accurate, firsthand information as quickly as possible. In situations like this, public information officers will often be available, getting the messages out to various distribution channels. By reporting to the scene, you can often obtain firsthand intelligence about the situation as well as potential resources to assist you.

If the crisis is likely to be prolonged it is also recommended that you establish and maintain a presence at the public information officer's command post, preferably equipped with communications support. Two-ways are preferable to cellular phones, as the demand for cellular service could overwhelm the service providers, rendering the service virtually unusable.

At a large-scale crisis response and recovery operation, local mobile phone service providers and equipment suppliers may install portable cell sites and deliver additional handsets to support the demand for increased calling capacity. Typically in such events, emergency personnel get priority access to wireless services

2. Media strategy

A very important community to address in both proactive and reactive modes is the media. An effective media management strategy and program can make an enormous difference in how a crisis is perceived, especially by the general public, clients, law enforcement, regulatory bodies, and governmental agencies. Clearly the strategy needs to incorporate activities prior to a crisis (proactive) and after it has occurred (reactive). Effective balancing of the activities in each area will ensure that the media becomes a partner, not an adversary.

Two issues relating to a media strategy need to be examined: the use of lawyers and the creation and use of pre-defined messages in response to emergency events.

The use of lawyers

This option is open to debate. Lawyers will almost always advise saying as little as possible as this tactic will make it easier to defend the company or organization from litigation. While this approach certainly has merit, especially if the situation is potentially damaging to the firm's reputation, it is also just as important to take positive steps such as releasing statements to the press as well as key clients, investors, financial institutions, and others. It is now widely accepted that a proactive release of information will help improve how the media perceives and subsequently handles an incident, and this can potentially reduce the number of lawsuits. It is important to realize that companies can always be candidates for some sort of litigation, no matter what products or services are offered. If an event, regardless of its severity, is handled with tact, honesty, diplomacy, and forthrightness, a potentially negative situation can be turned into a positive one. One effective technique is to enlist the company CEO or other high-ranking official as the company spokesperson. This will not work, however, if the spokesperson is not properly trained to deal with the media and other similar organizations.

Another important strategy where legal assistance may be useful is to set up a system to help the community cope with fallout from the incident. Investments made at this time could reduce the likelihood of lawsuits, particularly if the organization is viewed as taking a leadership position despite its own difficulties.

These suggested approaches can demonstrate that the company responded appropriately, and even may have sacrificed its own earnings and profitability, while trying to address the situation.

Predefined press materials

Often in law enforcement, the press is kept at a distance. In crisis management and business continuity planning, the press needs to be factored into the planning process. Assuming various press materials have been developed, custom tailor them to the situation at hand and provide them to the press as often as realistically possible. The media can help get your positive message out to the public—or it can portray your firm as insensitive, uncaring, and irresponsible. The choice is yours.

Most medium to large organizations should have someone assigned as the media liaison, especially during a crisis. Ideally, someone with a press background can be invaluable to the firm, but it's not mandatory. Prior experience with the media is important in helping properly to position the message, deliver it at opportune times, respond promptly to rumors, and actively "court" the media. This last issue is especially important when trying to deal with a serious, and potentially escalating, situation.

If your firm does not have a dedicated press officer, consider working with a public relations firm that has experience dealing with crisis situations. It may even be worthwhile to hire such a firm to train two or more employees as company spokespersons, one of which ought to be a company executive who can speak on behalf of the entire organization.

When preparing materials for the media, make sure the content is reviewed for legal accuracy, human resource issues, and other technical/operational issues. The statements should include basic information with blanks that can be filled in with event details, dates, times, and locations. The ability to prepare statements in real-time will be needed in a crisis. Key points for dealing with the media include the following:

- Who is the public information officer? Who supports that individual? Who backs that person up if he or she is unavailable?
- Who will be assigned to send and receive fax messages and answer telephones?
- Who will be assigned as runners, in case communications services are disrupted?
- Ensure that a work area is set aside for the media. If possible, make arrangements for communications and workspaces.

What is most important is that the media perceive that they are welcome.

- Who is designated as the primary company spokesperson? In the absence of this individual, who will coordinate with the media?
- Determine as quickly as possible what the message(s) will be to the media.
- Define key points that must be included in the press statement. These same points must be reflected in any comments made by a company spokesperson.
- Make sure that employees know in advance who the company spokesperson is. Reporters will seek out employees for their comments, which could be devastating if they are not trained on how to deal with the media. The "one-person, one message" rule should apply. Remember that the press will find their story regardless of whom they contact.

Other activities that must be addressed in connection with emergency communications operations include the following:

- Communicate with your employees, customers, vendors, investors, financial institutions, and others. If regular phone service and even cellular phone service are unavailable, use the media to disseminate information to these individuals and organizations by radio and/or television. Employees should be know that in an emergency they should tune to a specific channel or radio station to listen for instructions. If phone systems are working and available, configure emergency announcements on voice mail systems, with a local or toll-free number for convenient access. Local radio or cable stations are usually ready to assist. Use them in the same way as schools during snow emergencies, e.g., to announce school closings.
- Establish a public information officer's command post and use this to support the media. If possible, try to establish this facility near the main command center—for movement of messages—but try to keep it separate from that facility. This

provides better media management and minimizes the chance that reporters will invite themselves into your command center, which could disrupt operations.

- If an outside contractor is used to take photographs of the event, ensure that you maintain control of both the photographs and the negatives. If possible, develop the film internally. This will ensure that no unauthorized copies of photographs are released.
- Consider implementing an emergency notification system, which distributed pre-recorded messages to various individuals such as emergency team members and employees in general and to external agencies such as police and fire departments.

D. Vendor management

Another important issue from both proactive and reactive perspectives is vendor management. Make sure you have an accurate, up-to-date vendor list. During the planning process be sure to identify what your short- and long-term needs will be and have primary and alternate vendors that can support these requirements. Depending on the nature and severity of the crisis, obvious necessities include water and food supplies. Private water companies can provide potable drinking water. If necessary, arrange with portable toilet companies for portable toilets and hand washing stations. This equipment is rarely ordered and should really be a priority. Camping goods companies can supply "heater" meals and other items similar to military MREs (meals ready to eat). Work out agreements with suppliers in advance—before it's too late. Arrange in advance for storage areas for large-scale items. It's a good idea to establish preset spending limits for emergency team members and have credit lines pre-approved so that items can be purchased. Have purchase orders available and ready to use. Ensure access to supplies of cash, especially if ATMs are unavailable.

E. Proactive approaches and data-gathering intelligence from communications

A great source of intelligence data can be acquired from calls, letters, notes, and e-mails received by most organizations. While not every piece of mail should be considered a crucial piece of evidence, it is important to remember that it is a source. An effective technique is to allow the staff that handles the mail to make the decision. Since they handle mail all day, they have a very good idea as to what is normal and what is abnormal. By empowering them to screen the mail you have given them a task that they will be happy to perform, and by doing so they will provide a service that does not come out of your budget. When an item is brought to your attention, it is important to document a number of issues. The following is a worksheet to document and record the information necessary to track and identify potential problems.

29.4 Threat Assessment Worksheet

The following worksheet provides insight into the many issues that need to be addressed when conducting a threat assessment.

What type of threat occurred?
What method of action/assault did the person say he/she would use?
What time did he/she say the even would occur?
Where was the event going to occur?
Will it occur on a specific floor, in a specific office?
What police official took the threat report? Record the official's name.
What detective has been assigned to the case?
What gangs are operating in the area?
What have these organizations done in the past that may affect your operations?

How was the threat received? If by telephone

- What is number of the phone that received that threat?
- Where is that phone located?
- What information is available about the caller?
- Did the person give his or her name? (Ask for a name; it just may be provided.)
- Was the calling number identified via the Caller ID feature?
- What sex was the caller?
- What is caller's approximate age?
- What is the caller's ethnic background?
- What distinctive oral communication patterns were detected?
- Did the caller speak clearly?
- Did the caller have an accent?
- Did the caller appear to be on drugs?

Did the caller use profanity?

If the person making a threat walked into a public area of the company
- When did this occur?
- Where did the person enter the building?
- How did the person look?
- How was he/she dressed?
- Was the person under the influence of any controlled substance?
- Did the person have any tattoos or scars?
- What were the person's eye and hair color?
- What was the approximate height and weight?
- What is the person's address?

If the threat was received in the mail
- To whom is the threat addressed?
- What is the return address?
- What type of postage was used, e.g., a stamp or metered mail?
- What visual markings on the envelope could help determine its point of origin?

If the threat came via electronic mail
- What is the destination address?
- What is the sending address?
- What information can be gleaned from any header data?
- What was the actual message?
- How was it written?
- Was the writer of foreign origin?
- What foreign words were in the text?
- What word patterns can be identified?

If motor vehicles were involved
- What was the license plate number?
- What was the state?
- Provide the vehicle's color, make, model and year
- To whom does the vehicle belong?
- What markings could be identified, e.g., damage from previous accidents, different color paint?

What information is currently available that can help identify future threats?

Who is at risk, and what is that person's position in the company or organization?
Have they received threats in the past?
If so when was that threat received, and at what time?
Who recorded the information about the received threat?
Has the case been investigated?
What is the current status of that case?
What photos or additional information are on file?

The most important activity when performing a threat assessment is to gather as much information as possible. Even the most seemingly unimportant piece of information may prove invaluable later.

29.5 Trend Analysis Worksheet

Among the most important intelligence techniques are the identification of trends and analysis of patterns. The following worksheet provides guidance on trend analysis.

Attack Strategy
What is the name of the group that performed the attack?
What kind of presence does the group have in the area?
Historical data on the group:
- When was the group started?
- Where was it formed?
- What were the past attack scenarios?
- What key dates are associated with the group(s)?

What preferences does the group exhibit, particularly with respect to ethnic or religious groups?
What top officials in your company fit this profile?
How was the attack planned?
What period of surveillance was used?
What was the level of expertise with respect to performing the act?
What outside help, if any, was used?
What methods did the group use to obtain usable operational intelligence?
What type of device was used? Examples: bomb, chemical agent, biological agent, gun or fire
What secondary device was used? Examples: control devices, pressure sensitive switches

Analyze information from the threat assessment worksheet

After gathering information using the threat assessment worksheet review and examine the information. Some statistical analysis must be performed to identify patterns that might be developing.

29.6 Risk Assessment

Broken down into its component parts, risk assessments are valuable tools for security managers. Properly performed they can be used to justify purchase orders as well as identify areas for improvement. The three components of a risk assessment are:

- Capability and intent
- Threat and vulnerability
- Risk and capabilities

A. Capability and intent

Capability is defined as a person or group's ability to perform a desired act. The question to ask is whether the person or group can actually do what it claims it can do. Does the person/group have the means or technology to carry out the threat? *Intent is defined as a person or target group exhibiting the desire to perform the act.* Does the person/group have a history of performing such acts? For example, determine if they have acquired details needed to assess the target locations, and if they have obtained funding.

B. Threat and vulnerability

The potential damage caused by a threat is directly related to the vulnerability exhibited by your organization. *Vulnerability is defined as a site's potential inability to defend or sustain itself against anticipated threats.* Once a threat potential is identified it is necessary to compare the threat against known vulnerabilities. This analysis defines the potential risk.

C. Risk versus capability

Next, compare the identified risk against your existing capabilities. *Capability in this sense is defined as an individual's or firm's potential to defend itself from and respond effectively to a threat with available resources.* The capabilities defined here are your organization's assets and capabilities and not the capabilities described earlier regarding perpetrators. Matching the risks against your current capabilities identifies your needs. This process will outline the threat, the groups, vulnerabilities, and what is needed to deal with the threats. Although all your needs may not be met immediately, you will have a very good starting point in developing effective ways to minimize your risk.

D. Risk assessment worksheet

Facilities Assessment

Provide detail on the target location.
What is the total square footage?
How many floors exist, including underground levels?
How many parking levels exist?
How many occupants are in the building?
What is the building's construction? Different materials will exhibit different vulnerabilities.

Vehicle Access

What parking facilities are available?
Does the facility have underground parking?
Is it open to the public or is it restricted to employees only?
Are employee parking spaces identified with markings, or are all spaces available?
What access control systems are used for entering the parking facility?
Does the access control system grant public access to any part of the facility, such as the lobby?
What time period, if any, does the public have access?

Mail Service

How is incoming mail screened?
Are x-ray facilities available?
Who controls, monitors and tests these systems?
What training is provided to mail handlers to look for suspicious packages?

HVAC Systems

Where are air vents located?
Are they elevated or located at ground level?
What kind of air filtration system is used?
Does it have emergency shutdown and reversing capabilities?
Does the security staff know locations of air intakes?
Who manages the HVAC system?
What type of system manages overall HVAC operations?
Has the system ever been compromised or disrupted?
What provisions are in place to ensure uninterrupted operation of HVAC systems?
Assuming HVAC uses water chillers, how much water is available in an emergency?

Telecommunications

Where do telecom cables enter the building?
What kinds of cables enter the building? How many are copper, fiber?
How is service delivered to the building, e.g., a direct feed from the central office or via an intermediate switch?
How secure is the cable demarcation point?
Who has access to the demark area?
How is power delivered to communications systems?

Power Systems

What backup power supplies are in place?
Where are they located?
What sources of fuel are used? What alternate suppliers are available?
How secure are fuel storage areas?
How often are fuel levels checked?
How often are backup generators tested?
What power grid serves the building?
How many feeders can be disabled before your facility is affected?
Are there intrusion detection devices on your electrical panels?
What critical areas will need to be serviced by generator power?
Are backup facilities capable of exceeding emergency requirements?

Food and Water Supplies

What emergency water supplies are available? For how many days? For how many people?

What emergency food supplies are available? For how many days? For how many people?

What emergency toilet facilities are available? For how many days? For how many people?

First Aid

Where are first aid suppliers located?

Where is a defibrillator located? Who is trained to use it?

When were they last examined and updated?

Who is trained in first aid?

Who is trained in CPR?

Who is trained in emergency medical support?

What medical support is available?

What nursing support is available?

What facilities are available for triage?

What is the maximum number of people that can be supported?

Chapter 30

Background Investigations

Jay L. Groob

Synopsis

30.1 Introduction

The most fundamental element in all corporate investigations, as in virtually all criminal and civil cases, is centered on background investigations. This chapter will provide an overview of the different levels of background investigations, the complexities and pitfalls of conducting international background investigations, the laws pertaining to gathering and dissemination of personal data, and the necessity for providing adequate disclaimer to the end user.

When beginning the background investigation process, it is not necessary to expend the same level of resources on a mid- to lower-level employee as for the potential executive. Any applicant being considered for a position of trust, who will be a key holder, or who has been legally mandated to authorize a background check as a condition of employment, will definitely require close scrutiny.

Employers conduct background checks on potential and current employees for a number of reasons, the most important being to avoid negligent hiring lawsuits. **An employer can be held financially and criminally liable if an employee's actions result in harm or damage to another.** Employers lose 72 percent of all negligent hiring lawsuits, with the average jury award in excess of $1 million. Workplace theft costs employers in excess of $400 billion annually, with 30 percent of all business failures attributed to employee theft. As many as 40 percent of job applications and resumes contain misrepresentations in the areas of employment and academic history. Add to these statistics the fallout from a multitude of current events such as 9/11 and the Enron scandal and it is no wonder that employers are requiring more indepth background investigations for their potential hires. Most states require criminal background checks for anyone working with children, the elderly, or the disabled.

It would seem that with the proliferation of Internet accessible databases conducting a background check would be a relatively simple matter, involving only accessing a reputable source to verify information provided by the employee. However, an Internet database inquiry is only the first step towards a comprehensive background check. Recent federal legislation has dramatically increased the strictures on obtaining and disseminating personal data.

The following will provide you with important guidelines to follow when conducting an investigation in the corporate environment.

30.2 National (Domestic) Background Investigations

Generally speaking, the following are the essential elements of any background investigation conducted in the United States.

A. Social Security number verification

The most critical component in conducting the background investigation is first and foremost to verify the identity of the party being investigated. Wouldn't it be embarrassing for you to later find out after completing an exhaustive background, that the information you checked out was for a person that had his or her identity stolen or was not the true applicant? Therefore it is imperative to initiate your investigation with a diligent check of the Social Security number provided to verify identity.

How often have you been advised by daily media reports of the inherent problems associated with identity theft? Countless times we have been informed of unscrupulous persons selling Social Security numbers, credit cards, passports, and driver's licenses which on the surface may look authentic, but are in fact fraudulent. A potential applicant may provide accurate information regarding his or her name and date of birth, but fraudulent information regarding a Social Security number.

In one such instance, an applicant applied for a position of trust, providing his correct name and a Social Security number that matched his name. Only later it was discovered through an extensive investigation that the Social Security number did not match his date of birth. The investigation also revealed that this applicant had lost his driver's license for operating under the influence and obtained a new driver's license in another state by using the SSN of another person of approximately the same age from that state.

The Social Security Administration (SSA) has resources available to employers to verify correct names and to report whether the Social Security number was allocated. Knowing what Social Security numbers have been allocated will help you determine if a SSN is valid. The SSA has guidelines that will help you make this determination.

The SSA has also been piloting an Internet option that will provide immediate or next business day response to name/SSN verification requests. At the time of this writing, this program is available to a small number of pre-selected companies, but it is anticipated that this option may be open to all employers sometime in 2005.

The SSA will advise you if a name/SSN you submitted does not match their records. Their Employee Verification Service (EVS), can be used to verify current or previously employed workers and should be applied consistently to all workers. An employer that uses the information SSA provides regarding name/SSN verification to justify taking adverse action against an employee may violate state or federal law and be subject to legal consequences.[1]

B. Employment history

Verification of employment history is accomplished through direct contact with the applicant's former employers. Generally, former employers will verify dates of employment and the position held, but a thorough investigation will include eligibility for rehire, job performance, and salary, and the reason for leaving. Whenever possible, former supervisors and/or co-workers should be interviewed. In addition it is also highly beneficial to interview any other party who has had direct contact with the applicant in the workplace. Note that a co-worker may have been a friend/relative of the applicant and may show a bias that is not supported by another employee.

There are specific employee screening requirements for certain industries which are regulated by various government agencies, such as the Department of Defense, the Department of Transportation, the Drug Enforcement Administration, the Federal Aviation Administration, the Nuclear Regulatory Commission, and the Securities Exchange Commission. Unfortunately, request procedures and response turnaround times vary widely from source to source. For additional information regarding regulated employment history, we recommend accessing www.creativeservices.com, where a list of specialized background screening components for government entities is provided.

C. Education verification

Inquiry through the issuing educational institution or a reputable academic verification clearing house should be conducted to verify the highest degree earned by an applicant and the dates of attendance. One such clearing house is offered through Credentials Inc. at www.degreechk.com. This site has a list of many colleges that authorized it as their official agent.

If a graduate degree has been attained, there should be a diligent check for the applicant's thesis for further support and verification purposes. One company that provides this service is UMI, which gathers, indexes, films, and republishes doctoral dissertations in microform and print. In 2000, their Dissertation Abstracts database archived over 1.6 million dissertations and master's theses. One million of them are available in full text in print, microform, and digital format. Their website reflects the following:

> *"The UMI microfilm vault-now one of ProQuest Information and Learning's assets-constitutes the largest commercially available microform collection in the world. Its 5.5 billion page images deliver 500 years of information, drawn from thousands of literary, journalistic, and scholarly works. Every year we add another 37 million images of contemporary information.*
>
> *Today we digitize both current and retrospective content for inclusion in the ProQuest Digital Vault. Still, we continue to produce many products in microform and print, such as research collections, directories, dissertations, newspapers, periodicals, indexes, and out-of-print books.*
>
> *We now retain the UMI brand for our archival and retrospective products and services in all formats-microform, print, and electronic."*[2]

Additionally, any supplemental courses or training directly relating to the job applied for should also be verified.

D. Criminal history

There is no single, comprehensive source for accurate and current nationwide (or international), criminal conviction information, regardless of claims touted from sources on the Internet and elsewhere proclaiming to deliver nationwide criminal histories. There is no way for you to attest to your client that you have performed this comprehensive check. You absolutely cannot rely on these providers for these types of searches!

The only manner in which a comprehensive criminal check can be accomplished accurately is if your client is willing for you to conduct research in every courthouse throughout the country and internationally, when applicable. In most instances this would be cost prohibitive.

The most important aspect in conducting background investigations on any level centers on the criminal history of the subject of the investigation. A comprehensive criminal history investigation must include all residential addresses of the applicant/subject for the prior seven years. Regardless of the number of addresses and states in question, it is necessary to investigate each and every one. Inquiry should be made with the following governmental agencies, regardless of the amount of time the applicant/subject resided there:

1. County courthouses

Superior Courts or those with felony jurisdiction generally can be searched for warrants, pending cases, and felony and misdemeanor convictions. Again, your reliance on only database information may not provide you with the most up to date information. Also, it is not recommended to rely solely on third-party vendors (see **Due Diligence**). Unless you provide the client with a disclaimer, you may very well be in violation of the Fair Credit Reporting Act (FCRA) rules when the third-party information has been reported for pre-employment purposes. In-person research conducted by competent investigative firm or record retrieval agency at the superior court level is strongly encouraged.

2. District courts

In an effort to provide your client with a thorough and diligent check on potential criminal dockets, it would behoove the investigator to check the various district courts in person as well. The same criteria that were used for superior courts also apply to district courts.

The district court generally hears a wide range of cases, including criminal, civil, housing, juvenile, and mental health cases. Criminal jurisdiction may also extend to all felonies punishable by a sentence up to five years, and many other felonies with even greater potential penalties, all misdemeanors, and all violations of city and town ordinances and bylaws. District courts conduct probable cause hearings to determine if a defendant should be bound over to the superior court in the case of felonies not within their final jurisdiction. District court magistrates conduct hearings to issue criminal complaints and arrest warrants and to determine

CRIMINAL HISTORY
PROVIDE YOUR NAME, ADDRESS
AND TELEPHONE NUMBER HERE

REQUEST FOR PUBLICLY ACCESSIBLE MASSACHUSETTS CORI

IT IS LAWFUL TO REQUEST THIS AGENCY TO PROVIDE A COPY OF ANOTHER PERSON'S PUBLICLY ACCESSIBLE ADULT CONVICTION RECORD.

FOR THE ADULT CONVICTION RECORD TO BE "PUBLICLY ACCESSIBLE" THE PERSON WHOSE RECORD IS REQUESTED MUST HAVE BEEN CONVICTED OF A CRIME PUNISHABLE BY A SENTENCE OF FIVE YEARS OR MORE, OR HAS BEEN CONVICTED OF ANY CRIME AND SENTENCED TO ANY TERM OF IMPRISONMENT, AND AT THE TIME OF THE REQUEST:

1. IS SERVING A SENTENCE OF PROBATION OR INCARCERATION, OR IS UNDER THE CUSTODY OF THE PAROLE BOARD; OR

2. HAVING BEEN CONVICTED OF A MISDEMEANOR HAS BEEN RELEASED FROM ALL CUSTODY OR SUPERVISION NOT MORE THAN ONE YEAR; OR

3. HAVING BEEN CONVICTED FELONY, HAS BEEN RELEASED FROM ALL CUSTODY OR SUPERVISION FOR NOT MORE THAN TWO YEARS; OR

4. HAVING BEEN SENTENCED TO THE CUSTODY OF THE DEPARTMENT OF CORRECTION, HAS FINALLY BEEN DISCHARGED THEREFROM, EITHER HAVING BEEN DENIED RELEASE ON PAROLE OR HAVING BEEN RETURNED TO PENAL CUSTODY FOR VIOLATING PAROLE FOR NOT MORE THAN THREE YEARS.

DIRECTIONS: PLEASE FILL THIS REQUEST FORM OUT AS COMPLETELY AS POSSIBLE. THE MORE INFORMATION YOU ARE ABLE TO PROVIDE, THE MORE EASILY THIS AGENCY WILL BE ABLE TO PROCESS YOUR REQUEST. A NON-REFUNDABLE PROCESSING FEE OF $25.00 IS CHARGED FOR EACH RECORD REQUESTED AND MUST BE INCLUDED WITH YOUR REQUEST(S). THERE WILL BE NO EXCEPTIONS MADE TO THIS RULE. ONLY CHECKS OR MONEY ORDERS WILL BE ACCEPTED. MAKE THE CHECK OR MONEY ORDER PAYABLE TO THE COMMONWEALTH OF MASSACHUSETTS. A S IF-ADDRESSED STAMPED ENVELOPE MUST ALSO BE ENCLOSED WITH YOUR REQUEST(S).
WALKED-IN REQUESTS OR FAXED REQUESTS WILL NOT BE ACCEPTED. REQUESTS WILL BE PROCESSED IN THE ORDER IN WHICH THEY ARE RECEIVED. MAIL ALL REQUESTS TO: THE CRIMINAL HISTORY SYSTEMS BOARD, 200 ARLINGTON STREET, SUITE 2200, CHELSEA, MA 02150, AYVN: CORI UNIT

• ALL REQUESTS MUST BE TYPED. REQUESTS CONTAINING ANY ILLEGIBLE IDENTIFYING INFORMATION WILL BE RETURNED. IF YOU ARE MAKING MORE THAN ONE REQUEST, PLEASE COPY THIS FORM AND FILL IN THE REQUESTED IDENTIFYING INFORMATION ACCORDINGLY.

1\. ______ ______ ______
LAST NAME FIRST NAME MIDDLE INITIAL

______ ______
MAIDEN NAME

______ ______
DATE OF BIRTH (MM/DD/YY) SOCIAL SECURITY NUMBER

2\. ______ ______ ______
LAST NAME FIRST NAME MIDDLE INITIAL

______ ______
MAIDEN NAME

______ ______
DATE OF BIRTH (MM/DD/YY) SOCIAL SECURITY NUMBER

whether there is probable cause to detain persons arrested without a warrant. Both judges and magistrates issue criminal and administrative search warrants.

3. Statewide searches

Statewide searches are made in the state of the applicant's residence and will usually reveal warrants, pending cases, and felony and misdemeanor convictions. Many states have criminal record repositories, but they do not always include records from federal, county and district courts. There are some states, including Massachusetts that will search their statewide criminal records only after receipt of a request in writing accompanied by the appropriate fee. (Note that the agency responsible for maintaining criminal records also varies from state to state).

In the Commonwealth of Massachusetts, the Criminal History System Board is the repository for all statewide criminal records. However, the information that you may receive as a result of your request is by no means comprehensive or inclusive.

Access is limited to the level of security clearance your agency has attained. In order for you to receive a higher level of criminal history information then the general public, you must be certified as a criminal justice agency or an agency statutorily mandated to receive *CORI (Criminal Offense Record Information).*

There also are separate levels exclusively for law enforcement. Clearance level depends on who the requesting party is and the degree of authorization they have to request and receive criminal history information. As you can see from the above request form, there are numerous limitations and restrictions.

Remember, even requesting and obtaining a record reflecting that no record was found from the commonwealth or other state agency does not necessarily prove that your applicant does not posses a criminal record! As was explained with the preceding limitations, you have to be continually diligent with checking all available resources to affect an accurate and comprehensive search.

Your search should concentrate on the provided and developed names, as well as the counties and states associated with the applicant's residential and employment history.

4. Local law enforcement

It maybe appropriate for you to conduct an in-person visit to the local police department and/or sheriffs' offices. Your applicant may never have been arrested, but local law enforcement would have a record of any call responses to the applicant's home. Your applicant's name may also come up in an incident report not specifically related to the residential address, perhaps as a witness to an accident or other incident.

5. U.S. District Court

The U.S. District Court of the applicant's jurisdiction can be searched for warrants, pending cases, and convictions based on federal law, which are distinct from state and county violations. This search should include aliases provided or developed through investigation. Although these records are usually accurate and current, each search is limited to a single jurisdiction, and therefore a thorough investigation may require a search of multiple jurisdictions.

6. Felony conviction research

Your primary concern is with determining felony convictions since many employers are statutorily prohibited from hiring a person with recent felony conviction. Many states have different court systems and different protocols for checking these records. Larger states and commonwealths have county systems in addition to circuit and/or district courts and may share dual jurisdiction on felony charges.

The various methods used by the different courts to create, maintain, store, and access docket information make obvious the inherent problems in obtaining comprehensive statewide records.

Older records which are not accessible on the computer may require you to conduct a hand search of available indices or archives. We could write another entire chapter on the research methods required, not only from state to state, but county to county!

Conducting Internet database searches is only scratching the surface when conducting a thorough background investigation. In order to obtain the most accurate and up-to-date information, in-person searches at the individual county, district, and U.S. District courthouses must be conducted.

E. Civil litigation

Inquiry through county and/or federal courthouses in the jurisdiction of the applicant's residence determines the applicant's involvement in a civil matter, whether as plaintiff or defendant. At the county level, these records would include small claims disputes, breach of contract, and real estate foreclosures. At the federal level, litigation with regard to constitutional issues and bankruptcy records are available.

F. Credit worthiness

Credit history is available from three major sources, Trans Union, Experian, and Equifax, and is an essential component of a comprehensive background investigation. An applicant's credit history may reveal a pattern of late payments, foreclosures, or bankruptcy actions. A signed release from the applicant is necessary to obtain these records, and all information must be obtained and disseminated in compliance with the applicable laws (addressed later in this chapter). Following are the websites for these consumer credit reporters:

Equifax	http://www.equifax.com/
Experian	http://www.experian.com/
Trans Union	http://www.transunion.com/

G. Federal bankruptcy court

These records are an excellent resource to determine if the applicant has ever filed for bankruptcy. If so, the docket should be obtained to reveal the creditors and the level of the applicant's fiscal irresponsibility and indebtedness.

H. Driving history

The applicant's driving history may be obtained through the appropriate Registry of Motor Vehicles (RMV) and provides data regarding license class, restrictions, status, expirations date, violations, revocations, suspension, accidents, and insurance cancellations. In some states, a signed release may be necessary, and in other states access may not be allowed at all. This is a critical component of the investigation, particularly if the applicant is going to be operating company vehicles. Negligent hiring of a driver with a horrendous driver's history is tantamount to giving your company's keys to a hungry plaintiff's lawyer.

This information also may reveal criminal charges in jurisdictions other than those in which the subject/applicant has resided and for which a previous search had returned negative results. (Obviously your client should be advised of these findings and you should recommend that a review of the relevant docket information is in order.)

Another effective source for this information is through the National Highway Traffic Administration's National Drivers Register, located in Washington DC:

> "The National Driver Register (NDR) is a central repository of information on individuals whose privilege to drive has been revoked, suspended, canceled or denied or who have been convicted of serious traffic-related offenses. The records maintained at the NDR consist of identification information including name, date of birth, gender, driver license number, and reporting State. All of the substantive information, the reason for the suspension or conviction and associated dates, resides in the reporting State. All 50 States and the District of Columbia participate in the NDR. The system is also referred to as the Problem Driver Pointer System (PDPS)."[3]

There are a number of restrictions on who is legally authorized to obtain information from the National Driver Register. Authorized parties include:

- Any individual under the provisions of the Privacy Act
- State and federal driver's license officials
- Current or prospective employers of motor vehicle operators
- Air carriers for pilot applicants
- The Federal Railroad Administration and employers of railroad engineers
- The Federal Aviation Administration for airmen medical certification
- The U.S. Coast Guard for merchant mariner certification

- The National Transportation and Safety Board and the Federal Highway Administration for Accident Investigations.

For further information you can contact this agency at: http://www.nhtsa.dot.gov/toc.html.

I. Military history

The applicant's provided military history can be verified as to period and character of military service through request and receipt of a Form DD214 from the National Personnel Records Center and/or through contact with the applicant's last duty station.

J. Professional references

Any references provided by the applicant (or developed in the course of the investigation) should be interviewed to supply character information regarding the applicant and to verify any provided or developed information.

K. Professional licensure

It is of the utmost importance to verify any licensing through the appropriate board or issuing agency. Many states now offer online information regarding the status of a license from contractors to medical healthcare workers.

In several states you are now able to check to see if there are or have been any medical malpractice suits or disciplinary actions taken against a physician. You are also able to verify credentials and obtain information regarding where the physician attended undergraduate and medical school and with which hospitals he or she is associated.

L. Sex offender registry search

Most states now maintain a sex offender registry available to the public which identifies any individuals convicted of sexual assault, aggravated criminal sexual conduct, luring or enticing, and kidnapping, or who have been found to be repetitive and compulsive by experts and the court system. A search should be conducted using the applicant's name and any aliases in all jurisdictions where the applicant has resided.

M. Worker's compensation history

An investigator would be remiss in not checking state or regional records for prior worker's compensation claims made by the applicant. Use of worker's compensation information is strictly regulated by each state and often cannot be considered until after an offer of employment has been made. Some states also require signed and notarized release authorizing the search.

N. Media search

Any comprehensive, high-level background investigation should include a media search for any and all references to the applicant. There are reputable on-line services, such as *Lexis-Nexis*, *Factiva,* and *Dialogue NewsEdge* to name a few, which provide not only the source but often the content of any media reports in which the applicant's name appears. Direct contact of media sources within the applicant's known residential areas can sometimes provide more detailed information, and news clipping agencies should also be checked.

O. Internet search

(chat rooms, etc.)

P. Mode of living review

(when applicable)

Q. Neighborhood canvass

Only the most comprehensive background investigations include a neighborhood canvass, which entails an in-person visit to the applicant's neighborhood to assess and describe its character and the nature and condition of the applicant's abode. Information obtained from speaking with the applicant's neighbors can prove invaluable in assessing the applicant's character, social activities, apparent financial status and involvement in the community.

30.3 International Background Investigations

As the global community grows, many employers encounter the need to conduct background investigations of applicants from other countries who are applying for a position in the United States or a position in their own country for an American employer. Special challenges are encountered when conducting international investigations.

The most challenging aspect of conducting an international background investigation is that each country has its own laws, customs, and procedures with regard to how they store, maintain, and disseminate personal data. Techniques and information that we take for granted in the United States are frequently not available abroad where there is usually very limited access to public records, and criminal records particularly are extremely difficult to obtain. In some instances, no information can be obtained without retaining the services of a local private investigator who knows the ropes and has developed reliable resources.

Language is a huge barrier when attempting to conduct an international investigation. Even when the foreign sources speak English, or the investigator is fluent in that country's language, the potential for miscommunication and misunderstanding is enormous, not only when acquiring results but often when communicating the exact parameters of the information sought. The difference in how records are created, maintained, accessed, and interpreted varies greatly from country to country. Time differences can also hinder effective investigative efforts, and each country is apt to have its own official holidays, which can delay obtaining timely information.

Of particular importance is the legality of obtaining the information from abroad. If not in compliance with *Safe Harbor* rules in the EU (see "Applicable Laws" later in this chapter), the sources providing information can be in violation of laws in the country and can be subject to arrest. In fact, local law enforcement agencies in Great Britain have set up sting operations to nab investigators providing information across the pond illegally.

Should you be required to conduct an international investigation, we strongly recommend using a reliable and reputable investigator in the country where inquiry is to be made. The Council of International Investigators (CII), World Association of Detectives (WAD), World Investigators Network (WIN) and Intelnet[4] all provide contact information for all investigator members worldwide on their websites.[5]

30.4 Applicable Laws

Due to terrorist acts and other breaches of security and privacy such as identity theft, a number of laws have been enacted on the state, federal, and international levels which greatly affect the nature of information that can be obtained and the persons or entities to whom it can be disseminated. You must be armed with a fair amount of information about your subject and be able to navigate bureaucratic labyrinths in order to obtain fairly simple information. Once you have obtained that information, the fact that you are reporting to a third party (your client or company) triggers additional laws regarding how you provide that information to the "end user," and your responsibilities of disclosure to the subject of the investigation.

It is strongly recommended that, with any of the laws cited below, you obtain a copy, read it thoroughly to familiarize yourself with it, and be sure you understand your responsibilities under that law as well as your client's or company's responsibility regarding the information your have provided.

A. Fair Credit Reporting Act (FRCA)—15 U.S.C. § 1681 et seq.

The Fair Credit Reporting Act (FCRA) requires a potential employer to disclose to the applicant (consumer) that the employer intends to conduct a background investigation which will include the applicant's credit history. Following are the applicable definitions from § 603 of the FCRA:

> (e) The term **investigative consumer report** means a consumer report or portion thereof in which information on a consumer's character, general reputation, personal characteristics, or mode of living is *obtained through personal interviews with neighbors, friends, or associates of the consumer reported on or with others with whom he is acquainted or who may have knowledge concerning any such items of information*. However, such information shall not include specific factual information on a consumer's credit record obtained directly from a creditor of the consumer or from a consumer reporting agency when such information was obtained directly from a creditor of the consumer or from the consumer.
>
> (f) The term **consumer reporting agency** means any person which, for monetary fees, dues, or on a cooperative nonprofit basis, *regularly engages in whole or in part in the practice of assembling or evaluating consumer credit information or*

other information on consumers for the purpose of furnishing consumer reports to third parties, and which uses any means or facility of interstate commerce for the purpose of preparing or furnishing consumer reports.

(g) The term **file**, when used in connection with information on any consumer, means all of the information on that consumer recorded and retained by a consumer reporting agency regardless of how the information is stored.

(h) The term **employment purposes** when used in connection with a consumer report means a report used for the purpose of evaluating a consumer for employment, promotion, reassignment, or retention as an employee

Should an employer take adverse action with regard to the applicant or employee, the employer must provide the "consumer" (subject) with a copy of the "investigative consumer report" and a written description of the consumer's rights under the FCRA.

Effective March 30, 2004, the *Fair and Accurate Credit Transactions Act (FACTA)*, amended § 603 of the FCRA to provide that ***employers need not provide notice or obtain employee permission to order the investigation of suspected employee misconduct***. It is no longer necessary for investigators to obtain the employer's certification that the requisite notices have been given to the suspect(s).

The changes also provide that the employer need not provide the employee with a copy of the investigative report but rather, after taking adverse action,

" . . . the employer shall disclose to the consumer a summary containing the nature and substance of the communication upon which the adverse action is based, except that the sources of information acquired solely for use in preparing what would be but for subsection (d)(2)(D) an investigative consumer report need not be disclosed."[6]

B. United and Strengthening America by Providing Appropriate Tools Required to Intercept and Obstruct Terrorism Act of 2001—Public Law 107-56 (USA Patriot Act)

The Patriot Act requires certain defined businesses to establish "anti-money laundering programs," which include, at a minimum, (1) the development of internal policies, procedures, and control; (2) the designation of a compliance officer; (3) an ongoing employee training program; and (4) an independent audit function to test the program. The act only applies to "financial institutions," but that definition includes such businesses as credit unions, insurance companies, dealers in precious metals, stones or jewels, travel agencies, companies engaged in vehicle sales, and casinos and gaming establishments, to name but a few.[7]

C. Sarbanes-Oxley Act

The Sarbanes-Oxley Act is the single most important piece of legislation affecting corporate governance, financial disclosure, public accounting, and regulators since the inception of U.S. securities laws in 1933. There is a daunting amount of opinion and conjecture surrounding the interpretation of the act. More importantly, there is a total lack of consensus of what exactly must be done to fulfill the requirements of the act.[8] Therefore, we will not attempt to interpret the compliance issues involved in this legislation, but rather refer you to www.soxlaw.com for discussion of Sarbanes-Oxley Act issues.

D. Drivers Privacy Protection Act—18 U.S.C. § 2721 et. seq. Public Law 103-322

The Drivers Privacy Protection Act establishes prohibitions on release and use of certain personal information from state motor vehicle records. However, there are a number of permissible uses in the "normal course of business":

1) to verify the accuracy of personal information submitted by an individual to that company;
2) to correct information submitted (but only for the purposes of preventing fraud, pursuing legal remedies, or recovering debt);

3) for service of process, investigation in anticipation of litigation, or the execution or enforcement of judgments and orders;
4) for use by any insurer or insurance support organization in connection with claims, investigation activities, anti-fraud activities, rating or underwriting; or
5) for use by any licensed private investigative agency or licensed security service for any purpose permitted; or
6) use by an employer or its agents or insurer to obtain or verify information relating to a holder of a commercial driver's license; or
7) for use by any requester, if the requester demonstrates it has obtained the written consent of the individual to whom the information pertains.[9]

Once again, it is the responsibility of the investigating individual or agency to be familiar with the specifics of the Drivers Privacy Protection Act as it applies to the procurement and dissemination of personal data via motor vehicle records.

E. International Safe Harbor Privacy Law

The European Union (EU) enacted privacy legislation titled "Directive on Data Protection" in October of 1998. In essence, this law requires that transfer of personal data to non-EU countries is prohibited unless that country or entity can provide an "adequate" level of privacy protection. "Personal data" is defined as data about an identified or identifiable individual that is recorded in any form.

As a result, the U.S. Department of Commerce issued principles to foster, promote, and develop international commerce which are intended for use solely by U.S. organizations receiving personal data from the European Union for the purpose of qualifying for the safe harbor and the presumption of "adequacy" it creates. Decisions by organizations to qualify for safe harbor are entirely voluntary, but organizations that decide to adhere to these principles must comply with these principles in order to obtain and retain the benefits of the safe harbor and publicly declare that they do so.[10]

F. Due diligence

Although not a law, due diligence is a legal concept and commonly used term when referring to the extent and depth of an investigation, whether for pre-employment or in the case of acquisitions or mergers. At its most simple, due diligence is merely the measure of prudence properly expected from, and ordinarily exercised by, a reasonable and prudent person under the particular circumstances. It is an employer's first line of defense against a negligent hiring suit. The due diligence concept requires any employer or company to expend a reasonable amount of effort to identify and confirm any data which may have an effect on the hire or acquisition under consideration. If an employer's background investigation is well documented and can prove that the employer availed itself of the most up-to-date and accurate information and that any information obtained from a third-party vendor was confirmed or verified through an alternate source, then the employer has complied with the legal concept of due diligence.

30.5 Disclaimers

This chapter is in no way intended as an exhaustive treatise on the elements of conducting a legally compliant background investigation. The volume and complexity of applicable laws and concepts, both domestic and international, preclude the author from including all available information on the subject. The foregoing is intended simply as a guide, and should not be relied upon for interpretation of current applicable laws.

We are all familiar with the concept of disclaimers, as we encounter them on almost a daily basis. A disclaimer is merely a warning to the recipient of information that certain presumptions about the information provided cannot be made, and the above italicized paragraph is a prime example: the author's disclaimer to the reader. Usually associated with "the fine print" in a contract, a disclaimer protects the provider of information from legal repercussions as a result of the end-user's interpretation of that information. The most common disclaimers are associated with advertising and promotional activities (the rapid voice-over at the end of a radio or television commercial or the fine print on a coupon or certificate for products or services, for example).

As an investigator, it is incumbent upon you to provide an appropriate disclaimer to the client whenever providing information obtained as a result of your investigation. In other words, the client has a right to know, for example, that although no criminal records were found during the course of the investigation, that does not mean that they do not exist, as the investigator must rely on third-party recordkeepers and cannot guarantee that the recordkeepers have made no errors or omissions.

One of the most common disclaimers, familiar to us all, is the fine print at the bottom of a facsimile transmission cover sheet. The following is our own disclaimer used on all facsimile transmissions:

> *The information contained in this facsimile message is intended only for the use of the individual or entity named above. If the reader of this message is not the intended recipient, or the employee or agent responsible to deliver it to the intended recipient, you are hereby notified that any dissemination, distribution or copying of this communication is strictly prohibited. If you have received this communication in error, please notify us immediately by telephone and return the original message to us at the above address via first-class mail. Receipt by anyone other than the intended recipient is not a waiver of any investigator-client work-product privilege.*

Work product disclaimers regarding the results of your investigative efforts are crucial to protect you and your company from potential lawsuits by unhappy clients. By way of example, we provide the following background investigation disclaimer:

> *No cases found does not mean that none exist. Numerous cases are recorded in various counties by name and are not centrally searchable. Computer entry is limited by dates and many cases are not available through a computer search, making a lengthy hand search of records in individual courthouses necessary to positively determine whether any cases exist. It is often not practical or feasible to check all counties and/or possible cases for the subject; therefore, some listing may not have been detected and therefore would not be included in this report. All information contained in this report is subject to the limitations imposed by research data and data accuracy at the time of inquiry. Inasmuch as responsibility for the verification and maintenance of information obtained from various sources lies with the respective custodians of record, American Investigative Services accepts no responsibility for errors or omissions arising from, or malfeasance of, such record custodian, nor do we accept any responsibility for records not found that were*

beyond the scope and/or budget constraints of the investigation, or in counties, states or years that were not specifically request and included in the investigation by the client.

30.6 Budget Constraints

We have addressed the complexities of conducting an extensive and diligent background investigation, but not the fees associated with this form of investigation. In this industry, as in any other form of endeavor, the old adage certainly applies:

YOU GET WHAT YOU PAY FOR!

Many firms relay on affiliates in other states to assist them in completing assignments out of their specific territory. A basic fee structure should be predicated on the availability of the requested records, the travel time incurred, the number of specific jurisdictions that are to be included in the background check, and the fees charged by the local agencies for processing the request, among other factors. We structure our background investigations fees according to the level of information our clients require.

A background check for a low level sales position for a retail client of a teen-aged applicant may only require a minimal level of scrutiny, such as a county criminal check, reference check, and possibly driver's history. In contrast, a comprehensive investigation on a potential CEO may necessitate a more multi-layered approach and a more rigorous examination of his or her background. Depending on the requirements and scope delineated by the client, a "background investigation" can cost as little as $100, or more than $5,000.00 (if international investigation is required). It is good business practice to advise your client or company of the realistic expectations for both acquiring the requested information and the costs involved.

30.7 Conclusion

Even the most rigorous background investigation is subject to the pitfalls associated with the information providers and their indexing/reporting mechanism. It is therefore incumbent upon you to know: (1) what information is available, (2) the timeliness of said information, and (3) how and where to obtain the information. You must also be well versed with the local agencies in order to conduct your investigation with the utmost accuracy. Therefore, your disclaimer is a critical component in safeguarding you and your client from potential negligence suits.[11]

Endnotes

1. www.ssa.gov/employer/ssnv.htm#content

2. www.umi.com/division/PQDTmigration

3. www.nhtsa.dot.gov/toc.html

4. www.intelnetwork.org/index.asp

5. Council of International Investigators: www.cci2.org

6. National Council of Investigative and Security Services - www.nciss.com

7. Dykema Goeesett, PPLC - www.dykema.com

8. www.s-ox.com

9. www.accessreport.com/statutes

10. www.ita.doc.gov

11. Special thanks to Eli Whitney for her assistance with this project.

Chapter 31

Conducting a Threat Vulnerability Assessment

James Buckley, CHS III and Ed Petersen

Synopsis

31.1 Introduction

Increasingly, threat vulnerability assessments (TVA) are being performed in order to evaluate and measure the security posture at facilities and sites such as water treatment plants and dams, petro-chemical and storage locations, major sports venues, high-rise office buildings, buildings that house thousands of daily occupants, and many other sites that are considered to be part of critical infrastructures. TVAs provide the necessary information to implement security systems and programs that will "harden" the sites or facilities.

Many TVAs are voluntarily initiated on the part of business and industry. However, in some instances they are mandated by a governmental entity. Such is the case as it relates to state and federal government identified critical infrastructure elements in order to have these sites become compliant with industry best practice standards.

Physical security assessments are important because they can determine the current security standard at a specific location, note the lapses and potential vulnerabilities in the physical protection system, and also validate existing security measures that are in place and are compliant with industry best practice standards. Developing countermeasures to overcome existing weaknesses should be a part of the process.

When we speak of vulnerability, we are reminded of being susceptible to attack or physical injury. We must examine what this cause is and what threat exists that creates the vulnerability. Since the word "threat" implies an intention to cause harm or imminent danger, we must examine what factors together cause vulnerability and possibly an adverse impact on a facility.

The events surrounding September 11, 2001, have caused a heightened awareness when it comes to physical security. Prior to 9/11, not many believed that such an attack could or would take place against the World Trade Center, especially since security upgrades exceeding $60 million had been implemented in the aftermath of the 1993 WTC bombing. Security professionals were not actively focusing on identifying potential weaknesses or vulnerabilities by looking at potential targets from the adversary's perspective.

Terrorists' rules of engagement are not based on Marquis of Queensbury rules. Sensitivity about tactics or targets does not exist, nor will there be any fairness exhibited on behalf of a terrorist when planning or executing an attack. When a threat vulnerability/physical security assessment is conducted, consideration should be given to viewing the site through the eyes of a potential attacker. One must consciously and creatively think outside the box when looking for vulnerabilities. Do not overlook minute details and remember that years of planning went into the attack of 9/11. The target had already been attacked but not as successfully as the terrorists had imagined it would be. We now know that the fanaticism of the terrorists, tempered with their strategic mindset of patient determination, fueled the attack(s) and allowed for the unthinkable to happen on our soil.

When conducting a threat vulnerability/physical security assessment, considerations must be kept in mind that a natural or man-made event may have a critical effect on the facility. Further, obvious hazards may exist at the facility or on the facility property that might affect operations and employees. It is helpful to determine what, if any, countermeasures are in place to deal with such an event.

A physical protection system should be geared toward deterrence, detection, defense, and defeat. The threat(s) to the system include criminals, vandals, activists, radical extremists, and terrorists as well as the aforementioned natural and man-made disasters. Most often, if not always, natural disasters are not preventable through the implementation of physical security measures, though they will affect significantly the security systems and the facility operations.

31.2 Layers of Protection

An accepted method of conducting such an assessment is to apply the layers of protection or concentric rings of security concept when beginning the assessment. This method establishes rings around the operational core beginning with the surrounding area. Examination and evaluation is made of areas outside each ring.

1. The **surrounding area** includes all pertinent information within the immediate area of the outer property line of the facility and includes such considerations as transportations routes, highways, railroads and airports, medical facilities, emergency responder facilities, and potential hazardous industry sites.
2. The **outer perimeter** includes the property line of the facility and is normally the first physical barrier protection for the property. It includes access to/from the facility both pedestrian and vehicular, the location and types of utilities coming into the facility, private and public roadways, and the terrain.
3. The **middle perimeter** includes the areas between the property line and the exterior walls of the structure and details ac-

cess and accountability of people and vehicles, the location and type of utility services and identified vulnerabilities, potential hazards within the middle perimeter, terrain and landscape, delivery of goods and supplies, entryways into the structure, delay barriers, emergency access for fire, police, and medical situations.

4. The **inner perimeter**, which includes all areas contained within the exterior walls of the structure, covers communication systems, on-site medical capabilities, hazardous material storage, security and fire protection equipment, fire hazards, lighting, existing doors and locks, all utilities and backup systems and emergency procedures, such as the evacuation plan and crisis response.

Prior to the start of the assessment, members of the team should visit the site in order to familiarize themselves with the facility and operations and to develop the assessment plan. By doing this, the best use of team personnel is accomplished and every stage of the operation is examined.

Some points to consider and include when preparing a checklist are:

- **The Perimeter.** Fencing, gates, lighting, stand-off distance from/to the building.
- **The Parking Lot.** Is parking restricted? How many access points exist? Are vehicles examined by security officers at the access points? Are license plates recorded? Is the parking lot well lit? Are employee vehicles identified by way of company issued stickers? Does security patrol the parking lot to ensure safety to vehicles and to deter unauthorized parking? Is there assigned parking, i.e., numbered spaces?
- **Exterior Lighting.** What type of lighting exists? Is there backup power capability? What are the hours of use (dusk to dawn)? Are all luminaries functioning? Does the lighting complement and support the CCTV system? Are lighting fixtures easily accessible and prone to vandalism? Are there areas of the building that are not lit and present a potential danger due to lack of lighting?

- **Landscape.** Is the shrubbery overgrown, allowing for places of concealment? Do trees and other landscape features interfere with the CCTV coverage?
- **Access points.** How many entrances are there? Do employees, guests, and visitors enter though the same portal(s)? Does access control exist and if so, what type? Do the doors remain unlocked and unsecured during hours of operation? Do employees prop the doors open when egressing to allow for easy and convenient re-entry?
- **Ground level windows.** How are they secured? Do they have protective coverings, i.e., window grates?
- **Exterior doors.** How many are there? What are they made of? Do they contain glass panels, and if so, are the panels shatterproof? Are they properly aligned and positioned? Are the hinges located on the outside or inside?What type of locking mechanism is used and do they function properly?
- **Loading Dock.** Where is it located? Is it secure during hours of operation? How is it accessed? Are deliveries scheduled? Are vehicles examined by security personnel, and if so, what method is used? Do drivers have access into the building, and if so, is access limited or restricted to a certain area?
- **Air Vents.** Are they at ground level? Are they accessible to the public? Are there any protective coverings? Are vehicles allowed to park adjacent to or in close proximity to the vents? Are there any toxic or flammable items stored close to the air vents?
- **Reception area.** What is the sign-in policy for visitors? Are credentials required to be shown at time of sign-in? Is there a "guest list" provided to the reception desk personnel on a daily basis? Is there an escort policy? Is the visit confirmed with the company? Is there a food or other personal delivery policy? What is the sign-out policy? What type of communication exists between the reception desk personnel and security for emergency situations, i.e., walkie-talkie, direct line, duress/panic button?
- **Employees.** What is the method used to identify employees, i.e., building or company photo identification? How is em-

ployee entrance to the premises documented (card swipe, etc)? What is the policy for an employee who cannot produce the proper identification?

- **Packages, Bags, Briefcases.** Are these items examined prior to floor access? What method is employed? Is there an access denial policy for refusal?
- **Mail Room.** If applicable, where in the building is it located? How does it operate? Are packages scanned, and if so, what equipment is used? Is there a policy in place for suspicious packages/letters? If so, describe.
- **Elevators.** Are there separate elevator banks for employees and visitors? Can floors be locked against access after regular business hours? Do the elevator cabs have camera coverage?
- **Command Center/Operations Center.** Who staffs this area? Is there adequate personnel and relief? What systems are housed there? Are all systems functioning properly and efficiently? Are cameras capturing what they are supposed to capture, and what is the reporting mechanism? What are the capabilities of the security force? Are they proprietary, contract, or both?
- **Critical areas.** Identify all critical operations and areas located. How are these areas accessed and by whom? How are they protected? Are there backup systems in the event of power depletion or failure? Identify and describe the barriers and systems in place to deter an adversary's path.
- **Assessment of interior.** Examine the entire interior beginning with basement, mechanical and electrical rooms, telephone closets (BMS) and ending at the roof level. Identify security weaknesses and vulnerabilities. List any/all hazardous material stored on the premises and determine the safeguard policy.
- **Key Control.** What is the policy? Is the policy effective and adhered to by personnel? What is the policy for master and sub-master keys? Who is in charge of the keys and are they kept in a secure location? Do outside maintenance crews possess keys? Describe.

- **Fire suppression equipment.** Note all fire suppression equipment by type, compound, date of expiration, and date last inspected. Note any missing equipment and location.
- **Medical equipment.** Identify medical suite, if applicable, note equipment and supplies and method of protection.
- **Stairwells.** Identify locations and how they are identified, i.e., numbers, letters, directional (N, S, E, W). Note lighting and emergency lighting capability, ease of access, exit sign posting and the condition of signs.
- **Fire Doors.** Note locations, means of access and egress, locking mechanisms ("crash bars"), and how well they are functioning.
- **Roof Access/HVAC system.** How is the roof accessed? How many access points allow access to the roof? Is the door to the roof kept secure? Is the access door alarmed? Is the roof and HVAC covered by the physical protection system (CCTV)? Is the HVAC system protected by means of fencing? How is the building's air purged, if necessary? Note: An interview with the building engineer is recommended to determine air quality issues and purging procedures.
- **Evacuation Plans.** Do they exist? Determine if employees are familiar with the plans. Are the plans posted anywhere? If so, describe location(s). Where are the rally/gather points? If they are compromised, are there alternative locations, and if so, where? Describe the method in place that accounts for personnel in the event of an evacuation.
- **ADA.** Is the building/site compliant with ADA (Americans with Disabilities Act) standards? Describe.
- **Vendor Screening.** Identify the method for screening vendors such as cleaning crews, delivery personnel, independent contractors working on site, etc.

Needless to say, this list could be expanded and detailed significantly; in many cases it will be. This is not an all-encompassing list but is provided solely as a starting point and somewhat of a "go-by."

In addition to recording the team's findings, it has been proven helpful also to photograph areas or items of concern. The photographs should be made part of the report either by incorporating them with the text or as exhibits in an addendum section with proper identifiers.

Finally, based on the assessment findings, recommendations should be provided as to how countermeasures to any weaknesses or vulnerabilities can be implemented. It is helpful to provide more than one recommendation, if possible, thereby giving various options (cost factors) as to how to improve the current status of the vulnerability.

Through experience, we have found that it is helpful to provide a prioritized list of critical weaknesses and vulnerabilities (high, medium, low), thereby aiding the client in the decisionmaking process as to the urgency to correct or improve the noted deficiency.

31.3 Interview Process

The interview process focuses attention on the overall perception of safety and security from within. Interviews are conducted on a voluntary basis with a representative sampling of individuals who work at the facility, to include executive management, supervisory personnel, general staff, security personnel, facility management, system maintenance, and others covering a wide and diverse range of responsibilities. The individuals who are interviewed are given the opportunity to express their concerns and observations and to make recommendations regarding safety and security issues that may help to improve existing conditions. In order to ensure integrity throughout the process and to alleviate any concerns of the individual being interviewed, confidentiality is maintained. Our goal is to learn as much as possible, to ask the right questions, and to be good listeners in an effort to understand the concerns of the staff. We look to make recommendations that are logical and cost effective. We are sensitive to the importance of striking a balance between the appropriate level of security and the way security is perceived within the corporate culture.

Guidelines in conducting the interview

1. Identify yourself to the individual being interviewed and briefly describe your background. Determine his or her position and responsibilities within the company or corporation.
2. State the purpose of the interview as it relates to the threat vulnerability assessment.

3. In order to alleviate any concerns of the individual being interviewed, reinforce the integrity of the process and that the interview is voluntary and confidential.
4. Reinforce the value of the interview process, the importance of listening to their concerns as it pertains to safety and security. Drawing upon their experiences will enable us to be better informed in conducting the assessment.
5. Ask the question of the person being interviewed; if placed in charge of the facility, what changes would he or she make to enhance security?
6. Identify the location where the person being interviewed works. Does he or she feel safe in this location of the building?
7. If the security budget received a major increase in funding, what expenditures would make the facility safer? Prioritize in the order most critical.
8. Is unauthorized access to the facility a problem? How do you believe the vulnerability can be corrected? Based on your experience, how would you rate the access control system? Camera coverage? Overall technology?
9. Have you had any unfavorable experiences related to your personal safety and security at the facility? Do you know of any specific instances where security has been compromised? If so, describe what happened. How do you believe this vulnerability can be corrected?
10. Do you believe the communication system in the building is effective? How do you feel it could be enhanced? Are you able to reach security in an emergency? Do they respond in a timely fashion? How would you communicate in an emergency? PA system? walkie talkie? cell phone?
11. Is the security staff effective? Are they sufficiently staffed? Are they properly trained? Do they perform their job as professionals? Do you feel safe working overtime, after normal working hours? What could they do better? How could the overall system be improved?
12. Are there any areas of the building you believe to be unsafe? (i.e., stairwells, roof access, basement, bathrooms, etc.)

13. Are you aware of emergency evacuation plans? Have they been practiced? What about fire drills? Are you familiar with procedures and destination? Is there an alternate relocation site? Has anyone discussed the crisis management plan? What about the crisis management team? Have you seen the plan in action? Does it work?
14. Describe the visitor ID system. Is it effective? Is it enforced? How could it be improved? Do visitors go unchallenged? What about ID for maintenance, contractors, vendors?
15. How do you get to work? Where do you park? Do you feel safe in transit to and from work?

31.4 Crisis Management

There is no one definition regarding what constitutes a crisis, emergency, or disaster. These terms are often used interchangeably. What we do know is that by today's standards, crisis management is an important part of the threat vulnerability assessment process.

A crisis may be caused by nature or by people, such as:

- Fire emergency
- Flood
- Severe weather; hurricane, tornado, snow, ice
- Earthquake
- Chemical or hazardous materials
- Medical emergencies
- An act of violence
- Bomb threat
- Terrorism

31.5 Five Phases of Crisis Management

A. Awareness

Whenever a crisis occurs, the first questions asked are "Why did this happen? And why wasn't it prevented? It is important to recognize the need to have a crisis management plan that is practical and functional. An effective plan will provide the guidance needed to react in a positive way to a crisis situation. An alert and observant staff can provide a strong support system in helping to prevent and reduce the effect of a crisis situation. The plan will work best if it is customized to suit the culture, diversity, and philosophy of the corporation or company. The plan should be maintained in a location that will provide quick access and reference capabilities. Keep the plan basic and easy to follow. It is important to be aware of the different types of terrorist events that could affect your location; i.e. conventional explosives, bio-terrorism, chemical weapons, nuclear/radiological weapons, and cyber-terrorism.

B. Prevention

Knowing what to do when faced with a crisis situation can be the difference between success or failure, or even life and death. Don't wait until you are in a crisis situation to determine who is part of the crisis management team and what their responsibilities will be. Effective crisis management planning begins with good leadership.

- Crisis management plans should be developed in partnership with executive management, law enforcement, fire safety, emergency medical services, and neighboring facilities.
- Crisis plans need to be reviewed and revised on a regular basis.
- Conduct an assessment of your facility. Identify those factors that could place the facility, staff, and occupants at risk.
- The crisis management team; Who will be a part of the team? What are their responsibilities? Where do they meet? Who do they report to? How is information communicated? Where is the relocation site?

C. Preparation

Have site plans for the facility been made available and shared with first responders and agencies responsible for emergency response? Ensure there are multiple evacuation routes and rallying points; the first option maybe blocked or obstructed at the time of a crisis. Test communications, i.e., PA system, walkie talkies, cell phones. Communications are critical; ensure there is a back-up system that is reliable, and periodically inspect equipment to ensure it is operational. Test your crisis plan through exercises and practical drills. Being prepared involves an investment of time and resources, but the potential to save lives and reduce injury and damage is well worth the effort. Training and practice are essential for the successful implementation of the crisis plan.

D. Response

Have clarity in your plan regarding the basic steps to follow in responding to a crisis or emergency situation. Ensure that your supervisory staff and all personnel are familiar with the crisis management plan. They should know their specific responsibilities and how to help alleviate panic and anxiety. The chain of command should be clear. Flexibility and good common sense are necessary in a crisis situation. Identify who will handle the responsibility of documenting the actions taken during the response to the crisis and who has responsibility regarding equipment.

- Have individuals with special needs been appropriately addressed?
- What about cultural or language differences?
- Who will be the spokesperson for the facility?
- Who determines what information will be communicated to staff, family members, and the community?
- Are there adequate back-up and reserve staff members in place to handle responsibilities should a primary team member be unavailable during a crisis?
- Identify the resources available for transporting personnel. Where do they go if relocation is necessary?

Assess damage, activate your command centers, and establish lines of communication, keeping all critical entities informed of pertinent developments regarding the crisis. Institute effective liaison with authorities.

E. Recovery

If a crisis occurred would you be able to operate in a "business as usual mode?" Is there a plan in place regarding counseling and stress management for staff and if necessary family members subsequent to a crisis situation? Does the plan account for the whereabouts of all staff? Are provisions in place to evaluate and critique how a crisis was handled? What worked? What didn't? How could the plan be improved?

Be prepared to analyze the financial and operational effect of a crisis. Examine ways of protecting critical processes, resources, and vital records. Review plans on how to restore the work environment after the crisis. Restoring critical services that may have been cut off is essential. Are vital records, sensitive information, and other critical data protected at an off-site location? Protect your distribution chain, limit your potential economic losses, and reduce your business costs and insurance premiums. Protect all technical business operations (IT, data communications) with redundancy.

31.6 Crisis Response Outline

A. Assessment

Find out:

- **What** happened?
- **When** did it happen?
- **Who** was involved?
- **Were** there injuries?
- **Where** are they now?
- **What** is their condition?
- **What** do they need?
- **What** is the extent of the property damage?
- **Where** is the exact location of the incident?
- **Who** is at the scene and in charge?
- **What** equipment is necessary?
- **How** would it affect others (civilians, residents, businesses)?
- Add additional comments
- Assignment started by
- Assignment completed by

B. Call emergency and support services

1. **Emergency services:**

- Police department
- Fire department

- State police
- FBI
- EPA
- Emergency medical services/hospitals
- City governmental agencies; Mayor's office
- State governmental agencies; Governor's office
- County support services
- American Red Cross
- Emergency management agency/Homeland Security
- Haz-Mat
- Center for Disease Control
- Media list
- Local airports, FAA, port authority PD

2. Support services:

- Crisis response team

  Executive Management
  - Contact person (office and home)
  - Legal department (office and home)
  - Phone company
  - Gas and electric company
  - Water company

  Local Community Resources
  - Hospitals
  - Physicians
  - Pharmacies
  - General contractors
  - Electricians
  - Plumbers
  - Auto mechanics

C. Stabilize the situation in the area of the incident

1. Account for anyone involved in the incident
2. Ensure any injuries are quickly addressed
3. Deal with concerns of the surrounding neighborhood/businesses
4. Maintain leadership
5. Deal with hazards—identify, stabilize, remove everyone from dangerous conditions
6. Preserve the scene
7. Conduct interviews to determine cause
8. Interview to determine possible suspects, if any
9. Local hospital participation
10. First aid treatment and first aid/emergency kits

D. Establish crisis headquarters—operations room (plan contingency for off-site location)

1. Put emergency equipment in place
2. Prepare protocol for phone calls
3. Set up and maintain phone log book
4. Provide staffing of phones
5. Designate leader of the crisis center
6. Identify only personnel that needs to be there
7. Establish a hotline for family and friends
8. Assign person to determine back-up communication
    a. What are the existing communications' capabilities?
    b. Voice
    c. Data
    d. Take an inventory of existing back-up communications
        - *Walkie talkies*
        - *PA system*
        - *Cellular phones*
        - *Public telephones*
    e. Who will use the back-up communication during an incident?
    f. Where are your critical circuits?

g. What alternative communication or back-up protection exists there?
h. What systems have back-up power capabilities? Determine length of operability
i. Facilities – Prioritize who will need back-up communication at the time of an incident or disaster
j. Identify back-up personnel
k. It is recommended that alternate communications lines for each department be put in place
l. Mobile Operational Center

E. Mobilize the crisis management team (CMT)

1. Clarify team members' assignments, be sure to have back-up personnel available if needed
2. Assess the best plan of action for the particular incident

F. Follow-up

Assign members to gather facts, independent of each other:

- Talk to everyone directly or indirectly involved
- Describe conditions pre-and post-incident, e.g., weather, time of day, conditions in the area, other potential dangers
- Take photos and video if possible of any damage resulting from the incident (digital quality for downloading capabilities)

G. Deal with the media

1. Communication
   a. Prepare brief written statement/press release for media regarding pertinent facts about the incident
   b. Avoid speculation about why the crisis occurred
   c. Identify location to meet with and update the media

2. Interaction with the media
   a. in writing

b. by telephone, email, fax
c. in person

H. Post-incident actions (follow-up status)

Check status of:

- Persons involved in incident, injuries/treatment
- Others affected by the incident; make arrangements for counseling if needed
- Assess the damage – property
- Time factor involved in restoring order / recovery
- Community feedback
- Supplies
- Crisis response plan review

I. Organize files and prepare reports

1. Files should be complete and organized
2. Keep copies of all records
3. Reports (in conjunction with attorneys and insurance)
   a. Should be factual
   b. Should contain pertinent information regarding the response
   c. Should not be released to anyone unless unauthorized by appropriate officials, e.g., executive management/legal representative
   d. File appropriate forms/claims.
      - *Review liability insurance coverage*
      - *Other local, county, state and federal agency support*
      - *OSHA, EPA, if applicable*

J. Critique entire operation

Endnotes

1. Fischer, Robert J., Green, Gion. *Introduction to Security*. 6th ed. Butterworth-Heinemann. 2003.

2. Garcia, Mary Lynn. *The Design and Evaluation of Physical Protection Systems*. Butterworth-Heinemann. 2001.

3. Headquarters, Department of the Army. *Physical Security* (FM 3-19.30).

Part V

Geographics and Cultural Considerations

Chapter 32

Latin Investigations

Peter F. Wade

Synopsis

This chapter will familiarize the reader with some of the idiosyncrasies of conducting inquiries in Latin America and in seeking information concerning subjects of Latin American origin.

The intention is to provide sufficient information so that the investigator will know what to ask for when requesting assistance in a Latin American country and will know how to obtain accurate identifying data for subjects of Latin American origin. Some tips and cautions are also included to assist the investigator who travels to Latin America to follow investigative leads.

32.1 Surnames

There are several differences in the ways that people identify themselves in Latin America. Someone looking to conceal his or her true identity can use those differences to confuse the investigator without actually lying.

Traditionally, in Latin America, people use both the surnames of their father and of their mother's father. The "first last name" is the first last name of their father. This name stays with the person for life, whether male, female, married, or single. It is this first last name that is the principal personal identifier. The "second last name" is the first last name of the mother's father. All males, and all unmarried females, carry this second last name. It is an additional personal identifier. When females marry, they keep the first last name of their father but they change the second last name to the first last name of their husband. Does that sound confusing? It is. Here is a chart showing what happens:

Father before marriage: John Smith Jones
Mother before marriage: Mary Brown Miller
Father after marriage: John Smith Jones
Mother after marriage: Mary Brown Smith
Son before marriage: William Smith Brown
Daughter before marriage: Judy Smith Brown
Son after marriage to Betty Burton Davis: William Smith Brown
Daughter after marriage to Lou Ward Jensen: Judy Smith Ward

In common conversation, the son and daughter would be referred to as William Smith and Betty Smith. This is true even after Betty Smith weds.

Some confusion occurs in trying to establish information concerning a Latino who has moved to the United States, Often, it is the father's surname that gets dropped when information is taken from a Latino's documents. For example, when a Latino who applies for a Social Security card or driver's license fills out the application, he or she might misunderstand what is meant by middle name on the application. Take Juan Pueblo Gonzalez, for example. He puts the name Pueblo in the space for middle name.

Thus, his name in the official records becomes Juan P. Gonzalez. He is unable to explain and correct the error, and so his identity has changed. Another error is that most women adopt the American norm of using their husband's last name when they come to the United States. There would be nothing in their country of origin with that name as the prime identifier.

If you have an interest in someone of Latin American origin, be sure to obtain both his first and second last names. If he tells you he doesn't have a second last name, he is lying. If he tells you that both of his last names are the same, e.g., Juan Pueblo Pueblo, he may be telling the truth. To further assure that you have checked all possible leads, make inquiries for both name combinations: Juan Pueblo Gonzalez and Juan Gonzalez

Pueblo. In the case of married women, search for the surnames of both of her parents, and for both of her husband's surnames in those combinations.

32.2 Significant Dates

In Latin America, as in many parts of the world, the date is written: day/month/year. For example, October 12, 1982, is written 12/10/82. The stateside investigator tends to interpret 10/12/82 as December 10, 1982. Latinos tend to continue this date sequence custom after arriving in the United States. Whenever a day on an application is 12 or less, inquiry should be made for both possibilities. For instance, if you have a marriage date of 6/9/83, inquire for both June 9 and September 6. Knowledgeable aliens may transpose dates to conceal information. If they are discovered, they can say that they were merely confused.

32.3 National Identity Cards: *Cedulas*

A *cedula* is a national identity card. Most countries in Latin America require them. The *cedula* number is the person's national identity number. Like a Social Security number in the United States, it is the most accurate personal identifier. It will appear in such legal documents as property deeds, wills, arrest records, and civil suits. If you are doing a background investigation on a Latin foreign national who claims never to have had a *cedula* number in the country of origin, make a quick call to the U.S. Consulate General or Embassy in that country. This is an easy way to verify if the country requires a *cedula*. If the country issues *cedulas*, the person who denies having had one is trying to conceal something.

A *cedula juridical* is issued to businesses. This number functions like a Federal Employer Identification Number (FEIN) in the United States. In researching a company, one must obtain its *cedula juridical* number.

32.4 Identifying U.S. Citizens in Latin America

Social Security numbers are not used in Latin America. A legal resident alien is issued a *cedula number*. Nonresident aliens are identifiable by passport number. Most property leases and rental car contracts require a passport or *cedula* number from the renting party. Most hotels require this information at registration. Often, the contract will also include the party's date of birth. Remember that the day and month will be reversed from what you are used to seeing. When attempting to verify the foreign employment or personal history of a U.S. national, be sure that he or she provides a passport number and a *cedula*, or work permit, number for that country.

32.5 Public Record Research

There are several good websites for Latin American newspapers. Many of them have a good archive search. Many newspaper accounts of people identify them by their cedula number. In addition to a name search of the newspaper's archives, a search by *cedula*, *cedula juridica*, or passport number can often identify news articles about an individual or business.

While property records, marriages, divorces, births, criminal convictions and civil suits are generally available through government agencies much as they are in the United States, an investigator may not have easy access to them. Nothing slows a government clerk like a nervous looking gringo standing at the window. That clerk is deciding how much he's going to soak you for the information.

In large government buildings, you will find *tramitadores* or *expediters* who will guide you through the massive red tape for a fee. They are freelance line-jumpers. If you know what it is you are looking for, a *tramitador* may be the solution to your problem. One caution is that these people can be overly helpful and may obtain information to which you have no legal right. You don't want this kind of problem. You could wind up in jail or cause significant embarrassment to your client. If you don't know the nature of the documents you're seeking, it's better to deal with a local attorney.

When a complete business and personal history of a subject is needed, I use an attorney whose office is located near applicable record centers or close to the legislative branch of the government. Explaining my needs and asking what course of action the attorney suggests, I often find that he or she has local sources beyond my knowledge. I usually represent myself as an investor and try to leave the impression that I'll be doing a lot of business in the months to come. This way, perhaps the attorney won't feel that he or she has to take all my money at one time.

I give the attorney a complete list of everything I want to know, including all possible name combinations and date combinations. Instead of asking for particular documents, such as *planos catastros* (history of land title) or *escrituras* (deeds), I explain in simple language what I am trying to find out. I let the attorneys tell me what documents he or she can provide. If it's less than I know is available, I move on to another attorney.

If I'm not in a country where I have identified a trustworthy attorney, I always have at least two attorneys perform the search without letting either know that I've retained the other. If they give me different data, I have a third attorney perform the same search. A good starting point for locating an honest attorney with some command of English is the U.S. consulate in the country. They will provide you with a list of attorneys, with a clear disclaimer, but I've found many of those on the lists to be both competent and reasonable in the fees they charge.

The U.S. Consulate General or Embassy can provide American citizens with a wealth of local knowledge. Many of these offices are well prepared to help the U.S. businessman or investor looking to venture into Latin America. They can often caution the investor regarding areas of disputed land title and areas containing unexploded mines and munitions. They can also identify areas where squatters' rights are a problem for absentee landowners.

If your Spanish isn't fluent, obtain an impartial, professional translation of your documents before leaving the country. One prestigious stateside detective agency obtained what they believed to be public record information from an individual in Honduras only to discover after returning to the United States that they'd been given a rewrite of a magazine article about an automobile club's annual rally. The U.S. Consulate's office can provide a list of reliable translators.

32.6 Verification of Employment, Education, and Criminal and Civil Records

Privacy restrictions vary greatly from country to country. If the background investigation of an individual is overt, ask the individual to request his or her own records be sent to you through the embassy or consular office. Also, a signed release from the individual is helpful in obtaining records in a foreign country. Criminal convictions and civil judgments are generally matters of public record. Credit reports are also widely available.

32.7 Business Terms

The following business terminology is in general usage in Latin America:

Sociedad Anonimo. Most Latin American companies have the initials S.A. after their name. This literally means *anonymous society*. There is nothing sinister about this. An S.A. denotes the same thing that "Inc." or "Ltd." does for an English-language firm. In most countries, there will be public records of the company's address and directors. As with any other due diligence work, if there's no business address, phone listing, credit rating, and so forth, more work needs to be done. While disclosure varies from country to country, there is no automatic secrecy because the company is an S.A.

S.R.L. This means *Sociedad de Responsibilidad Limitado*, which in English is "a society with limited responsibility." This is just another form of S.A., with less strict rules concerning such things as annual stockholders' meetings. It could be compared to partnerships or proprietorships in the United States.

Cedula Juridica. This is a company's corporate tax identification number. In Latin America, it is common for a company to be required to have its invoices printed in consecutively numbered sequence at state-approved printers. This is an attempt to keep businesses from evading sales taxes. The *cedula juridica* number for a company should appear on their invoices. It's very helpful in researching a business.

Plano Catastro. Plano Catastro are official records of property ownership. Often, ownership can be traced to the days of the Spanish conquest.

Compraventa. This is a sales contract, most commonly a real estate sales contract.

Escritura. This is a property deed.

Licenciado. This is a term of respect for an educated person—usually an attorney, but in some countries the term also applies to teachers, architects, and others. If you see the title *Lic.* behind a name, this means *licenciado.*

Ingeneiro. In Latin America, engineers use the initials *Ing.* after their name to denote their professional credentials.

Diputado. This means representative or delegate in the same sense that "Congressman" means "U.S. Representative." If a person uses *Dip.* behind a name, he or she is representing himself or herself to be an elected national official.

32.8 A Word about the Police

It is as unfair to assume that all police in Latin America are corrupt, as it is unfair to assume that all snakes are poisonous—and every bit as prudent.

The police and military in Latin America are keepers of public order, not enforcers of laws. It is their function to maintain the status quo—that is, to keep those with power in power. Hence, if you, the outsider, are asking questions, they will want to know why. The best way for them to find out what you're up to is to ask the people in whom you've shown an interest. I never voluntarily speak to the police.

A word of caution regarding police knowledge of your whereabouts and activities: in many countries your passport, visa, and tourist card information must be reported to the police by your hotel, bus line, airline, and rental car agency. The police have daily access to this information. They can track your movements at will. If your work requires discretion, keep in mind how easy it is for someone with the right connections to trace your movements.

Chapter 33

Conducting Global Investigations and International Due Diligence

Jonathan Turner, CFE, CII

Synopsis

33.1 Introduction

In the three years since this chapter was initially written, globalization has dramatically affected the volume and necessity of international inquiries. Rapidly emerging laws and the security conscious world environment are a distinct change from the international privacy movements that dominated the 1990s. Companies and government, while still being mindful of privacy concerns, are much more focused on the need for accurate information about the people they deal with and the places they do business.

Not surprisingly, the increased globalization of business has also attracted a growing and ever more creative breed of scam artists. From traditional organized crime groups, to technology empowered grifters and confidence men, the explosion of business from a distance has created opportunities for schemes to be successful, and more importantly more opportunities to exploit weaknesses. In many cases the only defense that a company will have is its initial vetting of the vendor, employee, or business opportunity.

To that end, in today's multinational business climate investigators must take their tools around the globe to prevent and respond to allegations of theft, dishonesty, and other improprieties. But how well do those tools travel? What do you need to do to ensure that you and your team are prepared to handle investigations in the information age? Are you prepared to tackle global issues such as privacy, cultural idiosyncrasies, and changing legal standards that can alter investigative activities from legal to illegal?

Operating in a post September 11 world, businesses today are faced with an ever broadening range of investigative realities. Business partners are more often going to be around the globe than on the other side of town. In addition to time zones, organizations cross cultures and languages. The need to properly investigate allegations is also increasing. On the legal front, companies are required to investigate improprieties, but the laws that define a proper investigation vary from state to state and even more drastically from country to country.

With the expansion of business and commercial activities around the globe, business crime has also increased. From industrial espionage to embezzlement, there are people, inside and outside of the organizations, who are actively looking for ways to capitalize on our mistakes. When they find them, they act. Incidences of fraud, misuse of company information, insider trading, and other white-collar crimes are all increasing.

33.2 Globalization Brought Changes

The globalization of business has done more than scatter these cases around the globe. In addition to geographic separation, investigators now have to contend with a wide range of different environments, all throughout a single organization. Companies today are quite likely to have differing language, cultural, and ethnic issues and diverse legal environments. These all affect your ability to investigate otherwise similar allegations.

A. Language, culture, and ethnicity

A person's language, culture, and ethnicity are more than the way that person speaks, looks, and dresses. They reflect core values, ideals, and ways of looking at the world. The structure of a language directly affects the way a person thinks. One of the most common blunders made by early explorers was failing to understand these differences. While we talk about the world shrinking, the reality is that it still contains a wide range of viewpoints and beliefs—factors that affect an employee's propensity to steal and willingness to cooperate with investigators.

Understanding that there may be another viewpoint is half the battle. If you receive allegations or information that involves a distant or international business unit, take time to understand the cultural landscape. No matter how "politically correct" the United States tries to be, the reality is that the rest of the world is not.

Successful international investigators have to recognize that all people are not interchangeable. For example, an investigator who is fluent in a language is not the same as a native speaker, though both are far better than trying to conduct an important interview through an interpreter. Similarly, some cultures respond better to certain types of people, and others clash with specific types of people. Asking direct questions is considered rude in many Asian countries. Questioning a man's honor can put your life in danger in the Middle East. Not only is the technique important, but attention must also be paid to the investigative personnel used in the field. Being of the wrong race, sex, or citizenship can impede an investigator's progress in many developing counties. Knowing the cultural rules will not guarantee success, but it does make the process much faster and easier.

In addition to the language and culture, ethnicity can also be an issue. While there are a few racial groups and more language groups, there are even more ethnic groups. Most countries contain more than one ethnic group, and many contain dozens.

To send an investigator to look into theft allegations in Nigeria, with no understanding of the various linguistic, cultural, and ethnic issues in that country, would limit the probability of success. Nigeria's borders, like many African countries, were created during the colonial period. As such, it contains several very different groups, primarily divided into the North and South. Each group has differing tribal, linguistic, and religious affiliations. Specific local knowledge is necessary for success in any investigation. Sending properly prepared investigators into the region allows them to capitalize on the undercurrents and attributes of the employee base, enabling them to identify the information necessary for management to take action.

B. The legal landscape

Understanding the legal climate is just as important. All countries have legal processes for dealing with internal and external theft matters. How you resolve them, and what actions, mechanisms, and procedures are legal, varies tremendously from region to region.

Applying a standard operating procedure globally makes sense from an efficiency standpoint but will embroil your investigation in a legal quagmire. *There is no single standard, level of proof, or operating protocol that will be accepted globally.* Instead, you will need to think outside of the box and apply your investigative needs and priorities to the current situation in that country or region.

Criminal background checks are a part of many investigations, but the standards for these change radically across the globe. Many European countries restrict data to the individual concerned and law enforcement; there simply are no public records for convictions. To combat this, many employers require applicants to provide a copy of their criminal record. But that does not always work. In Austria, as well as other European countries, criminal records are even purged from the state system after only a few years, meaning that a thief could legitimately provide a clean record to an employer only five years after being convicted.

Active investigation is illegal in parts of the Middle East and Asia, as well as some specific tax havens and other locations. Most countries have specific prohibitions on how investigations are conducted (including the United States). Since we are most familiar with our home turf rules, each one of us typically uses them as defaults. When we go abroad, we have to start from ground zero and ask knowledgeable people, what is legal? If I can prove this, then what happens? What are the ramifications if we terminate this employee?

In addition, any legal analysis must include extralegal considerations. Firing a popular local employee could lead to worker unrest. Having a "foreigner" accuse a "local" can cause "difficulties" for companies operating in some countries. This can be especially problematic in small countries. Feeling "pushed around" by large companies or citizens of bigger countries can create a backlash that must be factored into the investigation.

On the positive side, getting government involvement, even at the highest levels, is often much easier in smaller countries. Understanding these elements can help you guide your company into making the best decision for the specific situation, rather than simply applying the same solution you might use at home. This is not to imply that theft should be tolerated. But rather it is a reminder that there are many paths to the same destination, and alternative legal environments require finding alternative investigative solutions.

C. Geography: distance matters

By the same token, do not underestimate the power of distance. Even within the same country or region, isolated operations quickly develop localized "personalities" of their own. Hard-to-get-to locations, unpopular facilities, and other "unimportant" locations can have very different viewpoints from the corporate headquarters. Especially when you add in the cultural and legal differences discussed above, geography can be a powerful force to deal with in managing international investigations.

Psychologically, distance translates into independence. Many times, the first thing an investigator hears upon landing at a distant office is some variant of, "Dorothy, you are not in Kansas anymore." While this can be intimidating or even threatening, it can also be an asset. Not only are the benefits of your familiar structure gone, but its limitations as well. Many times this distance will translate into flexibility that can work for you in investigating the case.

Also remember that the interest and effectiveness of law enforcement and prosecutors vary across the range of legal systems. Working with a foreign company against local people is not a politically popular move anywhere. To combat this urge, be sure to identify local contributions made by your organization and emphasize the benefits of action.

Witnesses may fear local managers or employees but often have little or no fear of corporate retribution. They may feel that certain types of investigations are improper or even immoral. However, they may provide other types of records or critical information that support your case.

D. Managing international investigations

This globalization of business has created enhanced opportunities for fraud schemes perpetrated against all types of business organizations. These risks can be generally separated into three categories: international or state sponsored schemes; schemes specific to a foreign locale; and insider or employee schemes that take advantage of the holes in the control processes.

There are a growing number of schemes based upon the combination of growing acceptance of international business practices and continued ignorance of the cultural and legal differences between countries. This is compounded by the spectacular growth in the investment arena. Together these factors have produced an explosion in international business arrangements.

The sheer volume of funds that has flown into these arrangements has encouraged the rise of specific ethnic and state sponsored schemes. These include industrial espionage, copyright, patent and trademark infringement, and specific fraud schemes aimed primarily at American and Western European businesses. The fraud schemes are designed to take advantage of the vagaries and risks inherent in an emerging market, as well as the basic greed found in financially motivated individuals (i.e., high-risk investors).

The most amazing attribute common to most of the industrial espionage and international fraud schemes is the lack of preparation or defenses on the part of the victim organizations. Many of these schemes involve highly speculative or fanciful predictions that should be obvious to experienced executives. Yet they dangle extraordinary returns that entice numerous executives and their companies into fairly obvious schemes.

The most common area involves the simple globalization of traditional advance fee, bank instrument, and Ponzi-style schemes. These schemes, perpetrated by either insiders or outsiders, simply exploit control process failures. Established control processes do not translate well to the variety of legal and cultural systems that permeate the international business community. Thus, your business, whether it has numerous international locations or even one key foreign trading partner, has opportunities for failure in the control process.

One of the most easily abused areas involves international currency transfers and the ensuing need for various types of reserve accounts. Current events are always causing fluctuations in the markets, and therefore they provide easy cover for discrepancies. It will be interesting to see how many of these schemes survive the implementation of the Euro, which eliminated the need for many of these accounts.

By the same token, the increased number of foreign vendors and supply outlets has made it easier for fraudsters to create dummy companies for payable/receivable schemes. The varied nature of the world's tax codes has also contributed to the problem by encouraging companies to create complex structures that minimize taxes rather than straightforward and more transparent arrangements. These elements combine to make it simply more difficult to police worldwide operations effectively.

These issues almost guarantee that every business with international dealings will encounter at least one of these issues on a regular basis. How they are dealt with can be another risk area altogether. For companies with a presence in the United States, two sets of laws and regulations are relevant. The first is the Federal Corporate Sentencing Guidelines, spelling out the range of criminal sanctions for businesses that violate federal law. The second is the Foreign Corrupt Practices Act (15 U.S.C.§§78dd-1; 78m, 78f), which can place severe penalties on companies found to have been involved in corruption or bribery of foreign public officials.

Since many fraud schemes involve official corruption at some level, participation in them can create an exposure under these acts. While this chapter does not include a full discussion of these acts, suffice it to say that they spell out the key items that can either increase or reduce the criminal sanctions that may be imposed on those found guilty. The single most important reducing factor is the level and effectiveness of the controls that the company had in place and the company's action (or inaction) in investigating possible violations.

E. "419" scams: Nigerian fraud letters

One of the best illustrations of these points is also one of the most blatant of the international fraud schemes. This involves an unsolicited letter from a foreign individual (usually in a developing nation) who claims to have access to some large fund that he or she needs help in transferring out of the country by either a legitimate or illegitimate means. These letters are very often from Nigeria, and they have developed a reputation in the

United States for using commercially available mailing lists to mass mail, fax, and e-mail these letters to thousands of people across the country.

The gist of the letters, Nigerian and otherwise, is that they need your cooperation to access the funds and that they will pay you a fee for helping them. In some cases they ask the receiver to create an invoice, in others they simply ask for the wiring details for the account that the receiver wants the funds deposited into. The more dangerous letters require that the receiver travel to their country to access the funds, possibly setting the stage for a kidnapping incident.

The following letters demonstrate the range and variety of these enticements:

Example 1

Tue, 14 Dec 2004 20:11:47 -0800
From:Mrs. Funmi Jacobs
ATTENTION:

I am the above named person from Liberia. I am married to Mr. Cletus John who worked with Liberian embassy in Lome-Togo for nine years before he died in the year 2002. We were married for eleven years without a child. He died after a brief illness that lasted for only four days. Before his death we were both born again Christian, we gave our life to christ, maybe because we were looking for a child.

Since his death I decided not to remarry or get a child outside my matrimonial home which the Bible is against. When my late husband was alive he deposited the sum of US $5.3 Million (Five Million,three hundred thousand United States Dollars) with one Bank in Africa. Presently, this money is still with the Bank in Africa. Recently, my Doctor told me that I would not last for the next six months due to my cancer problem the one that disturbs me most is my stroke sickness. Having known my condition I decided to keep this fund in the Bank where it would be safe.

I want an organization or an individual that will use this fund for orphanages, widows, propagating the word of God and to endeavor that the house of God is maintained. The Bible made us to understand that Blessed is the hand that giveth. I took this decision because I don't have any child that will inherit this money and my husband relatives are not Christians and I don't want my husbands efforts to be used by unbelievers.

I don't want a situation where this money will be used in an unGodly way. This is why I am taking this decision. I am not afraid of death hence I know where I am going. I know that I am going to be in the bosom of the Lord. Exodus 14 VS 14 says that the lord will fight my case and I shall hold my peace. I will need to talk to you personally on the telephone, although i am seriously lying down restlessly but at least i can still talk to you on phone to instruct you on what to do in this regard because of my health.

But mostly we will communicate through mails always because of the presence of my husband's relatives around me always. I don't want them to know about this development. With God all things are possible. As soon as I receive your reply I shall inform the security company that you are the beneficiary of the said consignment you will need to claim this funds. I will also issue you an authority letter that will prove you the present beneficiary of this fund. I want you and your organization or family to always pray for me because the lord is my shepherd. My happiness is that I lived a life of a worthy Christian. Whoever that wants to serve the Lord must serve him in spirit and truth. Please always be prayerful all through your life and have the fear of GOD in you.

Any delay in your reply will give me room in sourcing another person for this same purpose. Please assure me that you will act accordingly as I stated herein. for immediate commencement on this transaction, contact me, you can mail me at funmijacobs000@mail2world.com

Please upon your acceptance to help, i will instruct my lawyer to give you all neccessary documents to claim these fund.

Hoping to receive your reply and Remain blessed in the name of the Lord Almighty.

Yours in Christ,
MRS. FUNMI JACOBS

ps: please make sure you send your response to my private email box for security purpose, this is my private box, reply me here: funmijacobs000@mail2world.com, and kindly send your personal number for clearer explanation to you.

Example 2

Tue, 14 Dec 2004 18:57:17 +0200
PRESIDENT/CEO

INVESTMENT PROPOSAL OF FIFTEEN MILLION US DOLLARS US$15,000,000 IN YOUR COMPANY.

I am pleased to write you in order to inform you of my good intention to invest or form a joint partnership business with you. I am one of the directors in security and stock exchange commission in charge of payment of dividends of stock market and am Dr. Mark Johnson.

We have investors both local and foreign who deposited Millions of Dollars in stock market. By virtue of my position as director incharge of payment of dividend to investors, I discovered that one of our clients a (foreigner)who deposited Fifteen million dollars with the commission (stock market) died two years ago and no records to show that he had a relation or next of kin to claim this dividends. All efforts to trace his relative proved abortive.

Now, we have initiated an arrangement to transfer Fifteen Million Dollars (US$15,000,000) accrued as dividends and interest on deposit of Fifteen Million Dollars in reliable foreigner who is willing and able to receive this money as a bonafide next of kin, or relations to the late investor.

We have concluded arrangement to support and prove that whoever receive this fund is a bonafide relation or next of kin to the late investor, this is why I have decided to contact you for assistance to receive this money (US$15M) and invest it in your company for a period of one year or more as may be subject to negotiation.

I strongly believe this is an opportunity for you to increase your capital base of your company. If this proposal is accepted by you, kindly forward you honest response to the email address below for more information and of cause your opinion shall be welcomed concerning this transaction.

Please treat us urgent and confidential.

Regards.
Directors- in charge of payment of dividends of stock market
NB. PLEASE SEND ALL YOUR REPLY TO MY ALTERNAIVE EMAIL ADDRESS: < mark_johnson2008@k.ro >

Example 3

Tue, 30 Nov 2004 13:15:16 +0100
C/CORDOBA NO 21 PLANTA 2-A
28204 MADRID -SPAIN.
FROM: THE DESK OF THE VICE PRESIDENT
INTERNATIONAL PROMOTIONS/PRIZE AWARD DEPT
REF NO: EGS/2551256003/03
BATCH NO: 14/0017/IPD

ATTN: WINNER.

AWARD NOTIFICATION, FINAL NOTICE.

We are pleased to inform you, that as a result of our RECENT LOTTERY DRAWS HELD on the 21th of Nov 2004.Your e-mail address attached to ticket number:11 23 34 38 48 49 46 with serial number:2113 ? 05 drew lucky numbers:13 15 ? 22? 37 39 which consequently won in the 2nd category. you have therefore been approved for a lump sum pay of US$3,715,810.00 (THREE MILLION SEVEN HUNDRED AND FIFTEEN THOUSAND, EIGHT HUNDRED AND TEN US DOLLARS ONLY)

Note that All participants in this lottery program have been selected randomly through a computer ballot system drawn from over 20,000 companies and 30,000,000 individual email addresses from all search engines and web sites. This promotional program takes place every year, and is promoted and sponsored by eminent personalities like the Sultan of Brunei, Bill Gates of microsoft inc and other corporate organisations. This is to encourage the use of the internet and computers worldwide.

For security purpose and clarity, we advise that you keep your winning information confidential until your claims have been processed and your money remitted to you. This is part of our security protocol to avoid double claims and unwarranted abuse of this program by some participants. We look forward to your active participation in our next 4 million euro's slot.

You are requested to contact your clearance/cliam agent MR JUAN DEPEDRO, Foreign Operations Manager, EUROCITY GRUPO SEGURIDAD S.A ON (Email:juandepedro@tsamail.co.za) for processing and remittance of your prize money to a designated account of your choice.

All winnings must be claimed not later than one month After the date of this notice. Please note, in order to avoid unnecessary delays and complications, remember to quote your reference number and batch numbers in all correspondence. Furthermore, should there be any change of address do inform our agent as soon as possible.

Congratulations!!!once more and thank you for being part of our promotional program.

NOTE: YOU ARE AUTOMATICALLY DISQUALIFIED IF YOU ARE BELOW 18 YEARS OF AGE.

Sincerely,
MRS. TINA TOMMY.
VICE PRESIDENT.
INTL LOTERIA PRIMITIVA

Example 4

Date: Tue, 14 Dec 2004 18:23:02 +0100

Dear Sir,
I am Kennedy mboma and I represent Mr. Mikhail Khordokovsky the former C.E.O of Yukos Oil Company in Russia. I have a very sensitive and confidential brief from this top (oligarch) to ask for your partnership in re-profiling funds over US$450 million. I will give the details, but in summary, the funds are coming via Bank Menatep. This is a legitimate transaction. You will be paid 4% for your \\\"management fees\\\".

If you are interested, please write back by email kennedymboma@yahoo.com and provide me with your confidential telephone number, fax number and email address and I will provide further details and instructions. Please keep this confidential; we can't afford more political problems. Finally, please note that this must be concluded within two weeks. Please write back promptly. I will also suggest you visit these news sites on the internet to be better informed about this project.

http://www.winne.com/topinterviews/khodorkovsky.htm
http://newsfromrussia.com/main/2003/11/13/51215.html
http://www.supportmbk.com/mbk/mbk_bio.cfm

http://www.disinfopedia.org/wiki.phtml?title=Mikhail_B._Khodorkovsky

http://www.pbs.org/frontlineworld/stories/moscow/khodorkovskyinterview.html

http://www.forbes.com/finance/lists/75/2004/LIR.jhtml?passListId=75&passYear=2004&passListType=Person&uniqueId=M1IF&datatype=Person

http://mikhail_khodorkovsky_society.blogspot.com/

Write me back. I look forward to it.

Regards
Mr. Kennedy

These letters are uniformly directed to senior executives, business owners, and others who fall into certain profiles. The groups that sponsor them are all based in countries that have limited legal procedures for controlling or punishing the fraudsters. As the sample letters indicate, they play to the sense of adventure and greed in the recipient—evoking images of Humphrey Bogart's Casablanca, where great rewards are possible to people of action.

In fact, there are no such funds, and if the appeal were made for a few thousand dollars the letter would be instantly discarded. But when the stakes are raised, a certain percentage of the population will become involved in these schemes. Interestingly, it is typically educated and successful business people who fall prey to these schemes, sometimes even dragging their companies into the resulting mess.

This scheme depends on a variety of factors, and each letter is styled to accentuate these key points, masking the obvious deficiencies behind the request with pleas for secrecy, secret codes, and large sums. The net effect is that the victim has to participate actively in the scheme, including international travel, the establishment of foreign bank accounts, and other activities. The frantic pace set by the letter writer ensures that each of the respondents acts quickly and in secrecy, thus limiting the amount of objective counsel and scrutiny that is sought.

The final key is the introduction of fear and greed into the transaction. "Hurry," "They are trying to stop us," "If we don't act quickly, the funds will be gone," and other related prompts are designed to encourage the victim's participation and limit the likelihood of telling others about the scheme. This is so successful that many victims refuse to report the crime even after they have been taken, and others refuse to cooperate with authorities because of their perceived participation and gullibility.

The schemers focus on specific target groups and the use the psychology of mass marketing. They send mailings to people throughout the developed nations based around profiles and industry groups. Highly visible people are likely to be targeted, as are entrepreneurs, senior managers, and small business owners. The second level of the scheme is often more subtle, when they may ask the victims to refer others in the course of the scheme, thus further making the victim into an active participant.

The scheme resolves in one of two outcomes. Either the victim has gotten off of the hook in the process or has been relieved of his or her bank balance. In the case of corporate involvement, businesses have found entire operating and benefits accounts cleaned out by international wire, with the funds rapidly moved across the globe. **In the above letter, the groundwork is clearly being laid to demand that the respondent travel to Nigeria to consummate the deal. This will probably lead to the respondent's kidnapping because the resulting ransom demand is much simpler for the fraudster to pursue.**

Although these schemes seem amazingly transparent to some, a number of intelligent and experienced business people are taken in by them every year. In some notable instances, this has involved the use of corporate proceeds at substantial organizations.

F. International "investment" groups

Another type of scam that is becoming very common involves investment plans, groups, or schemes that promise large rewards with minimal risk. These are directed at individual investors and combine several elements that are especially effective when dealing with Americans.

In the typical case, the target is introduced to a "restricted" investment. The "deal" usually involves some sort of esoteric transaction, in some faraway locale, which is grounded in real estate or currency transactions. The fraudster's pitch almost always includes a section designed to play upon conspiracy theories. This can range from the simple "How do you think Rockefeller got rich" type to the play on fears of the New World Order conspiracy.

The final key is that the investment requires little or no understanding of the industry yet delivers a complex return, usually ranging from 200 percent to 10,000 percent in a short time. It is this simple hook of greed, and the willingness to believe in convoluted conspiracy theories, that leads otherwise intelligent people into these deals. These scams have been successfully perpetrated against businesses large and small, and even some legitimate investment groups.

Two recent examples illustrate how these schemes can infiltrate otherwise legitimate channels. In the first scheme, a foreign holding company was purportedly established to fund small growing concerns through private bond placements. The bond funds were to be used to fund an expansion and growth, following which the bonds would be repaid by the proceeds from an IPO. The scam provided a source for the exponentially increasing volume of funds available to bond mutual funds, retirement account managers, and pension funds.

With the explosion of investment funds in the 1990s this scheme found an abundance of investors seeking "undiscovered" opportunities. By portraying the note as a bond offering, this scheme successfully led investors into a false sense of security. The key to selling most of these vehicles was the elaborate risk reduction the scheme entailed. A certificate of insurance from a reputable insurance company accompanied the bonds, apparently bonding the entire proceeds of the project. Telephone calls to the various insuring companies revealed that the bonds were active legitimate policies. At closing, a significant portion of the proceeds was expensed to cover "insurance," further validating the implied protection.

In fact, the policies provided only performance bonding for management contracts, not credit enhancement as they were presented. Often purchased for under $2,000, these bonds provided no protection to the note holders and actually provided little protection to the contracting company. By presenting the matter as insured, the scheme convinced numerous reputable investment houses to market these bonds as low-risk products.

The proceeds from the scheme never made it to the intended company. Instead, the funds were used to provide cash flow to a foreign business owned by the fraudster. The maintenance on the bonds was covered through a traditional "lapping" mechanism in which the proceeds from each successive offering were used to pay the debt on the prior (ostensibly unrelated) issue. Over the course of five years, this scheme involved at least twelve public bond offerings ultimately leading to the default of over $23,000,000 in notes.

A similar, but unrelated, scheme involved purported investment and trading activities in the Far East. Under this "investment program" the funds were to be housed in an international bank until they built up sufficiently to enter the international trading market. At that point they would be used to fund mortgage and development groups that were secured though real estate. The whole transaction was guaranteed to be risk free, because "the money would never leave the bank."

To guide the investors through the maze of complex financing terminology this scheme also used a very effective strategy. The investors' greed was aroused by an elaborate conspiracy theory. They were told that all of the "real money" in international investing was made through only six traders and everyone else was limited to 10 to 20 percent returns. The scheme further described how, up to this point, only governments and large institutional investors had been able to make these trades.

Stage two of the scheme involved the alleged return. The original cycle promised to return all money invested in ninety international banking days, with 40 percent interest. However, the complex paperwork stated that the investment would undergo six cycles, and that investors could remain as long as they wished. With the principal and interest reinvested for all of the cycles, the scheme's documentation promised a return of the original principal and over 8,400 percent interest in only eighteen months.

The final key to this scheme was the subtle sales mechanism. The fraudster would introduce one person to the scheme. He would then casually mentioned that opportunities were still available before the fund closed. This investor would then contact several friends and introduce them to the scheme. They, in turn, would bring in others. One cell, over three months, generated hundreds of investors who wired an average of $35,000 each into the scheme. The entire fraud contained at least twelve of these cells, bringing the volume to over $25,000,000 within a few months.

These frauds all center on specific targets, usually successful professionals, entrepreneurial executives, and owners of small to medium-sized businesses. By playing on fear and greed, the scheme captures the target's attention and encourages him or her to overlook the otherwise obvious deficiencies. The typical target is approached under a variety of guises, usually through friends or family members, further obscuring the sales pitch of the scheme. Finally, for skeptics, the fraudster seems to have tremendous funds at his disposal, typically hosting meetings at his home or in sophisticated offices and calling from various places around the world. In one case the fraudster had set up international telephone numbers that forwarded to his home. He would then call various potential investors and ask them to call him in "Rome," "Paris," or "on his private plane."

Frauds of this type are often accompanied by volumes of official-looking paperwork, typically including letters of introduction, seals, stamps from foreign governments, and other such emblems designed to inspire confidence. In both of the above cases, each prospectus was accompanied by signed personal guarantees from the scheme's sponsor. In a particularly novel approach, one set of documents was accompanied by the sponsor's passport number; this was meaningless, yet it imputed legitimacy to his foreign business connections.

As can be expected neither of the examples yielded any return to the investors. How does personal investment naïveté affect investigations? In both of these cases, investors involved their business entities or business funds in the investment scheme. Alongside these risks are the increased pressures that can arise from such failed investments. Executives involved in fraud against their own companies often cite personal financial failure as the reason they initiated the fraud. Further, as they become financially exposed and more involved with these fraudsters, their companies face increased risk of being directly targeted in these schemes.

G. South American division of a U.S.-based multinational

A third potential source of fraud arises through the risk from a company's own employees and contractors working abroad. These employees are often empowered far beyond corresponding domestic positions, and there are many barriers to thorough oversight. The leading reason for improper management review is profitability. Companies accept any number of different business practices in the countries they operate in. However, it is not until the unit shows sign of unprofitability that the company really examines its local business practices.

Take, for instance, the case of a U.S.-based manufacturing conglomerate that has operating units in several South and Central American countries. These units produced finished goods for local sale and were primarily small, locally staffed companies. During a standard review of one of the South American units, the auditors discovered a number of unreconciled accounts. This was deemed to be an accounting error because the income and balance statements were consistent and the unit was producing a cash profit each period.

They followed up with the local controller, asking for clarification and reconciliation of these accounts. When clarification was not forthcoming, they released the controller from his position. The new controller, working with corporate accountants from the parent company, quickly discovered that the problems extended well beyond accounting irregularities.

A detailed analysis of the books and records was difficult because of the condition of the records, the large number of missing documents, and the language barrier. However, after several weeks the team was able to identify the obvious areas of abuse, including inventory, sales, receivables, and ghosting. They then tackled the final irregularities—in the foreign exchange area.

Their analysis revealed substantial shortages in the foreign currency cash accounts. The records also indicated an extensive network of foreign currency vendors, including some questionable entities. Further analysis revealed that the controller had been coding payments to the foreign exchange categories, while diverting the payments to his family members and their personal accounts.

The key to the scheme lay in the deliberate abuse of the coding and booking processes in the company's accounts. By coding the various equations improperly, he was able to keep each of the categories in balance. He then expanded his scheme, coding payments to accounts including customs and duties fees, employee advances, inventories and others. By using asset and expense accounts, as well as those that reflected directly on the income statement, he was able to adjust his books and minimize suspicion.

Upon discovery of the fraud, a number of employees came forward, telling management about his activities and their concerns. Several admitted to having been involved in the scheme, though the controller received the majority of the benefit. They gave statements that recounted how the controller had capriciously ordered the staff about, ordering them to comply with his nonsensical dictates or lose their jobs. Since the region was economically depressed, they had no recourse and were compelled to comply. Some received some small benefits for their roles, and many did not even know that the controller had involved them until the scheme was uncovered. Through his various schemes the controller converted over $6,000,000 to his use over a five-year period.

All companies are vulnerable to this type of fraud—perhaps not in the same way, or through that same type of scheme, but every organization has a weakness that a senior insider can exploit. Typically, this type of scheme affects larger companies, especially those with operational units in emerging regions. These companies rely on a network of professionals to manage their operations, develop business, and identify sustainable markets in diverse conditions. Under these circumstances, it can be easier for controls to fail, and for policies and procedures to be violated without being noticed.

33.3 Key Controls Are Weakened

Even if the proper controls are theoretically in place, several key controls are weakened, at least to some extent, in the international arena.

The first cause for this is simple geography. The farther apart people are, the more difficult it is to guard properly against dishonesty. Factoring in the complication of cultural, legal, and language differences, the chances for successful dishonesty increase dramatically.

The next cause is in the strength of external controls. The effectiveness of legal systems and law enforcement varies from country to country, as do external auditing standards.

Companies that rely on external audits of international locations will find that this does not provide any real protection against such schemes. The company in the previous example learned (and Enron subsequently demonstrated) that having an international accounting firm audit the books provided no real protection, because the annual audits failed to identify the irregularities and financial theft. In that case, the company initiated litigation against the auditors for negligence in auditing the accounts. The subsequent review of the auditors' work papers identified numerous areas in which they had not even tested the numbers and schedules provided. In other instances, they signed off on documents that never existed.

Finally, the restructuring wave that has swept through the world's businesses has created an environment in which time is precious. Given this, corporate management and internal auditors have ever more limited resources to explore the substance behind reported results. When there are large differences in time zone, language, or culture, managers often simply accept the operational results—especially when the results indicate the projected profitability.

33.4 Merger and Acquisition (M&A) Activities

Dramatic growth followed by the sudden contraction of the global economy led to a dazzling number of high-profile corporate marriages. From the automotive, banking, and natural resources industries to technology, insurance, energy, and manufacturing, this round of consolidations has brought together larger companies than ever before, merging diverse cultural and linguistic differences.

In fact, with companies racing to join the crowd with larger and more aggressive mergers, it was simply a matter of time before some went bad. As it happens, there have now been several mergers, both vertical and horizontal, in which the benefits were never realized, and the costs make the whole effort appear to be a waste of management time. Recent reports in the *Wall Street Journal*, as well as other business periodicals, describe an astoundingly high rate of failures in the high-profile combinations. Shareholders are finally starting to question the value of this tremendous commitment of management time and corporate resources.

Change is the single best enabler of fraud schemes. By altering the traditional processes and procedures, companies create opportunities for a dishonest person to carry out a scheme successfully. In the flurry of M&A activity, companies are radically and rapidly restructuring whole operational processes in their effort to consolidate functional responsibilities. This quest for operational efficiencies through growth, merger, and acquisition creates these opportunities. Management and control functions are simply overwhelmed by the pace and rate of change, leaving holes in the company's armor.

To enable these integrations, many merger scenarios include the divestiture of certain units. Either to accommodate certain anti-competition requirements or to streamline core competencies, these strategic divestitures create the identical opportunities for change based fraud schemes as the M&A side of the equation. In fact, companies are often much less concerned about the operational performance of a unit that is being spun off, even to the extent of dumping poor performers and problem issues into the unit before letting it go. While this may seem an expedient method of getting rid of problems, it will create enhanced opportunity for fraud schemes. Should the divestiture fail or be cancelled, the company could end up with "Frankenstein's monster."

33.5 Limiting Your Risk

While it is impossible to stop motivated and dishonest people from targeting your company, there are steps that you can take to limit your risk of acquiring these problems in the course of a merger or acquisition.

The key is in the make up and intent of the due diligence process. For many companies due diligence efforts are limited to key operations management personnel, assisted by limited audit and legal resources. These efforts are usually inadequate to protect the company's interests from deliberate fraud schemes. *The due diligence process should be a team-based review that analyzes all aspects of the proposed venture, including all of the negative ramifications.*

- Internal audit members should be looking for compliance with current control procedures.
- Legal members should be looking at known and anticipated liabilities. (Who really wants to acquire large known liabilities in this litigious culture?)
- Operational members should be looking at ease of integration and potential synergies.
- Investigators should be looking for unanticipated problems, including both deliberate and systemic issues. Too often, the modern due diligence exercise consists of a hasty verification of known information, rather than a detailed review of the situation. *By adding investi-*

gative due diligence elements, companies can mitigate risks on the front end.

Despite the seemingly obvious risks inherent in M&A activity, companies often overlook the risks in their haste to complete the process. Every fraud scheme is customized to the organization and the opportunities available to the criminal.

In preparing to evaluate potential fraud vulnerability, the investigator should be prepared to conduct a "pre-fraud" analysis to determining the reasonably possible actions by each potential player and establishing whether or not proper controls are in place.

Similarly, if your organization is undergoing even small amounts of M&A activity, analyzing the due diligence areas in the process will forewarn the investigators. Incorporation of these risk-mitigation techniques can help minimize fraud opportunities. Practically, however, all M&A activity involves turmoil and opportunities for fraud.

The most common type of change based fraud comes from employees. These may be people who are disillusioned by the process or believe that they are slated for termination. The stresses of the transition may push them past their ordinary boundaries. Whatever the cause, these disaffected persons pose the greatest risk to the company.

While some frauds are committed by one person, it is difficult for a single employee, regardless of his or her position, to perpetrate a complex fraud. However, a combination of persons, acting in concert, can damage any organization if they are properly positioned. To assess the risk factor for employee fraud properly the potential combinations of people and positions must be analyzed for early warning signs.

Unfortunately, in many organizations, management is often predisposed to find fault or expect problems with lower-level employees and, equally, to not see problems with upper-level or executive employees. Fraud prevention should focus on identifying the potential abuses in a given position and ensuring that preventive measures are in place, especially with regard to senior level positions. This is especially true in M&A activities, where midlevel and senior managers are vital to the transition process.

Investigators can position themselves to anticipate, control, and manage the risk of potential losses by appreciating the full extent of the damage that can be done by the dishonest employee, damage that escalates according to the level of the employee. Most established employee frauds, with the exception of petty cash theft, exceed $1 million. Many exceed $5 million.

In planning for these contingencies and preparing preventive measures, the company must anticipate a financial loss, the possible participation of one or more executives, and the loss of business activity stemming from the efforts devoted to discovery and investigation.

While many people still associate industrial espionage with "James Bond," an increasing number of companies are discovering that they have been attacked precisely at these key transition points. The attacks are focused and structured with specific objectives. Unfortunately, many of them are never discovered.

What is important in implementing preventive planning or handling fraud cases is that these people strike from the inside at the vulnerable areas in your organization. By identifying those particular areas where controls are either not in place or are ineffective, the dishonest employee begins to conceive a specific plan. "20/20 hindsight" is a phrase that is often used in discussing these cases. Once uncovered, the scheme becomes so apparent that people often wonder how it was possible that no one caught on. However, it is important to remember that the key to a successful fraud is that honest persons should not suspect anything. Employee schemes and espionage cases alike depend on this failure of the control process.

33.6 Due Diligence

The key to maximizing success is the establishment of sound due diligence investigation procedures in the evaluation of potential candidates. In addition to the standard audit and operational components, companies are increasingly including what are typically called investigative or risk management elements, designed to address areas of concern.

Under the due diligence investigation model, the standard verification tools are supplemented by a fraud and abuse audit process. Rather than approach the candidate from the verification perspective, these tests are designed to ferret out specific control weaknesses and failures, as well as identify active schemes.

A team of specialists, who should have operational knowledge of the business and expert knowledge in the prevention and detection of fraud schemes and related employee dishonesty issues, typically reviews these elements. During the pre-acquisition phase their review will include audit, inspection, and testing elements, as well as competitive intelligence, blind testing, and background related elements. The team focuses on the identification of potential exposure areas and then aggressively tests those areas for signs of active or potential fraud schemes. This combination of symptom and source testing provides the most effective set of quantifiable results.

A multidisciplinary team, including representation from the internal operations, audit, risk management and legal departments, as well as specialists in fraud detection and control process testing, should handle the due dilligence investigation. This team, working independently or as part of the pre-integration team, can isolate and test the key vulnerability areas effectively and efficiently.

Similar to an annual physical, these reviews can produce surprising results. In many cases they reveal information that can alter purchase terms, sometimes substantially. It is important to remember that these reviews serve as management tools, providing valuable intelligence even if fraud is not detected.

The investigative team, while its duties will be customized to each particular project, will review four areas that produce the greatest numbers of red flags in the fraud auditing process. Likewise, they provide the fastest means for testing and identifying red flags in an M&A candidate.

Management backgrounds are an often-overlooked aspect of the process. Conducting objective research into the background and history of the current management team can provide essential information in the decisionmaking process. Attributes such as lifestyle, habits, and circumstances, while not necessarily relating to fraud, can provide hints of potential weaknesses and vulnerabilities. Especially important in dealing with industrial espionage issues, executive foibles can lead to corporate losses.

Purchasing and production flow paths provide a blueprint of the operational approach of the unit. Review of these functions will provide access to the key bottlenecks and processes in the system; locations where careful review will reveal active fraud schemes. Analysis of these trends, along with interviews of the key personnel, typically provides a comprehensive listing of the unit's weaknesses and potential failures. This is the most detailed section of the investigative review, and the area in which most active frauds are discovered.

Competitive intelligence refers to industry and competitor benchmarking and comparison. Rather than dealing with confidential matters, this deals with a comparison of the subject unit to the industry, market, and sector trends, providing the acquirer the ability to verify that the unit will perform at the expected level. In recent years some spectacular failures have occurred when recently acquired divisions collapsed soon after the deal closed.

The fourth element is *customized testing*. Because each business unit is different, testing must be customized accordingly. It is usually a mistake for due diligence exercises to ignore this component of a successful business. Instead, as part of the due diligence investigation, the review includes identification and inspection of these features to establish risk and fraud potentialities.

As important as the results of the tests are the responses of management and staff to the findings. Experienced fraud investigators can spot problematic responses and learn to give inappropriate management reactions as much if not more credence that the original test results. In contrast to the standard audit, in which the goal is to clear the issues, this exercise is designed to raise the acquiring company's awareness and allow it to evaluate fully the potential problems before accepting responsibility and closing the deal.

33.7 Mergers

The most disruptive of these processes is the merger of one company with another. There have been several recordbreaking mergers of this type lately, including DaimlerChrysler and Exxon/Mobil. Under the traditional model, the two organizations combine to form one. In the modern variation, the two companies combine to form an entirely new entity with a dual management structure. The key risks lie in the separate phases: picking a partner, evolution of the merger, management of the process, and birth of the resultant entity. At each point there are risks for internal and external schemes.

Picking a merger partner should be approached with at least at much care as picking a spouse. Instead, in many cases it is approached like picking up a date in a singles bar—the best of those present and available. In today's whirlwind atmosphere of mergers, companies are quickly joining up with organizations they hardly know, companies with limited track records or a history of management turbulence. Does this make these companies unworthy suitors? No, but it does give pause for concern.

As several recent, spectacular collapses have shown, there is more to a company than a collection of business operations or a stock price. Investors and customers can be fickle. The current trend for "roll-ups" and industry consolidation has created a market for "made for the sale" companies. These can in turn consist of little more than momentum, as the new partner quickly learns. The key areas here are in the selection process. Any merger built upon speed and hasty decisionmaking will have resultant fraud costs; the question is, to what extent.

Having selected a merger partner, companies begin the process that can lead to the establishment of a new model of efficiency or the destruction of their legacy. It is this evolutionary process that takes the two companies from where they begin to where they aim to end up that holds the most opportunity for fraud and espionage. As the two companies meet each other and begin to blend it will quickly become apparent that there are two of everything that matters, and more in the middle and lower levels. These employees will be faced with close scrutiny to see who keeps their jobs and who moves on.

Disaffected employees, from the shop floor to the executive suite, are the keys to employee fraud schemes and corporate espionage efforts. Even in the most innocent of cases, where are the soon-to-be-let-go employees going to go? They will go to a company's competitors, because they can demonstrate value through knowledge of the industry and, of course, its operations. On the other hand, believing that they are on the way out, they can easily sabotage or subvert key corporate initiatives, even if they do not commit outright fraud.

Recognizing these risks, companies are working to establish a viable integration plan before announcing the merger. This helps by identifying in advance the potential areas of concern. Successful fraud neutralization depends on both early notification and active suppression throughout the process. The key positions that are being consolidated or eliminated must be identified and controlled to minimize the risk of fraud.

With investigators playing a role in the merger analysis process, companies afford themselves the opportunity to test for potential hidden problems in advance and thus mitigate their exposure through the process. Investigative due diligence is a tool that can be easily integrated into the standard process with minimal invasiveness. Further, there is no reason the other party will ever be aware of the investigation.

33.8 Acquisitions

In contrast to mergers, acquisitions involve companies acquiring additional smaller companies, new ventures, start-ups, and other operating units. These are often reviewed much less carefully than a merger candidate, often using low-level audit exercises and operations personnel only in the due diligence process. By far, the leading indicator of potential fraud comes in the juxtaposition of contrasting cultures. Typically this occurs when a much larger, bureaucratic organization absorbs a smaller, more entrepreneurial company. In these instances, common in emerging technology sectors, a single disaffected employee can easily cause significant losses both in value and market position.

Analyzing the acquired company's culture and structure from a fraud-risk perspective provides insight into potential problems. In one recent example, a multinational corporation was acquiring an operating unit of another multinational corporation. The initial due diligence investigation revealed the transition to be a turnkey opportunity. However, the investigation also identified several significant concerns, including the lack of unit-based financial controls and a high degree of interdependence with the former parent. While these were not necessarily indicators of fraud, they did isolate several core areas that would not longer exist after the transfer. In the absence of these controls during the transition, a window of opportunity for internal or external fraud schemes would exist. Since the unit was culturally and geographically independent, the risk of this type of scheme seemed significant.

This is especially true, as in this case, if the unit in question is in another country, especially one with a different language and legal framework. The identification of these elements, and the evaluation of the risk factors in advance of the purchase, allowed both multinationals to structure the process to provide for uninterrupted control procedures, ensuring that all of the potential loopholes were closed. Had they not realized these risks at the outset, the acquiring company would have created control failures for at least some period of time. Culturally this is significant, because the acquired unit had tremendous loyalty to the prior owner, and there were strong feelings among the employees regarding the transfer. Since the change was also going to involve restructuring responsibilities, their company correctly identified the potential for abuse.

According to the business press over the past few months, an astounding 70 percent of acquisitions fail to meet their stated goals. Some of these fail because potential synergies do not develop as quickly as anticipated; others should have been obvious from the beginning. Almost weekly, business periodicals feature stories of failed ventures, typically focusing on easily identifiable elements: culture, strategic fit, and market placement. What is less often discussed is the role that investigative due diligence and analysis could have had in the evaluation process. Using these tools in the M&A process, companies can explore and mitigate the possible downsides in advance.

33.9 Conclusions

As your company evaluates potential companies for either merger or acquisition, consider looking into the due diligence process. While many companies are revamping their procedures to take these modern tools into consideration, many others are going in the opposite direction, hastily consummating marriages only to seek annulment a few days later. While there is strong pressure to move promptly and react to changing market conditions, companies have the ability to protect themselves on the front end.

Using the due diligence investigation during the standard pre-deal process usually takes no more calendar time than does the traditional method, though it does increase the size of the project team. The difference in financial commitment is immaterial and becomes inexpensive insurance for those instances when significant issues are raised. In a recent case, the acquiring company was able to restate the purchase terms based on the findings of the due diligence investigation. While no significant fraud was discovered, the resulting savings paid for the review process 1,000 times over. That company is sold on the process having seen it in action.

About the Compilers

Reginald J. Montgomery, CPP, PSP, CLI, CFE, CP, CST. Following retirement from local law enforcement in 1979, Mr. Montgomery became a New Jersey licensed private investigator. He is President of R.J. Montgomery Associates in Saddle River, New Jersey. He has served as vice-chair for ASIS International's Standing Investigations Council and as the chairman of the Northern New Jersey Chapter. He is a life member and past assistant national director for the National Association of Legal Investigators. He is a life member of the Association of Certified Fraud Examiners. He currently serves on the board of directors of Intelnet as well as the Council of International Investigators. Mr. Montgomery served as president of New Jersey Licensed Private Investigators Association from June 1996 to June 2000.

Mr. Montgomery specializes in corporate asset protection and criminal defense investigations. He has given hundreds of speeches for national and international associations on a number of subjects ranging from product diversion and protecting intellectual property to workplace violence investigations. He has conducted interview and polygraph workshops. He teaches a number of subjects such as "The Laws of Inadequate Security" and the CPP Review program. He is an adjunct professor at New Jersey City University. Mr. Montgomery has been accepted as an expert in virtually every aspect of criminal defense, corporate security and investigative related matters. He is a certified polygraphist, protection professional, physical security professional, legal investigator, fraud examiner, security trainer and international investigator. He has appeared on dozens of network television programs as a polygraph and investigative expert and was featured in the business section of the *New York Times*. Mr. Montgomery was a contributor to *Advanced Forensic Criminal Defense Investigations* (Lawyers & Judges Publishing Co.).

William (Bill) J. Majeski is a former New York City police detective, who served with distinction for twenty-one years. He has a Bachelor of Science degree from John Jay College of Criminal Justice and is a graduate of the FBI National Academy, Quantico, Virginia. Over the eighteen years since his retirement from NYPD, he has owned and operated Majeski Associates Inc. (www.Majeski.Net), a full service investigative firm. Bill has successfully completed numerous complex investigations, becoming a recognized specialist in areas of corporate litigation, corporate and small business risk analysis and white collar crime. He also has extensive experience with criminal defense and prosecution. Bill is a recognized expert in interviewing techniques and body language, and developed the "Power Interview."

He is a former adjunct professor in the Graduate Criminal Justice Program of Long Island University, and for ten years directed academic programs as the chief instructor for the New York Institute of Polygraph Science. Mr. Majeski lectures on interviewing techniques, investigative procedures, polygraph methodology and a host of other topics to corporate, private and government sectors. He has written many articles for professional journals and has been published in *Parade* magazine. He has had the distinction of being featured in many publications including *Time* magazine, the *Sunday New York Times* and the *New York Daily News*. He is also the author of *The Lie Detection Book*, a Ballantine publication. Mr. Majeski has appeared on a variety of television shows and radio programs in connection with the interpretation of body language and his expertise on polygraph techniques and procedures.

Over the past three years Mr. Majeski has been a frequent guest on FOX News, MSNBC, CNN and Court TV. He is called upon for his insight and opinion on current high profile criminal and civil cases, as well as his evaluation of the investigative procedures being employed in the course of those investigations. Some of the shows Bill has appeared on include; Hannity and Colmes, Catherine Crier Live, Closing Arguments with Nancy Grace and the Abrams Report.

For more than thirty years Bill has taken an active roll in the polygraph profession. Mr. Majeski is a certified polygraph examiner and has conducted thousands of interviews, interrogations and polygraph examinations. He currently holds membership in a number of national polygraph organizations. He is the former president of the New York State Polygraph Association, a position he held for three years. He also sat, for two years, on the board of directors for the American Association of Police Polygraphists.

About the Contributors

John S. Belrose has twenty-six years of experience in the security industry and brings a high level of expertise in most areas of security and investigations. A licensed investigator in Massachusetts, Mr. Belrose has directed and trained field investigators and undercover agents, foreign and domestic, for American International Investigations, Inc., and is experienced in covert operations in multiple countries, and was a field investigator, undercover agent and supervisor of investigations for Burns International Investigations. He was a member of the U.S. Air Force from 1958 to 1961, a member of the presidential protection team for Michael Dukakis during his campaign for the U.S. presidency, and for Vice-President Spiro Agnew. He has conducted investigations and security consulting in Middle Eastern nations, and has conducted nuclear plant background investigations. Mr. Belrose has had extensive specialized training in intelligence gathering and analysis, nuclear security, bomb search and sabotage, and fire and arson investigations.

Julius Bombet, certified legal investigator and certified fraud examiner, was formerly with the Louisiana State Police and served as chief investigator for the Baton Rouge District Attorney's office for five years. He also has nine years of experience as a staff investigator for a large personal injury law firm. He served as national director of the National Association of Legal Investigators and served as chairman and board member of the Louisiana State Board of Private Investigator Examiners, the state's investigative licensing authority. He is the second vice president for the National Council Of Investigation and Security Services. Julius Bombet was presented with the "Investigator of the Year Award" in 1994 by the Louisiana Private Investigators Association and the "Investigator of the

Year Award" in 1998 by the Global Investigators Network. In 1999 at the Northeast Super Conference, he was awarded the first "Julius Bombet Lifetime Achievement Award" for service to the investigative profession.

Gerald R. (Gary) Brown, after over two decades as an Air Force officer and special agent of the AF Office of Special Investigations, opened his statement analysis and questioned document examination business, G. Brown & Associates, in 1988. His business serves the federal, corporate, legal and private investigative communities in thirty-five states and six countries. He also works pro-bono, cold-case homicides as a member of the Vidocq Society. His analyses of the Clinton deposition in the Paula Jones case and the anthrax letter have been published nationally by the *Washington Post/Los Angeles Times* news service and he has been interviewed on radio and TV throughout the country. He has been a speaker at seminars sponsored by corporations, federal investigative agencies, local law enforcement agencies, and private investigative associations in the United States, Canada and the United Kingdom.

Mr. Brown has a B.A. in international affairs from Texas Christian University, an M.S. in general studies (specializing in investigative techniques) from George Washington University and has done additional graduate work toward an M.P.A. at the University of Southern California. He is also a distinguished AFROTC graduate at TCU and a graduate of the AF Squadron Officer School and the AF Command and Staff College. He is a member of Intelnet, the American Society for Industrial Security International, the Federal Investigators Association, the Northwest Fraud Investigators Association, the Air Force Association and the Association of Former Office of Special Investigation Special Agents.

Matthew Buchert was employed as an investigator working at the home office of Bombet, Cashio, and Associates in Baton Rouge, Louisiana. A native of the area, Matthew left to serve in the United States Coast Guard, both in the states and abroad. Upon returning to Louisiana, he graduated from Southeastern Louisiana University in Hammond, Louisiana, with a bachelor's degree in criminal justice and a minor in mathematics. From there, he returned to Baton Rouge and began employment as a staff investigator with Bombet, Cashio & Associates. Matthew then gained a position as a private consultant in the Los Angeles, California area, where he works today.

James R. Buckley completed a distinguished career in law enforcement of more than thirty-two years, serving as the chief of detectives for the City of Paterson, New Jersey. Upon retirement from the Paterson Police Department, Mr. Buckley accepted a position as the advisor to the Special Agent in Charge of the Drug Enforcement Agency (DEA). In this capacity, Mr. Buckley was responsible for analyzing and drafting the agency's long-term strategies, future initiatives, management plans and corporate policies. As co-founder of Buckley Petersen Global (BPG), Mr. Buckley has conducted numerous high profile security assessments throughout the New York/New Jersey metropolitan area.

James P. Carino, CPP, VSM, a graduate of Colgate University, with an M.A. from the University of Hawaii, is president of Executive Security Consultants, Inc. (ESC), a company he formed in 1982. ESC specializes in conducting security surveys, training and major investigations. He also provides expert witness testimony in civil suits involving claims of security negligence. Based in Pennsylvania, some of his specific engagements have involved design of total security programs and systems for U.S. business and industrial firms, universities, hospitals, licensed nuclear facilities, and the aerospace industry, as well as development of executive security protection programs and guard force qualifications and training standards, worldwide. Mr. Carino is a retired Lt. Colonel, U.S. Air Force. He served as a special agent with the Air Force Office of Investigations for twenty years with his last position being director of criminal investigations. He is the founder and executive director of Intelnet, a worldwide network of investigators and security professionals, co-founder and chairman of the board of the Pennsylvania Association of Licensed Investigators, and a member of numerous other professional associations. He has served as an adjunct professor at Alvernia College and St. Joseph's University in the undergraduate and graduate programs.

Grace Elting Castle, CLI, is the former editor of *P.I. Magazine*. She owned and operated Castle Investigations in Oregon for several years before moving to Chicago, where she was employed for over six years by Paul J. Ciolino & Associates, LLC., first as investigations manager, and then as the executive managing director and Innocence Project Coordinator. A former newspaper editor, reporter and photographer, she has edited several professional journals and newsletters, including *The Legal Investigator* and *The Docket Sheet.* In addition, she created and edits *Cluesonline*, the original online newsletter for professional investigators. As a civil litigation investigator, she has worked with the attorneys who pioneered sexual exploitation cases against youth organizations, as well as assisting victims of all-terrain vehicle (ATV) collisions prove claims against the manufacturers. Her work in criminal defense has included high profile, as well as indigent defense, cases, particularly on behalf of minority defendants. Castle is a past president of the Oregon Association of Licensed Investigators, Inc. (OALI). She was the editor and co-author of *Advanced Forensic Civil Investigations* and *Advanced Forensic Criminal Defense Investigations.*

Paul J. Ciolino, CFE, BCFE, CII, who is a lifelong resident of the Chicago area, owns Paul J. Ciolino & Associates, LLC, and Dearborn Process Service, Inc. He specializes in complex criminal defense and fraud investigations, as well as wrongful conviction investigations. A stunning videotaped homicide confession that he obtained from a double murder suspect in February 1999 has been seen on most major television outlets in the Western Hemisphere. He has been featured in numerous publications in the U.S., Canada, Europe, South America and Australia. CBS News Anchor Dan Rather has called Ciolino, "One of America's top five investigators." Licensed in Illinois, Louisiana and Wisconsin, Mr. Ciolino is a popular lecturer at investigative seminars and conferences, as well as at Yale Law School. Mr. Ciolino is a past national director of the National Association of Legal Investigators, Inc. (NALI), and a past president and life member of the Special Agents Association in Chicago. He has been the recipient of numerous special awards, including being named CII's 1999 "Investigator of the Year." He was the compiler and a co-author of the investigative textbooks, *Advanced Forensic Civil Investigations* and *Advanced Forensic Criminal Defense Investigations.*

Steven Cooper is a staff investigator employed in the home office of Bombet, Cashio and Associates, Baton Rouge, Louisiana. A native of Louisiana, Steven obtained a bachelor's degree in criminal justice with a minor in sociology from the University of Louisiana at Lafayette. From there Steven attended law school where he earned a Juris Doctorate from the Southern University Law Center and has been admitted to practice in the State of Louisiana.

Harold F. Coyne, Jr., PPS, is the president and director of operations for Coyne Consulting Group, Inc. With fifteen years in the industry, Mr. Coyne has combined experience in technical, investigations and security solutions. A Massachusetts private detective and licensed firearms instructor, Mr. Coyne is a member of the Intelligence and Security Firm of the United Kingdom, the International Executive Guild, the Nine Lives Association, the International Foundation for Protection Officers, and the International Association of Counter Terrorism and Security Professionals. Among Mr. Coyne's major case assignments were the design and implementation of the security for a billion-dollar shipyard that was expected to produce under government contracts; the design and implementation of the protective services and security system for a major telephone communication corporation; serving as an expert witness on ballistics and facility security for an entertainment industry leader to investigate a multiple shooting; providing protection and transportation for members of the Bush family, and other governors, congressmen and representatives during the recent presidential debates, and providing protection to visiting dignitaries and high government officials from the Republic of China.

Robert DiPasquale, CPA, CFE, is a partner in the Business Investigation Services (BIS) Department at J.H. Cohn LLP. He is the past chairman of the board of regents of the Association of Certified Fraud Examiners, and is a past president of the New Jersey Chapter of the Association of Certified Fraud Examiners (three terms). In the year 2004, Bob was admitted as a "Fellow" by the Association of Certified Fraud Examiners and named "Certified Fraud Examiner of the year." Bob has been retained to perform investigatory services involving embezzlements, criminal and civil matters, including tax evasion, money laundering, Ponzi schemes and investment schemes, kickbacks, stockholder disputes, matrimonial and malpractice issues, economic damage computations, and healthcare and bankruptcy fraud. Bob has authored numerous articles and also lectures extensively on the area of white collar crime. Bob also has been appointed by federal and state courts as a forensic accountant and expert witness. Bob received a B.S. in accounting from Fairleigh Dickinson University.

Robert A. Dudash is retired from the U.S. Air Force, having served for over thirty years on active duty. During the last eighteen years of his career, he was a Special Agent for the Air Force Office of Special Investigations (OSI) until his retirement in May 1989.

After retiring from active duty, he continued working in the investigations field as a Contract Investigator for several federal government agencies, conducting background investigations for these federal agencies. In mid-1989, he founded Investigative Services, Incorporated and is licensed as a Private Investigator in both Iowa and Nebraska.

He is a Certified Fraud Examiner (CFE), a member and a Regional Director of the Council of International Investigators (CII), a member of National Council of Investigation and Security Services (NCISS), a member and Regional Director of Intelnet and a member and an Assistant Regional Director of the National Association of Legal Investigators (NALI). He is currently the President for the Association of Former OSI Special Agents.

Jay L. Groob, president and managing director of American Investigative Services, is considered one of the foremost authorities on investigative techniques in the Northeast. He has provided testimony in both federal and state courts on drug and homicide cases and has been classified as an expert on auto fraud investigations.

Mr. Groob is the 2002 recipient of the International Investigator of the Year Award from the Council of International Investigators (CII), an elite organization for private investigators whose members include officers from Scotland Yard, the FBI and Interpol. He is also the newly elected first vice president of CII and was the regional director and Internet committee chairman. As past chairman of the Council's Strategic Plan Committee, Mr. Groob has been instrumental in enhancing public awareness of the Council, and has forged strategic alliances with members around the world.

Mr. Groob is a graduate of Northeastern University's College of criminal justice, where he received a Bachelor of Science degree cum laude. In furtherance of his education, Mr. Groob has completed the Interviewing and Interrogation Course, the Kinesic Interview Technique Seminar offered through the Justice Department and the Vehicle Theft Investigation program at Montgomery County Community College, as well as various other seminars and workshops. Mr. Groob has also appeared in numerous publications and has been a guest lecturer at the Boston Bar Association, Boston University Law School and at other professional seminars.

Serving the investigative profession for over twenty years, Jay Groob brings a wealth of experience in all areas of investigation to the management of AIS and cases.

Kitty Hailey, CLI, has been an investigator for more than thirty years. Her early career involved the roles of chief investigator, manager and educator of a large New Jersey-based agency specializing in family law and personal injury work. During her career she has expanded her areas of expertise to include multi-plaintiff litigation, malpractice and criminal defense investigations. Ms. Hailey is a frequent writer and contributor to investigative journals and magazines. She is a contributing writer to the textbooks *Advanced Forensic Civil Investigations, Advanced Forensic Criminal Defense Investigations* and the first edition of *Corporate Investigations*. She has authored a compilation of her articles in a volume entitled *The Professional Investigator*. *Code of Professional Conduct: Standards and Ethics for the Investigative Profession* is her most important work. It establishes the criterion against which all investigative actions can be based. Ms. Hailey was the winner of the 2004 Investigator of the Year Award for the New Jersey Licensed Private Investigators Association (NJLPIA). She was the winner of the 2001 Julius "Buddy" Bombet Lifetime Achievement Award. She has won five industry-related Editor/Publisher awards as well.

Bruce H. Hulme, CFE, is a past president of the National Council of Investigation and Security Services (NCISS) and of the Associated Licensed Detectives of New York State (ALDONYS). He is also chairman of, or liaison to, several professional association legislative committees representing licensed private investigators, security professionals and certified fraud examiners. He serves as a member of the executive board as legislative liaison of the New York Chapter of Certified Fraud Examiners, and has lectured extensively at seminars presented by the profession's leading associations. Mr. Hulme assisted in drafting a provision of the federal Drivers Privacy Protection Act of 1994, with respect to obtaining access for licensed private investigators and security firms. He testified before the Federal Trade Commission on behalf of the private investigation industry's position on consumer information privacy. His participation helped create the record that formed the basis of the FTC's analysis of computer database services. He has testified before Congressional committee hearings including the House Committee on Banking and Financial Services on Identity Theft and Gramm-Leach-Bliley Act Implementation with respect to privacy issues. He was appointed by Governor George E. Pataki to serve as a member of the New York State Security Guard Advisory Council, and is an advisory board member of John Jay College of Criminal Justice. Mr. Hulme is president of Special Investigations, Inc., in New York City and is a licensed private investigator and a certified fraud examiner.

Don C. Johnson, CLI, CII has over twenty years experience as a professional investigator. He is the founder and owner of Trace Investigations in Bloomington, Indiana, a private investigations firm serving south central Indiana's business and legal community since 1990. Indiana's first certified legal investigator, he is a past president of the Indiana Society of Professional Investigators and edits *The NCISS Report*, the quarterly journal of the National Council of Investigation and Security Services. In 2003, Mr. Johnson was awarded NCISS' prestigious "Wayne Wunder Memorial Award" for distinguished service to his profession. A well known association delegate, writer and lecturer, Mr. Johnson is also a member of the National Association of Legal Investigators, the Council of International Investigators and an associate member of the Association of Certified Fraud Examiners. He is the editor of *PI Magazine*, the *Journal of Professional Investigators*, and a contributing author to *Advanced Forensic Civil Investigations* and *Advanced Forensic Criminal Defense Investigations*, both published by Lawyers & Judges Publishing Company. In 2001, Mr. Johnson was appointed by the governor of Indiana to the Private Detective Licensing Board, a division of the Indiana Professional Licensing Agency in Indianapolis, and he was elected president of the licensing board in January 2004. He is a former intelligence analyst with the U.S. Air Force Security Service, now known as the Air Intelligence Agency.

Sal Lifrieri, CEO and president, served as the Director of Security and Intelligence Operations for the Office of Emergency Management under Rudolph Giuliani, was the head of the Protective Operations Unit of New York City's prestigious Municipal Security Section, and is a retired "Detective First Grade" of the New York Police Department (NYPD). Mr. Lifrieri retired from the NYPD in January 2001 after twenty years of service. He received numerous decorations and awards, and was specially assigned to the Intelligence Division, where he developed and led the department's "Russian Organized Crime Project." His previous experience provides Mr. Lifrieri with the background and expertise he now utilizes in his leadership of Protective Countermeasures & Consulting, Inc.

Robyn R. Mace, Ph.D. is a visiting assistant professor at the University of Memphis. Her educational achievements include a Ph.D. in Criminal Justice from Rutgers University; an M.S. in Criminology from the University of Pennsylvania; and B.S. in Economics from the University of Pennsylvania. Dr. Mace is a principal at Intellitech Security Group in Jersey City, New Jersey.

Before being employed at the university, Dr. Mace was principal planner/program development specialist with the Jersey City Police Department. Her dissertation on prosecuting computer crime was partially supported by the National Institute of Justice.

Dr. Mace is a professional law enforcement trainer and regularly addresses national and regional business, and criminal justice audiences on a variety of topics, including strategic planning, police management and supervision, computer crime, crime analysis and external funding.

Michael C. McDermott has been working in the field of forensic audio analysis and voice identification since 1978. He has received training in forensic audio analysis from Rockwell International, Voice Identification, Inc., Kay Elemtrics, the Michigan State Department of State Police, the New York Institute of Forensic Audio to name just a few. Mr. McDermott is a member of the American College of Forensic Examiners. He is a past chairman of the Board of Recorded Evidence of the American College of Forensic Examiners, past chairman of the Voice Identification and Acoustical Analysis Subcommittee of the International Association for Identification, past chairman for the Certification Board for Voice Identification Examiners of the International Association for Identification. He is a certified expert in Voice Identification and Acoustical Analysis by the American College of Forensic Examiners, the International Association of Identification and the International Association of Voice Identification. Mr. McDermott is also a certified expert in the field of Audio Authentication by the American College of Forensic Examiners.

Mr. McDermott's presentations of aural and spectrographic voice identification analysis results have been accepted in federal and state courts, in arbitration hearings, and administrative hearings. He has worked for individuals as well as private, corporate and governmental entities, including federal and state law enforcement agencies. The accuracy of this analytical method has even allowed Mr. McDermott to distinguish the voices of identical twins.

His work using aural and spectrographic sound and voice analysis has not been limited to just the identification of human voices. He has used this technology in his work in the area of aviation accident analysis to identify aircraft transmission sources and pilot's voices. In the analysis of cockpit voice recordings, he has used this technique to identify mechanical events such as switches and circuit breaker pops in an aircraft cockpit as well as gun shots.

Kevin D. Murray, CPP, CFE, BCFE has been solving electronic eavesdropping, security and counterespionage matters for business and government since 1973. His many written works include the "Electronic Eavesdropping Detection" section of *The Protection of Assets Manual*; articles for *Security Management* magazine; and *Business Snoops and the Top 10 Spybusting Tips They Don't Want You To Know* (available at www.spybusters.com).

His chapter forms the basis for his college course, "Electronic Eavesdropping Detection and Industrial Espionage," created for the John Jay College of Criminal Justice in New York City.

Mr. Murray is a board certified forensic examiner; a board member of the International Association of Professional Security Consultants; on the advisory board of the Business Espionage Controls & Countermeasures Association; and is a certified protection professional (American Society for Industrial Security).

He maintains a detailed web site: www.counterespionage.org, (for those with a sense of humor it's, www.spybusters.com).

Tom Owen, a nationally known expert, served for many years on the board of The International Association for Voice Identification. He currently serves as chairman of the Audio Engineering Society's Standards Group WG-12 on Forensic Audio, and is the chairman of the American Board of Recorded Evidence. Tom Owen is also the head instructor for the New York Institute of Forensic Audio from 1992 to the present.

A graduate of Bellarmine College in Louisville, Kentucky, Mr. Owen worked eleven years at New York City's Lincoln Center Archives as chief engineer, and has appeared on network television and on radio discussing audio and video matters. Mr. Owen has lectured in the U.S., Japan, China, Canada and England, and has had publications in the *Audio Engineering Society Journal*, the *International Association for Identification Journal,* and the College of Forensic Examiners, among others.

Mr. Owen's qualifications as an expert witness have been demonstrated in more than twenty states for both prosecution and defense.

John J. Palmatier, Ph.D., is a retired Michigan state trooper and military officer. For seventeen years he served in the Forensic Science Division of the Michigan State Police as a lie detection/polygraph examiner. Following his graduation from Saginaw Valley State University, Dr. Palmatier completed an interdisciplinary doctoral program in social science with cognates in developmental and experimental psychology, and criminal justice. While a member of the Michigan State Police, Dr. Palmatier finished his collection and analysis of voice data and then worked for a short time for Integritek Systems, Inc. in Florida. He is currently a visiting expert and lie detection researcher with the Institute of Automation, in the Chinese Academy of Sciences in Beijing, PR China.

Edwin H. Petersen, served with the Federal Bureau of Investigation (FBI) for more than twenty-seven years handling a variety of responsibilities including the investigation of domestic and international terrorism matters. After retirement Mr. Petersen became the director of security and facility management for Major League Baseball, Office of the Commissioner. In this capacity, he worked with all thirty major league clubs regarding integrity of the game issues, as well as facility security. As co-founder of Buckley Petersen Global (BPG), Mr. Petersen has also been involved with numerous security assessments.

Raymond M. Pierce retired as a "Detective First Grade" from the New York City Police Department (NYPD) in 1998. A longtime member of the NYPD, he had received an Federal Bureau of Investigation (FBI) fellowship in psychological profiling with the Behavioral Science Unit at the FBI National Academy. He then established the Criminal Assessment and Profiling Unit, and the Detective Bureau's Training Unit responsible for the yearly in-service training of New York City's three thousand detectives. He also was the primary lecturer and coordinator of the NYPD's Homicide Investigator's course from 1986 to 1998. Mr. Pierce holds a bachelor's degree in behavioral science and a master's degree in forensic psychology from John Jay College of Criminal Justice. He is a contributing author to the *Criminal and Civil Investigation Handbook,* second edition, and has been the subject of two books and numerous media interviews. Among the specialties of his firm, RMP International, are psychological profiling, equivocal and wrongful death evaluation, statement and document analysis, expert testimony, and corporate fraud. He is a consultant to corporate security and private investigators, and to local, state and federal law enforcement agencies.

Jeffery Richardson, Sr. attended Michigan State University from 1963 to 1967 and then had a brief career in professional football with the world champion New York Jets, the Cincinnati Bengals, and the Miami Dolphins. In 1970, Mr. Richardson started working in the loss prevention field as an investigator in distribution security for Pathmark Stores, Inc. After mastering distribution and transportation security, he entered the retail arena in Brooklyn, the Bronx and Manhattan, where he helped to develop Pathmark's in-house plainclothes security staff, which has grown from a staff of four to a present store detective staff of over 245. As the vice-president of loss prevention for Pathmark Stores, Inc., one of Jeff's duties is to keep Pathmark's Loss Prevention Department up-to-date with the most modern techniques and equipment available. Mr. Richardson was the treasurer of the Northern New Jersey Chapter of ASIS from 1995 to 2000, has served on FMI's Loss Prevention Committee, and was the chairman of the New Jersey Food Council's Loss Prevention Committee for four years. Currently, he is serving on the Certified Forensic Interviewer advisory committee for the Center for Interviewer Standards and Assessment, Ltd. (CISA).

Al Ristuccia is an owner and principal of Larsen AVR Group, Inc., a California Corporation. He is retired from the Internal Revenue Service, Criminal Investigation Division, where he enjoyed more than twenty-two years as a special agent and supervisory special agent. Mr. Ristuccia has personally conducted and directed hundreds of investigations relating to a variety of matters including income tax fraud, bank fraud, wire fraud, stock fraud, money laundering and Bank Secrecy Act violations. He has participated in many federal trials resulting from his investigative activities. His participation has included assisting government counsel to prepare for trials and grand jury proceedings. He has also testified extensively during trials and before federal grand juries. Mr. Ristuccia is currently in private practice with his partner, Lynda Larsen. They operate a full-service, private investigations firm that specializes in all aspects of litigation support, serious financial fraud investigations and internal corporate investigations. They also deal with environmental and product liability issues.

David P. Roberts, FIPI, CSC, is an international investigative and security management consultant, and owner of British-American Consultants, the specialist investigative and consultancy division of Eastern Associates, Inc. The former owner of Churchill Consultancy Group, PLC, in the United Kingdom, he has also been responsible for the executive and personal protection of members of the royal families of Britain, Saudi Arabia and other middle-eastern countries. He has provided such services on a global basis for diplomats, heads of commerce of Fortune 500 companies and high profile entertainment industry clients. Mr. Roberts is a former police officer of the Royalty & Diplomatic Protection Department at new Scotland Yard in London, is a graduate of Police College and the Royal Air Force Academy. A member of numerous professional associations, Mr. Roberts has also written several training manuals on personal protection and security diciplines.

Ben Scaglione has a Masters Degree from Rutgers University. He is a certified protection professional (CPP) and a certified healthcare safety professional (CHSP). Currently, Ben is the director of security at New York Presbyterian Hospital/Weill Cornell Medical Center in New York. From 1985 until 1996 Ben was the director of safety and security at Mountainside Hospital in New Jersey, the director of hospital police at Bellevue Hospital in New York, the director of safety, security and risk management at St. Mary's Hospital in New Jersey and the assistant director of security at Beth Israel Medical Center in New York.

Todd Sheffer, CFE, a certified fraud examiner since 1993, has been a senior fraud and diversion consultant with Washington, D.C.-based law firm deKieffer & Horgan since 1999. At deKieffer & Horgan, Mr. Sheffer directs an international investigative and consulting division that specializes in anti-diversion and anti-counterfeiting matters. He also manages and markets a trade compliance database that is available through the Internet. Prior to joining deKieffer & Horgan, Mr. Sheffer worked as director of the Fraud Prevention Department of the National Association of Credit Management (NACM) where he uncovered an unprecedented number of frauds that ranged from a $500 million dollar Ponzi scheme to numerous multi-million dollar "bust-out" scams. Mr. Sheffer has also worked closely with multiple law enforcement agencies and has been instrumental in the apprehension of numerous white-collar criminals. Sheffer was formerly a senior business analyst with Dun & Bradstreet. He is a graduate of York College of Pennsylvania.

Herbert Simon, CPP, has more than twenty years loss prevention experience and is Vice President at R.J. Montgomery Associates in Allendale, New Jersey. Licensed (as private investigator) in 1999, Herbert conducts and supervises corporate, legal defense and domestic investigations. Herbert is the executive vice president of The New Jersey Licensed Private Investigators Association.

Before joining R.J. Montgomery Associates, Herbert started his career in physical security operations for several years and then moved to the corporate side as safety and security manager for both Emerson Radio Corp. and Gemini Industries, Inc. Herbert served as chairman for ASIS International's Northern New Jersey Chapter (1993 and 1994) as assistant regional vice president (1995) and from that time to the present as placement and law enforcement liaison committee chairs.

Herbert has served on three Northeast Super Conference Committees (Atlantic City 1999, 2000 and 2003) and the Annual Convention Committee for the National Association of Legal Investigators.

Larry R. Troxel, CLI, REA, is the owner of Verdict Resources, a research and investigations company located near Los Angeles, California. He specializes in environmental pollution liability investigations. A past national director of the National Association of Legal Investigators, Inc. (NALI), Troxel has twenty-three years of investigative experience with the Ventura County (California) District Attorney's Office, where he directed an aggressive environmental crimes investigation unit. During the eight years before establishing Verdict Resources in 1996, he worked for two widely known environmental consulting companies, where he managed both national and international projects. Having a degree in criminal justice, he has trained extensively with federal and state agencies, authored numerous articles, and has lectured at environmental investigations seminars and conferences at the University of California, the California Specialized Training Institute, and throughout the country. He was a contributing author to *Advanced Forensic Criminal Defense Investigations*.

Jonathan Turner, CFE, CII, is a founder and managing director with Wilson & Turner Incorporated, where he specializes in the prevention and detection of financial fraud and employee crime issues. Mr. Turner was educated at at Tulane University (BA, International Relations) and the University of Leicester (MSc, Security & Risk Management). Prior to cofounding WTI, he served in investigations management positions with regional, national and international investigations firms, with operational responsibility for thousands of investigations. Mr. Turner is an expert in the investigation and documentation of financial fraud and computer crime matters. He concentrates on the prevention, detection and resolution of financial fraud schemes, and specializes in commercial crime and fidelity bond claims. Working with Fortune 500 and other leading companies, his efforts have led to numerous multi-million-dollar recoveries from fraud losses. He has been retained to give expert testimony regarding fraud on behalf of governmental, public and private organizations for matters before U.S. state, federal and bankruptcy courts, as well as international courts. Seen on national news programs, he is a commentator on fraud related topics, including financial fraud schemes, employee fraud issues and complex fraud schemes. He has written and contributed to over three-dozen articles for professional publications of the risk management, security, investigation and claims industries. He regularly lectures in programs for the American Society for Industrial Security, the Association of Certified Fraud Examiners, and other professional groups. Mr. Turner is a certified fraud examiner (CFE), a certified international investigator (CII), and is licensed as a private investigator. He is an active member of the American Society for Industrial Security, the Association of Certified Fraud Examiners, the American Bar Association, the Investigators Network, and the National Council of Investigative & Security Services. He serves on the editorial boards of *Fraud Magazine* and *The John Liner Review*, and on the Audit Committee for a not-for-profit organization.

Peter F. Wade was a U.S. postal inspector for twenty-five years. At the time of his retirement he was assistant regional chief inspector for ciriminal investigations in the northeastern United States, Europe and the Caribbean. Previously, Mr. Wade was postal inspector in charge of the San Juan, Puerto Rico Division. For the past ten years he has been a private detective based in San Jose, Costa Rica and has specialized in due diligence investigations in Latin America.

Index

A

B

C

F

G

H

I

Q

R

S

T

U

V

W

X